KT-554-285

Guide to the Usage

The aim of this book is to help learners of English to choose the right words and structures for the meaning they want to communicate. Each entry is based on the latest evidence from the Collins Corpus®, which now totals over 4.5 billion words. Both learners and teachers will find the book useful as an authoritative reference on how English is actually used today.

To help you find what you want more easily, this new edition of Collins COBUILD English Usage has been divided into three sections: Usage and Grammar, Topics, and the Reference section. The following pages look at each of these in turn. You will also find an index at the back of the book to show you where to find specific items.

1. The Grammar and Usage section

There are several types of **Usage** entry, and these are explained below.

Entries for individual words

The entries for individual words explain how to use the word, for example by saying which preposition should be used after it, or whether you should use a *to*-infinitive or an *-ing* form after it. For example, at the entry for **agree**:

---

3 'agree to'

If you **agree to** a suggestion or proposal, you say that you will allow it to happen.
He had agreed to the use of force.

This book deals with words that often cause problems for learners. Notes often mention what learners should *not* say, as well as what they should say. Common errors are clearly marked like this:

! BE CAREFUL

Both **homework** and **housework** are uncountable nouns. Don't talk about 'a homework' or 'houseworks'.

The correct word or expression is also given, followed by examples of correct usage:

If someone has a bad injury, don't say that they are 'very hurt'. Say that they are **badly hurt** or **seriously hurt**.
The soldier was badly hurt.
Last year 5,000 children were seriously hurt in car accidents.

Entries for easily confused words

If two or more words are sometimes confused with each other, all the words are given in the entry heading. For example, the entry headed **accept – except** explains the differences between *accept* and *except*:

---

accept – except

Don't confuse **accept** /æk'sept/ with **except** /ɪk'sept/.

1 'accept'

Accept is a verb. If someone offers you something and you **accept** it, you agree to take it.

I never accept presents from clients.

→ See **accept**

2 'except'

Except is a preposition or conjunction. You use it to show that a statement does not include a particular thing or person.

All the boys except Paul started to giggle.

→ See **except**

Other entries distinguish between words which have similar basic meanings, but are used in slightly different ways:

---

called – named

You use **called** or **named** when you are giving the name of someone or something. **Named** is less common than **called**, and is not usually used in conversation.

Did you know a boy called Desmond?
We passed through a town called Monmouth.
A man named Richardson confessed to the theft.

You can use **called** either after a noun or after **be**.

She starred in a play called Katerina.
The book was called The Goalkeeper's Revenge.

You usually use **named** immediately after a noun.

The victim was an 18-year-old girl named Marinetta Jirkowski.

Grammar Finder entries

The **Grammar Finder** entries in this book contain grammatical information on all of the main grammatical points that you may need to refer to in your studies.

The longer Grammar Finder entries have a 'menu' at the start of the entry to help you find what you need easily. For example:

Questions

1	yes/no questions	**6**	wh-questions
2	'be'	**7**	wh-word as subject
3	'have'	**8**	wh-word as object or adverb
4	negative yes/no questions	**9**	questions in reply
5	answers to yes/no questions	**10**	indirect ways of asking questions

There is also a Glossary of grammatical terms on pages 763 to 773.

If you want to study English grammar in greater depth, or if you require more detail on a particular point, you should turn to COBUILD English Grammar.

2. The Topics section

The Topic entries in this book deal with two types of topic: (1) straightforward topics such as 'Meals', 'Places', and 'Transport' **(Section A: Subject areas)**, and (2) functional aspects of English such as 'Agreeing and disagreeing', 'Apologizing', 'Thanking', and 'Warning' **(Section B: Communication skills)**. The section also covers certain areas of written English such as writing emails and letters.

The longer Topic entries have a 'menu' at the beginning to help you to find what you need easily:

Agreeing and disagreeing

1	asking for agreement	**5**	expressing ignorance or uncertainty
2	expressing agreement		
3	strong agreement	**6**	expressing disagreement
4	partial agreement	**7**	strong disagreement

In Topic entries, formal and informal ways of saying something are often described. People use informal expressions when they are speaking to friends and family members. They use formal expressions when they are speaking to people they do not know well, or when they are in a formal situation such as a meeting.

3. The Reference section

Entries in the Reference section tell you about particular groups of words that are used in a particular way, for example abbreviations or words that are used to refer to nationalities. There are also entries on spelling and punctuation.

4. General points

Register information

Sometimes, information is given explaining which words and expressions are used in conversation and informal writing, and which are mainly used in formal speech or writing:

> **2** 'a couple of'
>
> In conversation and informal writing, you can refer to two people or things as **a couple of** people or things.
>
> *I asked a couple of friends to help me.*
> *We played a couple of games of tennis.*

When a word, expression, or structure occurs only in novels and written descriptions, we say that it occurs only 'in stories'. For example *dress* is used to mean 'put on your clothes' in stories, but in conversation you would say *get dressed*. Words described as 'literary', such as the adverb *seldom*, are used in poetical writing and passionate speeches.

If a word or expression is described as not being used 'in modern English', this means that you may come across it in a book written some time ago, but it would not sound natural in writing today, and should definitely not be used in conversation. For example, in modern British English, *go swimming* is used in preference to *bathe*. If a word is described as 'old-fashioned', it occurs in old books and may still be used by older people today, but is becoming uncommon.

If a word or expression is described as not being used 'in standard English', this means that speakers of some varieties of English use it, but it would be regarded as incorrect by most people.

A word that is described as 'neutral' is used simply to show that someone or something has a particular quality. A word that 'shows approval' shows that you admire the person you are describing. A word that 'shows disapproval' shows that you disapprove of the person.

American English

There is often a difference between British and American usage. The US flag symbol highlights information about these differences. For example:

> In American English, the floor which is level with the ground is called the **first floor**, the floor above it is the **second floor**, and so on.

Orton 8113

Peterborough City Council
Community School Libraries

WITHDRAWN FROM STOCK

PETERBOROUGH LIBRARIES

~~24 Hour renewal line 08458 505606~~

This book is to be returned on or before the latest date shown above, but may be renewed up to three times if the book is not in demand. Ask at your local library for details.

Please note that charges are made on overdue books

60000 0001 07053

HarperCollins Publishers
Westerhill Road
Bishopbriggs
Glasgow
G64 2QT

Third Edition 2012

Reprint 10 9 8 7 6 5 4 3 2 1 0

© HarperCollins Publishers 1992,
2004, 2011, 2012

ISBN 978-0-00-742374-3

Collins® and COBUILD®
are registered trademarks of
HarperCollins Publishers Limited

www.collinslanguage.com

A catalogue record for this book is
available from the British Library

Typeset by Davidson Publishing
Solutions, Glasgow

Printed and bound in China by
South China Printing Co. Ltd

Acknowledgements
We would like to thank those authors
and publishers who kindly gave
permission for copyright material
to be used in the Collins Corpus.
We would also like to thank Times
Newspapers Ltd for providing
valuable data.

All rights reserved. No part of this
book may be reproduced, stored in a
retrieval system, or transmitted in
any form or by any means, electronic,
mechanical, photocopying,
recording or otherwise, without the
prior permission in writing of the
Publisher. This book is sold subject
to the conditions that it shall not,
by way of trade or otherwise, be
lent, re-sold, hired out or otherwise
circulated without the Publisher's
prior consent in any form of binding
or cover other than that in which it
is published and without a similar
condition including this condition
being imposed on the subsequent
purchaser.

Entered words that we have reason
to believe constitute trademarks have
been designated as such. However,
neither the presence nor absence of
such designation should be regarded
as affecting the legal status of any
trademark.

HarperCollins does not warrant
that www.collinsdictionary.com,
www.collinslanguage.com or any
other website mentioned in this title
will be provided uninterrupted, that
any website will be error free, that
defects will be corrected, or that the
website or the server that makes it
available are free of viruses or bugs.
For full terms and conditions please
refer to the site terms provided on the
website.

Peterborough City Council	
60000 0001 07053	
Askews & Holts	Aug-2013
428.24	£20.00

Third Edition

Managing Editor
Penny Hands

Senior Editor
Kate Wild

Project Management
Gavin Gray
Lisa Sutherland

Contributors
Sandra Anderson
Rosalind Combley
Lucy Hollingworth
Laura Wedgeworth

American English Consultant
Orin Hargraves

Computing Support
Thomas Callan

For the Publishers
Lucy Cooper
Kerry Ferguson
Elaine Higgleton

Founding Editor-in-Chief
John Sinclair

We would like to thank the following people for their contributions
to previous editions of the text:

Maree Airlie, Mona Baker, Maksymilian Baranowski, Michela Clari, Sue Crawley,
Abkarovits Endre, Gwyneth Fox, Gill Francis, Bob Grossmith, Ann Hewings, Zoe James,
Yuan Kele, Lorna Knight, Ramesh Krishnamurthy, Paul Laurent, Alison Macaulay,
Elizabeth Manning, Francisco Gomes de Matos, Alyson McGee, Sue Ogden,
Wolf Paprotté, Liz Potter, Christina Rammell, Louise Ravelli, Maggie Seaton,
Keith Stuart, John Todd, Martin Warren

Contents

Introduction   vi
Guide to the Usage   viii
Pronunciation Guide   xiv

Usage and Grammar section   **1–613**

Among the Usage notes are the following **Grammar Finders**:
Adjectives   9
Adverbs and adverbials   15
Auxiliary verbs   67
Broad negatives   100
Clauses   124
Comparative and superlative adjectives   131
Comparative and superlative adverbs   136
Complements   138
Conjunctions   144
Contractions   149
Determiners   171
–ed participles   189
Ellipsis   193
Future time   237
The imperative   273
Infinitives   277
–ing forms   279
Inversion   289
Modals   330
Modifiers   331
Noun modifiers   357
Nouns   358
Objects   366
The passive   391
The past   393
Phrasal modals   397
Phrasal verbs   397
Possessive determiners   403
Prepositions   407
The present   409
The progressive form   414
Pronouns   416
Quantity   423
Questions   429
Question tags   432
Relative clauses   440
Reporting   447
Sentence connectors   476
The subjunctive   511
Subordinate clauses   512
That–clauses   531
Verb forms   559
Verbs   562
Wh–words   587

Topics section — 615

Section A: Subject areas

Age — 616
Meals — 619
Money — 621
Names and titles — 623
Pieces and amounts — 627
Places — 629
Time — 636
Transport — 642

Section B: Communication skills

Addressing someone — 643
Advising someone — 646
Agreeing and disagreeing — 648
Apologizing — 651
Asking for repetition — 653
Complimenting and congratulating someone — 654
Criticizing someone — 655
Emailing — 656
Greetings and goodbyes — 658
Intentions — 660
Introducing yourself and other people — 662
Invitations — 664
Letter writing — 666
Offers — 669
Opinions — 671
Permission — 676
Reactions — 678
Replies — 683
Requests, orders, and instructions — 685
Structuring your ideas — 690
Suggestions — 694
Telephoning — 697
Thanking someone — 700
Warning someone — 703

Reference section — 705

Abbreviations — 706
Capital letters — 708
Days and dates — 710
Irregular verbs — 716
Measurements — 719
Nationality words — 725
Numbers and fractions — 728
Plural forms of nouns — 737
Punctuation — 741
Spelling — 749
Verb forms (formation of) — 760

Glossary of grammatical terms — 763

Index — 775

Introduction

Welcome to the new edition of Collins COBUILD English Usage, for students from intermediate to advanced level, and for teachers of English. With the help of the Collins Corpus®, now totalling 4.5 billion words, we have been able to update and revise this title so that it describes how people actually use English now.

What is 'usage'? Usage deals with the essential details of language, involving aspects of grammar, meaning, idiom, and purpose. It looks at the way words are arranged to express a particular meaning or to do a particular job. Most of the statements in this book are not generalizations, because usage deals with all the things that are not covered by the general rules.

However, there is no strict dividing line between grammar and usage. For this reason, you will also find entries on the most important grammatical points in English, integrated into the main usage section of the book. Extensive cross-referencing helps you to move easily between entry-types.

The book is divided into three main sections: Usage and Grammar, Topics, and a Reference section. The Topics and Reference sections are clearly marked in the shaded area at the side of each page.

The Usage section

A large number of the entries in the Usage section consist of short notes on individual words and phrases. Two words like *although* and *though* may be easily confused; or one word may need to go with another, for example *afford* needs to be preceded by *can*, *could*, or *be able to*.

Other entries are longer: they might deal with words that have a lot of meanings, or they might focus on 'function words'; these are small words like *and* and *that*, which serve to express grammatical relationships between parts of a sentence. You can find out more about any of the grammatical terms that are used in the explanations by looking at the relevant Grammar Finder entry.

Using the evidence from our American corpus, we have also updated the coverage of American English for this new edition.

The Topics section

The Topics section is divided into two subsections: (1) straightforward topics such as 'Meals', 'Places', and 'Transport', and (2) functional aspects of English such as 'Agreeing and disagreeing', 'Apologizing', 'Thanking', and 'Warning'. It also covers certain areas of written English such as writing emails and letters.

The Reference section

The Reference section gives information on layout, rules, and formation in the following essential areas of English:

- Abbreviations
- Capital letters
- Days and dates
- Irregular verbs
- Measurements
- Nationality words
- Numbers and fractions
- Plural forms of nouns
- Punctuation
- Spelling
- Verb forms (formation of)

All the entries in each section are arranged in alphabetical order, and related areas are cross-referenced throughout.

The examples

Thousands of real extracts from the constantly updated Collins Corpus® are used to demonstrate the usage points. Where appropriate, they have been cut down or simplified, so that they help you to focus on the usage point that they illustrate.

Our intention is that this should be a practical, comprehensive, and accessible guide to English usage. As well as being an easy-to-use reference book, we hope that it is written in a way that will encourage you to learn while browsing and enjoying at your leisure.

COBUILD is always keen to know how the reference books and dictionaries are appreciated, and we have set up an email address (collins.elt@harpercollins.co.uk) for your comments and criticisms, so that future editions can continue to meet your needs.

Be Careful

'Be Careful' highlights points where people often have problems with a particular aspect of English, often because it is a feature where English is different from many other languages. For example:

> **BE CAREFUL**
>
> Don't say that someone '~~has difficulty to do~~' something.

Spoken English

The speech bubble symbol identifies paragraphs describing structures that are most commonly found in spoken English. For example:

> In conversation, you can use '**I mean**' to explain or correct something that you have just said.

Examples

Collins COBUILD English Usage gives thousands of examples of usage, all of which are taken from the Collins Corpus®, and show English as it is really used today. The corpus is contantly updated which ensures that the examples used in this book are up to date and relevant.

Cross-references

When information about the use of a word, or additional related information, is to be found in another entry, a cross-reference is given, explaining which section of the book to look in:

> **2** '**bare**'
>
> **Bare** is usually an adjective. Something that is **bare** has no covering.
>
> *The grass was warm under her <u>bare</u> feet.*
> *The walls were <u>bare</u>.*
>
> → See **bare – barely**

Pronunciation guide

British English vowel sounds

ɑː	heart, start, calm
æ	act, mass, lap
aɪ	dive, cry, mine
aɪə	fire, tyre, buyer
aʊ	out, down, loud
aʊə	flour, tower, sour
e	met, lend, pen
eɪ	say, main, weight
eə	fair, care, wear
ɪ	fit, win, list
iː	feed, me, beat
ɪə	near, beard, clear
ɒ	lot, lost, spot
əʊ	note, phone, coat
ɔː	more, cord, claw
ɔɪ	boy, coin, joint
ʊ	could, stood, hood
uː	you, use, choose
ʊə	sure, pure, cure
ɜː	turn, third, word
ʌ	but, fund, must
ə	(the weak vowel in) butter, about, forgotten

American English vowel sounds

ɑ	calm, drop, fall
ɑː	draw, saw
æ	act, mass, lap
ai	drive, cry, lie
aiər	fire, tire, buyer
au	out, down, loud
auər	flour, tower, sour
e	met, lend, pen
ei	say, main, weight
eər	fair, care, wear
ɪ	fit, win, list
i	feed, me, beat
ɪər	cheer, hear, clear
ou	note, phone, coat
ɔ	more, cord, sort
ɔi	boy, coin, joint
ʊ	could, stood, hood
u	you, use, choose
ʊər	sure, pure, cure
ɜr	turn, third, word
ʌ	but, fund, must
ə	(the weak vowel in) about, account, cancel

consonant sounds

b	bed	l	lip	v	van	tʃ	cheap
d	done	m	mat	w	win	θ	thin
f	fit	n	nine	x	lo<u>ch</u>	ð	then
g	good	p	pay	z	zoo	dʒ	joy
h	hat	r	run	ʃ	ship		
j	yellow	s	soon	ʒ	mea<u>s</u>ure		
k	king	t	talk	ŋ	si<u>ng</u>		

Letters

These are vowel letters:

a e i o u

These are consonant letters:

b c d f g h j k l m n p q r s t v w x y z

The letter y is sometimes used as a vowel, for example in 'shy' and 'myth'.

USAGE
AND
GRAMMAR

Aa

a – an

1 'a' and 'an'

You usually use **a** and **an** when it is not clear or important which specific thing or person you are referring to. You only use **a** and **an** with singular countable nouns. When you are talking about a specific person or thing, you usually use **the**.

She decided to buy a car.
He parked the car in front of the bakery.

→ See **Determiners**

→ See **the**

You can describe someone or something using **a** or **an** with an adjective and a noun, or with a noun followed by more information.

His brother was a sensitive child.
The information was contained in an article on biology.

! BE CAREFUL

Don't omit **a** or **an** in front of a noun when the noun refers to someone's profession or job. For example, you say 'He is **an** architect'. Don't say 'He is architect'.

She became a lawyer.

2 'a' or 'an'?

You use **a** in front of words beginning with consonant sounds and **an** in front of words beginning with vowel sounds.

Then I saw a tall woman standing by the window.
We live in an old house.

You use **an** in front of words beginning with 'h' when the 'h' is not pronounced. For example, you say '**an honest** man'. Don't say 'a honest man'.

The meeting lasted an hour.

An is used in front of the following words beginning with 'h':

heir	heirloom	honorary	honourable	hourly
heiress	honest	honour	hour	

You use **a** in front of words beginning with 'u' when the 'u' is pronounced /juː/ (like 'you'). For example, you say '**a unique** occasion'. Don't say 'an unique occasion'.

He was a university professor.
She became a union member.

A is used in front of the following words:

ubiquitous	uniform	unilateral	unisex
unanimous	uniformed	unilateralist	unit
unicorn	uniformity	union	united
unification	unifying	unique	universal

universe	usable	user	utilitarian
university	usage	usual	utility
uranium	use	usually	utopian
urinal	used	usurper	
urinary	useful	utensil	
urine	useless	uterus	

You use **an** in front of an abbreviation when the letters are pronounced separately and the first letter begins with a vowel sound.

Before she became an MP, she was a social worker.
He drives an SUV.

3 'a' meaning 'one'

A and **an** are used to mean 'one' in front of some numbers and units of measurement.

→ See **Reference** sections **Numbers and fractions**, **Measurements**

ability – capability – capacity

Do not confuse **ability** with **capability** and **capacity**.

1 'ability'

You often use **ability** to say that someone can do something well.

He had remarkable ability as a musician.
...the ability to bear hardship.

2 'capability'

A person's **capability** is the amount of work they can do and how well they can do it.

...a job that was beyond the capability of one man.
...the director's ideas of the capability of the actor.

3 'capacity'

If someone has a particular **capacity**, a **capacity** for something, or a **capacity** to do something, they have the qualities required to do it. **Capacity** is a more formal word than **ability**.

...their capacity for hard work.
...his capacity to see the other person's point of view.

a bit

→ See **bit**

able – capable

Able and **capable** are both used to say that someone can do something.

1 'able'

If someone is **able** to do something, they can do it either because of their knowledge or skill, or because it is possible.

He wondered if he would be able to climb over the fence.
They were able to use their profits for new investments.

If you use a past tense, you mean that someone has actually done something.

We were able to reduce costs.

→ See **can – could – be able to**

2 'capable'

If someone is **capable of** doing something, they have the knowledge and skill to do it.

The workers are perfectly capable of running the organization themselves.

You can say that someone is **capable of** a particular feeling or action.

He's capable of loyalty.
I don't believe he's capable of murder.

You can also use **capable of** when you are talking about what something such as a car or machine can do.

The car was capable of 110 miles per hour.

3 'able' or 'capable'

If you describe someone as **able** or **capable**, you mean that they do things well.

He's certainly a capable gardener.
Naomi was a hard-working and able student.

about

1 'about'

You use **about** when you mention what someone is saying, writing, or thinking.

Manuel told me about his new job.
I'll have to think about that.

You can say that a book is **about** a particular subject or that it is **on** that subject.

She is writing a book about politics.
I'm reading Anthony Daniels' book on Guatemala.

You can also use **about** to say what a novel or play deals with. Don't use 'on'.

This is a novel about ethics.
They read a story about growing up.

2 'about to'

If you are **about to do** something, you are going to do it soon.

You are about to cross the River Jordan.
I was about to go home.

! BE CAREFUL

Don't use an *-ing* form in sentences like these. Don't say, for example, 'You are about crossing the River Jordan'.

→ See **around – round – about**

above – over

1 used for talking about position and height

If something is higher than something else, you can say that the first thing is **above** or **over** the second thing.

He opened a cupboard above the sink.
There was a mirror over the fireplace.

If one thing is much higher than another thing, or there is a lot of space between them, you usually use **above**.

We heard a noise in the apartment above ours.

You usually use **over** when one thing is at a higher level than another thing, and the first thing is moving.

A plane flew over the city.

2 used for talking about measurements and quantities

Above and **over** are both used to talk about measurements, for example, when you are talking about a point that is higher than another point on a scale.

Any money earned over that level is taxed.
The temperature rose to just above forty degrees.

! BE CAREFUL

Don't use **above** in front of a number when you are talking about a quantity or number of things or people. For example, don't say 'She had above thirty pairs of shoes'. You say 'She had **over** thirty pairs of shoes' or 'She had **more than** thirty pairs of shoes'.

They paid out over 3 million pounds.
He saw more than 800 children, dying of starvation.

3 used for talking about distance and time

You use **over** to say that a distance or period of time is longer than the one mentioned.

The mountain is over twelve thousand feet high.
Our relationship lasted for over a year.

absent

1 'absent'

If someone is **absent from** a meeting, ceremony, or place, they are not there.

Gary O'Neil has been absent from training because of a stomach virus.
Their children are frequently absent from school.

You use **from** after **absent** in sentences like these. Don't use 'at'.

If it is clear what meeting, ceremony, or place you are talking about, you can simply say that someone is **absent**.

The Mongolian delegate to the assembly was absent.

2 'not at' and 'not there'

Absent is a fairly formal word. In conversation and in less formal writing, you say that someone is **not at** a meeting, ceremony, or place, or that they are **not there**.

She wasn't at Molly's wedding.
I looked in the kitchen but Magda wasn't there.

accept

If someone offers you something and you **accept** it, you agree to take it.

Jane accepted a slice of cake.

1 advice and suggestions

If you **accept** someone's advice or suggestion, you decide to do what they advise or suggest.

I knew that they would accept my proposal.

! BE CAREFUL

However, don't say that you 'accept to do' what someone suggests. You say that you **agree to do** it.

The princess agreed to go on television.
She agreed to let us use her flat while she was away.

2 situations and people

If you **accept** a difficult or unpleasant situation, you recognize that it cannot be changed.

They refused to accept poor working conditions.
Astronauts accept danger as part of their job.

accept – except

Don't confuse **accept** /æk'sept/ with **except** /ɪk'sept/.

1 'accept'

Accept is a verb. If someone offers you something and you **accept** it, you agree to take it.

I never accept presents from clients.

→ See **accept**

2 'except'

Except is a preposition or conjunction. You use it to show that a statement does not include a particular thing or person.

All the boys except Paul started to giggle.

→ See **except**

acceptable

You say that something is **acceptable** when it is satisfactory, or when people do not object to it.

To my relief he found the article acceptable.
Are we saying that violence is acceptable?

You do not say that someone is 'acceptable' to do something. You say that they are **willing** to do it.

Ed was quite willing to let us help him.
Would you be willing to go to Berkhamsted?

accommodation

Accommodation is where you live or stay, especially when you are on holiday or when you are staying somewhere for a short amount of time. In British English, **accommodation** is an uncountable noun. Don't talk about 'accommodations' or 'an accommodation'.

There is plenty of student accommodation in Edinburgh.
We booked our flights and accommodation three months before our holiday.

 Speakers of American English usually talk about **accommodations**.

The hotel provides cheap accommodations and good food.

! **BE CAREFUL**

Don't talk about 'an accommodation' in either British English or American English. Don't say, for example, ~~'I'm looking for an accommodation near the city centre'~~. Say 'I'm looking for **accommodation** near the city centre' or in American English, 'I'm looking for **accommodations** near the city centre'.

accompany

If you **accompany** someone to a place, you go there with them.

She asked me to accompany her to the church.

Accompany is a fairly formal word. In conversation and in less formal writing, you use **go with** or **come with**.

I went with my friends to see what it looked like.
He wished Ellen had come with him.

However, there is no passive form of **go with** or **come with**. If you want to use a passive form, you must use **accompany**.

He was accompanied by his wife.
She came out of the house accompanied by Mrs Jones.

accord

If you do something **of** your **own accord**, you do it freely and because you want to do it.

She knew they would leave of their own accord.

! **BE CAREFUL**

You must use 'own' in sentences like these. You do not say, for example, ~~'She had gone of her accord'~~.

You also do not say that someone does something 'on' their own accord.

according to

1 'according to'

You can use **according to** when you want to report what someone said.

According to Dr Santos, the cause of death was drowning.

You can also use **according to** when you want to report information given in a book or a document.

The road was forty miles long, according to my map.

💬 In conversation, instead of saying 'According to George, the roads are very slippery this morning', you often say 'George **says** the roads are very slippery this morning'.

Arnold says they do this in Essex as well.
Car sales have fallen this year, the report says.

2 'in my opinion'

If you want to emphasize that what you are saying is your own opinion, you say '**In my opinion...**' or '**In our opinion...**'.

In my opinion we face a national emergency.
The temple gets crowded, and in our opinion it's best to visit it in the evening.

! BE CAREFUL

Don't say 'according to me' or 'according to us'.

Don't use **according to** and **opinion** together. Don't say, for example, 'According to the bishop's opinion, the public has a right to know'. You say '**The bishop's opinion is that** the public has a right to know'.

The psychiatrist's opinion was that John was suffering from depression.

→ See **Topic** entry **Opinions**

---

accuse – charge

1 'accuse'

If you **accuse** someone **of** doing something wrong, you say that they did it.

He accused them of drinking beer while driving.
He is accused of killing ten young women.

! BE CAREFUL

Don't say that you accuse someone 'for' doing something wrong.

2 'charge'

When the police **charge** someone **with** committing a crime, they formally accuse them of it.

He was arrested and charged with committing a variety of offences.

---

accustomed to

1 'accustomed to'

If you are **accustomed to** something, you have become familiar with it and you no longer find it strange. **Accustomed to** usually comes after linking verbs such as **be**, **become**, **get**, and **grow**.

It did not get lighter, but I became accustomed to the dark.
I am not accustomed to being interrupted.

! BE CAREFUL

Don't say that someone is 'accustomed with' something.

2 'used to'

In conversation and in less formal writing, you don't usually say that someone is 'accustomed to' something. You say that they are **used to** it. **Used to** usually comes after **be** or **get**.

The company is used to much stronger growth.
It's very noisy here, but you'll get used to it.

→ See **used to**

You can say that someone is **accustomed to doing** something or **used to doing** something.

The manager is accustomed to working late.
We are used to queueing.

! BE CAREFUL

Don't say that someone is 'accustomed to do' something or 'used to do' something.

actual

1 'actual'

You use **actual** to emphasize that the place, object, or person you are talking about is the real or genuine one.

The predicted results and the actual results are very different.
The interpretation bore no relation to the actual words spoken.

! BE CAREFUL

You only use **actual** in front of a noun. You do not say that something 'is actual'.

2 'current' and 'present'

You do not use 'actual' to describe something that is happening, being done, or being used at the present time. Instead you use **current** or **present**.

The store needs more than $100,000 to survive the current crisis.
Is the present situation really any different from many others in the past?

actually

You use **actually** when you want to emphasize that something is true, especially if it is surprising or unexpected.

All the characters in the novel actually existed.
Some people think that Dave is bad-tempered, but he is actually very kind.

You also use **actually** when you are mentioning something that is very surprising. You put **actually** in front of the surprising part of what you are saying.

He actually began to cry.
The value of oil has actually been falling in the last two years.

You can use **actually** if you want to correct what someone says.

'Mr Hooper is a schoolteacher.' – 'A university lecturer, actually.'

If someone suggests something and you want to suggest something different, you can say '**Actually, I'd rather...**', or '**Actually, I'd prefer to...**'.

'Shall we go out for dinner?' – 'Actually, I'd rather stay in tonight.'

> **!** **BE CAREFUL**
>
> Don't use **actually** when you want to say that something is happening now. Use **at present**, **at the moment**, or **right now**.
>
> *He's in a meeting at the moment.*

→ See **now**

GRAMMAR FINDER

Adjectives

1 form	**8** compound adjectives
2 qualitative adjectives	**9** position of adjectives
3 comparatives and superlatives	**10** coordination of adjectives
4 classifying adjectives	**11** order of adjectives
5 colour adjectives	**12** adjectives with prepositions and
6 emphasizing adjectives	other structures
7 postdeterminers	

An **adjective** is a word that is used to describe someone or something, or to give information about them.

1 form

The form of an adjective does not change: the same form is used for singular and plural and for male and female.

We were looking for a good place to camp.
Good places to fish were hard to find.

2 qualitative adjectives

Qualitative adjectives are adjectives that indicate that someone or something has a particular quality. For example, **sad**, **pretty**, **happy**, and **wise** are qualitative adjectives.

...a sad story.
...a small child.

Qualitative adjectives are sometimes called **gradable adjectives**. This means that the person or thing described can have more or less of the quality mentioned. One way of indicating the amount of a quality that something or someone has is by using adverbs such as **very** and **rather**.

→ See **Adverbs and adverbials** for a list of adverbs used to indicate degree

...an extremely narrow road.
...a very pretty girl.
...a rather clumsy person.

3 comparatives and superlatives

Another way in which adjectives can be graded is by the use of the **comparative** and **superlative** forms -er and -est and the comparatives **more** and **most**. The comparative is used to say that something has more of a quality than something else, or more than it used to have. The superlative is used to say that something has more of a quality than anything else of its kind, or more than anything else in a particular group or place.

→ See **Comparative and superlative adjectives**

4 classifying adjectives

Classifying adjectives are adjectives that are used to indicate that something is of a particular type. For example, if you say **financial help**, you are using the adjective **financial** to classify the noun **help**. There are many different kinds of help: **financial help** is one of them. These adjectives cannot be graded and do not have comparative or superlative forms. They are sometimes called **non-gradable adjectives**.

...my _daily_ shower.
..._Victorian_ houses.
..._civil_ engineering.

5 colour adjectives

Colour adjectives are used to indicate what colour something is.

...a small _blue_ car.
Her eyes are _green_.

To specify a colour more precisely, a word such as **light**, **pale**, **dark**, or **bright** is put in front of the adjective.

..._light brown_ hair.
...a _bright green_ suit.
...a _dark blue_ dress.

Colour words are also nouns. When they are nouns, they are typically used in the singular with no determiner.

I like _blue_.
Christina always wore _red_.
Yellow is my favourite colour.

The more frequent colour words can be used in the plural, or in the singular with a determiner, to refer to the different shades of a colour.

They blended in well with the _greens_ of the landscape.
The shadows had turned _a deep blue_.

6 emphasizing adjectives

Emphasizing adjectives are used in front of a noun to emphasize a description of something or the degree of something.

He made me feel like a _complete_ idiot.
Some of it was _absolute_ rubbish.
World Cup tickets are _dead_ expensive you know.
The redundancy of skilled workers is a _terrible_ waste.
It was the _supreme_ arrogance of the killer that dismayed him.

The following adjectives are emphasizing adjectives:

absolute	mere	real	total
awful	outright	sheer	true
complete	perfect	simple	utter
dead	positive	supreme	
entire	pure	terrible	

7 postdeterminers

There is a small group of adjectives called **postdeterminers** that you use to indicate precisely what you are referring to. These adjectives come after a determiner and in front of any other adjectives.

...the following brief description.
He wore his usual old white coat.

They also come in front of numbers.

What has gone wrong during the last ten years?

The following adjectives are used in this way:

additional	following	opposite	principal
certain	further	other	remaining
chief	last	particular	same
entire	main	past	specific
existing	next	present	usual
first	only	previous	whole

A large number of adjectives end in *-ed* or *-ing*.

8 compound adjectives

Compound adjectives are made up of two or more words, usually written with hyphens between them. They may be qualitative, classifying, or colour adjectives.

He was giving a very light-hearted talk.
Olivia was driving a long bottle-green car.
...a good-looking girl.
...a part-time job.

9 position of adjectives

Most adjectives can be used in front of nouns to give more information about something that is mentioned.

She bought a loaf of white bread.
There was no clear evidence.

! BE CAREFUL

Adjectives cannot usually be used after a determiner without being followed by either a noun or **one**. Don't say, for example, 'He showed me all of them, but I preferred the large'. Say 'He showed me all of them, but I preferred the large one'.

→ See **one**

→ See **the** for information on the use of **the** with an adjective to refer to a group of people

Most adjectives can also be used after a linking verb such as **be**, **become**, **get**, **seem**, or **feel**.

The room was large and square.
I felt angry.
Nobody seemed amused.
He was so exhausted that he could hardly keep awake.

Some adjectives are normally used only after linking verbs, not in front of nouns, when used with a particular meaning. For example, you can say '**She was alone**' but you cannot say 'an alone girl'.

The following adjectives are normally used only after linking verbs:

afraid	ashamed	ill	well
alike	asleep	ready	
alive	awake	sorry	
alone	glad	sure	

There are many other adjectives that are only used after a linking verb in one or more of their meanings.

Instead of using these adjectives in front of a noun, you can sometimes use an alternative word or expression. For example, instead of 'the afraid child' you can say '**the frightened child**'.

10 coordination of adjectives

When two adjectives are used after a linking verb, a conjunction (usually **and**) is used to link them. With three or more adjectives, the last two are linked with a conjunction, and commas are put after the others.

The day was hot and dusty.
The house was old, damp and smelly.

When more than one adjective is used in front of a noun, the adjectives are not usually separated by 'and'. Don't say 'a short, fat and old man'.

→ See **and** for more information on how to link adjectives

11 order of adjectives

When more than one adjective is used in front of a noun, the usual order is as follows:

qualitative adjective – colour adjective – classifying adjective

...a little white wooden house.
...rapid technological advance.
...a large circular pool of water.
...a necklace of blue Venetian beads.

However, classifying adjectives indicating shape, such as **circular** and **rectangular**, often come in front of colour adjectives.

...the rectangular grey stones.
...the circular yellow patch on the lawn.

▶ order of qualitative adjectives

The order of qualitative adjectives is normally as follows:

opinions – size – quality – age – shape

We're going to have a nice big garden with two apple trees.
Their cat had beautiful thick fur.
...big, shiny beetles.
He had long curly red hair.
She put on her dirty old fur coat.

When you refer to '**a nice big garden**' or '**a lovely big garden**', you usually mean that the garden is nice because it is big, not nice in some other way.

▶ order of classifying adjectives

If there is more than one classifying adjective in front of a noun, the normal order is:

age – shape – nationality – material

...a medieval French village.
...a rectangular plastic box.
...an Italian silk jacket.

Other types of classifying adjective usually come after a nationality adjective.

...the Chinese artistic tradition.
...the American political system.

▶ comparatives and superlatives

Comparatives and superlatives normally come in front of all other adjectives in a noun phrase.

Some of the better English actors have gone to live in Hollywood.
These are the highest monthly figures on record.

▶ noun modifiers

When a noun phrase contains both an adjective and a **noun modifier** (= a noun used in front of another noun), the adjective is placed in front of the noun modifier.

He works in the French film industry.
He receives a large weekly cash payment.

▶ adjectives after a noun

You don't usually put adjectives after nouns. However, there are some exceptions, which are explained below.

You can put an adjective after a noun if the adjective is followed by a prepositional phrase or a *to*-infinitive clause.

...a warning to people eager for a quick cure.
...the sort of weapons likely to be deployed against it.

The adjectives **alive** and **awake** can be put after a noun that is preceded by a superlative, an adverb, or **first**, **last**, **only**, **every**, or **any**.

Is Phil Morgan the only man alive who knows all the words to that song?
She sat at the window, until she was the last person awake.

A few formal adjectives are only used after a noun:

designate	emeritus	incarnate	par excellence
elect	extraordinaire	manqué	

...British Rail's chairman designate, Mr Robert Reid.
She was now the president elect.
Doctors, lawyers and engineers are professionals par excellence.

▶ adjectives before or after a noun

A few adjectives have a different meaning depending on whether they come in front of a noun or after it. For example, '**the concerned mother**' describes a mother who is worried, but '**the mother concerned**' simply refers to a mother who has been mentioned.

...the approval of interested and concerned parents.
The idea needs to come from the individuals concerned.

The following adjectives have different meanings in different positions:

concerned	present	responsible
involved	proper	

→ See **separate Usage entries at these words**

Some adjectives that describe size can come after a noun phrase consisting of a number or determiner and a noun that indicates the unit of measurement.

The following adjectives can be used like this:

deep	long	tall	wide
high	square	thick	

He was about <u>six feet tall</u>.
The island is only <u>29 miles long</u>.

Some of these adjectives can also be used after words like **knee**, **ankle**, and **waist**:

The grass was <u>knee high</u>.
The track ahead was <u>ankle deep</u> in mud.

→ See **Topic** entry **Measurements**

Old is used after noun phrases in a similar way.

→ See **Topic** entry **Age**

12 adjectives with prepositions and other structures

Some adjectives are usually followed by a particular preposition, a *to*-infinitive, or a *that*-clause, because otherwise their meaning would be unclear or incomplete. For example, you cannot simply say that someone is 'fond'. You have to say that they are **fond of** something.

They are very <u>fond of</u> each other.
The sky is <u>filled with</u> clouds.

The following lists show some of the adjectives that must be followed by the preposition given when used immediately after a linking verb.

accustomed to	conducive to	proportional to	subservient to
adapted to	devoted to	proportionate to	susceptible to
allergic to	impervious to	reconciled to	unaccustomed to
attributable to	injurious to	resigned to	
attuned to	integral to	resistant to	
averse to	prone to	subject to	

He seemed to be becoming <u>accustomed to</u> my presence.
For all her experience, she was still <u>prone to</u> nerves.

aware of	desirous of	illustrative of	reminiscent of
bereft of	devoid of	incapable of	representative of
capable of	fond of	indicative of	
characteristic of	heedless of	mindful of	

Smokers are well <u>aware of</u> the dangers to their own health.
We must be <u>mindful of</u> the consequences of selfishness.

unhampered by	rooted in	conversant with	tinged with
descended from	steeped in	filled with	
inherent in	swathed in	fraught with	
lacking in	contingent on	riddled with	

We recognize the dangers <u>inherent in</u> an outbreak of war.
Her homecoming was <u>tinged with</u> sadness.

In some cases, there is a choice between two prepositions. The following adjectives are usually or always used immediately after a linking verb and can be followed by the prepositions indicated:

burdened by/with dependent on/ upon	immune from/to inclined to/ towards	incumbent on/ upon intent on/upon	parallel to/with reliant on/upon stricken by/with

We are in no way immune from this danger.
He was curiously immune to teasing.

→ See **that-clauses** for lists of adjectives followed by a *that*-clause

GRAMMAR FINDER

Adverbs and adverbials

1	adverbs and adverbials	**11**	emphasis
2	manner	**12**	focus
3	viewpoint adverbs	**13**	probability
4	opinion	**14**	position: manner, place, time
5	place	**15**	putting the adverbial first
6	time	**16**	position: frequency, probability
7	frequency	**17**	position: degree, extent
8	duration	**18**	position: emphasizing
9	degree	**19**	position: focusing
10	extent		

1 adverbs and adverbials

It is important to know the difference between **adverbs** and **adverbials**. **Adverbials** are words or phrases that give information about when, how, where, or in what circumstances something happens. They have a functional role in a clause. An **adverb**, on the other hand, is a single word that may be used as an adverbial. In fact an adverbial is very often an adverb, but an adverbial may also be a phrase. A few noun phrases can also be used in this way.

The main types of adverbial indicate manner, aspect, opinion, place, time, frequency, duration, degree, extent, emphasis, focus, and probability. These are explained below, and then information is given on the position of adverbials in a clause.

→ See **Sentence connectors** for information on adverbials that are used to indicate connections between clauses

2 manner

Adverbials of manner are used to describe the way in which something happens or is done. They may be adverbs, adverb phrases, or prepositional phrases.

They looked anxiously at each other.
He did not play well enough to win.
She listened with great patience as he told his story.

Adverbials of manner are usually adverbs of manner. Most of these are formed by adding -ly to an adjective. For example, the adverbs **quietly** and **badly** are formed by adding -ly to the adjectives **quiet** and **bad**.

I didn't play badly.
He reported accurately what they had said.

Some adverbs of manner have the same form as adjectives and have similar meanings. These are the ones most commonly used:

direct	late	right	straight
fast	loud	slow	tight
hard	quick	solo	wrong

I've always been interested in fast cars.
The driver was driving too fast.

The adverb of manner related to the adjective **good** is **well**.

He is a good dancer.
He dances well.

Well can also be an adjective describing someone's health.

'How are you?' – 'I am very well, thank you.'

→ See **well**

3 viewpoint adverbs

Not all adverbs ending in *-ly* are adverbs of manner. You use *-ly* adverbs formed from classifying adjectives to focus on a particular aspect of the topic. For example, if you want to say that something is important from a political point of view, you can say that it is '**politically important**'. Here is a list of the most common of these adverbs:

biologically	geographically	politically	statistically
commercially	intellectually	psychologically	technically
economically	logically	racially	visually
emotionally	morally	scientifically	
financially	outwardly	socially	

It would have been politically damaging for him to retreat.
We've had a very bad year financially.

Speaking is sometimes added to these adverbs. For example, '**technically speaking**' can be used to mean 'from a technical point of view'.

He's not a doctor, technically speaking.
There are some signs of recovery, economically speaking, in the latest figures.

4 opinion

Other *-ly* adverbs are used as adverbials to show your reaction to, or your opinion of, the fact or event you are talking about. These are sometimes called **sentence adverbials**.

Surprisingly, most of my help came from the technicians.
Luckily, I had seen the play before so I knew what it was about.

→ See **Topic** entry **Opinions**

! BE CAREFUL

Some *-ly* adverbs have a different meaning from the adjective to which they seem to be related. For example, **hardly** has a different meaning from **hard**.

This has been a long hard day.
Her bedroom was so small she could hardly move in it.

→ See **bare – barely, hard – hardly, late – lately, scarce – scarcely, short – shortly – briefly, terrible – terribly**

5 place

Adverbials of place are used to say where something happens or where something goes. Again they are usually adverbs or prepositional phrases.

A plane flew overhead.
The children were playing in the park.
No birds or animals came near the body.

→ See **Topic** entry **Places**

6 time

Adverbials of time are used to say when something happens.

She will be here soon.
He was born on 3 April 1925.
Come and see me next week.

→ See **Topic** entries **Days and dates**, **Time**

7 frequency

Adverbials of frequency are used to say how often something happens.

Here is a list of adverbials of frequency, arranged from 'least often' to 'most often':

▶ never

That was a mistake. We'll never do it again.

▶ rarely, seldom, hardly ever, not much, infrequently

I very rarely wear a coat because I spend most of my time in a car.
We ate chips every night, but hardly ever had fish.
The bridge is used infrequently.

▶ occasionally, periodically, intermittently, sporadically, from time to time, now and then, once in a while, every so often

He still misbehaves occasionally.
Meetings are held periodically to monitor progress on the case.
Her daughters visited him from time to time when he was ill.
I go back to Yorkshire every now and then.
Once in a while she phoned him.

▶ sometimes

You must have noticed how tired he sometimes looks.

▶ often, frequently, regularly, a lot

They often spent Christmas in Brighton.
Iron and folic acid supplements are frequently given to pregnant women.
He also writes regularly for 'International Management' magazine.

▶ usually, generally, normally

They ate in the kitchen, as they usually did.
It is generally true that the darker the fruit the higher its iron content.
Normally, the public transport system in Paris carries 950,000 passengers a day.

▶ nearly always

They nearly always ate outside.

▶ always, all the time, constantly, continually

She's <u>always</u> late for everything.
He was looking at me <u>all the time</u>.
She cried almost <u>continually</u>.

Note that **regularly** and **periodically** show that something happens at fairly regular intervals. **Intermittently** and **sporadically** show that something happens at irregular intervals.

8 duration

Adverbials of duration are used to say how long something takes or lasts. Here is a list of adverbs used as adverbials of duration, arranged from 'least long' to 'longest':

▶ briefly

He paused <u>briefly</u>, then continued his speech.

▶ temporarily

The peace agreement has <u>temporarily</u> halted the civil war.

▶ long

Repairs to the cable did not take too <u>long</u>.

▶ indefinitely

I couldn't stay there <u>indefinitely</u>.

▶ always, permanently, forever

We will <u>always</u> remember his generous hospitality.
The only way to lose weight <u>permanently</u> is to completely change your attitudes toward food.
I think that we will live together <u>forever</u>.

! **BE CAREFUL**

Long is normally used only in questions and negative sentences.
Have you known her <u>long</u>?
I can't stay <u>long</u>.

→ See **long**

9 degree

Adverbials of degree are used to indicate the degree or intensity of a state or action. The following is a list of adverbs that are used as adverbials of degree and are used with verbs. They are arranged from 'very low degree' to 'very high degree'.

▶ little

On their way back to Marseille, they spoke very <u>little</u>.

▶ a bit, a little, slightly

This girl was <u>a bit</u> strange.
He complained <u>a little</u> of a pain between his shoulder blades.
Each person learns in a <u>slightly</u> different way.

▶ rather, fairly, quite, somewhat, sufficiently, adequately, moderately, pretty

I'm afraid it's <u>rather</u> a long story.
Both ships are <u>fairly</u> new.
A recent public opinion survey has come up with <u>somewhat</u> surprising results.
Thomson plays the part of a <u>moderately</u> successful actor.

I had a __pretty__ good idea what she was going to do.

▶ significantly, noticeably

The number of MPs now supporting him had increased __significantly__.
Standards of living were deteriorating rather __noticeably__.

▶ very much, a lot, a great deal, really, heavily, greatly, strongly, considerably, extensively, badly, dearly, deeply, hard, well

I like you __a lot__.
He depended __a great deal__ on his wife for support.
They were __really__ nice people.
He is __strongly__ influenced by Spanish painters such as Goya and El Greco.
Our meetings and conversations left me __deeply__ depressed.
It was snowing __hard__ by then.
Wash your hands __well__ with soap.

▶ remarkably, enormously, intensely, profoundly, immensely, tremendously, hugely, severely, radically, drastically

For his age, he was in __remarkably__ good shape.
The fast-food business is __intensely__ competitive.
Ten countries in Africa were __severely__ affected by the drought.
...two large groups of people with __radically__ different beliefs and cultures.
Services have been __drastically__ reduced.

Note that **quite** can also be used to indicate completeness or to emphasize a verb.

→ See **quite**

→ See **Adverbs and adverbials** for information on the use of adverbs of degree in front of adjectives and other adverbs

10 extent

Adverbials of extent are used to talk about how much something happens, or how true it is.

The following is a list of adverbs that are used as adverbials of extent and are used with verbs. They are arranged from 'smallest extent' to 'greatest extent'.

▶ partly, partially

It's __partly__ my fault.
Lisa is deaf in one ear and __partially__ blind.

▶ largely

His appeals have been __largely__ ignored.

▶ almost, nearly, practically, virtually

The beach was __nearly__ empty.
He'd known the old man __practically__ all his life.
It would have been __virtually__ impossible to research all the information.

▶ completely, entirely, totally, quite, fully, perfectly, altogether, utterly

This is an __entirely__ new approach.
The fire __totally__ destroyed the top floor.
They are __perfectly__ safe to eat.
When Andy stopped calling __altogether__, Julie found a new man.
These new laws are __utterly__ ridiculous.

11 emphasis

Emphasizing adverbials add emphasis to the action described by a verb. They are always adverbs. The following adverbs are used to add emphasis:

absolutely	just	quite	simply
certainly	positively	really	totally

I *quite* agree.
I *simply* adore this flat.

Some emphasizing adverbs are used to emphasize adjectives.

→ See **Adverbs and adverbials**

12 focus

Focusing adverbials are used to indicate the main thing involved in a situation. They are always adverbs. The following is a list of adverbs that can be used like this:

chiefly	mostly	predominantly	specially
especially	notably	primarily	specifically
mainly	particularly	principally	

I'm *particularly* interested in classical music.
We want *especially* to thank all of our friends who encouraged us.

Some focusing adverbs can be used to emphasize that only one thing is involved in what you are saying. The following adverbs can be used like this:

alone	just	purely	solely
exclusively	only	simply	

This is *solely* a matter of money.
It's a large canvas covered with *just* one colour.

The adverbs of extent **largely**, **partly**, and **entirely** can be used to focus on additional information.

The house was cheap *partly* because it was falling down.

Adverbs of frequency such as **usually** and **often** can also be used like this.

They often fought each other, *usually* as a result of arguments over money.

13 probability

Adverbials of probability are used to show how certain you are about something. The following adverbs and adverb phrases are used to show probability or certainty. They are arranged from 'least certain' to 'most certain'.

▶ conceivably

The mission could *conceivably* be accomplished within a week.

▶ possibly

Exercise will not only lower blood pressure but *possibly* protect against heart attacks.

▶ perhaps, maybe

Millson regarded her thoughtfully. *Perhaps* she was right.
Maybe she is in love.

▶ hopefully

Hopefully, you won't have any problems after reading this.

▶ probably

Van Gogh is <u>*probably*</u> *the best-known painter in the world.*

▶ presumably

He had gone to the reception desk, <u>*presumably*</u> *to check out.*

▶ almost certainly

The bombs are <u>*almost certainly*</u> *part of a much bigger conspiracy.*

▶ no doubt, doubtless

She's a very hardworking woman, as you <u>*no doubt*</u> *know by now.*
He will <u>*doubtless*</u> *try and persuade his colleagues to change their minds.*

▶ definitely

I'm <u>*definitely*</u> *going to get in touch with these people.*

14 position: manner, place, time

Adverbials of manner, place, and time usually come after the main verb. If the verb has an object, the adverbial comes after the object.

She sang <u>*beautifully*</u>.
Thomas made his decision <u>*immediately*</u>.

If more than one of these adverbials is used in a clause, the usual order is manner, then place, then time.

They were sitting <u>*quite happily*</u> <u>*in the car*</u>.
She spoke <u>*very well*</u> <u>*at the village hall*</u> <u>*last night*</u>.

If the object of the verb is a long one, the adverbial is sometimes put in front of it.

He could imagine <u>*all too easily*</u> *the consequences of being found by the owners.*
Later I discovered <u>*in a shop in Monmouth*</u> *a weekly magazine about horse-riding.*

You can also put an adverb of manner in front of the main verb.

She <u>*carefully*</u> *wrapped each glass in several layers of foam rubber.*
Dixon <u>*swiftly*</u> *decided to back down.*
Thousands of people <u>*silently*</u> *marched through the streets of London.*

Adverbs of manner are rarely put in front of the verb if the verb would then be the last word in the clause. For example, you would say, 'She listened carefully'. You would not say 'She carefully listened'. However, sentences such as 'Smith gladly obliged', where the adverb describes the attitude of the subject, are possible in stories and formal speech.

I <u>*gladly*</u> *gave in.*
His uncle <u>*readily*</u> *agreed.*

If the verb phrase contains one or more auxiliary verbs, you can put the adverb of manner in front of the main verb or after the first auxiliary verb, especially if that auxiliary verb is a modal.

The historical background has been <u>*very carefully*</u> *researched.*
She <u>*carefully*</u> *measured out his dose of medicine.*
They were all <u>*quietly*</u> *smiling.*
Still, Brian thought, one death would probably be <u>*quickly*</u> *forgotten.*
Arrangements can <u>*quickly*</u> *be made to reimburse you.*

Adverbs that show how well something is done go after the object of the verb if there is one. If there is no object, they go after the verb.

Thomas did everything <u>perfectly</u>.
You played <u>well</u>.

If the verb is in the passive, the adverb can also go in front of the verb, after any auxiliary verbs.

I was very <u>well</u> brought up.
Standing behind the trees, Bond was <u>well</u> hidden.

Most adverbs of manner that do not end in -*ly*, for example **hard** and **loud**, are only used after verbs or the objects of verbs.

You work <u>too hard</u>.

The exception is **fast**, which is also used in front of the -*ing* participles of verbs in the progressive form.

We are <u>fast</u> becoming a nation of screen addicts.

If the adverbial is a prepositional phrase, it is usually put at the end of the clause, not in front of the verb. For example, you say 'He looked at her in a strange way'. Don't say 'He in a strange way looked at her'.

The horse's teeth become worn down <u>in an unusual way</u>.
He had been taught <u>in the proper manner</u>.
It just fell out <u>by accident</u>.

15 putting the adverbial first

In stories and descriptive accounts, adverbials of manner are sometimes put at the beginning of a sentence. This position gives the adverbial more emphasis.

<u>Gently</u> I took hold of Mary's wrists to ease her arms away.
<u>Slowly</u> people began to leave.
<u>With a sigh</u>, he rose and walked away.

Similarly, adverbials of time and duration are often placed first in accounts of events.

<u>At eight o'clock</u> I went down for my breakfast.
<u>In 1937</u> he retired.
<u>For years</u> I had to hide what I was thinking.

Adverbials of place are often put first when describing a scene or telling a story, or when contrasting what happens in one place with what happens in another.

<u>In the kitchen</u> there was a message from his son.
<u>In Paris</u> there was a wave of student riots.

Note that in the following two examples, inversion occurs: that is, the verb is put in front of the subject.

<u>At the very top of the steps</u> was a large monument.
She rang the bell for Sylvia. <u>In</u> came a girl she had not seen before.

! BE CAREFUL

Inversion does not occur when the subject is a pronoun.

Off <u>they ran</u>.

You cannot use a pronoun and 'be' after an adverbial. For example, you cannot say 'At the top of the steps it was'. You say 'It was at the top of the steps'. When negative adverbials are put first, inversion occurs even when the subject is a pronoun.

Never have so few been commanded by so many.
On no account must they be let in.

→ See **Inversion**

Adverbials that indicate your opinion are sentence adverbials. They are usually put first in a sentence.

→ See **Topic** entry **Opinions**

16 position: frequency, probability

Adverbials of frequency and probability are often put after the first auxiliary verb, if there is one, or in front of the main verb. They are usually adverbs.

Landlords have *usually* been able to evade land reform.
I have *often* wondered what that means.
They can *probably* afford another one.
This *sometimes* led to trouble.

They can also be put first in a clause.

Sometimes people expect you to do more than is reasonable.
Presumably they were invited.

They are put after the linking verb **be** when there is no auxiliary verb.

They are *usually* right.
He was *definitely* scared.

Adverbs of probability are put in front of negative contractions such as **don't** and **won't**.

They *definitely don't* want their children breaking the rules.
He *probably doesn't* really want them at all.
It *probably won't* be that bad.

Maybe and **perhaps** are usually put first in a clause.

Maybe I ought to go back there.
Perhaps they just wanted to warn us off.

17 position: degree, extent

Some adverbs of degree and extent usually come in front of the main verb. If there are auxiliary verbs, they can come after the first auxiliary verb or in front of the main verb. The following adverbs are used like this:

almost	nearly	really	virtually
largely	rather	quite	

He *almost* crashed into a lorry.
She *really* enjoyed the party.
So far we have *largely* been looking at the new societies from the inside.
This finding has been *largely* ignored.

Other adverbs of degree and extent can come in front of the main verb, after the main verb, or after the object (if there is one). The following adverbs are used like this:

badly	heavily	severely
completely	little	strongly
greatly	seriously	totally

Mr Brooke <u>strongly</u> criticized the Bank of England.
I disagree <u>completely</u> with John Taylor.
That argument doesn't convince me <u>totally</u>.

Some adverbials of degree are always or nearly always used after a verb or the object of a verb. They are usually adverbs. The following adverbs and adverb phrases are used like this:

a bit	a lot	immensely	terribly
a great deal	hard	moderately	tremendously
a little	hugely	remarkably	

The audience enjoyed it <u>hugely</u>.
I missed you <u>terribly</u>.
Annual budgets varied <u>tremendously</u>.

18 position: emphasizing

Emphasizing adverbials usually come after the subject, after an auxiliary verb, or after **be**. They are always adverbs.

I <u>absolutely</u> agree.
I would <u>just</u> hate to have a daughter like her.
That kind of money is <u>simply</u> not available.

Emphasizing adverbials are put in front of negative contractions such as **don't** and **won't**.

It <u>just</u> can't be done.
That <u>simply</u> isn't true.

19 position: focusing

Focusing adverbials are generally put after the first auxiliary verb or in front of the main verb, or in front of the words you are focusing on. They are always adverbs.

Until now, the law has <u>mainly</u> had a positive role in this area.
We told him what he <u>chiefly</u> wanted to know.
I survive <u>mainly</u> by pleasing others.

If the verb is **be**, the focusing adverb is put after **be** if there is no auxiliary verb.

Economic development <u>is primarily</u> a question of getting more work done.

The focusing adverbs **alone** and **only** can be put in other positions in a clause.

→ See **alone – lonely**, **only**

! **BE CAREFUL**

You don't usually use an adverbial to separate a verb from its object. Don't say, for example, 'I like very much English'. You say 'I like English very much'.

---

advice – advise

1 'advice'

Advice /æd'vaɪs/ is a noun. If you give someone **advice**, you tell them what you think they should do.

Take my <u>advice</u> — stay away from him!
She promised to follow his <u>advice</u>.

Advice is an uncountable noun. Don't talk about 'advices' or 'an advice'. However, you can talk about **a piece of advice**.

What's the best piece of advice you've ever been given?
Could I give you one last piece of advice?

2 'advise'

Advise / æd'vaɪz/ is a verb. If you **advise** someone to do something, you say that you think they should do it.

He advised her to see a doctor.
He advised me not to buy it.

If you say to someone '**I advise you to...**', you are telling them that you think they should do it.

The operation will be tiring so I advise you to get some rest.

> **! BE CAREFUL**
>
> Don't use 'advise' without an object. Don't say, for example, 'He advised to leave as quickly as possible'. If you don't want to say who is receiving the advice, you say '**His advice was** to leave as quickly as possible'.
>
> *Diego's advice was to wait until the morning.*

affect – effect

1 'affect'

Affect /ə'fekt/ is a verb. To **affect** someone or something means to cause them to change, often in a negative way.

There are many ways in which computers can affect our lives.
The disease affected Jane's lungs.

2 'effect'

Effect /ɪ'fekt/ is usually a noun. An **effect** is something that happens or exists because something else has happened.

The report shows the effect of noise on people in the factories.
This has the effect of separating students from teachers.

You can say that something **has a** particular **effect on** something else.

Improvement in water supply can have a dramatic effect on health.
These changes will have a significant effect on our business.

Effect is sometimes a verb. If you **effect** something that you are trying to achieve, you succeed in achieving it. This is a formal use.

The new law will give us the power to effect change.

afford

If you **can afford** something, you have enough money to buy it. If you **can't afford** something, you don't have enough money to buy it.

It's too expensive — we can't afford it.
Do you think one day we'll be able to afford a new sofa?

Afford is almost always used with **can**, **could**, or **be able to**.

! BE CAREFUL

Don't say that someone 'affords' something. Don't say, for example, 'We afforded a new television'. Say 'We **were able to afford** a new television'.

You say that someone **can afford to have** something or **can afford to do** something.

Imagine a situation where everybody can afford to have a car.
I can't afford to rent this flat.

Don't say that someone 'can afford having' something or 'can afford doing' something.

Don't use a passive form of **afford**. Don't say that something 'can be afforded'. Instead you say that **people can afford** it.

We need to build houses that people can afford.

afloat

If someone or something is **afloat**, they are floating on water rather than sinking.

By kicking constantly he could stay afloat.
Her hooped skirt kept her afloat and saved her.

! BE CAREFUL

You do not use 'afloat' in front of a noun.

afraid – frightened

1 'afraid' and 'frightened'

If you are **afraid** or **frightened**, you feel fear because you think something bad will happen.

The children were so afraid that they ran away.
She felt frightened.

You can also say that you are **afraid of** someone or something, or **frightened of** them.

Tom is afraid of the dark.
They are frightened of their father.

If you don't want to do something because you think it might be harmful or dangerous, you can say that you are **afraid to do** it or **frightened to do** it.

Many crime victims are afraid to go to the police.
She was frightened to go out on her own.

! BE CAREFUL

Afraid is used only after linking verbs such as **be** and **feel**. Don't use it in front of a noun. For example, don't talk about 'an afraid child'. However, you can talk about 'a **frightened** child'.

He was acting like a frightened kid.

2 another meaning of 'afraid'

If you are worried about something, you can say that you are **afraid of** doing something wrong, or **afraid that** something will happen. You don't usually use 'frightened' in this way.

She was afraid that I might be embarrassed.
She was afraid of being late for school.

3 **'I'm afraid...'**

If you have to tell someone something and you think it might upset or annoy them, you can politely say **'I'm afraid...'**, **'I'm afraid so'**, or **'I'm afraid not'**. **'I'm afraid so'** means 'yes'. **'I'm afraid not'** means 'no', and both of these expressions are used as responses to questions.

'I'm afraid Sue isn't at her desk at the moment. Can I take a message?'
'I hear she's leaving. Is that right?' – 'I'm afraid so.'
'Can you come round this evening?' – 'I'm afraid not.'

after – afterwards – later

1 **'after'**

After is usually a preposition. If something happens **after** a particular time or event, it happens during the period that follows that time or event.

Vineeta came in just after midnight.
We'll hear about everything after dinner.

You can say that someone does something **after doing** something else.

After leaving school he worked as an accountant.
After completing and signing the form, please return it to me.

! **BE CAREFUL**

Don't say that someone is 'after' a particular age. You say that they are **over** that age.

She was well over fifty.

Don't use 'after' to say that something is at the back of something else. The word you use is **behind**.

I've parked behind the school.

2 **'afterwards'**

Afterwards is an adverb. If something happens **afterwards**, it happens after a particular event or time that has already been mentioned. You often use **afterwards** in expressions like **not long afterwards**, **soon afterwards**, and **shortly afterwards**.

She died soon afterwards.
Shortly afterwards her marriage broke up.

3 **'afterward'**

 Afterward is also sometimes used, especially in American English.

I left soon afterward.
Not long afterward, he made a trip from L.A. to San Jose.

4 **'later'**

Later is an adverb. You use **later** to refer to a time or situation that follows the time when you are speaking.

I'll go and see her later.

A little, **much**, and **not much** can be used with **later**.

A little later, the lights went out.
I learned all this much later.

You can use **after**, **afterwards**, or **later** following a phrase that mentions a period of time, in order to say when something happens.

I met him *five years after* his wife's death.
She wrote about it *six years afterwards*.
Ten minutes later he left the house.

after all

You use **after all** when you are mentioning an additional point that supports or helps explain what you have just said.

It had to be recognized, after all, that I was still a schoolboy.
I thought he might know where Sue is. After all, she is his wife.

You also use **after all** to say that something is true or may be true in spite of what had previously been thought.

Perhaps it isn't such a bad village after all.
I realised he was telling the truth after all.

! **BE CAREFUL**

Don't use 'after all' when you want to introduce a final point, question, or topic. Instead you use **finally** or **lastly**.

Finally I want to thank you all for coming.
Lastly I would like to ask about your future plans.

afternoon

The **afternoon** is the part of each day that begins at noon or lunchtime and ends at about six o'clock, or after it is dark in winter.

1 the present day

You refer to the afternoon of the present day as **this afternoon**.

I rang Pat this afternoon.
Can I see you this afternoon?

You refer to the afternoon of the previous day as **yesterday afternoon**.

Doctors operated on the injury yesterday afternoon.

You refer to the afternoon of the next day as **tomorrow afternoon**.

I'll be home tomorrow afternoon.

2 single events in the past

If you want to say that something happened during a particular afternoon in the past, you use **on**.

Olivia was due to arrive on Friday afternoon.
The box was delivered on the afternoon before my departure.

If you have been describing what happened during a particular day, you can then say that something happened **that afternoon** or **in the afternoon**.

That afternoon I phoned Bill.
I left Walsall in the afternoon and went by bus to Nottingham.

If you are talking about a day in the past and you want to mention that something had happened during the afternoon of the day before, you say that it had happened **the previous afternoon**.

He had spoken to me the previous afternoon.

If you want to say that something happened during the afternoon of the next day, you say that it happened **the following afternoon**.

I arrived at the village the following afternoon.

3 talking about the future

If you want to say that something will happen during a particular afternoon in the future, you use **on**.

The meeting will be on Wednesday afternoon.

If you are already talking about a day in the future, you can say that something will happen **in the afternoon**.

We will arrive at Pisa early in the morning, then in the afternoon we will go on to Florence.

If you are talking about a day in the future and you want to say that something will happen during the afternoon of the next day, you say that it will happen **the following afternoon**.

You leave on Thursday, arriving in Cairo at 9.45pm, then fly on to Luxor the following afternoon.

4 regular events

If something happens or happened regularly every afternoon, you say that it happens or happened **in the afternoon** or **in the afternoons**.

He is usually busy in the afternoons.
In the afternoon he would take a nap.

If you want to say that something happens regularly once a week during a particular afternoon, you use **on** followed by the name of a day of the week and **afternoons**.

She plays tennis on Saturday afternoons.

 In informal English, you can use **afternoons** without 'on' or 'in'.

She worked afternoons at her parents' shop.

5 exact times

If you have mentioned an exact time and you want to make it clear that you are talking about the afternoon rather than the early morning, you add **in the afternoon**.

We arrived at three in the afternoon.

→ See **Topic** entry **Time**

afterward

→ See **after – afterwards – later**

afterwards

→ See **after – afterwards – later**

aged

→ See **Topic** entry **Age**

ago

You use **ago** to say how much time has passed since something happened.
For example, if it is now Sunday and something happened on Thursday, it happened three days **ago**.

We met two months ago.
We got married about a year ago.

> **!** **BE CAREFUL**
>
> You use the past simple, not the present perfect, with **ago**. For example, you say 'He **died** four years ago'. Don't say 'He has died four years ago'.
>
> *Seven years ago, she gave birth to their daughter, Nelly.*
> *I did it just a moment ago.*

You use **ago** only when you are talking about a period of time measured back from the present. If you are talking about a period measured back from an earlier time, you use the past perfect with **before** or **previously**.

The centre had been opened some years before.
The accident had happened nearly two years previously.

Don't use **ago** and 'since' together. Don't say, for example, 'It is three years ago since it happened'. You say 'It happened **three years ago**' or '**It is three years since** it happened'.

He died two years ago.
It is two weeks since I wrote to him.

→ See **since**

> **!** **BE CAREFUL**
>
> Don't say, for example, 'It has been happening since three years ago'. You say 'It has been happening **for three years**'.
>
> *I have lived here for nearly twenty years.*
> *I have known you for a long time.*

→ See **for**

agree

1 **'agree'**

If someone says something and you say '**I agree**', you mean that you have the same opinion.

'That film was excellent.' – 'I agree.'

2 **'agree with'**

You can also say that you **agree with** someone or **agree with** what they say.

I agree with Mark.
He agreed with my idea.

> **!** **BE CAREFUL**
>
> Don't say that you 'agree something' or 'are agreed with' it. Also, when you use 'agree' in this sense, don't use the progressive. Don't say, for example, 'I am agreeing with Mark'.

3 'agree to'

If you **agree to** a suggestion or proposal, you say that you will allow it to happen.

He had agreed to the use of force.

However, don't say that someone 'agrees to' an invitation. You say that they **accept** it.

He accepted our invitation to the dinner party.

If someone asks you to do something and you **agree to do** it, you say that you will do it.

She agreed to lend me her car.
She finally agreed to come to the club on Wednesday.

! **BE CAREFUL**

Don't say that you 'agree doing' something.

4 'agree on'

If people reach a decision together about something, they **agree on** it.

We agreed on a date for the wedding.

5 'agree that'

You can say what the decision is using **agree** and a *that*-clause.

They agreed that the meeting should be postponed.

The passive form '**It was agreed that...**' is often used.

It was agreed that something had to be done.

aim

Someone's **aim** is what they intend to achieve.

My aim is to play for England.
It is our aim to have this matter sorted quickly.

You can say that someone does something **with the aim of** achieving a particular result. You do not say that someone does something 'with the aim to achieve' a result.

They had left before dawn with the aim of getting a grandstand seat.

The purpose of the meeting was to share information with the common aim of finding Louise safe and well.

alight

If something is **alight**, it is burning.

The fire was safely alight.
A candle was alight on the chest of drawers.

To **set** something **alight** means to cause it to start burning.

...paraffin that had been poured on the ground and set alight.

! **BE CAREFUL**

You do not use **alight** in front of a noun. You do not say, for example, 'People rushed out of the alight building'. You say 'People rushed out of the **burning** building'.

alike

If two or more things or people are **alike**, they are similar in some way.

They all looked alike to me.

> **!** **BE CAREFUL**
>
> Don't use 'alike' in front of a noun. Don't say, for example, 'They wore alike hats'. You say 'They wore **similar** hats'.
>
> *The two companies sell similar products.*

alive

If a person or animal is **alive**, they are not dead.

I think his father is still alive.
She knew the dog was alive.

> **!** **BE CAREFUL**
>
> Don't use 'alive' in front of a noun. Don't say, for example, 'I have no alive relatives' or 'They export alive animals'. Instead you use **living** to talk about people, or **live** /laɪv/ to talk about animals.
>
> *I have no living relatives.*
> *They export live animals.*

all

1 used as a determiner

You use **all** immediately in front of the plural form of a noun to talk about every thing or person of a particular kind. When you use **all** in front of the plural form of a noun, you use a plural form of a verb after it.

There is built-in storage space in all bedrooms.
All boys like to eat.

You can use **all** immediately in front of an uncountable noun when you are making a general statement about something. When you use **all** in front of an uncountable noun, you use a singular form of a verb after it.

All research will be done by experts.
All crime is serious.

2 used with other determiners

If you want to say something about every thing or person in a group, you use **all** or **all of**, followed by **the**, **these**, **those**, or a possessive determiner, followed by the plural form of a noun.

Staff are checking all the books to make sure they are suitable.
All my friends came to my wedding.
All of the defendants were proved guilty.

If you want to say something about the whole of a particular thing, you use **all** or **all of**, followed by **the**, **this**, **that**, or a possessive determiner, followed by an uncountable noun or the singular form of a countable noun.

They carried all the luggage into the hall.

I want to thank you for all your help.
I lost all of my money.

3 used in front of pronouns

You can use **all** or **all of** in front of the pronouns **this**, **that**, **these**, and **those**.

Oh dear, what are we going to do about all this?
Maybe all of that is true, but that's not what I asked.

However, in front of personal pronouns you must use **all of**. Don't use 'all'.

Listen, all of you.
It would be impossible to list all of it in one programme.

Don't use 'we' or 'they' after **all of**. Instead you use **us** or **them**.

He discussed it with all of us.
All of them were tired.

4 used after the subject

All can also be used after the subject of a clause. For example, instead of saying 'All our friends came', you can say 'Our friends **all** came'.

When there is no auxiliary verb, **all** goes in front of the verb, unless the verb is **be**.

We all felt guilty.

If the verb is **be**, **all** goes after **be**.

They were all asleep.

If there is an auxiliary verb, you put **all** after it.

It will all be over soon.

If there is more than one auxiliary verb, you put **all** after the first one.

The drawers had all been opened.

All can also come after the direct or indirect object of a verb when this object is a personal pronoun.

We treat them all with care.
I admire you all.

5 used as a pronoun

All can be a pronoun meaning 'everything' or 'the only thing'. It is often used like this in front of a relative clause.

It was the result of all that had happened previously.
All I remember is his first name.

6 'every'

Every has a similar meaning to **all**. '**Every** teacher was at the meeting' means the same as '**All** the teachers were at the meeting'.

However, there is a difference between **all** and **every** when you use them with expressions of time. For example, if you spend **all day** doing something, you spend the whole of one day doing it. If you do something **every day**, you keep doing it each day.

The airport was closed all morning after the accident.
She goes running every morning.

allow – permit – let – enable

Allow, **permit**, and **let** are all used to say that someone is given permission to do something, or is not prevented from doing something. **Permit** is a formal word.

1 'allow' and 'permit'

Allow and **permit** are followed by an object and a *to*-infinitive clause.

He allowed me to take the course.
They do not permit students to use calculators in exams.

You can say that people **are not allowed to** do something or **are not permitted to** do something.

Visitors are not allowed to take photographs in the museum.
Children are not permitted to use the swimming pool.

You can also say that something **is not allowed** or that it **is not permitted**.

Running was not allowed in the school.
Picnics are not permitted in the park.

2 'let'

Let is followed by an object and an infinitive without *to*.

Let me go to the party on Saturday. I won't be late.

You don't usually use 'let' in the passive. Don't say, for example, 'She was let go to the party'.

3 'enable'

Don't confuse any of these words with **enable**. To **enable** someone to do something means to give them the opportunity to do it. It does not mean to give them permission to do it.

Contraception enables women to plan their families.
The new test should enable doctors to detect the disease early.

all right

If you say that something is **all right**, you mean that it is satisfactory or acceptable.

Is everything all right, sir?

All right is the usual spelling. **Alright** is sometimes used, but many people think this spelling is incorrect.

almost – nearly

1 when you can use 'almost' or 'nearly'

Almost and **nearly** both mean 'not completely' or 'not quite'. They can be used in front of adjectives or noun phrases, or with verbs.

Dinner is almost ready.
We're nearly ready now.
I spent almost a month in China.
He worked there for nearly five years.
Jenny almost fainted.
He nearly died.

Almost and **nearly** can also be used in front of some time adverbials such as **every morning** and **every day**, and in front of some place adverbials such as **there**.

We go swimming almost every evening.
I drive to work nearly every day.
We are almost there.
I think we are nearly there.

If it is **almost** or **nearly** a particular time, it will be that time soon.

It was almost 10 p.m.
It's nearly dinner-time.

2 when you use 'almost'

Don't use 'nearly' in front of adverbs ending in '-ly'. You should use **almost** in front of these adverbs.

She said it almost angrily.
Your boss is almost certainly there.

You can say that one thing is **almost like** another. Don't say that one thing is 'nearly like' another.

It made me feel almost like a mother.

You can use **almost** in front of negative words such as **never, no, none, no-one, nothing**, and **nowhere**.

He almost never visits.
She speaks almost no English.

Don't use 'nearly' in front of negative words like these.

3 when you use 'nearly'

You can use **nearly** after **not** to emphasize a negative statement. For example, instead of saying 'The room is not big enough', you can say 'The room is **not nearly** big enough'.

It's not nearly as nice.
We don't do nearly enough to help.

Don't use 'almost' after **not** like this.

You can use **very** or **so** in front of **nearly**.

We were very nearly at the end of our journey.
She so nearly won the championship.

Don't use 'almost' with **very** or **so**.

alone – lonely

1 'alone'

If you are **alone**, you are not with any other people.

I wanted to be alone.
Barbara spent most of her time alone in the flat.

! BE CAREFUL

Don't use 'alone' in front of a noun. For example, don't talk about 'an alone woman'. Instead, you say 'a woman **on her own**'.

These holidays are popular with people on their own.

2 'lonely'

Don't confuse **alone** with **lonely**. If you are **lonely**, you are unhappy because you don't have any friends or anyone to talk to. **Lonely** is used either in front of a noun or after a linking verb like **be** or **feel**.

He was a lonely little boy.
She must be very lonely here.

along

If you look or move **along** something long and narrow such as a road, a river, or a corridor, you look or move towards one end of it.

Tim walked along the street.
He led me along a corridor.

If something is situated **along** something long and narrow such as a road, a river, or a corridor, it is situated in it or beside it.

There are trees all along the river.

! BE CAREFUL

Don't use 'along' to describe movement from one side of an area to another. For example, don't talk about going 'along' a desert. Instead you use **through** or **across**.

We cycled through the forest.
He wandered across Hyde Park.

a lot

→ See **lot**

aloud – loudly

1 'aloud'

If you say something **aloud**, you say it so that other people can hear you.

'Where are we?' Alex wondered aloud.

If you read **aloud** a piece of writing, you say the words so that people can hear what has been written.

She read aloud to us from the newspaper.

2 'loudly'

If you do something **loudly**, you make a lot of noise when you do it.

The audience laughed loudly.

already

1 referring to an action

You use **already** to say that something has happened before now, or that it has happened sooner than expected. When referring to an action, most speakers of British English use a perfect form with **already**. They put **already** after **have**, **has**, or **had**, or at the end of a clause.

He had already left when I arrived.
I've had tea already, thank you.

 Many speakers of American English, and some speakers of British English, use the past simple instead of the present perfect. For example, instead of saying 'I have already met him', they say 'I **already** met him' or 'I met him **already**'.

You already woke up the kids.
I told you already — he's a professor.

2 referring to a situation

Already is also used to say that a situation exists at an earlier time than expected.

If there is no auxiliary verb, you put **already** in front of the verb, unless the verb is **be**.

She already knows the answer.
By the middle of June the society already had more than 1000 members.

If the verb is **be**, you put **already** after it.

It was already dark.
Tickets are already available online.

If there is an auxiliary verb, you put **already** after the auxiliary verb.

This species is already considered endangered.

If there is more than one auxiliary verb, you put **already** after the first one.

Portable computers can already be plugged into TV sets.

You can put **already** at the beginning of a sentence for emphasis.

Already the company is three quarters of the way to the target.

alright

→ See **all right**

also – too – as well

You use **also**, **too**, or **as well** when you are giving more information about something.

1 'also'

Also is usually used in front of a verb. If there is no auxiliary verb, you put **also** immediately in front of the verb, unless the verb is **be**.

I also began to be interested in cricket.
They also helped out.

If the verb is **be**, you put **also** after it.

I was also an American.

If there is an auxiliary verb, you put **also** after the auxiliary verb.

The symptoms of the illness were also described in the book.

If there is more than one auxiliary verb, you put **also** after the first one.

We'll also be learning about healthy eating.

Also is sometimes put at the beginning of a clause.

She is very intelligent. Also, she is gorgeous.

> **!** **BE CAREFUL**
> Don't put **also** at the end of a clause.

2 **'too'**

You usually put **too** at the end of a clause.

Now the problem affects middle-class children, too.
I'll miss you, and Steve will, too.

💬 In conversation, **too** is used after a word or phrase when you are making a brief comment on something that has just been said.

'His father kicked him out of the house.' – 'Quite right, too.'
'They've finished mending the road.' – 'About time, too!'

Too is sometimes put after the first noun phrase in a clause.

I wondered whether I too would become ill.
Melissa, too, felt miserable.

However, the position of **too** can make a difference to the meaning of a sentence. '*I am an American too*' can mean either 'Like the person just mentioned, I am an American' or 'Besides having the other qualities just mentioned, I am an American'. However, '*I **too** am an American*' can only mean 'Like the person just mentioned, I am an American'.

Don't put **too** at the beginning of a sentence.

→ See **too**

3 **'as well'**

As well always goes at the end of a clause.

Filter coffee is better for your health than instant coffee. And it tastes nicer as well.
They will have a difficult year next year as well.

4 **negatives**

You don't usually use 'also', 'too', or 'as well' in negative clauses. Don't say, for example, '~~I'm not hungry and she's not hungry too~~'. You say 'I'm not hungry and she's not hungry **either**', 'I'm not hungry and **neither is she**', or 'I'm not hungry and **nor is she**'.

Edward wasn't at the ceremony, either.
'I don't normally drink coffee in the evening.' – 'Neither do I.'

→ See **either**, **neither**, **nor**

---

alternate – alternative

1 **'alternate'**

Alternate actions, events, or processes keep happening regularly after each other.

...the alternate contraction and relaxation of muscles.

If something happens on **alternate** days, it happens on one day, then does not happen on the next day, then happens again on the day after it, and so on. Things can also happen in **alternate** weeks, months, or years.

We saw each other on alternate Sunday nights.
The two courses are available in alternate years.

2 'alternative'

You use **alternative** to describe something that can be used, had, or done instead of something else.

But still people try to find <u>alternative</u> explanations.
There is, however, an <u>alternative</u> approach.

 Note that in American English, **alternate** is sometimes used with this meaning.

How would a clever researcher rule out this <u>alternate</u> explanation?

Alternative can also be a noun. An **alternative** to something is something else that you can have or do instead.

Food suppliers are working hard to provide organic <u>alternatives</u> to everyday foodstuffs.
A magistrate offered them a Domestic Education course as an <u>alternative</u> to prison.
There is no <u>alternative</u> to permanent storage.

You can also say that someone has two or more **alternatives**, meaning that they have two or more courses of action to choose from.

If a man is threatened with attack, he has five <u>alternatives</u>: he can fight, flee, hide, summon help, or try to appease his attacker.

Note that it used to be considered incorrect to talk about more than two alternatives.

alternately – alternatively

1 'alternately'

You use **alternately** to say that two actions or processes keep happening regularly after each other.

Each piece of material is washed <u>alternately</u> in soft water and coconut oil.
She became <u>alternately</u> angry and calm.

2 'alternatively'

You use **alternatively** to give a different explanation from one that has just been mentioned, or to suggest a different course of action.

It is on sale there now for just £9.97. <u>Alternatively</u>, you can buy the album by mail order for just £10.
<u>Alternatively</u>, you can use household bleach.

although – though

1 used as conjunctions

You use **although** or **though** to introduce a subordinate clause in which you mention something that contrasts with what you are saying in the main clause. **Though** is not used in very formal English.

I can't play the piano, <u>although</u> I took lessons for years.
It wasn't my decision, <u>though</u> I think I agree with it.

You can put **even** in front of **though** for emphasis.

She wore a coat, <u>even though</u> it was a very hot day.
*Don't put 'even' in front of **although**.*

> ❗ **BE CAREFUL**
>
> When a sentence begins with **although** or **though**, don't use 'but' or 'yet' to introduce the main clause. Don't say, for example, '~~Although he was late, yet he stopped to buy a sandwich~~'. You say 'Although he was late, **he stopped** to buy a sandwich'.
>
> *Although he was English, he spoke fluent French.*
> *Though he hadn't stopped working all day, he wasn't tired.*
>
> Don't use **although** or **though** in front of a noun phrase. Don't say, for example, '~~Although his hard work, he failed his exam~~'. You say '**In spite of** his hard work, he failed his exam' or '**Despite** his hard work, he failed his exam'.
>
> *In spite of poor health, my father was always cheerful.*
> *Despite her confidence, Cindy was uncertain what to do next.*

2 'though' used as an adverb

Though is sometimes an adverb. You use it when you are making a statement that contrasts with what you have just said. You usually put **though** after the first phrase in the sentence.

Fortunately though, this is a story with a happy ending.
For Ryan, though, it was a busy year.

💬 In conversation, you can also put **though** at the end of a sentence.

I can't stay. I'll have a coffee though.

Although is never an adverb.

---

altogether

1 'altogether'

Altogether means 'completely'.

The noise had stopped altogether.
We need an altogether different plan.

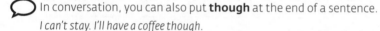 → See **Adverbs and adverbials** for a graded list of words used to indicate extent

You also use **altogether** to show that an amount is a total.

You will get £340 a week altogether.

2 'all together'

Don't confuse **altogether** with **all together**. You use **all together** to say that a group of people or things are together or do something together, and that none of them is missing.

It had been so long since we were all together — at home, secure, sheltered.

---

always

If something **always** happens, it happens at all times. If it has **always** happened, or will **always** happen, it has happened forever or will happen forever.

When **always** has one of these meanings, it is used with a simple form of a verb.

If there is no auxiliary verb, **always** goes in front of the verb, unless the verb is **be**.

Talking to Harold always cheered her up.
A man always remembers his first love.

If the verb is **be**, you usually put **always** after it.

She was always in a hurry.

If there is an auxiliary verb, you usually put **always** after it.

I've always been very careful.

If there is more than one auxiliary verb, you usually put **always** after the first one.

She had always been allowed to read whatever she wanted.

! **BE CAREFUL**

When you use **always** with this meaning, don't use it with a verb in a progressive form. Don't say, for example, 'Talking to Harold was always cheering her up'.

If you say that something is **always** happening, you mean that it happens often. When you use **always** like this, you use it with a progressive form of a verb.

Why are you always interrupting me?
The bed was always collapsing.
She's great — she's always laughing and smiling.

Don't use 'always' in comparisons, negative sentences, or questions to mean 'at any time in the past' or 'at any time in the future'. Instead you use **ever**. For example, don't say 'They got on better than always before'. You say 'They got on better than **ever** before'.

It was the biggest shooting star they had ever seen.
How will I ever manage to survive alone?

→ See **Adverbs and adverbials** for a graded list of words used to indicate frequency

---

a.m.

→ See **Topic** entry **Time**

---

among

1 groups

If you are **among** a group of people or things, you are surrounded by them.

Dev wandered among his guests.
Among his baggage was a medicine chest.

! **BE CAREFUL**

Don't say that you are 'among' two people or things. You say that you are **between** them.

Myra and Barbara sat in the back, the baby between them.
The island is midway between São Paulo and Porto Alegre.

→ See **between**

The form **amongst** is sometimes used, but is more formal than **among**.

The old farmhouse was hidden amongst orchards.

2 dividing

You can say that something is divided **among** or **between** a group of people. There is no difference in meaning.

He divided his money <u>among</u> his brothers and sisters.
Different scenes from the play are divided <u>between</u> five couples.

The form **amongst** is sometimes used, but is more formal than **among**.

I heard that flour was being distributed <u>amongst</u> the citizens.

3 differences

> **! BE CAREFUL**
>
> Don't use 'among' when you are talking about differences. Don't say, for example, 'I couldn't see any difference among the three chairs'. You say 'I couldn't see any difference **between** the three chairs'.

→ See **between**

amount

An **amount** of something is how much of it you have, need, or get.

They measured the <u>amount</u> of salt lost in sweat.
I was horrified by the <u>amount</u> of work I had to do.

You can talk about a **large amount** or a **small amount**. Don't talk about a 'big amount' or a 'little amount'.

Use only a <u>small amount</u> of water at first.
The army gave out <u>large amounts</u> of food.

When you use **amount** in the plural, you use a plural verb with it. For example, you say 'Large amounts of money **were** wasted'. Don't say 'Large amounts of money was wasted'.

Increasing amounts of force <u>are</u> necessary.
Very large amounts of money <u>are</u> required.

> **! BE CAREFUL**
>
> Don't talk about an 'amount' of things or people. For example, don't say 'There was an amount of chairs in the room'. You say 'There **were a number** of chairs in the room'. When you use **number** like this, you use a plural verb with it.
>
> *A <u>number</u> of offers <u>were</u> received.*

→ See **number**

an

→ See **a – an**

and

And can be used to link noun phrases, adjectives, adverbs, verbs, or clauses.

1 used for linking noun phrases

When you are talking about two things or people, you put **and** between two noun phrases.

I had a cup of tea <u>and</u> a biscuit.
The story is about a friendship between a boy <u>and</u> a girl.

When you are linking more than two noun phrases, you usually only put **and** in front of the last one.

They had fish, potatoes, and peas for dinner.
We need to build more roads, bridges and airports.

In lists like these, the comma before **and** is optional.

→ See **Reference** section **Punctuation**

2 used for linking adjectives

You put **and** between two adjectives when they come after linking verbs such as **be**, **seem**, and **feel**.

The room was large and square.
She felt cold and tired.

When there are more than two adjectives after a linking verb, you usually only put **and** in front of the last one.

We felt hot, tired, and thirsty.
The child is outgoing, happy and busy.

In lists like these, the comma before **and** is optional.

→ See **Reference** section **Punctuation**

When you use two or more adjectives in front of a noun, you don't usually put **and** between them.

She was wearing a beautiful pink dress.
We made rapid technological advance.

However, if the adjectives are colour adjectives, you must use **and**.

I bought a black and white swimming suit.

Similarly, if you are using adjectives that classify a noun in a similar way, you use **and**.

This is a social and educational dilemma.

You also use **and** when you put adjectives in front of a plural noun in order to talk about groups of things that have different or opposite qualities.

Both large and small firms deal with each other regularly.

! BE CAREFUL

Don't use 'and' to link adjectives when you want them to contrast with each other. For example, don't say 'We were ~~tired and happy~~'. You say 'We were tired **but** happy'.

They stayed in a small but comfortable hotel.

3 used for linking adverbs

You can use **and** to link adverbs.

Mary was breathing quietly and evenly.
They walked up and down, smiling.

4 used for linking verbs

You use **and** to link verbs when you are talking about actions performed by the same person, thing, or group.

I was shouting and swearing.
They sat and chatted.

If you want to say that someone does something repeatedly or for a long time, you can use **and** after a verb, and then repeat the verb.

They laughed and laughed.
Isaac didn't give up. He tried and tried.

 In conversation, you can sometimes use **and** after **try** or **wait** instead of using a *to*-infinitive clause. For example, instead of saying 'I'll try to get a newspaper', you say 'I'll try **and** get a newspaper'. In sentences like these you are describing one action, not two.

I'll try and answer the question.
I prefer to wait and see how things go.

You only use **and** like this when you are using a future form of **try** or **wait**, or when you are using the infinitive or imperative form.

If you **go and** do something or **come and** do something, you move from one place to another in order to do it.

I'll go and see him in the morning.
Would you like to come and stay with us?

5 used for linking clauses

And is often used to link clauses.

I came here in 1972 and I have lived here ever since.

When you are giving advice or a warning, you can use **and** to say what will happen if something is done. For example, instead of saying 'If you go by train, you'll get there quicker', you can say 'Go by train **and** you'll get there quicker'.

Do as you're told and you'll be all right.

You can put **and** at the beginning of a sentence when you are writing down what someone said, or writing in a conversational style.

I didn't mean to scare you. And I'm sorry I'm late.

6 leaving out repeated words

When you are linking verb phrases that contain the same auxiliary verb, you don't need to repeat the auxiliary verb.

John had already showered and changed.

Similarly, when you are linking nouns that have the same adjective, preposition, or determiner in front of them, you don't need to repeat the adjective, preposition, or determiner.

My mother and father worked hard.

7 'both' for emphasis

When you link two phrases using **and**, you can emphasize that what you are saying applies to both phrases by putting **both** in front of the first phrase.

They feel both anxiety and joy.

→ See **both**

8 negative sentences

You don't normally use 'and' to link groups of words in negative sentences.
For example, don't say 'She never reads and listens to stories'. You say 'She never reads **or** listens to stories'.

He was not exciting or good looking.

→ See **or**

However, you use **and** when you are talking about the possibility of two actions happening at the same time. For example, you say 'I can't think **and** talk at the same time'. You also use **and** if two noun phrases occur so frequently together that they are regarded as a single item. For example, **knife** and **fork** are always joined by **and** even in negative sentences such as 'I haven't got my knife **and** fork'.

Unions haven't taken health and safety seriously.

When two noun phrases are regarded as a single item like this, they almost always occur in a fixed order. For example, you talk about your **knife and fork**, not your 'fork and knife'.

angry

Angry is normally used to talk about someone's mood or feelings on a particular occasion. If someone is often angry, you can describe them as **bad-tempered**.

Are you angry with me for some reason?
She's a bad-tempered young lady.

If someone is very angry, you can describe them as **furious**.

Senior police officers are furious at the blunder.

If they are less angry, you can describe them as **annoyed** or **irritated**.

The Premier looked annoyed but calm.
...a man irritated by the barking of his neighbour's dog.

Typically, someone is **irritated** by something because it happens constantly or continually. If someone is often irritated, you can describe them as **irritable**.

anniversary – birthday

1 'anniversary'

An **anniversary** is a date when you remember something special that happened on that date in an earlier year.

It's our wedding anniversary today.
They celebrated the 400th anniversary of Shakespeare's birth.

2 'birthday'

Don't refer to the anniversary of the date when you were born as your 'anniversary'. You call it your **birthday**.

On my twelfth birthday I received a letter from my father.
It was 10 December, my daughter's birthday.

announcement – advertisement

1 'announcement'

An **announcement** is a public statement giving information about something.

The government made a public announcement about the progress of the talks.
The announcement gave details of small increases in taxes.

2 'advertisement'

An **advertisement** is an item in a newspaper, on television, on the internet, or in a public place, which tries to persuade you to buy something, or which gives you information about an event or job vacancy.

He bought the game after seeing an advertisement on TV.
They placed an advertisement for a sales assistant.

The abbreviated forms **advert** (in British English) and **ad** are also commonly used.

The advert is displayed at more than 4000 sites.
The agency is running a 60-second TV ad.

another

1 meaning 'one more'

Another thing or person means one more thing or person of the same kind. **Another** is usually followed by a singular countable noun.

Could I have another cup of coffee?
He opened another shop last month.

You can use **another** with 'few' or a number in front of a plural countable noun.

This will take another few minutes.
The woman lived for another ten days.

! BE CAREFUL

Don't use 'another' immediately in front of a plural countable noun or an uncountable noun. Don't say, for example, 'Another men came into the room'. You say '**More** men came into the room'.

We ought to have more police officers.
We need more information.

2 meaning 'different'

Another thing or person also means a different thing or person from the one you have been talking about.

It all happened in another country.
He mentioned the work of another colleague.

! BE CAREFUL

Don't use 'another' in front of a plural countable noun or an uncountable noun. Don't say, for example, 'They arrange things better in another countries'. You say 'They arrange things better in **other** countries'.

Other people had the same idea.
We bought toys, paints, books and other equipment.

3 used as a pronoun

Another is sometimes a pronoun.

I saw one girl whispering to another.

answer

1 used as a verb

When you **answer** someone who has asked you a question, you say something back to them. You can either say that someone **answers** a person or that they **answer** a question.

I didn't know how to answer her.
I tried my best to answer her questions.

! BE CAREFUL

You don't 'answer to' someone who has asked you a question, or 'answer to' their question.

2 used as a noun

An **answer** is something that you say to someone when they have asked you a question.

'Is there anyone here?' I asked. There was no answer.

An **answer to** a problem is a possible solution to it.

At first it seemed like the answer to all my problems.

! BE CAREFUL

Don't talk about an 'answer for' a problem.

anxious

1 'anxious about'

If you are **anxious about** someone or something, you are worried about them.

I was quite anxious about George.

2 'anxious to'

If you are **anxious to do** something, you want very much to do it.

We are very anxious to find out what really happened.
He seemed anxious to go.

! BE CAREFUL

Don't say that someone is 'anxious for doing' something.

3 'anxious for'

If you are **anxious for** something, you want to have it, or you want it to happen.

Many civil servants are anxious for promotion.
He was anxious for a deal, and we gave him the best we could.

4 'anxious that'

If you are **anxious that** something happen, or **anxious that** something **should** happen, you want it to happen very much.

My parents were anxious that I go to college.
He is anxious that there should be no delay.

5 'anxious' and 'nervous'

Don't confuse **anxious** with **nervous**. If you are **nervous**, you are rather frightened about something that you are going to do or experience.

I began to get nervous about crossing roads.
Both actors were very nervous on the day of the performance.

---

any

1 'any'

You use **any** in front of a singular countable noun to talk about each thing or person of a particular type.

Look it up in any large dictionary.
These are things that any man might do under pressure.

You use **any** in front of a plural countable noun to talk about all things or people of a particular type.

The patients know their rights like any other consumers.

You use **any** in front of an uncountable noun to talk about an amount of something.

Throw any leftovers in the bin.

When you use **any** in front of a singular countable noun or an uncountable noun, you use a singular form of a verb with it.

Any book that attracts children as much as this has to be taken seriously.
While any poverty remains, it must have the first priority.

When you use **any** in front of a plural countable noun, you use a plural form of a verb with it.

Before any decisions are made, ministers are carrying out a full enquiry.

2 'any of'

You use **any of** in front of a plural noun phrase beginning with **the**, **these**, **those**, or a possessive to talk about each thing or person belonging to a particular group.

It was more expensive than any of the other magazines.
You can find more information at any of our branches.

You can use either a plural or singular form of a verb with **any of** and a plural noun phrase. The singular form is more formal.

Find out if any of his colleagues were at the party.
There is no sign that any of these limits has been reached.

You use **any of** in front of a singular noun phrase beginning with **the**, **this**, **that**, or a possessive to talk about each part of something.

I'm not going to give you any of the money.
I feel guilty taking up any of your time.

You can also use **any of** in front of the pronouns **this**, **that**, **these**, **those**, **it**, **us**, **you**, or **them**.

Has any of this been helpful?
I don't believe any of it.

❗ BE CAREFUL

Don't use **any** without **of** in front of these pronouns. Don't say, for example, ~~Has any this been helpful?~~'

You can use either a plural or singular form of a verb with **any of** and the pronouns **these**, **those**, **us**, **you**, and **them**.

It didn't seem that any of us were ready.
I don't think any of us wants that.

③ used in questions and negatives

Any is used, especially after **have**, in questions and negative sentences.

Do you have any suggestions?
We don't have any sugar.

→ See **some**

④ used as a pronoun

Any can also be a pronoun.

Discuss it with your female colleagues, if you have any.
The meeting was different from any that had gone before.

anybody

→ See **anyone – anybody**

any more

If you want to say that something that happened in the past does not happen now, you say that it does not happen **any more**. **Any more** usually comes at the end of a clause.

There was no noise any more.
He can't hurt us any more.
I don't drive much any more.

❗ BE CAREFUL

Don't say that something does not happen 'no more'. Don't say, for example, ~~He can't hurt us no more~~.

 Any more is sometimes spelled **anymore**, especially in American English. Some speakers of British English think this spelling is incorrect.

The land isn't valuable anymore.

anyone – anybody

① 'anyone' and 'anybody'

You use **anyone** or **anybody** to talk about people in general, or about each person of a particular kind.

Anyone can miss a plane.
Anybody can go there.
If anyone asks where you are, I'll say you've just gone out.
If anybody calls, tell them I'll be back soon.

There is no difference in meaning between **anyone** and **anybody**, but **anybody** is more common in spoken English.

2 used in questions and negatives

Anyone and **anybody** are very commonly used in questions and negative sentences.

Was there anyone behind you?
There wasn't anybody in the room with her.

→ See **someone – somebody**

3 'any one'

Don't confuse **anyone** with **any one**. You use **any one** to emphasize that you are referring to only one of something.

There are about 350,000 properties for sale at any one time in Britain.

anyplace

→ See **anywhere**

anything

1 'anything'

You use **anything** to talk about something that might happen.

He was ready for anything.

You use **anything** to talk about each thing of a particular kind.

'Do you like chocolate?' – 'I like anything sweet.'

2 used in questions and negatives

Anything is very commonly used in questions and negative sentences.

Why do we have to show him anything?
I did not say anything.

→ See **something**

any time

If you can do something **any time** or **at any time**, you can do it whenever you want to.

If you'd like to give it a try, just come any time.
They can leave at any time.

When you use **any time** without 'at', you can spell it **anytime**.

I could have left anytime.
We'll be hearing from him anytime now.

If you want to say that something can be done whenever a particular thing is needed, you can use **any time** with a ***that*-clause**, usually without 'that'.

Any time you need him, let me know.
Any time the banks need to increase rates on loans they are passed on very quickly.

Any time is also used in negative sentences to mean 'some time'.

We mustn't waste <u>any time</u> in Athens.
I haven't had <u>any time</u> to learn how to use it properly.

When you use **any time** to mean 'some time', you do not spell it 'anytime'.

anyway

1 'anyway'

You use **anyway** when you are adding a remark to something you have just said. Usually the remark is something you have just thought of, and makes your previous statement seem less important or relevant.

If he doesn't apologize, I'm going to resign. I'm serious. That's what I feel like doing, <u>anyway</u>.
Mary doesn't want children. Not yet, <u>anyway</u>.

 You also use **anyway** to change the topic of a conversation, or to show that you want to end a conversation.

'I've got a terrible cold.' – 'Have you? That's a shame. <u>Anyway</u>, so you won't be coming this weekend?'
'<u>Anyway</u>, I'd better go and make dinner. I'll call you again tomorrow.'

2 'any way'

Don't confuse **anyway** with **any way**. You usually use **any way** in the phrase **in any way**, which means 'in any respect' or 'by any means'.

I am not connected <u>in any way</u> with the medical profession.
If I can help <u>in any way</u>, please ask.

anywhere

1 'anywhere' and 'anyplace'

Anywhere means in any place, or in any part of a particular place.

It is better to have it in the kitchen than <u>anywhere</u> else.
They are the oldest rock paintings <u>anywhere</u> in North America.

 Some speakers of American English say **anyplace** instead of 'anywhere'.

We're afraid to go <u>anyplace</u> alone.
Airports were more closely watched than <u>anyplace</u> else.

2 used in questions and negatives

Anywhere is very commonly used in questions and negative statements.

Is there a phone <u>anywhere</u>?
I decided not to go <u>anywhere</u> on holiday.

→ See **somewhere**

apart

1 'apart'

If two people are **apart**, they are not in each other's company.

They could not bear to be <u>apart</u>.

! **BE CAREFUL**

Don't use **apart** in front of a noun.

2 **'apart from'**

You use **apart from** when you mention an exception to a statement that you are making.

Apart from Ann, the car was empty.
She had no money, apart from the five pounds that Christopher had given her.

When **apart** is used in sentences like these, it must be followed by **from** and not by any other preposition.

 Note that in American English **aside from** is often used instead of **apart from**.

Aside from the location, we knew little about this park.

apologize

1 **'apologize'**

If you **apologize to** someone, you say you are sorry.

Afterwards George apologized to him personally.

! **BE CAREFUL**

Apologize must be followed by **to** in sentences like these. Don't say, for example, ~~'George apologized him'~~.

If you **apologize for** something you have done, or **apologize for** something someone else has done, you say you are sorry about it.

Later, Brad apologized to Simon for his rudeness.

2 **'I apologize' and 'I'm sorry'**

If you are sorry for something you have done, you can say **I apologize**. This is a formal use. In informal conversation, you are more likely to say **I'm sorry** or **Sorry**.

I apologize for being late.
Sorry I'm late.

→ See **Topic** entry **Apologizing**

appeal

In British English, if someone **appeals against** a legal decision or sentence, they formally ask a court to change the decision or reduce the sentence.

He appealed against the five year sentence he had been given.

 Speakers of American English do not use 'against' after **appeal**. They say that someone **appeals** a decision.

Casey's lawyer said he was appealing the interim decision.

appear

1 **'appear'**

When someone or something **appears**, they move into a position where you can see them.

A boat appeared on the horizon.

You also use **appear** to say that something becomes available for people to read or buy.

His second novel appeared under the title 'Getting By'.
It was about the time that smartphones first appeared in the shops.

2 'appear to'

If something **appears to** be true, it seems to be true. Similarly, if something **appears to** be a particular thing, it seems to be that thing. **Appear to** is more formal than 'seem to'.

The aircraft appears to have crashed near Kathmandu.
Their offer appears to be the most attractive.

apply

1 request formally

If you **apply to** have something or **apply for** something, you write asking formally to be allowed to have it or do it.

I've applied for another job.
Sally and Jack applied to adopt another child.

2 another meaning of 'apply'

Apply has another meaning. If you **apply** something to a surface, you put it onto the surface or rub it into it. This is a formal use of **apply**, which often occurs in written instructions.

Apply the cream evenly.
She applied a little make-up.

In conversation and in most kinds of writing, don't say that you **apply** something. You say that you **put** it **on**, **rub** it **on**, **rub** it **in**, or **spread** it **on**.

She put some cream on to soothe her sunburn.
Rub in some oil to darken it.

appreciate

If you **appreciate** something that someone has done for you, you are grateful to them because of it.

Thanks. I really appreciate your help.
We would appreciate guidance from an expert.

You can use **appreciate** with **it** and an *if*-clause to say politely that you would like someone to do something. For example, you can say 'I would **appreciate it if** you would deal with this matter urgently'.

We would really appreciate it if you could come.

! BE CAREFUL

You must use **it** in sentences like these. Don't say, for example, 'I would appreciate if you would deal with this matter urgently'.

approach

If you **approach** something, you get nearer to it.

He approached the front door.
...Nancy heard footsteps approaching the galley.

> **! BE CAREFUL**
>
> **Approach** is not followed by 'to'. You do not say, for example, ~~'He approached to the front door'~~.

approve

1 'approve of'

If you **approve of** someone or something, you have a good opinion of them.

His mother did not approve of Julie.
Stefan approved of the whole affair.

> **! BE CAREFUL**
>
> Don't say that you ~~'approve to'~~ someone or something.

2 'approve'

If someone in authority **approves** a plan or idea, they formally agree to it and say that it can happen.

The White House approved the proposal.
The directors quickly approved the new deal.

Don't use 'of' for this meaning of **approve**. Don't say, for example, ~~'The directors quickly approved of the new deal'~~.

arise – rise

Both **arise** and **rise** are irregular verbs. The other forms of **arise** are **arises**, **arising**, **arose**, **arisen**. The other forms of **rise** are **rises**, **rising**, **rose**, **risen**.

1 'arise'

When an opportunity, problem, or situation **arises**, it begins to exist.

He promised to help Rufus if the occasion arose.
A serious problem has arisen.

2 'rise'

When something **rises**, it moves upwards.

Several birds rose from the tree-tops.

If an amount **rises**, it increases.

Unemployment has risen sharply.
Their profits rose to $1.8 million.

armchair

→ See **chair – armchair**

army

→ See **Nouns** for information on collective nouns

around – round – about

1 **talking about movement: 'around', 'round', and 'about' as prepositions or adverbs**

When you are talking about movement in many different directions, you can use **around**, **round**, or **about**. You can use these words as adverbs.

It's so romantic up there, flying around in a small plane.
We wandered round for hours.
Police walk about patrolling the city.

You can also use these words as prepositions.

I've been walking around Moscow.
I spent a couple of hours driving round Richmond.
He looked about the room but couldn't see her.

 Speakers of American English usually use **around**, rather than 'round' or 'about', in this sense.

2 **talking about position: 'around' and 'round' as prepositions**

When one thing is **around** or **round** another thing, it surrounds it or is on all sides of it. In this sense, these words are prepositions. You can't use 'about' in this sense.

She was wearing a scarf round her head.
He had a towel wrapped around his head.
The earth moves round the sun.
The satellite passed around the earth.

 Speakers of American English usually use **around**, rather than 'round', in this sense.

3 **being present or available: 'around' and 'about' as adverbs**

When you are talking about something being generally present or available, you can use **around** or **about**, but not 'round', as adverbs.

There is a lot of talent around at the moment.
There are not that many jobs about.

4 **'around' and 'round' used in phrasal verbs**

You can also use **around** or **round** as the second part of some phrasal verbs, including **come (a)round**, **turn (a)round**, **look (a)round**, and **run (a)round**.

Don't wait for April to come round before planning your vegetable garden.
When interview time came around, Rachel was nervous.
Imogen got round the problem in a clever way.
A problem has developed and I don't know how to get around it.
He turned round and faced the window.
The old lady turned around angrily.

 American English uses only **around** in these cases.

5 'around', 'about' and 'round about' meaning 'approximately'

In conversation, **around**, **about** and **round about** are sometimes used to mean 'approximately'.

He owns <u>around</u> 200 acres.
She's <u>about</u> twenty years old.
I've been here for <u>round about</u> ten years.

! BE CAREFUL

Don't use 'round' like this. Don't say, for example, '~~He owns round 200 acres~~.'

arrival

When someone arrives at a place, you can talk about their **arrival** there. This is a rather formal use.

His <u>arrival</u> was hardly noticed.
A week after her <u>arrival</u>, we had a General School Meeting.

If you want to say that something happens immediately after someone arrives at a place, you can use a phrase beginning with **on**. Note that you must use **on**, not 'at', in sentences like these. You do not say, for example, '~~At his arrival in London, he went straight to Oxford Street~~'. You can say '**On his arrival** in London, he went straight to Oxford Street'.

<u>On his arrival</u> in Singapore he hired a secretary and rented his first office.
The British Council will book temporary hotel accommodation <u>on your arrival</u> in London.

The possessive determiner is often omitted. For example, instead of saying 'on their arrival', you can just say **on arrival**.

The principal guests were greeted <u>on arrival</u> by the Lord Mayor of London.
<u>On arrival</u> at the Station hotel in Dumfries he acknowledges a few familiar faces.

arrive – reach

1 'arrive'

You use **arrive** or **reach** to say that someone comes to a place at the end of a journey.

I'll tell Professor Sastri you<u>'ve arrived</u>.
He <u>reached</u> Bath in the late afternoon.

You usually say that someone **arrives at** a place.

We <u>arrived at</u> Victoria Station at 3 o'clock.

However, you say that someone **arrives in** a country or city.

He had <u>arrived in</u> France slightly ahead of schedule.
The ambassador <u>arrived in</u> Paris today.

! BE CAREFUL

Don't say that someone '~~arrives to~~' a place.

Don't use a preposition after **arrive** in front of **home**, **here**, **there**, **somewhere**, or **anywhere**.

We <u>arrived home</u> and I carried my suitcases up the stairs.
I <u>arrived here</u> yesterday.
She rarely <u>arrives anywhere</u> on time.

2 'reach'

Reach always takes a direct object. Don't say that someone 'reaches at' a place or that they 'have just reached'.

It was dark by the time I <u>reached</u> their house.

---

as

1 used in time clauses

If something happens **as** something else happens, it happens while the other thing is happening.

She cried <u>as</u> she told her story.
The play started <u>as</u> I got there.

You also use **as** to say that something is done whenever something happens.

Parts are replaced <u>as</u> they grow old.

! BE CAREFUL

Don't use 'as' simply to mean 'at the time that'. For example, don't say 'As I started work here, the pay was £20 an hour'. You say '**When** I started work here, the pay was £20 an hour'.

→ See **when**

2 meaning 'because'

As is often used to mean 'because' or 'since'.

She bought herself an iron <u>as</u> she felt she couldn't keep borrowing Anne's.
<u>As</u> he had been up since 4 a.m. he was now very tired.

→ See **because**

3 used with adjectives

You can use **as** in front of an adjective to say how someone or something is regarded or described.

They regarded manual work <u>as degrading</u>.
His teachers described him <u>as brilliant</u>.

! BE CAREFUL

Don't use 'as' after comparative adjectives. Don't say, for example, 'The trees are taller as the church'. You say 'The trees are taller **than** the church'.

She was much older <u>than</u> me.

4 used in prepositional phrases

You can also use **as** in prepositional phrases to say how someone or something is regarded, described, treated, or used.

Pluto was originally classified <u>as a planet</u>.
I treated business <u>as a game</u>.
I wanted to use him <u>as an agent</u>.

You can also use **as** in prepositional phrases to say what role or function someone or something has.

He worked <u>as a clerk</u>.
Bleach acts <u>as an antiseptic</u>.

5 **used in comparisons**

In writing, **as** is sometimes used to compare one action to another.

He looked over his shoulder as Jack had done.
She pushed him, as she had pushed her son.

Like and **the way** are used in a similar way.

→ See **like – as – the way**

! **BE CAREFUL**

You don't usually use 'as' in front of a noun phrase when you are comparing one thing or person to another. Don't say, for example, 'She sang as a bird'. You say 'She sang **like** a bird'.

He swam like a fish.
I am a worker like him.

However, you can make a comparison using **as**, an adjective or adverb, and another **as**. For example, you can say 'You're just **as bad as** your sister'.

→ See **as … as**

---

as … as

1 **in comparisons**

When you are comparing one person or thing to another, you can use **as** followed by an adjective or adverb followed by another **as**.

The ponds were as big as tennis courts.
I can't run as fast as you can.

After these expressions, you can use either a noun phrase and a verb, or a noun phrase on its own.

François understood the difficulties as well as Mark did.
I can't remember it as well as you.

If you use a personal pronoun on its own, it must be an object pronoun such as **me** or **him**. However, if the personal pronoun is followed by a verb, you must use a subject pronoun such as **I** or **he**.

He looked about as old as me.
You're as old as I am.

2 **using modifiers**

You can put words and expressions such as **almost**, **just**, and **at least** in front of **as … as** structures.

I could see almost as well at night as I could in sunlight.
He is just as strong as his brother.

3 **used with negatives**

You can use **as … as** structures in negative sentences.

They aren't as clever as they seem to be.
I don't notice things as well as I used to.
You've never been as late as this before.

So is sometimes used instead of the first **as**, but this use is not common.

Strikers are <u>not so important as</u> a good defence.

4 used for describing size or extent

You can use expressions such as **twice**, **three times**, or **half** in front of **as ... as** structures. You do this when you are indicating the size or extent of something by comparing it to something else.

The volcano is <u>twice as high as</u> Everest.
Water is <u>eight hundred times as dense as</u> air.

5 using just one 'as'

If it is quite clear what you are comparing someone or something to, you can omit the second **as** and the following noun phrase or clause.

A megaphone would be <u>as good</u>.
This fish is <u>twice as big</u>.

ashamed – embarrassed

1 'ashamed'

If you are **ashamed**, you feel sorry about something you did wrong.

He upset Dad, and he feels a bit <u>ashamed</u>.
They were <u>ashamed</u> to admit that they had lied.

You say that someone is **ashamed of** something, or **ashamed of** themselves.

Jen feels <u>ashamed of</u> the lies she told.
I was <u>ashamed of</u> myself for getting so angry.
It's nothing to be <u>ashamed of</u>.

2 'embarrassed'

If you are **embarrassed**, you are worried that people will laugh at you or think you are foolish.

*He looked a bit **embarrassed** when he noticed his mistake.*
She had been too <u>embarrassed</u> to ask her friends.

You say that someone is **embarrassed by** something or **embarrassed about** it.

He seemed <u>embarrassed by</u> the question.
I felt really <u>embarrassed about</u> singing in public.

! **BE CAREFUL**

Don't use 'of' in sentences like these. Don't say, for example, 'He seemed embarrassed of the question.'

as if

1 'as if' and 'as though'

You can use **as if** or **as though** at the beginning of a clause when you are describing how someone or something looks, or how someone behaves.

It's a wonderful item and in such good condition that it looks <u>as though</u> it was bought yesterday.
He lunged towards me <u>as if</u> he expected me to aim a gun at him.

Many people think it is incorrect to use 'was' in clauses of this type. They say you should use **were** instead.

He looked at me as if I were mad.
She remembered it all as if it were yesterday.

However, in conversation people usually use **was**.

The secretary spoke as though it was some kind of password.
He gave his orders as if this was only another training exercise.

You can use **was** or **were** in conversation, but in formal writing you should use **were**.

2 'like'

Some people say **like** instead of 'as if' or 'as though'.

He looked like he felt sorry for me.
Shaerl put up balloons all over the house like it was a six-year-old's party.

This use is generally regarded as incorrect.

---

ask

1 'ask'

You say that someone **asks** a question.

The police officer asked me a lot of questions.

> **!** **BE CAREFUL**
>
> Don't say that someone 'says a question'.

2 reporting questions

When you report a *yes/no*-question, you usually use **ask** with an *if*-clause.

She asked him if he spoke French.
Someone asked me if the work was going well.

You can also use a clause beginning with 'whether'.

I asked Brian whether he agreed.

When you report a *wh*-question, you usually use **ask** with a *wh*-clause.

I asked him what he wanted.
He asked me where I was going.

> **!** **BE CAREFUL**
>
> In the *wh*-clause, the subject and the verb do not change places. Don't say, for example, 'He asked me when was the train leaving'. You say 'He asked me when **the train was** leaving'.

You can say that someone **asks** someone else their name or their age.

He asked me my name.

You can say that someone **asks** someone else's opinion.

I was asked my opinion about the new car.

You don't need to say who a question is addressed to if this is clear from the context.

A young man asked if we were students.
I asked whether they liked the film.

Don't use 'to' when mentioning who a question is addressed to. Don't say, for example, 'He asked to me my name'.

3 direct reporting

You can use **ask** when reporting directly what someone says.

'How many languages can you speak?' he asked.
'Have you met him?' I asked.

4 reporting requests

When someone says that they want to be given something, you report this using **ask** and **for**. For example, if a man says to a waiter 'Can I have a glass of water?', you report this as 'He **asked for** a glass of water' or 'He **asked the waiter for** a glass of water'.

We asked for the bill.

When someone says that they want to speak to another person on the telephone, you say that they **ask for** that person.

He rang the office and asked for Cynthia.

When someone tells another person that they want them to do something, you report this using **ask** and either a *to*-infinitive clause or an *if*-clause.

He asked her to marry him.
I asked him if he could help.

→ See **Reporting**

---

asleep

→ See **sleep – asleep**

---

as long as

1 used in conditionals

You can use **as long as** or **so long as** to say that one thing is true only if another thing is true. For example, if you say '**As long as** you are under 16, you can take part in activities', you mean 'If you are under 16, you can take part in activities'.

You use a simple form after **as long as** and **so long as**.

We were all right as long as we kept quiet.
The president need not resign so long as the elections are supervised.

2 duration

You also use **as long as** to say that something lasts for a long period of time, or for as much time as possible.

Any stomach ache that persists for as long as one hour should be seen by a doctor.
I love football and I want to keep playing as long as I can.

Don't use 'so long as' in this way.

! BE CAREFUL

Don't use 'as long as' when you are talking about distances. Don't say, for example, 'I followed him as long as the bridge'. You say 'I followed him **as far as** the bridge'.

assignment – homework

1 'assignment'

An **assignment** is a task that someone is given to do, usually as part of their job.

My first major assignment as a reporter was to cover a large-scale riot.

An **assignment** is also a piece of academic work given to students.

The course has heavy reading assignments.
When class begins, he gives us an assignment and we have seven minutes to work at it.

 In American English, an **assignment** is also a piece of work given to students to do at home.

2 'homework'

Work given to schoolchildren to do at home is also called **homework**.

He never did any homework.

> **!** **BE CAREFUL**
>
> **Homework** is an uncountable noun. You do not talk about 'homeworks' or 'a homework'. Note that you do not say 'I have made my homework'. You say 'I have **done** my homework'.

---

assist – be present

1 'assist'

If you **assist** someone, you help them. **Assist** is a formal word.

We may be able to assist with the tuition fees.
They are raising money to assist hurricane victims.

2 'be present'

If you want to say that someone is there when something happens, you say that someone **is present**.

He had been present at the dance.
There is no need for me to be present.

---

as soon as

As soon as is a conjunction. You use **as soon as** to say that something will happen immediately after something else has happened.

As soon as we get the tickets we'll send them to you.

> **!** **BE CAREFUL**
>
> You usually use the present simple after **as soon as**. Don't use a future form. Don't say, for example, 'I will call you as soon as I will get home'. You say 'I will call you as soon as I **get** home'.
>
> *Ask him to come in, will you, as soon as he arrives.*

When you are talking about the past, you use the past simple or the past perfect after **as soon as**.

As soon as she got out of bed the telephone stopped ringing.
As soon as she had gone, he started eating the cake.

assure – ensure – insure

1 'assure'

If you **assure** someone that something is true or will happen, you tell them that it is definitely true or will definitely happen, often in order to make them less worried.

"I can assure you that neither of our two goalkeepers will be leaving," O'Leary said.
The government assured the public that there would be no increase in taxes.

2 'ensure' and 'insure'

In British English, to **ensure** that something happens means to make certain that it happens.

His reputation was enough to ensure that he was always welcome.

In American English, this word is usually spelled **insure**.

I shall try to insure that your stay is a pleasant one.

3 'insure'

Insure has another meaning. In both British and American English, if you **insure** your property, you pay money to a company so that if the property is lost, stolen, or damaged, the company will pay you a sum of money. In this meaning, the spelling is always **insure**, not 'ensure'.

Insure your baggage before you leave home.

as though

→ See **as if**

as usual

→ See **usual – usually**

as well

→ See **also – too – as well**

as well as

1 linking noun phrases

If you say that something is true of one person or thing **as well as** another, you are emphasizing that it is true not only of the second person or thing but also of the first one.

Women, as well as men, have the right to work.

2 linking adjectives

When you use **as well as** to link adjectives, you are emphasizing that something has not only the second quality but also the first one.

He is disorganised as well as rude.

3 linking clauses

You can use **as well as** in a similar way to link clauses. However, the second clause must be a clause beginning with an -*ing* form.

She manages the budget as well as ordering the equipment.

> **! BE CAREFUL**
>
> Don't use a finite clause after **as well as**. Don't say, for example, 'She manages the budget as well as she orders the equipment'.

---

at

1 place or position

At is used to talk about where something is or where something happens.

There was a staircase at the end of the hallway.

You often use **at** to mean 'next to' or 'beside'.

He waited at the door.

You say that someone sits **at** a table or desk.

I was sitting at my desk, reading.

If you want to mention the building where something is or where something happens, you usually use **at**.

We had dinner at a restaurant in Attleborough.
He lived at 14 Burnbank Gardens, Glasgow.

In British English, you say that someone is **at** school or **at** university when you want to say that they study there.

He had done some acting at school.
After a year at university, Ben joined the army.

 Speakers of American English usually say that someone is **in** school.

They met in high school.

→ See **school – university**

You say that something happens **at** a meeting, ceremony, or party.

The whole family were at the funeral.
They met at a dinner party.

2 time

At is also used to say when something happens.

You use **at** when you are mentioning a precise time.

At 2.30 a.m. he returned.
The train leaves at 9 a.m.

If you want to know the precise time when something happened or will happen, you can say **At what time...?** but people usually say **What time...?** or **When...?**

When does the boat leave?
'We're having a party on the beach.' – 'What time?' – 'At nine.'

You can say that something happened or will happen '**at** dawn', '**at** dusk', or '**at** night'.

She had come in at dawn.
It was ten o'clock at night.

However, you say that something happened or will happen '**in the** morning', '**in the** afternoon', or '**in the** evening'.

If something happens **at** a meal time, it happens while the meal is being eaten.

Let's talk about it at dinner.

You say that something happens **at** Christmas or **at** Easter.

She sent a card at Christmas.

However, you say that something happens **on** a particular day during Christmas or Easter.

They played cricket on Christmas Day.

In British English, **at** is usually used with **weekend**.

I went home at the weekend.

 American speakers usually use **on** or **over** with **weekend**.

I had a class on the weekend.
What are you doing over the weekend?

at first

→ See **first – firstly**

athletics – athletic

1 '**athletics**'

Athletics consists of sports such as running, the high jump, and the javelin.

He has retired from active athletics.

Athletics is an uncount noun. You use a singular form of a verb with it.

Athletics was developing rapidly.

 Note that the American term for this is **track and field**.

She never competed in track and field.

2 '**athletic**'

Athletic is an adjective. It can mean 'relating to athletics'.

...athletic trophies.

However, when you use **athletic** to describe a person, you mean that they are fit, healthy, and active. You do not mean that they take part in athletics.

...athletic young men.

at last

→ See **last – lastly**

attempt

→ See **try – attempt**

attendant

An **attendant** is someone whose job is to help people in a place such as a petrol station, a car park, or a cloakroom.

She stopped the car and asked the <u>attendant</u> to fill it up.

Someone who works in a shop selling goods to customers is not an 'attendant'. A person like this is called a **shop assistant**.

I asked the <u>shop assistant</u> for a receipt.

 In American English, this person is called a **sales clerk**.

She worked as a <u>sales clerk</u> in a record store.

attention

If you give someone or something your **attention**, you look at them, listen to them, or think about them carefully.

When he had their <u>attention</u>, he began his lecture.
He turned his <u>attention</u> back to his magazine.

You can also say that someone **pays attention to** something.

Look, <u>pay attention to</u> what I'm saying.
The food industry is beginning to <u>pay attention to</u> young consumers.

! BE CAREFUL

Don't say that someone '~~pays attention at~~' something.

audience

→ See **Nouns** for information on collective nouns

aural – oral

1 'aural'

Aural means 'relating to your ears and your sense of hearing'. **Aural** is pronounced /ˈɔːrəl/ or /ˈaʊrəl/.

I have used written and <u>aural</u> material.

2 'oral'

Oral means 'relating to your mouth'. It also describes things that involve speaking rather than writing. **Oral** is pronounced /ˈɔːrəl/.

...an <u>oral</u> test in German.

Both **aural** and **oral** are fairly formal words. They are used mainly to talk about teaching methods and examinations.

autumn

In British English, **autumn** or **the autumn** is the season between summer and winter.

Saturday was the first day of <u>autumn</u>.
The vote will take place in <u>the autumn</u>.

If you want to say that something happens every year during this season, you say that it happens **in autumn** or **in the autumn**.

In <u>autumn</u> the berries turn orange.
Birth rates are lowest <u>in the autumn</u>.

> **! BE CAREFUL**
>
> Don't say that something happens '~~in the autumns~~'.

 In American English, autumn is referred to as **the fall**.

In <u>the fall</u> we are going to England.

GRAMMAR FINDER

Auxiliary verbs

1 forms and uses

An **auxiliary verb** is a verb that is used with a main verb to form a verb phrase. The auxiliary verbs **be** and **have** are used in perfect and progressive forms. **Be** is also used to form passive verb phrases. The auxiliary verb **do** is most commonly used in questions and negative clauses.

I <u>am</u> feeling tired tonight.
They <u>have been</u> looking for you.
Thirteen people <u>were</u> killed.
<u>Did</u> you see him?
I <u>do</u> not remember her.

→ See **Verb forms**, **Questions**

→ See **not**, **do** for the use of **do** to emphasize or focus on an action

You put the auxiliary verbs you want to use in the following order: **have** (for perfect forms), **be** (for progressive forms), **be** (for the passive).

Twenty-eight flights <u>have been</u> cancelled.
Three broad strategies <u>are being</u> adopted.

> **! BE CAREFUL**
>
> Don't use the auxiliary verb **do** in combination with other auxiliary verbs.

Auxiliary verbs are often used without a main verb when the verb has already been used.

I didn't want to go but a friend of mine <u>did</u>.
'Have you been there before?' – 'Yes, I <u>have</u>.'

→ See **Ellipsis**

→ See **Topic** entry **Replies**

The different forms of the auxiliary verbs **be**, **have**, and **do** are shown in the following table.

	be	have	do
Simple present: with **I**	am	have	do
with **you**, **we**, **they** and plural noun phrases	are		
with **he**, **she**, **it** and singular noun phrases	is	has	does
Simple past: with **I**, **he**, **she**, **it** and singular noun phrases	was	had	did
with **you**, **we**, **they** and plural noun phrases	were		
Participles: -*ing* participle	being	having	doing
-*ed* participle	been	had	done

2 modals

Modals, such as **can**, **should**, **might**, and **may**, are also auxiliary verbs. You put them in front of all other auxiliary verbs.

The law will be changed.
She must have been dozing.

→ See **Modals**

3 contractions

→ See **Contractions** for information on the contracted forms of auxiliary verbs

avoid

If you **avoid** something, you take action to prevent it from happening to you.

We learned how to avoid a heart attack.
The bus swerved to avoid a collision.

If you **avoid doing** something, you make sure that you don't do it.

Thomas turned his head, trying to avoid breathing in the smoke.
You must avoid giving any unnecessary information.

! **BE CAREFUL**

Don't say that you 'avoid to do' something.

If you can't control or change the way you behave, don't say that you 'can't avoid' it. You say that you **can't help** it or that you **can't help yourself**.

It was so funny, I couldn't help laughing.
You know what his temper's like, he just can't help himself.

If someone does not allow you to do what you want to do, don't say that they 'avoid' you doing it. You say that they **prevent** you **from** doing it.

I wanted to prevent him from speaking.

await

If you **await** something, you expect it to come or happen, and you are often not intending to take some action until it comes or happens.

Daisy had remained behind to await her return.
We will await developments before deciding whether he should be allowed to continue.
We must await the results of field studies yet to come.

Await is a fairly common word in formal writing, but you do not usually use it in conversation. Instead you use **wait for**, often followed by an object and a *to*-infinitive. For example, instead of saying 'I awaited her reply', you say 'I **waited for her to reply**'.

I waited for Kate to return.
They just waited for me to die.

awake

Awake, **wake**, **awaken**, and **wake up** can all be intransitive verbs to say that someone becomes conscious again after being asleep. They can also be transitive verbs to say that someone makes you conscious when you have been asleep.

Awake and **wake** are irregular verbs. Their past tense forms are **awoke** and **woke**, and their -*ed* participles are **awoken** and **woken**.

1 'awake' and 'wake'

Awake and **wake** are fairly common in writing, especially as intransitive verbs.

I awoke from a deep sleep.
I sometimes wake at four in the morning.

2 'wake up'

 In ordinary conversation, you use **wake up**.

Ralph, wake up!
They went back to sleep but I woke them up again.

3 'awake' used as an adjective

Awake can also be an adjective. If someone is **awake**, they are not asleep. **Awake** is usually used after linking verbs like **be**, **stay**, **keep**, and **lie**.

An hour later he was still awake.
Cho stayed awake for a long time.

Awake is sometimes used after a noun.

She was the last person awake.

! BE CAREFUL

Don't use **awake** in front of a noun. Don't say, for example, 'an awake child'. Say 'a child who is awake'.

Don't say that someone is 'very awake'. You say that they are **wide awake** or **fully awake**.

He was wide awake by the time we reached my flat.
She got up, still not fully awake.

away

If you want to state the distance of one place from another place, you can say that it is that distance **away**.

Durban is over 300 kilometres <u>away</u>.
The camp is hundreds of miles <u>away</u> from the border.

If a place is very distant, you can say that it is **a long way away**, or that it is **a long way from** another place.

It is <u>a long way from</u> London.
Anna was still <u>a long way away</u>.

! **BE CAREFUL**

Don't use 'far' when you are stating a distance. Don't say, for example, '~~Durban is over 300 kilometres far~~'.

→ See **far**

Bb

back

1 used with an intransitive verb

You use **back** with an intransitive verb to say that someone returns to a place where they were before.

In six weeks we've got to go back to West Africa.
I went back to the kitchen.
I'll come back after dinner.

2 'be back'

In conversation, instead of saying that someone will 'come back', you often say that they will **be back**.

I imagine he'll be back for lunch.
Pete will be back from holiday next week.

! BE CAREFUL

You never use 'back' with the verb **return**. You do not say, for example, 'He returned back to his office'. You say 'He **returned** to his office'.

I returned from the Middle East in 1956.

3 used with a transitive verb

You use **back** with a transitive verb to say that someone or something is taken or sent to a place where they were before. **Back** usually goes after the direct object.

We brought Dolly back.
He took the tray back.

When the direct object is a pronoun, **back** always goes after it.

I brought him back to my room.
She put it back on the shelf.

However, when the direct object is a long noun group, or a noun group followed by a relative clause, you put **back** in front of the noun group.

He recently sent back his rented television set.
He put back the silk sock which had fallen out of the drawer.
He went to the market and brought back fresh food which he cooked at home.

4 returning to a former state

Back can also be used to say that someone or something returns to a state they were in before.

He went back to sleep.
...a £30 million plant which will turn all the waste back into sulphuric acid.

5 used as a noun

Back is also a noun. Your **back** is the part of your body from your neck to your waist that is on the opposite side to your chest and stomach.

We lay on our <u>backs</u> under the ash tree.
She tapped him on the <u>back</u>.

The **back** of an object is the side or part that is towards the rear or farthest from the front.

Many relatives sat at the <u>back</u> of the room, some visibly upset.
Keep some long-life milk at the <u>back</u> of your refrigerator.

The **back** of a door is the side which faces into a room or cupboard.

Pin your food list on the <u>back</u> of the larder door.

The **back** of a piece of paper is the side which has no writing on, or the side which you look at second.

Sign on the <u>back</u> of the prescription form.

 Note that in British English you do not talk about the 'back side' of a door or piece of paper. However, in American English, this construction is common.

Be sure to read the <u>back side</u> of this sheet.

backwards

→ See **-ward – -wards**

back yard

→ See **yard**

bad – badly

1 **'bad'**

Something that is **bad** is unpleasant, harmful, or undesirable.

I have some very <u>bad</u> news.
Sugar is <u>bad</u> for your teeth.

The comparative and superlative forms of **bad** are **worse** and **worst**.

Her grades are getting <u>worse</u> and <u>worse</u>.
This is the <u>worst</u> day of my life.

2 **'badly'**

Don't use 'bad' as an adverb. Don't say, for example, '~~They did bad in the elections~~'. You say 'They did **badly** in the elections'.

I cut myself <u>badly</u>.
The room was so <u>badly</u> lit I couldn't see what I was doing.

When **badly** is used like this, its comparative and superlative forms are **worse** and **worst**.

We played <u>worse</u> than in our previous match.
The south of England was the <u>worst</u> affected area.

Badly has another different meaning. If you need or want something **badly**, you need or want it very much.

I want this job so <u>badly</u>.
We <u>badly</u> need the money.
I am <u>badly</u> in need of advice.

For this meaning of **badly**, don't use the comparative and superlative forms 'worse' and 'worst'. Instead you use the forms **more badly** and **most badly**.

She wanted to see him <u>more badly</u> than ever.
Basketball is the sport that <u>most badly</u> needs new players.

→ See **Adverbs and adverbials** for a graded list of words used to indicate degree

bag

A **bag** is a paper or plastic container that something is sold in.

I bought a <u>bag</u> of crisps and a drink.
They sell herbs in plastic <u>bags</u>.

A bag of something can refer either to a bag and its contents, or just to the contents.

She bought <u>a bag of flour</u>.
He ate <u>a whole bag of sweets</u>.

A **bag** is also a soft container that you use to carry things in.

Mia put the shopping <u>bags</u> on the kitchen table.

You can call a woman's handbag her **bag**.

She opened her <u>bag</u> and took out her keys.

You can call someone's luggage their **bags**.

They went to their hotel room and unpacked their <u>bags</u>.

A single piece of luggage is a **case** or **suitcase**.

The driver helped me with my <u>case</u>.
She was carrying a heavy <u>suitcase</u>.

baggage

→ See **luggage – baggage**

bake

→ See **cook**

band – tape

1 **'band'**

A **band** is a narrow strip of material such as cloth or metal which is joined at the ends so that it can be fitted tightly round something.

...a panama hat with a red <u>band</u>.
A man with a black <u>band</u> around his arm stood alone.
Her hair was in a pony tail secured with a rubber <u>band</u>.

2 **'tape'**

You do not refer to the magnetic strips on which sounds are recorded as 'bands'. You call them **tapes**.

Do you want to put on a <u>tape</u>?
His manager persuaded him to make a <u>tape</u> of the song.

bank – bench – seat

1 'bank'

The **bank** of a river or lake is the ground at its edge.

There are new developments along both banks of the Thames.
She left her shoes on the bank and dived into the lake.

A **bank** is also a place where you can keep your money in an account.

You should ask your bank for a loan.

2 'bench' and 'seat'

Don't call a long, narrow seat in a park or garden a 'bank'. You call it a **bench** or a **seat**.

Greg sat on the bench and waited.
She sat on a seat in the park and read her magazine.

banknote

→ See **note – bill**

bar

 In American English, a place where you can buy and drink alcoholic drinks is called a **bar**.

Leaving Rita in a bar, I made for the town library.

In British English, a place like this is called a **pub**.

We used to go drinking in a pub called the Soldier's Arms.

→ See **pub – bar**

In British English, the rooms in a pub where people drink are called the **bars**. In a hotel, club, or theatre, the place where you can buy and drink alcoholic drinks is also called a **bar**.

...the terrace bar of the Continental Hotel.

bare – barely

1 'bare'

Bare is an adjective. If something is **bare**, it is not covered or decorated with anything.

The room has bare wooden floors.

If a part of the body is **bare**, it has no clothing.

Meg's feet were bare.

2 'barely'

Barely is an adverb. It has a totally different meaning from **bare**. You use **barely** to say that something is only just true or possible. For example, if you can **barely** do something, you can only just do it. If something is **barely** noticeable, you can only just notice it.

It was so dark we could barely see.
His whisper was barely audible.

> **!** **BE CAREFUL**
>
> Don't use 'not' with **barely**. Don't say, for example, '~~The temperature was not barely above freezing~~'. You say 'The temperature was **barely** above freezing'.
>
> If you use an auxiliary verb or modal with **barely**, you put the auxiliary verb or modal first. You say, for example, 'He **can barely** read'. Don't say '~~He barely can read~~'.
>
> _The audience could barely hear him._
>
> You can use **barely** to say that one thing happened immediately after another. For example, you can say 'We had **barely** started the meal when Jane arrived'.
>
> You use **when** or **before** after **barely**. Don't use 'than'. Don't say, for example, '~~We had barely started the meal than Jane arrived~~'.
>
> _I had barely arrived before he led me to the interview room._
> _They had barely sat down when they were told to leave._

→ See **Broad negatives**

bass – base

These words are both usually pronounced /beɪs/.

1 **'bass'**

A **bass** is a male singer who can sing very low notes.

...the great Russian bass Chaliapin.

A **bass** saxophone, guitar, or other musical instrument is one that has a lower range of notes than other instruments of its kind.

The girl vocalist had been joined by the lead and bass guitars.

A **bass** is also an edible fish that is found in rivers and the sea. There are several types of **bass**.

They unloaded their catch of cod and bass.

> **!** **BE CAREFUL**
>
> Note that this sense of the word **bass** is pronounced /bæs/.

2 **'base'**

The **base** of something is its lowest edge or part.

...the switch on the lamp base.
I had back pain starting at the base of my spine and shooting up it.

---

bath – bathe

Bath and **bathe** both have the _-ing_ participle **bathing** and the past tense and _-ed_ participle **bathed**. However, these are pronounced differently, depending on which of the two verbs they are associated with. **Bathing** and **bathed** are pronounced as follows:

▶ /ˈbɑːθɪŋ/ and /bɑːθt/ when they relate to **bath**

▶ /ˈbeɪðɪŋ/ and /beɪðd/ when they relate to **bathe**.

1 'bath'

If you **bath** someone, you wash them in a long rectangular container

The nurse will show you how to bath the baby.

Don't say that people **bath** themselves. You say that someone **has a bath** or **takes a bath**.

I'm going to have a bath.
She took a long hot bath.

 Bath is not a verb in American English. Americans use **bathe** (see the next section).

2 'bathe'

 American speakers sometimes say that people **bathe** /beɪð/.

I went back to my apartment to bathe and change.

In both British and American English, if you **bathe** a cut or wound, you wash it.

He bathed the cuts on her feet.

In formal or old-fashioned British English, when someone **bathes**, they swim or play in a lake or river or in the sea.

It is dangerous to bathe in the sea here.

3 'go swimming'

In modern English, you usually say that someone **goes swimming** or **goes for a swim**. American speakers sometimes say that someone **takes a swim**.

Let's go for a swim.
I went down to the ocean and took a swim.

---

be

1 forms

Be is the most common verb in English. It is used in many different ways.

The present tense forms of **be** are **am**, **are**, and **is**, and the past tense forms are **was** and **were**. **Be** is both an **auxiliary** and a **main verb**.

...a problem which is getting worse.
It was about four o'clock.

→ See **Auxiliary verbs**

Am, **is**, and **are** are not usually pronounced in full. When you write down what someone says, you usually represent **am** and **is** using **'m** and **'s**.

'I'm sorry,' I said.
'But it's not possible,' Lili said.
'Okay,' he said. 'Your brother's going to take you to Grafton.'

You can also represent **are** using **'re**, but only after a pronoun.

'We're winning,' he said.

You can also use the forms **'m**, **'s** and **'re** when you are writing in a conversational style.

→ See **Contractions**

2 used as an auxiliary

Be is an auxiliary when forming continuous tenses and passives.

She was watching us.
Several apartment buildings were destroyed.

→ See **Verb forms**

In conversation, **get** is often used to form passives.

→ See **get**

3 used as a main verb

You use **be** as a main verb when you are describing things or people or giving information about them. After **be**, you use a **complement**. A complement is either an adjective or a noun group.

We were very happy.
He is now a teenager.

→ See **Complements**

4 indicating someone's job

When **be** is followed by a noun group indicating a unique job or position within an organization, you do not have to put 'the' in front of the noun.

At one time you wanted to be President.

❗ BE CAREFUL

Make is sometimes used instead of 'be' to say how successful someone is in a particular job or role. For example, instead of saying 'He will be a good president', you can say 'He will **make** a good president'.

5 indicating age and cost

You can talk about a person's age by using **be** followed by a number.

Rose Gibson is twenty-seven.

You can also use **be** to say how much something costs.

How much is it?
It's five pounds.

→ See **Topic** entries **Age** and **Money**

6 with prepositional phrases

You can use many kinds of prepositional phrase after **be**.

He was still in a state of shock.
I'm from Dortmund originally.
...people who are under pressure.

7 with *to*-infinitives

You sometimes use *to*-infinitive clauses after **be**.

The talks are to begin tomorrow.
What is to be done?

→ See **Infinitives**

8 in questions and negative clauses

When you use **be** as a main verb in questions and negative clauses, you do not use the auxiliary 'do'.

Are you OK?
Is she Rick's sister?
I was not surprised.
It was not an easy task.

9 in continuous tenses

Be is not usually a main verb in continuous tenses. However, you can use it in continuous tenses to describe someone's behaviour at a particular time.

You're being very silly.

10 'be' and 'become'

Do not confuse **be** with **become**. **Be** is used to indicate that someone or something has a particular quality or nature, or is in a particular situation. **Become** is used to indicate that someone or something changes in some way.

Before he became Mayor he had been a tram driver.
It was not until 1845 that Texas became part of the U.S.A.

→ See **become**

11 after 'there'

Be is often used after **there** to indicate the existence or occurrence of something.

Clearly there is a problem here.
There are very few cars on this street.
There was nothing new in the letter.

! **BE CAREFUL**

You cannot use **be** without **there** to indicate that something exists or happens. You cannot say, for example, 'Another explanation is' or 'Another explanation must be'. You must say '**There is** another explanation' or '**There must be** another explanation'.

→ See **there**

12 after 'it'

Be is often used after **it** to describe something such as an experience, or to comment on a situation.

It was very quiet in the hut.
It was awkward keeping my news from Ted.
It's strange you should come today.

→ See **it**

13 'have been'

If you have visited a place and have now come back from it, British speakers say that you **have been** there.

I have been to Santander many times.

→ See **go**

be able to

→ See **can – could – be able to**

beach – shore – coast

1 'beach'

A **beach** is an area along the edge of a sea, lake, or wide river that is covered with sand or small stones. You can relax or play on a beach, or use it as a place to swim from.

He walked along the beach.
Children were building sandcastles on the beach.

2 'shore'

Shore is a more general word for the land along the edge of a sea, lake, or wide river.

He swam towards the shore.

3 'coast'

The **coast** is the border between the land and the sea, or the part of a country that is next to the sea.

We stayed in a small village on the west coast of Scotland.
There are industrial cities along the coast.

bear

1 'bear'

The other forms of **bear** are **bears**, **bore**, **borne**. However, the past form and *-ed* participle are rarely used.

If someone **bears** pain or a difficult situation, they accept it in a brave way.

Boys are encouraged to be tough and bear pain, to prove they're a man.

2 'endure'

Endure is used in a similar way.

Many people have to endure pain without specialist help.

3 'can't bear'

Bear is often used in negative sentences. If you **can't bear** something or someone, you dislike them very much.

I can't bear him!

If you **can't bear** to do something, you cannot do it because it makes you so unhappy.

She couldn't bear to talk about it.

4 'can't stand'

If you **can't stand** something or someone, you dislike them very much.

He kept on asking questions and I couldn't stand it any longer.
I can't stand people who lie.

! BE CAREFUL

Don't say that you 'can't stand to do something.

5 'tolerate' and 'put up with'

If you **tolerate** or **put up with** something, you accept it, although you don't like it or approve of it. **Tolerate** is more formal than **put up with**.

The school does not <u>tolerate</u> bad behaviour.
The local people have to <u>put up with</u> a lot of tourists.

bear – bare

These words are both pronounced /beə/.

1 'bear'

Bear can be a noun or a verb.

A **bear** is a large, strong wild animal with thick fur and sharp claws.
The <u>bear</u> stood on its hind legs.

If you **bear** a difficult situation, you accept it and are able to deal with it.
This disaster was more than some of them could <u>bear</u>.

2 'bare'

Bare is usually an adjective. Something that is **bare** has no covering.
The grass was warm under her <u>bare</u> feet.
The walls were <u>bare</u>.

→ See **bare – barely**

beat

To **beat** someone or something means to hit them several times very hard.
His stepfather used to <u>beat</u> him.
The rain was <u>beating</u> against the window.

If you **beat** someone in a game, you defeat them.
She always <u>beats</u> me when we play chess.

The past tense of **beat** is **beat**. The -ed participle is **beaten**.
Arsenal <u>beat</u> Oxford United 5-1.
They were <u>beaten</u> to death.

because

1 'because'

You use **because** when you are giving the reason for something.

If someone asks a question beginning with 'Why?', you can reply using **because**.
'Why can't you come?' – '<u>Because</u> I'm too busy.'

You use **because** with a reason clause when you are explaining a statement.
I couldn't see Elena's expression, <u>because</u> her head was turned.
<u>Because</u> it's an area of outstanding natural beauty, you can't build on it.

> **! BE CAREFUL**
>
> When you use **because** at the beginning of a sentence, don't put a phrase such as 'that is why' at the beginning of the second clause. Don't say, for example, 'Because you have been very ill, that is why you will understand how I feel'. You simply say 'Because you have been very ill, **you will understand** how I feel'.

2 'because of'

You can use **because of** before a noun phrase when you are giving the reason for something.

Many couples break up because of a lack of money.
Because of the heat, the front door was open.

---

become

1 'become'

When something or someone **becomes** a particular thing, they start to be that thing. If you **become** a doctor, a teacher, or a writer, for example, you start to be a doctor, a teacher, or a writer.

Greta wants to become a teacher.

If someone or something **becomes** a certain way, they start to have that quality.

When did you first become interested in politics?

The past tense of 'become' is **became**.

We became good friends at once.
The smell became stronger and stronger.

The -ed participle is **become**.

Life has become a lot harder since James died.

When **become** is followed by a singular noun phrase, the noun phrase usually begins with a determiner.

I became an engineer.
The young man became his friend.

However, when the noun phrase refers to a unique job or position within an organization, the determiner can be omitted.

In 1960 he became Ambassador to Hungary.
He became CEO last July.

The following words can be used to mean 'become'. These words can be followed only by an adjective. Don't use a noun phrase after them.

2 'get'

 In conversation, **get** is often used to talk about how people or things change and start to have a different quality.

It was getting dark.
She began to get suspicious.

3 'grow'

In written English, **grow** is often used to talk about how people or things change and start to have a different quality.

Some of her colleagues are growing impatient.
The sun grew so hot that they had to stop working.

4 'come'

If a dream, wish, or prediction **comes true**, it actually happens.

My wish had come true.

→ See **true – come true**

5 'go'

Go is used to talk about a sudden change in someone's body.

I went numb.
He went cold all over.

You say that someone **goes** blind or deaf.

She went blind twenty years ago.

Go is always used in the phrases **go wrong** and **go mad**.

Something has gone wrong with our car.
Tom went mad and started shouting at me.

6 'go' and 'turn'

If you want to say that someone or something becomes a different colour, you use **go** or **turn**.

Her hair was going grey.
The grass had turned brown.
When she heard the news, she went pale.
He turned bright red with embarrassment.

 In American English, you usually use **turn**, not 'go'.

> **!** | BE CAREFUL
>
> Don't use 'get' or 'become' when you are talking about someone's face changing colour. Don't say, for example, that someone 'gets pale' or 'becomes pale'.

before

1 talking about time

If something happens **before** a time or event, it happens earlier than that time or event.

We arrived just before two o'clock.
Before the First World War, farmers used horses instead of tractors.

You also use **before** when you are talking about the past and you want to refer to an earlier period of time. For example, if you are describing events that took place in 2010, you refer to 2009 as 'the year **before**'.

They had met in Bonn the weekend before.
They had forgotten the argument of the night before.

You use **before last** to refer to a period of time that came before the last one of its kind. For example, if today is Wednesday 18th September, you refer to Friday 13th September as 'last Friday', and Friday 6th September as 'the Friday **before last**'.

We met them on a camping holiday <u>the year before last</u>.
I have not slept since <u>the night before last</u>.

2 talking about position

Before is sometimes used to mean **in front of**. This is a formal or old-fashioned use. It is more common to use **in front of** with the same meaning.

He stood <u>before</u> the door leading to the cellar.
She stood <u>in front of</u> a mirror, combing her hair.

You use **before** or **in front of** when you are talking about the order in which things appear in speech or writing. For example, if you are describing the spelling of the word 'friend', you can say that the letter 'i' comes **before** or **in front of** the letter 'e'.

If you are giving someone directions, and you say that one place is a certain distance **before** another place, you mean that they will come to the first place first. Don't use 'in front of' with this meaning.

The turning is about two kilometres <u>before</u> the roundabout.

begin

→ See **start – begin**

behaviour

Someone's **behaviour** is the way they behave.

I had been puzzled by his <u>behaviour</u>.
...the obstinate <u>behaviour</u> of a small child.

 Note that the American spelling of this word is **behavior**.

behind

1 used as a preposition

If you are **behind** something, you are at the back of it.

They parked the motorcycle <u>behind</u> some bushes.
Just <u>behind</u> the cottage there was a shed.

! BE CAREFUL

Don't use 'of' after **behind**. Don't say, for example, '~~They parked the motorcycle behind of some bushes~~'.

If a project is **behind schedule**, it is completed later than planned or expected.

The project is several months <u>behind schedule</u>.

2 used as an adverb

Behind can also be an adverb.

The other police officers followed <u>behind</u>.
Several customers have fallen <u>behind</u> with their payments.

believe

1 'believe'

If you **believe** someone or **believe** what they say, you think that what they say is true.

I don't believe you.
Don't believe anything you read in that newspaper.

If you **believe** that something is true, you think that it is true.

I believe some of those lakes are over a hundred feet deep.
Police believe that the fire was started deliberately.

! BE CAREFUL

Believe is not used in the progressive. Don't say, for example, 'I am believing you'. You say 'I **believe** you'.

I believe that these findings should be presented to your readers.

2 'don't believe'

Instead of saying that you 'believe that something is not' true, you usually say that you **don't believe that it is** true.

I just don't believe that Alan had anything to do with it.

3 passive forms

You can say either that **it is believed that** something is true, or that something **is believed to** be true. For example, you can say '**It is believed that** the building is 700 years old' or 'The building **is believed to** be 700 years old'.

It is believed that two prisoners have escaped.
This is widely believed to be the tallest tree in England.

4 'believe in'

If you **believe in** something, you think that it exists.

I don't believe in ghosts.
My children still believe in Father Christmas.

If you **believe in** an idea or policy, you think it is good or right.

We believe in freedom of speech.

belong

1 showing possession

If something **belongs to** you, you own it or it is yours.

Everything you see here belongs to me.
You can't take the laptop home because it belongs to the company.

! BE CAREFUL

When **belong** is used with this meaning, it must be followed by **to**. Don't say, for example, 'This bag belongs me'. You say 'This bag **belongs to** me'.

Belong is not used in the progressive. Don't say, for example, 'This money is belonging to my sister'. You say 'This money **belongs to** my sister'.

The flat belongs to a man called Jimmy Roland.

2 another meaning of 'belong'

You can also use **belong** to say that someone or something is in the right place. **Belong** is used on its own, or is followed by an adverbial phrase such as **here**, **over there**, or **in the next room**.

The plates don't <u>belong in that cupboard</u>.
They need to feel they <u>belong</u>.

below

→ See **under – below – beneath**

beneath

→ See **under – below – beneath**

beside – besides

1 'beside'

If one thing is **beside** another, it is next to it or at the side of it.

<u>Beside</u> the shed was a huge tree.
I sat down <u>beside</u> my wife.

2 'besides' used as a preposition

Besides means 'in addition to' or 'as well as'.

What languages do you know <u>besides</u> Arabic and English?
There was only one person <u>besides</u> Jacques who knew Lorraine.

3 'besides' used to link clauses

You can use **besides** to introduce a clause beginning with an *-ing* form.

He writes novels and poems, <u>besides working</u> as a journalist.
<u>Besides being</u> good company, he was always ready to try anything.

! BE CAREFUL

You must use an *-ing* form in sentences like these. Don't say, for example, 'He writes novels and poems besides he works as a journalist'.

4 'besides' used as an adverb

You can use **besides** when you are making an additional point or giving an additional reason that you think is important.

I'll only be gone for five days, and <u>besides</u>, you'll have fun while I'm away.
The house was too big. <u>Besides</u>, we couldn't afford it.

best

Best is the superlative form of both **good** and **well**.

→ See **good – well**

If you **do your best**, you try as hard as you can to achieve something.

better

1 used as a comparative

Better is the comparative form of both **good** and **well**. Don't say that something is 'more good' or is done 'more well'. You say that it is **better** or is done **better**.

The results were better than expected.
Some people could ski better than others.

You can use words such as **even**, **far**, **a lot**, and **much** in front of **better**.

Bernard knew him even better than Annette did.
I decided that it would be far better just to wait.
I always feel much better after a bath.

2 another meaning of 'better'

You can also say that someone is **better**, or is feeling **better**. This means that they are recovering, or that they have recovered, from an illness or injury.

Her cold was better.
The doctor thinks I'll be better by the weekend.

3 'had better'

If you say that someone **had better** do something, you mean that they ought to do it. **Had better** is always followed by an infinitive without *to*. People usually shorten **had** to **'d**. They say '**I'd better**', '**We'd better**', and '**You'd better**'.

I'd better introduce myself.
We'd better go.

> ⚠ **BE CAREFUL**
>
> You must use **had** or **'d** in sentences like these. Don't say 'I better introduce myself' or 'I better go'.
>
> In negative sentences, **not** goes after **had better**.
>
> *We'd better not tell him what happened.*
>
> Don't say that someone 'hadn't better' do something.

between

1 describing position

If something is **between** two things, it has one of the things on one side of it and the other thing on the other side of it.

Janice was standing between the two men.
Northampton is roughly halfway between London and Birmingham.

> ⚠ **BE CAREFUL**
>
> Don't say that something is 'between' several things. You say that it is **among** them.

→ See **among**

2 differences

You talk about a difference **between** two or more things or people. Don't use 'among'.

What is the difference between football and soccer?
There isn't much difference between the three parties.

3 choosing

When someone makes a choice, you say that they choose **between** two or more things or people. Don't use 'among'.

It was difficult to choose <u>between</u> the two candidates.
You can choose <u>between</u> tomato, cheese or meat sauce on your pasta.

You say that someone chooses between one thing or person **and** another.

She had to choose <u>between</u> work <u>and</u> her family.

beware

If you tell someone to **beware** of a person or thing, you are warning them that the person or thing may harm them.

<u>Beware</u> of the dog.
I would <u>beware</u> of companies which depend on one product only.

Beware is only an imperative or infinitive. It does not have any other forms such as 'bewares', 'bewaring', or 'bewared'.

bid

1 'bid' in offers of payment

If you **bid** for something that is being sold, you offer to pay a particular amount of money for it. When **bid** has this meaning, its past tense and past participle is **bid**.

He <u>bid</u> a quarter of a million pounds for the portrait.

2 'bid' in greetings and farewells

People used to use **bid** with expressions like **good day** and **farewell**. This use still occurs sometimes in stories. When **bid** has this meaning, its past tense is either **bid** or **bade** and its past participle is either **bid** or **bidden**.

The old woman brought him his coffee and shyly <u>bid</u> him goodbye.
We <u>bade</u> Nandron a goodbye which was not returned.
Tom <u>had bid</u> her a good evening.
We <u>had bidden</u> them good night.

In modern English, you use **say** instead of 'bid' in sentences like these.

I <u>said</u> good evening to them.
Gertrude had already had her supper and had <u>said</u> good night to Guy.

However, when you use **say**, the indirect object goes after the direct object. You do not say '~~I said them good evening~~'.

big – large – great

Big, **large**, and **great** are used to talk about size. They can all be used in front of countable nouns, but only **great** can be used in front of uncountable nouns.

1 describing objects

Big, **large**, and **great** can all be used to describe objects. **Big** is the word you usually use in conversation. **Large** is more formal. **Great** is used in stories to show that something is very impressive because of its size.

'Where is Mark?' – 'Over there, by that <u>big</u> tree.'

The driver swerved to avoid a large tree.
A great tree had fallen across the river.

2 describing amounts

When you are describing amounts, you usually use **large**.

She made a very large amount of money.
They export large quantities of corn.

! BE CAREFUL

Don't use 'big' to describe amounts. Don't say, for example, ~~'She made a very big amount of money'~~.

3 describing feelings

When you are describing feelings or reactions, you usually use **great**.

He has great hopes for the future.
It was a great relief when we finally got home.

When **surprise** is a countable noun, you can use either **big** or **great** in front of it.

The announcement was a big surprise.
It will be no great surprise if Ryan wins.

Don't use 'large' to describe feelings or reactions.

4 describing problems

When you are describing a problem or danger, you use **big** or **great**.

The biggest problem at the moment is unemployment.
Many species are in great danger.

Don't use 'large' to describe a problem or danger.

5 showing importance

Great is used to say that a person or place is important or famous.

He was one of the greatest engineers of this century.
We visited the great cities of Europe.

6 used with other adjectives

In conversation, you can use **great** and **big** together in order to emphasize the size of something. You always put **great** first.

There was a great big hole in the road.

! BE CAREFUL

You can say that someone is in **great** pain, but you don't usually use 'big', 'large', or 'great' to describe an illness. Instead you use adjectives such as **bad**, **terrible**, or **severe**.

He's off work with a bad cold.
I started getting terrible headaches.

---

bill – check

In British English, a **bill** is a piece of paper showing how much money you must pay for a meal in a restaurant.

We paid our bill and left.

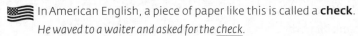 In American English, a piece of paper like this is called a **check**.

He waved to a waiter and asked for the check.

→ See **cheque – check** for another meaning of check

In both British and American English, a **bill** is a piece of paper that shows how much money you must pay for services such as electricity or gas.

If you are finding it difficult to pay your gas bill, please let us know quickly.
I ran up a huge phone bill.

 In American English, a **bill** is also a piece of paper money.

billfold

→ See **wallet**

billion

A **billion** is a thousand million, or 1,000,000,000.

The website gets almost a billion visits each month.

> **!** **BE CAREFUL**
>
> Don't add '-s' to **billion** when you put another number in front of it.
>
> *In January 1977, there were 4 billion people in the world.*

→ See **Reference** section **Numbers and fractions**

bit

1 'bit'

A **bit** is a small amount or a small part of something.

There's a bit of cake left.
He found a few bits of wood in the garage.

2 'a bit'

A bit means 'to a small degree'.

She looks a bit like her mother.
He was a bit deaf.

> **!** **BE CAREFUL**
>
> Don't use 'a bit' with an adjective in front of a noun. Don't say, for example, 'He was a bit deaf man'.

→ See **Adverbs and adverbials** for a graded list of words used to indicate degree

3 'a bit of'

In conversation and in less formal writing, you can use **a bit of** in front of **a** and a noun. You do this to make a statement seem less extreme.

Our room was a bit of a mess too.
His question came as a bit of a shock.

4 'a bit' and 'one bit' with negatives

You can add **a bit** or **one bit** at the end of a negative statement to make it stronger.

I don't like this one bit.
She hadn't changed a bit.

5 'not a bit'

You can use **not a bit** in front of an adjective to emphasize that someone or something does not have a particular quality. For example, if you say you are **not a bit** hungry, you mean you are not hungry at all.

They're not a bit interested.
I wasn't a bit surprised by the news.

6 'for a bit'

For a bit means 'for a short period of time'.

She was silent for a bit.
Why can't we stay here for a bit?

bite

When a person or animal **bites** something, they use their teeth to cut into it or through it. The past tense of **bite** is **bit**. The past participle is **bitten**.

My dog bit me.
You are quite liable to get bitten by an eel.

blame – fault

1 'blame' used as a verb

If you **blame** someone **for** something bad that has happened, you think that they made it happen.

Police blamed the bus driver for the accident.
Don't blame me!

You can **blame** something **on** someone.

Maya blames all her problems on her parents.

2 'to blame'

If someone is **to blame** for something bad that has happened, they caused it.

I knew I was partly to blame for the failure of the project.
The study found that schools are not to blame for the laziness of their pupils.

3 'fault'

Don't say that something is someone's 'blame'. You say that it is their **fault**.

This was all Jack's fault.
It's not our fault if the machine breaks down.

4 'at fault'

You can say that someone is **at fault**.

The other driver was at fault.

! **BE CAREFUL**
Don't say that someone is 'in fault'.

blind

Blind can be an adjective, a verb, or a noun.

1 used as an adjective

If someone is **blind**, they cannot see, because there is something wrong with their eyes.

He is ninety-four years of age and he is blind, deaf, and bad-tempered.

! **BE CAREFUL**
Don't say that 'someone's eyes are blind'.

2 used as a verb

If something **blinds** you, it makes you blind.

The acid went on her face and blinded her.

If something **blinds** you to a situation, it prevents you from being aware of it. This is the most common use of the verb **blind**.

He never let his love of his country blind him to his countrymen's faults.

3 used as a noun

You can refer to all the blind people in a country as **the blind**.

What do you think of the help that's given to the blind?

A **blind** is a wide roll of cloth or paper which you can pull down over a window in order to keep the light out, or to prevent people from looking in.

She slammed the window shut and pulled the blind.

 In American English, a device like this is sometimes called a **shade** or **window shade**.

blow up

→ See **explode – blow up**

board

1 'board'

If you **board** a bus, train, plane, or ship, you get on it or into it.

Gerry took a taxi to the station and boarded a train there.
I boarded the plane for San Diego.

2 'on board'

When you are **on board** a bus, train, plane, or ship, you are on it or in it.

There were 13 Britons on board the plane.
The crash killed all 57 passengers on board.

! **BE CAREFUL**
Don't use 'of' after **on board**. Don't say, for example, 'There were 13 Britons on board of the plane'.

boat – ship

1 'boat'

A **boat** is a small vessel for travelling on water, especially one that carries only a few people.

John took me down the river in the old boat.
...a fishing boat.

2 'ship'

A larger vessel is usually referred to as a **ship**.

The ship was due to sail the following morning.

However, in conversation large passenger ships which travel short distances are sometimes called **boats**.

She was getting off at Hamburg to take the boat to Stockholm.

> **!** **BE CAREFUL**
>
> When you are describing the way in which someone travels, you do not say that they travel 'by the boat' or 'by the ship'. You say that they travel **by boat** or **by ship**.
>
> *We are going by boat.*
> *They were sent home by ship.*

bonnet – hood

In British English, the metal cover over the engine of a car is called the **bonnet**.

I lifted the bonnet to see what the problem was.

 In American English, it is called the **hood**.

I looked under the hood to watch the mechanic at work.

boot – trunk

In British English, the **boot** of a car is the covered space, usually at the back, where you put things such as luggage or shopping.

Is the boot open?

 In American English, this part of a car is called the **trunk**.

We put our bags in the trunk.

border – frontier – boundary

1 'border'

The **border** between two countries is the dividing line between them.

They crossed the border into Mexico.
We stayed in a village near the German-Polish border.

2 'frontier'

A **frontier** is a border with official points for people to cross, often with guards.

Only three thousand soldiers were guarding the entire frontier.
They introduced stricter frontier controls.

You talk about one country's border or frontier **with** another.

She lives in a small Dutch town a mile from the <u>border</u> with Germany.
Spain reopened its <u>frontier with</u> Gibraltar.

3 **'boundary'**

The **boundary** of a region or area of land is its outer edge.

There are fences round the <u>boundary</u> of the National Park.

! BE CAREFUL

Don't talk about the 'boundary' of a country. Instead you talk about its **borders**.

These changes will be felt beyond the <u>borders</u> of Turkey.

---

bore

1 **'bore'**

Bore is a verb, and it is also the past tense of the verb **bear**.

→ See **bear**

If something or someone **bores** you, you don't find them interesting.

Life in the countryside <u>bores</u> me.
They used to enjoy his company, but now he <u>bored</u> them.

2 **'bored'**

You can say that you are **bored with** something or someone.

Tom was <u>bored with</u> the film.

If you have nothing to do, you can say that you are **bored**.

Many children get <u>bored</u> during the summer holidays.

3 **'boring'**

Don't confuse **bored** with **boring**. If you say that someone or something is **boring**, you mean that they bore you.

It's a very <u>boring</u> job.
He's a kind man, but he's a bit <u>boring</u>.

---

be born

When a baby **is born**, it comes out of its mother's body.

My mother was forty when I <u>was born</u>.

You often say that a person **was born** at a particular time or in a particular place.

Carla <u>was born</u> on April 10th.
Mary <u>was born</u> in Glasgow in 1999.

! BE CAREFUL

Don't say that someone 'has been born' at a particular time or in a particular place.

---

borrow – lend

If you **borrow** something that belongs to someone else, you use it for a period of time and then return it.

Could I borrow your car?
I borrowed this book from the library.

If you **lend** something you own to someone else, you allow them to have it or use it for a period of time. The past tense form and *-ed* participle of **lend** is **lent**.

I lent her £50.
Would you lend me your calculator?

> **! BE CAREFUL**
>
> You don't normally talk about borrowing or lending things that can't move. Don't say, for example, 'Can I borrow your garage next week?' You say 'Can I **use** your garage next week?'
>
> *You can use our washing machine.*
>
> Similarly, you don't usually say 'He lent me his office while he was on holiday'. You say 'He **let me use** his office while he was on holiday'.
>
> *She brought them mugs of coffee and let them use her bath.*

---

bosom

→ See **breast – bust – bosom**

---

both

1 used for emphasis

When you link two phrases using **and**, you can put **both** in front of the first phrase for emphasis. For example, if you want to emphasize that what you are saying is true of two things or people, you put **both** in front of the first of two noun phrases.

By that time both Robin and Drew were overseas.
Both she and the baby were completely safe.
They felt both anxiety and joy.

These changes will affect both teachers and students.

Similarly you can put **both** in front of the first of two adjectives, verb phrases, or adverbials.

Herbs are both beautiful and useful.
These headlines both worried and annoyed him.
She has won prizes both here and abroad.

The phrase after **both** should be of the same type as the phrase after **and**. For example, you say 'I told **both** Richard **and** George'. Don't say 'I both told Richard and George'.

2 used with one noun phrase

You can put **both** immediately in front of a single noun phrase when it refers to two people or things. For example, you can say '**Both boys** were Hungarian'. You can also say '**Both the boys** were Hungarian' or '**Both of the boys** were Hungarian'. There is no difference in meaning.

> **! BE CAREFUL**
>
> Don't say 'Both of boys were Hungarian' or 'The both boys were Hungarian'. Also, don't use 'two' after **both**. Don't say 'Both the two boys were Hungarian'.

You can use either **both** or **both of** in front of noun phrases beginning with **these**, **those**, or a possessive determiner.

The answer to <u>both these questions</u> is 'yes'.
I've got <u>both of their addresses</u>.

In front of personal pronouns you must use **both of**, not 'both'.

Are <u>both of you</u> ready?

Don't use 'we' or 'they' after **both of**. Instead you use **us** or **them**.

<u>Both of us</u> went to Balliol College, Oxford.
<u>Both of them</u> arrived late.

3 used after the subject

Both can also be used after the subject of a sentence. For example, instead of saying 'Both my sisters came', you can say 'My sisters **both** came'.

When there is no auxiliary verb, **both** goes in front of the verb, unless the verb is **be**.

They <u>both got</u> into the boat.

If the verb is **be**, **both** goes after **be**.

They <u>were both</u> schoolteachers.

If there is an auxiliary verb, you put **both** after it.

They <u>have both had</u> a good sleep.

If there is more than one auxiliary verb, you put **both** after the first one.

They <u>will both be sent</u> to prison.

Both can also come after a personal pronoun that is the direct or indirect object of the verb.

Rishi is coming to see <u>us both</u> next week.

4 negative sentences

You don't usually use 'both' in negative sentences. For example, don't say 'Both his students were not there'. You say '**Neither of** his students was there'.

→ See **neither**

Similarly, don't say 'I didn't see both of them'. You say 'I didn't see **either of** them'.

→ See **either**

5 used as a pronoun

Both can also be a pronoun.

A child should eat either meat or eggs daily, preferably <u>both</u>.

> **! BE CAREFUL**
> Don't use 'both' to talk about more than two things or people. Instead you use **all**.

→ See **all**

bottom

1 'bottom' and 'behind'

Your **bottom** is the part of your body that you sit on. You can use **bottom** in conversation and in most kinds of writing.

If she could change any part of her body, it would be her bottom.

 Speakers of American English usually say **behind** rather than 'bottom'.

My behind ached from cycling all day.

2 'buttocks'

In formal writing, you refer to this part of your body as your **buttocks**.

He strained the muscles on his shoulders and buttocks.

3 'bum' and 'butt'

 In conversation, some British speakers say **bum** instead of 'bottom', and some American speakers say **butt**. It is best to avoid both these words as many people think they are impolite.

boundary

→ See **border – frontier – boundary**

boxcar

→ See **carriage – car – truck – wagon**

brackets

→ See **Reference** section **Punctuation**

brake

→ See **break – brake**

brand – make

1 'brand'

A **brand** is a product that has its own name, and is made by a particular company. You usually use **brand** to talk about things that you buy in shops, such as food, drink, and clothes.

This is my favourite brand of cereal.
I bought one of the leading brands.

2 'make'

Don't confuse **brand** with **make**. You use **make** to talk about the names of products such as machines or cars, which last for a long time.

This is a very popular make of bike.

! **BE CAREFUL**

Don't use the plural form of a noun after **brand of** or **make of**. For example, don't talk about 'a make of vehicles'. Say 'a make of **vehicle**'.

Don't talk about the 'mark' of a product. For example, don't say 'What mark of coffee do you drink?' Say 'What **brand** of coffee do you drink?' Don't say 'What mark of car do you drive?' Say 'What **make** of car do you drive?'

break – brake

These words are both pronounced /breɪk/.

1 **'break'**

If you **break** something or it **breaks**, it divides into two or more pieces, often because it has been hit or dropped.

He fell through the window, breaking the glass.
Break the bread into pieces and place on a baking tray.

The past tense of **break** is **broke**. The -ed participle is **broken**.

She dropped the cup, which broke into several pieces.
Someone has broken the shop window.

→ See **broken**

2 **'brake'**

A **brake** is a device on a vehicle that makes it slow down or stop.

He took his foot off the brake.

Brake is also a verb. When a vehicle or its driver **brakes**, the driver makes the vehicle slow down or stop by using the brake.

The taxi braked suddenly.

breakfast

Your **breakfast** is your first meal of the day. You eat it in the morning, just after you get up.

They had eggs and toast for breakfast.
I open the mail immediately after breakfast.

! **BE CAREFUL**

You don't usually use 'a' with **breakfast**. Don't say, for example, She made a breakfast for everyone'. Say 'She made **breakfast** for everyone'.

→ See **Topic** entry **Meals**

breast – bust – bosom

1 **'breast'**

A woman's **breasts** are the two soft, round pieces of flesh on her chest that can produce milk to feed a baby.

...a beggar girl with a baby at her breast.
...women with small breasts.

2 **'bust'**

A woman's breasts can be referred to as her **bust**, especially when you are talking about their size. Note that **bust** refers to both breasts together. You do not talk about a woman's 'busts'.

She has a very large bust.

Bust is also used to talk about the measurement around the top part of a woman's body at the level of her breasts.

'Bust 34' means that the garment is a size 12.

3 **'bosom'**

A woman's breasts can also be referred to as her **bosom** /ˈbʊzəm/. This is an old-fashioned or literary word.

...hugging the cat to her bosom.

breathe – breath

1 **'breathe'**

Breathe /briːð/ is a verb. When people or animals **breathe**, they take air into their lungs and let it out again.

It was difficult for him to breathe.
Always breathe through your nose.

2 **'breath'**

Breath /breθ/ is a noun. Your **breath** is the air that you take into your lungs and let out again when you breathe.

She took a deep breath, then started to explain.
I could smell the coffee on his breath.

briefly

→ See **Adverbs and adverbials** for a list of words used to indicate duration

bring – take – fetch

1 **'bring'**

If you **bring** someone or something with you when you come to a place, you have them with you.

He would have to bring Judy with him.
Please bring your calculator to every lesson.

The past tense and -ed participle of **bring** is **brought**.

My secretary brought my mail to the house.
I've brought you a present.

If you ask someone to **bring** you something, you are asking them to carry or move it to the place where you are.

Can you bring me some water?

2 'take'

If you **take** someone or something to a place, you carry or drive them there. The past tense form of **take** is **took**. The -ed participle is **taken**.

He took the children to school.

If you **take** someone or something with you when you go to a place, you have them with you.

She gave me some books to take home.
Don't forget to take your umbrella.

3 'fetch'

If you **fetch** something, you go to the place where it is and return with it.

I went and fetched another glass.

---

bring up – raise – educate

1 'bring up'

When you **bring up** children, you look you look after them throughout their childhood, as their parent or guardian.

Tony was brought up in a working-class family.
When my parents died, my grandparents brought me up.

2 'raise'

Raise can be used to mean **bring up**.

Lynne raised three children on her own.
They want to get married and raise a family.

3 'educate'

Don't confuse **bring up** or **raise** with **educate**. When children are **educated**, they are taught different subjects over a long period, usually at school.

Many more schools are needed to educate the young.
He was educated in an English public school.

Britain – British – Briton

1 'Britain'

Britain or **Great Britain** consists of England, Scotland, and Wales. The **United Kingdom** consists of England, Scotland, Wales, and Northern Ireland. The **British Isles** refers to Britain, Ireland, and all the smaller islands around the coast.

2 'British'

The nationality of someone from the United Kingdom is **British**, although some people prefer to call themselves **English**, **Scottish**, **Welsh**, or **Northern Irish**. It is incorrect and may cause offence to call all British people 'English'.

You can refer to all the people who come from Britain as **the British**.

I don't think the British are good at hospitality.
The British have always displayed a healthy scepticism towards ideas.

The British can also be used to refer to a group of British people, for example the British representatives at an international conference.

The British have made these negotiations more complicated.
The British had come up with a bold and dangerous solution.

3 'Briton'

In writing, an individual British person can be referred to as a **Briton**.

The youth, a 17-year-old Briton, was searched and arrested.

→ See **Reference** section **Nationality words**

---

broad

→ See **wide – broad**

GRAMMAR FINDER

Broad negatives

1 broad negatives

A **broad negative** is one of a small group of words that are used to make a statement almost negative.

We were scarcely able to move.
Fathers and sons very seldom went together to football matches.

The five broad negatives are:

barely	rarely	seldom
hardly	scarcely	

The position of broad negatives within a clause is similar to that of **never**.

→ See **never**

2 with 'any' words

If you want to say that there is very little of something, you can use a broad negative with **any** or with a word that begins with '**any-**'.

There is rarely any difficulty in finding enough food.
Hardly anybody came.

3 'almost'

Instead of using a broad negative, you can use **almost** followed by a negative word such as **no** or **never**. For example, 'There was almost no food left' means the same as 'There was hardly any food left'.

They've almost no money for anything.
Sam almost never begins a conversation.

→ See **almost – nearly** for information on other uses of **almost**

4 question tags

If you make a **question tag** out of a statement that contains a broad negative, the tag at the end of the statement is normally positive, as it is with other negatives.

She's hardly the right person for the job, is she?
You rarely see that sort of thing these days, do you?

→ See **bare – barely, hard – hardly, scarce – scarcely, seldom**

broken

Broken is the past participle of the verb **break**.

He has broken a window with a ball.

Broken is also an adjective. A **broken** object has split into pieces or has cracked, for example because it has been hit or dropped.

He sweeps away the broken glass under the window.
...a long table covered in broken crockery.
He glanced at the broken lock he was still holding in his free hand.

If a machine or device is not functioning because there is something wrong with it, you do not usually say that it 'is broken'. You say that it **does not work** or **is not working**.

One of the lamps didn't work.
Chris sits beside him with sweaters on because the heater doesn't work.
The traffic lights weren't working properly.

bum

→ See **bottom**

burglar

→ See **thief – robber – burglar**

burgle – burglarize

In British English, if you **are burgled** or if your house **is burgled**, someone breaks into your house and steals things.

Our flat was burgled while we were on holiday.
Gail had recently been burgled.

 American speakers usually say that a house **is burglarized**.

Her home had been burglarized.

burst

When something **bursts** or when you **burst** it, it suddenly splits open, and air or some other substance comes out. The past tense and past participle of **burst** is **burst**, not 'bursted'.

As he braked, a tyre burst.

If you **burst** into tears, you suddenly begin to cry.

When the news was broken to Meehan he burst into tears.

! **BE CAREFUL**

Don't say that someone 'bursts in tears'.

Do not confuse **burst** with **bust**. If you **bust** something, you break or damage it so badly that it cannot be used.

→ See **bust**

bus – coach

A **bus** is a large motor vehicle that carries passengers by road from one place to another.

I'm waiting for the bus back to town.

In Britain, a comfortable bus that carries passengers on long journeys is called a **coach**.

The coach leaves Cardiff at twenty to eight.

 In America, a vehicle designed for long journeys is usually called a **bus**.

He took a bus from New York to Seattle.

→ See **Topic** entry **Transport**

business

1 **used as an uncountable noun**

Business is the work of making, buying, and selling goods or services.

Are you in San Francisco for business or pleasure?

! **BE CAREFUL**

When you use **business** in this sense, don't say 'a business'. Don't say, for example, 'We've got a business to do'. You say 'We've got **some business** to do'.

We may do some business with one of the major software companies in the United States.
We've still got some business to do. Do you mind waiting?

You can talk about a particular area of business using **the** followed by a noun followed by **business**.

Cindy works in the music business.
My brother is in the restaurant business.

2 **used as a countable noun**

A **business** is a company, shop, or organization that makes and sells goods or provides a service.

He set up a small travel business.

bust

Bust can be a verb, an adjective, or a noun. The past tense and past participle of the verb is either **bust** or **busted**.

1 **used as a verb**

If you **bust** something, you break or damage it so badly that it cannot be used. Note that you only use **bust** with this meaning in conversation. You do not use it in formal writing.

She found out about Jack busting the double-bass.

In informal English, if someone **is busted**, the police arrest them.

They were busted for possession of cannabis.

2 used as an adjective

In conversation, if you say that something is **bust**, you mean that it is broken or very badly damaged.

That clock's been <u>bust</u> for weeks.

 Note that in American English, the adjective is **busted** not 'bust'.

There he found a small writing table with a <u>busted</u> leg.

If a company **goes bust**, it loses so much money that it is forced to close down. You do not use this expression in formal English.

The company almost <u>went bust</u> in February.

3 used as a noun

A woman's **bust** is her breasts.

→ See **breast – bust – bosom**

but

You use **but** to introduce something that contrasts with what you have just said.

1 used to link clauses

But is usually used to link clauses.

It was a long walk <u>but</u> it was worth it.
I try to understand, <u>but</u> I can't.

You can put **but** at the beginning of a sentence when you are replying to someone, or writing in a conversational style.

'Somebody wants you on the telephone.' – '<u>But</u> nobody knows I'm here.'
I always thought that. <u>But</u> then I'm probably wrong.

2 used to link adjectives or adverbs

You can use **but** to link adjectives or adverbs that contrast with each other.

We stayed in a small <u>but</u> comfortable hotel.
Quickly <u>but</u> silently she ran out of the room.

3 used with negative words to mean 'only'

But is sometimes used after negative words such as **nothing**, **no-one**, **nowhere**, or **none**. A negative word followed by **but** means 'only'. For example, 'We have **nothing but** carrots' means 'We only have carrots'.

John had lived <u>nowhere but</u> the farm.
He cared about <u>no one but</u> himself.

4 meaning 'except'

But is also used after **all** and after words beginning with **every-** or **any-**. When **but** is used after one of these words, it means 'except'. For example, 'He enjoyed everything **but** maths' means 'He enjoyed everything **except** maths'.

There was no time for anything <u>but</u> work.
Could anyone <u>but</u> Wilhelm have done it?

butt

→ See **bottom**

buttocks

→ See **bottom**

buy

When you **buy** something, you get it by paying money for it. The past tense and -ed participle of **buy** is **bought**.

I'm going to buy everything that I need today.
He bought a first-class ticket.

If you pay for a drink for someone else, you say that you **buy** them a drink.

Let me buy you a drink.

> **!** **BE CAREFUL**
> Don't say 'Let me pay you a drink'.

by

① used in passives

By is most often used in passive sentences. If something is done or caused **by** a person or thing, that person or thing does it or causes it.

This view has been challenged by a number of researchers.
I was surprised by his anger.
He was knocked down by a bus.

When an -ed word is used like an adjective to describe a state rather than an action, it is not always followed by **by**. Some -ed words are followed by **with** or **in**.

The room was filled with flowers.
The walls of her flat are covered in dirt.

② used with time expressions

If something happens **by** a particular time, it happens at or before that time.

I'll be home by seven o'clock.
By 1995 the population had grown to 3 million.

> **!** **BE CAREFUL**
> **By** can only be used with this meaning as a preposition. Don't use it as a conjunction. Don't say, for example, 'By I had finished my lunch, we had to leave'. You say '**By the time** I had finished my lunch, we had to leave'.
> *By the time I went to bed, I was exhausted.*

③ used to describe position

You can use **by** to say that someone or something is at the side of a person or object.

I sat by her bed.
She lives in a cottage by the sea.

> **!** **BE CAREFUL**
>
> Don't use 'by' with the names of towns or cities. Don't say, for example, 'I was by Coventry when I ran out of petrol'. You say 'I was **near** Coventry when I ran out of petrol'.
>
> *Mandela was born near Elliotdale.*

4 **saying how something is done**

By can be used with some nouns to say how something is done. You don't usually put a determiner in front of the noun.

Can I pay by credit card?
I always go to work by bus.
He sent the form by email.

However, if you want to say that something is done using a particular object or tool, you often use **with**, rather than 'by'. **With** is followed by a determiner.

Clean the mirrors with a soft cloth.
He brushed back his hair with his hand.

You can use **by** with an -*ing* form to say how something is achieved.

Make the sauce by boiling the cream and stock together in a pan.
We saved a lot of money by booking our holiday online.

by far

→ See **very**

Cc

café – coffee

1 'café'

A **café** /'kæfeɪ/ is a place where you can buy drinks and simple meals or snacks. In Britain, **cafés** often don't sell alcoholic drinks. **Café** is sometimes spelled **cafe**.

Is there an internet café near here?
They've opened a cafe in the main square.

2 'coffee'

Coffee /'kɒfɪ/ is a hot drink.

Would you like a cup of coffee?

call

1 attracting attention

If you **call** something, you say it in a loud voice, usually because you are trying to attract someone's attention.

'Edward!' she called. 'Edward! Lunch is ready!'
I could hear a voice calling my name.
'Here's your drink,' Bob called to him.

2 telephoning

If you **call** a person or place, you telephone them.

Call me when you get home.
Greta called the office and complained.

When you use **call** like this, it is not followed by 'to'. Don't say, for example, 'I called to him at his London home'. You say 'I **called** him at his London home.

3 visiting

If someone **calls on** you, or if they **call**, they make a short visit in order to see you or deliver something.

He had called on Stephen at his London home.
The nurse calls at about 7 o'clock every morning.

 Call is not used like this without **on** in American English.

4 naming

If you **call** someone or something a particular name, you give them that name, or you address them by that name.

We decided to call our daughter Hannah.
'Pleased to meet you, Mr. Anderson.' – 'Please call me Mike.'

If you **call** someone or something a particular thing, you say they are that thing. You use **call** followed by a noun phrase, followed by an adjective or another noun phrase. You often use this construction when you are describing someone or something in a negative way.

He called the report unfair.
They called him a traitor.

> **! BE CAREFUL**
>
> Don't use 'as' with **call**. Don't say, for example, 'We decided to call our daughter as Hannah' or 'They called him as a traitor'.

called – named

You use **called** or **named** when you are giving the name of someone or something. **Named** is less common than **called**, and is not usually used in conversation.

Did you know a boy called Desmond?
We passed through a town called Monmouth.
A man named Richardson confessed to the theft.

You can use **called** either after a noun or after **be**.

She starred in a play called Katerina.
The book was called The Goalkeeper's Revenge.

You usually use **named** immediately after a noun.

The victim was an 18-year-old girl named Marinetta Jirkowski.

camp bed

→ See **cot – crib – camp bed**

can – could – be able to

These words are used to talk about ability, awareness, and possibility. They are also used to say that someone has permission to do something. These uses are dealt with separately in this entry. **Can** and **could** are called **modals**.

→ See **Modals**

Both **can** and **could** are followed by an infinitive without *to*.

I envy people who can sing.
I could work for twelve hours a day.

1 negative forms

The negative form of **can** is **cannot** or **can't**. **Cannot** is never written 'can not'. The negative form of **could** is **could not** or **couldn't**. To form the negative of **be able to**, you either put **not** or another negative word in front of **able**, or you use the expression **be unable to**.

Many elderly people cannot afford telephones.
I can't swim very well.
It was so dark you could not see anything.
They couldn't sleep.
We were not able to give any answers.
We were unable to afford the entrance fee.

2 **ability: the present**

Can, **could**, and **be able to** are all used to talk about a person's ability to do something. You use **can** or **be able to** to talk about ability in the present. **Be able to** is more formal than **can**.

You can all read and write.
The animals are able to move around, and they can all lie down.
Lisa nodded, unable to speak.

Could is also used to talk about ability in the present, but it has a special meaning. If you say that someone **could** do something, you mean that they have the ability to do it, but they don't in fact do it.

We could do much more in this country to educate people.

3 **ability: the past**

You use **could** or a past form of **be able to** to talk about ability in the past.

He could run faster than anyone else.
A lot of them couldn't read or write.
I wasn't able to answer their questions.

If you say that someone **was able to** do something, you usually mean that they had the ability to do it and they did it. **Could** does not have this meaning.

After two weeks in bed, he was able to return to work.
The farmers were able to pay their employees' wages.

If you want to say that someone had the ability to do something but did not in fact do it, you say that they **could have done** it.

You could have given it all to me.
You could have been a little bit more careful.

If you want to say that someone did not do something because they did not have the ability to do it, you say that they **could not have done** it.

I couldn't have gone with you, because I was in London at the time.

If you want to say that someone had the ability to do something in the past, although they don't now have this ability, you say that they **used to be able to** do it.

I used to be able to sleep anywhere.
You used to be able to see the house from here.

4 **ability: the future**

You use a future form of **be able to** to talk about ability in the future.

I shall be able to answer that question tomorrow.

5 **ability: reporting structures**

Could is often used in reporting structures. For example, if a woman says 'I can speak Arabic', you usually report this as 'She said she **could** speak Arabic'.

She said I could bring it back later.

→ See **Reporting**

6 **ability: 'be able to' after other verbs**

Be able to is sometimes used after modals such as **might** or **should**, and after verbs such as **want**, **hope**, or **expect**.

I might be able to help you.

You may be able to get extra money.
You should be able to see that from here.
She would not be able to go out alone.
Do you really expect to be able to do that?

Don't use **can** or **could** after any other verbs.

7 'being able to'

You can use an *-ing* form of **be able to**.

He liked being able to discuss politics with Veronica.

There is no *-ing* form of **can** or **could**.

8 awareness

Can and **could** are used with verbs such as **see**, **hear**, and **smell** to say that someone is or was aware of something through one of their senses.

I can smell gas.
I can't see her.
I could see a few stars in the sky.

9 possibility: the present and the future

Could and **can** are used to talk about possibility in the present or future.

You use **could** to say that there is a possibility that something is or will be true.

Don't eat it. It could be a toadstool.
He was jailed in February, and could be released next year.

Might and **may** can be used in a similar way.

It might be a trap.
Kathy's career may be ruined.

→ See **might – may**

! BE CAREFUL

Don't use 'could not' to say that there is a possibility that something is not true. Instead you use **might not** or **may not**.

It might not be possible.
It may not be easy.

If you want to say that it is impossible that something is true, you use **cannot** or **could not**.

You cannot possibly know what damage you caused.
It couldn't possibly be true.

You use **can** to say that something is sometimes possible.

Sudden changes can sometimes have a negative effect.

10 possibility: the past

You use **could have** to say that there is a possibility that something was true in the past.

He could have been in the house on his own.

Might have and **may have** can be used in a similar way.

She might have found the information online.
It may have been a dead bird.

You also use **could have** to say that there was a possibility of something being true in the past, although it was not in fact true.

It could have been worse.
He could have made a fortune as a lawyer.

! **BE CAREFUL**

Don't use 'could not have' to say that there is a possibility that something was not true. Instead you use **might not have** or **may not have**.

She might not have known the password.

If you want to say that it is impossible that something was true, you use **could not have**.

The decision couldn't have been easy.
The man couldn't have seen us at all.

11 permission

Can and **could** are used to say that someone is allowed to do something.

You can take out money at any branch of your own bank.
He could come and use my computer.

Cannot and **could not** are used to say that someone is or was forbidden to do something.

You can't bring strangers in here.
Her dad said she couldn't go out during the week.

→ See **Topic** entry Permission

cancel

→ See **delay – cancel – postpone – put off**

candy

→ See **sweets – candy**

cannot

→ See **can – could – be able to**

capability

→ See **ability – capability – capacity**

capacity

→ See **ability – capability – capacity**

car

→ See **carriage – car – truck – wagon**

care

1 'care'

If you **care** about something, you feel that it is very important or interesting, and you are concerned about it.

All he cares about is birds.
I'm too old to care what I look like.

If you don't **care** about something, it doesn't matter to you.

She didn't care what they thought.
Who cares where she is?

2 'care for'

If you **care for** people or animals, you look after them.

You must learn how to care for children.
With so many new animals to care for, larger premises were needed.

3 'take care'

To **take care of** someone or something or **take good care of** them means to look after them.

It is certainly normal for a mother to want to take care of her own baby.
He takes good care of my goats.

> **! BE CAREFUL**
>
> Don't say that someone ~~'takes care about'~~ someone else or ~~'takes a good care of'~~ them.

If you **take care of** a task or situation, you deal with it.

There was business to be taken care of.
If you'd prefer, they can take care of their own breakfast.

You also use **take care** when you are telling someone to be careful about something.

Take care what you tell him.
Take great care not to spill the mixture.

Take care is another way of saying goodbye.

'Night, night, Mr Beamish,' called Chloe. 'Take care.'

careful – careless – carefree

1 'careful'

If you are **careful**, you do something with a lot of attention.

She told me to be careful with the lawnmower.
He had to be careful about what he said.
This law will encourage more careful driving.

2 'careless'

If you are **careless**, you do things badly because you are not giving them enough attention. **Careless** is the opposite of **careful**.

I had been careless and let him wander off on his own.
Some parents are accused of being careless with their children's health.

3 'carefree'

Someone who is **carefree** has no worries and can therefore enjoy life.

When he was younger, he was <u>carefree</u>.
...his normally <u>carefree</u> attitude.

---

carriage – car – truck – wagon

'carriage'

Carriage is one of several nouns which are used to refer to vehicles pulled by railway engines.

In British English, a **carriage** is one of the separate sections of a train that carries passengers.

The man left his seat by the window and crossed the <u>carriage</u> to where I was sitting.

2 'car'

 In American English, these sections are called **cars**.

In British English, **car** used to be part of the name of some special kinds of railway carriage. For example, a carriage might be called a **dining car**, a **restaurant car**, or a **sleeping car**. These terms are no longer used officially, but people still use them in conversation.

3 'truck' and 'wagon'

In British English, a **truck** is an open vehicle used for carrying goods on a railway.

...a long <u>truck</u> loaded with bricks.

 In American English, this vehicle is called a **freight car** or a **flatcar**.

The train, carrying loaded containers on <u>flatcars,</u> was 1.2 miles long.
...the nation's third-largest railroad <u>freight car</u> maker.

In British English, a **wagon** is a vehicle with a top, sides and a sliding door, used for carrying goods on a railway.

The pesticides ended up at several sites, almost half of them in railway <u>wagons</u> at Bajza station.

 In American English, vehicles like these are usually called **boxcars**.

A long train of <u>boxcars,</u> its whistle hooting mournfully, rolled into town from the west.

A **truck** is also a large motor vehicle used for transporting goods by road.

→ See **lorry – truck**

---

carry – take

1 'carry' and 'take'

Carry and **take** are usually used to say that someone moves a person or thing from one place to another. When you use **carry**, you are showing that the person or thing is quite heavy.

He picked up his suitcase and <u>carried</u> it into the bedroom.
My father <u>carried</u> us on his shoulders.
She gave me some books to <u>take</u> home.

2 transport

You can also say that a ship, train, or lorry **is carrying** goods of a particular kind. Similarly you can say that a plane, ship, train, or bus **is carrying** passengers.

We passed tankers <u>carrying</u> crude oil.
The aircraft was <u>carrying</u> 145 passengers and crew.

Take can be used in a similar way, but only if you say where someone or something is being taken to. You can say, for example, 'The ship **was taking** crude oil **to Rotterdam**', but you can't just say '~~The ship was taking crude oil~~'.

This is the first of several aircraft to <u>take</u> British aid <u>to the area</u>.

You can say that a smaller vehicle such as a car **takes** you somewhere.

The taxi <u>took</u> him back to the station.

> **! BE CAREFUL**
>
> Don't say that a small vehicle 'carries' you somewhere.

case

1 'in case'

You use **in case** or **just in case** to say that someone has something or does something because a particular thing might happen.

I've got the key <u>in case</u> we want to go inside.
We tend not to go too far from the office, <u>just in case</u> there should be a bomb scare that would prevent us getting back.

> **! BE CAREFUL**
>
> After **in case** or **just in case**, you use a simple tense or **should**. You do not use 'will' or 'shall'.

You do not use 'in case' or 'just in case' to say that something will happen as a result of something else happening. You do not say, for example, '~~I will go in case he asks me~~'. You say 'I will go **if** he asks me'.

He qualifies this year <u>if</u> he gets through his exams.

2 'in that case'

You say **in that case** or **in which case** to refer to a situation which has just been mentioned and to introduce a statement or suggestion that is a consequence of it.

'The bar is closed,' the waiter said. '<u>In that case</u>,' McFee said, 'allow me to invite you back to my flat for a drink.'
I greatly enjoy these meetings unless I have to make a speech, <u>in which case</u> I'm in a state of dreadful anxiety.

3 'in this respect'

You do not use 'in this case' to refer to a particular aspect of something. For example, you do not say '~~Most of my friends lost their jobs, but I was very lucky in this case~~'. You say 'Most of my friends lost their jobs, but I was very lucky **in this respect**'.

The children are not unintelligent – in fact, they seem quite normal <u>in this respect</u>.
But most of all, there is that intangible thing, the value of the brand. <u>In this respect</u>, Manchester United, the most famous football club in the world, is unique.

cast

If you **cast** a glance in a particular direction, you glance in that direction.

Carmody casts an uneasy glance at Howard.
Out came Napoleon, casting haughty glances from side to side.

> ⚠ **BE CAREFUL**
>
> The verb **cast** has several other meanings. Note that for all its meanings its past tense and past participle is **cast**, not 'casted'.
>
> *He cast a quick glance at his friend.*
> *He cast his mind back over the day.*
> *He had cast doubt on our traditional beliefs.*
> *Will had cast his vote for the President.*

casualty

→ See **victim – casualty**

cause

1 used as a noun

The **cause of** an event is the thing that makes it happen.

Nobody knew the cause of the explosion.
He thought he had discovered the cause of her sadness.

You always use **of**, not 'for', after **cause**.

Don't use 'because of' or 'due to' with **cause**. Don't say, for example, 'The cause of the fire was probably due to a dropped cigarette'. You say 'The cause of the fire **was** probably a dropped cigarette'.

The report said the main cause of the disaster was the failure to secure doors properly.
The cause of the symptoms appears to be inability to digest gluten.

2 used as a verb

To **cause** something means to make it happen.

We are trying to find out what causes an earthquake.
Any acute infection can cause headaches.

You can say that something **causes someone to do** something.

A blow to the head had caused him to lose consciousness.
The experience had caused her to be distrustful of people.

Don't say that something 'causes that someone does' something.

certain – sure

1 having no doubts

If you are **certain** or **sure** about something, you have no doubts about it.

He felt certain that she would disapprove.
I'm sure she's right.

2 definite truths

If it is **certain** that something is true, it is definitely true. If it is **certain** that something will happen, it will definitely happen.

It is <u>certain</u> that he did not ask for the original of the portrait.
It seemed <u>certain</u> that they would succeed.

! **BE CAREFUL**

Don't say that it is 'sure' that something is true or will happen.

3 **'be certain to' and 'be sure to'**

Instead of saying that it is certain that someone or something will do something, you can say that they **are certain to do** it or **are sure to do** it.

I'm waiting for Cynthia. She'<u>s certain to be</u> late.
The growth in demand <u>is certain to drive up</u> the price.
These fears <u>are sure to go away</u> as the baby gets older.
The telephone stopped ringing. 'It'<u>s sure to ring</u> again,' Halle said.

Instead of saying that it is certain that someone will be able to do something, you often say that they **can be certain of** doing it or **can be sure of** doing it.

I chose this hospital so I <u>could be certain of</u> having the best care possible.
You <u>can always be sure of</u> controlling one thing – the strength with which you hit the ball.

4 **emphasis**

Don't use words such as 'very' or 'extremely' in front of **certain** or **sure**. If you want to emphasize that someone has no doubts or that something is true, you use words such as **absolutely** and **completely**.

We are not yet <u>absolutely certain</u> that this report is true.
Whether it was directed at Eddie or me, I couldn't be <u>completely certain</u>.
Can you be <u>absolutely sure</u> that a murder has been committed?
She felt <u>completely sure</u> that she was pregnant.

5 **negative structures**

Sure is more common that 'certain' in negative structures.

'Are you going to the party tonight?' – 'I'm not <u>sure</u>. Are you?'

certainly

1 **emphasizing and agreeing**

Certainly is used to emphasize statements. You often use **certainly** when you are agreeing with something that has been said or confirming that something is true.

It <u>certainly</u> looks wonderful, doesn't it?
Ellie was <u>certainly</u> a student at the university but I'm not sure about her brother.

! **BE CAREFUL**

Don't confuse **certainly** and **surely**. You use **surely** to express disagreement or surprise.

<u>Surely</u> you care about what happens to her.

 Both British and American speakers use **certainly** to respond positively to a question or statement.

'Do you see this as a good result?' – 'Oh, <u>certainly</u>.'

American speakers also use **surely** in this way.

'Can I have a drink?' – 'Why, <u>surely</u>.'

2 **position in sentence**

Certainly is usually used to modify verbs.

If there is no auxiliary verb, you put **certainly** in front of the verb, unless the verb is **be**.
It certainly gave some of her visitors a fright.

If the verb is **be**, **certainly** can go either in front of it or after it. It usually goes after it.
That certainly isn't true.

If there is an auxiliary verb, you usually put **certainly** after the auxiliary verb.
He'd certainly proved his point.

If there is more than one auxiliary verb, you usually put **certainly** after the first one.
Certainly can also go in front of the first auxiliary verb.
He will certainly be able to offer you advice.
The roadway certainly could be widened.

If you use an auxiliary verb without a main verb, you put **certainly** in front of the auxiliary verb.
'I don't know whether I've succeeded or not.' – 'Oh, you certainly have.'

You can also put **certainly** at the beginning of a sentence.
Certainly it was not the act of a sane man.

3 **'almost certainly'**

If you think that something is true, but you are not quite sure about it, you can use **almost certainly**.
She will almost certainly be left with some brain damage.

! **BE CAREFUL**

Don't put 'nearly' in front of **certainly**.

→ See **Adverbs and adverbials** for a graded list of words used to indicate probability

chair – armchair

1 **'chair'**

A **chair** is a piece of furniture for one person to sit on, with a support for the person's back. When a chair is a very simple one, you say that someone sits **on** it.
Anne was sitting on an upright chair.
Sit on this chair, please.

When a chair is a comfortable one, you usually say that someone sits **in** it.
He leaned back in his chair and looked out of the window.

2 **'armchair'**

An **armchair** is a comfortable chair with a support on each side for your arms. You always say that someone sits **in** an armchair.
He was sitting quietly in his armchair, smoking a pipe and reading the paper.

chair – chairperson – chairman – chairwoman

1 'chair' and 'chairperson'

The person in charge of a meeting or organization is referred to as the **chair**, or sometimes the **chairperson**. These words can be used to refer to either a man or a woman.

This is Ruth Michaels, <u>chairperson</u> of the Women Returners' Network.
You should address your remarks to the <u>chair</u>.

2 'chairman'

A **chairman** is a man who is in charge of a meeting or debate.

The vicar, full of apologies, took his seat as <u>chairman</u>.

The male head of an organization is often referred to as its **chairman**.

Sir John Hill, <u>chairman</u> of the Atomic Energy Authority, gave the opening speech.

3 'chairwoman'

In the past, **chairman** was used to refer to both men and women, but it is now not often used to refer to a woman. The woman in charge of a meeting or organization is sometimes referred to as the **chairwoman**.

Margaret Downes is this year's <u>chairwoman</u> of the Irish Institute.
Siobhan is a BBC radio journalist, and <u>chairwoman</u> of The Scottish Ballet.

chance

1 'chance'

If it is possible that something will happen, you can say that there is **a chance that it will happen** or **a chance of it happening**.

There is <u>a chance that I will have to stay longer</u>.
If we play well there is <u>a chance of winning</u> 5-0.

If something is fairly likely to happen, you can say that there is **a good chance** that it will happen.

There was <u>a good chance</u> that I would be discovered.
We've got <u>a good chance</u> of winning.

If something is unlikely to happen, you can say that there is **little chance** that it will happen. If you are sure that it will not happen, you can say that there is **no chance** that it will happen.

There's <u>little chance</u> that the situation will improve.
There's <u>no chance</u> of going home.

If someone is able to do something on a particular occasion, you can say that they have **the chance to do** it.

You will be given <u>the chance to ask</u> questions.
Visitors have <u>the chance to win</u> a camera.

2 'by chance'

If something happens **by chance**, it was not planned.

Many years later he met her <u>by chance</u> at a dinner party.

3 'luck'

If you say that something happens **by chance**, you are not saying whether it is a good thing or a bad thing. If something good happens without being planned, you refer to it as **luck**, not 'chance'.

I couldn't believe my luck.
Good luck!

charge

→ See **accuse – charge**

cheap – cheaply

1 'cheap' as an adjective

Cheap goods or services cost less than other goods or services of the same type.

...cheap red wine.
...cheap plastic buckets.
A solid fuel cooker is cheap to run.

2 'cheap' as an adverb

In conversation, **cheap** can also be an adverb, but only with verbs which refer to the buying, selling, or hiring of things.

I thought you got it very cheap.
You can hire boots pretty cheap.

3 'cheaply'

With other verbs, the adverb you use is **cheaply**.

You can play golf comparatively cheaply.
In fact you can travel just as cheaply by British Airways.

4 'low'

You do not say that things such as wages, costs, or payments are 'cheap'. You say that they are **low**.

If your family has a low income, you can apply for a student grant.
...tasty meals at a fairly low cost.

check

→ See **cheque – check, bill – check**

checkroom

→ See **cloakroom – checkroom**

cheerful

→ See **glad – happy – cheerful**

cheers

1 before drinking

People often say **cheers** to each other just before drinking an alcoholic drink.

I took a chair, poured myself a small drink and said 'Cheers!'
Cheers, Helen. Drink up.

2 thanking someone

British people sometimes say **cheers** instead of 'thank you' or 'goodbye'.

'Here you are.' – 'Oh, cheers. Thanks.'
'Thanks for ringing.' – 'OK, cheers.' – 'Bye bye.' – 'Cheers.'

chef – chief

1 'chef'

A **chef** /ʃef/ is a cook in a hotel or restaurant.

Her recipe was passed on to the chef.
He works as a chef in a large Paris hotel.

2 'chief'

The **chief** /tʃiːf/ of a group or organization is its leader.

The police chief has resigned.
I spoke to Jim Stretton, chief of UK operations.

chemist – pharmacist

1 'chemist'

In British English, a **chemist** is a person who is qualified to prepare and sell drugs and medicines.

...the pills the chemist had given him.

2 'pharmacist'

 In American English, someone like this is usually called a **pharmacist**.

The boy was eighteen, the son of the pharmacist at the Amity Pharmacy.

3 another meaning of 'chemist'

In both British and American English, a **chemist** is also a person who studies chemistry or who does work connected with chemical research.

...a research chemist.

chemist's – drugstore – pharmacy

1 'chemist's'

In Britain, a **chemist's** or **chemist** is a shop where you can buy medicine, cosmetics, and some household items.

She bought a couple of bottles of vitamin tablets at the chemist's.
He bought the perfume at the chemist in St James's Arcade.

2 'drugstore'

 In the United States, a shop where you can buy medicine and cosmetics is called a **drugstore**. In some drugstores, you can also buy simple meals and snacks.

3 'pharmacy'

A **pharmacy** is the place within a chemist's or drugstore, or within a supermarket or other business, where you can get prescription drugs.

Check in the pharmacy section of the drugstore.

In Britain, a chemist's is often referred to as a **pharmacy**.

cheque – check

1 'cheque'

In British English, a **cheque** is a printed form on which you write an amount of money and say who it is to be paid to. Your bank then pays the money to that person from your account.

Ellen gave the landlady a cheque for £80.

2 'check'

 In American English, this word is spelled **check**.

They sent me a check for $520.

In American English, a **check** is also a piece of paper showing how much money you owe for a meal in a restaurant.

He waved to a waiter and got the check.

In British English, a piece of paper like this is called a **bill**.

chief

→ See **chef – chief**

childish – childlike

1 'childish'

You say that someone is **childish** if you think they are behaving in a silly or immature way.

We were shocked by Josephine's selfish and childish behaviour.
Don't be so childish.

2 'childlike'

You describe someone's voice, appearance, or behaviour as **childlike** when it seems like that of a child.

Her voice was fresh and childlike.
'That's amazing!' he cried with childlike enthusiasm.

chips

 In British English, **chips** are long, thin pieces of potato that are fried in oil and eaten hot. Pieces of potato like these are called **fries** or **french fries** in American English.

We had fish and <u>chips</u> for dinner.
They went to a restaurant near the Capitol for a steak and <u>fries</u>.

 In American English, **chips** or **potato chips** are very thin slices of potato that have been fried until they are hard and crunchy and are eaten cold. Pieces of potato like these are called **crisps** in British English.

She ate a large bag of <u>potato chips</u>.
I bought a packet of <u>crisps</u> and a drink.

Chips made from foods other than potatoes usually have that word first.

There was a bowl of tortilla <u>chips</u> and salsa on the table.

choose

When you **choose** someone or something from a group of people or things, you decide which one you want.

Why did he <u>choose</u> these particular places?

The past tense of **choose** is **chose**, not 'choosed'. The past participle is **chosen**.

I <u>chose</u> a yellow dress.
Miles Davis <u>was chosen</u> as the principal soloist on both works.

1 'pick' and 'select'

Pick and **select** have very similar meanings to **choose**. **Select** is more formal than **choose** or **pick**, and is not usually used in conversation.

Next time let's <u>pick</u> somebody who can fight.
They <u>select</u> books that seem to them important.

2 'appoint'

If you **appoint** someone to a job or official position, you formally choose them for it.

It made sense to <u>appoint</u> a banker to this job.
The Prime Minister <u>has appointed</u> a civilian as defence minister.

3 'choose to'

If someone **chooses to do** something, they do it because they want to or because they feel it is right.

Some women <u>choose to manage</u> on their own.
The majority of people do not <u>choose to be</u> a single parent.
The way we <u>choose to bring up</u> children is vitally important.

You do not say that someone ~~picks to do~~ something or ~~selects to do~~ something.

chord – cord

These words are both pronounced /kɔːd/.

1 'chord'

A **chord** is a number of musical notes played or sung together to produce a pleasant sound.

He played some random <u>chords</u>.

2 'cord'

Cord is strong, thick string. A **cord** is a piece of this string.

She tied a cord around her box.

A **cord** is also a length of wire covered with plastic which connects a piece of electrical equipment to an electricity supply.

Christian name

→ See **first name – Christian name – forename – given name**

church

A **church** is a building in which Christians hold religious services.

The church has two entrances.
She goes to St Clement's Church, Oxford.

You use **church** with no determiner, and immediately after a preposition, when you are talking about a religious service in a church. For example, if someone goes to a service in a church, you say that they go **to church**.

None of the children goes to church regularly.
People had heard what had happened at church.
Will we see you in church tomorrow?
I saw him after church one morning.

A **mosque** is a building where Muslims hold religious services, and a **synagogue** is a building where Jewish people hold religious services. When you are talking about a religious service in a **mosque** or a **synagogue**, you usually use a preposition followed by a determiner, but sometimes the determiner is omitted.

He goes to the mosque to worship.
We went for morning prayers at the synagogue.
After synagogue, we had lunch together.

cinema

→ See **film**

class – form – grade – year

1 'class'

A **class** is a group of pupils or students who are taught together.

If classes were smaller, children would learn more.
I had forty students in my class.

2 'form'

In some British schools and in some American private schools, **form** is used instead of 'class'. **Form** is used especially with a number to refer to a particular class or age group.

I teach the fifth form.
She's in Form 5.

3 'year'

In British English, a **year** is a set of students of a similar age, who started school at around the same time.

'Which year are you in?' – 'I'm in the fifth year, and Krish is in the third year.'

4 'grade'

 A **grade** in an American school is similar to a **form** or a **year** in a British school.

A boy in the second grade won first prize.

---

classic – classical

1 'classic' used as an adjective

A **classic** example of something has all the features or characteristics that you expect something of its kind to have.

This statement was a classic illustration of British politeness.
It is a classic example of the principle of "less is more".

Classic is also used to describe films or books that are judged to be of very high quality.

This is one of the classic works of Hollywood cinema.
We discussed Brenan's classic analysis of Spanish history.

2 'classic' used as a noun

A **classic** is a book that is well-known and thought to be of a high literary standard.

We had all the standard classics at home.

Classics is the study of the ancient Greek and Roman civilizations, especially their languages, literature, and philosophy.

She got a first class degree in Classics.

3 'classical'

Classical music is music written by composers such as Mozart and Beethoven. Music of this kind is often complex in form, and is considered by many people to have lasting value.

I spend a lot of time reading and listening to classical music.
He is an accomplished classical pianist.

Classical is also used to refer to things connected with ancient Greek or Roman civilization.

We studied classical mythology.
Truffles have been eaten since classical times.

Clauses

A **clause** is a group of words containing a verb. A **simple sentence** has one clause.

I waited.
She married a young engineer.

1 main clauses

A **compound sentence** has two or more **main clauses** – that is, clauses that refer to two separate actions or situations that are equally important. Clauses in compound sentences are joined with a **coordinating conjunction** such as **and**, **but**, and **or**.

He met Jane at the station <u>and</u> they went shopping.
I wanted to go <u>but</u> I felt too ill.
You can come now <u>or</u> you can meet us there later.

The subject of the second clause can be omitted if it is the same as that of the first clause.

I wrote to him but received no reply.

2 subordinate clauses

A **complex sentence** contains a **subordinate clause** and at least one main clause. A subordinate clause gives more information about a main clause, and is introduced by a **subordinating conjunction** such as **because**, **if**, **whereas**, **that**, or a **wh**-word. Subordinate clauses can come in front of, after, or inside the main clause.

<u>When he stopped</u>, no one said anything.
They were going by car <u>because it was more comfortable</u>.
I said <u>that I should like to come</u>.
My brother, <u>who lives in New York</u>, is visiting us next week.

→ See **Subordinate clauses**, **Relative clauses**

→ See **Reporting** for more information on *that*-clauses and *wh*-clauses used after reporting verbs

3 finite clauses

Finite clauses always show the time at which something happened; they have a tense.

I <u>went</u> there last year.
<u>Did</u> you see him?

4 non-finite clauses

A **non-finite clause** is a subordinate clause that is based on a participle or an infinitive. Non-finite clauses do not show the time at which something happened; they have no tense.

Quite often <u>while talking to you</u> he would stand on one foot.
He walked about <u>feeling very important indeed</u>.
I wanted <u>to talk to her</u>.

→ See **-ing forms**, **-ed participles**

client

→ See **customer – client**

cloakroom – checkroom

A **cloakroom** is a room where you leave your hat and coat, especially in a place of entertainment.

 In American English, a room like this is sometimes called a **checkroom**.

In British English, **cloakroom** is also a polite word for a toilet.

→ See **toilet**

 In American English, a **checkroom** is also a place where luggage can be left for a short time, especially at a railway station.

close – closed – shut

1 **'close' or 'shut'**

If you **close** /kləʊz/ something such as a door, you move it so that it covers or fills a hole or gap.

He opened the door and <u>closed</u> it behind him.

You can also say that you **shut** something such as a door. There is no difference in meaning. The past tense and *-ed* participle of **shut** is **shut**.

I <u>shut</u> the door quietly.

Both **closed** and **shut** can be adjectives used after a linking verb.

All the other downstairs rooms are dark and the shutters are <u>closed</u>.
The windows were all <u>shut</u>.

You can use either **close** or **shut** to say that work or business stops for a short time in a shop or public building.

Many libraries <u>close</u> on Saturdays at 1 p.m.
What time do the shops <u>shut</u>?

2 **'close' or 'closed' only**

Only **closed** can be used in front of a noun. You can talk about a **closed** window, but not a 'shut' window.

He listened to her voice coming faintly through the <u>closed</u> door.

You can say that a road, border, or airport **is closed**.

The border <u>was closed</u> without notice around midnight.

Don't say that a road, border, or airport 'is shut'.

! **BE CAREFUL**

Don't confuse the verb **close** with the adjective **close** /kləʊs/. If something is **close** to something else, it is near to it.

→ See **near – close**

closet

→ See **cupboard – wardrobe – closet**

clothes – clothing – cloth

1 **'clothes'**

Clothes /kləʊðz/ are things you wear, such as shirts, trousers, dresses, and coats.

I took off all my clothes.

! BE CAREFUL

There is no singular form of **clothes**. In formal English, you can talk about a **garment**, a **piece of clothing**, or an **article of clothing**, but in ordinary conversation, you usually name the piece of clothing you are talking about.

2 **'clothing'**

Clothing /ˈkləʊðɪŋ/ is the clothes people wear. You often use **clothing** to talk about particular types of clothes, for example **winter clothing** or **warm clothing**. **Clothing** is an uncountable noun. Don't talk about 'clothings' or 'a clothing'.

Wear protective clothing.
Some locals offered food and clothing to the refugees.

3 **'cloth'**

Cloth /klɒθ/ is fabric such as wool or cotton that is used for making such things as clothes.

I cut up strips of cotton cloth.
The women wove cloth for a living.

When **cloth** is used like this, it is an uncountable noun.

A **cloth** is a piece of fabric used for cleaning or dusting. The plural form of **cloth** is **cloths**, not 'clothes'.

Clean with a soft cloth dipped in warm soapy water.
Don't leave damp cloths in a cupboard.

coach

→ See **bus – coach**

coast

→ See **beach – shore – coast**

coat

A **coat** is a piece of clothing with long sleeves which you wear over your other clothes, especially in order to keep warm.

She was wearing a heavy tweed coat.
Get your coats on.

You only use **coat** to refer to a piece of clothing which is worn outdoors. Knitted clothes which cover the upper part of your body and which you can wear indoors are called **cardigans**, **jumpers**, or **sweaters**.

coffee

→ See **café – coffee**

cold

If you want to emphasize how cold the weather is, you can say that it is **freezing**, especially in winter when there is ice or frost.

...*a freezing January afternoon*.

In summer, if the temperature is below average, you can say that it is **cool**. In general, **cold** suggests a lower temperature than **cool**, and **cool** things may be pleasant or refreshing.

This is the coldest winter I can remember.
A cool breeze swept off the sea; it was pleasant out there.

If it is very **cool** or too **cool**, you can also say that it is **chilly**.

It was decidedly pleasant out here, even on a chilly winter's day.

collaborate – co-operate

1 'collaborate'

When people **collaborate** on a project, they work together in order to produce something. For example, two writers can **collaborate** to produce a single piece of writing.

Anthony and I are collaborating on a paper for the conference.
The film was directed by Carl Jones, who collaborated with Rudy de Luca in writing it.

2 'co-operate'

When people **co-operate**, they help each other.

...an example of the way in which human beings can co-operate for the common good.

If you **co-operate** with someone who asks for your help, you help them.

The editors agreed to co-operate.
I couldn't get the RAF to co-operate.

 The spelling **cooperate** is sometimes used, and is preferred in American English.

They are willing to cooperate in the training of medical personnel.

college

A **college** is a place where students study after they have left school.

Computer Studies is one of the courses offered at the local technical college.
She got a diploma from the Royal College of Music.

You use **college** immediately after a preposition when you are talking about someone's attendance at a college. For example, you say that someone is **at college**.

He hardly knew Andrew at college.
He says you need the money for college.
What do you plan to do after college?

 In American English, you usually say that someone is **in college**, not 'at college'.

→ See **school – university**

colour

When you are describing the colour of something, you don't normally use the word **colour**. Don't say, for example, 'He wore a green colour tie'. You say 'He wore a **green** tie'.

She had blonde hair and green eyes.
She was wearing a bright yellow hat.

However, you sometimes use the word **colour** when you are asking about the colour of something, or when you are describing a colour in an indirect way.

What colour was the bird?
The paint was the colour of grass.

> **!** **BE CAREFUL**
>
> In sentences like these you use **be**, not 'have'. Don't say 'What colour has the bird?' or 'The paint has the colour of grass'.

You also use the word **colour** when you are using more unusual colour words. For example, you can say that something is **a bluish-green colour**.

The plastic is treated with heat until it turns a milky white colour.
There was the sea, a glittering blue-green colour.

You can also say, for example, that something is **bluish-green in colour**.

The leaves are rough and grey-green in colour.

You can also add the suffix **-coloured** to the name of a colour.

He bought me a cheap gold-coloured bracelet.
He selected one of his most expensive cream-coloured suits.

 The American spellings of 'colour' and '-coloured' are **color** and **-colored**.

---

come

1 'come'

You use **come** to talk about movement towards the place where you are, or towards a place where you have been or will be.

Come and look.
Eleanor had come to visit her.
You must come and see me about it.

The past tense of **come** is **came**. The -ed participle is **come**.

The children came along the beach towards me.
A ship had just come in from Turkey.

2 'come' or 'go'?

When you are talking about movement away from the place where you are, you use **go**, not 'come'. You also use **go** when you are describing movement that is neither towards you nor away from you.

You use **here** with **come** and **there** with **go**.

Alfredo, come over here.
I still go there all the time.

If you invite someone to accompany you somewhere, you usually use **come**, not 'go'.

Will you come with me to the hospital?
Come and meet Roger.

In some situations, you can use **come** or **go** to show indirectly whether you will be in a place that you are referring to. For example, if you say 'Are you **going** to John's party?', you are not showing whether you yourself are going to the party. However, if you say 'Are you **coming** to John's party?', you are showing that you will definitely be there.

3 'come and'

You use **come and** with another verb to say that someone visits you or moves towards you in order to do something.

Come and see me next time you're in London.
She would come and hold his hand.

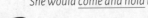 In informal American English you can leave out **and** in sentences like these.

*He has not had the courage to **come look** us in the eye.*

4 used to mean 'become'

Come is sometimes used to mean **become**.

One of my buttons came undone.
Remember that some dreams come true.

→ See **become**

come from

If you **come from** a particular place, you were born there, or it is your home.

'Where do you come from?' – 'India.'
I come from Zambia.

! BE CAREFUL

Don't use a progressive form in sentences like these. Don't say, for example, '~~Where are you coming from?~~' or '~~I am coming from Zambia~~'.

come with

→ See **accompany**

comic – comical – funny

1 'comical'

When people or things seem amusing or absurd, you can describe them as **comical**.

There is something slightly comical about him.

2 'comic'

Comic is used to describe things that are intended to make you laugh.

He is a great comic actor.
The novel is both comic and tragic.

! BE CAREFUL

Don't use 'comical' to describe things that are intended to make you laugh. Don't say, for example, '~~He is a great comical actor~~'.

3 'funny'

The word that you usually use to describe someone or something that makes you laugh is **funny**.

Let me tell you a funny story.
Farid was smart and good-looking, and he could be funny when he wanted to.

comment – commentary

1 'comment'

A **comment** is something you say that expresses your opinion of something.

People in the town started making rude comments.
It is unnecessary for me to add any comment.

2 'commentary'

A **commentary** is a description of an event that is broadcast on radio or television while the event is taking place.

We gathered round the radio to listen to the commentary.
The programme will include live commentary on the Cheltenham Gold Cup.

comment – mention – remark

1 'comment'

If you **comment on** a situation, or make a **comment** about it, you give your opinion on it.

Mr Cook has not commented on these reports.
I was wondering whether you had any comments.

2 'mention'

If you **mention** something, you say it, but only briefly, especially when you have not talked about it before.

He mentioned that he might go to New York.

3 'remark'

If you **remark on** something, or make a **remark** about it, you say what you think or what you have noticed, often in a casual way.

Visitors remark on how well the children look.
Martin made a rude remark about her t-shirt.

committee

→ See **Nouns** for information on collective nouns

common

If something is **common**, it is found in large numbers or it happens often.

His name was Hansen, a common name in Norway.
These days, it is common to see adults returning to study.

The comparative and superlative forms of **common** are usually **more common** and **most common**. **Commonest** is sometimes used instead of **more common** in front of a noun.

Job sharing has become more common.
The disease is most common in adults over 40.
Stress is one of the commonest causes of insomnia.

> **!** **BE CAREFUL**
>
> Don't use a *that*-clause after **common**. Don't say, for example, 'It is quite common that motorists fall asleep while driving'. You say 'It is quite common **for motorists to fall asleep** while driving'.
>
> *It is common for a child to become deaf after even a moderate ear infection.*

company

→ See **Nouns** for information on collective nouns

GRAMMAR FINDER

Comparative and superlative adjectives

1 comparative adjectives	**10** compound adjectives
2 superlative adjectives	**11** using comparatives
3 forming comparative and	**12** comparatives with 'than'
superlative adjectives	**13** linked comparatives
4 two syllables	**14** using superlatives
5 three or more syllables	**15** indicating group or place
6 irregular forms	**16** 'of all'
7 'little'	**17** with ordinal numbers
8 'ill'	**18** comparison with 'less' and 'least'
9 colour adjectives	

1 comparative adjectives

Comparative adjectives are used to say that something has more of a quality than something else, or more than it used to have. The comparative of an adjective is formed by adding *-er*, as in 'smaller', or by putting **more** in front of the adjective, as in 'more interesting'.

...the battle for safer and healthier working environments.
Diesel engines are more efficient than petrol engines.

2 superlative adjectives

Superlative adjectives are used to say that something has more of a quality than anything else of its kind, or more than anything else in a particular group or place. The superlative of an adjective is formed by adding *-est*, as in 'smallest', or by putting **most** in front of the adjective, as in 'most interesting'. Superlatives are usually preceded by **the**.

The cathedral is the oldest building in the city.
A house is the most suitable type of accommodation for a large family.

> **!** **BE CAREFUL**
>
> In conversation, people often use a superlative rather than a comparative when they are comparing just two things. For example, someone might say 'The train is quickest' rather than 'The train is quicker' when comparing a train service with a bus service. However, you should not use a superlative like this in formal writing.

3 forming comparative and superlative adjectives

The choice between adding -er and -est or using **more** and **most** usually depends on the number of syllables in the adjective.

With one-syllable adjectives, you usually add -er and -est to the end of the adjective.

tall – taller – tallest

quick – quicker – quickest

If the adjective ends in a single vowel letter and a single consonant letter, you double the consonant letter (unless the consonant is 'w').

big – bigger – biggest

fat – fatter – fattest

If the adjective ends in 'e', you remove the 'e'.

rare – rarer – rarest

wide – wider – widest

Dry usually has the comparative **drier** and the superlative **driest**. However, with the other one-syllable adjectives ending in 'y' (**shy**, **sly**, and **spry**), you don't change the 'y' to 'i' before adding -er and -est.

4 two syllables

You also add -er and -est to two-syllable adjectives ending in 'y', such as **angry**, **dirty**, and **silly**. You change the 'y' to 'i'.

dirty – dirtier – dirtiest

happy – happier – happiest

easy – easier – easiest

Other two-syllable adjectives usually have comparatives and superlatives formed with **more** and **most**. However, **clever** and **quiet** have comparatives and superlatives formed by adding -er and -est.

Some two-syllable adjectives have both kinds of comparative and superlative.

I can think of many pleasanter subjects.
It was more pleasant here than in the lecture room.
Exposure to sunlight is one of the commonest causes of skin cancer.
...five hundred of the most common words.

Here is a list of common adjectives that have both kinds of comparative and superlative:

angry	friendly	remote	stupid
costly	gentle	risky	subtle
cruel	narrow	shallow	

Bitter has the superlative form **bitterest** as well as **most bitter**. **Tender** has the superlative form **tenderest** as well as **most tender**.

5 **three or more syllables**

Adjectives that have three or more syllables usually have comparatives and superlatives with **more** and **most**.

dangerous – more dangerous – most dangerous

ridiculous – more ridiculous – most ridiculous

However, this does not apply to three-syllable adjectives formed by adding *un-* to the beginning of other adjectives, for example **unhappy** and **unlucky**. These adjectives have comparatives and superlatives formed by adding *-er* and *-est* as well as ones formed by using **more** and **most**.

He felt crosser and <u>unhappier</u> than ever.
He may be <u>more unhappy</u> seeing you occasionally.

6 **irregular forms**

A few common adjectives have irregular comparative and superlative forms.

good – better – best

bad – worse – worst

far – farther/further – farthest/furthest

old – older/elder – oldest/eldest

→ See **farther – further**, **elder – eldest – older – oldest**

7 **'little'**

People don't usually use comparative or superlative forms of **little**. To make a comparison, **smaller** and **smallest** are usually used.

→ See **little**

8 **'ill'**

Ill does not have a comparative or superlative form. When you want to use a comparative, you use **worse**.

Each day Katherine felt a little <u>worse</u>.

→ See **ill**

9 **colour adjectives**

Usually only qualitative adjectives have comparatives and superlatives, but a few basic colour adjectives also have these forms.

His face was <u>redder</u> than usual.
...some of the <u>greenest</u> scenery in America.

10 **compound adjectives**

The comparatives and superlatives of compound adjectives are usually formed by putting **more** and **most** in front of the adjective.

nerve-racking – more nerve-racking – most nerve-racking

Some compound adjectives have as their first part adjectives or adverbs with single-word comparatives and superlatives. The comparatives and superlatives of these compounds sometimes use these single-word forms, rather than 'more' and 'most'.

good-looking – better-looking – best-looking

well-known – better-known – best-known

The following compound adjectives have comparatives or superlatives using single-word forms:

good-looking	long-standing	well-behaved	well-off
high-paid	low-paid	well-dressed	
long-lasting	short-lived	well-known	

11 using comparatives

Comparatives can be used in front of nouns or after linking verbs.

Their demands for a bigger defence budget were refused.
To the brighter child, they will be challenging.
Be more careful next time.
His breath became quieter.

Comparatives normally come in front of all other adjectives in a noun phrase.

Some of the better English actors have gone to live in Hollywood.

12 comparatives with 'than'

Comparatives are often followed by **than** and a noun phrase or clause, to specify the other thing involved in the comparison.

My brother is younger than me.
I was a better writer than he was.
I would have done a better job than he did.

13 linked comparatives

You can show that the amount of one quality or thing is linked to the amount of another quality or thing by using two comparatives preceded by **the**.

The larger the organization, the less opportunity there is for decision.
The earlier you detect a problem, the easier it is to cure.

Note that you can use comparative adjectives or adverbs in this structure. You can also use **more**, **less**, and **fewer**.

14 using superlatives

Superlatives can be used in front of nouns, or after linking verbs.

He was the cleverest man I ever knew.
Now we come to the most important thing.
He was the youngest.

Superlatives normally come in front of all other adjectives in a noun phrase.

These are the highest monthly figures on record.

You usually put **the** in front of a superlative. However, 'the' is left out after a linking verb when the comparison does not involve a group of things. It is also sometimes left out in conversation or informal writing when comparing a group of things.

Beef is nicest slightly underdone.
Wool and cotton blankets are generally cheapest.

> **! BE CAREFUL**
>
> You cannot omit **the** when the superlative is followed by a structure indicating what group of things you are comparing. For example, you cannot say 'Amanda was youngest of our group'. You must say 'Amanda was **the** youngest of our group'.

You can use possessive determiners and nouns with **'s** instead of 'the' in front of a superlative.

...*the school's* most famous headmaster.
...*my* newest assistant.

15 indicating group or place

You can use a superlative on its own if it is clear what is being compared. However, if you need to indicate the group or place that is involved, you use:

▶ a prepositional phrase, normally beginning with **of** for a group or **in** for a place

Henry was the biggest of them.
These cakes are probably the best in the world.

▶ a relative clause

The visiting room was the worst I had seen.
That's the most convincing answer that you've given me.

▶ an adjective ending in -*ible* or -*able*

...*the longest possible gap.*
...*the most beautiful scenery imaginable.*

16 'of all'

If you want to emphasize that something has more of a quality than anything else of its kind or in its group, you can use **of all** after a superlative adjective.

The third requirement is the most important of all.
It's unlikely that we have discovered the oldest fossils of all.

17 with ordinal numbers

Ordinal numbers, such as **second**, are used with superlatives to say that something has more of a quality than nearly all other things of its kind or in its group. For example, if you say that a mountain is 'the second highest mountain in the world', you mean that it is higher than any other mountain except the highest one.

At one time, he owned the second biggest company in the United States.
Lyon is France's third largest city.

18 comparison with 'less' and 'least'

To show that something does not have as much of a quality as something else or as much of it as it had before, you can use **less** in front of an adjective.

→ See **less**

The cliffs here were less high.
As the days went by, Sita became less anxious.

To show that something has less of a quality than anything else or less than anything in a particular group or place, you use **least** in front of an adjective.

Mr Wilson is probably the least popular teacher in this school.

GRAMMAR FINDER

Comparative and superlative adverbs

Comparative and superlative adverbs are used to say how something happens or is done compared with how it happened or was done on a different occasion.

They are also used to say how something is done by one person or thing compared with how it is done by someone or something else.

1 forming comparative and superlative adverbs

The comparative of an adverb is usually formed by putting **more** in front of the adverb.

He began to speak more quickly.
The people needed business skills so that they could manage themselves more effectively.

The superlative of an adverb is usually formed by putting **most** in front of the adverb.

You are likely to have bills that can most easily be paid by post.
The country most severely affected was Holland.

2 single-word forms

Some very common adverbs have comparatives and superlatives that are single words and are not formed using 'more' and 'most'.

The comparative and superlative forms of **well** are **better** and **best**.

Over the year, I got to know him better.
Why don't you do what you do best?

The usual comparative and superlative forms of **badly** are **worse** and **worst**.

Most students performed worse in the second exam.
Those in the poorest groups are worst hit.

However, **badly** has a special meaning for which the comparative and superlative are **more badly** and **most badly**.

→ See **bad – badly**

Adverbs that have the same form as adjectives have the same comparatives and superlatives as the adjectives. The following words have the same comparative and superlative forms whether they are used as adverbs or adjectives:

close	fast	low	straight
deep	hard	near	tight
early	long	quick	wide
far	loud	slow	

They worked harder, and they were more honest.
George sang loudest.

The adverb **late** has the comparative form **later**, and the adverb **soon** has the comparative form **sooner**.

3 'the' with superlatives

It is possible to use **the** with single-word superlative adverbs, but this use is not common.

The old people work the hardest.
Sports in general are about who can run the fastest.

compare

1 'compare'

When you **compare** things, you consider how they are different and how they are similar.

It's interesting to compare the two products.

When **compare** has this meaning, you can use either **with** or **to** after it. For example, you can say 'It's interesting to compare this product **with** the old one' or 'It's interesting to compare this product **to** the old one'.

The study compared Russian children with those in Britain.
I haven't got anything to compare it to.

2 'be compared to'

If one thing **is compared to** or **can be compared to** another thing, people say they are similar.

As a writer he is compared frequently to Dickens.
A computer virus can be compared to a biological virus.

When you use **compare** like this, you must use **to** after it. Don't use 'with'.

complain

1 'complain about'

If you **complain about** something, you say that it is wrong or unsatisfactory.

Mothers complained about the lack of play space.
She never complains about the weather.

! BE CAREFUL

Don't use 'over' or 'on' after **complain**. Don't say, for example, '~~Mothers complained over the lack of play space~~' or '~~She never complains on the weather~~'.

2 'complain of'

If you **complain of** a pain, you say that you have it.

He complained of a headache.
Many patients complain of a lack of energy.

complement – compliment

These words can both be verbs or nouns. When they are verbs, they are pronounced /ˈkɒmplɪment/. When they are nouns, they are pronounced /ˈkɒmplɪmənt/.

1 'complement'

If one thing **complements** another, the two things increase each other's good qualities when they are brought together.

Nutmeg, parsley and cider all complement the flavour of these beans well.
Current advances in hardware development nicely complement British software skills.

2 'compliment'

If you **compliment** someone, you tell them that you admire something that they have or something that they have done.

They _complimented me on the way I looked._
She is to be complimented for handling the situation so well.

A **compliment** is something that you do or say to someone to show your admiration for them.

She took his acceptance as a great compliment.

You say that you **pay** someone a compliment.

He knew that he had just been paid a great compliment.

GRAMMAR FINDER

Complements

A **complement** is an adjective or noun phrase that comes after a **linking verb** such as **be**, and gives more information about the subject of the clause.

The children seemed frightened.
He is a geologist.

There are also complements that describe the object of a clause: see the section below on **object complements**.

1 adjectives as complements

Adjectives or **adjective phrases** can be used as complements after the following linking verbs:

appear	find	look	smell
be	get	pass	sound
become	go	prove	stay
come	grow	remain	taste
feel	keep	seem	turn

We were very happy.
The other child looked a bit neglected.
Their hall was larger than his whole flat.
She looked worried.
It smells nice.

! BE CAREFUL

Don't use an adverb after a linking verb. For example, say 'We felt very happy', not 'We felt very happily'.

Come, **go**, and **turn** are used with a restricted range of adjectives.

→ See **become**

2 noun phrases as complements

Noun phrases can be used as complements after the following linking verbs:

be	feel	prove	sound
become	form	remain	
comprise	look	represent	
constitute	make	seem	

He always seemed <u>a controlled sort of man</u>.
He'll make <u>a good president</u>.
I feel <u>a bit of a fraud</u>.

> ❗ **BE CAREFUL**
>
> Note that when you are saying what someone's job is, you use **a** or **an**. Don't just use the noun. For example, you say 'She's **a** journalist'. Don't say '~~She's journalist~~'.

3 **pronouns as complements**

Pronouns are sometimes used as complements to talk about identity, or to describe something.

It's <u>me</u> again.
This one is <u>yours</u>.
You're <u>someone who does what she wants</u>.

4 **other verbs with complements**

A small number of verbs that refer to actions and processes can be followed by complements. For example, instead of saying 'He returned. He had not been harmed', you can say 'He returned unharmed'.

The following verbs can be used with a complement like this:

arrive	escape	return	survive
be born	grow up	sit	watch
die	hang	stand	
emerge	lie	stare	

George <u>stood motionless</u> for at least a minute.
I used to <u>lie awake</u> watching the rain drip through the roof.
He <u>died young</u>.

A lot of adjectives with negative meanings are used as complements in this way, especially those with the prefix *un-* like **unannounced**, **unhurt** and **untouched**.

She often arrived <u>unannounced</u> at our front door.
The man's car was hit by a lorry but he escaped <u>unhurt</u>.

5 **object complements**

Some transitive verbs have a complement after their object when they are used with a particular meaning. This complement describes the object, and is often called the **object complement**. The following transitive verbs are used with an adjective as object complement:

believe	declare	label	rate
call	eat	leave	reckon
certify	find	make	render
colour	hold	presume	serve
consider	judge	pronounce	term
count	keep	prove	think

Willie's jokes made her <u>uneasy</u>.
He had proved them all <u>wrong</u>.
The journal 'Nature' called this book <u>dangerous</u>.
They held him <u>responsible</u> for the brutal treatment they had endured.

Some verbs are used with a very restricted range of object complements:

to burn someone alive	to open something wide	to plane something flat/smooth	to shoot someone dead
to drive someone crazy/mad	to paint something red, blue, etc	to rub something dry/smooth	to squash something flat
to get someone drunk/pregnant	to pat something dry	to scare someone stiff	to sweep something clean
to keep someone awake	to pick something clean	to send someone mad	to turn something white, black, etc
to knock someone unconscious		to set someone free	to wipe something clean/dry

She *painted* her eyelids *deep blue*.
Feelings of insecurity *kept* him *awake* at night.
He *wiped* the bottle *dry* with a towel.

The following transitive verbs are used with a noun phrase as object complement:

appoint	crown	judge	prove
believe	declare	label	reckon
brand	designate	make	term
bring up	elect	nominate	think
call	find	presume	
consider	hold	proclaim	

They *brought* him up *a Christian*.
They *consider* him *an embarrassment*.
His supporters *elected* him *president* in June.
In 1910 Asquith *made* him *a junior minister*.

The following transitive verbs are used with a name as object complement:

call	dub	nickname
christen	name	

Everyone *called* her *Molly*.

complete

Complete is usually an adjective. For some of its meanings, you can use words like **more** and **very** in front of it.

1 used to mean 'as great as possible'

You usually use **complete** to say that something is as great in degree, extent, or amount as possible.

You need a complete change of diet.
They were in complete agreement.

When **complete** has this meaning, you do not use words like **more** or **very** in front of it.

2 used to talk about contents

Complete is also used to say that something contains all the parts that it should contain.

I have a complete medical kit.
...a complete set of all her novels.

When two things do not contain all the parts that they should contain but one thing has more parts than the other, you can say that the first thing is **more complete** than the second one.

For a more complete picture of David's progress we must depend on his own assessment.

Similarly, if something does not contain all the parts that it should contain but contains more parts than anything else of its kind, you can say that it is the **most complete** thing of its kind.

...the most complete skeleton so far unearthed from that period.

3 used to mean 'thorough'

Complete is sometimes used to mean **thorough**. When **complete** has this meaning, you can use words like **very** and **more** in front of it.

She followed her mother's very complete instructions on how to organize a funeral.
You ought to have a more complete check-up if you are really thinking of going abroad.

4 used to mean 'finished'

Complete is also used to say that something such as a task or new building has been finished.

It'll be two years before the process is complete.
...blocks of luxury flats, complete but half-empty.

When **complete** has this meaning, you do not use words like 'more' or 'very' in front of it.

completely

→ See **Adverbs and adverbials** for a graded list of words used to indicate extent

compliment

→ See **complement – compliment**

composed

→ See **comprise**

comprehensible – comprehensive

1 'comprehensible'

If something is **comprehensible**, you can understand it.

The object is to make our research readable and comprehensible.
...language comprehensible only to the legal mind.

2 'comprehensive'

If something is **comprehensive**, it is complete and includes everything that is important.

...a comprehensive list of all the items in stock.
Linda received comprehensive training after joining the firm.

comprehension – understanding

■ 'comprehension'

Both **comprehension** and **understanding** can be used to talk about someone's ability to understand something.

He noted Bond's apparent lack of comprehension.
The problems of solar navigation seem beyond comprehension.
A very narrow subject would have become too highly technical for general understanding.

■ 'understanding'

If you have an **understanding** of something, you have some knowledge of it, or you know how it works or what it means.

The past decade has seen huge advances in our general understanding of how the ear works.
The job requires an understanding of Spanish.

You cannot use **comprehension** with this meaning.

Understanding has another meaning. If there is **understanding** between people, they are friendly towards each other and trust each other.

What we need is greater understanding between management and workers.

---

comprehensive

→ See **comprehensible – comprehensive**

---

comprise

■ 'comprise'

You say that something **comprises** particular things when you are mentioning all its parts.

The village's facilities comprised one public toilet and two telephones.

■ 'be composed of' and 'consist of'

You can also say that something **is composed of** or **consists of** particular things. There is no difference in meaning.

The body is composed of many kinds of cells, such as muscle, bone, nerve, and fat.
The committee consists of scientists and engineers.

■ BE CAREFUL

Don't use a passive form of **consist of**. Don't say, for example, 'The committee is consisted of scientists and engineers'.

■ 'constitute'

Constitute works in the opposite way to the verbs just mentioned. If a number of things or people **constitute** something, they are the parts or members that form it.

Volunteers constitute more than 95% of The Center's work force.

■ 'make up'

Make up can be used in either an active or passive form. In its active form, it has the same meaning as **constitute**.

Women made up two-fifths of the audience.

In its passive form, it is followed by **of** and has the same meaning as **be composed of**.

All substances are made up of molecules.
Nearly half the Congress is made up of lawyers.

> **!** **BE CAREFUL**
>
> Don't use a progressive form of any of these verbs. Don't say, for example,
> 'The committee is consisting of scientists and engineers'.

concentrate

If you **concentrate on** something, you give special attention to it, rather than to other things.

Concentrate on your driving.
He believed governments should concentrate more on education.

If someone **is concentrating on** something, they are spending most of their time or energy on it.

They are concentrating on saving lives.
One area Dr Gupta will be concentrating on is tourism.

> **!** **BE CAREFUL**
>
> Don't say that someone 'is concentrated on' something.

concerned

1 **used after a linking verb**

The adjective **concerned** is usually used after a linking verb such as **be**.

If you **are concerned about** something, you are worried about it.

He was concerned about the level of unemployment.
I've been concerned about you lately.

If a book, speech, or piece of information **is concerned with** a subject, it deals with it.

This chapter is concerned with recent changes.

> **!** **BE CAREFUL**
>
> Don't say that a book, speech, or piece of information 'is concerned about' a subject.
> Don't say, for example, 'This chapter is concerned about recent changes'.

2 **used after a noun**

When **concerned** is used immediately after a noun, it has a different meaning. You use it to refer to people or things involved in a situation that you have just mentioned.

We've spoken to the lecturers concerned.
Some of the chemicals concerned can cause cancer.

Concerned is often used with this meaning after the pronouns **all**, **everyone**, and **everybody**.

It was a perfect arrangement for all concerned.
This was a relief to everyone concerned.

concerto – concert

1 'concerto'

A **concerto** /kən'tʃeətəʊ/ is a piece of classical music written for one or more solo instruments and an orchestra.

...Beethoven's Violin Concerto.

2 'concert'

Note that you do not call a performance of music given by musicians a 'concerto'. You call it a **concert** /'kɒnsət/.

She had gone to the concert that evening.

confidant – confident

1 'confidant'

Confidant /'kɒnfɪdænt/ is a noun. A **confidant** is a person who you discuss your private problems and worries with. You use the spelling **confidante** when the person is a woman.

...Colonel House, a friend and confidant of President Woodrow Wilson.
She became her father's only confidante.

2 'confident'

Confident /'kɒnfɪdənt/ is an adjective. If you are **confident** about something, you are certain that it will happen in the way you want.

He was confident that the problem with the guidance mechanism could be fixed.
I feel confident about the future of British music.

People who are **confident** are sure of their own abilities.

... a witty, young and confident lawyer.
His manner is more confident these days.

conform

If you **conform**, you behave in the way that you are expected to behave.

You must be prepared to conform.

You also use **conform** to say that something is what is wanted or required. When you use **conform** like this, you use either **to** or **with** after it.

Such a change would not conform to the present wishes of the great majority of people.
Every home should have a fire extinguisher which conforms with British Standards.

GRAMMAR FINDER

Conjunctions

A **conjunction** is a word that links two clauses, groups, or words. There are two kinds of conjunction: coordinating conjunctions and subordinating conjunctions.

1 coordinating conjunctions

Coordinating conjunctions link clauses, groups, or words of the same grammatical type, for example two main clauses or two adjectives.

The coordinating conjunctions are:

and	nor	then
but	or	yet

Anna had to go into town and she wanted to go to Bride Street.
I asked if I could borrow her bicycle but she refused.
Her manner was hurried yet polite.

Nor, **then**, and **yet** can be used after **and**. **Nor** and **then** can be used after **but**.

Eric moaned something and then lay still.
It is a simple game and yet interesting enough to be played with skill.
Institutions of learning are not taxed but nor are they much respected.

When coordinating conjunctions are used to link clauses that have the same subject, the subject is not usually repeated in the second clause.

She was born in Budapest and raised in Manhattan.
He didn't yell or scream.
When she saw Morris she went pale, then blushed.

→ See **and**, **but**, **nor**, **or**

2 subordinating conjunctions

Subordinating conjunctions introduce **subordinate clauses**.

A subordinating conjunction can introduce the first clause in a sentence.

He only kept thinking about it because there was nothing else to think about.
When the jar was full, he turned the water off.
Although she was eighteen, her mother didn't like her to stay out late.

Some of the most frequent subordinating conjunctions are:

although	despite	though	when
as	if	unless	whenever
because	in spite of	whereas	while

→ See **Subordinate clauses**

conscious – consciousness – conscience – conscientious

1 'conscious'

Conscious is an adjective. If you are **conscious** of something, you are aware of it.

She became conscious of Rudolph looking at her.
I was conscious that he had changed his tactics.

If you are **conscious**, you are awake, rather than asleep or unconscious.

The patient was fully conscious during the operation.

2 'consciousness'

Consciousness is a noun. You can refer to your mind and thoughts as your **consciousness**.

Doubts were starting to enter into my consciousness.

If you **lose consciousness**, you become unconscious. If you **regain consciousness** or **recover consciousness**, you become conscious again after being unconscious. These are fairly formal expressions.

He fell down and <u>lost consciousness</u>.
He began to <u>regain consciousness</u> just as Kate was leaving.
She died in hospital without <u>recovering consciousness</u>.

In more informal English you can say that you **pass out** instead of 'lose consciousness', and **come round** instead of 'regain/recover consciousness'.

He felt sick and dizzy, then <u>passed out</u>.
When I <u>came round</u>, I was on the kitchen floor.

◼3 'conscience'

Conscience is a noun. Your **conscience** is the part of your mind that tells you whether what you are doing is right or wrong.

My <u>conscience</u> told me to vote against the others.
Their <u>consciences</u> were troubled by stories of famine and war.

◼4 'conscientious'

Conscientious is an adjective. Someone who is **conscientious** is very careful to do their work properly.

We are generally very <u>conscientious</u> about our work.
She seemed a <u>conscientious</u>, serious young woman.

consider

If you **consider** something, you think about it carefully.

He had no time to <u>consider</u> the matter.
The government is being asked to <u>consider</u> a plan to change the voting system.

You can say that someone **is considering doing** something in the future.

They <u>were considering opening</u> an office on the West Side of the city.
He <u>was considering taking</u> the bedside table downstairs.

❗ BE CAREFUL

Don't say that someone '~~is considering to do~~' something.

considerably

→ See **Adverbs and adverbials** for a graded list of words used to indicate degree

consist of

→ See **comprise**

constant – continual – continuous

You can use **constant**, **continual**, and **continuous** to describe things that happen or exist without stopping.

◼1 'constant'

You describe something as **constant** when it happens all the time or never goes away.

He was in <u>constant</u> pain.
I'm getting tired of Eva's <u>constant</u> criticism.

2 'continual' and 'continuous'

Continual is usually used to describe something that happens often over a period of time. If something is **continuous**, it happens all the time without stopping, or seems to do so. For example, if you say 'There was continual rain', you mean that it rained often. If you say 'There was continuous rain', you mean that it did not stop raining.

Continual can only be used in front of a noun. Don't use it after a verb. **Continuous** can be used either in front of a noun or after a linking verb.

There have been <u>continual</u> demands to cut costs.
He still smoked despite the <u>continual</u> warnings of his nurse.
There was a <u>continuous</u> background noise.
Breathing should be slow and <u>continuous</u>.

If you are describing something undesirable which continues to happen or exist without stopping, it is better to use **continual** rather than **continuous**.

Life is a <u>continual</u> struggle.
She was in <u>continual</u> pain.

3 'continual' or 'continuous'

If you are describing something undesirable which continues to happen or exist without stopping, it is better to use **continual** rather than **continuous**.

Life is a <u>continual</u> struggle.
It was sad to see her the victim of <u>continual</u> pain.

---

constantly

→ See **Adverbs and adverbials** for a list of words used to indicate frequency

---

constitute

→ See **comprise**

---

consult

If you **consult** someone, you ask them for their opinion or advice.

If your baby is losing weight, you should <u>consult</u> your doctor promptly.
She wished to <u>consult</u> him about her future.
If you are renting from a private landlord, you should <u>consult</u> a solicitor to find out your exact position.

 Some speakers of American English say **consult with** instead of 'consult'.

The Americans would have to <u>consult with</u> their allies about any military action in Europe.
They <u>consult with</u> companies to improve worker satisfaction and productivity.

---

content

Content can be a noun, an adjective, or a verb. When it is a noun, it is pronounced /ˈkɒntent/. When it is an adjective or verb, it is pronounced /kənˈtent/.

1 used as a plural noun

The **contents** /ˈkɒntents/ of something such as a box or room are the things inside it.

She emptied out the <u>contents</u> of the bag.

> ❗ **BE CAREFUL**
>
> **Contents** is a plural noun. Don't talk about ~~a content~~.

The **contents** of something such as a document or tape are the things written in it or recorded on it.

He couldn't remember the contents of the note.

2 used as an uncountable noun

The **content** of something such as a speech, piece of writing, website, or television programme is the information it gives, or the ideas or opinions expressed in it.

I was disturbed by the content of some of the speeches.
The website content includes issues of the newsletter.

3 used as an adjective

If you are **content** /kən'tent/ **to do** something or are **content with** something, you are willing to do it, have it, or accept it.

A few teachers were content to pay the fines.
Not content with running one business, Sally Green has bought another.

If you are **content**, you are happy and satisfied. You use this meaning of **content** after a linking verb. Don't use it in front of a noun.

He says his daughter is quite content.
I feel more content singing than at any other time.

4 'contented'

You can also use **contented** /kən'tentɪd/ to say that someone is happy and satisfied. **Contented** can be used in front of a noun or after a linking verb.

The firm has a loyal and contented labour force.
For ten years they lived like this and were perfectly contented.

5 'content' used as a verb

If you **content** /kən'tent/ **yourself with** doing something, you are satisfied with it and don't try to do other things.

Most manufacturers content themselves with updating existing models.

---

continent

1 'continent'

A **continent** is a very large area of land surrounded or almost surrounded by sea. A continent usually consists of several countries. Africa and Asia are continents.

They travelled across the South American continent.

2 'the Continent'

When people talk about **the Continent**, they mean the mainland of Europe, especially central and southern Europe.

On the Continent, the tradition has been quite different.
Sea traffic between the United Kingdom and the Continent was halted.

continual

→ See **constant – continual – continuous**

continually

→ See **Adverbs and adverbials** for a list of words used to indicate frequency

continuous

→ See **constant – continual – continuous**

GRAMMAR FINDER

Contractions

1 **basic forms**

A **contraction** is a shortened form in which a subject and an auxiliary verb, or an auxiliary verb and **not**, are combined to form one word.

I'm getting desperate.
She wouldn't believe me.

You use contractions when you are writing down what someone says, or when you are writing in a conversational style, for example in letters to friends.

The contracted forms of **be** are used when **be** is a main verb as well as when it is an auxiliary verb. The contracted forms of **have** are not usually used when **have** is a main verb.

The following table shows contractions of personal pronouns and **be**, **have**, **will**, **shall**, and **would**.

be – simple present		
I am	**I'm**	/aɪm/
you are	**you're**	/jɔː/, /jʊə/
he is	**he's**	/hiːz/
she is	**she's**	/ʃiːz/
it is	**it's**	/ɪts/
we are	**we're**	/wɪə/
they are	**they're**	/ðeə/
Also: **'s** added to names, singular nouns, and **wh-** words		
there's, here's, that's		

have – simple present

I have	**I've**	/aɪv/
you have	**you've**	/juːv/
he has	**he's**	/hiːz/
she has	**she's**	/ʃiːz/
it has	**it's**	/ɪts/
we have	**we've**	/wiːv/
they have	**they've**	/ðeɪv/

Also: **'s** added to names, singular nouns, and **wh-** words
there's, **there've** (not common), **that's**

have – simple past

I had	**I'd**	/aɪd/
you had	**you'd**	/juːd/
he had	**he'd**	/hiːd/
she had	**she'd**	/ʃiːd/
it had	**it'd**	/ɪtəd/
we had	**we'd**	/wiːd/
they had	**they'd**	/ðeɪd/

Also: **there'd**, **who'd**

will/shall

I shall/will	**I'll**	/aɪl/
you will	**you'll**	/juːl/
he will	**he'll**	/hiːl/
she will	**she'll**	/ʃiːl/
it will	**it'll**	/ɪtəl/
we will	**we'll**	/wiːl/
they will	**they'll**	/ðeɪl/

Also: **'ll** added to names and nouns (in speech)
there'll, **who'll**, **what'll**, **that'll**

would

I would	**I'd**	/aɪd/
you would	**you'd**	/juːd/
he would	**he'd**	/hiːd/
she would	**she'd**	/ʃiːd/
it would	**it'd**	/ɪtəd/
we would	**we'd**	/wiːd/
they would	**they'd**	/ðeɪd/

Also: **there'd**, **who'd**, **that'd**

! BE CAREFUL

You cannot use any of the above contractions at the end of a clause. You must use the full form instead. For example, you say 'I said I would', not 'I said I'd'.

2 negative contractions

The following table shows contractions of **be**, **do**, **have**, modals, and semi-modals with **not**.

be		
are not	**aren't**	/ɑːnt/
is not	**isn't**	/ɪznt/
was not	**wasn't**	/wɒznt/
were not	**weren't**	/wɜːnt/

do		
do not	**don't**	/dəʊnt/
does not	**doesn't**	/dʌznt/
did not	**didn't**	/dɪdnt/

have		
have	**haven't**	/hævnt/
has	**hasn't**	/hæznt/

modals		
cannot	**can't**	/kɑːnt/
could not	**couldn't**	/kʊdnt/
might not	**mightn't**	/maɪtnt/
must not	**mustn't**	/mʌsnt/
ought not	**oughtn't**	/ɔːtnt/
shall not	**shan't**	/ʃɑːnt/
should not	**shouldn't**	/ʃʊdnt/
will not	**won't**	/wəʊnt/
would not	**wouldn't**	/wʊdnt/

semi-modals		
dare not	**daren't**	/deənt/
need not	**needn't**	/niːdnt/

! BE CAREFUL

There is no contracted form of **am not** in standard English. In conversation and informal writing, **I'm not** is used. However, **aren't I?** is used in questions and question tags.

Aren't I brave?
I'm right, aren't I?

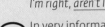 In very informal spoken English **ain't** is sometimes used with this meaning. However, many people consider this usage incorrect.

I certainly ain't going to retire.

In standard English, a pronoun followed by a negative contraction of a modal or **have** is more commonly used than a contraction followed by **not**. For example, **I won't**, **I wouldn't**, and **I haven't** are more common than 'I'll not', 'I'd not', and 'I've not'. However, in the case of **be**, both types of contraction are equally common. For example, **you're not** and **he's not** are used as commonly as **you aren't** and **he isn't**.

You aren't responsible.
You're not responsible.

3 **modals and 'have'**

The auxiliary verb **have** is not usually pronounced in full after **could**, **might**, **must**, **should**, and **would**. The contractions **could've**, **might've**, **must've**, **should've**, and **would've** are occasionally used in writing when reporting a conversation.

I must've fallen asleep.
You should've come to see us.

contrary

1 **'on the contrary'**

You say **on the contrary** when you are contradicting a statement that has just been made.

'You'll get tired of it.' – 'On the contrary. I'll enjoy it.'

You also use **on the contrary** when you have said that something is not the case, and you are going to say that the opposite is true.

There was nothing ugly about her dress: on the contrary, it was rather elegant.

2 **'on the other hand'**

Don't say 'on the contrary' when you are going to mention a situation that contrasts with one you have just described. Don't say, for example, 'I don't like living in the centre of the town. On the contrary, it's useful when you want to buy something'. You say 'I don't like living in the centre of the town. **On the other hand**, it's useful when you want to buy something'.

It's certainly hard work. But, on the other hand, the salary is good.

control

Control can be a verb or a noun.

1 **used as a verb**

If someone **controls** something such as a country or an organization, they have the power to take all the important decisions about the way it is run.

The Australian government at that time controlled the island.
His family had controlled the company for more than a century.

When **control** is a verb, it is not followed by a preposition.

2 **used as a noun**

Control is also used as a noun to refer to the power that someone has in a country or organization. You say that someone has control **of** a country or organization, or control **over** it.

Mr Ronson gave up control of the company.
The first aim of his government would be to establish control over the area.

3 **another meaning**

Control is used as a noun to refer to a place where your documents and luggage are officially checked when you enter a foreign country.

I went through passport control into the departure lounge.

Don't use **control** as a verb to mean 'check' or 'inspect'. Don't say, for example, ~~'My luggage was controlled'~~. You say 'My luggage **was checked**' or 'My luggage **was inspected**'.

I had to wait while the baggage <u>was being checked</u>.
The guard took his ID card and <u>inspected</u> it.

convince – persuade

1 'convince'

If you **convince** someone of something, you make them believe it is true.

These experiences <u>convinced</u> me of the drug's harmful effects.
It took them a few days to <u>convince</u> me that it was possible.

Some speakers use **convince** with a **to**-infinitive to say that one person makes another person decide to do something, by giving them a good reason for doing it.

Lyon did his best to <u>convince</u> me to settle in Tennessee.
I hope you will help me <u>convince</u> my father to leave.

2 'persuade'

Using 'convince' in this way is generally regarded as incorrect. Instead you should use **persuade**.

Marsha was trying to <u>persuade</u> Posy to change her mind.
They had no difficulty in <u>persuading</u> him to launch a new paper.

convinced

If you are **convinced** of something, you are sure that it is true or genuine.

I am <u>convinced</u> of your loyalty.
He was <u>convinced</u> that her mother was innocent.

You do not use words such as 'very' or 'extremely' in front of **convinced**. If you want to emphasize that someone has no doubts about something, you use words such as **fully** or **totally** in front of **convinced**.

To be <u>fully convinced</u> that reading is important, they have to find books they like.
I am <u>totally convinced</u> it was an accident.
We are <u>absolutely convinced</u> that this is the right thing to do.
Some people were <u>firmly convinced</u> that a non-human intelligence was attempting to make contact.

> **! BE CAREFUL**
>
> You do not use a '**to**'-infinitive after **convinced**. You do not say, for example, ~~'He is convinced to have failed'~~. You say 'He is **convinced that he has** failed'.

cook

1 'cook'

If you **cook** a meal or a particular type of food, you prepare it for eating and then heat it, for example in an oven or saucepan.

Lucas was in the kitchen, <u>cooking</u> dinner.
We <u>cooked</u> the pie in the oven.

Cook is only used to talk about food, not drinks.

Cook is also a noun.

→ See **cooker – cook**

2 'make'

If you **make** a meal or a drink, you combine foods or drinks together to produce something different. You can **make** a meal without heating anything.

I made his breakfast.
I'll make you a coffee.

3 'prepare'

Prepare is used in two ways. If you **prepare** food, you clean or cut it so that it is ready to be used.

Prepare the vegetables, cut into small chunks and add to the chicken.

To **prepare** a meal or drink means the same as to **make** it (see above). This is a fairly formal use.

Many elderly people are unable to prepare meals on their own.

4 'get'

If you **get** a meal, you prepare it or cook it. You can also say that someone **gets** a meal **ready**. If you **get** a drink, you either mix drinks together or pour a drink.

I'll get the dinner ready.
I was downstairs getting the drinks.

5 'fix'

 In American English, if you **fix** a meal or drink, you **make** it (see above).

Sarah fixed some food for us.
Manfred fixed himself a drink.

6 types of cooking

There are many verbs that refer to different ways of cooking things.

When you **bake** or **roast** something, you cook it in an oven without liquid. You **bake** bread and cakes, but you **roast** meat. When you **roast** potatoes, you cook them in an oven in some fat. You can also **roast** a large piece of meat or a bird over a fire.

Dave baked a cake for my birthday.
We roasted a whole chicken.

You use **roast**, not 'roasted', to describe meat and potatoes that have been roasted.

We had a traditional roast beef dinner.

When you **grill** or **toast** something, you cook it under or over strong heat. You **grill** meat and vegetables, but you **toast** slices of bread.

 Speakers of American English usually use **broil** rather than 'grill'.

Grill the meat for 20 minutes each side.
Toast the bread lightly on both sides.
I'll broil the lobster.

When you **boil** something, you cook it in boiling water.

I still need to boil the potatoes.

When you **fry** something, you cook it in hot fat or oil.
Fry the onions until they are brown.

cooker – cook

1 'cooker'

A **cooker** is a metal oven and hot plate that you use for boiling, grilling, or roasting food.
The food was warming in a saucepan on the cooker.

 In American English, this machine is called a **range**.
Can you cook fried chicken on an electric range?

2 'cook'

A **cook** is someone who cooks meals as their job.
They had a butler, a cook, and a maid.

You can also describe someone's ability to cook by using **cook** with an adjective. For example, you can say that someone is **a good cook** or **a bad cook**.
Abigail is an excellent cook.

> **! BE CAREFUL**
>
> Don't refer to a person who cooks meals as a 'cooker'. Don't say, for example, 'Abigail is an excellent cooker'.

co-operate

→ See **collaborate – co-operate**

cord

→ See **chord – cord**

corn

 In American English, **corn** is a long rounded vegetable covered in small yellow seeds. The seeds themselves are also called **corn**.
Serve with grilled corn or french fries.

In British English, this vegetable is usually called **sweetcorn**.
We had fish with peas and sweetcorn.

In British English, **corn** refers to any type of cereal plant growing in a particular area, for example wheat, barley, or maize.
We drove past fields of corn.

 Speakers of American English use **grain** for this meaning.
Grain harvests were delayed.

corner

A **corner** is a place where two sides or edges of something meet. You usually say that something is **in** a corner.

Put the television set in the corner.
Flowers were growing in one corner of the garden.

When two streets meet, you refer to each of the places where their edges meet as a **corner**. You use **on** when you are talking about the corner of a street.

There is a hotel on the corner of Main and Brisbane Streets.
We can't have police officers on every corner.

cost

→ See **price – cost**

cot – crib – camp bed

1 'cot' and 'crib'

 In British English, a **cot** is a bed for a baby. A cot has high sides to prevent the baby from falling out. In American English, a bed like this is called a **crib**.

Put your baby's cot beside your bed.
I asked for a crib to put the baby in.

2 'cot' and 'camp bed'

 In American English, a **cot** is a narrow bed for an adult. It is made of canvas fitted over a frame, and you can fold it up. You take it with you when you go camping, or you use it as a spare bed at home. In British English, a bed like this is called a **camp bed**.

His bodyguards slept on the cots.
I had to sleep on a camp bed in the living room.

could

→ See **can – could – be able to**

council – counsel

1 'council'

Council /ˈkaʊnsəl/ is a noun. A **council** is a group of people who run a local area such as a town, city, or county.

...Wiltshire County Council.

Some other groups of people who run organizations are also called **Councils**.

...the Arts Council.
...the British Council of Churches.

2 'counsel'

Counsel /ˈkaʊnsəl/ is usually a verb. If you **counsel** someone, you give them advice about their problems.

Part of her work is to counsel families when problems arise.

Someone's **counsel** is the lawyer who gives them advice on a legal case and speaks on their behalf in court.

Singleton's counsel said after the trial that he would appeal.

---

country

1 'country'

A **country** is one of the political areas that the world is divided into.

Indonesia is the fifth most populous country in the world.
Does this system apply in other European countries?

2 'the country'

Land that is away from towns and cities is **the country**.

We live in the country.
Many people moved away from the country to the towns.

❗ BE CAREFUL

When you use **country** like this, the only determiner you can use with it is **the**. Don't say, for example, '~~I like living in Paris, but my parents prefer to live in a country~~'. You say 'I like living in Paris, but my parents prefer to live in **the country**'.

3 'countryside'

Land that is away from towns and cities can also be called **the countryside**.

I've always wanted to live in the countryside.

Countryside can be used without 'the' when it is used after an adjective.

We are surrounded by beautiful countryside.

---

couple

→ See **pair – couple**

---

course

A **course** is a series of lessons or lectures on a particular subject. It usually includes reading and written work that a student has to do. You say that someone **takes** a course or **does** a course **in** a subject.

The department also offers a course in Opera Studies.
She took a course in Latin.

❗ BE CAREFUL

Don't say that someone takes a course 'of' a subject.

In British English, the people who are taking a course are referred to as the people **on** the course.

There were about 200 people on the course.

 In American English, they are also referred to as the people **in** the course.

How many are there in the course as a whole?

craft

A **craft** is an activity such as weaving, carving, or pottery that involves making things skilfully by hand, often in a traditional way. When **craft** has this meaning, its plural form is **crafts**.

It's a pity to see the old crafts dying out.

A **craft** is also a vehicle such as a boat, hovercraft, or submarine that carries people or things on or under water. When **craft** has this meaning, its plural form is **craft**.

There were eight destroyers and fifty smaller craft.

credible – credulous – creditable

1 'credible'

If something is **credible**, it can be believed.

His latest statements are hardly credible.
This is not credible to anyone who has studied the facts.

Credible is most commonly used in negative sentences.

2 'credulous'

People who are **credulous** are always ready to believe what other people tell them, and are easily deceived.

Credulous women bought the mandrake root to promote conception.

3 'creditable'

A performance, achievement, or action that is **creditable** is of a reasonably high standard.

He polled a creditable 44.8 percent.
Their performance was even less creditable.

crib

→ See **cot – crib – camp bed**

crime

A **crime** is an illegal action for which a person can be punished by law. You usually say that someone **commits** a crime.

A crime has been committed.
The police had no evidence of him having committed any crime.

! **BE CAREFUL**

Don't say that someone 'does a crime or 'makes a crime'.

crisps

→ See **chips**

criterion

A **criterion** is a standard by which you judge or evaluate something.

The most important criterion for entry is that applicants must design their own work.

The plural of **criterion** is **criteria**.

The Commission did not apply the same criteria to advertising.

critic – critical

1 'critic'

Critic /ˈkrɪtɪk/ is a noun. A **critic** is a person who writes reviews and gives opinions in newspapers or on television about books, films, music, or art.

What did the New York critics have to say about the production?
Most critics gave the play a good review.

2 'critical'

Critical is an adjective with several meanings.

A **critical** approach to something involves examining and judging it carefully. When **critical** has this meaning, you use it only in front of a noun.

I was planning a serious critical study of Shakespeare.

If you are **critical of** someone or something, you show that you disapprove of them. When **critical** has this meaning, it can be used in front of a noun or after a linking verb.

She apologized for her critical remarks.
His report is highly critical of the judge.

If a person is **critical** or in a **critical condition**, they are seriously ill.

Ten of the victims are said to be in a critical condition in hospital.

cry – weep

1 'cry'

Cry can be a verb or a noun. The other forms of the verb are **cries**, **crying**, **cried**. The plural of the noun is **cries**.

If you **cry**, tears come out of your eyes because you are unhappy, afraid, or in pain.

Helen began to cry.
Feed the baby as often as it cries.
If the baby cried at night, Nick would comfort him.
We heard what sounded like a little girl crying.

In conversation, you can say that someone has a **cry**.

She felt a lot better after a good cry.

2 'weep'

Weep means the same as **cry**. **Weep** is an old-fashioned word which is now used only in stories. The past tense and past participle of **weep** is **wept**, not 'weeped'.

The girl was weeping as she kissed him goodbye.
James wept when he heard the news.

3 another meaning of 'cry'

In a story, if someone **cries** something, they shout it.

'Come on!' he <u>cried.</u>
He <u>cried</u> out angrily, 'Get out of my house!'

A **cry** is something that someone shouts.

When she saw him she uttered a <u>cry</u> of surprise.
We heard <u>cries</u> of 'Help! Please help me!' coming from the river.

cup – glass – mug

1 'cup'

A **cup** is a small, round container, usually with a handle, from which you drink hot drinks such as tea and coffee. When you are not holding a cup, you usually rest it on a **saucer**.

John put his <u>cup</u> and saucer on the coffee table.

A **cup** is also a unit of measurement used in cooking.

Mix four <u>cups</u> of flour with a pinch of salt.

2 'glass'

A **glass** is a container made out of glass and used for cold drinks.

I put down my <u>glass</u> and stood up.
He poured Ellen a <u>glass</u> of juice.

3 'mug'

A **mug** is a large deep cup with straight sides and a handle, used for hot drinks. You don't rest a **mug** on a saucer.

He spooned instant coffee into two of the <u>mugs</u>.

4 containers and contents

You can use **cup**, **glass**, and **mug** to talk about either the containers or their contents.

I dropped the <u>cup</u> and it broke.
Drink eight <u>glasses</u> of water a day.

cupboard – wardrobe – closet

1 'cupboard'

A **cupboard** is a piece of furniture with doors at the front and usually shelves inside.

The kitchen <u>cupboard</u> is stocked with tins of soup.

 Cupboards in American English are built-in shelves behind doors. They are mainly found in kitchens.

She was in the kitchen, opening <u>cupboards</u>, moving boxes and cans to see what lay behind.

2 'wardrobe'

A **wardrobe** is a tall piece of furniture, usually in a bedroom, that has space for hanging clothes.

I hung my dress up in the <u>wardrobe</u>.

3 'closet'

 A wardrobe is sometimes built into the wall of a room, rather than being a separate piece of furniture. In American English, a built-in wardrobe is called a **closet**.

There's an iron in the closet.

curb – kerb

1 'curb'

Curb can be a noun or a verb.

If you **curb** something, you control it and keep it within definite limits.

...proposals to curb the powers of the Home Secretary.
You must curb your extravagant tastes.

You can say that someone imposes a **curb** on something.

This requires a curb on public spending.
Another year of wage curbs is inevitable.

2 'kerb'

 Curb is also the American spelling of the noun **kerb**. There is no difference in pronunciation. The **kerb** is the raised edge between a pavement and a road.

The taxi pulled into the kerb.
I pulled up at the curb.

curiosity

The following words can all be used to describe a person who is eager to find out about someone's life, or about an event or situation:

curious	interested	prying
inquisitive	nosy	

1 'curious'

Curious is a neutral word, which does not show approval or disapproval.

Steve was intensely curious about the world I came from.

2 'interested'

Interested is usually complimentary when it is used to talk about someone's interest in a person's life.

She put on a good show of looking interested.

3 'nosy' and 'prying'

Nosy and **prying** are used to show disapproval.

'Who is the girl you came in with?' – 'Don't be so nosy.'
Computer-based records can easily be protected from prying eyes by simple systems of codes.

Prying is usually used with **eyes**.

4 'inquisitive'

Inquisitive is sometimes used to show disapproval, but it can also be neutral or even complimentary.

Mr Courtney was surprised. 'A ring, you say?' He tried not to sound <u>inquisitive</u>.
Up close, he was a man with <u>inquisitive</u> sparkling eyes and a fresh, very down-to-earth smile.

currant – current

These words are both pronounced /'kʌrənt/.

▮1 'currant'

Currant is a noun. A **currant** is a small dried grape.

...dried fruits such as <u>currants</u>, raisins and dried apricots.

▮2 'current' used as a noun

Current can be a noun or an adjective.

A **current** is a steady and continuous flowing movement of some of the water in a river or lake, or in the sea.

The child had been swept out to sea by the <u>current</u>.

A **current** is also a steady flowing movement of air, or a flow of electricity through a wire or circuit.

I felt a <u>current</u> of cool air blowing in my face.
There was a powerful electric <u>current</u> running through the wires.

▮3 'current' used as an adjective

Current is used to describe things which are happening or being used now, rather than at some time in the past or future.

Our <u>current</u> methods of production are far too expensive.

custom

→ See **habit – custom**

customer – client

▮1 'customer'

A **customer** is someone who buys something, especially from a shop.

She's one of our regular <u>customers</u>.

▮2 'client'

A **client** is a person or company that receives a service from a professional person or organization in return for payment.

A solicitor and his <u>client</u> were sitting at the next table.

cut

If you **cut** something, you use something such as a knife or pair of scissors in order to remove a piece of it or damage it. The past tense and past participle of **cut** is **cut**, not 'cutted'.

She <u>cut</u> the cake and gave me a piece.
...the shiny crumpled pictures which she'd carefully <u>cut</u> out of the Sears catalogue.

Dd

dare

1 **used as an intransitive verb**

If you **dare** to do something, you have the courage to do it. You use **dare** on its own, or with an infinitive with or without *to*.

I went to see him as often as I dared.
It's remarkable that she dared to be so honest.

In this meaning, **dare** is often used in negative sentences and questions.

If someone **daren't** do something, they don't have enough courage to do it.

I daren't ring Jeremy again.

 In American English, the contraction 'daren't' is not used. American English uses the full form **dare not** instead.

I dare not leave you here alone.

! **BE CAREFUL**

You must use an infinitive without *to* after **daren't** and **dare not**. Don't say, for example, '<del>I daren't to ring Jeremy again</del>'.

If you are talking about the past, you say that someone **did not dare** do something or **didn't dare** do something. After **did not dare** and **didn't dare** you can use an infinitive with or without *to*.

She did not dare leave the path.
I didn't dare to speak or move.

In formal writing, you can say that someone **dares not** do something. **Dare not** is always followed by an infinitive without *to*.

He dared not show that he was afraid.

In other kinds of negative sentence, you can use an infinitive with or without *to* after **dare**.

No one dares disturb him.
No other manager dared to compete.

In *yes/no*-questions, you put the base form **dare** in front of the subject without using an auxiliary verb or modal. After the subject, you use an infinitive without *to*.

Dare she go in?

In *wh*-questions, you use a modal such as **would** in front of **dare**. After **dare**, you use an infinitive with or without *to*.

Who will dare to tell him?
What bank would dare offer such terms?

2 **used as a transitive verb**

If you **dare** someone to do something, you challenge them to prove that they are not frightened of doing it.

I dare you to swim across the lake.
She glared at Simon, daring him to disagree.

3 'I dare say'

You say **I dare say** or **I daresay** to show that you think that something is probably true.

It's worth a few pounds, I dare say, but no more.
Well, I daresay you've spent all your money by now.

! BE CAREFUL

I dare say is a fixed phrase. Don't say, for example, 'You dare say' or 'I dare to say'.

data

Data is information, usually in the form of facts or statistics that can be analysed.

Such tasks require the worker to process a large amount of data.
This will make the data easier to collect.

Data is usually regarded as an uncountable noun and is used with a singular form of a verb.

2010 is the latest year for which data is available.
The latest data shows that lending fell by 10% in May.

People usually say **this data**, rather than 'these data'.

Processing this data only takes a moment.

In some formal and scientific writing, **data** is used with a plural form of a verb, and **these data** is used instead of 'this data'.

The economic data are inconclusive.
To cope with these data, hospitals bought large mainframe computers.

In other kinds of writing and in conversation, people usually use **data** as an uncountable noun.

day

1 'day'

A **day** is one of the seven twenty-four hour periods in a week.

The attack occurred six days ago.
Can you go any day of the week? What about Monday?

You also use **day** to refer to the time when it is light and when people are awake and doing things. When **day** has this meaning, you can use it either as a countable noun or an uncountable noun.

The days were dry and the nights were cold.
How many meetings do you have on a typical working day?
The festivities went on all day.

2 'today'

You refer to the actual day when you are speaking or writing as **today**.

I hope you're feeling better today.
I want to get to New York today.

> **!** BE CAREFUL
>
> Don't use 'this day' to refer to the day when you are speaking or writing. Don't say, for example, 'I want to get to New York this day'.

3 **'the other day'**

You use **the other day** to show that something happened fairly recently.

We had lunch the other day at our favourite restaurant.
The other day, I got a phone call from Jack.

4 **referring to a particular day**

If you want to refer to a particular day when something happened or will happen, you usually use a prepositional phrase beginning with **on**.

We didn't catch any fish on the first day.
On the day after the race you should try to rest.

If you have already been talking about events that happened during a particular day, you can say that something else happened **that day**.

Then I took a bath, my second that day.
Later that day Amanda drove to Leeds.

You can also say that something had happened **the day before** or **the previous day**.

Kate had met him the day before.
My mobile had been stolen the previous day.

You can also say that something happened **the next day** or **the following day**.

The next day the revolution broke out.
We were due to meet Hamish the following day.

When you have been talking about a particular day in the future, you can say that something will happen **the following day** or **the day after**.

The board will meet tomorrow evening and the team will be named the following day.
I could come the day after.

5 **'every day'**

If something happens regularly on each day, you say that it happens **every day**.

She went running every day in the summer.
Eat at least five portions of fruit and vegetables every day.

> **!** BE CAREFUL
>
> Don't confuse **every day** with the adjective **everyday**.

→ See **everyday – every day**

6 **'these days' and 'nowadays'**

You use **these days** or **nowadays** when you are talking about things that are happening now, in contrast to things that happened in the past.

These days, more women become managers.
Why don't we ever see Jim nowadays?

7 **'one day'**

You use **one day** to say that something will happen at some time in the future.

Maybe he'll be Prime Minister one day.

I'll come back one day, I promise.

In stories, **one day** is used when a writer has just described a situation and is mentioning the first of a series of events.

One day a man called Carl came in to pay his electricity bill.

→ See **Reference** section **Days and dates**

dead

1 used as an adjective

Dead is usually an adjective. Someone who is **dead** is no longer living. You can use **dead** to talk about someone who has just died, or about someone who died a long time ago.

They covered the body of the dead woman.
He was shot dead in a gunfight.

You can also say that animals or plants are **dead**.

A dead sheep was lying on the road.
Ada threw away the dead flowers.

! BE CAREFUL

Don't confuse **dead** with **died**. **Died** is the past tense and -*ed* participle of the verb **die**. Don't use **died** as an adjective.

My dad died last year.

2 used as a noun

You can refer to a group of people who have died as **the dead**.

Among the dead was a five-year-old girl.

deal

1 'a great deal' and 'a good deal'

A great deal or **a good deal** of something is a lot of it. **A great deal** is more common than **a good deal**.

There was a great deal of concern about energy shortages.
She drank a good deal of coffee with him in his office.

! BE CAREFUL

These expressions can only be used with uncountable nouns. You can talk, for example, about **a great deal of money**, but not about 'a great deal of apples'.

If you do something **a great deal** or **a good deal**, you spend a lot of time doing it.

They talked a great deal.

→ See **Adverbs and adverbials** for a graded list of words used to indicate degree

2 'deal with'

When you **deal with** something, you give it your attention and often solve a problem concerning it.

They learned to deal with any sort of emergency.

The past tense and -ed participle of **deal** is **dealt** /delt/.

When they had dealt with the fire, another crisis arose.
Any queries will be dealt with immediately.

If a book, speech, or film **deals with** a particular subject, it is concerned with it.

Chapter 2 deals with contemporary Paris.
The film deals with a strange encounter between two soldiers.

definitely

→ See **surely – definitely – certainly – naturally**

delay – cancel – postpone – put off

1 'delay'

If you **delay** doing something, you do it at a later time.

The government delayed granting passports to them until a week before their departure.
Try and persuade them to delay some of the changes.

If a plane, train, ship, or bus **is delayed**, it is prevented from leaving or arriving on time.

The coach was delayed for about five hours.
The flight has been delayed one hour, due to weather conditions.

2 'cancel'

If you **cancel** something that was arranged, you decide officially that it will not take place.

The Russian foreign minister has cancelled his trip to Washington.
Over 80 flights were cancelled because of bad weather.

3 'postpone' and 'put off'

If you **postpone** or **put off** an event, you arrange for it to take place at a later time than was originally planned. **Postpone** is more formal than **put off**.

The crew did not know that the invasion had been postponed.
This is not a decision that can be put off much longer.
The Association has put the event off until October.

demand

Demand can be a noun or a verb.

1 used as a countable noun

A **demand** for something is a firm request for it.

There have been demands for better services.

2 used as an uncountable noun

Demand for a product or service is the amount of it that people want.

Demand for organic food rose by 10% last year.

3 used as a verb

If you **demand** something, you ask for it very forcefully.

They are demanding higher wages.
I demand to see a doctor.
She had been demanding that he visit her.

❗ BE CAREFUL

When **demand** is a verb, don't use 'for' after it. Don't say, for example, 'They are demanding for higher wages'.

deny

1 saying that something is not true

If you **deny** an accusation or a statement, you say that it is not true.

The accused women denied all the charges brought against them.
He denied that he was involved.
Gabriel denied doing anything illegal.

❗ BE CAREFUL

Deny must be followed by an object, a *that*-clause, or an *-ing* form. You say, for example, 'He accused her of stealing, but she **denied it**'. Don't say 'He accused her of stealing but she denied'.

If someone answers 'no' to an ordinary question in which they are not accused of anything, don't say that they 'deny' what they are asked. Don't say, for example, 'I asked him if the train had left, and he denied it'. You say 'I asked him if the train had left, and he **said no**'.

She asked if you'd been in and I said no.

2 refusing to let someone have something

If you **deny** someone something that they need or want, you refuse to let them have it.

His ex-wife denied him access to his children.
Don't deny yourself pleasure.

❗ BE CAREFUL

However, if someone says that they will not do something that someone asks them to do, don't say that they 'deny' it. You say that they **refuse to do** it or **refuse**.

Three employees were dismissed for refusing to join a union.
We asked them to play a game with us, but they refused.

depend

1 'depend on'

If you **depend on** someone or something or **depend upon** them, you need them in order to survive.

At college Julie seemed to depend on Simon more and more.
Uruguay's economy has depended heavily on its banking sector.
The factories depend upon natural resources.

If one thing **depends on** another thing, the first thing is affected by the second.

The success of the meeting depends largely on whether the chairperson is efficient.
The cooking time depends on the size of the potato.

> ❗ BE CAREFUL
>
> **Depend** is never an adjective. Don't say, for example, that someone or something 'is depend on' another person or thing. You say that they are **dependent** on that person or thing.
>
> *The local economy is dependent on oil and gas extraction.*

2 'depending on'

You use **depending on** to say that something varies according to particular circumstances.

There are, depending on the individual, a lot of different approaches.
They cost £20 or £25 depending on the size.

3 'it depends'

Sometimes people answer a question by saying 'It depends', rather than 'yes' or 'no'. They usually then explain what else affects the situation.

'What time will you arrive?' 'It depends. If I come by train, I'll arrive at 5 o'clock. If I come by bus, I'll be a bit later.'

describe

The verb **describe** can be used either with a direct object or with a *wh*-clause.

1 used with a direct object

When you **describe** someone or something, you say what they are like.

Can you describe your son?

You can use **describe** with a direct object and an indirect object. The direct object goes first.

He described the murderer in detail to the police officer.
She described the feeling to me.

2 used with a *wh*-clause

Describe can be used in front of various kinds of *wh*-clause.

The man described what he had seen.
He described how he escaped from prison.

You can use **describe** with an indirect object and a *wh*-clause. The indirect object goes first.

I can't describe to you what it was like.
I described to him what had happened in Patricia's house.

> ❗ BE CAREFUL
>
> When you use **describe** with an indirect object, you must put **to** in front of the indirect object. Don't say, for example, 'She described me the feeling' or 'I can't describe you what it was like'.

desert – dessert

1 'desert' as a noun

A **desert** /'dezət/ is a large area of land where there is very little water or rain, no trees, and very few plants.

They crossed the Sahara Desert.

2 'desert' as a verb

When people or animals **desert** /dɪ'zɜːt/ a place, they all leave it.

Poor farmers are deserting their fields and coming here looking for jobs.

If you **desert** someone, you leave them and no longer help or support them.

All our friends have deserted us.

3 'dessert'

Dessert /dɪ'zɜːt/ is sweet food served at the end of a meal.

For dessert there was ice cream.

despite

→ See **in spite of – despite**

dessert

→ See **desert – dessert**

destroy – spoil – ruin

1 'destroy'

If you **destroy** something, you cause so much damage to it that it can no longer be used or it no longer exists.

Several apartment buildings were destroyed by the fire.
I destroyed the letter as soon as I had read it.

2 'spoil' and 'ruin'

If someone or something prevents an experience from being enjoyable, don't say that they 'destroy' the experience. You say that they **spoil** it or **ruin** it.

The evening had been spoiled by their argument.
The weather had completely ruined their day.

detail – details

1 'detail'

A **detail** is an individual feature or element of something.

I can still remember every single detail of that night.
He described it down to the smallest detail.

2 'details'

If you obtain **details** of something, you obtain information about it.

You can get <u>details</u> of nursery schools from the local authority.
Further <u>details</u> are available online.

! BE CAREFUL

Don't say that you obtain 'detail' of something.

GRAMMAR FINDER

Determiners

A **determiner** is a word used in front of a noun to show whether you are talking about a specific thing or just something of a particular type. There are two types of determiner: definite determiners and indefinite determiners.

1 definite determiners

You use **definite determiners** when the person you are talking to knows which person or thing you are talking about. The definite determiners are:

▸ **the definite article: the**

<u>The</u> man began to run towards <u>the</u> boy.

▸ **demonstratives: this, that, these, those**

How much is it for <u>that</u> big box?
Young people don't like <u>these</u> operas.

▸ **possessive determiners: my, your, his, her, its, our, their**

I waited a long time to park <u>my</u> car.
<u>Her</u> face was very red.

→ See **Possessive determiners**

2 indefinite determiners

You use an **indefinite determiner** when you are mentioning people or things for the first time, or talking about them generally without saying exactly which ones you mean. The indefinite determiners are:

a	both	less	no
a few	each	little	other
a little	either	many	several
all	enough	more	some
an	every	most	
another	few	much	
any	fewer	neither	

There was <u>a</u> man in the lift.
You can stop at <u>any</u> time you like.
There were <u>several</u> reasons for this.

→ See **Quantity**

3 related pronouns

Most words used as determiners are also used as pronouns.

<u>This</u> is a very complex issue.
Have you got <u>any</u> that I could borrow?
There is <u>enough</u> for all of us.

However, **the**, **a**, **an**, **every**, **no**, **other**, and the possessive determiners cannot be used as pronouns. You use **one** as a pronoun instead of 'a' or 'an', **each** instead of 'every', **none** instead of 'no', and **others** instead of 'other'.

Have you got one?
Each has a separate box and number.
There are none left.
Some stretches of road are more dangerous than others.

die

When a person, animal, or plant **dies**, they stop living. When a person, animal, or plant **is dying**, they are so ill or injured they will not live much longer. The other forms of **die** are **dies**, **dying**, **died**.

Blake died in January, aged 76.
The elm trees are all dying.

When someone dies as a result of a disease or injury, you can say that they **die of** the disease or injury or **die from** it.

An old woman dying of cancer was taken into hospital.
Simon Martin died from brain injuries caused by blows to the head.

Don't use any preposition except **of** or **from** after **die** in sentences like these.

You say that someone **dies of** hunger or thirst, or **dies of** natural causes. Don't use 'die from'.

Millions of children are dying of hunger.

→ See **dead**

difference – distinction

1 'difference'

The **difference** between things is the way or ways in which they are not the same.

Is there much difference between British and European law?
There are many differences between computers and humans.

If something **makes a difference** to a situation, it affects it, usually in a positive way. If something **makes no difference** to a situation, it doesn't affect it.

The training certainly made a difference to staff performance.
The story about her past made no difference to his feelings for her.

2 'distinction'

If someone points out that two things are different, don't say that they 'make a difference' between the things. You say that they **make a distinction** or **draw a distinction** between them.

It is important to make a distinction between claimants who are over retirement age and those who are not.
He draws a distinction between art and culture.

different

1 'different'

If one thing is **different from** another, it is unlike the other thing in some way.

The meeting was different from any that had gone before.
Health is different from physical fitness.

Many British people say that one thing is **different to** another. **Different to** means the same as **different from**.

My methods are totally different to his.

! BE CAREFUL

Some people object to this use. In conversation and informal writing, you can use either **different from** or **different to**, but in formal writing it is better to use **different from**.

 In American English, you can say that one thing is **different than** another. This use is often considered incorrect in British English, but it is sometimes the simplest possibility when the comparison involves a clause.

I am no different than I was 50 years ago.

2 'very different'

If there is a great difference between two things, you can say that one thing is **very different from** the other.

The firm is now very different from the way it was ten years ago.

! BE CAREFUL

Don't say that one thing is 'much different' from another.

If two things are quite similar, you can say that one thing is **not very different from** the other or **not much different from** the other.

I discovered that things were not very different from what I had seen in New York.
The new model is not much different from the old one.

3 'no different'

If two things are alike, you can say that one thing is **no different from** the other.

He was no different from any other child his age.

! BE CAREFUL

Don't say that one thing is 'not different' from another.

difficulty

1 'difficulty'

A **difficulty** is a problem.

There are a lot of difficulties that have to be overcome.
The main difficulty is a shortage of time.

2 'have difficulty'

If you **have difficulty doing** something or **have difficulty in doing** something, you are unable to do it easily.

I often *have difficulty sleeping*.
She *had* great *difficulty in learning* to read and write.

! BE CAREFUL

Don't say that someone 'has difficulty to do' something.

dinner – lunch

1 'dinner'

People usually call their main meal of the day **dinner**. Some people have this meal in the middle of the day, and others have it in the evening.

We had roast beef and potatoes for dinner.
I haven't had dinner yet.

2 'lunch'

People who call their evening meal **dinner** usually refer to a meal eaten in the middle of the day as **lunch**.

I had soup and a sandwich for lunch.
I'm going out to lunch.

! BE CAREFUL

You don't usually use 'a' with **dinner** or **lunch**. Don't say, for example, 'I haven't had a dinner yet'.

→ See **Topic** entry **Meals**

directly – direct

1 'directly' and 'direct': giving, receiving, and communicating

If one thing or person interacts **directly** with another thing or person, there is nothing or nobody between them.

We deal directly with our suppliers.
Plants get their energy directly from the sun.
I shall be writing to you directly in the next few days.

Instead of saying that you receive something 'directly' from someone, you can say that you receive it **direct** from them.

Other money comes direct from industry.

Similarly, instead of saying that one person writes 'directly' to another, you can say that they write **direct** to them.

I should have written direct to the manager.

2 'directly' and 'direct': movement

If you go **directly** to a place, you go there by the shortest possible route, without stopping anywhere else.

I spent a few days in New York, then went directly to my apartment in Cardiff-by-the-Sea.

You can also say that someone goes **direct** to a place.

Why hadn't he gone direct to his office?

> ❗ **BE CAREFUL**
>
> If you can travel to a place by one plane, train, or bus, without changing to another plane, train, or bus, don't say that you can go there 'directly'. You say that you can go there **direct**.
>
> *You can't go to Manchester <u>direct</u>. You have to change trains at Birmingham.*

3 'directly': looking at something

If you look straight at a person or thing, you can say that you are looking **directly** at them.

She turned her head and looked <u>directly</u> at them.

> ❗ **BE CAREFUL**
>
> Don't use 'direct' with this meaning.

4 'directly': position

If something is **directly** above, below, opposite, or in front of something else, it is exactly in that position.

The sun was almost <u>directly</u> overhead.
I took a seat <u>directly</u> opposite the governor.

> ❗ **BE CAREFUL**
>
> Don't use 'direct' with this meaning.

5 'directly': saying when something happens

If something happens **directly after** something else, it happens immediately after it.

<u>Directly after</u> the meeting, a senior cabinet minister spoke to the BBC.

In British English (but not American English), **directly** is also used as a conjunction to say that one thing happens immediately after another.

<u>Directly</u> he heard the door close, he picked up the telephone.

> ❗ **BE CAREFUL**
>
> Don't use 'direct' with this meaning.

---

disabled – handicapped

Someone who is **disabled** has an illness, injury or condition that restricts the way they can live, especially by making it difficult for them to move about.

There are many practical problems encountered by <u>disabled</u> people in the workplace.

Some people use **handicapped** with this meaning, but many people find this offensive.

The most sensitive ways of referring to people with a restricting physical condition are to call them **people with disabilities** or **people with special needs**.

Those who will gain the most are <u>people with disabilities</u> and their carers.
Employers should pay for the training of <u>young people with special needs</u>.

disagree

If you **disagree with** a person, statement, or idea, you have a different opinion of what is true or correct.

I _disagree completely with John Taylor._
I _disagree with_ much of what he says.

Don't use any preposition except **with** when you are mentioning the person, statement, or idea that you disagree with.

You can say that you **disagree with** someone **about** something.

I _disagreed with_ them _about_ how we should spend the money.

You can also say that two or more people **disagree about** something.

He and I _disagree about_ it.
Historians _disagree about_ the date of his birth.

disappear

If someone or something **disappears**, they go or are taken to a place where they can't be seen or found.

I _saw the car disappear_ round the corner.
She _disappeared_ down the corridor.
Tools _disappeared_ and were never found.

! **BE CAREFUL**

Don't use **disappeared** as an adjective. If you can't find something because it is not in its usual place, don't say that it 'is disappeared'. You say that it **has disappeared**.

He discovered that a pint of milk _had disappeared_ from the fridge.
By the time the examiners got to work, most of the records _had disappeared_.

disc – disk

1 **'disc' or 'disk': a flat circular object**

In British English, a **disc** is a flat circular object.

A traffic warden pointed out that I had no tax _disc_ on the windscreen.

 In American English, this word is spelled **disk**.

2 **'compact disc'**

In both British and American English, a flat shiny object that stores music is called a **compact disc**. The abbreviation **CD** is often used.

The soundtrack will be released on _compact disc_ this summer.

3 **'disk': computer storage**

In both British and American English, a **disk** is a flat circular plate that is used to store large amounts of information for use by a computer.

The _disk_ is then slotted into a desktop PC.
The image data may be stored on your hard _disk_.

discover

→ See **find**

discuss

If you **discuss** something with someone, you talk to them seriously about it.

She could not discuss his school work with him.
We need to discuss what to do.
We discussed whether to call the police.

> **! BE CAREFUL**
>
> **Discuss** is always followed by a direct object, a *wh*-clause, or a *whether*-clause. Don't say, for example, 'I discussed with him' or 'They discussed'.

discussion – argument

1 'discussion'

If you have a **discussion** with someone, you have a serious conversation with them.

After the lecture there was a lively discussion.

You say that you have a discussion **about** something or a discussion **on** something.

We had long discussions about our future plans.
We're having a discussion on nuclear power.

2 'argument'

Don't use **discussion** to refer to a disagreement between people, especially one that results in them shouting angrily at each other. This kind of disagreement is usually called an **argument**.

We had a terrible argument, and now she won't talk to me.
I said no, and we got into a big argument over it.

disease

→ See **illness – disease**

disk

→ See **disc – disk**

dislike – not like

If you **dislike** someone or something, you find them unpleasant.

From what I know of him I dislike him intensely.
She disliked the theatre.

In conversation and in less formal writing, you don't normally use 'dislike'. Instead, you use a negative word with **like**.

She doesn't like tennis.
I've never liked him.

You can say that someone **dislikes doing** something or **doesn't like doing** something.

Many people dislike following orders.
I don't like working in a team.

You can also say that someone **doesn't like to do** something.

He doesn't like to be beaten.

! BE CAREFUL

However, don't say that someone 'dislikes to do' something.

dispose of – get rid of

1 'dispose of'

If you **dispose of** something that you no longer want or need, you throw it away or give it to someone.

Hundreds of used computers had to be disposed of.
This is the safest means of disposing of nuclear waste.

! BE CAREFUL

You must use **of** after **dispose**. Don't say that someone 'disposes something'.

2 'get rid of'

Dispose is a fairly formal word. In conversation and in less formal writing, you usually say that someone **gets rid of** something.

Now let's get rid of all this stuff.
There was a lot of rubbish to be got rid of.

distance

→ See **Reference** section **Measurements**

distinction

→ See **difference – distinction**

disturb – disturbed

1 'disturb'

If you **disturb** someone, you interrupt what they are doing and cause them inconvenience.

If she's asleep, don't disturb her.
Sorry to disturb you, but can I use your telephone?

2 'disturbed'

The adjective **disturbed** has a different meaning. A **disturbed** person is very upset emotionally and often needs special care or treatment. When **disturbed** has this meaning, it comes in front of a noun.

They help emotionally disturbed youngsters.

If someone **is disturbed**, they are very worried. When **disturbed** has this meaning, it comes after a linking verb.

He _was disturbed_ by the news of the attack.

do

Do is one of the most common verbs in English. Its other forms are **does**, **doing**, **did**, **done**. It can be an auxiliary verb or a main verb.

1 used as an auxiliary verb

→ See **Auxiliary verbs** for general information about the use of **do** as an auxiliary, **Questions** for information on **do** as an auxiliary in questions, **Question tags** for information on **do** as an auxiliary in questions, **Imperatives** for information on **do** as an auxiliary in negative clauses

→ See **not** for information on **do** as an auxiliary in negative clauses

Do has two other special uses as an auxiliary verb:

2 used for emphasis

You can use **do** to emphasize a statement. The forms **do**, **does**, and **did** can all be used in this way.

I _do feel_ sorry for Roger.
I wanted to go over to the Ramsey's. Later that day, I _did drive by_.

You can use **do** in front of an imperative when you are urging someone to do something or accept something.

Do help yourself to a biscuit
Do be careful.

3 used to focus on an action

You can also use **do** as an auxiliary verb to focus on an action.

When you use **do** like this, you put **what** at the beginning of the sentence, followed by a noun or noun phrase and the auxiliary verb **do**. After **do**, you put **is** or **was** and an infinitive with or without _to_.

For example, instead of saying 'Carolyn opened a bookshop', you can say '**What Carolyn did was to open** a bookshop' or '**What Carolyn did was open** a bookshop'.

What Stephen did was to interview a lot of teachers.
What it does is draw out all the vitamins from the body.

You can use **all** instead of 'what' if you want to emphasize that just one thing is done and nothing else.

All he did was shake hands and wish me luck.
All she ever does is make jam.

4 used as a main verb

Do is used as a main verb to say that someone performs an action, activity, or task.

We _did_ quite a lot of work yesterday.

Do is often used with -ing nouns referring to jobs connected with the home, and with nouns referring generally to work.

He *does all the shopping* and I *do the cooking*.
Have you *done your homework* yet?
The man who *did the job* had ten years' training.

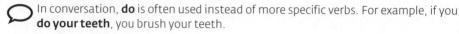

In conversation, **do** is often used instead of more specific verbs. For example, if you **do your teeth**, you brush your teeth.

Do I need to *do my hair*?
She had *done her breakfast dishes*.

! **BE CAREFUL**

You don't normally use 'do' when you are talking about creating or constructing something. Instead you use **make**.

I like *making* cakes.
Thuy *makes* all her own clothes.

→ See **make**

5 **repeating 'do'**

In questions and negative clauses, you often use **do** twice. You use it first as an auxiliary verb to form the question or negative verb phrase, and then repeat it as the main verb. The main verb is always in the infinitive form without *to*.

What *did* she *do* all day when she wasn't working?
If this exercise hurts your back *do not do* it.

---

doubt

Doubt can be a noun or a verb.

1 **'doubt' used as a noun**

If you have a **doubt** or **doubts** about something, you feel uncertain about it and you don't know if it is true or possible.

I had moments of *doubt*.
The report raises *doubts* about current methods.

2 **'no doubt'**

If you have **no doubts about** something, you are certain that it is true.

Francesca had *no doubts about* the outcome of the trial.

If you say **there is no doubt that** something is true, you mean that it is certainly true.

There's no doubt that it's going to be difficult.

You must use a *that*-clause after **there is no doubt**. Don't use an *if*-clause or a *whether*-clause.

You add **no doubt** to a statement to say that you are assuming that something is true, although you can't really be certain about it.

As Jennifer has *no doubt* told you, we are leaving tomorrow.
The contract for this will *no doubt* be widely advertised.

→ See **Adverbs and adverbials** for a graded list of words used to indicate probability

3 **'doubt' used as a verb**

If you **doubt** whether something is true or possible, you think it is probably not true or possible.

I doubt whether it would work.
I doubt if Alan will meet her.

If someone says that something is true, or asks you if something is true, you can show that you think it is unlikely by saying **I doubt it**.

'Do your family know you're here?' – 'I doubt it.'

> ❗ **BE CAREFUL**
> Don't say '~~I doubt so~~'.

downwards

→ See **-ward – -wards**

dozen

1 'dozen'

You can refer to twelve things as **a dozen** things.

We need a loaf of bread and a dozen eggs.
When he got there he found more than a dozen men having dinner.

> ❗ **BE CAREFUL**
> You use **a** in front of **dozen**. Don't talk about 'dozen' things.

You can talk about larger numbers of things by putting a number in front of **dozen**. For example, you can refer to 48 things as **four dozen** things.

On the trolley were two dozen cups and saucers.
They ordered three dozen cookies for a party.

You use the singular form **dozen** after a number. Don't talk about '~~two dozens cups and saucers~~'. Also, don't use 'of' after **dozen**. Don't say '~~two dozen of cups and saucers~~'.

2 'dozens'

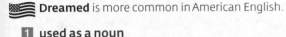In conversation, you can use **dozens** to emphasize that you are talking about a very large number of things. **Dozens** is followed by **of** when it is used in front of a noun.

She's borrowed dozens of books.
There had been dozens of attempts at reform.

dream

Dream can be a noun or a verb. The past tense and *-ed* participle of the verb is either **dreamed** /driːmd/ or **dreamt** /dremt/.

 Dreamed is more common in American English.

1 used as a noun

A **dream** is an imaginary series of events that you experience in your mind while you are asleep.

In his dream he was sitting in a theatre watching a play.

You say that someone **has** a dream.

The other night I had a strange dream.
Sam has bad dreams every night.

You don't usually say that someone 'dreams a dream'.

A **dream** is also a situation or event that you often think about because you would like it to happen.

My dream is to have a house in the country.
His dream of becoming a pilot had come true.

2 used as a verb

When someone experiences imaginary events while they are asleep, you can say that they **dream** something happens or **dream that** something happens.

I dreamed Marnie was in trouble.
Daniel dreamt that he was back in Minneapolis.

You can also say that someone **dreams about** someone or something or **dreams of** them.

Last night I dreamed about you.
I dreamt of him every night.

When someone thinks about a situation that they would like to happen, you can say that they **dream of having** something or **dream of doing** something.

He dreamt of having a car.
I've always dreamed of becoming a writer.

! BE CAREFUL

Don't say that someone 'dreams to have' something or 'dreams to do' something.

---

dress

1 'dress' and 'get dressed'

When someone **dresses**, they put on their clothes. This use of **dress** occurs mainly in stories.

When he had shaved and dressed, he went down to the kitchen.

In conversation and in less formal writing, you don't usually say that someone 'dresses'. You say that they **get dressed**.

Please hurry up and get dressed, Morris.
I got dressed and went downstairs.

If you say that someone **dresses** in a particular way, you mean that they usually wear clothes of a particular type.

She's over 40, but she still dresses like a teenager.
I really must try to make him change the way he dresses.

2 'dressed in'

If you want to describe someone's clothes on a particular occasion, you can say that they are **dressed in** something.

He was dressed in a black suit.

When a person's clothes are all the same colour, you can say that they are **dressed in** that colour.

All the girls were dressed in white.

3 'dress up'

If you **dress up**, you put on different clothes so that you look smarter than usual. People **dress up** in order to go, for example, to a wedding or to an interview for a new job.

You don't need to dress up for dinner.

You can say that someone is **dressed up**.

You're all dressed up. Are you going somewhere?

If someone **dresses up as** someone else, they wear the kind of clothes that person usually wears.

My daughter dressed up as a princess for the party.

> **! BE CAREFUL**
>
> You only use **dress up** to say that someone puts on clothes that are not their usual clothes. If someone normally wears smart or attractive clothes, don't say that they 'dress up well'. You say that they **dress well**.
>
> *They all had enough money to dress well and buy each other drinks.*
> *We are told by advertisers and fashion experts that we must dress well and use cosmetics.*

---

drink

Drink can be a verb or a noun.

1 used as a transitive verb

When you **drink** a liquid, you take it into your mouth and swallow it. The past tense of **drink** is **drank**.

You should drink water at every meal.
I drank some of my tea.

The -ed participle is **drunk**.

He was aware that he had drunk too much coffee.

2 used as an intransitive verb

If you use **drink** without an object, you are usually talking about drinking alcohol.

You shouldn't drink and drive.

If you say that someone **drinks**, you mean that they regularly drink too much alcohol.

Her mother drank, you know.

If you say that someone **does not drink**, you mean that they don't drink alcohol at all.

She doesn't smoke or drink.

3 used as a countable noun

A **drink** is an amount of liquid that you drink.

I asked her for a drink of water.
Lynne brought me a hot drink.

To **have a drink** means to spend some time, usually with other people, drinking alcoholic drinks.

I'm going to have a drink with some friends this evening.

Drinks usually refers to alcoholic drinks.

The drinks were served in the sitting room.

4 **used as an uncountable noun**

Drink is alcohol.

There was plenty of food and drink at the party.

drugstore

→ See **chemist's – drugstore – pharmacy**

during

1 **'during' and 'in'**

You use **during** or **in** to say that something happens continuously or often from the beginning to the end of a period of time.

We often get storms during the winter.
This music was popular in the 1960s.

In sentences like these, you can almost always use **in** instead of **during**. There is very little difference in meaning. When you use **during**, you are usually emphasizing that something is continuous or repeated.

→ See **in**

You can also use **during** to say that something happens while an activity takes place.

I met a lot of celebrities during my years as a journalist.
During her visit, the Queen will also open the new hospital.

You can sometimes use **in** in sentences like these, but the meaning is not always the same. For example, 'What did you do **during** the war?' means 'What did you do while the war was taking place?', but 'What did you do **in** the war?' means 'What part did you play in the war?'

2 **single events**

Both **during** and **in** can be used to say that a single event happened at some point in the course of a period of time.

He died during the night.
His father had died in the night.
She left Bengal during the spring of 1740.
Mr Tyrie left Hong Kong in June.

It is more common to use **in** in sentences like these. If you use **during**, you are usually emphasizing that you are not sure of the exact time when something happened.

! BE CAREFUL

Don't use **during** to say how long something lasts. Don't say, for example, 'I went to Wales during two weeks'. You say 'I went to Wales **for** two weeks'.

→ See **for**

duty

→ See **obligation – duty**

Ee

each

1 'each'

You use **each** in front of the singular form of a countable noun to talk about every person or thing in a group. You use **each** rather than 'every' when you are thinking about the members of a group as individuals.

Each applicant has five choices.
They interviewed each candidate.
Each country is divided into several districts.

2 'each of'

Instead of using 'each', you can sometimes use **each of**. For example, instead of saying 'Each soldier was given a new uniform', you can say '**Each of** the soldiers was given a new uniform'. **Each of** is followed by a determiner and the plural form of a countable noun.

Each of these phrases has a different meaning.
They inspected each of her appliances carefully.

You also use **each of** in front of plural pronouns.

They were all just sitting there, each of them thinking private thoughts.
Each of these would be a big advance in its own right.

When you use **each of** in front of a plural noun or pronoun, you use a singular form of a verb after the noun or pronoun.

Each of these cases was carefully locked.
Each of us looks over the passenger lists.

! BE CAREFUL

You never use **each** without **of** in front of a plural noun or pronoun. Don't say, for example, 'Each cases was carefully locked'.

Don't use words such as 'almost', 'nearly', or 'not' in front of **each**. Don't say, for example, 'Almost each house in the street is for sale'. You say 'Almost **every** house in the street is for sale'.

They show great skills in nearly every aspect of school life.
Not every lecturer wants to do research.

Don't use 'each' or 'each of' in a negative clause. Don't say, for example, 'Each boy did not enjoy football' or 'Each of the boys did not enjoy football'. You say '**None of** the boys enjoyed football'.

None of them are actually African.
None of these suggestions is very helpful.

→ See **none**

3 referring back to 'each'

You usually use a singular pronoun such as **he**, **she**, **him**, or **her** to refer back to an expression containing **each**.

Each boy said what he thought had happened.

However, when you are referring back to an expression such as **each person** or **each student** which does not indicate a specific sex, you usually use a form of **they**.

Each resident has their own bathroom.

---

each other – one another

1 uses

You use **each other** or **one another** to show that each member of a group does something to or for the other members. For example, if Simon likes Louise and Louise likes Simon, you say that Simon and Louise like **each other** or like **one another**. **Each other** and **one another** are sometimes called **reciprocal pronouns**.

Each other and **one another** are usually the direct or indirect object of a verb.

We help each other a lot.
They sent one another gifts from time to time.

You can also use them as the object of a preposition.

Pierre and Thierry were jealous of each other.
They didn't dare to look at one another.

2 possessives

You can form possessives by adding **'s** to **each other** and **one another**.

I hope that you all enjoy each other's company.
Apes spend a great deal of time grooming one another's fur.

3 differences

There is very little difference in meaning between **each other** and **one another**. **One another** is fairly formal, and many people do not use it at all. Some people prefer to use **each other** when they are talking about two people or things, and **one another** when they are talking about more than two. However, most people do not make this distinction.

---

easily

→ See **easy – easily**

---

east

1 'east'

The **east** is the direction that you look towards in order to see the sun rise.

A strong wind was blowing from the east.

An **east** wind blows from the east.

It has turned bitterly cold, with a cruel east wind.

The **east** of a place is the part that is towards the east.

She lives in a small flat in the east of Glasgow.

The plane travelled on to the east of the continent.

East occurs in the names of some countries and regions.

He comes from East Timor.
They travelled around East Africa.

→ See **Reference** section **Capital letters**

2 'eastern'

However, you don't usually talk about the 'east' part of a country. You talk about the **eastern** part.

Most of the parks are in the eastern part of the city.

Similarly, don't talk about 'east Europe' or 'east England'. You say **eastern** Europe or **eastern** England.

They discussed the economies of Central and Eastern Europe.
He took a flight from Dijon in eastern France.

---

eastwards

→ See **-ward – -wards**

---

easy – easily

1 'easy'

Something that is **easy** can be done or achieved without effort or difficulty, because it is not complicated and causes no problems.

Both sides had secured easy victories earlier in the day.
The task was not easy.

The comparative and superlative forms of **easy** are **easier** and **easiest**.

This is much easier than it sounds.
This was the easiest stage.

You can say that **it is easy to do** something. For example, instead of saying 'Riding a camel is easy', you can say '**It is easy to ride** a camel'. You can also say 'A camel **is easy to ride**'.

It is always very easy to be cynical about politics.
The house is easy to keep clean.

2 'easily'

Easy is not an adverb, except in the expressions **go easy**, **take it easy**, and **easier said than done**. If you want to say that something is done without difficulty, you say that it is done **easily**.

Put things in a place where you can find them quickly and easily.
Belgium easily beat Mexico 3-0.

The comparative and superlative forms of **easily** are **more easily** and **most easily**.

Milk is digested more easily when it is skimmed.
This is the format that is most easily understood by customers.

economic

→ See **economics**

---

economical

→ See **economics**

---

economics

1 'economics'

Economics is a noun. It usually refers to the study of the way in which money, industry, and trade are organized.

Paula has a degree in economics.

When **economics** has this meaning, it is an uncountable noun. You use a singular form of a verb with it.

Economics is a science.

If you want to say that something relates to the subject of economics, you use **economics** in front of another noun.

He has an economics degree.
I teach in the economics department.

! BE CAREFUL

Don't talk about an 'economic degree' or an 'economic department'.

The **economics** of an industry or project are the aspects of it that are concerned with making a profit.

This decision will change the economics of the project.

When **economics** is used with this meaning, it is a plural noun. You use a plural form of a verb with it.

The economics of the airline industry are dramatically affected by rising energy costs.

2 'economy'

Economy is also a noun. The **economy** of a country or region is the system by which money, industry, and trade are organized there.

New England's economy is still largely based on manufacturing.
Unofficial strikes were damaging the British economy.

Economy is also careful spending or the careful use of things in order to save money.

His home was small for reasons of economy.

3 'economies'

If you make **economies**, you try to save money by not spending it on unnecessary things.

It might be necessary to make a few economies.
They will make economies by hiring fewer part-time workers.

> **!** **BE CAREFUL**
> However, don't refer to the money that someone has saved as their 'economies'.
> You refer to this money as their **savings**.
>
> *She spent all her savings.*
> *He opened a savings account.*

4 **'economic'**

Economic is an adjective. You use it to describe things connected with the organization of money and trade in a country or region. When **economic** has this meaning, you only use it in front of a noun. Don't use it after a linking verb.

The chancellor proposed radical economic reforms.
What has gone wrong with the economic system during the last ten years?

If something is **economic**, it makes a profit, or does not result in money being lost. When **economic** has this meaning, it can go either in front of a noun or after a linking verb.

It is difficult to provide an economic public transport service.
We have to keep fares high enough to make it economic for the service to continue.

5 **'economical'**

Economical is also an adjective. If something is **economical**, it is cheap to operate or use.

We bought a small, economical car.
This system was extremely economical because it ran on half-price electricity.

economies
→ See **economics**

economy
→ See **economics**

GRAMMAR FINDER

-ed participles

1 **basic uses**

The *-ed* participle of a verb is used in perfect forms, passives, and, in some cases, adjectives. It is also called the *-ed* form, especially when it is used as an adjective.

Advances have continued, though productivity has fallen.
Jobs are still being lost.
We cannot refuse to teach children the required subjects.

→ See **Verb forms**

The *-ed* participle is usually the same as the past form of the verb, except in the case of irregular verbs.

→ See **Reference** section **Irregular verbs**

2 introducing a clause

In writing, an -ed participle can be used to begin a clause, with a passive meaning. For example, instead of writing 'She was saddened by their betrayal and resigned', you could write 'Saddened by their betrayal, she resigned'. The main clause can refer to a consequence of the situation mentioned in the -ed participle clause, or just to a related event that followed it.

Stunned by the sudden assault, the enemy were overwhelmed.
Arrested as a spy and sentenced to death, he spent three months in prison.

Alternative structures are **having been**, **after having been**, or **after being** followed by an -ed participle.

Having been left fatherless in early childhood he was brought up by his uncle.
After being left for an hour in the waiting room, we were led to the consultant's office.

You can use -ed participles in clauses introduced by a subordinating conjunction, with no subject or auxiliary verb, when the subject would be the same as the one in the main clause.

Dogs, when threatened, make themselves smaller and whimper like puppies.
Although now recognised as an important habitat for birds, the area has been cut in half since 1962.

3 after nouns

You can use a clause beginning with an -ed participle after a noun, **those**, or an indefinite pronoun to identify or describe someone by saying what happens or has happened to them.

...a successful method of bringing up children rejected by their natural parents.
Many of those questioned in the poll agreed with the party's policy on defence.
It doesn't have to be someone appointed by the government.

educate

→ See **bring up – raise – educate**

effect

→ See **affect – effect**

effective – efficient

1 'effective'

If someone or something is **effective**, they do something well and produce the results that were intended.

We need effective street lighting.
Simple antibiotics are effective against this virus.
She was very effective in getting people to communicate.

2 'efficient'

If someone or something is **efficient**, they do a job well and successfully, without wasting time or energy.

You need a highly efficient production manager if you want to reduce costs.
Engines and cars can be made more efficient.

> **! BE CAREFUL**
>
> **Effective** and **efficient** are often confused, but they have slightly different meanings. If you are **effective**, you do a job properly; if you are **efficient**, you do it quickly and easily.
>
> *Doing research at the library can be effective, but using the internet is often more efficient.*

efficient

→ See **effective – efficient**

effort

If you **make an effort** to do something, you try hard to do it.

Schmitt made one more effort to escape.
Little effort has been made to investigate this claim.

> **! BE CAREFUL**
>
> Don't say that someone 'does an effort'.

either

1 used as a determiner

You use **either** in front of the singular form of a countable noun to say that something is true about each of two people or things.

Many children don't resemble either parent.
In either case, Robert would never succeed.

2 'either of'

Instead of using **either**, you can use **either of** with a plural noun. For example, instead of saying 'Either answer is correct', you can say '**Either of** the answers is correct'. There is no difference in meaning.

You could hear everything that was said in either of the rooms.
They didn't want either of their children to know about this.

You use **either of** in front of plural pronouns.

I don't know either of them very well.
He was better dressed than either of us.

> **! BE CAREFUL**
>
> Don't use **either** without **of** in front of a plural noun or pronoun. Don't say, for example 'He was better dressed than either us.'

Some people use a plural form of a verb after **either of** and a noun phrase. For example, instead of saying 'I don't think either of you is wrong', they say 'I don't think either of you **are** wrong'.

I'm surprised either of you are here.

This use is acceptable in conversation and in less formal writing, but in formal writing you should always use a singular form of a verb after **either of**.

Either of these interpretations is possible.

3 used in negative statements

You can use **either** or **either of** in a negative statement to emphasize that the statement applies to both of two things or people. For example, instead of saying about two people 'I don't like them', you can say 'I don't like **either of** them'.

She could not see either man.
There was no sound from either of the rooms.
'Which one do you want – the red one or the blue one?' – 'I don't want either.'

4 used to mean 'each'

If there are things on **either side** of something or **either end** of something, they are on both sides or both ends.

There were trees on either side of the road.
There are toilets at either end of the train.

5 used as an adverb

When one negative statement follows another, you can put **either** at the end of the second one.

I can't play tennis and I can't play golf either.
'I haven't got that address.' – 'No, I haven't got it either.'

→ See **neither, nor**

either ... or

1 used in positive statements

You use **either** and **or** when you are mentioning two alternatives and you want to show that no other alternatives are possible. You put **either** in front of the first alternative and **or** in front of the second one.

Recruits are interviewed by either Mrs Darby or Mr Beaufort.
He must have thought that I was either stupid or rude.
I was expecting you either today or tomorrow.
People either leave or are promoted.
Either she goes or I go.

2 used in negative statements

You use **either** and **or** in negative statements when you are emphasizing that a statement refers to both of two things or qualities. For example, instead of saying 'I haven't been to Paris or Rome', you can say 'I haven't been to **either** Paris **or** Rome'.

He was not the choice of either Dexter or the team manager.
Dr Li, you're not being either truthful or fair.

→ See **neither ... nor**

elderly

→ See **old**

electric – electrical – electronic

1 'electric'

You use **electric** in front of nouns to talk about particular machines or devices that use electricity.

The boat runs on an electric motor.
I switched on the electric fire.

2 'electrical'

You use **electrical** when you are talking in a more general way about machines, devices, or systems that use or produce electricity. **Electrical** is typically used in front of nouns such as **equipment**, **appliance**, and **component**.

They sell electrical appliances such as dishwashers and washing machines.
We are waiting for a shipment of electrical equipment.

You also use **electrical** to talk about people or organizations connected with the production of electricity or electrical goods.

Jan is an electrical engineer.
They work in the electrical engineering industry.

3 'electronic'

You use **electronic** to talk about a device that has transistors or silicon chips that control and change the electric current running through the device, or to describe a process or activity using electronic devices.

Mobile phones, laptops and other electronic devices must be switched off.
They use electronic surveillance systems.

elevator

→ See **lift – elevator**

GRAMMAR FINDER

Ellipsis

1 used in place of a verb phrase	6 'dare' and 'need'
2 'be'	7 'would rather'
3 'have' used as a main verb	8 'had better'
4 'have' used as an auxiliary verb	9 in conversation
5 *to*-infinitive clauses	10 in coordinate clauses

1 used in place of a verb phrase

Ellipsis involves leaving out words that are understood from the context. In many cases you use an auxiliary verb in place of a full verb phrase, or in place of a verb phrase and its object. For example, you say 'John won't like it but Rachel will' instead of 'John won't like it but Rachel will like it'.

They would stop it if they could.
I never went to Stratford, although I probably should have.
This topic should have attracted more attention from philosophers than it has.

A full clause would sound unnatural in these examples.

You use **do**, **does**, or **did**, when the auxiliary verb already occurs in the first verb phrase or when the verb phrase is present simple or past simple:

Do farmers deserve a ministry all to themselves? I think they do.
I think we want it more than they do.
He went shopping yesterday; at least, I think he did.

2 'be'

However, don't use the auxiliary verb 'do' to stand for the linking verb **be**. You just use a form of **be**. You also use a form of **be** when it is used as an auxiliary verb in the first verb phrase:

'I think you're right.' – 'I'm sure I <u>am</u>.'
'He was driving too fast.' – 'Yes, I know he <u>was</u>.'

If the second verb phrase contains a modal, you usually put **be** after the modal.

'He thought that the condition was quite serious.' – 'Well, it <u>might be</u>.'

Be is sometimes used after a modal in the second clause to contrast with another linking verb such as **seem**, **look**, or **sound**.

'It <u>looks</u> like tea to me.' – 'Yes, it <u>could be</u>.'

With passives, **be** is often, but not always, kept after a modal.

He argued that if tissues could be marketed, then anything <u>could be</u>.

3 'have' used as a main verb

When you are using **have** as a main verb, for example to show possession, you can use a form of **have** or a form of **do** to refer back to it.

 American speakers usually use a form of **do**.

She probably has a temperature – she certainly looks as if she <u>has</u>.
The Earth has a greater diameter than the Moon <u>does</u>.

Note that in the second example you don't need to use any verb after **than**. You can just say 'The Earth has a greater diameter than the Moon'.

4 'have' used as an auxiliary verb

When **have** is used as an auxiliary verb in the first verb phrase in a perfect form, you repeat it in the second verb phrase and omit the main verb:

'Have you visited Rome? I have.'

When you use the auxiliary verb **have** to stand for a perfect passive, you don't usually add 'been'. For example, you say, 'Have you been interviewed yet? I have.'

However, when **have** is used after a modal, **been** cannot be omitted.

I'm sure it was repeated in the media. It <u>must have been</u>.
They were not working as hard as they <u>should have been</u>.

5 *to*-infinitive clauses

Instead of using a full *to*-infinitive clause after a verb, you can just use **to**, if the action or state has already been mentioned.

Don't tell me if you don't want <u>to</u>.
At last he agreed to do what I asked him <u>to</u>.

6 'dare' and 'need'

You can omit a verb after **dare** and **need**, but only when they are used in the negative.

'I don't mind telling you what I know.' – 'You <u>needn't</u>. I'm not asking you to'.
'You must tell her the truth.' – 'But, Neill, I <u>daren't</u>.'

 Speakers of American English do not use the contraction 'daren't'. Instead, they say **don't dare** or **dare not**.

I hear her screaming and I <u>don't dare</u> open the door.

⑦ 'would rather'

Similarly, the verb is only omitted after **would rather** when it is used in a negative clause or an *if*-clause.

It's just that I'd rather not.
We could go to your place, if you'd rather.

⑧ 'had better'

The verb is sometimes omitted after **had better**, even when it is used affirmatively.

'I can't tell you.' – 'You'd better.'

However, you don't usually omit **be**.

'He'll be out of town by nightfall.' – 'He'd better be.'

⑨ in conversation

Ellipsis often occurs in conversation in replies and questions.

→ See **Topic** entry **Agreeing and disagreeing**, **Reactions**, **Replies**, **Questions**

⑩ in coordinate clauses

Words are often left out of the second of two coordinate clauses, for example after **and** or **or**.

→ See **and**

---

else

① used with 'someone', 'somewhere', and 'anything'

You use **else** after words such as **someone**, **somewhere**, or **anything** to refer to another person, place, or thing, without saying which one.

She had borrowed someone else's hat.
Let's go somewhere else.
I had nothing else to do.

② used with wh-words

You can use **else** after most *wh*-words. For example, if you ask '**What else** did they do?', you are asking what other things were done besides the things that have already been mentioned.

What else do I need to do?
Who else was there?
Why else would he be so angry?
Where else could they live in such comfort?
How else was I to explain what had happened?

Don't use 'else' after 'which'.

③ 'or else'

Or else is a conjunction with a similar meaning to **or**. You use it to introduce the second of two possibilities.

She is either very brave or else she must be very stupid.
It's likely that someone gave her a lift, or else that she took a taxi.

You also use **or else** when you are saying that something bad will happen if someone does not do a particular thing.

We need to hurry or else we'll be late.

embarrassed

→ See **ashamed – embarrassed**

emigration – immigration – migration

1 'emigrate', 'emigration', 'emigrant'

If you **emigrate**, you leave your own country and go to live permanently in another country.

He received permission to emigrate to Canada.
He had emigrated from Germany in the early 1920's.

People who emigrate are called **emigrants**. The act of emigrating is called **emigration**. However, these words are less frequent than **immigrant** and **immigration**.

2 'immigrate', 'immigration', 'immigrant'

If you **immigrate** to a country, you go to live in that country permanently.

They immigrated to Israel.

However, it is more common to say that someone **emigrates from** a country than to say that someone **immigrates to** a country.

People that leave their own country to live in another country are called **immigrants**.

The company employs several immigrants.

The process by which people come to live in a country is called **immigration**.

The government has changed its immigration policy.

3 'migrate', 'migration', 'migrant'

When people **migrate**, they temporarily move to another place, usually a city or another country, in order to find work.

The only solution people can see is to migrate.
Millions have migrated to the cities.

This process is called **migration**.

New jobs are encouraging migration from the cities of the north.

People who migrate are called **migrants** or **migrant workers**.

She was a migrant looking for a place to live.
In South America there are three million migrant workers.

employ – use

1 'employ'

If you **employ** someone, you pay them to work for you.

The company employs 7.5 million people.
He was employed as a research assistant.

If something **is employed** for a particular purpose, it is used for that purpose. You can say, for example, that a particular method or technique **is employed**.

A number of ingenious techniques are employed.
The methods employed are varied, depending on the material in question.

You can also say that a machine, tool, or weapon **is employed**.

Similar technology could be employed in the major cities.
What matters most is how the tools are employed.

2 'use'

However, **employ** is a formal word when it is used to talk about such things as methods or tools. You usually say that a method or tool **is used**.

This method has been extensively used in the United States.
These weapons are used in training sessions.

enable

→ See **allow – permit – let – enable**

end

1 'end'

When something **ends** or when you **end** it, it stops.

The current agreement ends on November 24.
He wanted to end their friendship.

2 'end with'

If you **end with** something, it is the last of a series of things that you say, do, or perform.

He ended with the question: "When will we learn?"
The concert ended with a Bach sonata.

3 'end by'

If you **end by doing** something, it is the last of a series of things that you do.

I ended by saying that further instructions would be given to him later.
The letter ends by requesting a deadline.

4 'end up'

You use **end up** to say what happens at the end of a series of events, usually without being planned. You can say that someone or something **ends up** in a particular place, that they **end up** with something, or that they **end up** doing something.

A lot of computer hardware ends up in landfill sites.
She was afraid to close the window and ended up with a cold.
We missed our train, and we ended up taking a taxi.

endure

→ See **bear, Britain – British – Briton**

enjoy

1 'enjoy'

If you **enjoy** something, you get pleasure and satisfaction from it.

I enjoyed the holiday enormously.

2 used with a reflexive pronoun

If you experience pleasure and satisfaction on a particular occasion, you can say that you **enjoyed yourself**.

I've enjoyed myself very much.

People often say **Enjoy yourself** to someone who is going to a social occasion such as a party or a dance.

Enjoy yourself on Wednesday.

3 used with an -*ing* form

You can say that someone **enjoys doing** something or **enjoys being** something.

I used to enjoy going for long walks.
They enjoyed being in a large group.

> **!** **BE CAREFUL**
>
> Don't say that someone 'enjoys to do' or 'enjoys to be' something.

4 used as an imperative

Enjoy is normally only a transitive or reflexive verb. Don't say 'I enjoyed'. However, you can say **Enjoy**!, meaning 'Enjoy yourself' or 'Enjoy your meal'.

Here's your pizza. Enjoy!

---

enough

1 after adjectives and adverbs

You use **enough** after an adjective or adverb to say that someone or something has as much of a quality as is needed.

It's big enough.
We have a long enough list.
The student isn't trying hard enough.

If you want to say who the person or thing is acceptable to, you add a prepositional phrase beginning with **for**.

That's good enough for me.
Is the soup hot enough for you?

If someone has as much of a quality as they need in order to do something, you add a *to*-infinitive after **enough**.

The children are old enough to travel to school on their own.

You can also use a *to*-infinitive after **enough** to say that something has as much of a quality as is needed for someone to do something with it. If you want to make it clear who you are talking about, you can add a prepositional phrase beginning with **for**. For example, you can say 'The boat was **close enough to touch**' or 'The boat was **close enough for me to touch it**'.

The bananas are <u>ripe enough to eat</u>.
The music was just loud <u>enough for us to hear it</u>.

> **!** **BE CAREFUL**
>
> Don't use a *that*-clause after **enough** when you are saying what is needed for something to be possible. Don't say, for example, '~~The bananas are ripe enough that we can eat them~~'.

Enough is sometimes used after an adjective to confirm or emphasize that something or someone has a particular quality.

It's a <u>common enough</u> dilemma.

When you make a statement of this kind, you often add a second statement that contrasts with it.

She's <u>likeable enough</u>, but very ordinary.

2 used as a determiner

Enough is used in front of the plural form of a countable noun to say that there are as many things or people as are needed.

They need to make sure there are <u>enough bedrooms</u> for the family.
Do we have <u>enough chairs</u>?

You can also use **enough** in front of an uncountable noun to say that there is as much of something as is needed.

We had <u>enough room</u> to store all the information.
He hasn't had <u>enough exercise</u>.

3 'enough of'

Don't use **enough** immediately in front of a noun phrase beginning with a determiner, or in front of a pronoun. Instead you use **enough of**.

All parents worry about whether their child is getting <u>enough of the right foods</u>.
They haven't had <u>enough of it</u>.

When you use **enough of** in front of a plural noun or pronoun, you use a plural form of a verb with it.

Eventually enough of these shapes <u>were</u> collected.
There <u>were</u> enough of them to fill a large box.

When you use **enough of** in front of a singular or uncountable noun or a singular pronoun, you use a singular form of a verb with it.

Is there enough of a market for this product?
There <u>is</u> enough of it for everybody.

4 used as a pronoun

Enough can be used on its own as a pronoun.

I've got <u>enough</u> to worry about.
<u>Enough</u> has been said about this already.

5 'not enough'

Don't use **enough**, or **enough** and a noun, as the subject of a negative sentence. Don't say, for example, '~~Enough people didn't come~~'. You say '**Not enough** people came'.

<u>Not enough</u> has been done to help them.
<u>Not enough attention</u> is paid to young people.

6 modifying adverbs

You can use adverbs such as **nearly**, **almost**, **just**, **hardly**, and **quite** in front of **enough**.

At present there is just enough to feed them.
There was hardly enough time to have lunch.

You can also use these adverbs in front of an expression consisting of an adjective and **enough**.

We are all nearly young enough to be mistaken for students.
She is just old enough to work.

7 used with sentence adverbials

You can use **enough** after sentence adverbials like **interestingly** or **strangely** to draw attention to a surprising quality in what you are saying.

Interestingly enough, there were some questions that Brian couldn't answer.
I find myself strangely enough in agreement with Jamal for a change.

ensure

→ See **assure – ensure – insure**

entirely

→ See **Adverbs and adverbials** for a graded list of words used to indicate extent

equally

You use **equally** in front of an adjective to say that a person or thing has as much of a quality as someone or something else that has been mentioned.

He was a superb pianist. Irene was equally brilliant.

! BE CAREFUL

Don't use 'equally' in front of **as** when making a comparison. Don't say, for example, 'He is equally as tall as his brother'. You say 'He is **just as tall as** his brother'.

Severe sunburn is just as dangerous as a heat burn.
He was just as shocked as I was.

→ See **as ... as**

equipment

Equipment consists of the things you need for a particular activity.

We need some new kitchen equipment.
They fix tractors and other farm equipment.

Equipment is an uncountable noun. Don't talk about 'equipments' or 'an equipment'. You can refer to a single item as a **piece of equipment**.

This radio is an important piece of equipment.
The leader carried a number of pieces of equipment with him.

error

→ See **mistake**

especially – specially

1 'especially'

You use **especially** to show that what you are saying applies more to one thing or situation than to others.

He was kind to his staff, especially those who were sick or in trouble.
Double ovens are a good idea, especially if you are cooking several meals at once.
These changes are especially important to small businesses.

When **especially** relates to the subject of a sentence, you put it immediately after the subject.

Young babies, especially, are vulnerable to colds.

You can also use **especially** in front of an adjective to emphasize a characteristic or quality.

I found her laugh especially annoying.

2 'specially'

You use **specially** to say that something is done or made for a particular purpose.

They'd come down specially to see us.
She wore a specially designed costume.
The school is specially for children whose schooling has been disrupted by illness.

---

even

1 position

You use **even** to show that what you are saying is surprising. You put **even** in front of the surprising part of your statement.

Even Anthony enjoyed it.
She liked him even when she was arguing with him.
I shall give the details to no one, not even to you.

However, **even** usually goes after an auxiliary verb or modal, not in front of it.

You didn't even enjoy it very much.
I couldn't even see the shore.
They may even give you a lift in their van.

2 used with comparatives

You use **even** in front of a comparative to emphasize that someone or something has more of a quality than they had before. For example, you say 'The weather was bad yesterday, but it is **even worse** today'.

He became even more suspicious of me.

You also use **even** in front of a comparative to emphasize that someone or something has more of a quality than someone or something else. For example, you say 'The train is slow, but the bus is **even slower**'.

Barbara had something even worse to tell me.
The second task was even more difficult.

3 'even if' and 'even though'

Even if and **even though** are used to introduce subordinate clauses. You use **even if** to say that a possible situation would not prevent something from being true.

Even if you disagree with her, she's worth listening to.
I hope I can come back, even if it's only for a few weeks.

Even though has a similar meaning to 'although', but is more emphatic.

He went to work even though he was unwell.
I was always afraid of him, even though he was kind to me.

! BE CAREFUL

If you begin a sentence with **even if** or **even though**, don't put 'yet' or 'but' at the beginning of the main clause. Don't say, for example, 'Even if you disagree with her, yet she's worth listening to'.

However, you can use **still** in the main clause. This is a very common use.

Even though the news is six months old, staff are still in shock.
But even if they do change the system, they still face an economic crisis.

---

evening

The **evening** is the part of each day between the end of the afternoon and the time when you go to bed.

1 the present day

You refer to the evening of the present day as **this evening**.

Come and have dinner with me this evening.
I came here this evening because I wanted to be on my own.

You can refer to the evening of the previous day as **yesterday evening**, but it is more common to say **last night**.

'So you saw me in King Street yesterday evening?' – 'Yes.'
I met your husband last night.
I've been thinking about what we said last night.

You refer to the evening of the next day as **tomorrow evening** or **tomorrow night**.

Gerald's giving a little party tomorrow evening.
Will you be home in time for dinner tomorrow night?

2 single events in the past

If you want to say that something happened during a particular evening in the past, you use **on**.

She telephoned Ida on Tuesday evening.
On the evening after the party, Dirk went to see Erik.

If you have been describing what happened during a particular day, you can say that something happened **that evening** or **in the evening**.

That evening the children asked me to watch television with them.
He came back in the evening.

If you are talking about a day in the past and you want to mention that something had happened during the evening of the day before, you say that it had happened **the previous evening** or **the evening before**.

Douglas had spent the previous evening at a hotel.
Freya opened the gift Beth had given her the evening before.

If you want to say that something happened during the evening of the next day, you say that it happened **the following evening**.

Mopani arrived at their house the following evening.
I told Patricia that I would take her for dinner the following evening.

3 talking about the future

If you want to say that something will happen during a particular evening in the future, you use **on**.

The winning project will be announced on Monday evening.
I will write to her on Sunday evening.

If you are already talking about a day in the future, you can say that something will happen **in the evening**.

The school sports day will be on June 22 with prizegiving in the evening.

4 regular events

If something happens regularly every evening, you say that it happens **in the evening** or **in the evenings**.

In the evening I like to iron my clothes as this is one less job for the morning.
And what do you do in the evenings?

 In American English, **evenings** does not require 'in' or 'on'.

I like to go out evenings with friends.

If you want to say that something happens regularly once a week during a particular evening, you use **on** followed by the name of the day and **evenings**.

He plays chess on Monday evenings.
We would all gather there on Friday evenings.

 American English does not require 'on'.

Friday evenings he visited with his father.

5 exact times

If you have mentioned an exact time and you want to make it clear that you are talking about the evening rather than the morning, you add **in the evening**.

He arrived about six in the evening.

→ See **Topic** entry **Time**

eventually – finally

! BE CAREFUL

Don't use 'eventually' when you mean that something might be true. Use **possibly** or **perhaps**.

Perhaps he'll call later.

1 'eventually' or 'finally'

When something happens after a lot of delays or problems, you can say that it **eventually** happens or that it **finally** happens You use **eventually** when you want to emphasize that there were a lot of problems. You use **finally** when you want to emphasize the amount of time it took.

Eventually they got to the hospital.
I found Victoria Avenue eventually.
When John finally arrived, he said he'd lost his way.

2 'finally'

You can also use **finally** to show that something happens last in a series of events.

The sky turned red, then purple, and finally black.

Don't use 'eventually' with this meaning, unless you want to emphasize that it happened after a lot of delays or problems.

You can also use **finally** to introduce a final point, ask a final question, or mention a final item.

Finally, Carol, can you tell us why you want this job?
Combine the flour and the cheese, and finally, add the milk.

Don't use 'eventually' with this meaning.

---

ever

1 'ever'

Ever is used in negative sentences, questions, and comparisons to mean 'at any time in the past' or 'at any time in the future'.

Neither of us had ever skied.
I don't think I'll ever be homesick here.
Have you ever played football?
I'm happier than I've ever been.

2 'yet'

Don't use **ever** in questions or negative sentences to ask whether an expected event has happened, or to say that it has not happened so far. Don't say, for example, 'Has the taxi arrived ever?' or 'The taxi has not arrived ever'. The word you use is **yet**.

Have you had your lunch yet?
It isn't dark yet.

→ See **yet**

3 'always'

Don't use **ever** in positive sentences to say that there was never a time when something was not true. Don't say, for example, 'I've ever been happy here'. Use **always**.

She was always in a hurry.
Talking to Harold always cheered her up.

→ See **always**

4 'still'

Don't use **ever** to say that something is continuing to happen. Don't say, for example, 'When we left, it was ever raining'. Use **still**.

Unemployment is still falling.
I'm still a student.

→ See **still**

5 'ever since'

If something has been true **ever since** a particular time, it has been true all the time from then until now.

'How long have you lived here?' – 'Ever since I was married.'
We have been good friends ever since.

---

every

1 'every'

You use **every** in front of the singular form of a countable noun to show that you are referring to all the members of a group and not just some of them.

She spoke to every person at the party.
I agree with every word Peter says.
This new wealth can be seen in every village.

2 'every' and 'all'

You can often use **every** or **all** with the same meaning. For example, '**Every** student should attend' means the same as '**All** students should attend'.

However, **every** is followed by the singular form of a noun, whereas **all** is followed by the plural form.

Every child is entitled to free education.
All children love to build and explore.

→ See **all**

3 'each'

Instead of 'every' or 'all', you sometimes use **each**. You use **each** when you are thinking about the members of a group as individuals.

Each customer has the choice of thirty colours.
Each meal will be served in a different room.

→ See **each**

4 referring back to 'every'

You usually use a singular pronoun such as **he**, **she**, **him**, or **her** to refer back to an expression beginning with **every**.

Every businesswoman would have a secretary if she could.

However, when you are referring back to an expression such as **every student** or **every inhabitant** which does not indicate a specific sex, you usually use **they** or **them**.

Every employee knew exactly what their job was.

5 used with expressions of time

You use **every** to show that something happens at regular intervals.

They met every day.
Every Monday there is a staff meeting.

Every and **all** do not have the same meaning when they are used with expressions of time. For example, if you do something **every morning**, you do it regularly each morning. If you do something **all morning**, you spend the whole of one morning doing it.

He goes running every day.
I was busy all day.

6 **'every other'**

If something happens, for example, **every other** year or **every second** year, it happens one year, then does not happen the next year, then happens the year after that, and so on.

We only save enough money to take a real vacation every other year.
It seemed easier to shave every second day.

---

everybody

→ See **everyone – everybody**

---

everyday – every day

1 **'everyday'**

Everyday is an adjective. You use it to describe something that is normal and not exciting or unusual in any way.

...the everyday problems of living in the city.
Computers are a part of everyday life for most people.

2 **'every day'**

Every day is an adverbial phrase. If something happens **every day**, it happens regularly each day.

Shanti asked the same question every day.

---

everyone – everybody

1 **'everyone' and 'everybody'**

You usually use **everyone** or **everybody** to refer to all the people in a particular group.

The police had ordered everyone out of the office.
There wasn't enough room for everybody.

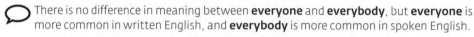 There is no difference in meaning between **everyone** and **everybody**, but **everyone** is more common in written English, and **everybody** is more common in spoken English.

You can also use **everyone** and **everybody** to talk about people in general.

Everyone has the right to freedom of expression.
Everybody has to die some day.

After **everyone** or **everybody** you use a singular form of a verb.

Everyone wants to find out what is going on.
Everybody is selling the same product.

2 **referring back**

When you are referring back to **everyone** or **everybody**, you usually use **they**, **them**, or **their**.

Will everyone please carry on as best they can.
Everybody had to bring their own paper.

3 'every one'

Don't confuse **everyone** with **every one**. You use **every one** to emphasize that something is true about each one of the things or people you are mentioning.

He read every one of her novels.
She thought about her friends. Every one had tried to help her.

evidence

Evidence is anything that you see, hear, or read that causes you to believe that something is true or has really happened.

We saw evidence everywhere that a real effort was being made to promote tourism.
There was no evidence of problems between them.

Evidence is an uncountable noun. Don't talk about '~~evidences~~' or '~~an evidence~~'. However, you can talk about a **piece of evidence**.

The finding is the latest piece of evidence that vaccines can help prevent cancer.
It was one of the strongest pieces of evidence in the Crown's case.

exam – examination

An **exam** or **examination** is an official test that shows your knowledge or ability in a particular subject. **Exam** is the word most commonly used. **Examination** is more formal and is used mainly in written English.

I was told the exam was difficult.
All students must take a three-hour written examination.

When someone takes part in an exam, you say that they **take** it or **sit** it.

Many children want to take these exams.
After the third term we'll be sitting the exam.

 Speakers of American English generally use **take** instead of 'sit'.

In conversation, you can also say that someone **does** an exam.

I did my exams last week.

If someone is successful in an exam, you say that they **pass** it.

If you want a good job, you'll have to pass your exams.

! BE CAREFUL

To **pass** an exam always means to succeed in it. It does not mean to take part in it.

If someone is unsuccessful in an exam, you say that they **fail** it.

He failed the entrance exam.
I passed the written part but then failed the oral section hopelessly.

You also say that someone **passes in** or **fails in** a particular subject.

I've been told that I'll probably pass in English and French.
I failed in a few other subjects.

example

1 'example'

If something has the typical features of a particular kind of thing, you can say that it is an **example of** that kind of thing.

It's a very fine example of traditional architecture.
This is yet another example of poor management.

When someone mentions an example of a particular kind of thing, you say that they are **giving** an example of that kind of thing.

Could you give me an example?
Let me give you an example of the sort of thing that happens.

! BE CAREFUL

Don't say that someone 'says an example'.

2 'for example'

When you mention an example of something, you often say **for example**.

Switzerland, for example, has four official languages.
There must be some discipline in the home. For example, I do not allow my daughter to play with my computer.

! BE CAREFUL

Don't say 'by example'.

except

You use **except** to introduce the only thing, person, or group that your main statement does not apply to.

1 used with a noun phrase

You usually use **except** in front of a noun phrase.

Anything, except water, is likely to block a sink.
All the boys except Peter started to laugh.

You can use **except** in front of object pronouns such as **me**, **him**, or **her**, or in front of reflexive pronouns such as **himself** or **herself**.

There's nobody except me.
Pedro didn't trust anyone except himself.

! BE CAREFUL

Don't use **except** in front of subject pronouns. Don't say, for example, 'There's nobody here except I'.

Don't confuse **except** with **besides** or **unless**. You use **except** when you mention something that a statement does not apply to. **Besides** means 'in addition to'.

What languages do you know besides Arabic and English?

→ See **beside – besides**

> **!** **BE CAREFUL**
>
> **Unless** is used to introduce the only situation in which something will take place or be true.
>
> *I won't speak to you <u>unless</u> you apologize.*

→ See **unless**

2 used with a verb

You can use **except** in front of a *to*-infinitive.

I never wanted anything <u>except to be an actor</u>.
She seldom goes out <u>except to go to church</u>.

After **do**, you can use **except** in front of an infinitive without *to*.

There was little I could <u>do except wait</u>.

3 used with a finite clause

You can use **except** in front of a finite clause, but only when the clause is introduced by **when**, **while**, **where**, **what**, or **that**.

I knew nothing about Judith <u>except what her dad told me</u>.
I can't remember what we ate, <u>except that it was delicious</u>.

> **!** **BE CAREFUL**
>
> Don't use 'except' immediately in front of a finite verb. Don't say, for example '~~I can't remember what we ate, except it was delicious~~'.

4 'except for'

You use **except for** in front of a noun phrase when you are mentioning something that prevents a statement from being completely true.

The classroom was silent, <u>except for the sound of pens on paper</u>.
The room was very cold and, <u>except for Mao</u>, entirely empty.

→ See **accept – except**

excited – exciting

1 'excited'

Excited is used to describe how a person feels when they are looking forward eagerly to an enjoyable or special event.

He was so <u>excited</u> he could hardly sleep.
There were hundreds of <u>excited</u> children waiting for us.

You say that someone is **excited about** something.

I'm very <u>excited about</u> the possibility of joining the team.

You can say that someone is **excited about doing** something.

Kendra was especially <u>excited about seeing</u> him after so many years.

When someone is looking forward to doing something, don't say that they are '~~excited to do~~' it.

2 'exciting'

Don't confuse **excited** with **exciting**. An **exciting** book or film is full of action, and an **exciting** idea or situation makes you feel very enthusiastic.

The film was a bit scary, and very exciting.
It did not seem a very exciting idea.

excursion

→ See **journey – trip – voyage – excursion**

excuse

Excuse can be a noun or a verb. When it is a noun, it is pronounced /ɪkˈskjuːs/. When it is a verb, it is pronounced /ɪkˈskjuːz/.

1 used as a noun

An **excuse** is a reason that you give in order to explain why something has been done, has not been done, or will not be done.

They are trying to find excuses for their failures.
There is no excuse for this happening in a new building.

You say that someone **makes** an excuse.

I made an excuse and left the meeting early.
You don't have to make any excuses to me.

! BE CAREFUL

Don't say that someone 'says an excuse'.

2 used as a verb

If someone **is excused** from doing something, they are officially allowed not to do it.

She is usually excused from her duties during the school holidays.
You can apply to be excused payment if your earnings are low.

In conversation, if you say you must **excuse** yourself or if you ask someone to **excuse** you, you are saying politely that you must leave.

Now I must excuse myself.
You'll have to excuse me; I ought to be saying goodnight.

If you **excuse** someone for something wrong they have done, you decide not to criticize them or be angry with them.

Such delays cannot be excused.
Please excuse my bad handwriting.

3 'forgive'

Forgive is used in a similar way. However, when you say that you **forgive** someone, you usually mean that you have already been angry with them or argued with them. You cannot use 'excuse' in this way.

I forgave him everything.

4 'excuse me'

People often say **Excuse me** as a way of politely apologizing for something they are going to do. For example, you can say **Excuse me** when you are interrupting someone, when you want to get their attention, or when you want to get past them.

Excuse me, but are you Mr Hess?

→ See **Topic** entry **Apologizing**

5 **'apologize'**

However, when people say they are sorry for something they have done, don't say that they 'excuse themselves'. You say that they **apologize**. If you want to say that you are sorry for something you have done, you say **Sorry, I'm sorry** or **I apologize**.

She apologized for being so unkind.
'You're late.' – 'Sorry.'

→ See **apologize**

---

exhausted – exhausting – exhaustive

1 **'exhausted'**

If you are **exhausted**, you are very tired.

At the end of the day I felt exhausted.
All three men were hot, dirty and exhausted.

Don't use words such as 'rather' or 'very' in front of **exhausted**. You can, however, use words such as **completely**, **absolutely**, or **utterly**.

'And how are you feeling?' – 'Exhausted. Completely exhausted.'
The guest speaker looked absolutely exhausted.

2 **'exhausting'**

If an activity is **exhausting**, it is very tiring.

It's a difficult and exhausting job.
Carrying bags is exhausting.

3 **'exhaustive'**

An **exhaustive** study or description is thorough and complete.

He studied the problem in exhaustive detail.
For a more exhaustive treatment you should read Margaret Boden's book.

---

exist

If something **exists**, it is actually present in the world.

It is clear that a serious problem exists.
They walked through my office as if I didn't exist.

When **exist** has this meaning, don't use it in a progressive form. Don't say, for example, 'It is clear that a serious problem is existing'.

You also use **exist** to say that someone manages to live under difficult conditions or with very little food or money.

How can we exist out here?
The whole band exist on a diet of chocolate and crisps.

When **exist** has this meaning, it can be used in a progressive form.

People were existing on a hundred grams of bread a day.

expect

1 'expect'

If you **expect** that something will happen, you believe that it will happen.

I expect you'll be glad when I leave.
They expect that about 1,500 people will attend.

You can sometimes use a *to*-infinitive after **expect** instead of a *that*-clause. For example, instead of saying 'I expect Johnson will come to the meeting', you can say '**I expect Johnson to come** to the meeting'. However, the meaning is not quite the same. If you say 'I expect Johnson will come to the meeting', you are simply saying that you think he will come. If you say 'I expect Johnson to come to the meeting', you are showing that you want Johnson to come to the meeting and that you will be annoyed or disappointed if he does not come.

Nobody expected the strike to succeed.
The talks are expected to last two or three days.

Instead of saying you 'expect something will not' happen, you usually say you **do not expect it will** happen or **do not expect it to** happen.

I don't expect it will be necessary.
I did not expect to be acknowledged.

If you **expect** something is true, you think it is probably true.

I expect they've gone.

Instead of saying you 'expect something is not' true, you usually say you **do not expect it is** true.

I don't expect you have much time for shopping.

If someone asks if something is true, you can say **I expect so**.

'Will Joe be here at Christmas?' – 'I expect so.'

! BE CAREFUL

Don't say 'I expect it'.

If you **are expecting** someone or something, you believe that they are going to arrive or happen.

They were expecting Wendy and the children.
Rodin was expecting an important letter from France.
We are expecting rain.

When **expect** is used like this, don't use a preposition after it.

2 'wait for'

Don't confuse **expect** with **wait for**. If you **are waiting for** someone or something, you are remaining in the same place or delaying doing something until they arrive or happen.

He sat on the bench and waited for Miguel.
Stop waiting for things to happen. Make them happen.

→ See **wait**

3 'look forward to'

When you **look forward to** something that is going to happen, you feel happy because you think you will enjoy it.

I'll bet you're looking forward to your holidays.
I always looked forward to seeing her.

→ See **look forward to**

expensive

If something is **expensive**, it costs a lot of money.

I get very nervous because I'm using a lot of expensive equipment.
It was more expensive than the other magazines.

Don't say that the price of something is 'expensive'. You say that it is **high**.

The price is much too high.
This must result in consumers paying higher prices.

experience – experiment

1 'experience'

If you have **experience** of something, you have seen it, done it, or felt it.

Do you have any teaching experience?
I've had no experience of running a business.

An **experience** is something that happens to you or something that you do.

Moving house can be a stressful experience.

You say that someone **has** an experience.

I had a strange experience last night.

! BE CAREFUL

Don't say that someone 'makes an experience'.

2 'experiment'

Don't use 'experience' to refer to a scientific test that is carried out in order to discover or prove something. Use **experiment**.

Laboratory experiments show that Vitamin D may slow cancer growth.
Try it out in an experiment.

You usually say that someone **does**, **conducts**, or **carries out** an experiment.

We decided to do an experiment.
Several experiments were conducted at the University of Zurich.

! BE CAREFUL

Don't say that someone 'makes an experiment'.

explain

If you **explain** something, you give details about it so that it can be understood.

The head teacher should be able to explain the school's teaching policy.

You say that you explain something **to** someone.

Let me explain to you about Jackie.
We explained everything to the police.

> **!** **BE CAREFUL**
>
> You must use **to** in sentences like these. Don't say, for example, 'Let me explain you about Jackie'.

You can use **explain** with a *that*-clause to say that someone tells someone else the reason for something.

I explained that I was trying to write a book.

---

explode – blow up

1 'explode'

When a bomb **explodes**, it bursts loudly and with great force, often causing a lot of damage.

A bomb had exploded in the next street.

You can say that someone **explodes** a bomb.

They exploded a nuclear device.

2 'blow up'

However, if someone destroys a building with a bomb, don't say that they 'explode' the building. You say that they **blow** it **up**.

He was going to blow the place up.

Ff

fabric

Fabric is cloth or other material produced by weaving cotton, nylon, wool, silk, or other threads together. Fabrics are used for making things such as clothes, curtains, and sheets.

A piece of white fabric was thrown out of the window.
They sell silks and other soft fabrics.

Don't use 'fabric' to refer to a building where machines are used to make things. A building like this is usually called a **factory**.

→ See **factory – works – mill – plant**

fact

1 'fact'

A **fact** is an item of knowledge or information that is true.

It may help you to know the full facts of the case.
The report is several pages long and full of facts and figures.

❗ BE CAREFUL

Don't talk about '~~true facts~~' or say, for example, '~~These facts are true~~'.

2 'the fact that'

You can refer to a whole situation by using a clause beginning with **the fact that**.

He tried to hide the fact that he was disappointed.
The fact that the centre is overcrowded is the main thing that people complain about.

❗ BE CAREFUL

You must use **that** in clauses like these. Don't say, for example, '~~He tried to hide the fact he was disappointed~~'.

3 'in fact'

You use **in fact** to show that you are giving more detailed information about what you have just said.

They've been having financial problems. In fact, they may have to close down.

factory – works – mill – plant

1 'factory'

A building where machines are used to make things is usually called a **factory**.

I work in a cheese factory.
He visited several factories which produce domestic electrical goods.

2 'works'

A place where things are made or where an industrial process takes place can also be called a **works**. A **works** can consist of several buildings and may include outdoor equipment and machinery.

There used to be an iron works here.

After **works** you can use either a singular or plural form of a verb.

The sewage works was closed down.
Engineering works are planned for this district.

3 'mill'

A building where a particular material is made is often called a **mill**.

He worked at a cotton mill.

4 'plant'

A building where chemicals are produced is called a chemical **plant**.

There was an explosion at a chemical plant.

A power station can also be referred to as a **plant**.

They discussed the re-opening of the nuclear plant.

---

fair – fairly

1 'fair'

You say that behaviour or a decision is **fair** when it is reasonable, right, or just.

It wouldn't be fair to disturb the children's education at this stage.
Do you feel they're paying their fair share?

2 'fairly'

Don't use 'fair' as an adverb, except in the expression **play fair**. If you want to say that something is done in a reasonable or just way, the word you use is **fairly**.

We want it to be fairly distributed.
He had not explained things fairly.

Fairly also has a completely different meaning. It means 'to quite a large degree'.

The information was fairly accurate.
I wrote the first part fairly quickly.

! BE CAREFUL

Don't use 'fairly' in front of a comparative form. Don't say, for example, 'The train is fairly quicker than the bus'. In conversation and less formal writing, you say 'The train is **a bit** quicker than the bus'.

Golf's a bit more expensive.
I began to understand her a bit better.

In more formal writing, you use **rather** or **somewhat**.

In short, the problems now look rather worse than they did a year ago.
The results were somewhat lower than expected.

Many other words and expressions can be used to show degree.

→ See **Adverbs and adverbials** for a graded list of words used to indicate degree

fair – fare

These words are both pronounced /feə/.

1 'fair'

Fair can be an adjective or a noun. If something is **fair**, it is reasonable, right, or just.

→ See **fair – fairly**

If someone is **fair** or has **fair** hair, they have light coloured hair.

My daughter has three children, and they're all fair.

A **fair** is an event held in a park or field for people's amusement.

We took the children to the fair.

2 'fare'

Your **fare** is the money you pay for a journey by bus, taxi, train, boat, or plane.

Coach fares are cheaper than rail fares.
Airline officials say they must raise fares in order to cover rising costs.

---

fall

Fall can be a verb or a noun.

1 used as a verb

When something **falls**, it moves quickly towards the ground by accident. The past tense of **fall** is **fell**. The -ed participle is **fallen**.

The cup fell from her hand and broke.
Several napkins had fallen to the floor.

When rain or snow **falls**, it comes down from the sky.

Rain was beginning to fall.

When someone who is standing or walking **falls**, they drop downwards so that they are kneeling or lying on the ground.

She fell and hurt her leg.

 In conversation, you don't usually say that someone 'falls'. You say that they **fall down** or **fall over**.

He fell down in the mud.
He fell over backwards and lay completely still.

You can also say that a tall object **falls down** or **falls over**.

The pile of books fell down and scattered all over the floor.
A tree fell over in the storm.

! BE CAREFUL

Fall is an intransitive verb. You can't say that someone 'falls' something. Don't say, for example, 'She screamed and fell the tray'. You say 'She screamed and **dropped** the tray'.

He bumped into a chair and dropped his plate.
Careful! Don't drop it!

Similarly, don't say that someone 'falls' a person. Don't say, for example, '~~He bumped into the girl and fell her~~'. You say 'He bumped into the girl and **knocked** her **down**' or 'He bumped into the girl and **knocked** her **over**'.

I nearly <u>knocked down</u> a person at the bus stop.
I got <u>knocked over</u> by a car when I was six.

2 **used as a noun**

Fall can also be a noun. If you **have** a **fall**, you lose your balance and drop on to the ground, hurting yourself.

He <u>had</u> a bad <u>fall</u> and was taken to hospital.

 In American English, **fall** is the season between summer and winter.

In the <u>fall</u>, I love going to Vermont.

British speakers call this season **autumn**.

→ See **autumn**

familiar

1 **'familiar'**

If someone or something is **familiar**, you recognize them because you have seen, heard, or experienced them before.

There was something <u>familiar</u> about him.
Gradually I began to recognize <u>familiar</u> faces.

2 **'familiar to'**

If something is **familiar to** you, you know it well.

His name is <u>familiar to</u> millions of people.
This problem will be <u>familiar to</u> many parents.

3 **'familiar with'**

If you know or understand something well, you can say that you are **familiar with** it.

I am of course <u>familiar with</u> your work.
These are statements which I am sure you are <u>familiar with</u>.

far

1 **distance**

You use **how far** when you are asking about a distance.

<u>How far</u> is it to Seattle?
He asked us <u>how far</u> we had come.

However, don't use 'far' when you are stating a distance. Don't say, for example, that something is 10 kilometres 'far' from a place. You say that it is 10 kilometres **from** the place or 10 kilometres **away from** it.

The hotel is just fifty metres <u>from</u> the ocean.
I was about five miles <u>away from</u> some hills.

You use **far** in questions and negative sentences to mean 'a long distance'. For example, if you say that it is **not far** to a place, you mean that the place is not a long distance from where you are.

Do tell us more about it, Lee. Is it far?
It isn't far now.
I don't live far from here.

Don't use 'far' like this in positive sentences. Don't say, for example, that a place is 'far'. You say that it is **far away** or **a long way away**.

He is far away in Australia.
That's up in the Cairngorms, which is quite a long way away.

→ See **away**

In modern English, 'far' is not used in front of a noun. Don't, for example, talk about 'far hills'. Instead you use **distant**, **faraway**, or **far-off**.

The bedroom has views of the distant mountains.
I heard the faraway sound of a waterfall.
She dreamed of travelling to far-off places.

2 degree or extent

You also use **far** in questions and negative sentences to talk about the degree or extent to which something happens.

How far have you got in developing this?
Prices will not come down very far.
None of us would trust them very far.

3 used as an intensifier

You use **far** in front of comparatives to say that something has very much more of a quality than something else. For example, if you say that one thing is **far bigger** than another, you mean that it is very much bigger than the other thing.

This is a far better picture than the other one.
The situation was far more dangerous than Woodward realized.

Far more in front of a noun means 'very much more' or 'very many more'.

He had to process far more information than before.
Professional training was provided in far more forms than in Europe.

You can also use **far** in front of **too**. For example, if you say that something is **far too big**, you mean that it is very much bigger than it should be.

I was far too polite.
It is far too early to judge.

You can use **far** in front of **too much** or **too many**. For example, if you say that there is **far too much** of something, you mean that there is a very much greater quantity than is necessary or desirable.

Teachers are being given far too much new information.
Every middle-class child gets far too many toys.

In informal English, you can use **way** instead of **far** as an intensifier.

It's way too early to say who will win.
You talk way too much.
I communicate way better with music than with words.

fare

→ See **fair – fare**

fault

→ See **blame – fault**

favourite

Your **favourite** thing or person of a particular type is the one you like most.

What is your favourite television programme?
Her favourite writer is Hans Christian Andersen.

Don't use 'most' with **favourite**. Don't say, for example, 'This is my most favourite book'. You say 'This is my **favourite** book'.

 The American spelling of 'favourite' is **favorite**.

feel

Feel is a common verb that has several meanings. Its past tense and *-ed* participle is **felt**.

1 awareness

If you **can feel** something, you are aware of it because of your sense of touch, or you are aware of it in your body.

I can feel the heat of the sun on my face.
I wonder if insects can feel pain.

! BE CAREFUL

You usually use **can** in sentences like these. You say, for example, 'I **can feel** a pain in my foot'. Don't say 'I feel a pain in my foot'. Also, don't use a progressive form. Don't say 'I am feeling a pain in my foot'.

If you want to say that someone was aware of something in the past, you use **felt** or **could feel**.

They felt the wind on their faces.
Through several layers of clothes I could feel his muscles.

However, if you want to say that someone suddenly became aware of something, you must use **felt**.

He felt a sting on his elbow.

You can use an *-ing* form after **felt** or **could feel** to show that someone was aware of something that was continuing to take place.

He could feel the sweat pouring down his face.

You can use an infinitive without *to* after **felt** to show that someone became aware of a single action.

She felt the boat move.

2 touching

When you **feel** an object, you touch it deliberately in order to find out what it is like.

The doctor felt her pulse.

3 impressions

The way something **feels** is the way it seems to you when you hold it or touch it.

The blanket felt soft.
How does it feel? Warm or cold?
It looks and feels like a normal fabric.

! BE CAREFUL

When you use **feel** like this, don't use a progressive form. Don't say, for example, 'The blanket was feeling soft'.

4 emotions and sensations

You can use **feel** with an adjective to say that someone is or was experiencing an emotion or a physical sensation. When you use **feel** like this, you use either a simple form or a progressive form.

I feel lonely.
I'm feeling terrible.
She felt happy.
I was feeling hungry.

You can also use **feel** with a noun phrase to say that someone experiences an emotion or a physical sensation. When you use **feel** with a noun phrase, you use a simple form.

She felt a sudden desire to scream.

! BE CAREFUL

When you use **feel** to say that someone experiences an emotion or a physical sensation, don't use a reflexive pronoun. Don't say, for example, 'I felt myself uncomfortable'. You say 'I **felt** uncomfortable'.

5 'feel like'

If you **feel like** a particular type of person or thing, you are aware of having some of the qualities or feelings of that person or thing.

If you want to feel like a star, travel like a star.
I feel like a mouse being chased by a cat.

If you **feel like doing** something, you want to do it.

Whenever I felt like talking, they were ready to listen.
Are there days when you don't feel like writing?

In sentences like these, you can sometimes use a noun phrase instead of an -*ing* form. For example, instead of saying 'I feel like going for a walk', you can say 'I **feel like** a walk'.

I feel like a cup of coffee.

! BE CAREFUL

Don't say that you 'feel like to do' something.

female – feminine

1 'female'

Female means 'relating to the sex that can have babies'. You can use **female** as an adjective to talk about either people or animals.

There has been a rise in the number of female employees.
A female toad may lay 20,000 eggs each season.

You can also use **female** as a noun to talk about animals.

The male fertilizes the female's eggs.
He saw a family of lions – a big male, a beautiful female, and two cubs.

In scientific contexts, **female** is sometimes used as a noun to refer to women or girls.

The condition affects both males and females.

People sometimes use **female** to talk about young women, in order to avoid using 'woman' or 'girl'.

He asked if a white female of a certain age had checked into the hotel.

2 'feminine'

Feminine means 'typical of women, rather than men'.

The bedroom has a light, feminine look.
She is a calm, reasonable and deeply feminine woman.

Don't use 'feminine' to talk about animals.

fetch

→ See **bring – take – fetch**

few – a few

1 used in front of nouns

Few and **a few** are both used in front of nouns, but they do not have the same meaning. You use **a few** simply to show that you are talking about a small number of people or things.

I'm having a dinner party for a few close friends.
Here are a few ideas that might help you.

When you use **few** without 'a', you are emphasizing that there are only a small number of people or things of a particular kind. So, for example, if you say 'I have **a few** friends', you are simply saying that you have some friends. However, if you say 'I have **few** friends', you are saying that you do not have enough friends and are lonely.

There were few resources available.

2 used as pronouns

Few and **a few** can be used in a similar way as pronouns.

Doctors work an average of 90 hours a week, while a few work up to 120 hours.
Many were invited but few came.

3 'not many'

In conversation and in less formal writing, people don't usually use **few** without 'a'. Instead they use **not many**. For example, instead of saying 'I have few friends', people usually say 'I **haven't got many** friends' or 'I **don't have many** friends'.

They haven't got many books.
I don't have many visitors.

> **BE CAREFUL**
>
> Don't use 'few' or 'a few' when you are talking about a small amount of something. Don't say, for example, 'Would you like a few more milk in your tea?' You say 'Would you like **a little** more milk in your tea?'

→ See **little – a little**

fewer

→ See **less**

film

A **film** consists of moving pictures that have been recorded so that they can be shown at a cinema or on television.

The film is based on a true story.
Do you want to watch a film tonight?

Films are called **movies**.

His last book was made into a movie.

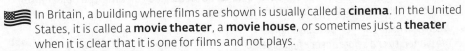 In Britain, a building where films are shown is usually called a **cinema**. In the United States, it is called a **movie theater**, a **movie house**, or sometimes just a **theater** when it is clear that it is one for films and not plays.

British people talk about going to the **cinema**. American speakers talk about going to the **movies**.

Everyone has gone to the cinema.
Some friends and I were driving home from the movies.

finally

→ See **eventually – finally**

find

1 result of a search

If you **find** something you have been looking for, you see it or learn where it is. The past tense and -ed participle of **find** is **found**.

I eventually found what I was looking for.
Have you found your keys yet?

> **BE CAREFUL**
>
> When **find** has this meaning, don't use 'out' after it. Don't say, for example, 'I eventually found out what I was looking for'.

2 'discover'

Discover is sometimes used instead of 'find'. **Discover** is a rather formal word.

The bodies of the family were discovered by police officers on Tuesday.

If you cannot see the thing you are looking for, you say that you **cannot find** it.

I think I'm lost – I can't find the bridge.

However, don't say that you 'cannot discover' something.

3 noticing something

You can use **find** or **discover** to say that someone notices an object somewhere.

Look what I've found!
A bomb could be discovered and that would ruin everything.

Come across has a similar meaning.

They came across the bones of an animal.

4 obtaining information

If you **find**, **find out**, or **discover** that something is the case, you learn that it is the case.

Researchers found that there was little difference between the two groups.
It was such a relief to find out that the boy was safe.
He has since discovered that his statement was wrong.

In clauses beginning with **when**, **before**, or **as soon as**, you can omit the object after **find out**. You can't do this with **find** or **discover**.

When Dad finds out, he'll be really angry.
You want it to end before anyone finds out.
As soon as I found out, I jumped into the car.

If you **find out** or **discover** some information that is difficult to obtain, you succeed in obtaining it.

Have you found out who killed my husband?
Police discovered that he was hiding out in London.

You can also say that someone **finds out** facts that are easy to obtain.

I found out the train times.

> **!** BE CAREFUL
>
> Don't say that someone 'discovers' facts that are easy to obtain.

5 another meaning of 'find'

You can use **find** followed by **it** and an adjective to give your opinion about something. For example, if you have difficulty doing something, you can say that you **find it difficult to do** it. If you think that something is funny, you can say that you **find it funny**.

I find it difficult to talk to the other parents.
'Was the exam hard?' – 'No, I found it quite easy.'

> **!** BE CAREFUL
>
> You must use **it** in sentences like these. Don't say, for example, 'I find difficult to talk to other parents'.

You can also use **find** followed by a noun phrase and an adjective, or two noun phrases, in order to give your opinion about something.

I found his behaviour extremely rude.
I'm sure you'll find him a good worker.

fine – finely

Fine is usually an adjective, but in conversation you can also use it as an adverb. **Fine** has three main meanings.

1 used to mean 'very good'

You can use it to say that something is very good or impressive.

He gave a <u>fine</u> performance.
From the top there is a <u>fine</u> view.

When you use **fine** like this, you can use words such as **very** or **extremely** in front of it.

He's intelligent and he'd do a <u>very fine</u> job.
This is an <u>unusually fine</u> piece of work.

You can't use **fine** as an adverb with this meaning, but you can use the adverb **finely** in front of an -*ed* participle.

This is a <u>finely</u> crafted story.

2 used to mean 'satisfactory'

You can also use **fine** to say that something is satisfactory or acceptable.

'Do you want more milk?' – 'No, this is <u>fine</u>.'

If you say that you are **fine**, you mean that your health is satisfactory.

'How are you?' – '<u>Fine</u>, thanks.'

When you use **fine** to mean 'satisfactory', don't use 'very' in front of it. However, you can use **just**.

Everything is <u>just fine</u>.
'Is she settling down in England?' – 'Oh, she's <u>just fine</u>.'

In conversation, you can use **fine** as an adverb to mean 'satisfactorily' or 'well'.

We got on <u>fine</u>.
I was doing <u>fine</u>.

! **BE CAREFUL**

Don't use 'finely' in sentences like these. Don't say, for example, '~~We got on finely~~'.

3 used to mean 'small' or 'narrow'

You can also use **fine** to say that something is very narrow, or consists of very small or narrow parts.

She has long, <u>fine</u> hair.

When you use **fine** like this, you can use words such as **very** in front of it.

These pins are <u>very fine</u> and won't split the wood.

You can use **finely** as an adverb with this meaning.

Put the mixture in the bowl and add a cup of <u>finely</u> chopped onions.

finish

When something **finishes**, it ends.

The concert <u>finished</u> at midnight.

When you **finish** what you are doing, you reach the end of it.

Have you finished the ironing yet?
When he had finished, he closed the file.

You can say that someone **finishes doing** something.

Jonathan finished studying three years ago.
I've finished reading your book.

! **BE CAREFUL**

Don't say that someone 'finishes to do' something.

first – firstly

1 'first' used as an adjective

The **first** thing, event, or person of a particular kind is the one that comes before all the others.

She lost 16 pounds in the first month of her diet.
Yuri Gagarin was the first man in space.

If you want to emphasize that a thing, event, or person is the first one of their kind, you can put **very** in front of **first**.

The very first thing I do when I get home is have a cup of tea.

2 'first' used as an adverb

If an event happens before other events, you say that it happens **first**.

Rani spoke first.
When people get their newspaper, which page do they read first?

! **BE CAREFUL**

Don't use 'firstly' with this meaning. Don't say, for example, 'Rani spoke firstly'.

3 'first' and 'firstly' used as sentence adverbials

You can use **first** or **firstly** to introduce the first point in a discussion, the first of a series of questions or instructions, or the first item in a list.

First, mix the eggs and flour.
There are two reasons why I'm angry. Firstly you're late, and secondly, you've forgotten your homework.

If you want to emphasize that an item is the first one you are going to mention, you can say **first of all**.

I have made a commitment, first of all to myself, and secondly to my family.
First of all, I'd like to thank you all for coming.

! **BE CAREFUL**

Don't say 'firstly of all'.

4 'at first'

When you are contrasting feelings or actions at the beginning of an event with ones that came later, you say **at first**.

At first I was reluctant.

At first I thought that the shop was empty, then from behind one of the counters a man appeared.

 **BE CAREFUL**

Don't use 'firstly' in sentences like these.

first floor

→ See **ground floor – first floor**

first name – Christian name – forename – given name

1 'first name'

Your **first name** is the name that was given to you when you were born. Your first name comes in front of your surname.

At some point in the conversation Brian began calling Philip by his first name.

2 'Christian name'

In British English, people sometimes use **Christian name** instead of **first name**. This use is rather old-fashioned.

Do all your students call you by your Christian name?

In American English, **Christian name** is not used.

3 'forename'

On official forms, you are usually asked to write your **surname** and your **first name** or **forename**. **Forename** is only used in writing.

4 'given name'

In American English, **given name** is sometimes used instead of 'first name' or 'forename'.

→ See **Topic** entry **Addressing someone**

fit – suit

1 'fit'

If clothes **fit** you, they are the right size, neither too big nor too small.

That dress fits you perfectly.
He was wearing pyjamas which did not fit him.

In British English, the past tense form of **fit** is **fitted**. In American English, the past tense form is **fit**.

The boots fitted him snugly.
The pants fit him well and were very comfortable.

2 'suit'

If clothes make you look attractive, don't say that they 'fit' you. You say that they **suit** you.

You look great in that dress, it really suits you.

flat – apartment

1 'flat'

In British English, a **flat** is a set of rooms for living in, usually on one floor of a large building.

She lived in a tiny furnished flat near Sloane Square.

2 'apartment'

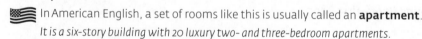 In American English, a set of rooms like this is usually called an **apartment**.

It is a six-story building with 20 luxury two- and three-bedroom apartments.

3 'block of flats'

In British English, a large building containing flats is usually called a **block of flats**.

The building was pulled down to make way for a block of flats.

4 'apartment block' and 'apartment building'

 In American English, and sometimes in British English, it is called an **apartment building** or an **apartment block**.

He lives on the ninth story of an apartment block on Charlesgate East.
Several apartment buildings were destroyed in the fire.

floor – ground

1 'floor'

The **floor** of a room is the flat part you walk on.

The book fell to the floor.

A **floor** of a building is all the rooms on a particular level.

I went up the stairs to the third floor.

You say that something is **on** a particular floor.

My office is on the second floor.

! BE CAREFUL

Don't say that something is 'in' a particular floor.

→ See **ground floor – first floor**

2 'ground'

You don't normally refer to the surface of the earth as the 'floor'. You call it the **ground**.

He set down his backpack on the ground.
The ground was very wet and muddy.

However, the surface of the earth in a forest is sometimes referred to as the **forest floor**, and the land under the sea is sometimes called the **sea floor** or the **ocean floor**.

The forest floor is not rich in vegetation.
Some species are mainly found on the sea floor.

foot

1 part of the body

Your **foot** is the part of your body at the end of your leg. Your foot includes your toes.

He kept on running despite the pain in his foot.

When you use **foot** with this meaning, its plural is **feet**.

She's got very small feet.

If someone goes somewhere **on foot**, they walk, rather than using some form of transport.

The city should be explored on foot.

2 measurements

A **foot** is also a unit for measuring length, equal to 12 inches or 30.48 centimetres. When **foot** has this meaning, its usual plural is **feet**.

We were only a few feet away from the edge of the cliff.
The planes flew at 65,000 feet.

However, you can use **foot** as the plural in front of words like **high**, **tall**, and **long**.

She's five foot eight inches tall.

You always use **foot** as the plural in front of another noun. For example, if a gap is twenty feet wide, you refer to it as a 'twenty **foot** gap'. Don't refer to it as a 'twenty feet gap'.

The prison was enclosed by a forty foot wall.

---

football

1 'football'

In Britain, **football** is a game played between two teams who kick a round ball around a field in an attempt to score goals. In America, this game is called **soccer**.

We met a group of Italian football fans.
There was a lot of pressure on the US soccer team.

2 'American football'

In North America, **football** is a game played between two teams who throw or run with an oval ball in an attempt to score points. In Britain, this game is called **American football**.

This year's national college football championship was won by Princeton.
He was an American football star.

3 'match'

In Britain, two teams play a football **match**. In America, they play a football **game**.

We watched the match between Arsenal and Manchester United.
Are you going to watch the football game Monday night?

for

If something is **for** someone, they are intended to have it or benefit from it.

He left a note for her on the table.
She held out the flowers and said, 'They're for you.'
I am doing everything I can for you.

You use **for** in front of a noun phrase or *-ing* form when you state the purpose of an object, action, or activity.

Some planes are for internal use, others for international flights.
The mug had been used for mixing flour and water.

You use **for** in front of a noun phrase when you are saying why someone does something.

We stopped for lunch by the roadside.
I went to the store for a newspaper.

! BE CAREFUL

Don't use 'for' with an *-ing* form when you saying why someone does something. Don't say, for example, 'He went to the city for finding work'. You say 'He went to the city **to find** work' or 'He went to the city **in order to find** work'.

People would stroll down the path to admire the garden.
He had to hurry in order to reach the next place on his schedule.

1 duration

You use **for** to say how long something lasts or continues.

I'm staying with Bob for a few days.

You also use **for** to say how long something has been the case.

I have known you for a long time.
He has been missing for three weeks.

! BE CAREFUL

When you use **for** to say how long something has been the case, you must use a perfect form. Don't say, for example, 'I am living here for five years'. You must say 'I **have lived** here for five years'.

2 'since'

Don't confuse **for** with **since**. You use **since** to say that something has been the case from a particular time in the past until now.

Exam results have improved rapidly since 1999.
I've known her since she was twelve.

→ See **since**

3 used to mean 'because'

In stories, **for** is sometimes used to mean 'because'. This use is rather old-fashioned, and is not used in conversation.

This is where he spent his free time, for he had nowhere else to go.

→ See **because**

forename

→ See **first name – Christian name – forename – given name**

forget

1 'forget'

The past tense of **forget** is **forgot**. The *-ed* participle is **forgotten**.

If you **forget** something, or **forget about** something, you stop thinking about it.

Alan, having <u>forgotten</u> his fear, became more confident.
Tim <u>forgot about</u> his problems for a few hours.

If you **have forgotten** something that you knew, you can no longer remember it.

I <u>have forgotten</u> where it is.
...a Grand Duke whose name I <u>have forgotten</u>.

If you **forget** something such as a key or an umbrella, you do not remember to take it with you when you go somewhere.

Sorry to disturb you – I <u>forgot</u> my key.

> **! BE CAREFUL**
>
> Don't use the verb 'forget' to say that you have put something somewhere and left it there. Instead you use the verb **leave**.
>
> *I <u>left</u> my bag on the bus.*

2 'forget to'

If you **forget to do** something that you had intended to do, you do not do it because you do not remember it at the right time.

She <u>forgot to lock</u> her door one day and two men got in.
Don't <u>forget to call</u> Dad.

> **! BE CAREFUL**
>
> Don't use an *-ing* form. Don't say, for example, '~~She forgot locking her door~~'.

form

→ See **class – form – grade – year**

fortnight

In British English, two weeks is often called a **fortnight**.

I went to Rothesay for a <u>fortnight</u>.
He borrowed it a <u>fortnight</u> ago.

 American speakers do not usually use this word.

forward – forwards

→ See **-ward – -wards**

free – freely

1 no controls

You use **free** as an adjective to describe activities that are not controlled or limited.

We believe in free speech.
The elections were free and fair.

Don't use 'free' as an adverb with this meaning. Use **freely**.

We are all friends here and I can talk freely.

2 no payment

If something is **free**, you can have it or use it without paying for it.

The coffee was free.
Many children are entitled to free school meals.

The adverb you use with this meaning is **free**, not 'freely'. For example, you say 'Pensioners can travel **free** on the buses'. Don't say 'Pensioners can travel freely on the buses'.

Children can get into the museum free.

3 releasing

If something is cut or pulled **free**, it is cut or pulled so that it is no longer attached to something or no longer trapped. Don't say that something is cut or pulled 'freely'.

She tugged to get it free.
I shook my jacket free and hurried off.

4 availability

If you are **free** at a particular time, you are not busy. **Free time** is time when you are not busy.

They spend most of their free time reading.
Are you free on Tuesday?

---

frequently

→ See **Adverbs and adverbials** for a graded list of words used to indicate frequency

---

friend

1 'friend'

Your **friends** are people you know well and like spending time with. You can refer to a friend who you know very well as a **good friend** or a **close friend**.

He's a good friend of mine.
A close friend told me about it.

If someone has been your friend for a long time, you can refer to them as an **old friend**. He or she is not necessarily an old person.

I went back to my hometown and visited some old friends.

2 'be friends with'

If someone is your friend, you can say that you are **friends with** them.

You used to be good <u>friends with</u> him, didn't you?
I also became <u>friends with</u> Melanie.

friendly

A **friendly** person is kind and pleasant.

The staff are very <u>friendly</u> and helpful.

If you are **friendly to** someone or **friendly towards** someone, you are kind and pleasant to them.

The women had been <u>friendly to</u> Lyn.
Your father is not as <u>friendly towards</u> me as he used to be.

If you are **friendly with** someone, you like each other and enjoy spending time together.

I became <u>friendly with</u> some of my neighbours.

Friendly is never an adverb. Don't say, for example, 'He behaved friendly'. You say 'He behaved **in a friendly way**'.

We talked to them <u>in a friendly way</u>.
She looked up at Boris, smiling at him <u>in such a friendly way</u>.

> **!** **BE CAREFUL**
>
> Don't confuse **friendly** and **sympathetic**. If you have a problem and someone is **sympathetic** or shows a **sympathetic** attitude, they show that they care and would like to help you.
>
> *When I told him how I felt, he was very <u>sympathetic</u>.*

fries

→ See **chips**

frighten – frightened

1 'frighten'

If something **frightens** you, it makes you feel afraid.

Rats and mice don't <u>frighten</u> me.

Frighten is almost always a transitive verb. Don't say that someone 'frightens'. If you want to say that someone is afraid because of something that has happened or that might happen, you say that they **are frightened**.

Miriam <u>was</u> too <u>frightened</u> to tell her family what had happened.
He told the children not to <u>be frightened</u>.

→ See **afraid – frightened**

2 'frightening'

Don't confuse **frightened** with **frightening**. Something that is **frightening** causes you to feel fear.

It was a very <u>frightening</u> experience.
It is <u>frightening</u> to think what damage could be done.

from

1 source or origin

You use **from** to say what the source, origin, or starting point of something is.

Smoke was rising from the fire.
Get the leaflet from a post office.
The houses were built from local stone.

When you are talking about the person who has written you a letter or sent a message to you, you say that the letter or message is **from** that person.

He got an email from Linda.

If you **come from** a particular place, you were born there, or it is your home.

I come from Scotland.

→ See **come from**

! BE CAREFUL

Don't use 'from' to say who wrote a book, play, or piece of music. Don't say, for example, 'Have you seen any plays from Ibsen?' You say 'Have you seen any plays **by** Ibsen?'

We listened to some pieces by Mozart.

2 distance

You can use **from** when you are talking about the distance between places. For example, if one place is fifty kilometres **from** another place, the distance between the two places is fifty kilometres.

How far is the hotel from here?

3 time

If something happens **from** a particular time, it begins to happen at that time.

Breakfast is available from 6 a.m.
We had no rain from March to October.

! BE CAREFUL

Don't use **from** to say that something began to be the case at a particular time in the past and is still the case now. Don't say, for example, 'I have lived here from 1984'. You say 'I have lived here **since** 1984'.

He has been chairman since 1998.

→ See **since**

front

1 'front'

The **front** of a building is the part that faces the street or that has the building's main entrance.

There is a large garden at the front of the house.
I knocked on the front door.

2 'in front of '

If you are between the front of a building and the street, you say that you are **in front of** the building.

A crowd had assembled in front of the court.
People were waiting in front of the art gallery.

> **!** BE CAREFUL
>
> Don't use 'the' before **front** in sentences like these. Don't say, for example, 'People were waiting in the front of the art gallery'.

3 'opposite'

If there is a street between you and the front of a building, don't say that you are 'in front of' the building. You say that you are **opposite** it.

The hotel is opposite a railway station.
Opposite is St Paul's Church.
There was a banner on the building opposite.

 Speakers of American English usually say **across from** rather than 'opposite'.

Stinson has rented a home across from his parents.

---

frontier

→ See **border – frontier – boundary**

---

fruit

Fruit is usually an uncountable noun. Oranges, bananas, grapes, and apples are all **fruit**.

You should eat plenty of fresh fruit and vegetables.
They import fruit from Australia.

→ See **Nouns** for information on uncountable nouns

You can refer to an individual orange, banana, etc as a **fruit**.

Each fruit contains many juicy seeds.

However, this use is not common. You usually refer to an individual orange, banana, etc as a **piece of fruit**.

Try to eat five pieces of fruit a day.

Don't use a plural form of **fruit** to refer to several oranges, bananas, etc. Instead you use **fruit** as an uncountable noun. For example, you say 'I'm going to the market to buy some **fruit**'. Don't say 'I'm going to the market to buy some fruits'.

There was a bowl with some fruit in it.
They gave me fruit, cake and wine.

---

full

If something is **full of** things or people, it contains a very large number of them.

They had a large garden full of pear and apple trees.
His office was full of people.

> **!** **BE CAREFUL**
>
> Don't use any preposition except **of** after **full** in sentences like these.

fun – funny

1 'fun'

If something is **fun**, it is pleasant, enjoyable, and not serious.

It's fun working for him.

If you have **fun**, you enjoy yourself.

We had great fun at the party.
She wanted a bit more fun out of life.

> **!** **BE CAREFUL**
>
> **Fun** is an uncountable noun. Don't say that someone 'has funs' or 'has a great fun'.

If you want to say that something is very enjoyable, you can say that it is **great fun** or **a lot of fun**.

The game was great fun.

In conversation and informal writing, you can use **fun** as an adjective. Don't use **fun** in this way in formal writing.

It was a fun evening.
She's a really fun person to be around.

2 'funny'

If something is **funny**, it is amusing and makes you smile or laugh.

She told funny stories.
Wayne could be very funny when he wanted to.

You can also say that something is **funny** when it is strange, surprising, or puzzling.

The funny thing is, we went to Arthur's house just yesterday.
Have you noticed anything funny about this plane?

furniture

Furniture consists of the large moveable objects in a room, such as tables and chairs.

She arranged the furniture.
All the furniture is made of wood.

Furniture is an uncountable noun. Don't talk about 'a furniture' or 'furnitures'. You can refer to a single item as a **piece of furniture**.

Each piece of furniture matched the style of the house.

→ See **Nouns** for information on uncountable nouns

GRAMMAR FINDER

Future time

→ See **Verb forms** for the formation of future forms

1 talking about the future

You can talk about future events in several different ways. You use **will** or **shall** when you are making predictions about the future. **Shall** is used less frequently than **will**, and usually only with **I** or **we**.

→ See **shall – will**

The weather tomorrow will be warm and sunny.
I'm sure you will enjoy your visit to the zoo.
He's been really good company. I shall miss him when he leaves.

You can also use the future progressive form when you are talking about something that will happen in the normal course of events.

You'll be starting school soon, I suppose.
Once the holiday season is over, they'll be cutting down on staff.

If you are certain that an event will happen, you can use **be bound to** in conversation and informal writing.

Marion's bound to be back soon.
The party's bound to be cancelled now.

Be sure to and **be certain to** are also sometimes used.

She's sure to find out sooner or later.
He's certain to be elected.

You use **be going to** when you are talking about an event that you think will happen fairly soon.

It's going to rain.
I'm going to be late.

You use **be about to** when you are talking about an event that you think will happen very soon.

Another 385 people are about to lose their jobs.
She seemed to sense that something terrible was about to happen.
I was just about to serve dinner when there was a knock on the door.

You can also refer to events in the very near future using **be on the point of**. You use an -*ing* form after it.

She was on the point of bursting into tears.
You may remember that I was on the point of asking you something else when we were interrupted by Doctor Gupta.

2 intentions and plans

When you are talking about your own intentions, you use **will** or **be going to**. **Will** is more commonly used when you are making the decision at the time of speaking. **Be going to** is more often used when you have made your decision some time before. When you are talking about someone else's intentions, you use **be going to**.

I'll call you tonight.

I'm going to stay at home.
They're going to have a party.

> **!** **BE CAREFUL**
>
> People tend to avoid using 'be going to' with the verb **go**. For example, they would probably say 'I'm going away next week' rather than 'I'm going to go away next week'.

→ See **Topic** entry **Intentions**

You can also talk about people's plans or arrangements for the future using the present progressive.

I'm meeting Bill next week.
They're getting married in June.

The future progressive is also sometimes used.

I'll be seeing them when I've finished with you.

Be due to is used in writing and more formal speech to show that an event is intended to happen at a particular time in the future.

He is due to start working as a waiter soon.
The centre's due to be completed in 1996.

The present simple is used to talk about an event that is planned to happen soon, or that happens regularly, following a timetable or schedule.

My flight leaves in half an hour.
Our next lesson is on Thursday.

In the news, *to*-infinitive clauses are used after **be** to say that something is planned to happen.

The Prime Minister is to visit Hungary and the Czech Republic in the autumn.
A national energy efficiency centre is to be set up in Milton Keynes.

3 using the future perfect

When you want to talk about something that will happen before a particular time in the future, you use the future perfect.

By the time we arrive, the party will already have started.
By 2002, he will have worked for twelve years.

4 verb forms in subordinate clauses

In some subordinate clauses, you use the present simple when you are referring to a future event. For example, in conditional clauses and time clauses, you normally use the present simple or the present perfect when you are talking about the future.

If he comes, I'll let you know.
Please start when you are ready.
We won't start until everyone arrives.
I'll let you know when I have arranged everything.

You also use the present simple in reason clauses introduced by **in case**.

It would be better if you could arrive back here a day early, just in case there are some last minute changes.

→ See **if**

→ See **Subordinate clauses**

In a defining relative clause, you use the present simple, not 'will', when you are referring to the future in the main clause.

Any decision that you make will need her approval.
Give my love to any friends you meet.
The next job I do is not going to be so time-consuming.

However, you use **will** in the relative clause when you need to make it clear that you are referring to the future, or when the relative clause refers to an even later time.

Thousands of dollars can be spent on something that will be worn for only a few minutes.
The only people who will be questioned are those who have knowledge that is dangerous to our cause.
They go to a good school so that they will meet people who will be useful to them later on.

You use the present simple in reported questions and similar clauses that refer to a future event when the event will happen at about the same time as the reporting or knowing.

I'll telephone you. If I say it's Hugh, you'll know who it is.

However, if the future event is going to happen after the reporting, you use 'will' in the reported question.

I'll tell you what I will do.

In a *that*-clause after the verb **hope**, you often use the present simple to refer to the future.

I hope you enjoy your holiday.

→ See **hope**

→ See **Reporting** for information on tenses in other *that*-clauses

Gg

gain – earn

1 'gain'

If you **gain** something such as an ability or quality, you gradually get more of it.

After a nervous start, the speaker began to gain confidence.
This gives you a chance to gain experience.

2 'earn'

If you **earn** wages or a salary, you are paid money for work that you do.

She earns $200 a week.

! BE CAREFUL

Don't say 'She gains $200 a week.'

garbage

→ See **rubbish**

gas – petrol

1 'gas'

In British and American English, the air-like substance that burns easily and that is used for cooking and heating is called **gas**.

In American English, the liquid that is used as fuel for vehicles is also called **gas**, or **gasoline**.

I'm sorry I'm late. I had to stop for gas.

2 'petrol'

In British English, this liquid is called **petrol**.

Petrol only costs 90p per gallon there.

gaze – stare

1 'gaze'

If you **gaze** at something, you look at it for a long time, often because you think it is beautiful or impressive.

The little girl gazed in wonder at the bright lights.

2 'stare'

If you **stare** at something or someone, you look at them for a long time, often because you think they are strange or shocking.

He stared at the scar on her face.

generally – mainly

1 'generally'

Generally means 'usually', 'in most cases', or 'on the whole'.

Paperback books are <u>generally</u> cheapest.
His answer was <u>generally</u> correct.

2 'mainly'

Don't use **generally** to say that something is true about most of something, or about most of the people or things in a group. Use **mainly**.

The bedroom is <u>mainly</u> blue.
The people in the audience were <u>mainly</u> from Senegal or Mali.

gently – politely

1 'gently'

If you do something **gently**, you do it carefully and without using force, in order to avoid hurting someone or damaging something.

I shook her <u>gently</u> and she opened her eyes.

2 'politely'

Don't use 'gently' to say that someone shows good manners. Use **politely**.

He thanked me <u>politely</u>.

get

 Get is a very common verb which has several different meanings. Its past tense is **got**. In British English its *-ed* participle is also **got**. American speakers also use **got**, but they usually use **gotten** as the *-ed* participle for meanings 1 to 5 below.

→ See **gotten**

1 meaning 'become'

Get is very often used to mean 'become'.

The sun shone and I <u>got</u> very hot.
I <u>was getting</u> quite hungry.

→ See **become**

2 used for forming passives

In spoken English and informal writing, you often use **get** instead of 'be' to form passives.

My husband <u>got</u> fired from his job.
Our car <u>gets</u> cleaned about once every two months.

Don't use **get** to form passives in formal English.

3 used for describing movement

You use **get** instead of 'go' when you are describing a movement that involves difficulty.

They had to <u>get</u> across the field without being seen.
I don't think we can <u>get</u> over that wall.

Get is also used in front of **in**, **into**, **on**, and **out** to talk about entering and leaving vehicles and buildings.

I got into my car and drove into town.
I got out of there as fast as possible.

→ See **go into – get into – get on, go out – get out – get off**

4 **'get to'**

When you **get to** a place, you arrive there.

When we got to the top of the hill we had a rest.

Get to is also used in front of a verb to talk about attitudes, feelings, or knowledge that someone gradually starts to have.

I got to hate the sound of his voice.
I got to know the town really well.

→ See **get to – grow to**

5 **transitive uses of 'get'**

If you **get** something, you obtain or receive it.

He's trying to get a new job.
I got the bike for Christmas.

6 **'have got'**

Got is also used in the expression **have got**.

→ See **have got**

get to – grow to

You use **get to** or **grow to** in front of another verb to say that someone gradually starts to have a particular attitude or feeling. **Grow to** is more formal than **get to**.

I got to like the idea after a while.
I grew to dislike working for him.

You also use **get to** to say that someone gradually starts to know or realize something.

I got to understand it more as I grew older.
You'll enjoy college when you get to know a few people.

If you **get to** do something, you have the opportunity to do it.

They get to stay in nice hotels.
We don't get to see each other very often.

get up

→ See **rise – raise**

give

1 **form and word order**

Give is a very common verb that has several meanings. Its past tense is **gave**. Its -ed participle is **given**.

Give usually takes an indirect object. For some meanings of **give**, the indirect object must go in front of the direct object. For other meanings, it can go either in front of the direct object or after it.

2 physical actions

Give is often used to describe physical actions. When you use **give** like this, put the indirect object in front of the direct object. For example, say 'He **gave the ball a kick**'. Don't say 'He gave a kick to the ball'.

He gave the door a push.
Ana gave Bal's hand a squeeze.

3 expressions and gestures

Give is also used to describe expressions and gestures. When **give** is used like this, the indirect object goes in front of the direct object.

He gave her a kind smile.
As he passed me, he gave me a wink.

4 effects

You can also use **give** to describe an effect produced by someone or something. Again, the indirect object goes in front of the direct object.

I thought I'd give you a surprise.
That noise gives me a headache.

5 things

If you **give** someone something, you offer it to them and they take it. When you use **give** like this, the indirect object can go either in front of the direct object or after it. When you put the direct object first, you put **to** in front of the indirect object.

She gave Ravinder the keys.
He gave the letter to the teacher.

However, when the direct object is a pronoun such as **it** or **them** and the indirect object is not a pronoun, you must put the direct object first. Say 'He **gave it to his father**'. Don't say 'He gave his father it'.

He poured some milk and gave it to Joseph.

6 information

You also say that you **give** someone information, advice, a warning, or an order. When **give** is used like this, the indirect object can go either in front of the direct object or after it.

Her secretary gave the caller the message.
He gave a strict warning to them not to look at the sun.
The captain gave an order to his team.

given name

→ See **first name – Christian name – forename – given name**

glad – happy – cheerful

1 'glad'

If you are **glad** about something, you are pleased about it.

I'm so glad that you passed the exam.
She seemed glad of the chance to leave early.

2 'happy'

You can also say that you are **happy** about something when you are pleased about it.

She was happy that his sister was coming.

If someone is contented and enjoys life, you say that they are **happy**.

She always seemed such a happy woman.

! BE CAREFUL

Don't use 'glad' with this meaning, and don't use 'glad' in front of a noun. Don't say, for example, 'She always seemed such a glad woman'.

3 'cheerful'

If someone shows that they are happy by smiling and laughing a lot, you say that they are **cheerful**.

The men stayed cheerful and determined even when things got difficult.

glasses

A person's **glasses** are two pieces of glass in a frame which they wear to help them to see better.

He took off his glasses.
Who is that girl with red hair and glasses?

Glasses is a plural noun. Don't talk about 'a glasses'. Instead say **a pair of glasses**.

Li has a new pair of glasses.

After **glasses** you use a plural form of a verb. After **a pair of glasses** you use a singular form.

Your glasses are on the table.
A pair of glasses costs a lot of money.

go

The past tense of **go** is **went**. The -ed participle is **gone**.

I went to Paris to visit friends.
Dad has gone to work already.

1 describing movement

You usually use the verb **go** to describe movement from one place to another.

→ See **come** for when you use **come** instead of **go**

2 leaving

Go is sometimes used to say that someone or something leaves a place.

'I must _go_,' she said.
Our train _went_ at 2.25.

3 **'have gone' and 'have been'**

If someone is visiting a place or now lives there, you can say that they **have gone** there.

He _has gone_ to Argentina.
She'd _gone_ to Tokyo to start a new job.

 If someone has visited a place and has now returned, you usually say that they **have been** there. American speakers sometimes say that they **have gone** there.

I've never _gone_ to Italy.
I've _been_ to his house many times.

4 **talking about activities**

You can use **go** with an _-ing_ form to talk about activities.

Let's _go shopping_!
They _go running_ together once a week.

You can also use **go** with **for** and a noun phrase to talk about activities.

Would you like to _go for a swim_?
We're _going for a bike ride_.
He _went for a walk_.

! **BE CAREFUL**

Don't use **go** with a _to_-infinitive to talk about activities. Don't say, for example, 'He went to walk'.

5 **'go and'**

To **go and** do something means to move from one place to another in order to do it.

I'll _go and_ see him in the morning.
I _went and_ fetched a glass from the kitchen.

6 **'be going to'**

If you say that something **is going to** happen, you mean that it will happen soon, or that you intend it to happen.

She told him she _was going to_ leave her job.
I'm _not going to_ let anyone hurt you.

→ See **Future time**

7 **used to mean 'become'**

Go is sometimes used to mean 'become'.

The water _had gone_ cold.
I'm _going_ bald.

→ See **become**

go into – get into – get on

1 'go into'

When you enter a building or room, you usually say that you **go into** it or **go in**.

I went into the church.
She took him to the kitchen, switching on the light as she went in.

2 'enter'

In formal English, you can also say that you **enter** a building or room.

Nervously he entered the classroom.

3 'get into'

When you enter a car or other small vehicle, you say that you **get into** it or **get in**.

I saw him get into a taxi.
He unlocked the van, got in and drove away.

You also say that you **get into** a lift, a small boat, or a small plane.

4 'get on' and 'board'

When you enter a bus, train, large plane, or ship, you say that you **get on** it or **board** it.

The bus stopped and several more people got on.
Rina boarded a train for Kyoto.

! BE CAREFUL

You never say that someone 'goes into' or 'enters' any kind of vehicle.

5 entering with difficulty

If you enter building or room with difficulty, you say that you **get into** it or **get in**.

Someone had got into his office and stolen some papers.
It cost $10 to get in.

good – well

1 'good'

Something that is **good** is pleasant, acceptable, or satisfactory. The comparative form of **good** is **better**. The superlative form is **best**.

Your French is better than mine.
This is the best cake I've ever eaten.

2 'well'

Good is never an adverb. If you want to say that something is done to a high standard or to a great extent, you use **well**, not 'good'.

She speaks English well.
I don't know him very well.

→ See **well**

The comparative form of **well** is **better**. The superlative form is **best**.

I changed seats so I could see better.
Use the method that works best for you.

→ See **better**

go on

If you **go on doing** something, you continue to do it.

I just went on eating like I hadn't heard anything.
Asif went on working until he had finished.

If you **go on to do** something, you do it after doing something else.

She went on to talk about her plans for the future.
He later went on to form a successful computer company.

go out – get out – get off

1 **'go out'**

When you leave a building or room, you usually say that you **go out** of it or **go out**

He threw down his napkin and went out of the room.
I went out into the garden.

2 **'get out'**

When you leave a car, you say that you **get out** of it or **get out**.

We got out of the taxi at the station.
I got out and examined the right rear wheel.

You also say that you **get out** of a lift, plane, or small boat.

3 **'get off'**

When you leave a bus or train, you say that you **get off**.

When the train stopped, he got off.
Get off at the next stop.

You can also say that you **get off** a plane.

! **BE CAREFUL**

You never say that someone 'goes out' of any kind of vehicle.

4 **leaving with difficulty**

If you leave a building or room with difficulty, you say that you **get out** of it or **get out**.

I managed to get out through a window.

gotten

 In American English, **gotten** is usually the -*ed* participle of **get**. It is used to mean 'obtained', 'received', 'become', or 'caused to be'.

He had gotten his boots out of the closet.
He has gotten something in his eye.
He had gotten very successful since she last saw him.
I had gotten quite a lot of work done that morning.

It is also used in many phrasal verbs and phrases.

He must have gotten up at dawn.
We should have gotten rid of him.

> **!** **BE CAREFUL**
>
> Don't use **have gotten** to mean 'possess'. For example, don't say '~~I have gotten a headache~~' or '~~He has gotten two sisters~~'.
>
> In British English, the *-ed* participle of **get** is **got**, not 'gotten'.

government

→ See **Nouns** for information on collective nouns

go with

→ See **accompany**

grade

→ See **class – form – grade – year**

great

→ See **big – large – great**

greatly

→ See **Adverbs and adverbials** for a graded list of words used to indicate degree

grill

→ See **cook**

ground floor – first floor

In British English, the floor of a building which is level with the ground is called the **ground floor**. The floor above it is called the **first floor**, the floor above that is the **second floor**, and so on.

 In American English, the floor which is level with the ground is called the **first floor**, the floor above it is the **second floor**, and so on.

grow

1 'grow'

When children or young animals **grow**, they become bigger or taller. The past tense of **grow** is **grew**. The *-ed* participle is **grown**.

The doctor will check that the baby is <u>growing</u> normally.
The plant <u>grew</u> to a height of over 1 metre.
Has he <u>grown</u> any taller?

2 'grow up'

When someone **grows up**, they gradually change from a child into an adult.

He <u>grew up</u> in Cambridge.
They <u>grew up</u> at a time when there was no television.

> **!** **BE CAREFUL**
>
> Don't confuse the verbs **grow up** and **bring up**. If you **bring up** a child, you look after it as it grows up. Don't say '~~grow up a child~~'.
>
> *We thought the village was the perfect place to bring up a family.*

→ See **bring up – raise – educate**

3 **used to mean 'become'**

Grow is also used to mean 'become'.

He's growing old.
The sky grew dark.

→ See **become**

4 **'grow to'**

If you **grow to** feel or think something, you gradually start to feel or think it.

After a few months, I grew to hate my job.

→ See **get to – grow to**

---

guess

1 **'guess'**

If you **guess** that something is true, you decide that it is probably true.

By this time they'd guessed that something was seriously wrong.

You also use **guess** to say that someone finds the correct answer to a problem or question without knowing that it is correct.

I guessed what was going to happen at the end of the film.

2 **'I guess'**

In conversation, you can say **I guess** when you think that something is true or likely.

I guess he got stuck in traffic.
'What's that?' – 'Some sort of blackbird, I guess.'

You can use **I guess so** in conversation as an informal way of answering **yes**. Don't say '~~I guess it~~'.

'Can you find some information for me?' – 'I guess so.'
'Does that answer your question?' – 'Yeah, I guess so.'

You can use **I guess not** in conversation as an informal way of answering **no**, or of answering **yes** to a negative question.

'So no one actually saw him arriving?' – 'No, I guess not.'

---

gymnasium

Gymnasium is a formal word for a building or large room used for physical exercise, with equipment such as bars, mats, and ropes in it. In normal spoken and written English, it is more usual to say **gym**.

I go to the gym twice a week.

! BE CAREFUL

Don't use **gymnasium** to refer to a British or American school for older pupils. In Britain, the general term for this kind of school is **secondary school**.

In America, it is **high school**.

→ See **high school**

Hh

habit – custom

1 'habit'

A **habit** is something that a person does often or regularly.

He had a nervous habit of biting his nails.
Try to get out of the habit of adding unnecessary salt in cooking.

2 'custom'

A **custom** is something that people in a society do at a particular time of year or in a particular situation.

It is the custom to take chocolates or fruit when visiting a patient in hospital.
My wife likes all the old English customs.

hair

Hair can be a countable noun or an uncountable noun.

1 used as a countable noun

Each of the thread-like things growing on your head and body is a **hair**. You can refer to several of these things as **hairs**.

These tiny needles are far thinner than a human hair.
There were black hairs on the back of his hands.

2 used as an uncountable noun

However, don't refer to all the hairs on your head as your 'hairs'. Refer to them as your **hair**.

I washed my hands and combed my hair.
Brigitte was a young woman with long blonde hair.

half – half of

1 used in front of noun phrases

Half or **half of** an amount or object is one of the two equal parts that together make up the whole amount or object.

You use **half** or **half of** in front of a noun phrase beginning with a determiner. **Half** is more common.

He had finished about half his drink.
She is allowed to keep half of her tips.
She'd known me half her life.
For half of his adult life he has lived in Tokyo.

! BE CAREFUL

Don't say 'the half of'.

In front of measurement words like **metre**, **kilogram**, or **hour**, you always use **half**, not 'half of'.

They were nearly half a mile away.
The fault was fixed in half an hour.
They had been friends for about half a century.

Use **half of** in front of pronouns. Don't use 'half'.

The waitress brought the drink, and Ellen drank half of it immediately.
More than half of them have gone back to their home towns.

Don't use 'they' or 'we' after **half of**. Instead use **them** or **us**.

Half of them have had no education at all.
If production goes down by half, half of us lose our jobs.

When you use **half** or **half of** in front of a singular noun or pronoun, you use a singular form of a verb after the noun or pronoun.

Half her property belongs to him.
Half of it was destroyed in a fire.

When you use **half** or **half of** in front of a plural noun or pronoun, you use a plural form of a verb after the noun or pronoun.

Half my friends have children.
Half of them were still married.

2 used as a pronoun

Half can be a pronoun.

Roughly half are French and roughly half are from North America.
Half of the money is for you, half is for me.

3 used as a noun

You can also use **half** as a noun to talk about a particular part of something.

The house was built in the first half of the eighteenth century.
Philip rented an apartment in the top half of a two-storey house.

hand

Your **hand** is the part of your body at the end of your arm. It includes your fingers and your thumb.

Don't refer to a particular person's hand as 'the hand'. Say **his hand** or **her hand**. You refer to your own hand as **my hand**.

The young man held a letter in his hand.
Louise was shading her eyes with her hand.
I raised my hand.
The guards put their hands on his shoulders and led him quickly away.

However, if you say that someone does something to someone else's hand, you usually use **the**.

I grabbed Carlos by the hand.
Ahmed took his wife by the hand.

happen

1 'happen'

When something **happens**, it takes place without being planned.

Then a strange thing <u>happened</u>.
There'll be an investigation into what <u>happened</u> and why.

> **!** BE CAREFUL
>
> **Happen** does not have a passive form. Don't say, for example, '~~Then a strange thing was happened~~'.

2 'take place', 'occur'

Happen is usually used after vague words like **something**, **thing**, **what**, or **this**. After words with a more precise meaning, you usually use **take place** or **occur**.

The incident <u>had taken place</u> many years ago.
Mrs Brogan was in the house when the explosion <u>occurred</u>.

Don't say that a planned event 'happens'. Say that it **takes place**.

The first meeting of the committee <u>took place</u> on 9 January.
The election will <u>take place</u> in June.

3 'happen to'

When something **happens to** someone or something, it takes place and affects them.

I wonder what<u>'s happened to</u> Jeremy?
If anything <u>happens to</u> the car, you'll have to pay for it.

In sentences like these, don't use any preposition except **to** after **happen**.

You use **happen** in front of a *to*-infinitive to show that something happens or exists by chance. For example, instead of saying 'The two people he wanted to speak to lived in the same street', you can say 'The two people he wanted to speak to **happened to live** in the same street'.

I just <u>happened to be</u> in the wrong place at the wrong time.
If you <u>happen to see</u> Jane, ask her to call me.

You often use **happen to be** in sentences beginning with **there**. For example, instead of saying 'A post office happened to be in the next street', you say '**There happened to be** a post office in the next street'.

<u>There happened to be</u> a policeman on the corner, so I asked him the way.

> **!** BE CAREFUL
>
> In sentences like these you must use **there**. Don't say, for example, '~~Happened to be a post office in the next street~~'.

hard – hardly

1 'hard'

Hard can be an adjective. If something is **hard**, it is not easy to do.

Coping with three babies is very <u>hard</u> work.

Hard can also be an adverb. For example, if you work **hard**, you work with a lot of effort.

Many elderly people have worked <u>hard</u> all their lives.

2 'hardly'

Hardly is an adverb. It has a totally different meaning from **hard**. You use **hardly** to modify a statement when you want to emphasize that only a small amount or detail makes it true, and it is best to consider the opposite as true. For example, if someone **hardly** speaks, they do not speak much. If something is **hardly** surprising, it is not very surprising.

I <u>hardly</u> knew him.
Nick <u>hardly</u> slept because he was so worried.

If you use an auxiliary verb or modal with **hardly**, you put the auxiliary verb or modal first. You say, for example, 'I **can hardly** see'. Don't say 'I hardly can see'.

Two years before, the wall <u>had hardly</u> existed.
She <u>can hardly</u> wait to begin.
We <u>could hardly</u> move.

! BE CAREFUL

Don't use 'not' with **hardly**. Don't say, for example, 'I did not hardly know him'. Say 'I **hardly** knew him'.

Hardly is sometimes used in longer structures to say that one thing happened immediately after another.

The local police had <u>hardly</u> finished their search when the detectives arrived.

In structures like these you use **when**, not 'than'. Don't say, for example, 'The local police had hardly finished their search than the detectives arrived'.

In stories, **hardly** is sometimes put at the beginning of a sentence, followed by **had** or the verb **be** and the subject.

<u>Hardly had he</u> uttered the words when he began laughing.

3 'hardly ever'

If something **hardly ever** happens, it almost never happens.

I <u>hardly ever</u> spoke to them.
Tim <u>hardly ever</u> met her friends.

→ See **Adverbs and adverbials** for a graded list of words used to indicate frequency, **Broad negatives**

---

have

Have is one of the most common verbs in English. It is used in many different ways. Its other forms are **has**, **having**, **had**.

1 used as an auxiliary verb

Have is often an auxiliary verb.

They <u>have</u> just bought a new car.
She <u>has</u> never been to Rome.
<u>Having</u> been warned beforehand, I knew how to react.

→ See **Auxiliary verbs**, **Verb forms**

Have, **has**, and **had** are not usually pronounced in full when they come after a pronoun or noun. When you write down what someone says, you usually represent **have**, **has**, and **had** as **'ve**, **'s**, and **'d** after a pronoun. You can also represent **has** as **'s** after a noun.

I've changed my mind.
She's become a teacher.
I do wish you'd met Guy.
Ralph's told you often enough.

→ See **Contractions**

2 'have to'

Have to is often used to say that someone must do something.

I have to speak to your father.
He had to sit down because he felt dizzy.

→ See **must**

3 actions and activities

Have is often used in front of a noun phrase to say that someone does something.

Did you have a look at the shop when you were there?
I'm going to have a bath.

→ See **have – take**

4 causing something to be done

Have can also be used to say that someone arranges for something to be done. When **have** is used like this, it is followed by a noun phrase and an *-ed* participle.

We've just had the house decorated.
They had him killed.

5 possession

Have is often used to show possession.

He had a small hotel.
You have beautiful eyes.
Do you have any brothers or sisters?

In conversation and less formal writing, **have got** can be used instead of 'have' to show possession.

She's got two sisters.
Have you got any information about bus times, please?

→ See **have got**

6 using a simple tense

Don't use a progressive form in any of the following ways:

▶ Don't use a progressive form when you are talking about ownership. For example, don't say 'I am having a collection of old coins'. Say 'I **have** a collection of old coins' or 'I **'ve got** a collection of old coins'.

We haven't got a car.

▶ Don't use a progressive form when you are talking about relationships. Don't say 'I am having three sisters' or 'I am having a lot of friends'.

They have one daughter.
I've got loads of friends.

▶ Don't use a progressive form to say that someone or something has a particular feature. For example, don't say 'He is having a beard'.

He has nice eyes.
He had beautiful manners.
The door's got a lock on it.

▶ Don't use a progressive form to say that someone has an illness or disease. For example, don't say 'She is having a bad cold'.

He had a headache.
Sam's got measles.

▶ Don't use a progressive form to say how much time someone has in which to do something. For example, don't say 'He is having plenty of time to get to the airport'.

I haven't got time to go to the library.
He had only a short time to live.
I hope I'll have time to finish it.

7 using a progressive form

Here are some ways in which you do use a progressive form of **have**:

▶ You use a progressive form to say that an activity is taking place. For example, you say 'He **is having** a bath at the moment'. Don't say 'He has a bath at the moment'.

The children are having a party.
I was having a chat with an old friend.

▶ You use a progressive form to say that an activity will take place at a particular time in the future. For example, you can say 'I**'m having** lunch with Barbara tomorrow'.

We're having a party tonight.
She's having a baby next month.

▶ You also use a progressive form to talk about continuous or repeated actions, events, or experiences. For example, you can say 'I **am having** driving lessons'.

I was already having problems.
Neither of us was having any luck.
You're having a very busy time.

have – take

Have and **take** are both commonly used with nouns as their objects to indicate that someone performs an action or takes part in an activity. With some nouns, you can use either **have** or **take** with the same meaning. For example, you can say '**Have** a look at this' or '**Take** a look at this'. Similarly, you can say 'We **have** our holidays in August' or 'We **take** our holidays in August'.

 There is often a difference between British and American usage. For example, British speakers usually say 'He **had** a bath', while American speakers say 'He **took** a bath'.

I'm going to have a bath.
I took a bath, my second that day.

 When talking about some activities, American speakers often use **take**. For example, they say 'He **took** a walk' or 'She **took** a nap'. British speakers would say 'He **went for** a walk' or 'She **had** a nap'.

Brody decided to take a walk.
I went out on the verandah and took a nap.

After dinner we <u>went for</u> a ride.
She's <u>going for</u> a swim.

have got

1 form and basic uses

Have got is often used in conversation and in less formal writing with the same meaning as **have**.

I <u>have got</u> three children.
You <u>have got</u> a problem.

Have got, **has got**, and **had got** are not usually pronounced in full. When you write down what someone says, you usually write **'ve got**, **'s got**, or **'d got**.

I've<u> got</u> her address.
He's<u> got</u> a beard now.
They'd<u> got</u> a special grant from the Institute.

 Have got is not used in formal written English, and is less common in American English than British English. The *-ed* participle for all the meanings below is **got** (not **gotten**) in both British and American English.

You cannot use **have got** for all meanings of **have**. You use it when you are talking about a situation or state, but not when you are talking about an event or action. For example, you say 'I**'ve got** a new car', but not 'I've got a bath every morning'.

Have got is usually used in the present tense. You don't usually use **have got** in future or past forms. Instead, you use **have**.

Will you <u>have</u> time to eat before you go?
I <u>had</u> a cold and couldn't decide whether to go to work.

2 possession

Have got is most commonly used to talk about possession, relationships, and qualities or features.

I've<u> got</u> a very small house.
She's<u> got</u> two sisters.
He's<u> got</u> a lovely smile.
It's a nice town. It's<u> got</u> a beautiful cathedral.

3 illness

You often use **have got** to talk about illnesses.

Sam's<u> got</u> measles.
I've<u> got</u> an awful headache.

4 availability

You also use **have got** to talk about the availability of something.

Come in and have a chat when you've<u> got</u> time.
I think we've<u> got</u> an enormous amount to offer.

5 future events

You can use **have got** with a noun phrase to mention a future event that you will be involved in.

I've<u> got</u> a date.
I've<u> got</u> an appointment at the dentist's.

You can use **have got** with a noun phrase and an *-ing* form to mention an event that you have arranged or that will affect you.

I've got two directors flying out first class.
I've got some more people coming.

You use **have got** with a noun phrase and a *to*-infinitive to say that there is some work that you must do.

I've got some work to do.
She's got the house to clean.

6 negatives

In negative sentences, **not** goes between **have** and **got**, and is almost always shortened to **n't**.

He hasn't got a moustache.
I haven't got much money.

 American speakers do not always use this form. Often they use the auxiliary verb **do**, followed by **not** and **have**. **Not** is usually shortened to **n't**.

I don't have a boyfriend.
I'm bored. I don't have anything to do.

7 questions

In questions, you put the subject between **have** and **got**.

Have you got enough money for a taxi?
I'd like a drink. What have you got?

 American speakers do not always use this form. Instead they use the auxiliary verb **do**, followed by the subject and **have**. Some British speakers also use **do** and **have**.

Do you have her address?
What kind of cakes do you have?

---

have got to

→ See **must**

---

have to

→ See **must**

---

he – she – they

1 'he'

He, **him**, **his**, and **himself** are sometimes used to refer back to an indefinite pronoun or to a word such as **person**, **child**, or **student**.

If anybody complained about this, he was told that things would soon get back to normal.
It won't hurt a child to have his meals at a different time.

Many people object to this use because it suggests that the person referred to is male.

2 'he or she'

You can sometimes use **he or she**, **him or her**, **his or her**, or **himself or herself**.

A parent may feel that <u>he or she</u> has nothing to give a child.
Anyone can call <u>himself or herself</u> a psychologist, even if untrained and unqualified.

Many people avoid these expressions because they think they sound clumsy and unnatural, especially when more than one of them is used in the same sentence.

In writing, some people use **s/he** to mean **he or she**.

3 'they'

Most people use **they**, **them**, and **their**.

Everyone thinks <u>they</u> know what the problems of living with a teenager are.
Often when we touch someone we are demonstrating our love for <u>them</u>.
Don't hope to change anyone or <u>their</u> attitudes.

This use used to be considered incorrect, but it is now the most common form in both spoken and written English, and is used in formal and informal writing.

It is often possible to avoid all the above uses. You can sometimes do this by using plurals. For example, instead of saying 'Every student has his own room', you can say '**All** the students have **their** own rooms'. Instead of saying 'Anyone who goes inside must take off his shoes', you can say '**People** who go inside must take off **their** shoes'.

headache

If you have a **headache**, you have a pain in your head.

I told Derek I had <u>a headache</u>.

Headache is a countable noun. Don't say that someone '~~has headache~~'.

headline

→ See **title – headline**

heap – stack – pile

1 'heap'

A **heap** of things is usually untidy, and often has the shape of a hill or mound.

The building collapsed into a <u>heap</u> of rubble.

2 'stack'

A **stack** is usually tidy, and often consists of flat objects placed directly on top of each other.

...a neat <u>stack</u> of dishes.
Eric came out of his room with a small <u>stack</u> of CDs in his hands.

3 'pile'

A **pile** of things can be tidy or untidy.

...a neat <u>pile</u> of clothes.
He reached over to a <u>pile</u> of newspapers and magazines

hear

1 'hear' in the present

If you **can hear** a sound, you are aware of it because it has reached your ears.

I can hear a car.

! BE CAREFUL

You usually use **can** in sentences like these. You say, for example, 'I **can hear** a radio'. Don't say 'I hear a radio'. Also don't use a progressive form. Don't say 'I am hearing a radio'.

The past tense and *-ed* participle of **hear** is **heard** /hɜːd/. If you want to say that someone was aware of something in the past, you use **heard** or **could hear**.

She heard no further sounds.
I could hear music in the distance.

2 'hear' in the past

However, if you want to say that someone suddenly became aware of something, you must use **heard**.

I heard a shout.

You can use an *-ing* form after **heard** or **could hear** to show that someone was aware of something that was continuing to take place.

He heard Hajime shouting and laughing.
I could hear him crying.

You can use an infinitive without *to* after **heard** to show that someone was aware of a complete event or action.

I heard him open the door.
I heard Amy cry out in fright.

! BE CAREFUL

You must use an infinitive without *to* in sentences like these. Don't say, for example, 'I heard him to open the door'.

help

1 'help' as a transitive verb

If you **help** someone, you make something easier for them. When **help** has this meaning, it can be followed by an infinitive, with or without *to*. For example, you can say 'I **helped him to move** the desk' or 'I **helped him move** the desk'. There is no difference in meaning.

We must try to help students to have confidence in their ability.
Something went wrong with his machine so I helped him fix it.

2 'help' as an intransitive verb

You can also use **help** as an intransitive verb, followed by an infinitive with or without *to*. If someone **helps do** something or **helps to do** it, they help other people to do it.

I used to help cook the meals for the children.
The taxi driver helped to carry the bags into the hotel.

If something **helps do** something or **helps to do** it, it makes it easier for that thing to be done.

The money helped pay the rent.
This policy helped to improve the competitiveness of American exports.

> **!** **BE CAREFUL**
> Don't use an *-ing* form after **help**. Don't say, for example, 'I helped moving the desk' or 'I helped him moving the desk'.

3 **'cannot help'**

If you **cannot help** doing something, you are unable to prevent yourself from doing it.

I couldn't help teasing him a little.

> **!** **BE CAREFUL**
> Don't use a *to*-infinitive after **cannot help**. Don't say, for example, 'I couldn't help to tease him a little'.

---

her

Her can be the object of a verb or preposition. You use **her** to refer to a woman, girl, or female animal that has already been mentioned, or whose identity is known.

They gave her the job.
I knew your mother. I was at school with her.

→ See **Pronouns**

> **!** **BE CAREFUL**
> Don't use 'her' as the indirect object of a sentence when you are referring to the same person as the subject. Instead use **herself**.
>
> *Rose bought herself a sandwich for lunch.*

---

here

1 **'here'**

Here refers to the place where you are.

I'm glad you'll still be here next year.
We're allowed to come here at any time.

> **!** **BE CAREFUL**
> 'To' is never used in front of **here**. Don't say, for example, 'We're allowed to come to here at any time'.

2 **'here is' and 'here are'**

You can use **here is** or **here are** at the beginning of a sentence when you want to draw attention to something or to introduce something. You use **here is** in front of a singular noun phrase and **here are** in front of a plural noun phrase.

Here's your coffee.
Here are the addresses to which you should apply.

here – hear

These words are both pronounced /hɪə/.

1 **'here'**

You use **here** to refer to the place where you are.

Come here!
She left here at eight o'clock.

→ See **here**

2 **'hear'**

When you **hear** a sound, you are aware of it through your ears.

Did you hear that noise?

→ See **hear**

high – tall

1 **'high'**

You use **high** to describe things which measure a larger distance than usual from the bottom to the top. For example, you talk about a **high hill** or a **high fence**.

...the high mountains of northern Japan.
...the high walls of the prison.

2 **'tall'**

You use **tall** to describe things which are higher than usual, but which are also much higher than they are wide. So, for example, you talk about a **tall tree** or a **tall chimney**.

Insects buzzed in the tall grass.
We saw several birds, including a tall heron standing on one leg.

You always use **tall** when you are talking about people.

Andreas was a tall handsome man.
She was a young woman, fairly tall and slim.

3 **another meaning of 'high'**

High also means 'a long way above the ground'. For example, you talk about a **high window** or a **high shelf**.

It was a large room with a high ceiling.

high school

 In America, and sometimes in the UK, a **high school** is a school for older students up to the age of 18. In Britain, the general term for a school of this kind is **secondary school**.

him

Him can be the object of a verb or preposition. You use **him** to refer to a man, boy, or male animal that has already been mentioned, or whose identity is known.

He asked if you'd call <u>him</u> when you got in.
There's no need for <u>him</u> to worry.

→ See **Pronouns**

 BE CAREFUL

Don't use 'him' as the indirect object of a sentence when you are referring to the same person as the subject. Instead use **himself**.

He poured <u>himself</u> a drink.

hire – rent – let

1 'hire' and 'rent'

If you pay a sum of money in order to use something for a short period of time, you can say that you **hire** it or **rent** it. **Hire** is more common in British English and **rent** is more common in American English.

We <u>hired</u> a car from a local car agency and drove across the island.
He <u>rented</u> a car for the weekend.

If you make a series of payments in order to use something for a long period, you say that you **rent** it. You do not usually say that you 'hire' it.

A month's deposit may be required before you can <u>rent</u> the house.

2 'hire out'

If you hire something from someone, you can say that they **hire** it **out** to you.

Companies <u>hiring out</u> boats do well in the summer months.

3 'rent out'

If you rent something from someone, you can say that they **rent** it **out** to you.

They had to <u>rent out</u> the upstairs room.

4 'let' and 'let out'

If you rent a building or piece of land from someone, you can say that they **let** it to you or **let** it **out** to you. The past tense and -ed participle of **let** is **let**.

The cottage <u>was let</u> to an actor from London.
I couldn't sell the house, so I <u>let</u> it <u>out</u>.

 This usage is more common in British English than American English. The usual American terms are **rent** and **rent out**.

The house was <u>rented</u> to a farmer.
He repaired the boat and <u>rented</u> it <u>out</u> for $150.

holiday – vacation

1 'holiday'

In British English, you refer to a period of time that you are allowed to spend away from work or school as the **holiday** or the **holidays**.

The school had undergone repairs during the <u>holiday</u>.
One day after the Christmas <u>holidays</u> I rang her up.

You refer to a period of time spent away from home enjoying yourself as a **holiday**.

He thought that Vita needed a holiday.
I went to Marrakesh for a holiday.

When you spend a long period of time like this each year, you refer to it as your **holidays**.

Where are you going for your holidays?

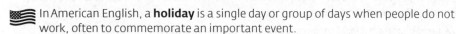 **BE CAREFUL**

You usually use a determiner or a possessive in front of **holiday** or **holidays**. Don't say, for example, 'I went to Marrakesh for holidays.'

If you are **on holiday**, you are spending a period of time away from work or school, or you are spending some time away from home enjoying yourself.

Remember to turn off the gas when you go on holiday.

 In American English, a **holiday** is a single day or group of days when people do not work, often to commemorate an important event.

In British English, a day like this is called a **bank holiday** or a **public holiday**.

 When Americans talk about **the holidays**, they mean the period at the end of the year that includes Christmas and the New Year; sometimes Thanksgiving (at the end of November) is also included in this.

Now that the holidays are over, we should take down our Christmas tree.

2 'vacation'

 The usual American word for a longer period of time spent away from work or school, or for a period of time spent away from home enjoying yourself, is **vacation**.

Harold used to take a vacation at that time.

home

Your **home** is the place where you live and feel that you belong. **Home** is most commonly used to refer to a person's house, but it can also be used to refer to a town, a region, or a country.

His father often worked away from home.
Dublin will always be home to me.

Don't refer to a particular person's home as 'the home'. Say **his home**, **her home**, or just **home**.

Victoria is selling her home in Ireland.
Their children have left home.

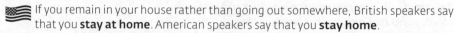 **BE CAREFUL**

You never use 'to' immediately in front of **home**. Don't say, for example, 'We went to home'. Say 'We went **home**'.

Come home with me.
The police officer escorted her home.

 If you remain in your house rather than going out somewhere, British speakers say that you **stay at home**. American speakers say that you **stay home**.

Oh, we'll just have to stay at home for the weekend.
What was Cindy supposed to do? Stay home all day and dust the house?

homework – housework

1 'homework'

Homework is work that school pupils are given to do at home. You say that pupils **do** homework. Don't say that they 'make homework'.

Have you done your English homework?

2 'housework'

Housework is work such as cleaning or washing that is done in a house.

She relied on him to do most of the housework.

! BE CAREFUL

Both **homework** and **housework** are uncountable nouns. Don't talk about 'a homework' or 'houseworks'.

→ See **Nouns** for information on uncountable nouns

hood

→ See **bonnet – hood**

hope

1 'basic meaning'

If you **hope** that something is true or will happen, you want it to be true or to happen.

She hoped she would have a career in the music industry.
I sat down, hoping to remain unnoticed.

2 'I hope'

You often use **I hope** to express a wish that someone will have a pleasant time. After **hope** you can use either the future form or the present simple. For example, you can say '**I hope you'll enjoy** the film' or '**I hope you enjoy** the film'.

I hope you'll enjoy your stay in Roehampton.
I hope you get well very soon.

If you say to someone that you **hope they are going to do** something, you are usually asking or reminding them to do something that they may not want to do.

I hope you're going to clean up this mess.
Next time I come I hope you're going to be a lot more entertaining.

3 'I hope so'

If someone says that something is true or will happen, or asks you whether something is true or will happen, you can express your wish that it is true or will happen by saying **I hope so**.

'I will see you in the church.' – 'I hope so.'
'You'll be home at six?' – 'I hope so.'

! BE CAREFUL

Don't say 'I hope it'.

4 **'I hope not'**

Similarly, you can express your wish that something is not true or will not happen by saying **I hope not**.

'You haven't lost the ticket, have you?' – 'I hope not.'

> **!** **BE CAREFUL**
>
> Don't say ~~'I don't hope so'~~.

hospital

A **hospital** is a place where sick people are looked after by doctors and nurses.

In British English, if you want to say that someone is in a hospital without mentioning which hospital they are in, you say they are **in hospital**.

I used to visit him in hospital.
She had to go into hospital for an operation.

 American speakers do not say 'in hospital'. They say **in the hospital**.

She broke her back and spent some time in the hospital.

In both British and American English, if you want to say that something happened in a particular hospital, you usually say **at the hospital**.

I was working at the hospital.

house

Your **house** is the building where you live and which you own or rent.

She has moved to a smaller house.

You do not usually say ~~'I am going to my house'~~ or ~~'She was in her house'~~. You say 'I am going **home**' or 'She was at **home**'.

Brody arrived home a little before five.
I'll finish the work at home.

→ See **home**

housework

→ See **homework – housework**

how

1 **ways of doing things**

You use **how** in questions and explanations when you are talking about the way something is done.

How do you spell his name?
Tell me how to get there.
This is how I make a vegetable curry.

! BE CAREFUL

Don't use 'how' to mean 'in the way that'. For example, don't say 'He walks to work every day, how his father did'. Instead you use **like**, **as**, or **the way**.

→ See **like – as – the way**

2 **asking about someone's health**

You use **how** with **be** to ask about someone's health.

How are you?
How is she? All right?

! BE CAREFUL

Don't use 'how' to ask what kind of person someone is. For example, if you are asking someone for a description of their boss, don't say 'How is your boss?' Say '**What** is your boss **like**?'

What's his mother like?

3 **asking about impressions**

You use **how** with **be** to ask whether someone likes or enjoys something or not.

How was your trip?
How was the smoked trout?

! BE CAREFUL

Don't use 'how' to ask for a description of a thing or place. For example, if you say 'How is Birmingham?', you are not asking someone what kind of place Birmingham is; you are asking them if they are enjoying living or working there. If you want them to give you a description of Birmingham, you say '**What** is Birmingham **like**?'

What is Fiji like?

Don't say 'How do you think of Birmingham?' Say '**What do you think of** Birmingham?'

What do you think of his writing style?
What did you think of Tokyo?

4 **commenting on a quality**

People often use **how** with an adjective when they are commenting on what someone has just said.

'She has a house there as well.' – 'How nice!'
'To my surprise, I found her waiting for me at the station.' – 'How kind!'

→ See **Topic** entry **Reactions** for other ways of commenting on what someone has just said

however

You use **however** when you are adding a comment that contrasts with what has just been said.

Some of the food crops failed. However, the cotton did quite well.
Losing at games doesn't matter to some women. Most men, however, can't stand it.

You also use **however** to say that it makes no difference how something is done.

You can do it however you want.

However we add that up, it does not make a dozen.
However we prepare for retirement there are undeniably risks.

> **! BE CAREFUL**
>
> Don't use 'however' as a conjunction. For example, don't say ~~'John always cooks dinner, however I usually wash up afterwards'~~. You can start a new sentence or clause, for example 'John always cooks dinner. However, I usually wash up afterwards'. Or you can use a conjunction such as **but** or **although**, for example 'John always cooks dinner, although I usually wash up afterwards.'

how much

You use **how much** when you are asking about the price of something. For example, you say '**How much** is that T-shirt?'

I like that dress – how much is it?

> **! BE CAREFUL**
>
> Don't say ~~'How much is the price of that T-shirt?'~~
>
> You only use **how much** with **be** when you are asking about the price of something. Don't use it to ask about other amounts of money. Don't say, for example, ~~'How much is his income?'~~ Say '**What is his income?**', '**What does he earn?**', or '**How much does he earn?**'
>
> Similarly, don't say ~~'How much is the temperature outside?'~~ or ~~'How much is the population of Tokyo?'~~ You say '**What** is the temperature outside?' or '**What** is the population of Tokyo?'
>
> *What is the basic rate of income tax?*
> *What is the lowest temperature it's possible to reach?*

hundred

A hundred or **one hundred** is the number 100.

→ See **Reference** section **Numbers and fractions**

You can say that there are **a hundred** things or **one hundred** things.

She must have had a hundred pairs of shoes at least.
The group claimed the support of over one hundred MPs.

> **! BE CAREFUL**
>
> Don't say that there are 'hundred' things.
>
> Don't add '-s' to the word **hundred** when you put another number in front of it.
>
> *There are more than two hundred languages spoken in Nigeria.*

 For numbers greater than 100, most speakers add **and** before pronouncing the second part of the number, but speakers of American English sometimes leave out the **and**. For example, 370 is expressed as **three hundred and seventy** in British English and sometimes as **three hundred seventy** in American English.

He got nine hundred and eighty-three votes.
Eduardo won a hundred fifty dollars.

hurt

Hurt can be a verb or an adjective.

1 used as a verb

If you **hurt** yourself or **hurt** a part of your body, you accidentally injure yourself. The past tense and -*ed* participle of **hurt** is **hurt**.

The boy fell down and hurt himself.
How did you hurt your finger?

If a part of your body **hurts**, you feel pain there.

My leg was beginning to hurt.

 In American English, you can also say that a person **hurts**.

When that anesthetic wears off, you're going to hurt a bit.

Some British speakers also use **hurt** like this, but this use is not generally accepted in British English.

2 used as an adjective

You can use **hurt** as an adjective to describe an injured person.

He was hurt in a serious accident.
Luckily no-one was hurt but both vehicles were badly damaged.

If someone has a bad injury, don't say that they are 'very hurt'. Say that they are **badly hurt** or **seriously hurt**.

The soldier was badly hurt.
Last year 5,000 children were seriously hurt in car accidents.

In British English you do not usually use 'hurt' in front of a noun. Don't, for example, talk about 'a hurt soldier'. You say 'an **injured** soldier'.

hyphen

→ See **Reference** sections **Punctuation**, **Spelling**

I i

I

A speaker or writer uses **I** to refer to himself or herself. **I** is the subject of a verb. It is always written as a capital letter.

I will be leaving soon.
I like your dress.

You can also use **I** as part of the subject of a verb, along with another person or other people. You mention the other person first. Say 'My friend **and I**', not '~~I and my friend~~'.

My mother and I stood beside the road and waited.
My brothers and I go to the same school.

> **!** **BE CAREFUL**
> Don't use 'I' after **is**. Say 'It's me', not '~~It's I~~'.

→ See **me**

if

1 possible situations

You use **if** to introduce a conditional clause in which you mention a possible situation.

If you get tired, have a rest.
If the machine stops working, call this number.

You can use **if** to mention a situation that might exist in the future. In the conditional clause, you use the present simple form. Don't use a future form.

If all goes well, we will arrive by lunchtime.
If you make a mistake, you will have to start again.

You sometimes use **if** in a conditional clause to suggest that someone does something. You usually use the present simple in the conditional clause.

If you turn to page 15, you will see a list of questions.

You can use **if** to mention a situation that sometimes existed in the past. You usually use the past simple in the conditional clause.

They ate outside if it was sunny.
If we had enough money, we used to go to the cinema.

You can also use **if** to mention something that might have happened in the past, but did not in fact happen. In the conditional clause, you use the past perfect. Don't use the past simple.

If he had known the truth, he would have run away.
If they had not met, this book would never have been written.

2 unlikely situations

You also use **if** in conditional clauses to mention situations that do not exist, or events that are unlikely to happen. In the conditional clause, you use the past simple. Don't use a present tense.

They would find it difficult to get a job if they left the farm.
If she wanted to, she could be a dancer.

In formal writing, when the subject of the conditional clause is **I**, **he**, **she**, **it**, **there**, or a singular noun, you use **were** in the clause instead of 'was'.

If a problem were to arise, she would be able to resolve it.
Employees would be more productive if better resources were provided.

In conversation or informal writing people usually use **was** (except in the expression **If I were you**).

If I was a painter, I'd paint this garden.
We would prefer it if the test was a bit easier.

Sometimes **was** is used in formal writing too, but this is considered incorrect by many people.

3 in reported questions

If is also used in reported questions.

I asked her if I could help her.
I wonder if you understand what I mean.

→ See **Reporting**

ill – sick

1 'ill' and 'sick'

Ill and **sick** are both used for saying that someone has a disease or some other problem with their health. You can use either **ill** or **sick** after a linking verb.

Manjit is ill and can't come to school.
Your uncle is very sick.

You usually use **sick**, rather than 'ill', in front of a noun.

She was at home looking after her sick baby.

However, you often use **ill** in front of a noun when you are also using an adverb such as **seriously**, **chronically**, or **terminally**.

This ward is for terminally ill patients.

! BE CAREFUL

The usual comparative form of **ill** is **worse**.

The next day I felt worse.

2 'be sick'

To **be sick** means to bring up food from your stomach.

Cristina ate so much that she was sick.

→ See **sick**

! BE CAREFUL

Don't use 'ill' or 'sick' to say that someone has received an injury. Say that they are **injured** or **hurt**.

Two people were injured and taken to hospital after the car crash.

→ See **hurt**

illness – disease

1 'illness'

If you have an **illness**, there is something wrong with your health. An illness can last for a long time or a short time, and its effects can be serious or not serious.

The doctor thought that Bae's illness was caused by stress.

You can use the adjectives **long** and **short** in front of **illness**, but not in front of **disease**.

He died last month after a long illness.

2 'disease'

A **disease** is a particular kind of illness caused by bacteria or an infection. Diseases can often be passed from one person to another.

Glaucoma is an eye disease.
Children should be immunised against dangerous diseases.

Animals and plants can also have **diseases**, but not **illnesses**.

Scrapie is a disease that affects sheep.
The trees were killed by Dutch Elm disease.

imagine

If you **imagine** a situation, you think about it and your mind forms a picture or idea of it.

It is difficult to imagine such a huge building.
Try to imagine you're on a beautiful beach.

You can use an *-ing* form after **imagine**.

It is hard to imagine anyone being so cruel.
She could not imagine living with Daniel.

! BE CAREFUL

Don't use a *to*-infinitive after **imagine**. Don't say, for example, 'She could not imagine to live with Daniel'.

If you **imagine** something is true, you think it is probably true.

I imagine it would be difficult to make money from a business like that.
I imagine that he finds his work very satisfying.

You can say '**I imagine so**' or '**I would imagine so**' if someone asks you if something is true and you think that it probably is.

'Could he get through that window?' – 'I imagine so.'
'Was that why she left?' – 'I would imagine so.'

Don't say 'I imagine it'.

Instead of saying that you 'imagine something is not' true, you usually say that you **don't imagine it is** true.

I don't imagine we'll have a problem, anyway.

immediately

If something happens **immediately**, it happens without delay.

We have to leave immediately. It's very urgent.

Rishi read the letter, and immediately started to cry.

If something happens **immediately after** something else, it happens as soon as the other thing is finished.

He had to go out immediately after lunch.
She left for the airport immediately after I spoke to her.

If something is **immediately above** something else, it is above it and very close to it. You can use **immediately** in a similar way with other prepositions such as **under**, **opposite**, and **behind**.

There is a window immediately above the door.
The man immediately behind me in the photograph is my father.

immigrant

→ See **emigration – immigration – migration**

immigration

→ See **emigration – immigration – migration**

GRAMMAR FINDER

The imperative

You use the **imperative** form of a verb when you are telling someone to do something or not to do something. A statement in the imperative usually has no subject.

1 form

The imperative form of a verb is the same as its base form.

Come here.
Take two tablets every four hours.

For a **negative imperative**, you use **don't** and the base form of the verb. In formal English, you use **do not** and the base form.

Don't touch that wire!
Don't be afraid of them.
Do not forget to leave the key on the desk.

2 emphasis and politeness

An imperative form usually comes at the beginning of a sentence. However, you can put **always** or **never** first for emphasis.

Always check that you have enough money first.
Never believe what he tells you.

You can also use **do** to add emphasis.

Do be careful!

You can add **please** to the beginning or end of the clause in order to be more polite.

Please don't do that.
Follow me, please.

Question tags are sometimes added after imperative clauses to make them sound more like requests, or to express impatience or anger.

Post that letter for me, will you?
Hurry up, can't you?

→ See **Topic** entry **Requests, orders, and instructions**

The subject **you** is sometimes used when people want to show which person they are talking to, or want to add emphasis or express anger.

You get in the car this minute!

! **BE CAREFUL**

An imperative can often sound rude or abrupt.

→ See **Topic** entries **Advising someone**, **Invitations**, **Requests, orders, and instructions**, **Suggestions**, **Warning someone**

3 **conditional use**

Sometimes, when an imperative is followed by **and** or **or**, it has a meaning similar to a conditional clause beginning 'If you...'. For example, 'Take that piece away, and the whole lot falls down' means 'If you take that piece away, the whole lot falls down'. 'Go away or I'll call the police' means 'If you don't go away, I'll call the police'.

Say that again, and I'll leave.
Hurry up, or you'll be late for school.

important

Something that is **important** is very significant, valuable, or necessary.

This is the most important part of the job.
It is important to study for your exams.

! **BE CAREFUL**

Don't use 'important' to talk about a large sum or amount. Use **considerable**, **substantial**, or **large**.

He was paid a substantial sum of money for the information.
A considerable amount of rain had fallen.

in

1 **used for saying where something is**

You use **in** as a preposition to say where someone or something is, or where something happens.

Carlos was in the bath.
I wanted to play in the park.
In New York we saw the Statue of Liberty.

In is sometimes used with superlatives.

The Ueno Zoo is the oldest zoo in Japan.
His company is one of the biggest in the world.

2 **used for saying where something goes**

You use **in** as an adverb to say that someone goes into a place, or that something is put into a container.

Someone knocked at the door, and Hana called 'Come in!'.
She opened her bag and put her phone in.

In is sometimes a preposition meaning **into**.

She threw both letters in the fire.

→ See **into**

3 used with expressions of time

In is often used with expressions of time.

You use **in** to say how long something takes.

He learned to drive in six months.
The food was all eaten in a few minutes.

You also use **in** to say how long it will be before something happens in the future.

In another hour it will be dark.

You use **in** to say that something happens during a particular year, month, or season.

In 1872, there was a terrible fire in Chicago.
Her birthday is in April.
We plan to go camping in the summer.

You use **in** with **the** to say that something happens regularly each morning, afternoon, or evening.

I often go swimming in the morning.
Dad used to sit there in the evening and listen to the radio.

→ See **morning**, **afternoon**, **evening**

Don't say 'in the night' to mean that something happens regularly each night. Use **at night**.

There were no lights in the street at night.

→ See **night**

! BE CAREFUL

Don't say that something happens 'in' a particular day or date. Say that it happens **on** that day or date.

On Tuesday they went shopping.
Ali was born on April 10th.

American speakers sometimes omit the **on**.

I'm going to a party Wednesday.

Don't say that something lasts or continues 'in' a period of time. Say that it lasts or continues **for** that time.

I have known you for a long time.
I worked for the same company for ten years.

→ See **for**

4 meaning 'wearing'

In is sometimes used when saying what someone is wearing.

The bar was full of men in baseball caps.

→ See **wear**

> ❗ **BE CAREFUL**
>
> Don't use 'in' when you are talking about someone's ability to speak a language. Don't say, for example, 'She speaks in Russian'. Say 'She speaks Russian'.

→ See **speak – talk**

in case

→ See **case**

indicate – show

1 talking about evidence and results

You can use **indicate** and **show** in a similar way when you are talking about evidence or the results of research.

Evidence indicates that the experiments were unsuccessful.
Research shows that doctors are working harder.

2 talking about objects

If you **show** an object to someone, you hold it up or give or take it to them, so that they can look at it. When **show** has this meaning, it always takes an indirect object. You can say '**show** someone something' or '**show** something to someone'.

I showed Ayeisha what I had written.
Show your drawing to the teacher.

'Indicate' is not usually used with this meaning.

indoors – indoor

1 'indoors'

Indoors is an adverb. If you go **indoors**, you go into a building.

It started to rain, so we went indoors.

If something happens **indoors**, it happens inside a building.

The children were playing indoors.

2 'indoor'

Indoor is an adjective used in front of a noun. You use it to describe objects or activities that exist or happen inside a building.

The hotel has an indoor swimming pool.
We'll think of some indoor games to play if it's wet.

industrious – industrial

1 'industrious'

An **industrious** person works very hard.

He was industrious and always trying to improve himself.
Michael was an intelligent, industrious man.

2 'industrial'

Don't use 'industrious' to describe things related to making goods in factories.
Use **industrial**.

They have increased their <u>industrial</u> production in recent years.
The company is located in an <u>industrial</u> zone to the east of the city.

GRAMMAR FINDER

Infinitives

1 infinitives with and without *to*

There are two types of infinitive. One kind is called the *to*-infinitive. It consists of **to** and the base form of a verb.

I wanted <u>to escape</u> from here.
I asked Don <u>to go</u> with me.

The other kind of infinitive is sometimes called the **infinitive without *to*** or the **bare infinitive**. It is the same as the base form of a verb. Its uses are explained in this entry.

They helped me <u>get</u> settled here.

2 used after other verbs

You use an infinitive without *to* to talk about a completed action that someone sees, hears, or notices.

She heard him <u>fall</u> down the stairs.
The teachers here just don't want to let anybody <u>speak</u>.

An infinitive without *to* is used in this way after the object of the following verbs:

feel	listen to	see
hear	notice	watch

I <u>felt her touch</u> my hand.
Chandler did not <u>notice him enter</u>.

These verbs can also have an *-ing* form after their object.

→ See *-ing* forms

3 'have', 'let', and 'make'

You use an infinitive without *to* after the object of **have**, **let**, and **make** when it means 'cause or force someone to do something'.

Have the children <u>work in pairs</u>.
Don't let Tim <u>go</u> by himself!
They made me <u>write</u> all the details down again.

4 'know'

 In British English, an infinitive without *to* can be used after the object of **know** in negative, past simple clauses or in perfect clauses, but American English uses a *to*-infinitive.

I never knew him <u>go jogging</u> before breakfast.
Have you ever known him <u>buy</u> someone a coffee?
I've never known him <u>to be</u> unkind.

5 'help'

You can also use an infinitive without *to* with **help**. You can leave out the object if you do not think it is necessary to mention the person who is being helped.

John helped the old lady carry the bags upstairs.
We stayed and helped clear up.

Help can also be used with a *to*-infinitive.

→ See **help**

! **BE CAREFUL**

When you are using the verbs mentioned above in passive clauses, don't use an infinitive without *to* after them. Use a *to*-infinitive instead.

I resent being made to feel guilty.
These people need to be helped to liberate themselves.

6 used after modals

You use an infinitive without *to* after all modals except 'ought'.

I must go.
Can you see him?

→ See **Modals**

You use an infinitive without *to* after the expressions **had better** and **would rather**.

I had better go.
Would you rather do it yourself?

You sometimes use an infinitive without *to* after **dare** and **need**.

I daren't leave before six.
Need you pay him right now?

→ See **dare, need**

7 other uses

You can use an infinitive without *to* after **Why** to show that you think that an action is not worth doing.

Why wait until then?

You can use an infinitive without *to* after **Why not** to suggest what someone should do.

Why not come with us?

You can use an infinitive without *to* after **be** when you are explaining what someone or something does or should do. The subject must be a clause beginning with **all** or **what**.

All he did was open the door.
What it does is cool the engine.

! **BE CAREFUL**

You cannot use infinitives without *to* after prepositions. You can, however, use an *-ing* form.

→ See *-ing* **forms**

inform

→ See **tell**

information – news

1 'information'

Information is facts that you learn or discover.

You can get more <u>information</u> about our products on our website.

> **! BE CAREFUL**
>
> **Information** is an uncountable noun. Don't say '~~an information~~ or '~~informations~~'.
> You can say a **piece of information**.
>
> *I found out an interesting <u>piece of information</u>.*
>
> You **give** people information.
>
> *She <u>gave</u> me some useful information.*
>
> Use **give**, not 'tell'. Don't say '~~She told me some useful information.~~'
>
> You refer to information **about** something or **on** something.
>
> *We don't have any information <u>about</u> him.*
> *I'm looking for information <u>on</u> the history of the town.*

2 'news'

Don't use 'information' to refer to descriptions of recent events in newspapers or on television or radio. Use **news**.

Our town was in the <u>news</u> when it was visited by the Pope.
The story was on the <u>news</u> this evening.

→ See **news**

GRAMMAR FINDER

-ing forms

1 form	**7** separate *-ing* clauses
2 progressive forms	**8** active meaning
3 after verbs	**9** passive meaning
4 choice of *-ing* form and *to*-infinitive	**10** after a noun
5 after the object of a verb	**11** used like nouns
6 *-ing* forms after conjunctions	**12** other uses

1 form

-ing forms are sometimes called **present participles**. Most *-ing* forms are formed by adding *-ing* to the base form of a verb, for example **asking**, **eating**, and **passing**. Sometimes there is a change in spelling, as in **dying**, **making**, and **putting**.

→ See **Reference** section **Verb forms** formation of

→ See **it** for the use of *-ing* forms in sentences such as 'It was difficult saying goodbye'

2 **progressive forms**

One common use of *-ing* forms is as part of the progressive verb form.

He *was sleeping* in the other room.
Cathy *has been looking* at the results.

→ See **Verb forms, The progressive form**

3 **after verbs**

When you are talking about someone's behaviour in relation to an action, or their attitude towards doing it, you often use a verb followed by a clause beginning with an *-ing* form (an *-ing* clause.) The following verbs can be followed by an *-ing* clause:

admit	describe	imagine	resent
adore	detest	involve	resist
avoid	dislike	keep	risk
chance	dread	mind	stop
commence	enjoy	miss	suggest
consider	escape	postpone	
delay	fancy	practise	
deny	finish	recall	

He *avoided mentioning the incident*.
They *enjoy working together*.
You must *keep trying*.

 Need, **require**, and **want** can be followed by an *-ing* form that has a passive meaning. For example, if you say that something **needs doing**, you mean that it needs to be done. These constructions are less common in American English, where a passive *to*-infinitive is commonly used.

It *needs dusting*.
The beans *want picking*.
The room *needs to be cleaned*.

Deserve and **merit** are also sometimes used in this way.

4 **choice of *-ing* form and *to*-infinitive**

After some verbs, you can use an *-ing* clause or a *to*-infinitive clause without greatly changing the meaning.

It *started raining* soon after we set off.
Then it *started to rain*.

Here are some common verbs that can be followed by an *-ing* clause or a *to*-infinitive clause:

begin	continue	intend	omit
bother	deserve	like	prefer
cease	hate	love	start

After the verbs **go on**, **regret**, **remember**, and **try**, an *-ing* form has a different meaning from a *to*-infinitive.

→ See **go on, regret – be sorry, remember – remind, try – attempt**

5 **after the object of a verb**

Some verbs, particularly verbs of perception, are used with an object and an *-ing* clause. The *-ing* clause indicates what the person or thing referred to by the object is doing.

I saw him looking at me.
He was caught stealing.

The following verbs are commonly used with an object and an -*ing* clause:

bring	keep	picture	show
catch	leave	prevent	spot
feel	listen to	save	watch
find	notice	see	
have	observe	send	
hear	photograph	set	

Some of these verbs can also be used with an object and an infinitive without *to*.

→ See **Infinitives**

6 -*ing* forms after conjunctions

You can use -*ing* forms after some subordinating conjunctions, with no subject or auxiliary verb. You can only do this when the subject would be the same as the one in the main clause, or when it is not specific.

I didn't read the book before going to see the film.
When buying a new car, it is best to seek expert advice.

→ See **Subordinate clauses**

7 separate -*ing* clauses

When you are describing two actions done by the same person at about the same time, you can use an -*ing* clause in front of the main clause. You can also put the -*ing* clause after the main clause, if it is clear who the subject is.

Walking down Newbury Street, they spotted the same man again.
He looked at me, suddenly realising that he was talking to a stranger.

If you want to say that someone did one thing immediately after another, you can mention the first thing they did in an -*ing* clause in front of the main clause.

Leaping out of bed, he ran downstairs and answered the phone.

! BE CAREFUL

You should not use an -*ing* clause in front of a main clause when the subject of the -*ing* clause is not the same as the subject of the main clause. If you say 'Driving home later that night, the streets were deserted', you are suggesting that the streets were driving.

8 active meaning

When an -*ing* form is used to begin a clause, it has an active meaning.

'You could play me a tune,' said Simon, sitting down.
Glancing at my clock, I saw that it was midnight.

Combinations beginning with **having** are sometimes used, especially in writing. For example, instead of writing 'John, who had already eaten, left early', you could write 'John, having already eaten, left early'.

Ash, having forgotten his fear, was becoming bored.
Having beaten Rangers the previous week, Aberdeen were confident about their match with Celtic.

9 passive meaning

-*ing* clauses beginning with **having been** and an -*ed* participle have a passive meaning.

Having been born and brought up in Spain, she presumed that she was of Spanish nationality.

In writing, you can use a clause containing a subject and an -*ing* form when you want to mention a fact or situation that is relevant to the fact stated in the main clause, or is the reason for it.

Bats are long-lived creatures, some having a life-expectancy of around twenty years.
Ashton being dead, the whole affair must now be explained to Colonel Browne.
The subject having been opened, he had to go on with it.

You do this when the subject of the -*ing* clause is closely connected with the subject of the main clause, or when the -*ing* form is **being** or **having**.

With is sometimes added at the beginning of clauses of this type.

The old man stood up with tears running down his face.

With is always used when the two subjects are not closely connected, and the -*ing* form is not 'being' or 'having'.

With the weather conditions improving, they had plenty of chances to take the boat out.
Our correspondent said it resembled a city at war, with helicopters patrolling overhead.

10 after a noun

You can use an -*ing* clause after a noun, **those**, or an indefinite pronoun to identify or describe someone by saying what they do or are doing.

She is now a British citizen working for the Medical Research Council.
It is a rare sight that greets those crossing Malawi's southwest border.
Anyone following this advice could find themselves in trouble.

The -*ing* clause has a similar function to a relative clause.

11 used like nouns

You can use -*ing* forms like nouns. When used like this, they are sometimes called **gerunds** or **verbal nouns**. They can be the subject, object, or complement of a clause.

Does slow talking indicate slow mental development?
Most men regarded shopping as boring.
His hobby was collecting old coins.

They can be used after prepositions, including **to**.

They get pleasure from taking it home and showing it to their parents.

When you are not using a determiner in front of an -*ing* form, the -*ing* form can have a direct object. When you are using a determiner, you use **of** to introduce the object.

This interview was recorded during the making of Karel Reisz's film.

The object of the verb is put in front of the -*ing* form to form a compound noun if you are referring to a common type of activity, such as a type of job or hobby.

He regarded film-making as the most glamorous job on earth.
As a child, his interests were drawing and stamp collecting.

Note that you use a singular form for the object. For example, you refer to **stamp collecting**, not **stamps collecting**.

You can use an -*ing* form with a possessive. This is rather formal.

Your being in the English department means that you must have chosen English as your main subject.
'I think _my mother's being_ American had considerable advantage,' says Lady Astor's son.

You can use an _-ing_ form in a similar way with a pronoun or noun. This is less formal.
_What do you think about _him being_ elected again?_

A few nouns ending in _-ing_, particularly ones referring to leisure activities, are not related to verbs, but are formed from other nouns, or are much commoner than the related verbs.

ballooning	hang-gliding	power-boating	skydiving
caravanning	pot-holing	skateboarding	tobogganing

_Camping and _caravanning_ are increasingly attractive._
Skateboarding has come back into fashion._

12 other uses

A few _-ing_ forms are used as subordinating conjunctions:

assuming	presuming	supposing
considering	providing	

_The payments would gradually increase to £1,298, _assuming_ interest rates stayed the same._
Supposing you won, what would you do with the money?_

A few _-ing_ forms are used as prepositions or in compound prepositions:

according to	considering	excluding	owing to
barring	depending on	following	regarding
concerning	excepting	including	

_The property tax would be set _according to_ the capital value of the home._
_There seems no reason why, _barring_ injury, Carson should not win._
_We had already ended the party just after midnight, _following_ complaints from neighbours._

---

in front of

→ See **front**

---

injured

→ See **hurt**

---

inside

1 used as a preposition

When someone or something is in a building, vehicle, or container, you can say that they are **inside** it.

_They heard loud music coming from _inside_ the building._
_Jaya wondered what was _inside_ the box._

! BE CAREFUL

Don't say that someone or something is 'inside of' something.

2 **used as an adverb**

Inside can also be an adverb.

Marta opened the door and invited him inside.
He gave me a package with something soft inside.

insist

If someone **insists on doing** something, they say very firmly that they will do it, and they do it.

He insisted on paying for the meal.
Akito always insists on sitting in the front seat of the car.

! **BE CAREFUL**

Don't say that someone 'insists to do' something.

in spite of – despite

1 **'in spite of'**

You use **in spite of** when you are mentioning something that surprisingly does not prevent something else from being true. The spelling is **in spite of**, not 'inspite of'.

The air was clear and fresh, in spite of all the traffic.
In spite of his ill health, my father was always cheerful.

! **BE CAREFUL**

Don't use 'in spite of' to say that something is not affected by any circumstances. Don't say, for example, 'Everyone can take part, in spite of their ability'. Say 'Everyone can take part **regardless of** their ability' or 'Everyone can take part **whatever** their ability'.

If she is determined to do something, she will do it regardless of what her parents say.
The gardens look beautiful whatever the time of year.

Don't use 'in spite of' as a conjunction. Don't say, for example, 'In spite of we objected, they took our phones away'. Say '**Although** we objected, they took our phones away'.

Maria kept her coat on, although it was warm in the room.

2 **'despite'**

Despite means the same as **in spite of**. Don't say 'despite of'.

Despite the difference in their ages, they were close friends.
The school is going to be closed despite protests from local people.

instead – instead of

1 **'instead'**

Instead is an adverb. You use it when saying what someone does rather than doing something else.

Hema did not answer. Instead she looked out of the taxi window.
I felt like crying, but I managed to smile instead.

2 **'instead of'**

Instead of is a preposition. You use it to introduce something that is not done, not used, or not true, in contrast to something that is done, is used, or is true.

Why not use your bike to get to work instead of your car?
  You can have rice instead of potatoes.

You can say that someone does something **instead of doing** something else.

You could always go camping instead of staying in a hotel.
Why don't you help, instead of standing there and watching?

> **!** **BE CAREFUL**
> Don't say that someone does something 'instead to do' something else.

insure

→ See **assure – ensure – insure**

intention

1 **'intention to' and 'intention of'**

When someone intends to do something, you can talk about their **intention to do** it or their **intention of doing** it.

He declared his intention to apply for the job.
They announced their intention of starting a new business.

You can say that **it is** someone's **intention to do** something.

It had been her intention to go for a walk.
It was not my intention to offend anyone.

> **!** **BE CAREFUL**
> Don't say that 'it is someone's intention of doing' something.

2 **'with the intention'**

You can say that someone does something **with the intention of doing** something else, when they intend to do the second thing.

He had come with the intention of talking to Paco.

> **!** **BE CAREFUL**
> Don't say that someone does something 'with the intention to do' something else.

3 **'no intention'**

You can say that someone **has no intention of doing** something.

She had no intention of telling him what really happened.

> **!** **BE CAREFUL**
> Don't say that someone 'has no intention to do' something.

interested – interesting

1 **'interested'**

If you want to know more about something or someone, you can say that you are **interested in** them.

I am very interested in politics.
Kanako seemed genuinely interested in him and his work.

> **! BE CAREFUL**
>
> Don't use any preposition except **in** after **interested**.

If you want to do something, you can say that you are **interested in doing** it.

I was underline{interested in visiting} different parts of the world.
We're only underline{interested in finding out} the facts.

Don't say that you are '~~interested to do~~' something.

2 'interesting'

Do not confuse **interested** with **interesting**. If someone or something is **interesting**, they have qualities which make you want to know more about them.

I've met some very underline{interesting} people.
There are some underline{interesting} old buildings in the village.

> **! BE CAREFUL**
>
> Don't use 'interesting' to describe things which make a lot of money. For example, '**an interesting job**' is one that is enjoyable because it makes you feel interested, not one in which you earn a large salary. For a job that earns a lot of money, use **well-paid**.

People with university degrees usually end up with well-paid jobs.
Looking after children is not usually very well-paid.

---

into

The preposition **into** is usually used with verbs of movement. You use **into** to say where someone or something goes, or where something is put.

I went into the yard.
He poured tea into the cup.

After verbs meaning **put**, **throw**, **drop**, or **fall**, you can use **into** or **in** with the same meaning.

Chen put the letter into his pocket.
She put the key in her purse.
He fell into a pond.
One of the boys fell in the river.

Before **here** and **there**, use **in**, not 'into'.

Come underline{in} here.
Put your bags underline{in} there.

---

invite

If you **invite** someone **to** a party or a meal, you ask them to come to it.

The Lees underline{invited} me underline{to} dinner.
He underline{invited} her underline{to} a party.

> **! BE CAREFUL**
>
> Don't say '~~He invited her a party~~'. You must use **to**.

You can also **invite** someone **for** a meal.

My new neighbors underline{invited} me underline{for} lunch on Sunday.

You can **invite** someone **to do** something that you think they will enjoy.

He *invited* Axel *to come* to the concert with him.
I *invited* my friends *to stay* one weekend.

Don't say that you '~~invite someone for doing~~' something.

involved

1 used after a linking verb

The adjective **involved** is usually used after a linking verb such as **be** or **get**.

If you are **involved in** an activity, you take part in it.

He doesn't think sportsmen should get involved in *politics.*
Many different companies are involved in *producing these aircraft.*

2 used after a noun

The people **involved** in something are the people affected by it or taking part in it.

It is difficult to make a decision when there are so many people involved.
The play was a great success and we'd like to thank everyone involved.

You also use **involved** immediately after a noun when you are mentioning an important aspect of something.

There is quite a lot of work involved.
She had no real understanding of the problems involved.

irritated

→ See **nervous – anxious – irritated – annoyed**

it

1 referring to things

You use **it** to refer to an object, animal, or other thing that has just been mentioned.

He brought a tray with drinks on it.
The horse was so tired it *could hardly walk.*
The noise went on for hours, then it *suddenly stopped.*

❗ BE CAREFUL

When the subject of a sentence is followed by a relative clause, don't use 'it' in front of the main verb. Don't say, for example, '~~The town where I work, it is near London~~'. Say 'The town where I work **is** near London'.

2 referring to situations

You can also use **it** to refer to a situation, fact, or experience.

I like it *here.*
She was frightened, but tried not to show it.

❗ BE CAREFUL

You often express an opinion using an *-ing* form or *to*-infinitive after a verb such as **like**. When you do this, don't use 'it' in front of the *-ing* form or infinitive.

For example, don't say '~~I like it, walking in the park~~'. Say 'I like walking in the park'.
Don't say '~~I prefer it, to make my own bread~~'. Say 'I prefer to make my own bread'.

3 with linking verbs

It is often the subject of a linking verb such as **be**.

You can use **it** as the subject of **be** to say what the time, day, or date is.

It's seven o'clock.
It's Sunday morning.

You can also use **it** as the subject of a linking verb to describe the weather or the light.

It was a windy day.
It's getting dark.

4 describing an experience

You can use **it** with a linking verb and an adjective to describe an experience. After the adjective, you use an *-ing* form or a *to*-infinitive. For example, instead of saying 'Walking by the lake was nice', people usually say '**It was** nice walking by the lake'.

It's lovely hearing your voice again.
It was sad to see her in so much pain.

You can use **it** with a linking verb and an adjective to describe the experience of being in a particular place. After the adjective, you use a phrase referring to the place.

It's very quiet here.
It was warm in the restaurant.

5 commenting on a situation

You can use **it** with an adjective or noun phrase to comment on a whole situation. After the adjective or noun phrase, you use a *that*-clause.

It is lucky that he didn't hear you.
It's a pity you can't stay longer.

After an adjective, you can sometimes use a *wh*-clause instead of a *that*-clause.

It's funny how people change.
It's amazing what you can discover in the library.

! BE CAREFUL

Don't use 'it' with a linking verb and a noun phrase to say that something exists or is present. Don't say, for example, '~~It's a lot of traffic on this road tonight~~'. Say '**There's** a lot of traffic on this road tonight'.

There's a teacher at my school called Miss Large.
There was no space for me to park my car.

→ See **there**

its – it's

1 'its'

Its is a possessive determiner. You use **its** to show that something belongs or relates to a thing, place, animal, or child.

The chair fell over on its side.
A bird was building its nest.
The baby dropped its toy and started to cry.

2 'it's'

It's is a shortened form of 'it is' or 'it has'.

It's just like riding a bike.
It's been nice talking to you.

GRAMMAR FINDER

Inversion

Inversion means changing the normal word order in a sentence by putting part or all of the verb phrase in front of the subject. Usually an auxiliary verb is put in front of the subject, and the rest of the verb phrase is put after the subject. If no other auxiliary verb is used, a form of **do** is used, unless the verb is **be**.

1 **in questions**

Inversion is normal in questions.

Are you ready?
Can John swim?
Did he go to the fair?
Why did you fire him?
How many are there?

You don't need to use inversion when you are expecting someone to confirm what you are saying, or when you want to express a reaction such as surprise, interest, doubt, or anger about what has just been said.

You've been having trouble?
She's not going to do it?
'She's gone home.' – 'She's gone back to Montrose?'

! **BE CAREFUL**

You must use inversion in a question that begins with a *wh*-word, unless the *wh*-word is the subject. For example, you must say 'What did she think?', not ~~'What she thought?'~~ If the *wh*-word is the subject, there is no need for inversion. For example, you say 'Who was at the party?'

Inversion is not used in reported questions. Don't say, for example, ~~'She asked what was I doing'~~. Say 'She asked what I was doing'.

→ See **Reporting**

2 **after place adverbials**

Inversion occurs in descriptions of a place or scene when an adverbial of place is put at the beginning of a clause. This type of structure is found mainly in writing.

On the ceiling hung dustpans and brushes.
Beyond them lay the fields.
Behind the desk was a middle-aged woman.

Inversion is used in speech after **here** and **there** when you are drawing attention to something.

Here's the money. Go and buy yourself a watch.
Here comes the cloud of smoke.
There's another one!

> **!** **BE CAREFUL**
>
> Don't use inversion when the subject is a personal pronoun.
> *Here he comes.*
> *There she is.*

3 **after negative adverbials**

Inversion occurs when broad negative adverbs or other negative adverbials are put at the beginning of a clause for emphasis. This structure is used in formal speech and writing.

Never have I experienced such pain.
Seldom have enterprise and personal responsibility been more needed.
Rarely has so much time been wasted by so many people.

Inversion also occurs in formal speech and writing after adverbials preceded by **only**.

Only then would I ponder the contradictions inherent in my own personality.

→ See **only**

4 **after 'neither' and 'nor'**

You use inversion after **neither** and **nor** when you are saying that the previous negative statement also applies to another person or group.

'I can't remember.' – 'Neither can I.'
Research assistants don't know how to do it, and nor do qualified tutors.

5 **after 'so'**

You use inversion after **so** when you are saying that the previous positive statement also applies to another person or group.

'I've been to Australia twice.' – 'So have I.'
'I hate it when people are late.' – 'So do I.'
'Skating's just a matter of practice.' – 'Yes; so is skiing.'
Jeff went to jail. So did his son.

When **so** is used to express surprise or to emphasize that someone should do something, inversion does not occur.

'It's on the table behind you.' – 'So it is!'
'I feel very guilty about it.' – 'So you should.'

6 **other uses**

Inversion occurs in conditional clauses that are not introduced by a conjunction. This structure is formal.

Had the two teams drawn, victory would have gone to Todd.

Inversion can occur in comparisons after **as**.

The piece was well and confidently played, as was Peter Maxwell Davies' 'Revelation and Fall'.
Their father, George Churchill, also made jewellery, as did their grandfather.

Inversion is often used after a quote.

→ See **Reporting**

Jj

jam

→ See **marmalade – jam – jelly**

job

→ See **work**

joke

When someone **makes** or **cracks** a joke, they say something in order to make people laugh.

She would make jokes about her appearance.
We stayed up for hours, laughing and cracking jokes.

A **joke** is also a clever or funny story that you repeat in order to make people laugh. When **joke** has this meaning, you say that someone **tells** a joke.

Tell Uncle Henry the joke you told us.

A **joke** is also something that is done to make someone appear foolish. When **joke** has this meaning, you say that someone **plays** a joke **on** someone else.

They're playing a joke on you.

❗ BE CAREFUL
Don't say that someone 'says a joke' or 'does a joke'.

journal

A **journal** is a magazine that deals with a specialized subject. Many magazines have **Journal** as part of their name.

...the British Medical Journal.
All our results are published in scientific journals.

A **journal** is also a kind of diary in which you keep a record of events or progress.

My doctor told me to keep a journal of everything I ate.

❗ BE CAREFUL
Don't refer to a newspaper as a 'journal'.

journey – trip – voyage – excursion

1 'journey'

A **journey** is the process of travelling from one place to another by land, air, or sea.

There is a direct train from London Paddington to Penzance. The journey takes around 5 hours.
This service will save thousands of long-distance lorry journeys on Britain's roads.

2 'trip'

A **trip** is the process of travelling from one place to another, staying there, usually for a short time, and coming back again.

Lucy is away on a business trip to Milan.
They went on a day trip to the seaside.

3 'voyage'

A **voyage** is a long journey from one place to another in a ship or spacecraft.

The ship's voyage is over.
...the voyage to the moon in 1972.

4 'excursion'

An **excursion** is a short trip made either as a tourist or in order to do a particular thing.

The tourist office organizes excursions to the palace.

5 verbs used with 'journey', 'trip', 'voyage' and 'excursion'

You **make** or **go on** a journey.

He made the long journey to India.

You **take** or **go on** a trip.

We took a bus trip to Manchester.

You **make** a voyage.

The ship made the 4,000-kilometre voyage across the Atlantic.

You **go on** an excursion.

Students went on an excursion to the Natural History Museum.

> ❗ **BE CAREFUL**
> Don't use 'do' with any of these words. Don't say, for example, '~~We did a bus trip~~'.

---

just

You use **just** to say that something happened a very short time ago. British speakers usually use the present perfect with **just**. For example, they say 'I**'ve just** arrived'.

I've just bought a new house.

 American speakers usually use the past simple. Instead of saying 'I've just arrived', they say 'I **just** arrived'.

His wife just died.
I just broke the pink bowl.

Some British speakers also use the past simple, but in Britain this use is usually regarded as incorrect.

> ❗ **BE CAREFUL**
> Don't use 'just' with adverbs such as **partly** to give the meaning 'not completely'. Don't say, for example, '~~The job is just partly done~~'. You say 'The job is **only partly** done'.

He was only partially successful.
The bus was only half full.

just now

→ See **now**

Kk

keep

1 used as a transitive verb

If you **keep** something or someone in a place, you cause them to remain in that place. The past tense and -ed participle of **keep** is **kept**.

Where do you keep your keys?
The doctors kept her in hospital for another week.

To **keep** someone or something in a particular state means to cause them to remain in that state.

The fire kept them warm.
They had been kept awake by birds.

2 used as an intransitive verb

To **keep** in a particular state means to remain in that state.

They've got to hunt for food to keep alive.

3 used with an *-ing* form

Keep can be used in two different ways with an *-ing* form.

You can use it to say that something is repeated many times.

The phone keeps ringing.
My mother keeps asking questions.

You can also use it to say that something continues to happen and does not stop.

I turned back after a while, but he kept walking.
The fire is still burning. I think it'll keep going all night.

For emphasis, you can use **keep on** instead of 'keep'.

Did he give up or keep on trying?

> **!** **BE CAREFUL**
>
> Don't say that someone or something 'keeps to do' something.

kerb

→ See **curb – kerb**

kind

You use **kind** to talk about a class of people or things. **Kind** is a countable noun. After words like **all** and **many**, you use **kinds**, not 'kind'.

It will give you an opportunity to meet all kinds of people.
The trees were filled with many kinds of birds.

After **kinds of** you can use either the plural or singular form of a noun. For example, you can say 'I like most kinds of **cars**' or 'I like most kinds of **car**'. The singular form is more formal.

People have been working hard to produce the kinds of courses that we need.
There will be two kinds of certificate.

After **kind of** you use the singular form of a noun.

I'm not the kind of person to get married.
She makes the same kind of point in another essay.

In conversation, **these** and **those** are often used with **kind**. For example, people say 'I don't like these kind of films' or 'I don't like those kind of films'. This use is generally thought to be incorrect, and it is best to avoid it. Instead you should say 'I don't like **this kind of film**' or 'I don't like **that kind of film**'.

There are problems with this kind of explanation.
How will we answer that kind of question?

In more formal English, you can also say 'I don't like films **of this kind**'.

This is the best way of interpreting data of this kind.

You can also use **like this**, **like that**, or **like these** after a noun. For example, instead of saying 'this kind of film', you can say 'films **like this**'.

I hope we see many more enterprises like this.
I'd read a few books like that.
Companies like these represent an important part of our economy.

Sort is used in a similar way to **kind**.

→ See **sort**

You can also use **kind of** to describe something in a vague or uncertain way.

→ See **sort of – kind of**

---

know

1 **awareness of facts**

If you **know** that something is true, you are aware that it is true. The past tense of **know** is **knew**. The -ed participle is **known**.

I knew that she had recently graduated from law school.
I should have known that something was seriously wrong.

! **BE CAREFUL**

Don't use a progressive form with **know**. Don't say, for example, 'I am knowing that this is true'. You say 'I **know** that this is true'.

2 **'I know'**

If someone tells you a fact that you already know, or if they say something and you agree, you say '**I know**'.

'That's not their fault, Peter.' – 'Yes, I know.'
'This pizza is great' – 'I know.'

 In American English you can also say '**I know it**' in this situation. However, this often indicates that you are angry or annoyed.

'The speed limit here is 35.' – 'Yeah, I know it.'

3 'let...know'

If you say that you will **let** someone **know** something, you mean that you will give them some information when you receive it, or if you receive it.

I'll find out about the car and let you know what's happened.
Let me know if she calls.

4 acquaintance and familiarity

If you **know** a person, place, or thing, you are acquainted with them or are familiar with them.

Do you know David?
He knew London well.
Do you know the poem 'Kubla Khan'?

5 'get to know'

If you want to say that someone gradually becomes acquainted with a person or gradually becomes familiar with a place, you say that they **get to know** the person or place.

I got to know some of the staff quite well.
I really wanted to get to know America.

! BE CAREFUL

Don't use **know** without **get to** to mean 'become acquainted with'.

6 'know how to'

If you **know how to** do something, you have the necessary knowledge to do it.

No one knew how to repair it.
Do you know how to drive?

Don't say that someone 'knows to' do something.

Ll

lack

Lack can be a noun or a verb.

1 used as a noun

If there is a **lack of** something, there is not enough of it, or it does not exist at all.

I hated the lack of privacy in the hostel.

2 used as a verb

If someone or something **lacks** a quality, they do not have it.

Often new mothers lack confidence in their ability to look after their newborn baby properly.
Our little car lacked the power to pass other cars.

! BE CAREFUL

Don't say that someone or something 'lacks of a quality'.

You can't use a passive form of 'lack'. Don't say, for example, 'Resources are lacked in this school'. Say 'This school **lacks** resources.'

lady

→ See **woman – lady**

landscape

→ See **scene – sight – view – landscape – scenery**

large

→ See **big – large – great**

last – lastly

Last can be an adjective or an adverb.

1 'last' used as an adjective

The **last** thing, event, or person of a particular kind is the one that comes after all the others.

He missed the last bus.
They met for the last time just before the war.
He was the last person to see Rebecca alive.

If you want to emphasize that someone or something is the last one of their kind, you can put **very** in front of **last**.

Those were his very last words.
I changed my mind at the very last minute.

Latest is sometimes used in a similar way.

2 'last' used as an adverb

If something **last** happened on a particular occasion, it has not happened since then.

They last saw their homeland nine years ago.
It's a long time since we met last.

If an event is the final one in a series of similar events, you can say that it happens **last**. You put **last** at the end of a clause.

He added the milk last.
Mr Ross was meant to have gone first, but in fact went last.

3 'lastly'

You can also use **lastly** to say that an event is the final one in a series. You put **lastly** at the beginning of a clause.

They wash their hands, arms and faces, and lastly, they wash their feet.

However, **last** and **lastly** are not always used in the same way. You usually use **last** to say that an event is the final one in a series of similar events. You use **lastly** when you are talking about events which are not similar.

For example, if you say 'George phoned his aunt **last**', you usually mean that George had phoned several people and that his aunt was the last person he phoned. If you say '**Lastly** George phoned his aunt', you mean that George had done several things and that the last thing he did was to phoned his aunt.

Lastly has a much more common use. You use it to introduce a final point in a discussion, ask a final question, give a final instruction, or mention a final item in a list.

Lastly, I would like to thank Mr. Mark Collins for his advice, assistance and patience.
Lastly I would like to ask about your future plans.

4 'at last'

At last and **at long last** are used to show that something that you have been waiting for or expecting for a long time has happened. These expressions usually go at the beginning or end of a clause.

The journey had taken a long time, but they had arrived at last.
At long last I've found a woman who really loves me.

5 'last' with time expressions

You use **last** in front of a word such as **week** or **month** to say when something happened. For example, if it is August and something happened in July, you say that it happened **last month**.

Wolfgang and I had lunch with her last month.
The group held its first meeting last week.

! BE CAREFUL

Don't say that something happened 'the last month' or 'the last week'.

Last can be used in a similar way in front of the names of festivals, seasons, months, or days of the week.

Last Christmas we received more than a hundred cards.
She died last summer.
I bought these shoes last Saturday.

Don't, however, say 'last morning' or 'last afternoon'. Say **yesterday morning** or **yesterday afternoon**.

It's warmer this morning than it was yesterday morning.
Yesterday afternoon I had lunch with Cameron.

Don't say 'last evening'. Say **yesterday evening** or **last night**.

Yesterday evening another British soldier was killed.
I've been thinking about what we said last night.

6 'previous' and 'before'

When you are describing something that happened in the past and you want to refer to an earlier period of time, you use **previous** or **before** instead of 'last'. For example, if you are talking about events that happened in 2005 and you want to mention something that happened in 2004, you say that it happened **the previous year** or **the year before**.

We had had an argument the previous night.
He had done some work on the farmhouse the previous summer.
The two women had met in Bonn the weekend before.

7 'before last'

You use **before last** to refer to the period of time immediately before the most recent one of its kind. For example, **the year before last** means 'the year before last year'.

We went camping the summer before last.
I have not slept since the night before last.

8 'the last'

You can also use **last** to refer to any period of time measured back from the present. For example, if it is July 23rd and you want to refer to the period from July 2nd to the present, you refer to it as **the last three weeks**. Note that you must use **the**. If you want to say that something happened during this period, you say that it happened **in the last three weeks** or **during the last three weeks**.

He had asked himself that question at least a thousand times in the last eight days.
All this has happened during the last few years.

> **! BE CAREFUL**
>
> Note the order of words in these examples. Don't say 'the eight last days' or 'the few last years'.

Don't use 'in the last' or 'during the last' on their own with a plural noun such as 'years' or 'days'. For example, don't say 'Many changes have been made in the last years'. Use a quantity word or a number. For example, say 'Many changes have been made **in the last few years**'. Or use **recent** instead. For example, you can say 'Many changes have been made **in recent years**'.

---

late – lately

1 'late'

Late can be an adjective or an adverb.

If you are **late** for something, you arrive after the time that was arranged.

I was ten minutes late for my appointment.

You can also say that someone arrives **late**.

Etta arrived late.

Don't say that someone 'arrives lately'.

2 'lately'

You use **lately** to say that something has been happening since a short time ago.

As you know, I've lately become interested in psychology.
Have you talked to Marianne lately?

later

→ See **after – afterwards – later**

latter – former

The latter should only be used to refer to the second of two things or people which have already been mentioned.

Given the choice between working for someone else and working for the family business, she'd prefer the latter.

You use **the former** to talk about the first of two things already mentioned.

These two firms are in direct competition, with the former trying to cut costs and increase profits.

If you are talking about three or more things or people, don't use 'the latter' or 'the former'. Use an expression with **the last** or **the first**.

The company has three branches, in Birmingham, Plymouth, and Greenock. The last of these will close next year.

If you are mentioning things for the first time, don't use 'the former' or 'the latter'. Use **the first** or **the second**.

There will be two matches next week. The first will be in Brighton, and the second in London.

lay – lie

1 'lay'

Lay is a transitive verb, and it is also a past tense of another verb, **lie**.

To **lay** something somewhere means to put it there carefully or neatly.

Lay a sheet of newspaper on the floor.

The other forms of **lay** are **lays**, **laying**, **laid**.

Michael laid the box on the table gently.
'I couldn't get a taxi,' she said, laying her hand on Nick's sleeve.

2 'lie'

Lie is an intransitive verb with two different meanings.

To **lie** somewhere means to be there in a horizontal position, or to get into that position.

She would lie on the floor, listening to music.

When **lie** is used like this, its other forms are **lies**, **lying**, **lay**, **lain**. The *-ed* participle **lain** is rarely used.

The baby was <u>lying</u> on the table.
I <u>lay</u> in bed listening to the rain.

To **lie** means to say or write something which you know is untrue. When **lie** is used like this, its other forms are **lies**, **lying**, **lied**.

Why did he <u>lie</u> to me?
Robert was sure that Thomas <u>was lying</u>.
He <u>had lied</u> about where he had been that night.

learn

1 knowledge and skills

When you **learn** something, you obtain knowledge or a skill as a result of studying or training.

 The past tense and *-ed* participle of **learn** can be either **learned** or **learnt**. However, **learnt** is rarely used in American English.

We first <u>learned</u> to ski at les Rousses.
He <u>had</u> never <u>learnt</u> to read and write.

2 'teach'

Don't say that you 'learn someone something' or 'learn someone how to do something'. The word you use is **teach**.

My sister <u>taught</u> me how to read.

→ See **teach**

3 learning from experience

You can use **learn** to say that someone becomes wiser or becomes better at doing something as the result of an experience.

Industry and commerce <u>have learned</u> a lot in the last few years.

You say that someone **learns** something **from** an experience.

They <u>had learned</u> a lot <u>from</u> their earlier mistakes.

! BE CAREFUL
Don't use any preposition except **from** in a sentence like this.

4 information

Learn can also be used to say that someone receives some information. After **learn**, you use **of** and a noun phrase, or you use a *that*-clause.

He <u>had learned of</u> his father's death in Australia.
She <u>learned that</u> her grandmother had been a nurse.

lend

→ See **borrow – lend**

less

1 **used in front of nouns**

You use **less** in front of an uncountable noun to say that one quantity is not as big as another, or that a quantity is not as big as it was before.

A shower uses less water than a bath.
His work gets less attention than it deserves.

Less is sometimes used in front of plural nouns.

This proposal will mean less jobs.
Less people are going to university than usual.

Some people think this use is wrong. They say that you should use **fewer** in front of plural nouns, not 'less'.

There are fewer trees here.
The new technology allows products to be made with fewer components than before.

However, **fewer** sounds formal when used in conversation. As an alternative to 'less' or 'fewer', you can use **not as many** or **not so many** in front of plural nouns. These expressions are acceptable in both conversation and writing.

There are not as many cottages as there were.
There aren't so many trees there.

After **not as many** and **not so many** you use **as**, not 'than'.

2 **'less than' and 'fewer than'**

You use **less than** in front of a noun phrase to say that an amount or measurement is below a particular point or level.

It's hard to find a house in Beverly Hills for less than a million dollars.
I travelled less than 3000 miles.

Less than is sometimes used in front of a noun phrase referring to a number of people or things.

The whole of Switzerland has less than six million inhabitants.
The country's army consisted of less than a hundred soldiers.

Some people think this use is wrong. They say that you should use **fewer than**, not 'less than', in front of a noun phrase referring to people or things.

He had never been in a class with fewer than forty children.
In 1900 there were fewer than one thousand university teachers.

You can use **less than** in conversation, but you should use **fewer than** in formal writing.

However, **fewer than** can only be used when the following noun phrase refers to a number of people or things. Don't use 'fewer than' when the noun phrase refers to an amount or measurement. Don't say, for example, 'I travelled fewer than 3000 miles'.

3 **'less' used in front of adjectives**

Less can be used in front of an adjective to say that someone or something has a smaller amount of a quality than they had before, or a smaller amount than someone or something else has.

After I spoke to her, I felt less worried.
Most of the other plays were less successful.

! BE CAREFUL

Don't use 'less' in front of the comparative form of an adjective. Don't say, for example, 'It is less colder than it was yesterday'. Say 'It is **less cold** than it was yesterday'.

4 'not as ... as'

In conversation and informal writing, people don't usually use 'less' in front of adjectives. They don't say, for example, 'It is less cold than it was yesterday'. They say 'It is **not as cold as** it was yesterday'.

The region is not as pretty as the Dordogne.

Not so is also sometimes used, but this is less common.

The officers here are not so young as the lieutenants.

After **not as** and **not so**, you use **as**, not 'than'.

let

Let is used to say that someone allows someone else to do something. After the object, you use an infinitive without *to*.

The farmer lets me live in a caravan behind his barn.
Her Dad never lets her have ice-cream.
They sit back and let everyone else do the work.

! BE CAREFUL

Don't use a *to*-infinitive or an *-ing* form after **let**. Don't say, for example, 'He lets me to use his telephone' or 'He lets me using his telephone'.

The past tense and *-ed* participle of **let** is **let**.

He let Jack lead the way.
She had let him borrow her pen.

There is no passive form of **let**. Don't say, for example, 'He was let go' or 'He was let to go'. If you want to use a passive form, use a different verb, such as **allow** or **permit**.

He had been allowed to enter Italy as a political refugee.
Laurent was only permitted to leave his room at mealtimes.

1 'let ... know'

If you **let** someone **know** something, you tell them about it.

I'll find out about the meeting and let you know when it is.
If the pain gets worse, let your doctor know immediately.

2 'let me'

People often use **let me** when they are offering to do something for someone.

Let me show you.
Let me help you carry your bags.

→ See **Topic** entry **Offers**

let's – let us

1 let's

You use **let's** when you are suggesting that you and someone else should do something. **Let's** is short for 'let us'. It is followed by an infinitive without *to*.

Let's go outside.
Let's decide what we want.

The full form **let us** is used with this meaning only in formal English.

Let us postpone the matter.

If you are suggesting that you and someone else should not do something, you say **let's not**.

Let's not talk about that.
Let's not waste time.

2 'let us'

When you are talking about you and someone else being allowed to do something, use **let us**.

They wouldn't let us leave.
His mum let us stay there for free.

You can use **let us** when you are making a request on behalf of yourself and someone else. In sentences like these, don't shorten **let us** to 'let's'.

Let us know what progress has been made.

lettuce

→ See **salad – lettuce**

library – bookshop

1 'library'

A **library** is a building where books are kept that people can look at or borrow.

You can borrow the book from your local library.

A **library** is also a private collection of books, or a room in a large house where books are kept.

I once stayed in one of his houses and saw his library.

2 'bookshop'

 Don't refer to a shop where you can buy books as a 'library'. In Britain, a shop like this is called a **bookshop**. In America, it is called a **bookstore**.

I went into the bookshop to buy a present for my son.
My wife works in a bookstore.

lie

→ See **lay – lie**

lift – elevator

1 'lift'

In British English, a **lift** is a device that moves up and down inside a tall building and carries people from one floor to another.

I took the lift to the eighth floor.

2 'elevator'

 In American English, a device like this is called an **elevator**.

like

1 'like'

If you **like** someone or something, you find them pleasant or attractive.

She's a nice girl, I like her.
Very few people liked the idea.

> ❗ **BE CAREFUL**
>
> Don't use a progressive form of **like**. Don't say, for example, 'I am liking peanuts'. Say 'I **like** peanuts'.

You can use **like** in front of an -*ing* form to say that you enjoy an activity.

I like reading.
I just don't like being in crowds.

You can add **very much** to emphasize how much you like someone or something, or how much you enjoy an activity.

I like him very much.
I like swimming very much.

You must put **very much** after the object, not after **like**. Don't say, for example, 'I like very much swimming'.

If someone asks you if you like something, you can say 'Yes, I **do**.' Don't say 'Yes, I like.'

'Do you like walking?' – 'Yes I do, I love it.'

Don't use 'like' immediately in front of a clause beginning with 'when' or 'if'. For example, don't say 'I like when I can go home early'. Say 'I **like it** when I can go home early'.

The guests don't like it when they can't use the pool.
I'd like it if we were friends again.

2 'would like'

You say '**Would you like...?**' when you are offering something to someone.

Would you like some coffee?

> ❗ **BE CAREFUL**
>
> Don't say 'Do you like some coffee?'

You say '**Would you like...**' followed by a *to*-infinitive when you are inviting someone to do something.

Would you like to meet him?

Don't not use an -*ing* form after '**Would you like...**'. Don't say, for example, '~~Would you like meeting him?~~'

→ See **Topic** entry **Invitations**

You can say '**I'd like...**' when asking for something in a shop or café.

I'd like some apples, please.

→ See **Topic** entry **Requests, orders, and instructions**

You say '**I'd like you to...**' when you are telling someone to do something in a fairly polite way.

I'd like you to tell them where I am.

→ See **Topic** entry **Requests, orders, and instructions**

like – as – the way

1 used as conjunctions

You can use **like**, **as**, or **the way** as conjunctions when you are comparing one person's behaviour or appearance to another's. In the clause which follows the conjunction, the verb is usually **do**.

For example, you can say 'He walked to work every day, **like** his father had done', 'He walked to work every day, **as** his father had done', or 'He walked to work every day, **the way** his father had done'.

I never behave like she does.
They were people who spoke and thought as he did.
Start lending things, the way people did in the war.

2 used as prepositions

Like and **as** can be prepositions, but their meaning is not usually the same. For example, if you do something **like** a particular kind of person, you do it the way that kind of person would do it, although you are not that kind of person.

We worked like slaves.

If you do something **as** a particular kind of person, you are that kind of person.

Over the summer she worked as a waitress.
I can only speak as a married man without children.

likely

1 used as an adjective

Likely is usually an adjective. You say, for example, that something is **likely to** happen.

These services are likely to be available to us all before long.

You can also say that **it is likely that** something will happen.

It is likely that his symptoms will disappear without treatment.
If this is your first baby, it's far more likely that you'll get to the hospital too early.

2 used as an adverb

In conversation and in informal writing, **likely** is sometimes an adverb with **most**, **more than**, or **very** in front of it, or as part of the phrase **more likely than not**. Don't use it as an adverb on its own.

Profits will <u>most likely</u> have risen by about $25 million.
<u>More than likely</u>, the cause of her illness is stress.
<u>More likely than not</u> they would kill him if they found out who he really was.

listen to

If you **listen to** a sound or **listen to** a person who is talking, you pay attention to the sound or to what the person is saying.

I do my ironing while <u>listening to</u> the radio.
<u>Listen</u> carefully <u>to</u> what he says.
They wouldn't <u>listen to</u> me.

! BE CAREFUL

Listen is not a transitive verb. Don't say that someone '~~listens a sound~~' or '~~listens a person~~'.

If you have been to a musical performance, you don't usually say that you 'listened to' the music or 'listened to' the performer. You say that you **heard** them.

That was the first time I ever <u>heard</u> Jimi Hendrix.

→ See **hear**

! BE CAREFUL

Don't confuse **listen to** and **hear**. If you **hear** something, you become aware of it without trying. If you **listen to** something, you deliberately pay attention to it. For example, you would say 'Suddenly I **heard** a noise', not '~~Suddenly I listened to a noise~~'.

little – a little

◾1 'little' used as an adjective

Little is usually an adjective. You use it to talk about the size of something.

He took a little black book from his pocket.

→ See **small – little**

◾2 'a little' used as an adverb

A little is usually an adverb. You use it after a verb, or in front of an adjective or another adverb. It means 'to a small extent or degree'.

They get paid for it. Not much. Just <u>a little</u>.
The local football team is doing <u>a little</u> better.
The celebrations began <u>a little</u> earlier than expected.

! BE CAREFUL

Don't use 'a little' in front of an adjective when the adjective comes in front of a noun. Don't say, for example, '~~It was a little better result~~'. Say 'It was a **slightly** better result' or 'It was a **somewhat** better result'.

→ See **Adverbs and adverbials** for a graded list of words used to indicate degree

◾3 used in front of nouns

Little and **a little** are also used in front of nouns to talk about quantities. When they are used like this, they do not have the same meaning.

You use **a little** to show that you are talking about a small quantity or amount of something. When you use **little** without 'a', you are emphasizing that there is only a small quantity or amount of something.

So, for example, if you say 'I have **a little** money', you are saying that you have some money. However, if you say 'I have **little** money', you mean that you do not have enough money.

I had made a little progress.
It is clear that little progress was made.

4 used as pronouns

Little and **a little** can be used in similar ways as pronouns.

Beat in the eggs, a little at a time.
Little has changed.

5 'not much'

In conversation and in less formal writing, people do not usually use 'little' without 'a'. Instead they use **not much**. For example, instead of saying 'I have little money', they say 'I **haven't got much** money' or 'I **don't have much** money'.

I haven't got much appetite.
We don't have much time.

> **!** **BE CAREFUL**
>
> Don't use 'little' or 'a little' when you are talking about a small number of people or things. Don't say, for example, 'She has a little hens'. Say 'She has **a few** hens'. Similarly, don't say 'Little people attended his lectures'. Say '**Few** people attended his lectures', or '**Not many** people attended his lectures'.

→ See **few – a few**

live

If you **live** in a particular place, it is your home.

I have some friends who live in Nairobi.
I live in a house just down the road from you.

If you want to say that a place is someone's home, don't use a progressive form of **live**. You only use a progressive form when you are saying that someone has just moved to a place, or that it is their home for a temporary period.

Her husband had been released from prison and was now living at the house.
Remember that you are living in someone else's home.
We had to leave Ziatur, the town where we had been living.

If you want to say how long you have been living in a place, you use **for** or **since**. You say, for example, 'I have been living here **for** four years', 'I have been living here **since** 2007', or 'I have lived here **since** 2007'. Don't say 'I am living here for four years' or 'I am living here since 2007'.

He has been living in France now for almost two years.
She has lived there since she was six.

→ See **for, since**

long

1 used to talk about length

You use **long** when you are talking about the length of something.

The pool is ninety feet long by twenty feet wide.
How long is that side of the triangle?

2 talking about distance

You use **a long way** to talk about the distance from one place to another. You say, for example, 'It's **a long way** from here to Birmingham'.

I'm a long way from London.

> ! **BE CAREFUL**
>
> Don't say 'It's long from here to Birmingham' or 'I'm long from London'.

In negative sentences, you use **far**. You say, for example, 'It's **not far** from here to Birmingham'.

We rented a villa not far from the beach.

You also use **far** in questions. You say, for example, 'How **far** is it from here to Birmingham?'

How far is Tokyo from here?

Don't use 'long' in negative sentences and questions like these.

When you are talking about the extent of a journey, you use **as far as**, not 'as long as'. You say, for example, 'We walked **as far as** the church'.

We went with Harold as far as Bologna.

3 used to talk about time

In a negative sentence or a question, you can use **long** as an adverb to mean 'a long time'.

Wilkins hasn't been with us long.
Are you staying long?

You can also use **long** to mean 'a long time' after **too** or in front of **enough**.

He's been here too long.
You've been here long enough to know what we're like.

However, don't use 'long' with this meaning in any other kind of positive sentence. Instead use **a long time**.

We may be here a long time.
It may seem a long time to wait.

The comparative and superlative forms **longer** and **longest** can be used with this meaning in any kind of positive sentence.

Reform in Europe always takes longer than expected.
The study found that people who walk a lot live longest.

→ See **Adverbs and adverbials** for a graded list of words used to indicate duration

4 'no longer'

When something that happened in the past does not happen now, you can say that it **no longer** happens or that it does not happen **any longer**.

The factory no longer builds cars.
I noticed that he wasn't sitting by the door any longer.

---

look

1 'look at'

If someone directs their eyes towards something, you say that they **look at** it.

Lang looked at his watch.
She looked at the people around her.

When **look** has this meaning, it must be followed by **at**. Don't say, for example, '~~Lang looked his watch~~'.

! **BE CAREFUL**

Don't confuse **look** with **see** or **watch**.

→ See **see – look at – watch**

If you want to say that someone shows a particular feeling when they look at someone or something, use an adverb, not an adjective. For example, you say 'She looked **sadly** at her husband'. Don't say '~~She looked sad at her husband~~'.

Jack looked uncertainly at Ralph.
He looked adoringly at Keiko.

2 'look and see'

If you intend to use your eyes to find out if something is true, you say that you will **see** or **look and see** if it is true.

Have a look at your wife's face to see if she's blushing.
Now let's look and see whether that's true or not.

! **BE CAREFUL**

Don't say that you will 'look' if something is true.

You can use **see** to say that you will find out about something, even if you are not talking about using your eyes. For example, you can say 'I'll **see** if Li is in her office', and then find out whether Li is in her office by making a phone call there.

I'll just see if he's at home.
I'll see if I can borrow a car for the weekend.

3 used to mean 'seem'

Look can also be used to mean 'seem' or 'appear'. When you use **look** like this, you use an adjective after it, not an adverb. For example, you say 'She looked **sad**'. Don't say '~~She looked sadly~~'.

You look very pale.
The place looked a bit dirty.

! **BE CAREFUL**

You only use **look** to mean 'seem' when talking about the appearance of something.

look after – look for

1 'look after'

If you **look after** someone or something, you do what is necessary to keep them healthy, safe, or in good condition.

She will look after the children during their holidays.
You can borrow my laptop as long as you look after it.

2 'look for'

If you **look for** someone or something, you try to find them.

Were you looking for me?
He looked for his shoes under the bed.

look forward to

1 used with a noun

If you **are looking forward to** something that you are going to experience, you are pleased or excited about it.

I'm really looking forward to his visit.
Is there any particular thing you are looking forward to next year?

! BE CAREFUL

Don't use this expression without **to**. Don't say, for example, 'I'm really looking forward his visit'. Also don't say that someone 'is looking forwards to' something.

2 used with an -ing form

You can use an -ing form after **look forward to**.

I was so much looking forward to talking to you.
I look forward to seeing you in Washington.

! BE CAREFUL

Don't use an infinitive after **look forward to**. Don't say, for example, 'He's looking forward to go home'.

There is a difference between 'I look forward to…' and 'I'm looking forward to…'. In formal English, people use 'I look forward to…' and in less formal English, people usually use 'I'm looking forward to…'

I look forward to receiving your report this afternoon.
I'm really looking forward to seeing you, Carol.

loose – lose

1 'loose'

Loose /luːs/ is an adjective. It means 'not firmly fixed', or 'not tight'.

The handle is loose.
Mary wore loose clothes.

2 'lose'

Lose /luːz/ is a verb. If you **lose** something, you no longer have it, or you cannot find it.

I don't want to lose my job.
If you lose your credit card, let the company know immediately.

The other forms of **lose** are **loses**, **losing**, **lost**.

They were willing to risk losing their jobs.
He had lost his passport.

lorry – truck

1 'lorry'

In British English, a **lorry** is a large vehicle used for transporting goods by road.

The lorries were carrying 42 tonnes of sand.

2 'truck'

 In American English, a vehicle like this is called a **truck**. In British English, small open lorries are sometimes called **trucks**.

A blue truck drove up and delivered some boxes.

lose

→ See **loose – lose**

lot

1 'a lot of' and 'lots of'

You use **a lot of** in front of a noun when you are talking about a large number of people or things, or a large amount of something.

We have quite a lot of newspapers.
There's a lot of research to be done.

In conversation, you can use **lots of** in the same way.

Lots of people thought it was funny.
You've got lots of time.

When you use **a lot of** or **lots of** in front of a plural countable noun, you use a plural form of a verb with it.

A lot of people come to our classes.
Lots of people think writing is based on ideas, but it's much more than that.

When you use **a lot of** or **lots of** in front of an uncountable noun, you use a singular form of a verb with it.

A lot of money is spent on marketing.
There is lots of money to be made in advertising.

2 'a lot' and 'lots'

You use **a lot** to refer to a large quantity or amount of something.

I'd learnt a lot.
I feel that we have a lot to offer.

You use **a lot** as an adverb to mean 'to a great extent' or 'often'.

You like Ralph a lot, don't you?
They talk a lot about equality.

→ See **Adverbs and adverbials** for a graded list of words used to indicate degree

You also use **a lot** in front of comparatives. For example, if you want to emphasize the difference in age between two things, you can say that one thing is **a lot older** than the other.

The weather's a lot warmer there.
I've known people who were in a lot more serious trouble than you.

You also use **a lot** with **more** to emphasize the difference between two quantities or amounts.

He earns a lot more money than she does.

 In conversation, you can use **lots** with the same meaning.

She meets lots more people than I do.

loudly

→ See **aloud – loudly**

love

The verb **love** is usually used to express a strong feeling of affection for a person or place.

She loved her husband deeply.
He had loved his aunt very much.
He loved his country above all else.

If you want to say that something gives you pleasure, or that you enjoy a person's company, you usually say **like**, not 'love'.

I like reading.
We liked him very much.

In conversation and in less formal writing, people sometimes use **love** to emphasize that they like a thing or activity very much.

I love your dress.
I love reading his plays.

 Love is usually used in simple rather than progressive forms. For example, you say 'I love you', not 'I'm loving you'. However, in informal spoken English, **love** is sometimes used in the progressive.

I'm loving your new hairdo!

lucky – happy

1 'lucky'

You say that someone is **lucky** when something nice happens to them, or when they always seem to have good luck.

You're a lucky girl to have so many friends.
The lucky winners were given £5000 each.

2 **'happy'**

Don't use 'lucky' to say that someone has feelings of pleasure and contentment. The word you use is **happy**.

Sarah's such a <u>happy</u> person – she's always laughing.
Barbara felt tremendously <u>happy</u> when she heard the news.

luggage – baggage

In British English, both these words refer to the bags and suitcases that you take with you when you travel, together with their contents. **Luggage** is more common than **baggage**.

 In American English, **luggage** refers to empty bags and suitcases. **Baggage** refers to bags and suitcases with their contents.

There has been a decline in sales of hand-sized <u>luggage</u>.
The passengers went through immigration control and collected their <u>baggage</u>.

Both these words are uncountable nouns. Don't talk about 'luggages' or 'a baggage'.

lunch

→ See **dinner – lunch**

Mm

machinery

You can refer to machines in general as **machinery**.

The company makes tractors and other farm machinery.
If you are taking this medication, you should not drive a car or operate machinery.

Machinery is an uncountable noun. Don't say 'machineries' or 'a machinery'. You can talk about a **piece of machinery**.

He was called out to fix a piece of machinery that had broken down.

→ See **Nouns** for information on uncountable nouns

mad

1 'mad'

In conversation and informal writing, people often describe a foolish action or idea as **mad**.

Camping in winter was a mad idea.
You would be mad to refuse such a great offer.

In conversation, **mad** is sometimes used to mean 'angry'. If you are **mad at** someone, you are angry with them.

When she told him she wouldn't go, he got mad.
My parents were mad at me for waking them up so early.

2 'mad about'

If you are **mad about** something that has happened, you are angry about it.

He's really mad about being lied to.

In conversation, you can say that someone is **mad about** an activity, when they like it very much.

Her daughter is mad about dancing.
The whole family is mad about football.

3 mental illness

If someone has a mental illness that makes them behave in strange ways, don't say that they are 'mad'. You should use the phrase **mentally ill**.

She spent time in hospital when she was mentally ill.
The drug is used to treat mentally ill patients.

made from – made of – made out of

Made is the past tense and -ed participle of the verb **make**.

→ See **make**

You can use **made from**, **made out of**, or **made of** to say that something has been produced using a substance or object, so that the original substance or object is completely changed.

They sailed on a raft made from bamboo.
The plates were made out of solid gold.
Her dress was made of a light, floaty material.

If something has been produced from another thing in an unusual or surprising way, you usually use **made out of**.

She was wearing a hat made out of plastic bags.

If you are mentioning the parts or materials from which something is constructed, you use **made of** or **made out of**. Don't use 'made from'.

My cabin was made of logs.

magazine – shop

1 'magazine'

A **magazine** is a collection of articles, photographs, and advertisements published every week or every month.

Her face was on the cover of every magazine.
Tanya read a magazine while she waited.

2 'shop'

Don't use 'magazine' to refer to a building or part of a building where things are sold. The word you use is **shop** or **store**.

There is a row of shops on the High Street.

mail

→ See **post – mail**

majority

1 'majority'

If something is true of **the majority** of the people or things in a group, it is true of more than half of them.

The majority of students in the class will go on to study at college.
In the majority of cases, the illness can be treated successfully.

When **the majority** is not followed by 'of', you can use either a singular or plural form of a verb after it.

The majority is still undecided about which way to vote.
The majority were in favour of the proposal.

However, when you use **the majority of** followed by a plural noun or pronoun, you must use a plural form of a verb after it.

The majority of cars on the road have only one person in them.

2 **'most of'**

Don't use 'the majority' when you are talking about an amount of something or part of something. Don't say, for example, 'The majority of the forest has been cut down'. Say '**Most of** the forest has been cut down'.

Most of the food was good.
Katya did most of the work.

→ See **most**

make

Make is a very common verb which is used in many different ways. The past tense and -*ed* participle of **make** is **made**.

1 **performing an action**

Make is most often used to say that someone performs an action. For example, if someone suggests something, you can say that they **make** a suggestion. If someone promises something, you can say that they **make** a promise.

I think that I made the wrong decision.
He made a short speech.

Here is a list of common nouns that you can use with **make** in this way:

arrangement	enquiry	point	suggestion
choice	journey	promise	tour
comment	mistake	remark	trip
decision	noise	sound	visit
effort	plan	speech	

Don't use 'make' when you are talking generally about action, rather than referring to a particular action. Instead use **do**. For example, if you are unsure what action to take, don't say 'I don't know what to make'. Say 'I don't know what to **do**'.

What are you going to do at the weekend?
You've done a lot to help us.

2 **making an object or substance**

If you **make** an object or substance, you construct or produce it.

Asha makes all her own clothes.
They make furniture out of recycled plastic.

You can also say that someone **makes** a meal or a drink.

I made some breakfast.

→ See **cook**

When **make** is used to talk about constructing or producing something, it can have an indirect object. You say that you **make** someone something, or **make** something **for** them.

I'll make you a drink.
She made a copy for her colleague.

3 **making someone do something**

If someone forces you to do something, you can say that they **make you do** it.

You've got to *make him listen*.
Mom *made us clean up* the mess.

> **!** **BE CAREFUL**
>
> In active sentences like these, don't use a *to*-infinitive after **make**. Don't say, for example, '~~You've got to make him to listen~~'.
>
> However, in passive sentences you must use a *to*-infinitive.
>
> They *were made to pay* for the damage.
> One woman *was made to wait* more than an hour.

4 used to mean 'be'

Make is sometimes used instead of 'be' to say how successful someone is in a particular job or role. For example, instead of saying 'He will be a good prime minister', you can say 'He will **make** a good prime minister'.

You'll *make* a great teacher.
They *made* a good team.

→ See **brand – make**

---

make up

→ See **comprise**

---

male – masculine

1 'male'

Male means 'relating to the sex that cannot have babies'. You can use **male** as an adjective to describe either people or animals.

A *male* nurse came to take my temperature.
Male dogs tend to be more aggressive.

You can use **male** as a noun to refer to an animal.

They protect their territory from other *males*.

In scientific contexts, **male** is sometimes used as a noun to refer to men or boys.

The condition affects both *males* and females.

People sometimes use **male** to talk about men, in order to avoid using 'man' or 'boy'.

I looked in through the window and saw only *males*.
The police are looking for a tall white *male* in his mid-twenties.

2 'masculine'

Masculine means 'typical of men, rather than women'.

He was tall, strong, and very *masculine*.
They painted the room in dark, *masculine* colours.

> **!** **BE CAREFUL**
>
> Don't use 'masculine' to talk about animals.

man

1 'man'

A **man** is an adult male human being. The plural of **man** is **men**.

Larry was a handsome man of about 50.
Two men got on the bus.

Man is sometimes used to refer to human beings in general. For example, instead of saying 'Human beings are destroying the environment', you can say '**Man** is destroying the environment'. When **man** has this meaning, don't use 'the' in front of it.

Man is always searching for new knowledge.
Massage is one of the oldest forms of treatment known to man.

Men is sometimes used to refer to all human beings, considered as individuals.

All men are born equal.
Darwin concluded that men were descended from apes.

2 'mankind'

Mankind is used to refer to all human beings, considered as a group.

His only desire is to help mankind.

Some people do not like the use of **man**, **men**, and **mankind** to refer to human beings of both sexes, because they think it suggests that men are more important than women. You can use **people** instead.

All people are born equal.

manage – arrange

1 'manage'

If you **manage to do** something, you succeed in doing it.

Manuel managed to finish the work on time.
How did you manage to convince her?

> **! BE CAREFUL**
> Use a *to*-infinitive, not an *-ing* form, after **manage**. Don't say, for example, 'How did you manage convincing her?'

2 'arrange'

Don't use a *that*-clause after **manage**. Don't say, for example, that you 'manage that something is done'. Say that you **arrange for something to be done**.

He had arranged for me to be met at the airport.

Don't say that you 'manage that someone does something'. Say that you **arrange for someone to do something**.

I had arranged for a photographer to take pictures of the team.

mankind

→ See **man**

manufacture – factory

1 'manufacture'

Manufacture refers to the process of making goods using machines. **Manufacture** is an uncountable noun.

The chemical is used in the manufacture of plastics.

2 'factory'

Don't use 'manufacture' to refer to a building where machines are used to make things. Use **factory**.

She works at the chocolate factory.

→ See **factory – works – mill – plant**

---

many

1 'many' used in front of a plural noun

You use **many** immediately in front of the plural form of a noun to talk about a large number of people or things.

Many young people worry about their weight.
Her music is popular in many countries.

In positive statements, 'many' is slightly formal, and **a lot of** is often used instead.

A lot of people agree with this view.

→ See **lot**

In questions and negative statements, **many** is usually used rather than 'a lot of'.

Do many people in your country speak English?
There are not many books in the library.

2 'many of'

To refer to a large number of the people or things in a particular group, you use **many of** in front of a plural pronoun, or in front of a plural noun phrase beginning with **the**, **these**, **those**, or a possessive such as **my** or **their**.

Many of them were forced to leave their homes.
Many of the plants had been killed by cold weather.
Many of his books are still available.

3 'many' used as a pronoun

Many is sometimes used as a pronoun to refer to a large group of people or things. This is a fairly formal use.

Many have asked themselves whether this was the right thing to do.

! BE CAREFUL

Don't use 'many' or 'many of' before an uncountable noun, to talk about a large quantity or amount of something. Use **much** or **much of**.

→ See **much**

4 'many more'

You can use **many** with **more** to emphasize the difference in size between two groups of people or things.

I have many more friends here than I did in my home town.
We have had many more problems recently than before.

marmalade – jam – jelly

1 'marmalade'

Marmalade is a sweet food made from oranges, lemons, limes, or grapefruit. In Britain, people spread it on bread or toast and eat it as part of their breakfast.

I love toast with orange marmalade.

2 'jam' and 'jelly'

 In English **marmalade** refers only to a food made from oranges, lemons, limes, or grapefruit. Don't use it to refer to a similar food made from other fruits, for example blackberries, strawberries, or apricots. A food like this is called **jam** in British English, and **jam** or **jelly** in American English.

I bought a jar of raspberry jam.
She made us jelly sandwiches.

marriage – wedding

1 'marriage'

Marriage refers to the state of being married, or to the relationship between a husband and wife.

I wasn't interested in marriage or children.
They have a very happy marriage.

You can also use **marriage** to refer to the act of getting married.

Her family did not approve of her marriage to David.

2 'wedding'

You don't usually use 'marriage' to refer to the ceremony in which two people get married. Use **wedding**.

He was not invited to the wedding.

married – marry

1 'married to'

If you are **married to** someone, they are your husband or wife.

Her daughter was married to a Frenchman.

2 'marry'

When you **marry** someone, you become their husband or wife during a special ceremony.

I wanted to marry him.

> ❗ **BE CAREFUL**
> Don't use 'to' after **marry**. Don't say '~~I wanted to marry to him~~'.

3 **'get married'**

Marry is not usually used without an object. Don't say, for example, that a person 'marries' or that two people 'marry'. Say that they **get married**.

Lisa and Kunal are getting married next month.
My parents want me to get married and settle down.

Marry is sometimes used without an object, but this is a literary or old-fashioned use.

Jane swore that she would never marry.

masculine

→ See **male – masculine**

match

If one thing has the same colour or design as another thing, you say that it **matches** the other thing, or that the two things **match**.

The cushions match the carpet.
He sometimes wore socks which did not match.

> ❗ **BE CAREFUL**
> Don't use 'to' with **match**. Don't say, for example, '~~The cushions match to the carpet~~'.

mathematics – maths – math

 Mathematics is the study of numbers, quantities, and shapes. When mathematics is taught as a subject at school, it is usually called **maths** in British English, and **math** in American English.

Maths is my best subject at school.
Julio teaches math at a middle school.

> ❗ **BE CAREFUL**
> **Mathematics**, **maths**, and **math** are uncountable nouns and are used with a singular verb. Don't say, for example, '~~Maths are my best subject~~'.

When you are referring to a science rather than a school subject, use **mathematics**.

According to the laws of mathematics, this is not possible.

matter

1 **talking about a problem**

The matter is used after **what**, **something**, **anything**, or **nothing** to talk about a problem or difficulty. You use **the matter** in the same way as an adjective like **wrong**. For example, instead of saying 'Is something wrong?' you can say 'Is something **the matter**?'

What's the matter?
There's something the matter with your eyes.

> **!** **BE CAREFUL**
>
> Don't use 'the matter' with this meaning in other types of sentence. Don't say, for example, 'The matter is that we don't know where she is'. Say '**The problem** is that we don't know where she is' or '**The trouble** is that we don't know where she is'.
>
> *The problem is that she can't cook.*
> *The trouble is there isn't enough money.*

2 **'It doesn't matter'**

When someone apologizes to you, you can say '**It doesn't matter**.' Don't say 'No matter'.

'I've only got dried milk.' – 'It doesn't matter.'

→ See **Topic** entry **Apologizing**

3 **'no matter'**

You use **no matter** in expressions such as **no matter what** and **no matter how** to say that something happens or is true in all circumstances.

He does what he wants, no matter what I say.
Call me when you get home, no matter how late it is.

Don't use **no matter** to mention something that makes your main statement seem surprising. Don't say, for example, 'No matter the rain, we carried on playing'. Say '**In spite of** the rain, we carried on playing' or '**Despite** the rain, we carried on playing'

In spite of his ill health, my father was always cheerful.

→ See **in spite of – despite**

4 **used as a countable noun**

A **matter** is a situation that someone has to deal with.

I wanted to talk to you about a personal matter.
This is a matter for the police.

You can use the plural form **matters** to refer to a situation that has just been discussed.

There is only one applicant for the job, which makes matters easier.
His attitude did not help matters.

> **!** **BE CAREFUL**
>
> When **matters** has this meaning, don't put 'the' in front of it. Don't say, for example 'His attitude did not help the matters.'

may

→ See **might – may**

→ See **Adverbs and adverbials** for a graded list of words used to indicate probability

me

1 **'me'**

Me can be the object of a verb or preposition. You use **me** to refer to yourself.

Sara told me about her new job.
He looked at me curiously.

> **!** BE CAREFUL
>
> In standard English, 'me' is not used as the indirect object of a sentence when '**I**' is the subject. Don't say, for example, 'I got me a drink'. Say 'I got **myself** a drink'.
>
> *I poured myself a cup of tea.*
> *I had set myself a time limit of two hours.*

> 💬 In conversation, people sometimes use **me** as part of the subject of a sentence.
>
> *Me and my dad argue a lot.*
> *Me and Marcus are leaving.*

Don't use 'me' as part of the subject of a sentence in formal or written English. Use **I**.

My sister and I were very disappointed with the service.
Brad and I got engaged last year.

2 'it's me'

If you are asked 'Who is it?', you can say 'It's **me**', or just '**Me**'.

'Who is it?' – 'It's me, Frank.'

---

mean

The past tense and -*ed* participle of the verb **mean** is **meant** /ment/.

You use **mean** when you are talking or asking about the meaning of a word or expression.

What does 'imperialism' mean?
'Pandemonium' means 'the place of all devils'.

> **!** BE CAREFUL
>
> You must use the auxiliary verb **does** in questions like these. Don't say, for example, 'What means 'imperialism'?'

You can use **mean** with an -*ing* form to say what an attitude or type of behaviour involves.

Healthy living means being physically and mentally healthy.
I've got to do the right thing, even if it means taking a risk.

What someone **means** is what they are referring to or intend to say.

That friend of Sami's was there. Do you know the one I mean?
I thought you meant that you wanted some more to eat.

Don't use 'mean' to talk about what people think or believe. Don't say, for example, 'Most people mean he should resign'. Say 'Most people **think** he should resign'.

I think a woman has as much right to work as a man.
Most scientists believe that climate change is caused by human activity.

> 💬 In conversation, you can use '**I mean**' to explain or correct something that you have just said.
>
> *So what happens now? With your job, I mean.*
> *I don't want to go. I mean, I want to, but I can't.*

meaning – intention – opinion

1 '**meaning**'

The '**meaning**' of a word, expression, or gesture is the thing or idea that it refers to or represents.

The word 'guide' is used with various meanings.
This gesture has the same meaning throughout Italy.

The **meaning** of what someone says is what they intend to express.

The meaning of his remark was clear.

2 '**intention**'

Don't use '**meaning**' to refer to what someone intends to do. Don't say, for example, 'His meaning was to leave without paying'. Say 'His **intention** was to leave without paying'.

Their intention is to finish the work by Friday.

3 '**opinion**'

Don't use 'meaning' to refer to what someone thinks about something. Don't say, for example, 'I think he should go. What's your meaning?' You say 'I think he should go. What's your **opinion**?'

My opinion is that this is completely the wrong thing to do.

media

Media is a noun, and it is also a plural form of another noun, **medium**.

1 '**the media**'

You can refer to television, radio, and newspapers as **the media**.

She refused to talk to the media.

It is usually regarded as correct to use a plural form of a verb with **the media**, but people often use a singular form.

The media are very powerful in influencing opinions.
The media was full of stories about the singer and her husband.

You can use a singular or plural form in conversation and in less formal writing, but you should use a plural form in formal writing.

2 '**medium**'

A **medium** is a way of expressing your ideas or communicating with people. The plural of **medium** is either **mediums** or **media**.

She is an artist who uses various mediums including photography and sculpture.
They advertise through a range of different media – radio, billboards, and the internet.

meet

Meet is usually a verb. Its past tense and *-ed* participle is **met**.

When you **meet** someone, you are in the same place and you start talking to each other.

I met a Swedish girl on the train.
I have never met his wife before.

When you intend to meet someone, you can say that you **meet**, **meet with**, or **meet up with** them.

This is an opportunity for parents to <u>meet</u> their child's teachers.
She's <u>meeting up with</u> some of her friends on Saturday to go shopping.

 Meet with is especially common in American English.

We can <u>meet with</u> the professor Monday night.

memory

→ See **souvenir – memory**

mention

→ See **comment – mention – remark**

merry-go-round

→ See **roundabout**

might – may

Might and **may** are used mainly to talk about possibility. They can also be used to make a request, to ask permission, or to make a suggestion. When **might** and **may** are used with the same meaning, **may** is more formal than **might**. **Might** and **may** are called **modals**.

→ See **Modals**

 In conversation, the negative form **mightn't** is often used instead of 'might not'. The form **mayn't** is much less common. People usually use the full form **may not**.

He <u>mightn't</u> have time to see you.
It <u>may not</u> be as hard as you think.

1 **possibility: the present and the future**

You can use **might** or **may** to say that it is possible that something is true or that something will happen in the future.

I <u>might</u> see you at the party.
This <u>may</u> be why she enjoys her work.

You can use **could** in a similar way, but only in positive sentences.

Don't eat it. It <u>could</u> be poisonous.

→ See **can – could – be able to**

You can use **might well** or **may well** to show that it is fairly likely that something is true.

You <u>might well</u> be right.
I think that <u>may well</u> be the last time we see him.

You use **might not** or **may not** to say that it is possible that something is not true.

He <u>might not</u> like spicy food.
That <u>may not</u> be the reason she left.

! BE CAREFUL

Don't use 'might not' or 'may not' to say that it is impossible that something is true. Instead you use **could not**, **cannot**, or **can't**.

She could not have known what happened unless she was there.
He cannot be younger than me.
You can't talk to the dead.

Don't use 'may' when you are asking if something is possible. Don't say, for example, 'May he be right?' Say '**Might** he be right?' or, more usually, '**Could** he be right?'

Might we have got the date wrong?
Could this be true?

Don't say 'What may happen?' You usually say 'What **is likely to** happen?'

What are likely to be the effects of these changes?

2 possibility: the past

You use **might** or **may** with **have** to say that it is possible that something happened in the past, but you do not know whether it happened or not.

Jorge didn't play well. He might have been feeling tired.
I may have been a little unfair to you.

Could have can be used in a similar way.

It could have been one of the staff that stole the money.

! BE CAREFUL

However, if something did not happen and you want to say that there was a possibility of it happening, you can only use **might have** or **could have**. Don't use 'may have'. For example, you say 'If he hadn't fallen, he **might have** won the race'. Don't say 'If he hadn't hurt his ankle, he may have won the race'.

A lot of men died who might have been saved.

You use **might not** or **may not** with **have** to say that it is possible that something did not happen or was not true.

They might not have got your message.
Her parents may not have realized what she was doing.

Don't use 'might not have' or 'may not have' to say that it is impossible that something happened or was true. Instead you use **could not have** or, in British English, **cannot have**.

They could not have guessed what was going to happen.
The measurement can't have been wrong.

3 requests and permission

In formal English, **may** and **might** are sometimes used for making a request, or asking or giving permission.

Might I ask a question?
You may leave the table.

→ See **Topic** entry **Requests, orders, and instructions**

→ See **Topic** entry **Permission**

4 **suggestions**

Might is often used in polite suggestions.

You might like to read this and see what you think.
I think it might be better to switch off your phones.

→ See **Topic** entry **Suggestions**

migrate – migration – migrant

→ See **emigration – immigration – migration**

mill

→ See **factory – works – mill – plant**

million

A million or **one million** is the number 1,000,000.

Profits for 2010 were over $100 million.

! **BE CAREFUL**

Don't add '-s' to the word **million** when you put another number in front of it. Don't say, for example, 'five millions dollars'. Say 'five **million** dollars'.

Over five million people visit the country every year.

→ See **Reference** section **Numbers and fractions**

mind

Mind can be a noun or a verb.

1 **used as a noun**

Your **mind** is your ability to think.

Psychology is the study of the human mind.
I did a crossword puzzle to occupy my mind.

2 **'make up one's mind'**

If you **make up your mind**, you make a decision. If you **make up your mind to** do something, you decide to do it.

I couldn't make up my mind whether to stay or go.
She made up her mind to look for a new job.

! **BE CAREFUL**

You use a to-infinitive after this expression. Don't say, for example 'She made up her mind looking for a new job'.

3 **used as a verb**

If you have no objection to doing something, you can say that you **don't mind doing** it.

I don't mind walking.

! **BE CAREFUL**

You use an -ing form with this expression. Don't say, for example, 'I don't mind to walk'.

If you do not object to a situation or proposal, or if you do not prefer any particular option, you can say '**I don't mind**'.

It was raining, but we didn't mind.
'Would you rather go out or stay in?' – 'I don't mind.'

Don't say 'I don't mind it' with this meaning.

If you want to politely ask someone to do something, you can use **Would you mind** followed by an -ing form.

Would you mind turning your music down a little?
He asked us if we would mind waiting outside.

mistake

1 **'mistake' and 'error'**

A **mistake** is something incorrect or unfortunate that someone does. You say that someone **makes** a mistake.

He made a terrible mistake.
We made the mistake of leaving our bedroom window open.

In more formal English, you can use **error** with the same meaning. You also say that someone **makes** an error.

The letter contained several spelling errors.
He made a serious error in sending the man to prison.

! **BE CAREFUL**

Don't say that someone 'does' a mistake or an error. Don't say, for example, 'He did a terrible mistake'.

You say that someone does something **by mistake** or, in more formal English, **in error**. Don't say 'in mistake or 'by error'.

I went into the wrong room by mistake.
She was given another student's report in error.

2 **'fault'**

Don't use 'mistake' or 'error' to refer to something wrong in a machine or system. Use **fault**.

The machine has developed a fault.
I tried to call him on the phone, but there was some sort of fault on the line.

GRAMMAR FINDER

Modals

1 word order and form

Modals are a type of auxiliary verb. They are used, for example, to talk about the possibility or necessity of an event, and to make requests, offers, and suggestions. They can also be used to make what you are saying more polite.

The following words are modals:

can	may	need	will
could	might	shall	would
dare	must	should	

A modal is always followed by the base form of a verb (the infinitive without *to*), unless the verb has already been mentioned.

I must leave fairly soon.
Things might have been so different.
People may be watching.

→ See **Ellipsis**

The modals **dare** and **need** also occur as main verbs. In 'He doesn't dare climb the tree', **dare** is a main verb, but in 'He dare not climb the tree', **dare** is a modal.

→ See **dare, need**

Modals have only one form. There is no *-s* form for the third person singular of the present tense, and there are no *-ing* or *-ed* forms.

There's nothing I can do about it.
I'm sure he can do it.

2 short forms

Shall, **will**, and **would** are not usually pronounced in full. When you write down what someone says, or write in a conversational style, you usually represent 'shall' and 'will' using **'ll**, and 'would' using **'d**, after pronouns.

→ See **Contractions**

I'll see you tomorrow.
Patricia said she'd love to stay.

You can also represent 'will' as **'ll** after a noun.

My car'll be outside.

! BE CAREFUL

Shall, **will**, and **would** are never shortened if they come at the end of a sentence.

Paul said he'd come, and I hope he will.

In questions, too, you use the full form of **shall**, **will**, and **would**.

Shall I open the door for you?
Will you hurry up!
Would you like an apple?

Remember that **'d** is also the short form of the auxiliary verb **had**.

I'd heard it many times.

The auxiliary verb **have** is not usually pronounced in full after **could**, **might**, **must**, **should**, and **would**. The contractions **could've**, **might've**, **must've**, **should've**, and **would've** are occasionally used in writing when reporting a conversation.

I must've fallen asleep.
You should've come to see us.

Not is not usually pronounced in full after a modal. You usually represent what someone says using **n't** after the modal.

→ See **Contractions**, **Phrasal modals** for information about modals that consist of more than one word

For more information about the uses of modals, see the individual Usage entries for each word.

→ See **Topic** entries **Advising someone**, **Invitations**, **Offers**, **Opinions**, **Permission**, **Suggestions**

→ See **The Future** for information on the use of **will** to talk about the future, **The Past** for information on the use of **would** to talk about the past

GRAMMAR FINDER

Modifiers

A **modifier** is a word or group of words that comes in front of a noun and adds information about the thing that the noun refers to. Modifiers can be:

▶ **adjectives**

This is the <u>main</u> bedroom.
After the crossroads look out for the <u>large white</u> building.

→ See **Adjectives**

▶ **nouns**

...the <u>music</u> industry.
...<u>tennis</u> lessons.

→ See **Noun modifiers**

→ See **Topic** entry **Possession**

▶ **place names**

...a <u>London</u> hotel.
...<u>Arctic</u> explorers.

→ See **Topic** entry **Places**

▶ **place and direction adverbs**

...the <u>downstairs</u> television room.
The <u>overhead</u> light went on.

→ See **Topic** entry **Places**

▶ **times**

Colin was usually able to catch the <u>six thirty-five</u> train from Euston.
Every morning she would set off right after the <u>eight o'clock</u> news.

→ See **Topic** entry **Time**

moment

1 'moment'

A **moment** is a very short period of time.

She hesitated for only a moment.
A few moments later he heard footsteps.

2 'the moment'

The moment is often used as a conjunction to say that something happens or is done at the same time as something else, or immediately after it.

The moment I heard the news, I rushed over to her house.

When you use **the moment** in this way to talk about the future, you use the present simple after it. Don't use a future form.

The moment he arrives, ask him to come and see me.

3 'at the moment'

At the moment means now, at the present time.

I'm very busy at the moment.

! BE CAREFUL

Don't say ~~'I'm very busy in the moment'~~ or ~~'I'm very busy in this moment'~~.

4 'in a moment'

You can use **in a moment** to mean 'soon'.

Wait there – I'll be back in a moment.

---

money

Money is the coins or bank notes that you use to buy things. **Money** is an uncountable noun. Don't talk about ~~'moneys'~~ or ~~'a money'~~.

I spent all my money on clothes.
They don't have much money.

→ See **Nouns** for information on uncountable nouns

After **money** you use a singular form of a verb.

My money has all gone.
Money isn't the most important thing.

---

more

1 talking about a greater number or amount

You use **more** or **more of** to talk about a larger number of people or things, or a larger amount of something.

You use **more** in front of a noun which does not have a determiner, such as 'the' or 'a', or possessive, such as 'my' or 'our', in front of it.

There are more people going to university than ever before.
They were offered more food than they needed.

You use **more of** in front of a pronoun, such as **us** or **it**, or in front of a noun which has a determiner or possessive in front of it.

There are more of them looking for work now.
I've read more of his novels than anybody else's.

2 talking about an additional number or amount

You also use **more** or **more of** to talk about an additional number of people or things, or an additional amount of something.

More police officers will be brought in.
We need more information.
More of the land is needed to grow crops.
I ate some more of her cookies.

3 used with modifiers

You can use words such as **some** and **any** and expressions such as **a lot** in front of **more** and **more of**.

We need to buy some more milk.
I don't want to take up any more of your time.
She plans to invite a lot more people.

These words and expressions can be used in front of **more** and **more of** when they are followed by a plural form:

any	many	some	a great many
far	no	a few	a lot
lots	several	a good many	

These words and expressions can be used in front of **more** and **more of** when they are followed by an uncountable noun or a singular pronoun:

any	much	some	a great deal
far	no	a bit	a little
lots	rather	a good deal	a lot

! BE CAREFUL

Don't use 'many', 'several', 'a few', 'a good many', or 'a great many' in front of **more** or **more of** when they are followed by an uncountable noun or a singular pronoun. Don't say, for example, '~~I need a few more money~~'. Say '~~I need a bit more money~~' or '~~I need a little more money~~'.

4 'more than'

If you want to say that the number of people or things in a group is greater than a particular number, you use **more than** in front of the number.

Police arrested more than 70 people.
He had been awake for more than forty-eight hours.

When you use **more than** in front of a number and a plural noun, use a plural form of a verb after it.

More than 100 people were injured.
More than a thousand cars pass over this bridge every day.

5 used in comparatives

More is also used in front of adjectives and adverbs to form comparatives.

My children are more important than my job.
Next time, I will choose more carefully.

→ See **Comparative and superlative adjectives**, **Comparative and superlative adverbs**

---

morning

The **morning** is the part of each day which begins when you get up or when it becomes light outside, and which ends at noon or lunchtime.

→ See **Topic** entry **Time**

1 the present day

You refer to the morning of the present day as **this morning**.

His plane left this morning.
'When did the letter come?' – 'This morning.'

You refer to the morning of the previous day as **yesterday morning**.

They held a meeting yesterday morning.

If something will happen during the morning of the next day, you can say that it will happen **tomorrow morning** or **in the morning**.

I've got to go to work tomorrow morning.
Phone him in the morning.

2 single events in the past

If something happened during a particular morning in the past, use **on** and mention the particular morning, for example, '**on Monday morning**'.

We left after breakfast on Sunday morning.
On the morning of the exam, she felt sick.

If something happened earlier in the morning during a particular day in the past that you are describing, you can say that it happened **that morning** or **in the morning**.

I was late because that morning I had missed my train.
There had already been a meeting in the morning.

If something happened during the morning of the day before a particular day in the past, you can say that it happened **the previous morning**.

I remembered what she had told me the previous morning.

If something happened during the morning of the day after a day in the past, you say that it happened **the next morning**, **in the morning**, **next morning**, or **the following morning**.

The next morning I got up early.
In the morning we decided to go out for a walk.
Next morning we drove over to Grandma's.
The ship was due to sail the following morning.

In stories, if you want to say that something happened during a morning in the past, without saying which morning, you say that it happened **one morning**.

One morning, I was walking to school when I met Dan.
He woke up one morning and found she was gone.

3 talking about the future

If you want to say that something will happen during a particular morning in the future, you use **on** and mention the particular morning, for example, '**on Monday morning**'.

They're coming to see me on Friday morning.
He will probably feel very nervous on the morning of the wedding.

If something will happen in the morning during a particular day in the future that you are describing, you can say that it will happen **in the morning**.

Our plane leaves at 4 pm on Saturday, so we will have time to pack our bags in the morning.

If something will happen during the morning of the day after a particular day in the future, you can say that it will happen **the following morning**.

I will finish the report on Tuesday evening and send out copies the following morning.

4 regular events

If something happens or happened regularly every morning, you say that it happens or happened **in the morning** or **in the mornings**.

Chris usually went swimming in the morning.
The museum is only open in the mornings.

If something happens or happened once a week during a particular morning, you use **on** followed by the name of a day of the week and **mornings**.

The post office is closed on Wednesday mornings.
She did her grocery shopping on Saturday mornings.

 In American English, you can say that something happens **mornings**, without 'on'.

Mornings, she went for a walk if the weather was fine.

5 exact times

You can use **in the morning** with times of day to make it clear that you are talking about the period between midnight and noon rather than the period between noon and midnight.

They sometimes had meetings at seven in the morning.
We didn't get to bed until four in the morning.

most

1 used to mean 'the majority' or 'the largest part'

You use **most** or **most of** to talk about the majority of a group of things or people, or the largest part of something.

You use **most** in front of a plural noun which does not have a determiner, such as 'the' or 'a', or a possessive, such as 'my' or 'our', in front of it.

Most people agree that stealing is wrong.
In most schools, sports are compulsory.

You use **most of** in front of a pronoun, such as **us** or **it**, or in front of a noun which has a determiner or possessive noun in front of it.

Most of them enjoy music.
   He used to spend most of his time in the library.

! BE CAREFUL

When you use **most** like this, don't use a determiner in front of it. Don't say, for example, 'The most of them enjoy music'.

Don't talk about 'the most part' of something. Don't say, for example, 'She had eaten the most part of the pizza'. Say 'She had eaten **most of** the pizza'.

2 used to form superlatives

Most is used in front of adjectives and adverbs to form superlatives.

It was the most interesting film I'd seen for a long time.
These are foods the body can digest most easily.

→ See **Comparative and superlative adjectives**, **Comparative and superlative adverbs**

movie

→ See **film**

much

1 'very much'

You use **very much** to say that something is true to a great extent.

I enjoyed it very much.

When **very much** is used with a transitive verb, it usually goes after the object. Don't use it immediately after the verb. Don't say, for example, 'I enjoyed very much the party'. Say 'I enjoyed the party **very much**'.

! BE CAREFUL

In positive sentences, don't use **much** without **very**. Don't say, for example, 'I enjoyed it much' or 'We much agree' Say 'I enjoyed it **very much**' or 'We **very much** agree'.

In negative sentences, you can use **much** without 'very'.

I didn't like him much.
The situation is not likely to change much.

2 'much' meaning 'often'

You can also use **much** in negative sentences and questions to mean 'often'.

She doesn't talk about them much.
Does he come here much?

! BE CAREFUL

Don't use 'much' in positive sentences to mean 'often'. Don't say, for example, 'He comes here much'.

Many other words and expressions can be used to indicate degree.

→ See **Adverbs and adverbials** for a graded list of words used to indicate degree

3 **used with comparatives**

You often use **much** or **very much** in front of comparative adjectives and adverbs. For example, if you want to emphasize the difference in size between two things, you can say that one thing is **much bigger** or **very much bigger** than the other.

She was much older than me.
Now I can work much more quickly.

Much more and **very much more** can be used in front of a noun to emphasize the difference between two quantities or amounts.

She needs much more time to finish the job.
We had much more fun than we expected.

4 **'much too'**

You use **much too** in front of an adjective to say that something cannot be done or achieved because someone or something has too much of a quality.

The bedrooms were much too cold.
The price is much too high for me.

! **BE CAREFUL**

In sentences like these you put **much** in front of **too**, not after it. Don't say, for example, '~~The bedrooms were too much cold~~'.

5 **used as a determiner**

You use **much** in front of an uncountable noun to talk about a large quantity or amount of something. **Much** is usually used like this in negative sentences, in questions, or after **too**, **so**, or **as**.

I don't think there is much risk involved.
Is this going to make much difference?
The President has too much power.
My only ambition is to make as much money as possible.

In positive sentences, **a lot of** is usually used instead of 'much', especially in conversation and less formal writing.

There is a lot of risk involved in what he's doing.

→ See **lot**

In more formal writing, **much** is sometimes used, especially before abstract nouns such as **discussion**, **debate**, or **attention**.

Much emphasis has been placed on equality of opportunity in education.

6 **'much of'**

In front of **it**, **this**, or **that**, use **much of**, not 'much'.

We saw a film but I don't remember much of it.
Much of this is already possible.

You also use **much of** in front of a noun phrase which begins with a determiner, such as **the** or **a**, or a possessive, such as **my** or **his**.

Much of the food was vegetarian.
Carla spends much of her time helping other people.

In positive sentences, **a lot of** is usually used instead of 'much of', especially in conversation and less formal writing.

She spends a lot of her free time reading.

→ See **lot**

7 used as a pronoun

You can use **much** as a pronoun to refer to a large quantity or amount of something.

There wasn't much to do.
Much has been learned about how the brain works.

! BE CAREFUL

You don't usually use 'much' as an object pronoun in positive sentences. Instead you use **a lot**. For example, don't say 'He knows much about butterflies'. Say 'He knows **a lot** about butterflies'.

She talks a lot about music.
I've learned a lot from him.

→ See **lot**

8 'how much'

You use **how much** when you are asking the price of something.

I like that dress – how much is it? .

→ See **how much**

! BE CAREFUL

Don't use 'much' or 'much of' with plural countable nouns, to talk about a large number of people or things. Use **many** or **many of**.

→ See **many**

---

must

Must is usually used to say that something is necessary. It can also be used to say that you believe that something is true. **Must** is called a '**modal**'.

→ See **Modals**

1 'must', 'have to', 'have got to', and 'need to'

The expressions **have to**, **have got to**, and **need to** can sometimes be used with the same meaning as **must**.

The negative form of **must** is **must not** or **mustn't**. The negative forms of **have to** and **have got to** are **don't have to** and **haven't got to**. The negative form of **need to** is **need not**, **needn't** or **don't need to**. However, these negative forms do not all have the same meaning. This is explained below under **negative necessity**.

2 necessity in the present

Must, **have to**, **have got to**, and **need to** are all used to say that it is necessary that something is done.

I must go now.
You have to find a solution.

We've got to get up early tomorrow.
A few things need to be done before we can leave.

After **must** you use an infinitive without *to*. Don't use a *to*-infinitive. Don't say, for example, 'I must to go now.'

If someone is required to do something regularly, for example as a job or duty, say that they **have to** do it. Don't use 'must'.

She has to do all the cooking and cleaning.
We always have to write to our grandparents to thank them for our birthday gifts.

 If someone is required to do something on a particular occasion, say that they **have got to** do it or, in formal English and American English, that they **have to** do it.

I've got to go and see the headmaster.
We have to take all these boxes upstairs.

In formal English, **must** is used to say that someone is required to do something by a rule or law.

You must submit your application by the end of this month.

3 necessity in the past

If you want to say that something was necessary in the past, you use **had to**. Don't use 'must'.

She couldn't stay because she had to go to work.
We had to sit in silence.

4 necessity in the future

If you want to say that something will be necessary in the future, you use **will have to**.

He'll have to go to hospital.
We will have to finish this tomorrow.

5 negative necessity

You use **must not** or **mustn't** to say that it is important that something is not done.

You must not be late.
We mustn't forget the tickets.

If you want to say that it is not necessary that something is done, you use **don't have to**, **haven't got to**, **needn't**, or **don't need to**.

You don't have to eat everything on your plate.
I haven't got to work tomorrow, so I can sleep late.
You don't need to explain.

> **! BE CAREFUL**
>
> Don't use 'must not', 'mustn't', or 'have not to' to say that it is not necessary that something is done. Don't say, for example 'You mustn't explain' when you mean that it is not necessary to explain.

To say that it was not necessary for something to be done on a particular occasion in the past, use **didn't have to** or **didn't need to**.

Fortunately, she didn't have to choose.
I didn't need to say anything at all.

→ See **need**

6 strong belief

You use **must** to say that you strongly believe that something is true, because of particular facts or circumstances.

There must be some mistake.
Oh, you must be Gloria's husband.

Have to and **have got to** can also be used in this way, but not when the subject is **you**.

There has to be way out.
Money has got to be the reason.

You can use **must** with **be** and an *-ing* form to say that you believe something is happening.

He isn't in his office. He must be working at home.
You must be getting tired.

> **!** BE CAREFUL
>
> Don't use **must** with an infinitive to say that you believe something is happening. Don't say, for example, 'He isn't in his office. He must work at home'.

To say that you believe something is not true, use **cannot** or **can't**. Don't use 'must' or 'have to' with **not**.

The two statements cannot both be correct.
You can't have forgotten me.

→ See **can – could – be able to**

Nn

named

→ See **called – named**

nation

You use **nation** to refer to a country, together with its social and political structures.

These policies require cooperation between the world's industrialized nations.

You can also use **nation** to mean the people who live in a country.

He asked the nation to be patient.

Nation can also to refer to a group of people who are part of the same linguistic or historical group, even if they are not politically independent.

We studied the traditions and culture of the Great Sioux Nation.

> ❗ **BE CAREFUL**
>
> Don't use 'nation' simply to refer to a place. Don't say, for example, '~~What nation do you come from?~~' When you are referring to a place, use **country**, not 'nation'.
>
> *There are over a hundred edible species growing in this country.*
> *Have you any plans to leave the country in the next few days?*

nationality

You use **nationality** to say what country someone legally belongs to. For example, you say that someone 'has Belgian **nationality**'.

He's got British nationality.
They have the right to claim Hungarian nationality.

> ❗ **BE CAREFUL**
>
> Don't use 'nationality' to talk about things. Don't say, for example, that something 'has Swedish nationality'. You say that it **comes from** Sweden or **was made in** Sweden.
>
> *The best vanilla comes from Mexico.*
> *All of the trucks that Ford sold in Europe were made in Britain.*

nature

◼ 'nature'

Nature is used for talking about all living things and natural processes.

I am interested in science and learning about nature's secrets.
We must consider the ecological balance of nature.

When **nature** has this meaning, don't use 'the' in front of it.

2 **'the country'**

Don't use 'nature' to refer to land outside towns and cities. You refer to this land as **the country** or **the countryside**.

We live in the country.
We missed the English countryside.

---

near – close

1 **talking about short distances**

If something is **near**, **near to**, or **close to** a place or thing, it is a short distance from it. When **close** has this meaning, it is pronounced /kləʊs/.

I live in Reinfeld, which is near Lübeck.
I stood very near to them.
They owned a cottage close to the sea.

When **near** and **close** have this meaning, don't use them immediately in front of a noun. Instead use **nearby**.

He was taken to a nearby hospital.
He threw the bag into some nearby bushes.

However, the superlative form **nearest** can be used immediately in front of a noun.

They hurried to the nearest exit.

2 **meaning 'almost'**

You can use **near** immediately in front of a noun to say that something is almost a particular thing.

The country is in a state of near chaos.
We drove to the station in near silence.

You can also use **near** immediately in front of an adjective and a noun to say that something almost has a particular quality.

It was a near fatal accident.
The Government faces a near impossible dilemma.

You can use **near**, **near to**, or **close to** immediately in front of a noun to say that someone or something is almost in a particular state.

Her father was angry, her mother near tears.
When she saw him again, he was near to death.
She was close to tears.

3 **talking about friends and relatives**

You can refer to someone you know well as a '**close** friend'.

His father was a close friend of Peter Thorneycroft.

Don't refer to someone as a 'near friend'.

You can refer to someone who is directly related to you as a '**close** relative'.

She had no very close relatives.

You can also refer to someone as a '**near** relative', but this is less common.

! BE CAREFUL

Don't confuse the adjective 'close' with the verb **close** /kləʊz/. If you **close** something, you move it so that it fills a hole or gap.

→ See **close – closed – shut**

nearly

→ See **almost – nearly**

necessary

1 **used with an infinitive**

If **it is necessary to do** a particular thing, that thing must be done.

It is necessary to act fast.
It is necessary to examine the patient carefully.

2 **used with 'for'**

You can say that it is necessary **for someone** to do something.

It was necessary for me to keep active and not think about Sally.
It is necessary for management and staff to work together positively.

! BE CAREFUL

If you use **necessary** in sentences like these, the subject must be **it**. Don't say, for example, 'She was necessary to make several calls'. Say '**It was necessary for her to** make several calls'. However, in conversation and in less formal writing, people normally say '**She had to** make several calls'.

→ See **must**

If one thing is **necessary for** another, the second thing can only happen or exist if the first one happens or exists.

Total rest is necessary for the muscle to repair itself.

need

Need has the negative forms **need not** and **do not need**. The contracted forms **needn't** and **don't need** are also used. However, you cannot use all these forms for all meanings of **need**. This is explained below.

1 **used as a transitive verb**

If you **need** something, it is necessary for you to have it.

These animals need food throughout the winter.
He desperately needed money.

For this meaning of **need**, the negative form is **do not need**.

You do not need special tools for this job.
I don't need any help, thank you.
I didn't need any further encouragement.

! BE CAREFUL

Don't use a progressive form of 'need'. Don't say, for example, 'We are needing some milk'. Say 'We **need** some milk'.

2 **used as an intransitive verb or modal**

If you **need to do** something, it is necessary for you to do it.

You'll need to work hard to pass this exam.
For an answer to these problems we need to look elsewhere.

→ See **Modals**

You must use **to** in sentences like these. Don't say, for example, 'You'll need work hard to pass this exam'.

3 **questions and negatives**

In negative statements you usually use **do not need to**. You say, for example, 'He **doesn't need to** go'. You can also use **need not** as the negative form. For example, you can say 'He **needn't** go'. However, this is less common and more formal. Don't say 'He doesn't need go' or 'He needn't to go'.

You don't need to shout.
You needn't talk about it unless you want to.

In questions, you almost always use **do** and **need to**. You usually only use **need** on its own in a few set phrases, such as 'Need I say more?' and 'Need I remind you?'

Do you need to go?
Need I remind you that you owe the company money?

4 **'must not'**

If you tell someone that they **don't need to** or **need not** do something, you are saying that it is not necessary for them to do it. If you want to say that it is necessary for someone **not** to do something, don't use 'need'. Instead you use **must not** or **mustn't**.

You must not accept it.
We mustn't forget the tickets.

→ See **must**

5 **talking about the past**

If you want to say that it was not necessary for someone to do something at a time in the past, you say that they **didn't need to** do it or they **didn't have to** do it. Don't say that they 'needn't' do it.

I didn't need to say anything at all.
Fortunately, she didn't have to choose.

However, in a reporting structure you can use **needn't**.

They knew they needn't worry about me.

If someone has done something and you want to say that it was not necessary, you can say that they **needn't have** done it.

I was wondering whether you were eating properly, but I needn't have worried, need I?

6 **'need' with -ing forms**

You can use **need** with an -*ing* form to say that something should have something done to it. For example, you can say 'The cooker **needs cleaning**', rather than 'The cooker needs to be cleaned'.

The plan needs improving.
We made a list of things that needed doing.

neither

1 'neither' and 'neither of'

You use **neither** or **neither of** to make a negative statement about two people or things. You use **neither** in front of the singular form of a countable noun. You use **neither of** in front of a plural pronoun or a plural noun phrase beginning with **the**, **these**, **those**, or a possessive.

So, for example, you can say '**Neither child** was hurt' or '**Neither of the children** was hurt'. There is no difference in meaning.

Neither man spoke or moved.
Neither of them spoke for several moments.

! BE CAREFUL

Don't use 'neither' without **of** in front of a plural form. Don't say, for example, 'Neither the children was hurt'. Also, don't use 'not' after **neither**. Don't say, for example, 'Neither of the children wasn't hurt'.

People sometimes use a plural form of a verb after **neither of** and a noun phrase. For example, they say 'Neither of the children **were** hurt'.

Neither of them are students.
Neither of them were listening.

This use is acceptable in conversation and in less formal writing, but in formal writing you should always use a singular form of a verb after **neither of**.

2 'neither' in replies

When a negative statement has been made, you can use **neither** to show that this statement also applies to another person or thing. You put **neither** at the beginning of the clause, followed by an auxiliary verb, a modal, or **be**, then the subject. You can also use **nor** in the same way with the same meaning.

'I didn't invite them.' – 'Neither did I.'
If your printer does not work, neither will your fax or copier.
Douglas can't do it, and nor can Gavin.

neither ... nor

In writing and formal speech, **neither** and **nor** are used for linking two words or expressions in order to make a negative statement about two people, things, qualities, or actions. You put **neither** in front of the first word or expression and **nor** in front of the second one.

For example, instead of saying 'The President did not come and the Vice-President did not come' you can say '**Neither** the President **nor** the Vice-President came'.

Neither he nor Melanie owe me an apology.
He neither drinks nor smokes.

In conversation and in less formal writing, people sometimes use **or** after **neither**. For example, they say 'He neither drinks or smokes'. However, in formal writing you should always use **nor**.

You always put **neither** immediately in front of the first of the words or expressions that are linked by **nor**. Don't put it any earlier in the sentence. Don't say, for example, 'She neither ate meat nor fish'. You say 'She ate **neither meat nor fish**'.

In conversation, people do not usually use **neither** and **nor**. Instead of saying 'Neither the President nor the Vice-President came', you normally say 'The President didn't come and **neither did** the Vice-President'.

Margaret didn't talk about her mother and <u>neither did</u> Rosa.
I won't give up, and <u>neither will</u> my colleagues.

Instead of saying 'She ate neither meat nor fish', you normally say 'She **didn't** eat meat **or** fish'. Instead of saying 'She neither smokes nor drinks', you say 'She **doesn't** smoke **or** drink'.

Karin's from abroad and <u>hasn't any relatives or friends</u> here.
You <u>can't run or climb</u> in shoes like that.

---

nervous – anxious – irritated – annoyed

1 'nervous'

If you are **nervous**, you are rather frightened about something that you are going to do or experience.

My daughter is <u>nervous</u> about starting school.

2 'anxious'

If you are worried about something that might happen to someone else, don't say that you are 'nervous'. Say that you are **anxious**.

It's time to be going home – your mother will be <u>anxious</u>.
I had to deal with calls from <u>anxious</u> relatives.

→ See **anxious**

3 'irritated' and 'annoyed'

If something makes you angry and impatient because you cannot stop it continuing, don't say that it makes you 'nervous'. Say that you are **irritated** or **annoyed** by it.

Perhaps they were <u>irritated</u> by the sound of crying.
I was <u>annoyed</u> by his questions.

---

never

1 uses

You use **never** to say that something did not, does not, or will not happen at any time.

She <u>never</u> asked him to lend her any money.
I will <u>never</u> give up.

! BE CAREFUL

Don't use 'do' in front of **never**. Don't say, for example, 'He does never write to me'. Say 'He **never writes** to me'.

He <u>never complains</u>.
He <u>never speaks</u> to you, does he?

You don't usually use another negative word with '**never**'. Don't say, for example, 'I haven't never been there' or 'They never said nothing'. Say 'I have **never** been there' or 'They **never** said **anything**'.

It was an experience I will <u>never</u> forget.
I've <u>never</u> seen <u>anything</u> like it.

Similarly, don't use 'never' if the subject of a clause is a negative word such as **nothing** or **no one**. Instead use **ever**. You say, for example, 'Nothing will **ever** happen'. Don't say 'Nothing will never happen'.

Nothing ever changes.
No one will ever know.

2 **position in clause**

If you are not using an auxiliary verb or modal, you put **never** in front of the verb, unless the verb is **be**.

He never allowed himself to lose control.
They never take risks.

▶ If the verb is **be**, you usually put **never** after it.

The road by the river was never quiet.

▶ If you are using an auxiliary verb or modal, you put **never** after it.

I have never known a year quite like this.
My husband says he will never retire.

▶ If you are using more than one auxiliary verb or modal, you put **never** after the first one.

He said he had never been arrested.
The answer to this question might never be known.

▶ If you are using an auxiliary verb on its own, you put **never** in front of it.

I do not want to marry you. I never did. I never will.

▶ In stories, **never** is sometimes put first for emphasis, followed by an auxiliary verb and the subject of the clause.

Never had Dixon been so glad to see Margaret.
Never had two hours gone so slowly.

3 **'never' with an imperative**

You can use **never** with an imperative instead of 'do not'. You do this when you want to emphasize that something should not be done at any time.

Never attempt to do this without a safety net.
Never use your credit card as personal identification.

news

News is information about a recent event or a recently changed situation.

I've got some good news for you.
Sabine was at home when she heard news of the disaster.

→ See **information – news**

You also use **news** to refer to descriptions of recent events on television or radio or in a newspaper.

They continued to broadcast up-to-date news and pictures of these events.

News looks like a plural noun but is in fact an uncountable noun. You use a singular form of a verb after it.

The news is likely to be bad.
I was still in the office when the news was brought to me.

You talk about **this news**, not ~~'these news'~~.

I had been waiting at home for this news.

> **!** **BE CAREFUL**
>
> Don't talk about ~~'a news'~~. You refer to a piece of information as **some news**, **a bit of news**, or **a piece of news**.

I've got some good news for you.
I've had a bit of bad news.
A respectful silence greeted this piece of news.

A description of an event on television or in a newspaper is **a news item** or **an item of news**.

This was a small news item in The Times last Friday.
An item of news in the Sunday paper caught my attention.

---

next

Next is usually used for saying when something will happen. It can also be used for talking about the position of something, either physically, or in a list or series.

1 talking about the future

You use **next** in front of words such as **week**, **month**, or **year** to say when something will happen. For example, if it is Wednesday and something is going to happen on Monday, you can say that it will happen **next week**.

I'm getting married next month.
I don't know where I will be next year.

> **!** **BE CAREFUL**
>
> Don't use 'the' or a preposition in front of **next**. Don't say, for example, that something will happen ~~'the next week'~~ or ~~'in the next week'~~.

You can also use **next** without 'the' or a preposition in front of **weekend** or in front of the name of a season, month, or day of the week.

You must come and see us next weekend.
He'll be seventy-five next April.
Let's have lunch together next Wednesday.

Don't say that something will happen 'next day'. Say that it will happen **tomorrow**. Similarly, don't say that something will happen 'next morning', 'next afternoon', 'next evening', or 'next night'. Say that it will happen **tomorrow morning**, **tomorrow afternoon**, **tomorrow evening**, or **tomorrow night**.

Can we meet tomorrow at five?
I'm going down there tomorrow morning.

You don't usually use 'next' to refer to a day in the same week. For example, if it is Monday and you intend to ring someone in four days' time, don't say ~~'I will ring you next Friday'~~. You say 'I will ring you **on Friday**'.

He's going camping on Friday.

If you want to make it completely clear that you are talking about a day in the same week, you use **this**.

The film opens this Thursday at various cinemas in London.

Similarly, you can say that something will happen **this weekend**.

I might be able to go skiing this weekend.

Use **the next** to refer to any period of time measured forward from the present. For example, if it is July 2nd and you want to say that something will happen between now and July 23rd, you say that it will happen **in the next three weeks** or **during the next three weeks**.

Mr MacGregor will make the announcement in the next two weeks.
Plans will be finalized during the next few months.

2 talking about the past

When you are talking about the past and you want to say that something happened on the day after events that you have been describing, you say that it happened **the next day** or **the following day**.

I telephoned the next day and made a complaint.
The following day I went to speak at a conference in Scotland.

Next, **the next**, and **the following** can also be used in front of **morning**.

Next morning he began to work.
The next morning, a letter arrived for me.
The following morning he checked out of the hotel.

However, in front of **afternoon**, **evening**, or the name of a day of the week you normally only use **the following**.

I arrived at the village the following afternoon.
He was supposed to start the following Friday.

3 talking about physical position

You use **next to** to say that someone or something is by the side of a person or object.

She sat next to him.
There was a lamp next to the bed.

If you talk about **the next room**, you mean a room that is separated by a wall from the one you are in.

I can hear my husband talking in the next room.

Similarly, if you are in a theatre or a bus, **the next seat** is a seat by the side of the one that you are sitting in.

The girl in the next seat was looking at him with interest.

You can use **next** like this with a few other nouns, for example **desk**, **bed**, or **compartment**.

! BE CAREFUL

However, don't use 'next' simply to say that a particular thing is the closest one. Don't say, for example, 'They took him to the next hospital'. You say 'They took him to **the nearest hospital**'.

The nearest town is Brompton.
The nearest beach is 15 minutes' walk away.

4 talking about a list or series

The **next** one in a list or series is the one that comes immediately after the one you have been talking about.

Let's go on to the next item on the agenda.

In British English, the **next** thing **but one** in a list or series is the one that comes after the next one.

The next entry but one is another recipe.

night

1 'night', and 'at night'

Night is the period during each twenty-four hours when it is dark. If something happens regularly during this period, you say that it happens **at night**.

The doors were kept closed at night.
I used to lie awake at night, listening to the rain.

→ See **Topic** entry **Time**

A **night** is one of these periods of darkness. You usually refer to a particular period as **the night**.

He went to a hotel and spent the night there.
I got a phone call in the middle of the night.

2 the previous night

If something happened during the night before the present day, you say that it happened **in the night**, **during the night**, or **last night**.

I didn't hear Sheila in the night.
I had the strangest dream last night.

You can also say that a situation existed **last night**.

I didn't manage to sleep much last night.

Last night is also used for saying that something happened during the previous evening.

I met your husband last night.

If you are talking about a day in the past and you want to say that something happened the night before that day, you say that it happened **in the night**, **during the night**, or **the previous night**.

His father had died in the night.
This was the hotel where they had stayed the previous night.

3 exact times

If you want to make it clear that you are talking about a particular time in the early part of the night rather than the morning, you add **at night**.

This took place at eleven o'clock at night on our second day.

However, if you are talking about a time after midnight and you want to make it clear that you are talking about the night and not the afternoon, you say **in the morning**.

It was five o'clock in the morning.

no

1 used as a reply

No can be a negative reply.

'Is he down there already?' – 'No, he's not there.'

'Did you come alone?' – *'No. John's here with me.'*

No is a negative reply to negative questions. For example, if you are Spanish and someone says to you 'You aren't Italian, are you?', you say '**No**'. Don't say ~~Yes~~.

'You don't like pasta, do you?' – *'No'.*
'It won't take you more than ten minutes, will it?' – *'No'.*

2 'not any'

No is used in front of nouns to mean 'not any'. For example, instead of saying 'She doesn't have any friends', you can say 'She has **no friends**'.

I have no complaints.
My children are hungry. We have no food.

3 used with comparatives

No is used in front of comparative adjectives instead of 'not'. For example, instead of saying 'She isn't taller than her sister', you say 'She is **no taller** than her sister'.

The woman was no older than Kate.
We collected shells that were no bigger than a fingernail.

However, don't use 'no' and a comparative in front of a noun. Don't say, for example, '~~a no older woman~~' or '~~a no bigger shell~~'.

4 used with 'different'

No is used in front of **different** instead of 'not'.

The local people say Kilkenny is no different from other towns.

5 'not allowed'

No is often used on notices to tell you that something is not allowed. **No** is followed by an *-ing* form or a noun.

No smoking.
No entry.
No vehicles beyond this point.

nobody

→ See **no one**

noise

→ See **sound – noise**

none

1 'none of'

You use **none of** in front of a plural noun phrase to make a negative statement about all the things or people in a particular group.

None of these suggestions is very helpful.
None of the others looked at her.

You use **none of** in front of a noun phrase containing an uncountable noun to make a negative statement about every part of something.

None of the furniture was out of place.

You can use **none of** in front of a singular or plural pronoun.

None of this seems to have affected him.
We had none of these at home.

Don't use 'we' or 'they' after **none of**. Instead you use **us** or **them**.

None of us had written our reports.
None of them had learned anything that day.

When you use **none of** in front of a plural noun or pronoun, you can use either a plural or singular form of a verb after it. The singular form is more formal.

None of his books have been published in England.
None of them is real.

When you use **none of** in front of an uncountable noun or a singular pronoun, you use a singular form of a verb after it.

None of the wheat was ruined.
Yet none of this has seriously affected business.

2 used as a pronoun

None can be used on its own as a pronoun.

There were none left.
He asked for some proof. I told him that I had none.

! BE CAREFUL

You don't usually use any other negative word after **none of** or **none**. Don't say, for example, 'None of them weren't ready'. Say 'None of them **were** ready'. Similarly, don't use 'none of' or 'none' as the object of a sentence that already has a negative word in it. Don't say, for example, 'I didn't want none of them'. Say 'I didn't want **any** of them'.

You only use **none of** or **none** to talk about a group of three or more things or people. If you want to talk about two things or people, you use **neither of** or **neither**.

→ See **neither**

---

no one

No one or **nobody** means 'not a single person', or 'not a single member of a particular group'. In British English, **no one** can also be written **no-one**. **Nobody** is always written as one word.

 There is no difference in meaning between **no one** and **nobody**. However, **nobody** is more common in spoken English and **no one** is more common in written English.

You use a singular form of a verb with **no one** or **nobody**.

Everyone wants to be a hero, but no one wants to die.
Nobody knows where he is.

! BE CAREFUL

You don't usually use any other negative word after **no one** or **nobody**. Don't say, for example, 'No one didn't come'. Say 'No one **came**'. Similarly, don't use 'no one' or 'nobody' as the object of a sentence which already has a negative word in it. Don't say, for example, 'We didn't see no one'. You say 'We didn't see **anyone**' or 'We didn't see **anybody**'.

You mustn't tell <u>anyone</u>.
He didn't trust <u>anybody</u>.

Don't use 'of' after 'no one' or 'nobody'. Don't say, for example, 'N̶o̶ ̶o̶n̶e̶ ̶o̶f̶ ̶t̶h̶e̶ ̶c̶h̶i̶l̶d̶r̶e̶n̶ c̶o̶u̶l̶d̶ ̶s̶p̶e̶a̶k̶ ̶F̶r̶e̶n̶c̶h̶'. Say '**None of** the children could speak French'.

<u>None of</u> the women will talk to me.
It was something <u>none of</u> us could possibly have guessed.

→ See **none**

nor

1 'neither ... nor'

You can use **nor** with **neither** to make a negative statement about two people or things.

Neither Maria <u>nor</u> Juan was there.
He spoke <u>neither</u> English <u>nor</u> French.

→ See **neither ... nor**

2 used for linking clauses

Nor is also used for linking negative clauses. You put **nor** at the beginning of the second clause, followed by an auxiliary verb, a modal, or **be**, followed by the subject and the main verb, if there is one.

The officer didn't believe me, <u>nor did the girls</u> when I told them.
We cannot give personal replies, <u>nor can we guarantee</u> to answer letters.

3 'nor' in replies

You can reply to a negative statement using **nor**. You do this to show that what has just been said also applies to another person or thing. You can use **neither** in the same way with the same meaning.

'I don't like him.' – '<u>Nor do I.</u>'
'I can't stand much more of this.' – '<u>Neither can I.</u>'

normally

→ See **Adverbs and adverbials** for words used to indicate frequency

north – northern

1 'north'

The **north** is the direction that is on your left when you are looking towards the direction where the sun rises.

The land to the <u>north</u> and east was very flat.
There is a possibility of colder weather and winds from the <u>north</u>.

A **north** wind blows from the north.

The <u>north</u> wind was blowing straight into her face.

The **north** of a place is the part that is towards the north.

The violence started in the <u>north</u> of the country.
The best asparagus comes from the Calvados region in the <u>north</u> of France.

North occurs in the names of some countries, states, and regions.

They have hopes for business in North Korea.
They crossed the mountains of North Carolina.
We are worried about possible ecological damage in North America.

2 'northern'

However, you don't usually talk about a 'north' part of a country or region. You talk about a **northern** part.

Hausa is a language spoken in the northern regions of West Africa.
We travelled to the northern tip of Caithness.

Similarly, don't talk about 'north Europe' or 'north England'. You say **northern** Europe or **northern** England.

Preston had flown over northern Canada.

northwards

→ See **-ward – -wards**

not

Not is used with verbs to form negative sentences.

1 position of 'not'

You put **not** after the first auxiliary verb or modal, if there is one.

They are not seen as major problems.
They might not even notice.
Adrina realised that she had not been listening to him.

If there is no other auxiliary verb, you use **do** as the auxiliary verb. After **not** you use the base form of a verb.

The girl did not answer.
He does not speak English very well.

In conversation, when **not** is used after **be**, **have**, **do**, or a modal, it is not usually pronounced in full. When you write down what someone says, you usually represent **not** as **n't** and add it to the verb in front of it. In some cases, the verb also changes its form.

→ See **Contractions**

You nearly always use an auxiliary verb when you want to make a negative form of a verb using **not**. Don't say, for example, 'I not liked it' or 'I liked not it'. You say 'I **didn't like** it'.

There are two exceptions to this. When you use **not** with **be**, don't use an auxiliary verb. You simply put **not** after **be**.

I'm not sure about this.
The program was not a success.

When **have** is a main verb, **not** is sometimes added without an auxiliary verb, but only in the short forms **hasn't**, **haven't**, and **hadn't**.

You haven't any choice.
The sky hadn't a cloud in it.

However, it is more common to use the forms **doesn't have**, **don't have**, and **didn't have**.

This question doesn't have a proper answer.
We don't have any direct control of the prices.
I didn't have a cheque book.

> **! BE CAREFUL**
>
> When you use **not** to make what you are saying negative, you don't usually use another negative word such as 'nothing', 'never', or 'none'. Don't say, for example, 'I don't know nothing about it'. You say 'I don't know **anything** about it'.

2 'not really'

You can make a negative statement more polite or less strong by using **really** after **not**.

It doesn't really matter.
I don't really want to be part of it.

You can reply to some questions by saying '**Not really**'.

→ See **Topic** entry **Replies**

3 'not very'

When you make a negative statement using **not** and an adjective, you can make the statement less strong by putting **very** in front of the adjective.

I'm not very interested in the subject.
That's not a very good arrangement.

> **! BE CAREFUL**
>
> Although you can say that something is **not very good**, don't use 'not' in front of other words meaning 'very good'. Don't say, for example, that something is 'not excellent' or 'not marvellous'.

4 used with *to*-infinitives

You can use **not** with a *to*-infinitive. You put **not** in front of **to**, not after it.

The Prime Minister has asked us not to discuss the issue publicly any more.
I decided not to go in.

5 'not' in contrasts

You can use **not** to link two words or expressions. You do this to point out that something is the case, and to contrast it with what is not the case.

So they went by plane, not by car.
He is now an adult, not a child.

You can make a similar contrast by changing the order of the words or expressions. When you do this, you put **not** in front of the first word or expression and **but** in front of the second one.

This story is not about the past, but about the future.
He was caught, not by the police, but by a man who recognised him.

6 used with sentence adverbials

You can use **not** with **surprisingly** and **unexpectedly** to make a negative comment about a statement.

Laura, not surprisingly, disliked discussing the subject.
The great man had died, not unexpectedly and very quietly, in the night.

7 'not all'

Not is sometimes used with **all** and with words beginning with **every-** to form the subject of a sentence. For example, instead of saying 'Some snakes are not poisonous', you can say '**Not all** snakes are poisonous'.

Not all the houses have central heating.
Not everyone agrees with me.

8 'not only'

Not only is often used with **but** or **but also** to link two words or phrases.

→ See **not only**

9 'not' in short replies

You can use **not** at the end of a short reply in order to give your opinion. For example, you can say '**I hope not**', '**Probably not**', or '**Certainly not**'.

'Will it happen again?' – 'I hope not.'
'I hope she won't die.' – 'Die? Certainly not!'

note – bill

1 'note'

In British English, a **note** is a piece of paper money.

He handed me a ten pound note.

2 'bill'

 A piece of American paper money is called a **bill**, not a 'note'.

He took out a five dollar bill.

nothing

1 'nothing'

Nothing means 'not a single thing', or 'not a single part of something'. You use a singular form of a verb with **nothing**.

Nothing is happening.
Nothing has been discussed.

❗ BE CAREFUL

You don't usually use any other negative word such as 'not' after **nothing**. Don't say, for example, 'Nothing didn't happen'. You say '**Nothing happened**'. Similarly, don't use 'nothing' as the object of a sentence which already has a negative word in it. Don't say, for example, 'I couldn't hear nothing'. Say 'I couldn't hear **anything**'.

I did not say anything.
He never seemed to do anything at all.

2 'nothing but'

Nothing but is used in front of a noun phrase or an infinitive without *to* to mean 'only'. For example, instead of saying 'In the fridge there was only a piece of cheese', you can say 'In the fridge there was **nothing but** a piece of cheese'.

For a few months I thought of <u>nothing but</u> Jeremy.
He did <u>nothing but</u> complain.

---

not only

1 used with 'but' or 'but also'

You use **not only** to link two words or phrases that refer to things, actions, or situations. You put **not only** in front of the first word or group, and **but** or **but also** in front of the second one. The second thing is usually more surprising, interesting, or important than the first one.

The government radio <u>not only</u> reported the demonstration, <u>but</u> announced it in advance.
We asked <u>not only</u> what the children had learnt <u>but also</u> how they had learnt it.

2 used with a pronoun

When you are linking phrases that begin with a verb, you can omit 'but' or 'but also' and use a personal pronoun instead. For example, instead of saying 'Margaret not only came to the party but brought her aunt as well', you can say 'Margaret not only came to the party, **she** brought her aunt as well'.

Her interest in this work <u>not only</u> continued, <u>it</u> increased.

3 putting 'not only' first

For emphasis, you can put **not only** first, followed by an auxiliary verb or **be**, then the subject, then the main verb.

<u>Not only did they send</u> home large amounts, but they also saved money.
<u>Not only do they rarely go</u> on school trips, they rarely, if ever, leave Brooklyn.

Not only must come first when you are linking two clauses which have different subjects.

Not only were <u>the local people</u> old, but <u>the women</u> still dressed in long black dresses.
Not only were <u>many of the roads</u> closed, <u>many bridges</u> had also been blown up.

GRAMMAR FINDER

Noun modifiers

A **noun modifier** is a noun that is used in front of another noun to give more specific information about someone or something. It is nearly always singular.

...the <u>car</u> door.
...a <u>football</u> player.
...a <u>surprise</u> announcement.

A few plural nouns remain plural when used as modifiers.

→ See **Nouns** for more information on plural nouns

The use of noun modifiers is very common in English. You can use noun modifiers to show a wide range of relationships between two nouns. For example, you can indicate:

▸ what something is made of, as in **cotton socks**

▸ what is made in a particular place, as in **a glass factory**

▸ what someone does, as in **a football player**

▶ where something is, as in **my bedroom curtains** and **Brighton Technical College**

▶ when something happens, as in **the morning mist** and **her childhood experiences**

▶ the nature or size of something, as in **a surprise attack** and **a pocket chess-set**

→ See **Topic** entry **Possession and other relationships**

Noun modifiers can be used together.

...*car body repair* kits.
...*a family dinner* party.
...*a Careers Information* Officer.

Adjectives can be put in front of a noun modifier.

...*a long* car journey.
...*a new red* silk handkerchief.
...*complex* business deals.

GRAMMAR FINDER

Nouns

1 countable nouns	**7** collective nouns	
2 uncountable nouns	**8** proper nouns	
3 variable nouns	**9** compound nouns	
4 mass nouns	**10** abstract and concrete nouns	
5 singular nouns	**11** nouns followed by prepositions	
6 plural nouns		

A **noun** is used to identify a person or thing. Nouns can be classified into eight main grammatical types: countable nouns, uncountable nouns, variable nouns, mass nouns, singular nouns, plural nouns, collective nouns, and proper nouns.

1 countable nouns

Nouns referring to things that can be counted are called **countable nouns**. They have two forms, singular and plural. The plural form usually ends in '**s**'.

→ See **Reference** section **Plural forms of nouns** for full information on how to form plurals

The singular form of a countable noun is usually preceded by a determiner such as **a**, **another**, **every**, or **the**.

They left the house to go for a walk after tea.

When you use a singular form as the subject of a verb, you use a singular verb form.

My son likes playing football.
The address on the letter was wrong.

The plural form of a countable noun can be used with or without a determiner. Don't use a determiner if you are referring to a type of thing in general.

Does the hotel have large rooms?

You use a determiner such as **the** or **my** if you are talking about a particular group of things.

The rooms at Watermouth are all like this.

You use a determiner such as **many** or **several** when you are talking about how many things there are.

The house had many rooms and a terrace with a view of Etna.

When you use a plural form as the subject of a verb, you use a plural verb form.

These cakes are delicious.

Countable nouns can be used after numbers.

...underline{one} table.
...underline{two} cats.
...underline{three hundred} pounds.

2 uncountable nouns

Nouns that refer to things such as substances, qualities, feelings, and types of activity, rather than to individual objects or events, are called **uncountable nouns**. These nouns have only one form.

I needed help with my homework.
The children had fun playing with the puppets.

> ! **BE CAREFUL**
>
> Some nouns that are uncountable nouns in English are countable nouns or plural nouns in other languages.

advice	furniture	knowledge	money
baggage	homework	luggage	news
equipment	information	machinery	traffic

Uncountable nouns are not used with 'a' or 'an'. They are used with **the** or possessive determiners such as **his** and **our** when they refer to something that is specified or known.

I liked the music, but the words were boring.
Eva clambered over the side of the boat into the water.
She admired his intelligence.

When you use an uncountable noun as the subject of a verb, you use a singular verb form.

Electricity is dangerous.
Food was expensive in those days.

Uncountable nouns are not used after numbers. It is possible to refer to a quantity of something that is expressed by an uncountable noun by using a word like **some** or a phrase like **a piece of**.

→ See **Quantity**

I want some privacy.
I took the two pieces of paper out of my pocket.

> ! **BE CAREFUL**
>
> Some uncountable nouns end in '**-ics**' or '**-s**' and therefore look like plural countable nouns.

Mathematics is too difficult for me.
Measles is in most cases a harmless illness.

These nouns usually refer to:

▶ subjects of study and activities

acoustics	classics	gymnastics	obstetrics
aerobics	economics	linguistics	physics
aerodynamics	electronics	logistics	politics
aeronautics	ethics	mathematics	statistics
athletics	genetics	mechanics	thermodynamics

▶ games

billiards	cards	darts	skittles
bowls	checkers	draughts	tiddlywinks

▶ illnesses

diabetes	mumps	rickets
measles	rabies	shingles

3 variable nouns

Variable nouns are nouns that combine the behaviour of countable and uncountable nouns. They are like countable nouns when they refer to an instance or more than one instance of something, for example **an injustice**; **injustices** or to individual members of a class, for example **a cake**; **cakes**. Otherwise they behave like uncountable nouns, referring to something in more general terms.

He has been in <u>prison</u> for ten years.
Staff were called in from <u>a prison</u> nearby to help stop the violence.
... the problems of British <u>prisons</u>.
They ate all their chicken and nearly all the stewed <u>apple</u>.
She brought in a tray on which were toast, butter, <u>an apple</u>, and some jam.
There was a bowl of red <u>apples</u> on the table.

4 mass nouns

Mass nouns are nouns that behave like uncountable nouns when they refer to a substance, for example '**detergent**', and like countable nouns when they refer to types or brands of substance, for example '**a strong detergent**'; '**more detergents**'.

I passed a shop where <u>perfume</u> is sold.
I found <u>an</u> interesting new <u>perfume</u> last week.
Department stores are finding that French <u>perfumes</u> are selling slowly.
The chicken is filled with <u>cheese</u> and spinach.
I was looking for <u>a cheese</u> that was soft and creamy.
There are plenty of delicious <u>cheeses</u> made in the area.

5 singular nouns

There are some nouns, and some particular meanings of nouns, that are used only in the singular form. **Singular nouns** are always used with a determiner and take a singular verb.

<u>The sun</u> was shining.
He's always thinking about <u>the past</u> and worrying about <u>the future</u>.
There was <u>a note</u> of satisfaction in his voice.

6 plural nouns

Some nouns have only a plural form. For example, you can buy **goods**, but not 'a good'. Other nouns have only a plural form when they are used with a particular meaning. They take a plural verb.

Take care of your <u>clothes</u>.
The weather <u>conditions</u> *were the same.*

> ! **BE CAREFUL**
>
> Plural nouns are not usually used after numbers. For example, don't say '~~two clothes~~'
> or '~~two goods~~'.

Some plural nouns refer to single items that have two linked parts: things that people wear or tools that people use. These plural nouns are:

▶ things that people wear

glasses	leggings	pyjamas	trousers
jeans	panties	shorts	
knickers	pants	tights	

▶ things that people use

binoculars	pliers	scissors	tweezers
pincers	scales	shears	

You use **some** in front of these words when you are talking about one item.

I wish I had brought <u>some scissors</u>.

You can also use **a pair of** when you are talking about one item, and **two pairs of**, **three pairs of**, and so on when you are talking about more than one item.

I went out to buy <u>a pair of scissors</u>.
Liza gave me <u>three pairs of jeans</u>.

Many plural nouns lose their '-s' and '-es' endings when they are used in front of other nouns.

...my <u>trouser</u> *pocket.*
... <u>pyjama</u> *trousers.*

However, some plural nouns keep the same form when they are used in front of other nouns.

arms	clothes	jeans
binoculars	glasses	sunglasses

...a <u>glasses</u> *case.*
... <u>clothes</u> *pegs.*

7 collective nouns

Some nouns, called **collective nouns**, refer to a group of people or things.

army	enemy	group	staff
audience	family	herd	team
committee	flock	navy	
company	gang	press	
crew	government	public	

 The singular form of these nouns can be used with a singular or plural verb form, depending on whether the group is seen as one thing or as several things. It is more common to use a plural form in British English. The singular form of the verb is nearly always preferred in American English.

Our <u>family</u> *isn't poor any more.*
My <u>family</u> *are perfectly normal.*

When you are referring back to a collective noun, you usually use a singular pronoun or determiner if you have used a singular verb. You use a plural pronoun or determiner if you have used a plural verb.

The government has said it would wish to do this only if there was no alternative.
The government have made up their minds that they're going to win.

However, plural pronouns and determiners are sometimes used to refer back to a collective noun even when a singular verb has been used. This is done especially in a separate clause.

The team was not always successful but their success often exceeded expectations.
His family was waiting in the next room, but they had not yet heard the news.

 Names of organizations and groups such as football teams also behave like collective nouns in British English, but in American English they are usually regarded as singular.

Liverpool is leading 1–0.
Liverpool are winning.
Sears is struggling to attract shoppers.

> **!** **BE CAREFUL**
>
> Although you can use a plural verb after the singular form of a collective noun, these singular forms do not behave exactly like plural countable nouns. Numbers cannot be used in front of them. For example, you cannot say 'Three crew were killed'. You have to say 'Three of the crew were killed' or 'Three members of the crew were killed'.

Most of the collective nouns listed above have ordinary plural forms, which refer to more than one group. However, **press** (meaning 'newspapers' or 'journalists') and **public** (meaning 'the people of a country') do not have plural forms.

8 **proper nouns**

Names of people, places, organizations, institutions, ships, magazines, books, plays, paintings, and other unique things are **proper nouns** and are spelled with initial capital letters. A proper noun is sometimes used with a determiner but normally has no plural.

→ See **Topic** entries **Names and titles**, **Places**

...Mozart.
...Romeo and Juliet.
...the President of the United States.
...the United Nations.
...the Seine.

9 **compound nouns**

Compound nouns are made up of two or more words. Some are written as separate words, some are written with hyphens between the words, and some have a hyphen between the first two words.

His luggage came sliding towards him on the conveyor belt.
There are many cross-references to help you find what you want.
It can be cleaned with a drop of washing-up liquid.

Some compound nouns can be written in several ways. A COBUILD dictionary will tell you how you should write each compound noun.

→ See **-ing forms** for information on compound nouns ending in *ing*

→ See **Reference** section **Plural forms of nouns** for information on the plurals of compound nouns

10 abstract and concrete nouns

An **abstract noun** is a noun that refers to a quality, idea, or experience rather than something that can be seen or touched.

...a boy or girl with <u>intelligence</u>.
We found Alan weeping with <u>relief</u> and <u>joy</u>.
I am stimulated by <u>conflict</u>.

Abstract nouns are often variable nouns. They behave like countable nouns when they refer to a particular instance of something. Otherwise they behave like uncountable nouns, referring to something in more general terms.

→ See section above on **variable nouns**

The island had been successful in previous <u>conflicts</u>.

A **concrete noun** is a noun that refers to something that can be seen or touched. Nouns referring to objects, animals, and people are usually countable.

...a broad <u>road</u> lined with tall <u>trees</u>.

A few nouns that refer to groups of objects, such as **furniture** and **equipment**, are uncountable.

→ See section above on **uncountable nouns**

Nouns referring to substances are usually uncountable.

There is not enough <u>water</u>.

However, when they refer to a particular type or brand of a substance, they behave like countable nouns.

→ See section above on **mass nouns**

11 nouns followed by prepositions

Some nouns, especially abstract nouns, are often followed by a prepositional phrase to show what they relate to. There is often little or no choice about which preposition to use after a particular noun.

I demanded <u>access to</u> a telephone.
...his <u>authority over</u> them.
...the <u>solution to</u> our energy problem.

▶ The following nouns usually or often have **to** after them:

access	antidote	immunity	resistance
addiction	approach	incitement	return
adherence	aversion	introduction	sequel
affront	contribution	preface	solution
allegiance	damage	prelude	susceptibility
allergy	devotion	recourse	threat
allusion	disloyalty	reference	vulnerability
alternative	exception	relevance	witness
answer	fidelity	reply	

▶ The following nouns usually or often have **for** after them:

admiration	craving	desire	disrespect
appetite	credit	disdain	hunger
aptitude	cure	dislike	love
bid	demand	disregard	need

provision	remedy	substitute	thirst
quest	respect	sympathy	
recipe	responsibility	synonym	
regard	room	taste	

▶ The following nouns usually or often have **on** or **upon** after them:

assault	constraint	embargo	restriction
attack	crackdown	hold	stance
ban	curb	insistence	tax
comment	dependence	reflection	
concentration	effect	reliance	

▶ The following nouns usually or often have **with** after them:

affinity	dealings	familiarity	intersection
collusion	dissatisfaction	identification	sympathy

▶ The following nouns usually or often have **with** or **between** after them:

collision	correspondence	link	relationship
connection	encounter	parity	
contrast	intimacy	quarrel	

Many other nouns are usually or often followed by a particular preposition. The following list shows which preposition follows each noun.

authority over	excerpt from	insurance against	safeguard against
control over	foray into	quotation from	
departure from	freedom from	reaction against	
escape from	grudge against	relapse into	

As you can see from the lists given above, it is often the case that words with a similar meaning are typically followed by the same preposition.

For example, **appetite**, **craving**, **desire**, **hunger**, and **thirst** are all followed by **for**.

Acceleration, **decline**, **fall**, **drop**, and **rise** are all followed by **in**.

now

1 'now'

Now is usually used for contrasting the present with the past.

She gradually built up energy and is now back to normal.
He knew now that he could rely completely on Paul.
Now he felt safe.

2 'right now' and 'just now'

In conversation and in less formal writing, you use **right now** or **just now** to say that a situation exists at present, although it may change in the future.

The new car market is in chaos right now.
I'm awfully busy just now.

You also use **right now** to emphasize that something is happening now.

The crisis is occurring right now.

If you say that something happened **just now**, you mean that it happened a very short time ago.

Did you feel the ship move just now?
I told you a lie just now.

If you intend to do something **now** or **right now**, you intend to do it immediately, without any delay.

He wants you to come and see him now, in his room.
I guess we'd better do it right now.

! BE CAREFUL
Don't use 'right now' or 'just now' in formal writing.

---

nowhere

You use **nowhere** to say that there is no place where something happens or can happen.

There's nowhere for either of us to go.
There was nowhere to hide.

Nowhere is sometimes put first for emphasis, followed by **be** or an auxiliary verb and the subject of the clause.

Nowhere is language a more serious issue than in Hawaii.
Nowhere have I seen this written down.

! BE CAREFUL
You don't usually use another negative word with 'nowhere'. Don't say, for example, 'I couldn't find her nowhere'. You say 'I couldn't find her **anywhere**'.

I changed my mind and decided not to go anywhere.

---

number

1 'a number of'

A **number of** things or people means several things or people. You use a plural form of a verb after **a number of**.

A number of key questions remain unanswered.
An increasing number of women are learning self-defence.

2 'the number of'

When you talk about **the number of** people or things of a particular kind, you are talking about an actual number. After **the number of** you use a singular form of a verb.

In the last 30 years, the number of electricity consumers has risen by 50 per cent.

When you use **number** in either of these ways, you can use **large** or **small** with it.

His private papers included a large number of unpaid bills.
The problem affects a relatively small number of people.

However, don't use 'big' or 'little' with **number** in sentences like these.

Oo

object

Object can be a noun or a verb. When it is a noun, it is pronounced /ˈɒbdʒekt/. When it is a verb, it is pronounced /əbˈdʒekt/.

1 used as a noun

You can refer to anything that has a fixed shape and that is not alive as an **object**.

I looked at the shabby, black <u>object</u> he was carrying.
The statue was an <u>object</u> of great beauty.

A person's **object** is their aim or purpose.

My <u>object</u> was to publish a new book on Shakespeare.
The <u>object</u>, of course, is to persuade people to remain at their jobs.

2 used as a verb

If you **object to** something, you do not approve of it, or you say that you do not approve of it.

Residents can <u>object to</u> these developments if they wish.
Many people <u>objected to</u> the film.

If you **object to doing** something, you say that you don't think you should do it.

I <u>object to paying</u> for services that should be free.
This group did not <u>object to returning</u>.

You use an *-ing* form, not an infinitive, after **object to**.

If it is clear what you are referring to, you can use **object** without 'to'.

The men <u>objected</u> and the women supported their protest.
Other workers will still have the right to <u>object</u>.

If you want to say why someone does not approve of something or does not agree with something, you can use **object** with a *that*-clause. For example, you can say 'They wanted me to do some extra work, but I **objected that** I had too much to do already'. This is a fairly formal use.

The others quite rightly <u>object that he is holding back the work</u>.

GRAMMAR FINDER

Objects

1 The direct object

The **object** of a verb or clause is a noun phrase that refers to the person or thing that is involved in an action but does not perform the action. The object comes after the verb. It is sometimes called the **direct object**.

He closed <u>the door</u>.
It was dark by the time they reached <u>their house</u>.
Some of the women noticed <u>me</u>.

2 **The indirect object**

Some verbs have two objects. For example in the sentence 'I gave John the book', 'the book' is the direct object, and 'John' is the **indirect object**. The **indirect object** usually refers to the person who benefits from an action or receives something as a result of it.

You can put an **indirect object** in front of the direct object or in a prepositional phrase after the direct object.

Dad gave <u>me</u> a car.
He handed his room key to <u>the receptionist</u>.

→ See **Verbs**

3 **prepositional objects**

Prepositions also have objects. The noun phrase after a preposition is sometimes called the **prepositional object**.

I climbed up <u>the tree</u>.
Miss Burns looked calmly at <u>Marianne</u>.
Woodward finished the second page and passed it to <u>the editor</u>.

→ See **Prepositions**

obligation – duty

1 **'obligation' and 'duty'**

If you say that someone has an **obligation to do** something or a **duty to do** something, you mean that they ought to do it, because it is their responsibility. When **obligation** and **duty** are used like this, they have the same meaning.

When teachers assign homework, students usually feel an <u>obligation to do</u> it.
Perhaps it was his <u>duty to tell</u> the police what he had seen.

2 **'duties'**

Your **duties** are the things that you do as part of your job.

She has been given a reasonable time to learn her <u>duties</u>.
They also have to carry out many administrative <u>duties</u>.

! BE CAREFUL

Don't refer to the things that you do as part of your job as 'obligations'.

obtain

1 **'obtain'**

If you **obtain** something that you want or need, you get it.

I made another attempt to <u>obtain</u> employment.
He <u>had obtained</u> the papers during his visits to Berlin.

2 **'get'**

'Obtain' is a formal word. You don't usually use it in conversation. Instead you use **get**.

I <u>got</u> a job at the factory.
He had been having trouble <u>getting</u> a hotel room.

In writing, **obtain** is often used in the passive.

All the above items can be obtained from most supermarkets.
You need to know where this kind of information can be obtained.

> **!** BE CAREFUL
>
> You don't usually use 'get' in the passive. Don't say, for example, '~~Maps can be got from the Tourist Office~~'. Say 'Maps **can be obtained** from the Tourist Office' or, in conversation, '**You can get** maps from the Tourist Office'.

occasion – opportunity – chance

1 'occasion'

An **occasion** is a particular time when something happens.

I remember the occasion very well.
There are occasions when you must refuse.

You often say that something happens **on** a particular occasion.

I think it would be better if I went alone on this occasion.
I met him only on one occasion.

An **occasion** is also an important event, ceremony, or celebration.

It was a wonderful end to an unforgettable occasion.
They have fixed the date for the big occasion.

2 'opportunity' and 'chance'

Don't use **occasion** to refer to a situation in which it is possible for someone to do something. Instead, use **opportunity** or **chance**.

I am very grateful to have had the opportunity of working with Paul.
She put the phone down before I had a chance to reply.

→ See **chance**

occasionally

→ See **Adverbs and adverbials** for words used to indicate frequency

occur

You can say that an event **occurs**.

The accident occurred at 8:40 a.m.
Mistakes are bound to occur.

However, you only use **occur** to talk about events which are not planned.

Occur is a fairly formal word. In conversation and in less formal writing, you usually say that an event **happens**.

You might have noticed what happened on Tuesday.
A curious thing has happened.

→ See **happen**

> **!** BE CAREFUL
>
> Don't say that a planned event 'occurs' or 'happens'. Say that it **takes place**.

The first meeting of this committee took place on 9 January.
These lessons took place twice a week.

Don't use 'occur to' to say that someone is affected by an event. Don't say, for example, '~~I wonder what's occurred to Jane~~'. Say 'I wonder what**'s happened to** Jane'.

She no longer cared what happened to her.
It couldn't have happened to a nicer man.

of

1 possession and other relationships

Of is used for showing possession. It can also be used to show other types of relationship between people or things.

It was the home of a schoolteacher.
She was the sister of the Duke of Urbino.
At the top of the hill Jackson paused for breath.

You can use **of** in front of a possessive pronoun such as **mine**, **his**, or **theirs**. You do this to show that someone is one of a group of people or things connected with a particular person. For example, instead of saying 'He is one of my friends', you can say 'He is a friend **of mine**.'

He's a very good friend of ours.
I talked to a colleague of yours recently.

You can use **of** like this in front of other possessives.

He's a friend of my mother's.
She was a cousin of Lorna Cook's.

 The 's is sometimes omitted, especially in American English.

He's a close friend of the President.

! **BE CAREFUL**

Don't use 'of' in front of a personal pronoun such as 'me', 'him', or 'them'. Don't say, for example, '~~the sister of me~~'. Instead you use a **possessive determiner** such as **my**, **his**, or **their**.

My sister visited us last week.
He had his hands in his pockets.
Consider the future of our society.

→ See **Possessive determiners**

You don't usually use 'of' in front of short noun phrases. Instead you use **'s** or the apostrophe **'**. For example, instead of saying 'the car of my friend', you say '**my friend's** car'.

I can hear Raoul's voice.
This is Mr Duffield's sister.
We watched the President's speech.
The notice is in all our colleagues' offices.

→ See **'s**

2 descriptions

You can sometimes use **of** and a noun phrase to describe something, instead of using an adjective and a grading adverb. For example, instead of saying that something is 'very interesting', you can say that it is **of great interest**. This is a rather formal use.

It will be of great interest to you.
The result is of little importance.

When you use an adjective to comment on an action, you can put **of** and a pronoun after the adjective. The pronoun refers to the person who has performed the action. For example, you can say 'That was **stupid of you**'.

It was brave of them.
I'm sorry, that was silly of me.

3 works of art

Don't talk about a book 'of' a particular author, or a piece of music 'of' a particular composer. Instead, use **by**.

Have you read the latest book by Hilda Offen?
We'll hear some pieces by Mozart.

Similarly, you use **by** to indicate who painted a picture. A picture **of** a particular person shows that person in the picture.

We saw the famous painting by Rubens, The Straw Hat.
The museum owns a 16th century painting of Henry VIII.

4 places

You can talk about the capital **of** a country, state, or province.

We went to Ulan Bator, the capital of Mongolia.

However, don't talk about a town or village 'of' a particular country or area. Instead, use **in**.

He lives in a small town in Southern Ecuador.
My favourite town in Shropshire is Ludlow.

You also use **in**, rather than 'of', after superlatives. For example, you talk about 'the tallest building **in** Europe'. Don't say 'the tallest building of Europe'.

These are the biggest lizards in the world.

→ See **Comparative and superlative adjectives**

offer – give – invite

1 'offer'

If you **offer** something to someone, you ask them if they would like to have it or use it.

He offered me a chocolate. I shook my head.

2 'give'

If you put something in someone's hand expecting them to take it, and they do take it, don't say that you 'offer' it to them. You say that you **give** it to them.

She gave Minnie the keys.
He gave me a red jewellery box.

3 **'offer to'**

If you **offer to do** something, you say that you are willing to do it.

He _offered to take_ her home in a taxi.
I _offered to answer_ any questions.

4 **'invite'**

If someone asks you to do something that they think you will want to do, don't say that they 'offer' you to do it. You say that they **invite** you to do it.

I _was invited_ to attend future meetings.
She _invited_ me to come for dinner.

often

If something happens **often**, it happens many times.

1 **position in clause**

▶ If there is no auxiliary verb, you put **often** in front of the verb, unless the verb is **be**. If the verb is **be**, you put **often** after it.

We _often get_ very cold winters here.
They _were often_ hungry.

▶ If there is an auxiliary verb, you put **often** after it.

She _has often written_ about human rights.

▶ If there is more than one auxiliary verb, you put **often** after the first one.

The idea _had often been discussed_.

▶ If a sentence is fairly short, you can put **often** at the end of it.

He's in London _often_.

▶ In writing, **often** is sometimes put at the beginning of a long sentence.

Often in the evening the little girl would be sitting at my knee while I held the baby.

! BE CAREFUL

Don't use 'often' to talk about something that happens several times within a short period of time. Don't say, for example, 'I often phoned her yesterday'. You say 'I phoned her **several times** yesterday' or 'I **kept phoning** her yesterday'.

That fear was expressed _several times_ last week.
Rather than correct her, I _kept trying_ to change the subject.

→ See **Adverbs and adverbials** for a graded list of words used to indicate frequency

2 **other uses of 'often'**

You use **often** with **how** when you are asking about the number of times that something happens or happened.

How often do you need to weigh the baby?
How often have you done this programme?

Often can also be used for saying that something is done just once by many people, or that something is true about many people.

People _often_ asked me why I didn't ride more during the trip.
Older people _often_ catch this disease.

old

1 'old'

Old is most commonly used for describing the age of a person or thing. For example, you say that someone 'is forty years **old**'.

Legally, witnesses must be at least fourteen years old.
They found bits of bone which are three-and-a-half million years old.

You can also describe someone as, for example, 'a **forty-year-old** man'. Don't say 'a forty-years-old man'.

She married a sixty-year-old man.
Sue lives with her five-year-old son John in the West Country.

You can also say that someone is 'a man of forty'. However, don't say 'a man of forty years old'.

Maya is a tall, strong woman of thirty.
Actually, he looks good for a man of 62.

→ See **Topic** entry **Age**

2 asking about age

You use **old** after **how** when you are asking about the age of a person or thing.

'How old are you?' – 'I'll be eight next year.'
'How old is the Taj Mahal?' – 'It was built in about 1640, I think.'

3 another meaning of 'old'

You can also use **old** to describe someone who has lived a very long time.

She was a very old lady.
He was very thin and he looked really old.

4 'elderly'

This use of **old** can sometimes sound rude. **Elderly** is a more polite word.

I look after my elderly mother.
Like many elderly people, Mrs Carstairs could remember voices better than faces.

You can talk about old people as **the elderly**.

This is one of the many organizations which help the elderly.

5 old friends

An **old** friend is someone who has been your friend for a long time. He or she is not necessarily an old person.

Some of us took the opportunity to visit old friends.

6 'old' used for describing objects

An **old** building or other object was built or made a long time ago.

The museum is a massive old building.
The drawers were full of old clothes.

7 'former'

Old can sometimes mean 'former'. For example, your '**old** teacher' is someone that used to be your teacher. He or she is not necessarily an old person.

Jane returned to her old boyfriend.
I still like to visit my old school.

on

1 used for saying where something is

On is usually a preposition. You use **on** to say where someone or something is by mentioning the object or surface that is under them.

When I came back, she was sitting on the stairs.
There was a photograph of a beautiful girl on Deepak's desk.

On is used in some other ways to say where someone or something is. For example, you use it to mention an area of land where someone works or lives, such as a farm, building site, or housing estate.

He briefly worked on a building site in Seoul.

You also use **on** to mention an island where something exists or happens.

She lives on a Caribbean island.

→ See **in** for a common way of saying where something is, **at** for a common way of saying where something is

2 used for saying where something goes

You can use **on** to say where someone or something falls or is put.

He fell on the floor.
I put a hand on his shoulder.

Onto is used in a similar way.

→ See **onto**

You use **on** after **get** to say that someone enters a bus, train, or ship.

George got on the bus with us.

→ See **go into – get into – get on**

3 used for talking about time

You say that something happens **on** a particular day or date.

She came to see the play on the following Friday.
Caro was born on April 10th.

→ See **Reference** section **Days and dates**

You can sometimes use **on** to say that one thing happens immediately after another. For example, if something happens **on** someone's arrival, it happens immediately after they arrive.

'It's so unfair,' Clarissa said on her return.

4 used as an adverb

On is sometimes an adverb, usually showing that something continues to happen or be done.

She walked on, silently thinking.
I flew on to California.

once

1 meaning 'only one time'

If something happens **once**, it happens only one time.

I've been out with him once, that's all.
I have never forgotten her, though I saw her only once.

When **once** is used with this meaning, it usually goes at the end of a clause.

2 used about the past

You also use **once** to say that something happened at some time in the past.

I once investigated this story and I don't think it's true.
'Once I saw a shooting star here,' Jeffrey says.

When **once** is used with this meaning, it usually goes in front of a verb or at the beginning of a clause.

You also use **once** to say that something was true in the past, although it is no longer true.

These walls were once brightly coloured.
She was a teacher once.

When **once** is used with this meaning, it usually goes after **be** or an auxiliary verb, or at the end of a clause.

! BE CAREFUL

Don't use 'once' to show that something will happen at some time in the future. Instead you use **one day** for events in the distant future, or **sometime** for things that might happen fairly soon.

One day, you'll be very glad we stopped you.
I'll give you a ring sometime.

3 'at once'

If you do something **at once**, you do it immediately.

She stopped playing at once.
I knew at once that something was wrong.

---

one

1 used instead of a noun phrase

You can use **one** instead of a noun phrase beginning with **a** when it is clear what sort of thing you are talking about. For example, instead of saying 'If you want a drink, I'll get you a drink', you say 'If you want a drink, I'll get you **one**'.

Although she wasn't a rich customer, she looked and acted like one.
The cupboards were empty except for one at the top of the bookshelves.

! BE CAREFUL

You can't use a plural form of 'one' in this kind of sentence. Don't say, for example, 'If you like grapes, I'll get you ones'. Say 'If you like grapes, I'll get you **some**'.

The shelves contained Daisy's books, mostly novels but some on history and philosophy too.
We need more helicopters. There are some, but we need more.

2 used instead of a noun

You can use **one** or **ones** instead of a countable noun when the noun comes after an adjective. For example, instead of saying 'I've had this car a long time, and I'm thinking of getting a new car', you say 'I've had this car a long time, and I'm thinking of getting **a new one**'.

I got this trumpet for thirty pounds. It's quite a good one.
This idea has become a very popular one.
We made money from buying old houses and building new ones.

You can also use **one** or **ones** instead of a countable noun in front of a relative clause or a prepositional phrase.

Of all the subjects, science was the one I loved best.
Could I see that map again – the one with lines across it?

You can use **one** instead of a singular countable noun when the noun comes immediately after any determiner except 'a'. For example, instead of saying 'I bought these masks when I was in Africa. That mask came from Kenya', you say 'I bought these masks when I was in Africa. **That one** came from Kenya'.

We need to buy a new car. This one's too small.
He took the glasses and wrapped each one carefully.
She had a bowl of soup, then went back for another one.

! BE CAREFUL

Don't use 'the one' in front of 'of' and a name. Don't say, for example, '~~This is my mug.~~ ~~That's the one of Jane~~'. You say 'This is my mug. That's **Jane's**'.

He has a northern accent like Brian's.

→ See **one – you – we – they**

---

one – you – we – they

1 'one'

One is sometimes an impersonal pronoun, showing that something is generally done or should generally be done.

One doesn't talk about politics at parties.

You can also use the possessive determiner **one's** and the reflexive pronoun **oneself**.

Naturally, one wants only the best for one's children.
We all understood the fear of making a fool of oneself.

One, **one's**, and **oneself** are fairly formal. Here are some other ways in which you can say that something is generally done or should be done:

2 'you'

You can use **you**, **your**, **yours** and **yourself**, as we usually do in this book.

There are things that have to be done and you do them and you never talk about them.
Ignoring your neighbours is rude.

3 'we'

You can use **we**, **us**, **our**, **ours**, and **ourselves** to say that something is generally done by a group of people that includes yourself.

We say things in the heat of an argument that we don't really mean.
There are things we can all do to make ourselves and our children happier.

4 'they'

They can sometimes mean people in general, or a group of people whose identity is not actually stated.

They found the body in the river.

Some people use **they** when they are mentioning a saying or repeating a piece of gossip.

They say that the camera never lies – but it doesn't always show the full picture.
He made a fortune, they say.

They, **them**, **their**, **theirs**, and **themselves** are also used to refer to words such as **everyone** and **anyone**, **person**, **child**, and **student**.

→ See **he – she – they**

5 'people'

You can use **people**. This is also a fairly common use.

People shouldn't leave jobs unfinished.
I don't think people should make promises they don't mean to keep.

6 the passive

Instead of using one of these words and an active verb, you can sometimes use a passive verb. This is a fairly common use in formal writing.

If there is increasing pain, medical advice should be taken.
Bookings must be made before the end of December.

one another

→ See **each other – one another**

only

Only can be an adjective or an adverb.

1 used as an adjective

You use **only** in front of a noun or **one** to say that something is true about one person, thing, or group and not true about anyone or anything else. In front of **only** you put **the** or a possessive.

Grace was the only survivor.
I was the only one listening.
'Have you a spare one?' – 'No, it's my only copy unfortunately.'

When **only** has this meaning, you must use a noun or **one** after it. You cannot say, for example, 'He was the only to escape'. If you don't want to use a more specific noun, you can use **person** or **thing**. You can say, for example, 'He was **the only person** to escape'.

He was the only person allowed to issue documents of that sort.
It was the only thing they could do.

If you use another adjective or a number, you put **only** in front of it.

The only English city he enjoyed working in was Manchester.
So I probably have the only three copies of the album in existence.

'Only' is not normally used after **an**. There is one common exception: if you say that someone is **an only child**, you mean that they have no brothers or sisters.

As an only child she is accustomed to adult company.

2 used as an adverb

Only is used as an adverb to say that something is the one thing that is done, that happens, or that is relevant in a particular situation, in contrast to all the other things that are not done, do not happen, or are not relevant.

▸ If **only** applies to the subject of a clause, you put it in front of the subject.

Only his close friends knew how much he worried about his daughters.
We believe that only a completely different approach will be effective.

▸ If the verb is **be**, you put **only** after it.

There is only one train that goes from Denmark to Sweden by night.

▸ If the verb is not 'be' and **only** does not apply to the subject, you usually put it in front of the verb or after the first auxiliary verb, regardless of what it applies to. For example, instead of saying 'I see my brother only at weekends', you usually say 'I **only** see my brother at weekends'.

Drivers only find serious traffic jams in the city centre.
We could only choose two of them.
New technology will only be introduced by agreement with the unions.

3 used for emphasis

However, if you want to be quite clear or emphatic, you put **only** immediately in front of the word, word phrase, or clause it applies to.

He played only classical music.
You may borrow only one item at a time.
We film only when something interesting is found.

For extra emphasis, you can put **only** after the word or word phrase that it applies to.

We insisted on being interviewed by women journalists only.
This strategy was used once only.

In writing and formal speech, you can put **only** at the beginning of a sentence, followed by the word, phrase, or clause it applies to. After this word, phrase, or clause, you put an auxiliary verb or **be** followed by the subject of the main clause.

Only here was it safe to prepare and handle hot drinks.
Only then did Ginny realize that she still hadn't phoned her mother.

Another way of emphasizing is to start with '**It is only...**' or '**It was only...**' and the word or words that you want to emphasize. You put the rest of the sentence in a *that*-clause.

It was only much later that I realized what had happened.
It was only when he started to take photographs that he was stopped.

4 'not only'

You use **not only** with **but** or **but also** as a way of linking words or word groups.

→ See **not only**

onto

You usually use the preposition **onto** to say where someone or something falls or is put.

He fell down onto the floor.
Place the bread onto a large piece of clean white cloth.

After many verbs you can use either **onto** or **on** with the same meaning.

I fell with a crash onto the road.
He fell on the floor with a thud.
She poured some shampoo onto my hair.
Carlo poured ketchup on the beans.

However, after verbs meaning **climb** or **lift** you should use **onto**, rather than 'on'.

She climbed up onto his knee.
The little boy was helped onto the piano stool.

If you hold **onto** something, you put your hand round it or against it in order to avoid falling. After verbs meaning **hold**, you use **onto** as a preposition and **on** as an adverb.

She had to hold onto the edge of the table.
I couldn't put up my umbrella and hold on at the same time.
We were both hanging onto the side of the boat.
He had to hang on to avoid being washed overboard.

Onto is sometimes written as two words **on to**.

She sank on to a chair.

open

Open can be a verb or an adjective.

1 used as a verb

If you **open** something such as a door, you move it so that it no longer covers a hole or gap.

She opened the door with her key.
He opened the window and looked out.

> **!** **BE CAREFUL**
>
> When you use **open** with a person as the subject, you must put an object after it. Don't say, for example, 'I went to the door and opened'. You say 'I went to the door and **opened it**'.
>
> *I went to the front door, opened it, and looked out.*

2 used as an adjective

When a door or window is not covering the hole or gap it is intended to cover, you say that it is **open**.

The door was open.
He was sitting by the open window of the office.

> **!** **BE CAREFUL**
>
> When a door or window is in this position, don't say that it is 'opened'. **Opened** is the past form or -ed participle of the verb **open**. You only use it when you are describing the action of opening a door or window.
>
> *The front door was opened, then suddenly shut again.*

3 used after other verbs

Open can be used after other verbs of position or movement.

The doors of the ninth-floor rooms hung open.
Bernard pushed the door fully open.
He noticed the way the drawer slid open.

Open is one of several words that can be used after verbs of position or movement like this. Others are **closed**, **shut**, **free**, **loose**, **straight**, and **upright**. These words are sometimes considered to be adverbs and sometimes adjectives.

! BE CAREFUL

Don't use **open** as a verb or adjective to talk about electrical equipment. For example, if someone makes some electrical equipment work by pressing a switch or turning a knob, don't say that they 'open' it. Say that they **put** it **on**, **switch** it **on** or **turn** it **on**.

Do you mind if I put the light on?
I went across and switched on the TV.
I turned on the radio as I did every morning.

---

opinion

Your **opinion** of something is what you think about it.

We would like to have your opinion.
The students wanted to express their opinions.

When you want to show whose opinion you are giving, you can use an expression such as '**in my opinion**', '**in Sarah's opinion**', or '**in the opinion of the voters...**'.

In my opinion, there are four key problems that have to be addressed.
In Lee's opinion, the protests were 'unnecessary'.
In the opinion of the Court of Appeal the sentence was too severe.

→ See **according to**

In formal speech or writing, people sometimes say '**It is my opinion that...**' or '**It is our opinion that...**'.

It is my opinion that high school students should have the vote.

! BE CAREFUL

Don't say 'To my opinion...' or 'According to my opinion...'.

→ See **point of view – view – opinion**

---

opposite

Opposite can be a preposition, a noun, or an adjective.

1 used as a preposition

If one building or room is **opposite** another, they are separated from each other by a street or corridor.

The hotel is opposite a railway station.
The bathroom was located opposite my room.

If two people are **opposite** each other, they are facing each other, for example when they are sitting at the same table.

Lynn was sitting opposite him.
He drank half his coffee, still staring at the Englishman opposite him.

 Speakers of American English usually say **across from** rather than 'opposite' in both of the above senses.

Stinson has rented a home across from his parents.
He took a seat on one side of the table, and Judy sat across from him.

2 used as a noun

If two things or people are totally different from each other in some way, you can say that one is **the opposite of** the other.

The opposite of right is wrong.
He was the exact opposite of Ariel, of course.

You can use **the opposite** without 'of', if it is clear what you are making a contrast with.

Well, whatever he says you can be sure he's thinking the opposite.
They believe the statement because the opposite is unimaginable.

! BE CAREFUL

You cannot express difference by saying that one thing or person is 'opposite' another.

3 used as an adjective

Opposite can be an adjective either in front of a noun or after a noun, but with different meanings.

You use **opposite** in front of a noun when you are mentioning one of two sides of something.

I was moved to a room on the opposite side of the corridor.
On the opposite side of the room a telephone rang.

You also use **opposite** in front of a noun when you are talking about something that is totally different from something else in some way.

Holmes took the opposite point of view.
Too much pressure would produce overheating, whereas too little would produce the opposite result.

You use **opposite** after a noun when you are mentioning someone or something that is on the other side of a street, corridor, room, or table from yourself.

The elderly woman opposite glanced up at the window.
In one of the new houses opposite, a party was in progress.

A building can be referred to as, for example, 'the house on **the opposite** side of the street' or 'the house **opposite**'. Don't refer to it as 'the opposite house'.

4 'opposed'

Don't confuse **opposite** with **opposed**. If someone is **opposed to** something, they disagree with it or disapprove of it.

I am opposed to capital punishment.

or

1 basic uses

You use **or** when you are mentioning two or more alternatives or possibilities. You use **or** to link words, phrases, or clauses.

Would you like some coffee or tea, Dr Floyd?
It is better to delay planting if the ground is very wet or frosty.
Do you want to go to the beach or spend time at home?

2 used with negative words

You use **or** instead of 'and' after using a negative word. For example, say 'I do not like coffee **or** tea'. Don't say '~~I do not like coffee and tea~~'.

The situation is not fair on the children or their parents.
It is not poisonous and will not harm any animals or birds.
The house is not large or glamorous.

3 verb agreement

When you link two or more nouns using **or**, you use a plural verb after plural countable nouns, and a singular verb after singular countable or uncountable nouns.

Even minor changes or developments were reported in the press.
If your son or daughter is failing at school, it is no use being angry.

4 'either ... or'

You use **either** with **or** when you are mentioning two alternatives and you want to say that no other alternatives are possible. **Either** goes in front of the first alternative and **or** goes in front of the second one.

Replace it with a broadband access device, either rented or costing around $500.

→ See **either ... or**

After **neither**, you usually use **nor**.

He speaks neither English nor German.

→ See **neither ... nor**

5 linking more than two items

When you are linking more than two items, you usually only put **or** in front of the last one. After each of the others you put a comma. Often the comma is omitted in front of **or**.

Flights leave from Heathrow, Manchester, Gatwick, or Glasgow.
Students are asked to take another course in English, science or mathematics.

6 beginning a sentence with 'or'

You don't normally put **or** at the beginning of a sentence, but you can sometimes do so when you are reporting what someone says or thinks.

I may go home and have a steak. Or I may have some spaghetti.

7 used for correcting

You can use **or** when you are correcting a mistake you have made, or when you think of a better way of saying something.

We were considered by the others to be mad, or at least very strange.

oral

→ See **aural – oral**

ordinary

→ See **usual – usually**

or else

→ See **else**

other

1 'the other'

When you are talking about two people or things and have already referred to one of them, you refer to the second one as **the other** or **the other one**.

They had two little daughters, one a baby, the other a girl of twelve.
He blew out one of the candles and moved the other one.

2 'the others'

When you are talking about several people or things and have already referred to one or more of them, you usually refer to the remaining ones as **the others**.

Jack and the others paid no attention.
First, concentrate only on the important tasks, then move on to the others.

3 'others'

When you have been talking about some people or things of a particular type, you refer to more people or things of this type as **others**.

Some players are better than others in these weather conditions.
The couple had one biological child and adopted three others.

! BE CAREFUL

Don't use 'the' with **others** in sentences like these. Don't say, for example, 'Some players are better than the others'.

4 'another'

When you have been talking about people or things of a particular type, you can refer to one more person or thing of this type as **another** or **another one**.

I saw one girl whispering to another.
There was something wrong with the car he had hired and he had to hire another one.

→ See **another**

5 used in front of nouns

The other, **other**, and **another** can be used in a similar way in front of countable nouns.

The other girls followed, thinking there may be some news for them too.
The roof was covered with straw and other materials.
He opened another shop last month.

ought to

→ See **should – ought to**

out

1 'out of'

When you go **out of** a place or get **out of** something such as a vehicle, you leave it, so that you are no longer inside it.

She rushed out of the house.
He got out of the car.
She's just got out of bed.

In conversation and in less formal writing, you can use **out** without 'of' in sentences like these.

'Come on, get out the car,' she said.

! BE CAREFUL

Some people think this is incorrect. In formal English, you must use **out of**.

→ See **go out – get out – get off** for more information about 'go out' and 'get out'

You don't usually use 'from' after **out**. However, you use **from** in front of some other prepositions such as **behind** or **under**.

He came out from behind the table.

2 'out' used as an adverb

You can use **out** as an adverb to say that someone leaves a place.

I ran out and slammed the door.
Why don't we go out into the garden?

If someone is **out**, they are not at home.

He came when I was out.

outdoors – outdoor

1 'outdoors'

Outdoors is an adverb. If something happens **outdoors**, it does not happen inside a building.

He spent a lot of his time outdoors.
School classes were held outdoors.

When someone goes out of a building, you don't usually say that they go 'outdoors'. You say that they go **outside**.

→ See **outside**

2 'outdoor'

Outdoor is an adjective used in front of a noun. You use it to describe things or activities that exist or happen in the open air, rather than inside a building.

There is also an outdoor play area.
If you enjoy outdoor activities, this is the trip for you.

outside

Outside can be a preposition or an adverb.

1 used as a preposition

When someone or something is close to a building but not actually inside it, you say that they are **outside** the building.

I parked outside the hotel.
There are queues for jobs outside the main offices.

! BE CAREFUL

Don't say that someone is 'outside of' a building.

2 used as an adverb

You can also say that someone or something is **outside** or that something is happening **outside**.

The shouting outside grew louder.
Please could you come and fetch me in 20 minutes? I'll be waiting outside.

When you go **outside**, you leave a building and go into the open air, but stay quite close to the building.

When they went outside, snow was falling.
Go outside and play for a bit.

If you leave a building in order to go some distance from it, don't say that you go 'outside'. Say that you go **out**.

When it got dark he went out.
I have to go out. I'll be back late tonight.

You can also say that someone is **outside** when they are close to a room, for example in a hallway or corridor.

I'd better wait outside in the corridor.

3 another meaning of 'outside'

You can also talk about someone or something being **outside** a country. When **outside** is used like this, it does not have 'near' as part of its meaning. If you are **outside** a country, you can be near the country or a long way away from it.

You'll know this if you have lived outside Britain.

---

over

Over is a preposition used in several different ways.

1 position

If one thing is **over** another thing, it is directly above it.

I had reached the little bridge over the stream.
His name is on the monument over the west door.

2 movement

If you go **over** something, you cross it and get to the other side.

Sayeed climbed over the fence.
The sea was rough on the way back over the Channel.

3 age

If someone is **over** a particular age, they are older than that age.

She was well over fifty.

4 time

If something happens **over** a period of time, it happens during that time.

He'd had flu over Christmas.
There have been many changes over the last few years.

If you do something **over** a meal, you do it while you are eating the meal.

It's often easier to discuss difficult ideas over lunch.

→ See **above – over**

overseas

Overseas can be an adverb or an adjective.

1 used as an adverb

If you go **overseas**, you visit a foreign country which is separated from your own country by sea.

Roughly 4 million Americans travel overseas each year.

2 used as an adjective

Overseas is used in front of a noun to describe things relating to countries across the sea from your own country. **Overseas** has a similar meaning to 'foreign', but is more formal. You use it especially when talking about trade, finance, and travel.

We organize major programmes of overseas aid.
I met him on a recent overseas visit.

> **! BE CAREFUL**
>
> Don't use 'overseas' after 'be' with this meaning. If you say that someone **is overseas**, you do not mean that they are foreign; you mean that they are visiting a foreign country.

own

1 used after a possessive

If you want to emphasize that something belongs or relates to a particular person or thing, you use **own** after a possessive.

These people have total confidence in their own ability.
Now the nuclear industry's own experts support these claims.

2 'own' with a number

If you are also using a number, you put the number after **own**. You say, for example, 'She had given the same advice to her **own three** children'. Don't say 'She had given the same advice to her three own children'.

She was younger than my own two daughters.

3 'of your own'

Don't use **own** after 'an'. Don't say, for example, ~~'I've got an own place'~~. You say 'I've got **my own** place' or 'I've got a place **of my own**'.

By this time Laura had got her own radio.
It's a clear lemonade with little flavour of its own.

4 emphasizing 'own'

You can use **very** in front of **own** for emphasis.

We heard the prison's very own pop group.
Accountants have a language of their very own.

5 'own' without a noun

You can use **own** without a noun after it, when it is clear what you are talking about. However, there must always be a possessive in front of it.

These people's ideas were the same as their own.
I was given no clothes other than my own to wear.

6 'on your own'

If you are **on your own**, you are alone.

She lived on her own.

If you do something **on your own**, you do it without any help from anyone else.

We can't solve this problem on our own.

Pp

package

→ See **parcel – package – packet**

packet

→ See **parcel – package – packet**

pair – couple

1 'a pair of'

A pair of things are two things of the same size and shape that are used together, such as shoes.

Someone has dropped a pair of gloves.
He bought a pair of hiking boots.

When you use **a pair of** like this, you can use either a singular or a plural form of a verb.

He wore a pair of shoes that were given to him by his mother.
A pair of shoes was stolen.

You also use **a pair of** to refer to something that has two main parts of the same size and shape, such as trousers, glasses, or scissors.

She has a new pair of glasses.
Do you have a pair of scissors I could use?

When you use **a pair of** like this, you use a singular form of a verb.

Who does this pair of jeans belong to?
A good pair of binoculars is essential for watching birds.

2 'a couple of'

In conversation and informal writing, you can refer to two people or things as **a couple of** people or things.

I asked a couple of friends to help me.
We played a couple of games of tennis.

You use a plural form of a verb with **a couple of**.

A couple of guys were standing by the car.
On the table were a couple of mobile phones.

❗ BE CAREFUL

Don't use 'a couple of' in formal writing.

3 referring to two people as a 'couple'

A **couple** consists of two people who have a romantic or sexual relationship, for example a husband and wife or boyfriend and girlfriend.

In Venice we met a South African couple.
Married couples will get tax benefits.

You usually use a plural form of a verb with **couple**.

A couple <u>were</u> sitting together on the bench.

pants – shorts

In British English, **pants** are a piece of clothing worn by men, women, or children under their other clothes. Pants have two holes to put your legs through and elastic round the waist or hips to keep them up.

Men's pants are sometimes referred to as **underpants**. Women's pants are sometimes referred to as **panties** or **knickers**.

 In American English, a piece of clothing like this for men is usually referred to as **shorts** or **underpants**. For women, they are usually called **panties**.

 In American English, the word **pants** is used to refer to men's or women's trousers.

He wore brown corduroy <u>pants</u> and a white cotton shirt.

In both British and American English, **shorts** are also trousers with very short legs that people wear in hot weather or for taking part in sports.

I usually wear <u>shorts</u> and a T-shirt when I play tennis.

Both **pants** and **shorts** are plural nouns. You use a plural form of a verb with them.

The pants <u>were</u> white with a lace trim.
His grey shorts <u>were</u> far too big.

> **!** **BE CAREFUL**
>
> Don't say '<s>a pants</s>' or '<s>a shorts</s>'. You can say **a pair of pants** or **a pair of shorts**.
> *It doesn't take long to choose <u>a pair of pants</u>.*
> *He is wearing <u>a pair of shorts</u> and a T-shirt.*

You use a singular form of a verb with **a pair of pants** or **a pair of shorts**.

Why <u>is</u> this pair of pants on the floor?

paper

Paper is a material that you write things on or wrap things in.

Bring a pencil and some <u>paper</u>.

You can refer to several sheets of paper with information on them as **papers**.

This filing cabinet is where we keep important <u>papers</u>.

Don't refer to a single sheet of paper as '<s>a paper</s>'. You refer to it as a **sheet of paper** or, if it is small, a **piece of paper**.

He wrote his name at the top of a blank <u>sheet of paper</u>.
The floor was covered in little <u>pieces of paper</u>.

A newspapers is often referred to as a **paper**.

Dad was reading the daily <u>paper</u>.
His picture was in the <u>papers</u>.

parcel – package – packet

1 'parcel' and 'package'

A **parcel** or **package** is an object or group of objects wrapped in paper, that can be carried somewhere or sent by post. The two words have almost exactly the same meaning in British English, but a **parcel** usually has a more regular shape than a **package**.

Charities sent parcels of food and clothes to the refugees.
I am taking this package to the post office.

 In American English, **package** is usually used rather than 'parcel'.

2 'packet'

In British English, a **packet** is a small container in which a quantity of something is sold. Packets are either small boxes made of thin cardboard, or bags or envelopes made of paper or plastic.

There was an empty cereal packet on the table.
Cook the pasta according to the instructions on the packet.

 In American English, a container like this is usually called a **package** or **pack**.

A packet of or **a package of** something can refer either to the container and its contents, or to the contents only.

The shelf was stacked with packages of rice and dried peas.
He ate a whole a packet of biscuits.

pardon

You can apologize to someone by saying '**I beg your pardon**'.

'You're sitting in my seat.' – 'Oh, I beg your pardon.'

 Some American speakers say '**Pardon me**'.

'Pardon me!' said a man who had bumped into her.

British speakers sometimes say '**Pardon?**' when they have not heard or understood what someone has said.

'His name is Hardeep.' – 'Pardon?' – 'I said, his name is Hardeep.'

→ See **Topic** entry **Apologizing**

parking – car park

 Don't use the word 'parking' to refer to a place where cars are parked. Instead, say **car park** in British English and **parking lot** in American English.

We parked in the car park next to the theatre.
The high school parking lot was filled with cars.

A building with several levels for parking cars is called a **parking garage** in American English, and a **multi-storey car park** in British English.

Parking is used only to refer to the action of parking your car, or to the state of being parked.

Parking in the city centre is very difficult.
He put a 'No Parking' sign on the gates.

part

1 'part of'

Part of or **a part of** something is one of the pieces or elements that it consists of. You use **part of** or **a part of** in front of the singular form of a countable noun, or in front of an uncountable noun.

I've told her part of the story, but not all of it.
Using the internet is a part of everyday life for most people.

2 'some of' and 'many of'

Don't use 'part of' or 'a part of' in front of a plural noun phrase. Don't say, for example, 'Part of the students have no books'. Say '**Some of** the students have no books'.

Some of the players looked very tired.
Some of us have finished.

Don't say 'A large part of the houses have flat roofs'. Say '**Many of** the houses have flat roofs'.

Many of the old people remember the war.

→ See **some, many**

partly

→ See **Adverbs and adverbials** for a graded list of words used to indicate extent

party

A **party** is a social event where people enjoy themselves by eating, drinking, dancing, talking, or playing games. You use **have**, **give**, or **throw** to say that someone organizes a party.

We are having a party on Saturday.
They gave a party to celebrate their daughter's graduation.
We threw her a huge birthday party.

! BE CAREFUL

Don't use 'make'. Don't say, for example, 'We are making a party'.

pass

The verb **pass** is used with several different meanings.

1 movement

If you **pass** someone or something, you go past them.

We passed the New Hotel.
They stood aside to let him pass.

If you **pass** something to someone or **pass** someone something, you take it in your hand and give it to them.

She passed me her glass.
I passed the picture to Lia so she could see it.

2 **time**

If you **pass** time in a particular way, you spend it doing something.

They passed the time until dinner talking and playing cards.

→ See **spend – pass**

3 **tests and exams**

If you **pass** a test or exam, you are successful in it.

I passed my driving test on my first attempt.
If you pass, you can go to college.

→ See **exam – examination**

! BE CAREFUL

Don't use 'pass' to say that someone has completed a test or exam, without mentioning the result. Say that they have **taken** it.

I'm taking my driving test next week.
Where did she take her degree?

GRAMMAR FINDER

The passive

1 **form and usage**

The passive refers to verb phrases whose subject is the person or thing that is affected by an action. For example, 'He was helped by his brother' contains a passive verb. With **active** verb phrases, the subject is the person or thing doing the action, as in 'His brother helped him'.

You use the passive when you are more interested in the person or thing affected by the action than in the person or thing doing the action, or when you do not know who performed the action. When you use the passive, you don't have to mention the performer of the action, as in 'He was helpful'.

Passive verb phrases consist of a tense of **be**, followed by the -*ed* participle of the main verb.

For example, if you want to use the passive of the past simple of 'eat', you use the past simple of 'be' (**was** or **were**) and the -*ed* participle of 'eat' (**eaten**).

You can have passive infinitives, such as **to be eaten** and passive -*ing* forms, such as **being eaten**.

→ See **Verb forms**

Nearly all transitive verbs (verbs that can have an object) can be used in the passive.

The room has been cleaned.
Some very interesting work is being done on this.
The name of the winner will be announced tomorrow.

> **!** **BE CAREFUL**
>
> A few transitive verbs are rarely or never used in the passive:
>
> | | | | |
> |---|---|---|---|
> | elude | get | like | suit |
> | escape | have | race | |
> | flee | let | resemble | |

Many phrasal verbs that consist of an intransitive verb and a preposition can also be used in the passive.

In some households, the man was referred to as the master.
Sanders asked if these people could be relied on to keep quiet.

Note that the preposition is still placed after the verb, but it is not followed by a noun phrase because the noun phrase it applies to is being used as the subject.

2 'by' and 'with'

In a passive sentence, if you want to mention the person or thing that performs an action, you use the preposition **by**.

He had been poisoned by his girlfriend.
He was brought up by an aunt.

If you want to mention the thing that is used to perform an action, you use the preposition **with**.

A circle was drawn in the dirt with a stick.
Moisture must be drawn out first with salt.

3 the object complement

Some verbs can have a complement after their object. The complement is an adjective or noun phrase that describes the object.

→ See **Complements**

When these verbs are used in the passive, the complement is put immediately after the verb.

In August he was elected Vice President of the Senate.
These days, if a person talks about ghosts, they are considered ignorant or mad.

4 'get'

 In conversation, **get** is sometimes used instead of 'be' to form the passive.

Our car gets cleaned about once every two months.
My husband got fined in Germany for crossing the road.

5 in reporting structures

→ See **Reporting** for information on the use of reporting verbs in the passive

---

past

Past can be a noun or adjective referring to a period of time before the present.

He never discussed his past.
I've spent most of the past eight years looking after children.

1 telling the time

In British English, when you are telling the time, you use **past** to say how many minutes it is after a particular hour.

It's ten past five.
I slept until quarter past ten.

 American speakers also say **after**.

It's ten after five.
I arrived around a quarter after twelve.

→ See **Topic** entry **Time** for other ways of telling the time

2 going near something

Past is also used as a preposition or adverb to say that someone goes near something when they are moving in a particular direction.

He walked past the school.
People ran past laughing.

3 'passed'

Don't use 'past' as the past tense or *-ed* participle of the verb **pass**. Use **passed**.

As she passed the library door, the telephone began to ring.
A new law was passed by Parliament.

GRAMMAR FINDER

The past

→ See **Verb forms** for formation of past forms

1 talking about the past

The **past simple** is used to refer to an event in the past.

She opened the door.
One other factor influenced him.

In order to say exactly when something happened, or to say that something happened for a period of time or took place regularly, it is necessary to use additional words and expressions.

The Prime Minister flew to New York yesterday.
He thought for a few minutes.
They went for picnics most weekends.

When you want to talk about something that had been happening for some time when an event occurred, or that continued to happen after the event, you use the **past progressive**.

We were driving towards the racetrack when a policeman stepped in front of our car to ask for identification.
While they were approaching the convent, a couple of girls ran out of the gate.

You also use the past progressive to talk about a temporary state of affairs in the past.

Our team were losing 2—1 at the time.
We were staying with friends in Italy.

2 regular events

Would or **used to** can be used instead of the past simple to talk about something that occurred regularly in the past.

We would normally spend the winter in Miami.
She used to get quite cross with Lilly.

Used to is also used to talk about situations that no longer exist.

People used to believe that the earth was flat.

'Would' is not used like this.

3 perfect forms

When you are concerned with the present effects of something that happened at some time in the past, you use the **present perfect** form.

I'm afraid I've forgotten my book, so I don't know.
Have you heard from Jill recently? How is she?

You also use the present perfect when you are talking about a situation that started in the past and still continues.

I have known him for years.
He has been here since six o'clock.

You use the **present perfect progressive** when you want to emphasize the fact that a recent event continued to happen for some time.

She's been crying.
I've been working hard all day.

When you are looking back to a point in the past, and you are concerned with the effects of something that happened at an even earlier time in the past, you use the **past perfect** form.

I apologized because I had left my wallet at home.
The fence between the two properties had been removed.

You use the **past perfect progressive** when referring to a situation or event that started at an earlier time and continued for some time, or was still continuing.

I was about twenty. I had been studying French for a couple of years.
He had been working there for ten years when the trouble started.

4 future in the past

When you want to talk about something that was in the future at a particular moment in the past, you can use **would**, **was/were going to**, or the past progressive.

He thought to himself how wonderful it would taste.
Her daughter was going to do the cooking.
Mike was taking his test the week after.

pay

The past tense and -ed participle of the verb **pay** is **paid**.

If you **pay for** something which has been done or provided, you give money to the person who does or provides it.

You should be paid for the work you do.
Roberto paid for the tickets.

! BE CAREFUL

You must use **for** after **pay** in sentences like these. Don't say, for example, 'Roberto paid the tickets'.

Don't say 'pay someone a drink' or 'pay someone a meal'. Say that you **buy someone a drink** or **buy someone a meal**.

The boss <u>bought</u> us all a drink to celebrate.
Come on, I'll <u>buy</u> you lunch.

You can also say that you **take someone out for a meal**.

My aunt <u>took me out for</u> dinner on my birthday.

people – person

1 **'people'**

People is a plural noun. You use a plural form of a verb after it.

People is most commonly used to refer to a particular group of men and women, or a particular group of men, women, and children.

The <u>people</u> at my work mostly wear suits.
Two hundred <u>people</u> were killed in the fire.

You often use **people** to refer to all the men, women, and children of a particular country, tribe, or race.

The British <u>people</u> elect a new government every four or five years.

2 **'peoples'**

When you are referring to several countries, tribes, or races, you can use the plural form **peoples**.

They all belong to the ancient group of Indo-European <u>peoples</u>.

3 **another use of 'people'**

People can also be used to say that something is generally done.

I don't think <u>people</u> should drive so fast.
She always tried to help <u>people</u>.

→ See **one – you – we – they**

4 **'person'**

Person is a countable noun. A **person** is an individual man, woman, or child.

There was far too much food for one <u>person</u>.
Chen is a good <u>person</u> to ask if you have a computer problem.

The usual plural of 'person' is **people**, but in formal English **persons** is sometimes used.

No unauthorized <u>persons</u> may enter the building.

percentage – per cent

When you express an amount as a **percentage** of a whole, you say how many parts the amount would have if the whole had 100 equal parts. You write a percentage as a number followed by **per cent** or by the symbol %. So, for example, if there are 1000 people living in a village and 250 of them are children, you say that **25 per cent** or **25%** of the people in the village are children.

What is the <u>percentage</u> of nitrogen in air?
He won 28.3 <u>per cent</u> of the vote.

Per cent is sometimes written as one word, especially in American English.

Remember that 90 percent of most food is water.

You also use **percentage** to show approximately how large or small an amount is as a proportion of a whole. For example, you can say that an amount is **a large percentage** or **a small percentage** of the whole.

The illness affects only a tiny percentage of babies.

When **percentage** is used like this in front of the plural form of a noun, you use a plural form of a verb after it.

A large percentage of the students do not speak English at home.

When **percentage** is used in front of a singular form or an uncountable noun, you use a singular form of a verb after it.

Only a small percentage of the money is given to charity.
A high percentage of their income was spent on rent.

permission

If someone gives you **permission** to do something, they say they will allow you to do it.

My parents gave me permission to go.
You can't do it without permission.

Permission is an uncountable noun. Don't talk about 'permissions' or 'a permission'.

When you ask for permission to do something and are given it, you say that you **get** or, in more formal English, **obtain** permission to do it.

She got permission to leave early.
The school has obtained permission to build a new science block.

! **BE CAREFUL**

Don't use 'take'. Don't say, for example, 'She took permission to leave early'.

When you have been given permission to do something, you say that you **have** or **have got** permission to do it.

Students don't have permission to leave the school grounds at lunchtime.
You can only copy these documents if you've got permission.

permit

→ See **allow – permit – let – enable**

person

→ See **people – person**

persuade

→ See **convince – persuade**

petrol

→ See **gas – petrol**

pharmacist

→ See **chemist – pharmacist**

pharmacy

→ See **chemist's – drugstore – pharmacy**

phone

When you **phone** someone, you dial their phone number and speak to them by phone.

I need to phone my mother.
Luis phoned us to say he had arrived.

You can also **phone** a place.

He phoned work to tell them he was ill.
I'll phone the cinema and find out what time the film starts.

! **BE CAREFUL**

Don't use 'to' after **phone**. Don't say, for example, '~~I need to phone to my mother~~'.

GRAMMAR FINDER

Phrasal modals

A **phrasal modal** is a phrase that forms a single verb phrase with another verb and that affects the meaning of that verb in the same way that a modal verb does.

Some phrasal modals begin with **be** or **have**, for example **be able to**, **be bound to**, **be going to**, **have got to**, and **have to**. The first word in these phrases changes its form depending on the subject and the tense, in the way that 'be' and 'have' normally do. You say 'We have to leave tonight' and 'They had to leave last night'. The other phrasal modals do not change in this way. You say 'I would rather go by bus' and 'He would rather go by bus'.

The phrasal modals are:

be able to	have got to	would rather	be unable to
had best	have to	would just as soon	used to
had better	be liable to	would sooner	would do well to
be bound to	be meant to	be supposed to	
be going to	ought to	be sure to	

It was supposed to last for a year and actually lasted eight.
She is able to sit up in a wheelchair.
He used to shout at people.

GRAMMAR FINDER

Phrasal verbs

1 phrasal verbs

A **phrasal verb** is a combination of a verb and an adverb, a verb and a preposition, or a verb, an adverb, and a preposition, which together have a single meaning.

The adverb or preposition is sometimes called a **particle**. Phrasal verbs extend the usual meaning of the verb or create a new meaning.

The pain gradually <u>wore off</u>.
I had to <u>look after</u> the kids.
They <u>broke out of</u> prison.
Kevin tried to <u>talk</u> her <u>out of</u> it.

2 **position of objects**

▶ With phrasal verbs consisting of a transitive verb and an adverb, the object of the verb can usually be put in front of the adverb or after it.

Don't give <u>the story</u> away, silly!
I wouldn't want to give away <u>any secrets</u>.

▶ However, when the object of the verb is a pronoun, the pronoun must go in front of the adverb.

He cleaned <u>it</u> up.
I answered <u>him</u> back and took my chances.

▶ With phrasal verbs consisting of a transitive verb and a preposition, the object of the verb is put after the verb, and the object of the preposition is put after the preposition.

They agreed to let <u>him</u> into <u>their little secret</u>.
The farmer threatened to set <u>his dogs</u> on <u>them</u>.

▶ With phrasal verbs where a verb and a preposition act as one transitive unit, the object is put after the verb and the preposition.

I love looking after <u>the children</u>.
Elaine wouldn't let him provide for <u>her</u>.
...friends who stuck by <u>me</u> during the difficult times.

▶ With phrasal verbs consisting of a transitive verb, an adverb, and a preposition, the object of the verb is usually put in front of the adverb, not after it.

Multinational companies can play <u>individual markets</u> off against each other.
I'll take <u>you</u> up on that generous invitation.

▶ With phrasal verbs where a verb, an adverb, and a preposition act as one transitive unit, The object is put after the verb, adverb, and preposition.

They had to put up with <u>their son's bad behaviour</u>.
He was looking forward to <u>life after retirement</u>.
Look out for <u>the symptoms of flu</u>.

3 **passives**

With transitive phrasal verbs that can be used in the passive, the verb and the preposition or adverb stay together.

She died a year later, and I <u>was taken in</u> by her only relative.
I <u>was dropped off</u> in front of my house.
The factory <u>was closed down</u> last year.

pick

→ See **choose**

pile

→ See **heap – stack – pile**

---

place

1 used in descriptions

You can use **place** after an adjective when you are describing a building, room, town, or area of land. For example, instead of saying 'Paris is nice', you can say 'Paris is a nice **place**'.

I love this village – it's a beautiful place.
Their new house is a really comfortable place.

2 saying where something is

You can say where something is using **the place where...**. For example, you can say 'This is **the place where** I parked my car'.

He reached the place where I was standing.
This is the place where we leave our school bags.

> **!** **BE CAREFUL**
>
> Don't use a *to*-infinitive after **a place where**. Don't say, for example, ~~'I'm looking for a place where to park my car'~~. Say 'I'm looking for **a place to park** my car' or 'I'm looking for **a place where I can park** my car'. You can also say 'I'm looking for **somewhere to park** my car'.
>
> *He was looking for a place to hide.*
> *Is there a place where you can go swimming?*
> *We had to find somewhere to live.*

3 'anywhere'

In British English, you don't usually use 'place' after 'any' in questions or negative statements. Don't say, for example, ~~'She never goes to any place alone'~~. You say 'She never goes **anywhere** alone'.

I decided not to go anywhere in the summer holidays.
Is there a spare seat anywhere?

 In American English, **anyplace** is sometimes used instead of **anywhere**.

He doesn't stay anyplace for very long.

4 'there'

Don't use 'that place' to refer to somewhere that has just been mentioned. Don't say, for example, ~~'I threw my bag on the ground and left it in that place'~~. You say 'I threw my bag on the ground and left it **there**'.

I moved to London and soon found a job there.
I must go home. Bill is there on his own.

5 'room'

Don't use 'place' as an uncountable noun to refer to an open or empty area. Use **room** or **space** instead. **Room** is more likely to be used when you are talking about space inside an enclosed area.

There's not enough room in the car for all of us.
We need plenty of space for the children to play.

play

1 children's games

When children **play**, they spend time amusing themselves with toys or taking part in games.

The kids went off to play in the park.

2 sports and games

If you **play** a sport or game, you take part in it regularly.

Raja and I play tennis at least once a week.
Do you play chess?

If someone **plays in** a game, match, or competition, they take part in it on a particular occasion.

He hopes to play in England's match against France next week.

3 CDs and DVDs

If you **play** something such as a CD or DVD, you put it in a piece of equipment and listen to it.

She played me a tape of the interview.
She plays her CDs too loudly.

Don't say that someone 'plays' a film or a television programme. Say that they **show** it.

The teacher showed us a film about tigers.
Many news programmes showed the clip.

4 musical instruments

If you **play** a musical instrument, you produce music from it.

There is a piano in the hall, but nobody ever plays it.

If you want to say that someone is able to play a particular instrument, you can use **play** with or without **the**. For example, you say 'She **plays the piano**' or 'She **plays piano**'.

Uncle Rudi played the cello.
He wanted to learn to play guitar.

point

1 'point'

A **point** is something you say that expresses an idea, opinion, or fact.

That's a very good point.
I want to make a quick point about safety.

A **point** is also an aspect or detail of something, or a part of a person's character.

The two books have many points in common.
One of his best points is his confidence.

2 'the point'

The point is the most important fact in a situation.

The point is that everyone is welcome to join.
I'll come straight to the point. You didn't get the job.

The point of doing something is the reason for doing it.

What was the point of asking him when you knew he'd say no?
I don't see the point of learning all this boring stuff.

3 'no point'

If you say that **there is no point in doing** something, you mean that it has no purpose or will not achieve anything.

There's no point in talking to you if you won't listen.
There was not much point in thinking about it.

! BE CAREFUL

Don't say 'there is no point to do' something or 'it is no point in doing' something.

4 'full stop'

Don't refer to the punctuation mark (.) which comes at the end of a sentence as a 'point'. In British English, it is called a **full stop**. In American English, it is called a **period**.

→ See **Reference** sections **Punctuation**, **Numbers and fractions**

point of view – view – opinion

1 'point of view'

When you are considering one aspect of a situation, you can say that you are considering it from a particular **point of view**.

From a practical point of view it is quite easy.
The movie was very successful from a commercial point of view.

A person's **point of view** is their general attitude to something, or the way they feel about something.

We understand your point of view.
I tried to see things from Frank's point of view.

2 'view' and 'opinion'

Don't refer to what someone thinks or believes about a particular subject as their 'point of view'. Refer to it as their **view** or **opinion**.

Leo's view is that there is not enough evidence.
If you want my honest opinion, I don't think it will work.

View is most commonly used in the plural.

We are happy to listen to your views.
He was sent to jail for his political views.

You talk about someone's opinions or views **on** or **about** a subject.

He always asked for her opinions on his work.
I have strong views about education.

You can use expressions such as **in my opinion** or **in his view** to show that something is an opinion, and may not be a fact.

He's not doing a very good job in my opinion.
These changes, in his view, would be very damaging.

police

The police are the official organization responsible for making sure that people obey the law. They also protect people and property and arrest criminals.

He called the police to report a robbery.
Contact the police if you see anything suspicious.

Police is a plural noun. You use a plural form of a verb after it.

The police were called to the scene of the crime.

! | **BE CAREFUL**

Don't refer to an individual member of the police force as a 'police'. You usually refer to him or her as a **police officer**. You can also say **policeman** or **policewoman**.

A police officer stood outside the building.

politics – policy – political

1 **'politics'**

The noun **politics** is usually used to refer to the methods by which people get, keep, and use power in a country or society.

She is interested in a career in politics.
Her parents never discussed politics.

When **politics** is used like this, you can use either a singular or plural form of a verb with it. It is more common to use a singular form.

Politics is sometimes about compromise.
American politics are very interesting.

Politics can refer to a particular set of beliefs about how countries should be governed or power should be used. When you use **politics** like this, you use a plural form of a verb with it.

I think his politics are are quite conservative.

Politics can also refer to the study of the ways in which countries are governed, and of the ways in which people get and use power. When you use **politics** like this, you must use a singular form of a verb with it.

Politics is often studied together with Economics.

2 **'policy'**

There is no noun 'politic'. To refer to a course of action or plan that has been agreed upon by a government or political party, use **policy**.

He criticized the government's education policy.

3 **'political'**

Don't use 'politic' as an adjective to mean 'relating to politics'. Use **political**.

The government is facing a political crisis.
Do you belong to a political party?

position – post – job

1 'position' and 'post'

Someone's job can be referred to in formal English as their **position** or **post**. When advertising or applying for a job, you usually use **position** or **post**.

We are looking for someone to fill a senior management position.
I am writing to apply for the post of clerical assistant.

2 'job'

In conversation, don't use 'position' or 'post'. Use **job**.

He's afraid of losing his job.
She's got a really interesting job.

GRAMMAR FINDER

Possessive determiners

1 possessive determiners

Possessive determiners show who or what something belongs to or is connected with.

The possessive determiners are:

	singular	plural
1st person	my	our
2nd person	your	
3rd person	his her its	their

You choose a possessive determiner according to the identity of the person or thing who has the thing you are talking about. For example, if you are talking about a pen belonging to a woman, you say '**her** pen', but if the pen belongs to a man, you say '**his** pen'.

Come round to my house this evening.
Sir Thomas More built his house there.
I stayed at her house last week.
Sometimes I would sleep in their house all night.

The same determiner is used whether the noun after the possessive determiner is singular or plural, or refers to a person or a thing.

I just went on writing in my notebook.
My parents don't trust me.

! BE CAREFUL

Don't use another determiner with a possessive determiner. For example, don't say 'I took off the my shoes'. Say 'I took off my shoes'.

② 'the' instead of possessive

Sometimes the determiner **the** is used when there is an obvious possessive meaning, particularly when you are talking about someone doing something to a part of someone else's body.

She patted him on the head.
He took his daughters by the hand and led them away.

You can also use **the** when referring to one of your possessions. For example, you can say 'I'll go and get **the** car' instead of 'I'll go and get my car'.

I went back to the house.
The noise from the washing-machine is getting worse.

However, you cannot use 'the' like this when referring to something that someone is wearing. For example, you say 'My watch is slow'. Don't say 'The watch is slow'. It is not usual to use 'the' with a possessive meaning when referring to a relative such as an uncle or a sister. However, people often refer to their children as '**the** children' or '**the** kids'.

When the children had gone to bed I said, 'I'm going out for a while'.

Possessive determiners are more commonly used to show that something belongs to a person than to a thing. For example, it is more usual to say '**the** door' than to say 'its door' when referring to the door of a room.

→ See **Topic** entry **Possession and other relationships** for more information on when to use a possessive determiner

possibility – opportunity

① 'possibility'

If there is a **possibility** of something happening or being true, it might happen or be true.

There was a possibility that they had taken the wrong road.
We must accept the possibility that we might be wrong.

If there is **no possibility** of something happening or being true, it cannot happen or be true.

There was now no possibility of success.
There is no possibility that he did that accidentally.

If you talk or think about the **possibility of doing** something, you are considering whether to do it.

He talked about the possibility of getting married.

! BE CAREFUL

Don't say 'He talked about the possibility to get married.'

② 'opportunity'

When a situation makes it possible for someone to do something, don't say that they have 'the possibility to do' it. Say that they have the **opportunity to do** it or the **opportunity of doing** it.

You will have the opportunity to study several different subjects in your first year.
Sadly, I never had the opportunity of meeting him.

possible – possibly

1 'possible'

Possible is an adjective. If something is **possible**, it can be done or achieved.

It is possible for us to measure the amount of rain.
Some improvement may be possible.

Possible is often used in expressions such as **as soon as possible** and **as much as possible**. If you do something **as soon as possible**, you do it as soon as you can.

I like to know as much as possible about my patients.
He sat as far away from me as possible.

> **!** **BE CAREFUL**
>
> Don't say 'as soon as possibly'.

You also use **possible** to say that something may be true or correct.

It is possible that he made a mistake.
That's one possible answer.

2 'possibly'

Possibly is an adverb. You use **possibly** to show that you are not sure about something.

Television is possibly to blame for this.
She is always cheerful, which is possibly why people like her.

→ See **Adverbs and adverbials** for a list of words used to indicate probability

You also use **possibly** when you are asking someone to do something in a very polite way. For example, you say '**Could you possibly** carry this for me?'

Could you possibly meet me there tomorrow at ten?

→ See **Topic** entry **Requests, orders, and instructions**

---

post – mail

1 'post' and 'mail' as nouns

 The public service by which letters and parcels are collected and delivered is usually called the **post** in British English and the **mail** in American English. **Mail** is also sometimes used in British English, for example in the name **Royal Mail**.

Winners will be notified by post.
Your reply must have been lost in the mail.

 British speakers usually refer to letters and parcels delivered to them as their **post**. American speakers refer to these letters and parcels as their **mail**. **Mail** is also sometimes used in British English, especially in phrases such as **junk mail** and **direct mail**.

Has the post arrived yet?
I would never open someone else's mail.

In both British and American English, **mail** is used to mean 'email'.

I switched on my laptop to check my mail.
Did you get that mail I sent you this morning?

In both British and American English, **post** is used to refer to a comment or message that someone puts on a website.

I read his latest post on his blog.

2 'postage'

Don't use 'post' or 'mail' to refer to the amount of money that you pay to send a letter or parcel. In both British and American English, this money is called **postage**.

Send £1.50 extra for postage and packing.

3 'post' and 'mail' as verbs

 British speakers talk about **posting** a letter or parcel. Americans usually say that they **mail** it.

The letter had already been posted.
She mailed the picture to a friend.

In both British and American English, you can say that someone **mails** something to mean that they send it by email.

I'll mail it to you as an attachment.
He mailed to cancel the meeting.

In both British and American English, you can say that someone **posts on** or **posts** something **on** the internet or on a website, to mean that they put a message, comment, or item there.

She regularly posts on a music blog.
I posted the photo on my Facebook page.

postpone

→ See **delay – cancel – postpone – put off**, **pore – pour**

power – strength

1 'power'

If someone has **power**, they are able to control other people and their activities.

People in positions of power, such as teachers, must act responsibly.
He believes the President has too much power.

2 'strength'

Don't use 'power' to refer to someone's physical energy, or their ability to move heavy objects. Use **strength**.

It took me some time to recover my strength after the illness.
This sport requires a lot of physical strength.

practically

→ See **Adverbs and adverbials** for a list of words used to indicate extent

practice – practise

In British English, **practice** is a noun and **practise** is a verb.

1 **used as an uncountable noun**

Practice involves doing something regularly in order to improve your ability at it.

Your skiing will get better with practice.
He has to do a lot of music practice.

2 **used as a countable noun**

A **practice** is something that is done regularly, for example as a custom.

Our usual practice is to keep a written record of all meetings.
The ancient practice of yoga is still popular today.

3 **used as a verb**

If you **practise** something, you do it or take part in it regularly.

I had been practising the piece for months.
His family practised traditional Judaism.

 In American English, the spelling 'practise' is not normally used. The verb and noun are both spelled **practice**.

I practiced throwing and catching the ball every day.

---

prefer

If you **prefer** one person or thing **to** another, you like the first one better.

I prefer art to sports.
She preferred cooking at home to eating in restaurants.

! **BE CAREFUL**

Don't use any preposition except **to** in sentences like these. Don't say, for example 'I prefer art than sports'.

Prefer is rather formal. In ordinary conversation, you often use expressions such as **like...better** and **would rather...** instead. For example, instead of saying 'I prefer football to tennis', you can say 'I **like** football **better** than tennis'. Instead of saying 'I'd prefer an apple', you can say 'I'**d rather** have an apple'.

GRAMMAR FINDER

Prepositions

1 **with a following noun phrase**

A **preposition** is a word like **at**, **in**, **on**, or **with** which is normally followed by a noun phrase, forming a **prepositional phrase**. The noun phrase after a preposition is sometimes called the **prepositional object**.

Prepositions are often used in phrases which indicate place and time.

She waited at the bus stop for twenty minutes.
Tell me if you're coming to my party on Saturday.
They arrived at York in the morning.

→ See **Topic** entries **Places**, **Time**

Prepositions are also used after nouns, adjectives, and verbs to introduce phrases that give more information about a thing, quality, or action.

→ See **Nouns, Adjectives, Verbs**

2 without a following noun phrase

There are some cases where a preposition is not followed by a noun phrase. The noun phrase it relates to comes earlier in the sentence. These cases are:

▶ **questions and reported questions**

What will you talk about?
She doesn't know what we were talking about.

→ See **Questions, Reporting**

▶ **relative clauses**

This was the job which I'd been training for.

→ See **Relative clauses**

▶ **passive structures**

Those findings have already been referred to.

→ See **The passive**

▶ **after a complement and** *to*-**infinitive**

She's very difficult to get on with.
The whole thing was just too awful to think about.

3 complex prepositional object

After a preposition, you can sometimes use another prepositional phrase or a *wh*-clause.

I had taken his bag from under the kitchen table.
I walked across the room to where she was sitting.
We discussed the question of who should be the new chairperson.

4 prepositions and adverbs

Some words that are used as prepositions are also used with a similar meaning as adverbs (that is, without a noun phrase after them).

I looked underneath the bed, but the box had gone.
Always put a sheet of paper underneath.
The door was opposite the window.
The kitchen was opposite, across a little landing.

The following words can be used as prepositions or adverbs with a similar meaning:

aboard	behind	inside	round
about	below	near	since
above	beneath	off	through
across	beside	on	throughout
after	beyond	on board	under
against	by	opposite	underneath
along	down	outside	up
alongside	in	over	within
before	in between	past	

present

You use **present** in front of a noun to show that you are talking about something that exists now, rather than about something in the past or future.

When did you start working in your present job?
The present system has many faults.

You also use **present** in front of a noun to show that you are talking about the person who has a job, role, or title now, rather than someone who had it in the past or will have it in the future.

The present director of the company is a woman.
Who is the present team captain?

When **present** is used after **be**, it has a different meaning. If someone is **present at** an event, they are there.

Several reporters were present at the event.
He was not present at the birth of his child.

! BE CAREFUL

Don't use any preposition except **at** in sentences like these. Don't say, for example ~~'Several reporters were present in the event'~~.

If it is clear what event you are talking about, you can just say that someone **is present**.

The Prime Minister and his wife were present.

You can also use **present** with this meaning immediately after a noun.

There was a photographer present.
He should not have said that with so many children present.

GRAMMAR FINDER

The present

→ See **Verb forms** for formation of present forms

The **present simple** is usually used for talking about long-term situations that exist at the present time, regular or habitual actions currently taking place, and general truths.

My dad works in Saudi Arabia.
I wake up early and eat my breakfast in bed.
Water boils at 100 degrees Celsius.

The **present progressive** is used to talk about something which is regarded as temporary or something which is happening at the present moment.

I'm working in London at the moment.
Wait a moment. I'm listening to the news.

! BE CAREFUL

There are a number of verbs which are not used in the present progressive, even when talking about the present moment.

→ See **The progressive form**

Present tenses are sometimes used to talk about future events.

→ See **The Future**, **The Past** for the use of present perfect

press

→ See **Nouns** for information on collective nouns

previous

→ See **last – lastly**

price – cost

1 'price' and 'cost'

The **price** or **cost** of something is the amount of money you must pay to buy it.

The price of oil doubled in a few months.
They are worried about the rising cost of food.

You can also use **cost** to refer to the amount of money needed to do or make something.

The cost of raising a child is very high.
The building was recently restored at a cost of £500,000.

> **! BE CAREFUL**
>
> Don't use 'price' in this way. Don't say, for example, '~~The price of raising a child is very high~~.'

2 'costs'

You use the plural noun **costs** when you are referring to the total amount of money needed to run something such as a business.

We need to cut our costs in order to make a profit.
Stores have had to raise their prices to cover increased costs.

3 'cost' used as a verb

You use **cost** as a verb to talk about the amount of money that you must pay for something.

The dress costs $200.
How much do these new phones cost?

You can use **cost** with two objects to say how much money someone pays for something on a particular occasion. The past tense and *-ed* participle of **cost** is **cost**.

A two-day stay there cost me $125.
How much did that haircut cost you?

> **! BE CAREFUL**
>
> Don't use 'to' after **cost** in a sentence like this. Don't say, for example, '~~How much did that haircut cost to you?~~'

price – prize

1 'price'

The **price** /praɪs/ of something is the amount of money that you must pay to buy it.

The price of a cup of coffee is almost five dollars.

The price is shown on the label.

→ See **price – cost**

2 'prize'

A **prize** /praɪz/ is something given to someone for winning a competition or game, or for doing good work.

He won a prize in a painting competition.
She was awarded the Nobel Prize for Peace.

principal – principle

1 'principal'

Principal can be an adjective or a noun.

The **principal** thing or person in a group is the most important one.

His principal interest in life was money.
The principal character in the film was played by John Hurt.

The **principal** of a school or college is the person in charge of it.

The teacher sent me to the principal's office.
Lodge was Principal of Birmingham University.

2 'principle'

Principle is always a noun. A **principle** is a general rule that someone's behaviour or ideas are based on.

She did not eat meat because it was against her principles.
We follow the principle that everyone should be treated equally.

prison

1 used as a countable noun

A **prison** is a building where criminals or other people are kept and are not allowed to leave.

The prison housed almost 500 inmates.
The castle was used as a prison at one time.

2 used as an uncountable noun

Prison is used without an article when talking about the punishment of going to prison, without mentioning which particular prison. For example, you can say that someone is **in prison**, is sent **to prison**, or is released **from prison**.

They were threatened with prison if they did not pay.
It can be hard to find work after coming out of prison.

! BE CAREFUL

Don't use 'the' in front of **prison** unless you are referring to a particular prison.

prize

→ See **price – prize**

probably

You use **probably** to say that a statement is very likely to be true.

▶ With a verb phrase consisting of an auxiliary verb and a main verb, put **probably** after the auxiliary verb. For example, say 'He **will probably come** soon'. Don't say 'He probably will come soon'.

He's probably left by now.
Chaucer was probably born here.

▶ If you are using more than one auxiliary verb, put **probably** after the first auxiliary verb.

Next year I will probably be looking for a job.
They've probably been asked to leave.

▶ When there is no auxiliary verb, put **probably** in front of the verb unless the verb is **be**.

He probably misses the children.
She probably feels sorry for you.

▶ If the verb is **be**, put **probably** after it.

You're probably right.
He is probably a businessman.

▶ In a negative sentence, if you are using a contraction such as **won't** or **can't**, you put **probably** in front of the contraction.

They probably won't help.
They probably don't want you to go.

▶ You can also put **probably** at the beginning of a clause.

Probably it was just my imagination.
Hundreds of people were killed, and probably thousands more injured.

! BE CAREFUL

Don't put **probably** at the end of a clause. For example, don't say 'They won't help probably'.

→ See **Adverbs and adverbials** for a graded list of words used to indicate probability

problem

The noun **problem** has two common meanings.

1 an unsatisfactory situation

A **problem** is an unsatisfactory situation that needs to be dealt with.

They discussed the problem of bullying in schools.

You can say that someone **has a problem** or **has problems**.

We have a problem with our car.
They are having financial problems at the moment.

You can also say that someone **has problems doing** something.

Many people are having problems paying their rent.
The company has problems finding suitably qualified staff.

> **!** | **BE CAREFUL**
>
> Don't say that someone 'has problems to do' something. Don't say, for example, 'Many people are having problems to pay their rent'.

2 'reason'

Don't use 'problem' with **why** when you are explaining why a situation has occurred. Don't say, for example, 'The problem why he couldn't come is that he is ill'. You say 'The **reason** why he couldn't come is that he is ill'.

The reason why the project failed is lack of money.

→ See **reason**

produce – product

1 'produce' used as a verb

Produce is usually a verb, pronounced /prəˈdjuːs/.

To **produce** a result or effect means to cause it to happen.

His comments produced an angry response.
The talks failed to produce an agreement.

To **produce** goods or food means to make or grow them, usually to be sold.

The factory produces goods for export.
They use all the available land to produce crops.

2 'produce' used as a noun

Food that is grown to be sold is called **produce**, pronounced /ˈprɒdjuːs/.

She has a market stall selling organic produce.

3 'product'

Goods that are made and sold in large quantities are called **products**.

Manufacturers spend huge sums of money advertising their products.

---

professor – teacher

1 'professor'

In a British university, a **professor** is the most senior teacher in a department.

Professor Cole is giving a lecture today.
She was professor of English at Strathclyde University.

 In an American or Canadian university or college, a **professor** is a senior teacher. He or she is not necessarily the most senior teacher in a department.

He's a physics professor at Harvard.
My professor allowed me to retake the test.

2 'teacher'

Don't use 'professor' to refer to a person who teaches at a school or similar institution. Use **teacher**.

I'm a qualified French teacher.
The teacher set us some homework.

programme – program

A **programme** is a plan which has been developed for a particular purpose.

The company has begun a major new research programme.

 This word is spelled **program** in American English.

There has been a lot of criticism of the nuclear power program.

A television or radio **programme** is a single broadcast, for example a play, discussion, or show.

I watched a programme on education.

 This word, too, is spelled **program** in American English.

This is mom's favorite TV program.

A computer **program** is a set of instructions that a computer uses to perform a particular operation. This word is spelled **program** in both British and American English.

It's important to have an anti-virus program on your computer.
There must be a bug in the program.

progress

You say that there is **progress** when something improves gradually, or when someone gets nearer to achieving or completing something.

Many things are now possible due to technological progress.
His doctors are very pleased with his progress.

Progress is an uncountable noun. Don't talk about 'progresses' or 'a progress'.

You can say that someone or something **makes progress**.

She is making good progress with her studies.
We haven't solved the problem yet, but we are making progress.

! **BE CAREFUL**

Don't use 'do'. Don't say, for example, 'She is doing good progress.'

GRAMMAR FINDER

The progressive form

1 **The progressive form**

The **progressive form** is made up of a form of the verb **be** and an *-ing* participle. The progressive form is used when talking about temporary situations at a particular point in time.

→ See **Verb forms**

Verbs that can be used in the progressive form are sometimes called **dynamic verbs**.

The industry has been developing rapidly.
He'll be working abroad next week.

2 stative verbs

There are a number of verbs that are not normally used in the progressive form. Verbs of this kind are sometimes called **stative verbs**.

The verbs in the following list are not normally used in the progressive form when they are used with their commonest or basic meaning.

admire	envy	last	resemble
adore	exist	like	satisfy
appear	fit	look like	see
astonish	forget	love	seem
be	hate	matter	sound
believe	have	mean	stop
belong to	hear	owe	suppose
concern	imagine	own	surprise
consist of	impress	please	survive
contain	include	possess	suspect
deserve	interest	prefer	understand
desire	involve	reach	want
despise	keep	realize	wish
detest	know	recognize	
dislike	lack	remember	

Do you <u>like</u> football?
I <u>want</u> to come with you.
Where <u>do</u> you <u>keep</u> your keys?
Then I <u>heard</u> a noise.

Generally, these sentences cannot be expressed as, for example, 'Are you liking football?', 'I'm wanting to come with you', 'Where are you keeping your keys?' or 'Then I was hearing a noise'.

 However, a few of these verbs are sometimes used with present and past progressive forms, particularly in informal spoken English. You can use the progressive form with these verbs when you want to emphasize that a state is new or temporary, or when you want to focus on the present moment.

Rachel <u>is loving</u> one benefit of the job – the new clothes.
I'm <u>liking</u> grapes these days too.
I'm <u>wanting</u> the film to be deliberately old-fashioned.

Some people think this usage is incorrect, and it is usually avoided in formal texts.

Here is a list of verbs that are traditionally considered to be stative verbs, but that are sometimes used with present and past progressive forms.

forget	imagine	like	remember
guess	lack	love	want

You can use the present perfect progressive or past perfect progressive with some stative verbs in both formal and informal contexts.

I've <u>been wanting</u> to speak to you about this for some time.
John <u>has been keeping</u> birds for about three years now.
Then she heard it. The sound she <u>had been hearing</u> in her head for weeks.

3 'be'

Be is not usually used as a main verb in the progressive form. However, you use the progressive form when you are describing someone's behaviour at a particular time.

You're being naughty.

4 'have'

Have is not used in the progressive form to talk about possession. However, you can use the progressive form to say that someone is doing something.

We were just having a philosophical discussion.

→ See **have**

5 other verbs

Some verbs have very specific senses in which they are not used in the progressive form. For example, **smell** is sometimes used in the progressive form when it means 'to smell something deliberately', but not when it means 'to smell of something'.

She was smelling her bunch of flowers.
The air smelled sweet.

The following verbs are not usually used in the progressive form when they have the meanings shown:

depend (be related to)	measure (have length)	taste (of something)	weigh (have weight)
feel (have an opinion)	smell (of something)	think (have an opinion)	

GRAMMAR FINDER

Pronouns

1 pronouns

Pronouns are words such as **it**, **this**, and **nobody** that are used in a sentence like noun phrases containing a noun. Some pronouns are used in order to avoid repeating nouns. For example, you would not say 'My mother said my mother would phone me this evening'. You would say 'My mother said **she** would phone me this evening'.

! BE CAREFUL

You use a pronoun instead of a noun phrase containing a noun, not in addition to a noun phrase. For example, don't say 'My mother she wants to see you'. You say either 'My mother wants to see you' or 'She wants to see you'.

In this entry, information is given on **personal pronouns**, **possessive pronouns**, **reflexive pronouns**, and **indefinite pronouns**.

→ See **this – that** for information on demonstrative pronouns, **each other – one another** for information on reciprocal pronouns

→ See **Wh-words**

Words such as **many** and **some** that are used to refer to quantities of people or things can also be used as pronouns.

→ See **Quantity** section on pronoun use

One can be used to replace a noun phrase, but can also be used to replace a noun within a noun phrase.

→ See **one**

2 **personal pronouns**

Personal pronouns are used to refer to something or someone that has already been mentioned, or to the speaker or hearer. There are two sets of personal pronouns: **subject pronouns** and **object pronouns**.

Subject pronouns are used as the subject of a verb. The subject pronouns are:

	singular	plural
1st person	I	we
2nd person	you	
3rd person	he she it	they

I do the cleaning; he does the cooking; we share the washing-up.
My father is huge – he is almost two metres tall.

Object pronouns are used as the direct or indirect object of a verb, or after a preposition. The object pronouns are:

	singular	plural
1st person	me	us
2nd person	you	
3rd person	him her it	them

The nurse washed me with cold water.
I'm going to read him some of my poems.

Don't use an object pronoun as the indirect object of a verb when you are referring to the same person as the subject. Instead you use a **reflexive pronoun**.

He cooked himself an omelette.

Me, not 'I', is used after **it's** in modern English.

'Who is it?' – 'It's me.'

→ See **me**

We and **us** can be used either to include the person you are talking to or not to include the person you are talking to. For example, you can say 'We must meet more often', meaning that you and the person you are talking to must meet each other more often. You can also say 'We don't meet very often now', meaning that you and someone else do not meet very often.

You and **they** can be used to refer to people in general.

If you want to be a doctor, you have to have good communication skills.
They say she's very clever.

→ See **one – you – we – they**

They and **them** are sometimes used to refer back to indefinite pronouns referring to people.

→ See **he – she – they**

It is used as an impersonal pronoun in general statements about the time, the date, the weather, or a situation.

→ See **it**

3 possessive pronouns

Possessive pronouns show who the person or thing you are referring to belongs to or is connected with. The possessive pronouns are:

	singular	plural
1st person	mine	ours
2nd person	yours	
3rd person	his hers	theirs

Is that coffee yours or mine?
It was his fault, not theirs.
'What's your name?' – 'Frank.' – 'Mine's Laura.'

! BE CAREFUL

There is no possessive pronoun 'its'.

Possessive pronouns are sometimes confused with **possessive determiners**, which are quite similar in form.

→ See **Possessive determiners**

Possessive pronouns can be used after **of**.

→ See **of**

He was an old friend of mine.

4 reflexive pronouns

Reflexive pronouns are used as the object of a verb or preposition when the person or thing affected by an action is the same as the person or thing doing it. The reflexive pronouns are:

	singular	plural
1st person	myself	ourselves
2nd person	yourself	yourselves
3rd person	himself herself itself	themselves

She stretched herself out on the sofa.
The men formed themselves into a line.

→ See **Verbs** for more information about this use of reflexive pronouns

Reflexive pronouns are also used after nouns or pronouns to emphasize them.

I myself have never read the book.
The town itself was so small that it didn't have a bank.

They are also used at the end of a clause to emphasize the subject.

I find it a bit odd myself.

Reflexive pronouns are also used at the end of a clause to say that someone did something without any help from anyone else.

Did you make those yourself?

You can also show that someone did something without any help, or that someone was alone, by using a reflexive pronoun after **by** at the end of a clause.

Did you put those shelves up all by yourself?
He went off to sit by himself.

5 indefinite pronouns

Indefinite pronouns are used to refer to people or things without indicating exactly who or what they are. The indefinite pronouns are:

anybody	everybody	nobody	somebody
anyone	everyone	no one	someone
anything	everything	nothing	something

Everyone knows that.
Jane said nothing for a moment.
Is anybody there?

You always use singular verbs with indefinite pronouns.

Is anyone here?
Everything was ready.

However, the plural pronouns **they**, **them**, or **themselves** are often used to refer back to an indefinite pronoun referring to a person.

→ See **he – she – they**

You can use adjectives immediately after indefinite pronouns.

Choose someone quiet.
There is nothing extraordinary about this.

proper

The adjective **proper** is used with several different meanings.

1 used to mean 'real'

You use **proper** in front of a noun to emphasize that someone or something really is the thing referred to by the noun.

It's important to have a proper breakfast in the morning, not just a cup of tea.
He's never had a proper job.

2 used to mean 'correct'

You also use **proper** in front of a noun to say that something is correct or suitable.

Everything was in its <u>proper</u> place.
The <u>proper</u> word is 'lying', not 'laying'.

> **!** **BE CAREFUL**
>
> Don't use 'proper' when you are saying that something belongs to you. Use **own** instead. Don't say, for example, '~~I've got my proper car~~'. Say 'I've got my **own** car.'

protest

Protest can be a verb or a noun, but with different pronunciations.

1 used as a verb

Protest /prə'test/ is used as a verb to say that someone shows publicly that they do not approve of something. You can say that someone **protests about** something or **protests against** something.

Women's groups <u>protested about</u> the way women were portrayed in commercials.
Students marched in the streets to <u>protest against</u> the arrests.

 In American English, you can use **protest** as a transitive verb. You say that someone **protests** something.

Environmental campaigners <u>protested</u> the decision.

Protest can also be a reporting verb. If you **protest** that something is true, you insist that it is true, when someone has said or suggested the opposite.

They <u>protested</u> that they had nothing to do with the incident.
'You're wrong,' I <u>protested</u>.

2 used as a noun

The noun is pronounced /'prəʊtest/. **Protest** or a **protest** is behaviour in which someone shows publicly that they do not approve of something.

They joined in the <u>protests</u> against the government's proposals.
We wrote a letter of <u>protest</u> to the newspaper.

prove – test

1 'prove'

If you **prove** that something is true or correct, you provide evidence showing that it is definitely true or correct.

He was able to <u>prove</u> that he was an American.
Tests <u>proved</u> that the bullet was not fired from a police weapon.

2 'test'

When you use a practical method to try to find out how good or bad someone or something is, don't say that you 'prove' them. Say that you **test** them.

I will <u>test</u> you on your knowledge of French.
A number of new techniques <u>were tested</u>.

provide

1 'provide with'

To **provide** something that someone needs or wants means to give it to them or make it available to them. You say that you **provide** someone **with** something.

They provided him with money to buy new clothes.
We can provide you with information that may help you to find a job.

> **! BE CAREFUL**
>
> You must use **with** in sentences like these. Don't say, for example, 'They provided him money to buy new clothes'.

2 'provide for'

You can also say that you **provide** something **for** someone.

The animals provide food for their young.
The hospital provides care for thousands of sick children.

> **! BE CAREFUL**
>
> Don't use any preposition except **for** in sentences like these. Don't say, for example, 'The animals provide food to their young'.

If you **provide for** someone, you regularly give them the things they need, such as money, food, or clothing.

Parents are expected to provide for their children.
If he dies, will the family be provided for?

You must use **for** in sentences like these. Don't say, for example, 'Parents are expected to provide their children'.

---

pub – bar

1 'pub'

In Britain, a **pub** is a building where people meet friends and have drinks, especially alcoholic drinks, and sometimes food.

John was in the pub last night and he bought me a drink.

In formal English, this can also be called a **public house**.

The Green Man is often seen as a name or sign on public houses.

2 'bar'

 In American English, a place where you can buy and drink alcoholic drinks is usually called a **bar**.

After work they went to a bar downtown.

In British English, the word **bar** is sometimes used, especially to refer to a place serving alcoholic drinks that is part of a larger building, or in expressions such as **wine bar** and **cocktail bar**.

I'll meet you in the hotel bar in 20 minutes.

→ See **bar**

public

→ See **Nouns** for information on Collective nouns

public house

→ See **pub – bar**

pupil

→ See **student**

purse

In British English, a **purse** is a small container that a woman carries money in.

I always have my phone, purse, and keys in my handbag.

 In American English, this is called a **change purse**, **coin purse**, **pocketbook**, or **wallet**.

Eva searched her change purse and found fifty cents.

The word **wallet** is also used in British English, but only to refer to a container that a man carries money in.

Dad opened his wallet and gave me a ten pound note.

 In American English, a **purse** is a woman's handbag.

She reached in her purse for her diary.

put off

→ See **delay – cancel – postpone – put off**

put up with

→ See **bear**

Qq

quality

When you are talking about things that have been made or produced, you can use **quality** to say how good or bad they are.

The quality of the photograph was poor.
Over the years they have received many awards for the high quality of their products.

You can say that something is **of good quality** or **of poor quality**.

The treatment and care provided were also of poor quality.
Television ensures that films of high quality are shown to large audiences.

You can also use expressions such as **good quality** and **high quality** in front of nouns.

I've got some good quality paper.
Teaching is backed up by the highest quality research.

You can also use **quality** on its own in front of a noun. When you do this, you are showing that something is of a high standard.

They publish quality fiction.
The employers don't want quality work any more.

GRAMMAR FINDER

Quantity

1 numbers	**12**	with specific plural noun phrases
2 indefinite determiners	**13**	with all singular noun phrases
3 with singular nouns	**14**	with all uncountable noun phrases
4 with plural and uncountable nouns	**15**	with all plural noun phrases
5 with plural countable nouns	**16**	pronoun use
6 with uncountable nouns	**17**	fractions
7 with all types of noun	**18**	quantifiers used with abstract nouns
8 words used in front of determiners	**19**	partitives
9 quantifiers	**20**	measurement nouns
10 with specific or general noun phrases	**21**	containers
11 with specific uncountable nouns	**22**	-ful
	23	countable nouns

1 numbers

Quantities and amounts of things are often referred to using **numbers**.

→ See **Reference** sections **Numbers and fractions**, **Measurements**

2 indefinite determiners

You can use **indefinite determiners** such as **some**, **any**, **all**, **every**, and **much** to talk about quantities and amounts of things.

There is <u>some</u> chocolate cake over there.
He spoke <u>many</u> different languages.
<u>Most</u> farmers are still using the old methods.

3 with singular nouns

The following indefinite determiners can only be used in front of singular countable nouns:

a	another	either	neither
an	each	every	

Could I have <u>another cup</u> of coffee?
I agree with <u>every word</u> Peter says.

4 with plural countable and uncountable nouns

The following indefinite determiners are only used with plural forms of nouns and with uncountable nouns:

all	enough	more	most

He has <u>more books</u> than I do.
It had <u>enough room</u> to store all the information.

5 with plural countable nouns

The following indefinite determiners are only used with plural forms of nouns:

a few	fewer	many	several
few	fewest	other	

The town has <u>few monuments</u>.
He wrote <u>many novels</u>.

6 with uncountable nouns

Much, **little**, and **a little** are only used with uncountable nouns.

Do you watch <u>much television</u>?
We've made <u>little progress</u>.

! BE CAREFUL

There are restrictions on using **much** in positive statements.

→ See **much**

Some people think that **less** and **least** should only be used with uncountable nouns, not with plural forms of nouns.

→ See **less**

7 with all types of noun

Any, **no**, and **some** are used with all types of noun.

Cars can be rented at almost <u>any US airport</u>.
He had <u>no money</u>.
They've had <u>some experience</u> of teaching.

Any is not generally used in positive statements.

→ See **any**

8 words used in front of determiners

A few words used to indicate amounts or quantities can come in front of definite determiners such as **the**, **these**, and **my**. These are also called **predeterminers**.

all	double	twice
both	half	

All the boys started to laugh.
I invited both the boys.
She paid double the sum they asked for.

Half can also come in front of **a** or **an**.

I read for half an hour.

What is a predeterminer that can only be used before **a** or **an**.

What a lovely day!
What an awful thing to do.

→ See **all**, **both**, **half – half of**

9 quantity words + 'of'

Quantities and amounts are also referred to using a word or phrase such as **several**, **most**, or **a number** linked with **of** to the following noun phrase.

I am sure both of you agree with me.
I make a lot of mistakes.
In Tunis there are a number of art galleries.

When you use a quantity word + **of** as the subject of a verb, you use a singular verb form if the noun phrase after **of** is singular or uncountable, and a plural verb form if the noun phrase after **of** is plural.

Some of the information has already been analysed.
Some of my best friends are policemen.

10 with specific or general noun phrases

Quantity words + **of** are often used to refer to part of a particular amount, group, or thing. The noun phrase after **of** begins with a definite determiner such as **the**, **these**, or **my**, or consists of a pronoun such as **us**, **them**, or **these**.

Nearly all of the increase has been caused by inflation.
Very few of my classes were interesting.
Several of them died.

Sometimes quantity words + **of** are used to refer to part of something of a particular kind. The noun phrase after **of** is a singular countable noun preceded by an indefinite determiner such as **a**, **an**, or **another**.

It took him the whole of an evening to get her to agree.

Often, quantity words + **of** are used simply to show how many or how much of a type of thing you are talking about. In this case, the noun phrase after **of** is a general plural or uncountable noun phrase, without a determiner.

I would like to ask you a couple of questions.
There's a great deal of money involved.

◼ with specific uncountable nouns

The following quantity words + **of** are used with specific uncountable noun phrases, but not general ones:

all of	little of	none of	the remainder of
any of	more of	part of	the rest of
enough of	most of	some of	the whole of
less of	much of	a little of	

Most of my hair had to be cut off.
Ken and Tony did much of the work.

◼ with specific plural noun phrases

The following quantity words + **of** are used with specific plural noun phrases, but not general ones:

all of	enough of	none of	a good many of
another of	few of	one of	a great many of
any of	fewer of	several of	the remainder of
both of	many of	some of	the rest of
certain of	more of	various of	
each of	most of	a few of	
either of	neither of	a little of	

Start by looking through their papers for either of the two documents.
Few of these organizations survive for long.

◼ with all singular noun phrases

The following quantity words + **of** are used with specific and general singular noun phrases:

all of	most of	an abundance of	a lot of
any of	much of	an amount of	a quantity of
enough of	none of	a bit of	a trace of
less of	part of	a good deal of	the majority of
little of	plenty of	a great deal of	the remainder of
lots of	some of	a little bit of	the rest of
more of	traces of	a little of	the whole of

Part of the farm lay close to the river bank.
Much of the day was taken up with classes.
Meetings are quarterly and take up most of a day.

◼ with all uncountable noun phrases

The following quantity words + **of** are used with definite and indefinite uncountable noun phrases:

heaps of	quantities of	a bit of	the majority of
loads of	tons of	a little bit of	a quantity of
lots of	traces of	a good deal of	a trace of
masses of	an abundance of	a great deal of	
plenty of	an amount of	a lot of	

These creatures spend a great deal of their time on the ground.
A lot of the energy that is wasted in negotiations could be directed into industry.

There had been <u>plenty of action</u> that day.
There was <u>a good deal of smoke</u>.

15 with all plural noun phrases

The following quantity words + **of** are used with definite and indefinite plural noun phrases:

heaps of	numbers of	an abundance of	a minority of
loads of	plenty of	a couple of	the majority of
lots of	quantities of	a lot of	a number of
masses of	tons of	a majority of	a quantity of

I picked up <u>a couple of the pamphlets</u>.
<u>A lot of them</u> were middle-aged ladies.
They had <u>loads of things to say to each other</u>.

Numbers of and **quantities of** are very often preceded by adjectives such as **large** and **small**.

The report contained <u>large numbers of</u> inaccuracies.
Chemical batteries are used to store <u>relatively small quantities of</u> electricity.

BE CAREFUL

Heaps of, **loads of**, **lots of**, **masses of**, and **tons of** are used only in conversation. When these quantity words + **of** are used with an uncountable noun or a singular noun phrase as the subject of a verb, the verb is singular, even though the quantity word sounds plural.

<u>Masses of evidence has</u> been accumulated.
<u>Lots of it isn't</u> relevant, of course.

16 pronoun use

Most of the words and expressions listed so far in this entry can be used as pronouns when it is clear who or what you are referring to.

<u>Many</u> are shareholders in companies.
<u>A few</u> crossed over the bridge.

However, **a**, **an**, **every**, **no**, and **other** are not used as pronouns.

17 fractions

Fractions such as **a fifth** and **two-thirds** can be used with **of** in the same way as **all of** and **some of**.

→ See **Reference** section **Numbers and fractions**

18 quantity words + 'of' used with abstract nouns

The following quantity words + **of** are used only or mainly when referring to qualities or emotions:

an element of	a measure of	a touch of
a hint of	a modicum of	

There was <u>an element of danger</u> in using the two runways together.
I must admit to <u>a tiny touch of envy</u> when I heard about his success.

A trace of is also often used when referring to an emotion.

She spoke without <u>a trace of embarrassment</u> about the problems that she had had.

19 partitives

You can refer to a particular quantity of something using a **partitive** such as **piece** or **group** linked by **of** to a noun. Partitives are all countable nouns. Often a partitive indicates the shape or nature of the amount or group.

Some partitives are used with **of** and an uncountable noun.

Who owns this bit of land?
...portions of mashed potato.

Some are used with **of** and a plural noun.

...a huge heap of stones.
It was evaluated by an independent team of inspectors.

→ See **Topic** entry **Pieces and amounts** for more information about partitives used with uncountable nouns

When you use a singular partitive as the subject, you use a singular verb form if the noun after **of** is an uncountable noun.

A piece of paper is lifeless.

If the noun after **of** is a plural countable noun, you can use a plural verb form or a singular verb form. A plural verb form is more commonly used.

The second group of animals were brought up in a stimulating environment.
Each small group of workers is responsible for their own production targets.

When you use a plural partitive, you use a plural verb form.

Two pieces of metal were being rubbed together.

20 measurement nouns

Nouns referring to units of measurement are often used as partitives.

He owns only five hundred square metres of land.
I drink a pint of milk a day.

→ See **Reference** section **Measurements**

21 containers

You can use the names of containers as partitives when you want to refer to the contents of a container, or to a container and its contents.

I drank a bottle of water.
I went to buy a bag of chips.

22 '-ful'

You can add '**-ful**' to partitives referring to containers.

He brought me a bagful of sweets.
Pour a bucketful of cold water on the ash.

When people want to make a noun ending in '**-ful**' plural, they usually add an '**-s**' to the end of the word, as in **bucketfuls**. However, some people put the '**-s**' in front of '**-ful**', as in **bucketsful**.

She ladled three spoonfuls of sugar into my tea.
...two teaspoonsful of milk.

You can also add '**-ful**' to some parts of the body to form partitives. The commonest partitives of this kind are **armful**, **fistful**, **handful**, and **mouthful**.

Eleanor was holding an <u>armful of</u> roses.
He took another <u>mouthful of</u> juice.

23 countable nouns

Instead of using a partitive and **of**, you can sometimes use a noun that is usually uncountable as a countable noun. For example, **two teas** means the same as 'two cups of tea', and **two sugars** means 'two spoonfuls of sugar'.

I asked for two <u>coffees</u> with milk.

→ See **Nouns**

GRAMMAR FINDER

Questions

1	yes/no questions	**6**	wh-questions
2	'be'	**7**	wh-word as subject
3	'have'	**8**	wh-word as object or adverb
4	negative yes/no questions	**9**	questions in reply
5	answers to yes/no questions	**10**	indirect ways of asking questions

There are two main types of question: *yes/no*-questions and *wh*-questions.

1 yes/no-questions

Questions which can be answered by 'yes' or 'no' are called *yes/no*-questions.

'Are you ready?' – 'Yes.'
'Have you read this magazine?' – 'No.'

Yes/no-questions are formed by changing the order of the subject and the verb phrase.

If the verb phrase consists a main verb and one or more **auxiliary verbs**, you put the first auxiliary verb at the beginning of the sentence, in front of the subject. You put the rest of the verb phrase after the subject.

<u>Will you</u> have finished by lunchtime?
<u>Has he</u> been working?

If you are using a simple form (present simple or past simple), you use an appropriate form of the auxiliary verb **do** in front of the subject. You put the base form of the main verb after the subject.

<u>Do the British take</u> sport seriously?
<u>Does David do</u> this sort of thing often?
<u>Did you meet</u> George in France?

2 'be'

However, if the main verb is **be**, you put a form of **be** at the beginning of the clause, followed by the subject. Don't use 'do'.

<u>Are you</u> okay?
<u>Was it</u> lonely without us?

3 **'have'**

You can use a structure such as **Have you got...?** or a structure such as **Do you have...?**

→ See **have got**

People no longer say 'Have you...?' when using **have** as the main verb.

! **BE CAREFUL**

If you want to ask a yes/no-question, you don't usually use the normal word order of a statement. However, you can use the normal word order of a statement if you want to express surprise, or to check that something is true.

You've flown this machine before?
You've got two thousand already?

4 **negative yes/no-questions**

You use a negative yes/no-question when you think the answer will be, or should be, 'Yes'. For example, you say 'Didn't we see Daphne last weekend?' if you think you saw Daphne last weekend. You say 'Haven't you got a pen?' if you think the person you are speaking to should have a pen.

'Wasn't he French?' – 'Yes.'
'Didn't you say you'd done it?' – 'Yes.'

5 **answers to yes/no-questions**

When you answer a yes/no-question, you can just say '**Yes**' or '**No**', or you can follow '**Yes**' or '**No**' with a subject and auxiliary verb. For example, if you are asked a question like 'Have you finished?', you can say '**Yes, I have**' or '**No, I haven't**'. You use the auxiliary verb that was used in the question. However, if the main verb is **be** you can use the same form of **be** in your answer.

'Did you enjoy the film?' – 'Yes I did'.
'Have you met him yet?' – 'No I haven't.'
'Were you late?' – 'Yes I was.'

6 **wh-questions**

Wh-questions are used to ask about the identity of the people or things involved in an action, or about the circumstances of an action. Wh-questions begin with a wh-word. The wh-words are:

▶ the adverbs **how**, **when**, **where**, and **why**

▶ the pronouns **who**, **whom**, **what**, **which**, and **whose**

▶ the determiners **what**, **which**, and **whose**

Whom is only used as the object of a verb or preposition, not as a subject.

→ See **who – whom**

7 **wh-word as subject**

When a wh-word is the subject of a question, the wh-word comes first, followed by the verb phrase. The word order of the clause is the same as that of an ordinary statement.

What happened?
Who could have done it?

The form of a question is similar when the *wh*-word is part of the subject.

Which men had been ill?

8 *wh*-word as object or adverb

When a *wh*-word is the object of a verb or preposition, or when it is an adverb, the *wh*-word comes first. The formation of the rest of the clause is the same as for *yes/no*-questions; that is, the subject is put after the first auxiliary verb in the verb phrase, and the auxiliary verb **do** is used for simple forms.

Which do you like best?
When would you be coming down?

The form of a question is similar when the *wh*-word is part of the object.

Which graph are you going to use?

If there is a preposition, it usually comes at the end of the clause.

What are they looking for?
Which country do you come from?

However, if a phrase such as **at what time** or **in what way** is being used, the preposition is put at the beginning.

In what way are they different?

If **whom** is used, the preposition is always put first. **Whom** is only used in formal speech and writing.

With whom were you talking?

9 questions in reply

When you are asking a question in reply to what someone has said, you can often just use a *wh*-word, not a whole clause, because it is clear what you mean.

'There's someone coming.' – 'Who?'
'Maria! We won't discuss that here.' – 'Why not?'

10 indirect ways of asking questions

When you ask someone for information, it is more polite to use the expressions **'Could you tell me...?'** or **'Do you know...?'**

Could you tell me how far it is to the bank?
Do you know where Jane is?

Note that the second part of the question has the form of a reported question.

→ See **Reporting**

People sometimes use expressions like **'May I ask...?'** and **'Might I ask...?'** to ask a question indirectly. However, it is best not to use this way of asking a question, as it can sound hostile or aggressive.

May I ask what your name is?
Might I inquire if you are the owner?

GRAMMAR FINDER

Question tags

A **question tag** is a short phrase that you add to the end of a statement to turn it into a *yes/no*-question. You usually do this when you expect the other person to agree with the statement. For example, if you say 'It's cold, **isn't it?**', you expect the other person to say 'Yes'. If you say 'It isn't very warm, **is it?**', you expect the other person to say 'No'.

You form a question tag by using the same auxiliary verb or form of **be** as in the statement, followed by a personal pronoun. The pronoun refers to the subject of the statement.

You've never been to Spain, <u>have you</u>?
David's school is quite nice, <u>isn't it</u>?

If the statement is in a simple form (that is, it does not contain an auxiliary verb or **be**), the verb **do** is used in the question tag.

You <u>like</u> it here, <u>don't you</u>?
He <u>won</u>, <u>didn't he</u>?

You usually add a negative tag to a positive statement, and a positive tag to a negative statement. However, you add a positive tag to a positive statement when checking that you have guessed something correctly, or to show interest, surprise, or anger.

You've been to North America before, <u>have you</u>?
Oh, <u>he wants</u> us to make films as well, <u>does he</u>?

If you add a tag to a statement that contains a broad negative such as **hardly**, **rarely**, or **seldom**, the tag is normally positive, as it is with other negatives.

She's <u>hardly</u> the right person for the job, <u>is she</u>?
You <u>seldom</u> see that sort of thing these days, <u>do you</u>?

If you are making a statement about yourself and you want to check if the person you are talking to has the same opinion or feeling, you can put a tag with **you** after your statement.

I <u>think</u> this is the best thing, <u>don't you</u>?
I <u>love</u> tea, <u>don't you</u>?

→ See **Topic** entries **Agreeing and disagreeing**, **Invitations**, **Requests, orders, and instructions**, **Suggestions**

quiet – quite

1 'quiet'

Quiet is an adjective. Someone or something that is **quiet** makes only a small amount of noise.

Bal said in a <u>quiet</u> voice, 'I have resigned.'
The airlines have invested a lot of money in new, <u>quieter</u> aircraft.

If a place is **quiet**, there is very little noise there.

It was very <u>quiet</u> there; you could just hear the wind moving in the trees.

2 'quite'

Don't confuse **quiet** /ˈkwaɪət/ with **quite** /kwaɪt/. You use **quite** to show that something is the case to a fairly great extent.

→ See **quite**

---

quite

1 meaning 'to some extent'

You use **quite** in front of an adjective or adverb to show that something is the case to a fairly great extent but not to a very great extent. **Quite** is less emphatic than **very** and **extremely**.

He was quite young.
The end of the story can be told quite quickly.

 In American English, this use of **quite** is not as common as it is in British English. Speakers of American English tend to use **fairly** instead.

This example is fairly typical.

You can also use **quite** in front of **a**, an adjective, and a noun. For example, instead of saying 'It was quite cold', you can say 'It was **quite a cold day**'.

It's quite a good job.
She was quite a talented girl.

! BE CAREFUL

In sentences like these you put **quite** in front of **a**, not after it. Don't say, for example, 'It was a quite cold day'.

Don't use 'quite' in front of comparative adjectives or adverbs. Don't say, for example, 'The train is quite quicker than the bus'. Instead you use **a bit**, **a little**, or **slightly**.

I ought to do something a bit more ambitious.
He arrived a little earlier than he expected.
The risk of epidemics may be slightly higher in crowded urban areas.

→ See **Adverbs and adverbials** for graded lists of words used to indicate degree and extent

2 meaning 'very much' or 'completely'

Quite can be used with a different meaning. You can use it in front of an adjective, adverb, or verb to emphasize that something is completely the case or very much the case.

You're quite right.
I saw the driver quite clearly.
I quite understand.

→ See **Adverbs and adverbials** for a list of adverbs to emphasize a verb

Rr

raise

→ See **rise – raise**

rarely

→ See **Adverbs and adverbials** for a graded list of words used to indicate frequency

rather

1 used as adverb of degree

Rather means 'to a small extent'.

It's a rather sad story.

You can use **rather** in front of **like** when you are using **like** as a preposition.

This animal looks and behaves rather like a squirrel.
She imagined a life rather like that of the Kennedys.

Rather in this sense is mainly used in writing. In conversation you would normally use **a bit**.

I'm a bit confused
It tastes a bit like a tomato.

Several words and expressions can be used to say that something is the case to a smaller or greater extent.

→ See **Adverbs and adverbials** for a graded list of words used to indicate degree

Rather is also used to soften the effect of the word or expression that follows it. For example, if someone asks you to do something, you might say 'I'm rather busy'. You mean that you are busy, but **rather** makes your reply seem more polite.

I'm rather puzzled by this question.
He did it rather badly.

 Rather is more common in British than American English in the above senses.

2 'would rather'

If you say that you **would rather do** something, you mean that you would prefer to do it. In speech, **would rather** is usually contracted to **'d rather**. If you write down what someone says, you usually write **'d rather**.

I'll order tea. Or perhaps you'd rather have coffee.
'What was all that about?' – 'I'm sorry, I'd rather not say.'

In sentences like these you use an infinitive without **to** after **would rather**.

You can also use **would rather** followed by a clause to say that you would prefer something to happen or be done. In the clause you use the past simple.

Would you rather she came to see me?
'May I go on?' – 'I'd rather you didn't.'

3 'rather than'

Rather than is used to link words or expressions of the same type. You use **rather than** when you have said what is true and you want to compare it with what is not true.

I have used familiar English names rather than scientific Latin ones.
It made him frightened rather than angry.

4 correcting a mistake

You can also use **rather** when you are correcting a mistake you have made, or when you think of a better word than the one you have just used.

There'd been a message, or rather a series of messages, on Dalziel's answering machine.
He explained what the Crux is, or rather, what it was.

reach

→ See **arrive – reach**

read

1 reading to yourself

When you **read** /riːd/ a piece of writing, you look at it and understand what it says.

Why don't you read your letter?

The past tense and *-ed* participle of **read** is **read** /red/.

I read through the whole paper.
Have you read that article I gave you?

2 reading to someone else

If you **read** something such as a book to someone, you say the words so that the other person can hear them. When you use **read** like this, it has two objects. If the indirect object is a pronoun, it usually goes in front of the direct object.

I'm going to read him some of my poems.
I read her the two pages dealing with plants.

If the indirect object is not a pronoun, it usually goes after the direct object. When this happens, you put **to** in front of the indirect object.

Read books to your baby – this helps to develop language and listening skills.

You also put the indirect object after the direct object when the direct object is a pronoun.

You will have to read it to him.

You can also omit the direct object.

I'll go up and read to Sam for five minutes.

ready

1 used after a verb

If you are **ready**, you have prepared yourself for something.

Are you ready now? I'll take you back home.
We were getting ready for bed.

If something is **ready**, it has been prepared and you can use it.

Lunch is ready.
Go and get the boat ready.

! BE CAREFUL

Don't use '**ready**' with either of these meanings in front of a noun.

2 used in front of a noun

You use **ready** in front of a noun to show that something is available to be used very quickly and easily.

Many supermarket ready meals contain high levels of salt.
I have no ready explanation for this fact.

Ready money is in the form of notes and coins rather than cheques, and so can be used immediately.

He had £3000 in ready cash.

realize

→ See **understand – realize**

really

You use **really** in conversation and in less formal writing to emphasize something that you are saying.

Really usually goes in front of a verb, or in front of an adjective or adverb.

I really enjoyed that.
It was really good.
He did it really carefully.

You can put **really** in front of or after an auxiliary verb. For example, you can say 'He **really is** coming' or 'He **is really** coming'. There is no difference in meaning.

We really are expecting it to be a best-seller.
It would really be too much trouble.

! BE CAREFUL

'Really' is not usually used in formal writing. Words such as **very** or **extremely** are usually used instead.

 You can say '**Really?**' to show that you are surprised by something that someone has said.

'I think he likes you.' – 'Really? He hardly spoke to me all day.'

reason

The **reason for** something is the fact or situation which explains why it happens, exists, or is done.

I asked the reason for the decision.
The reason for this relationship is clear.

! BE CAREFUL

Don't use any preposition except **for** after **reason** in sentences like these.

You can talk about a person's **reason for doing** something.

One of his reasons for coming to England was to make money.

You can also talk about the **reason why** something happens or is done.

There are several reasons why we can't do that.

However, if you are actually stating the reason, don't use 'why'. Instead you use a *that*-clause.

The reason that they liked the restaurant was its relaxed atmosphere.
The reason I'm calling you is that I know Larry talked with you earlier.

Note that the second clause in these sentences is also a *that*-clause. Instead of a *that*-clause, some speakers use a clause beginning with **because**.

The reason they are not like other boys is because they have been brought up differently.

This use of **because** is fairly common in spoken and informal English. However, some people think that it is incorrect, and you should avoid it in formal English.

receipt – recipe

1 'receipt'

A **receipt** /rɪˈsiːt/ is a piece of paper that confirms that money or goods have been received.

We've got receipts for each thing we've bought.

2 'recipe'

Don't use 'receipt' to refer to a set of instructions telling you how to cook something. The word you use is **recipe** /ˈresəpi/.

This is an old Polish recipe for beetroot soup.

receive

When you **receive** something, someone gives it to you, or it arrives after it has been sent to you. **Get** is used in a similar way. You use **receive** in formal writing and **get** in conversation and in less formal writing.

For example, in a business letter you might write 'I **received** a letter from Mr Jones', but in conversation and in less formal writing you would say or write 'I **got** a letter from Mr Jones'.

The police received a call from the house at about 4.50 a.m.
I got a call from my father.

You can say that someone **receives** or **gets** a wage, salary, or pension.

His mother received no pension or compensation.
He was getting a very low salary.

You can also say that someone **receives** or **gets** help or advice.

She has received help from friends.
Get advice from your local health department.

recognize – realize

1 'recognize'

If you **recognize** someone or something, you know who or what they are because you have seen them before, or because they have been described to you.

She didn't recognize me at first.
Doctors are trained to recognize the symptoms of depression.

If you **recognize** something such as a problem, you accept that it exists.

Governments are beginning to recognize the problem.
We recognize this as a genuine need.

2 'realize'

If you become aware of a fact, don't say that you 'recognize' it. Say that you **realize** it.

I realized Martha was right.
She realized that she was going to be late.

recommend

If you **recommend** someone or something, you praise them and advise other people to use them or buy them.

I asked my friends to recommend a doctor who is good with children.
We strongly recommend the publications listed on the back page of this leaflet.

You can say that you **recommend** someone or something **for** a particular job or purpose.

Nell was recommended for a job as a cleaner.
I recommend running for strengthening your leg muscles.

If you **recommend** a particular action, you say that it is the best thing to do in the circumstances.

They recommended a merger of the two biggest supermarket groups.
The doctor may recommend limiting the amount of fat in your diet.

You can recommend **that someone does** something or recommend **that someone should do** something.

Waugh was examined by a doctor who recommended that he see an orthopaedic surgeon.
It is strongly recommended that you should attend this course if possible.

You can also recommend **someone to do** something.

Although they have eight children, they do not recommend other couples to have families of this size.

Some people consider this use to be incorrect, and say that you should say 'Although they have eight children, they do not **recommend that other couples should have** families of this size'.

! BE CAREFUL

Don't say that you 'recommend someone' a particular action. Don't say, for example, 'I recommend you a visit to Paris'. Say 'I **recommend a visit** to Paris', 'I **recommend visiting** Paris', or 'I **recommend that you visit** Paris'.

recover

If you **recover**, you become well again after an illness or injury.

It was several weeks before he fully recovered.

Recover is a fairly formal word. In conversation and in less formal writing, you usually say that someone **gets better**.

He soon got better after a few days in bed.

→ See **better**

You can say that someone **recovers from** an illness.

How long do people take to recover from an infection of this kind?

> **!** **BE CAREFUL**
> Don't say that someone ~~gets better from~~ an illness.

regret – be sorry

1 sadness and disappointment

Regret and **be sorry** are both used to say that someone feels sadness or disappointment about something that has happened, or about something they have done. **Regret** is more formal than **be sorry**.

You can say that you **regret** something or **are sorry about** it.

I immediately regretted my decision.
Astrid was sorry about leaving abruptly.

You can also say that you **regret** or **are sorry** that something has happened.

Pisarev regretted that no real changes had occurred.
He was sorry he had agreed to stay.

You can also say that you **regret doing** something.

None of the women I spoke to regretted making this change.

> **!** **BE CAREFUL**
> Don't say that you 'are sorry doing' something.

2 apologizing

When you are apologizing to someone for something that has happened, you can say that you **are sorry about** it.

I'm sorry about the mess – I'll clean up.

You can also report someone's apology by saying that they **are sorry about** something.

She was very sorry about all the trouble she'd caused.

> **!** **BE CAREFUL**
> Don't say that you are 'sorry for' something.

In conversation, don't apologize by saying that you 'regret' something. **Regret** is only used in formal letters and announcements.

London Transport regrets any inconvenience caused by these delays.

→ See **Topic** entry **Apologizing**

3 giving bad news

When you are giving someone some bad news, you can begin by saying 'I**'m sorry to** tell you...'. In a formal letter, you say 'I **regret to** inform you...'.

I'm very sorry to tell you this, but she's dead.
I regret to inform you that your application has not been successful.

---

relation – relative – relationship

These words are used to refer to people or to connections between people.

1 'relation' and 'relative'

Your **relations** or **relatives** are the members of your family.

I said that I was a relation of her first husband.
I'm going to visit some relatives.

The **relations** between people or groups are the contacts between them and the way they behave towards each other.

Relations between the two men had not improved.
Britain has close relations with the US.

2 'relationship'

You can talk in a similar way about the **relationship** between two people or groups.

The old relationship between the friends was quickly re-established.
Senor Zapatero has shown that he is keen to have a close relationship with Britain.

A **relationship** is also a close friendship between two people, especially one involving sexual or romantic feelings.

When the relationship ended two months ago, he was very upset.

GRAMMAR FINDER

Relative clauses

1 relative pronouns	9 referring to a situation
2 defining relative clauses	10 prepositions with relative
3 referring to people	pronouns
4 referring to things	11 'of whom' and 'of which'
5 not using a relative pronoun	12 'whose' in relative clauses
6 non-defining relative clauses	13 'when', 'where', and 'why'
7 referring to people	14 referring to the future
8 referring to things	

A **relative clause** is a subordinate clause that gives more information about someone or something mentioned in the main clause. The relative clause comes immediately after the noun that refers to the person or thing being talked about.

The man who came into the room was short and thin.
Opposite is St. Paul's Church, where you can hear some lovely music.

1 relative pronouns

Many relative clauses begin with a **relative pronoun**. The relative pronouns are:

that	which	who	whom

The relative pronoun usually acts as the subject or object of a verb in the relative clause.

...a girl who wanted to go to college.
There was so much that she wanted to ask.

There are two kinds of relative clause: **defining relative clauses** and **non-defining relative clauses**.

2 defining relative clauses

Defining relative clauses give information that helps to identify the person or thing being spoken about. For example, in the sentence 'The woman who owned the shop was away', the defining relative clause 'who owned the shop' makes it clear which particular woman is being referred to.

The man who you met yesterday was my brother.
The car which crashed into me belonged to Paul.

Defining relative clauses are sometimes called **identifying relative clauses**.

3 referring to people

When you are referring to a person or group of people in a defining relative clause, you use **who** or **that** as the subject of the defining clause.

We met the people who live in the cottage.
He was the man that bought my house.

You use **who**, **that**, or **whom** as the object of a defining clause.

...someone who I haven't seen for a long time.
...a woman that I dislike.
...distant relatives whom he had never seen.

Whom is a formal word.

→ See **who – whom**

4 referring to things

When you are referring to a thing or group of things, you use **which** or **that** as the subject or object of a defining clause.

...pasta which came from Milan.
There are a lot of things that are wrong.
...shells which my sister has collected.
The thing that I really liked about it was its size.

In general, **that** is more common in American English, in defining relative clauses of this type, but both forms are found in both varieties.

5 not using a relative pronoun

You don't have to use a relative pronoun as the object of the verb in a defining relative clause. For example, instead of saying 'a woman that I dislike', you can say 'a woman I dislike'.

The woman you met yesterday lives next door.
The car I wanted to buy was not for sale.

However, when the relative pronoun is the subject of the verb in a defining relative clause, the relative pronoun cannot be omitted.

The man who did this was a criminal.

> **❗ BE CAREFUL**
>
> The relative pronoun in a relative clause acts as the subject or object of the clause. This means that you should not add another pronoun as the subject or object. For example, you say 'There are a lot of people that want to be rich'. Don't say 'There are a lot of people that they want to be rich'.
>
> Similarly, you say 'This is the book which I bought yesterday'. Don't say 'This is the book which I bought it yesterday'. Even if you don't use a relative pronoun, as in 'This is the book I bought yesterday', don't put in another pronoun.

6 non-defining relative clauses

Non-defining relative clauses are used to give further information about someone or something, not to identify them. For example, in 'I'm writing to my mother, who's in hospital', the relative clause 'who's in hospital' gives more information about 'my mother' and is not used to show which mother you mean.

He was waving to the girl, who was running along the platform.
He walked down to Broadway, the main street of the town, which ran parallel to the river.

Note that you put a comma in front of a non-defining relative clause.

7 referring to people

When a non-defining clause relates to a person or group of people, you use **who** as the subject of the clause, or **who** or **whom** as the object of the clause.

Heath Robinson, who died in 1944, was a graphic artist and cartoonist.
I was in the same group as Janice, who I like a lot.
She was engaged to a sailor, whom she had met at Dartmouth.

8 referring to things

When a non-defining clause relates to a thing or a group of things, you use **which** as the subject or object.

I am teaching at the local college, which is just over the road.
He had a lot of money, which he mainly spent on cars.

> **❗ BE CAREFUL**
>
> Don't use 'that' to begin a non-defining relative clause. For example, don't say 'She sold her car, that she had bought the year before'. You must say 'She sold her car, **which** she had bought the year before'. Non-defining clauses cannot be used without a relative pronoun. For example, you cannot say 'She sold her car, she had bought the year before'.

9 referring to a situation

Non-defining relative clauses beginning with **which** can be used to say something about the whole situation described in the main clause.

I never met Brendan again, which was a pity.
Small computers need only small amounts of power, which means that they will run on small batteries.

10 prepositions with relative pronouns

In both types of relative clause, a relative pronoun can be the object of a preposition. In conversation, the preposition usually comes at the end of the clause, with no noun phrase after it.

I wanted to do the job which I'd been trained for.
...the world that you are interacting with.

Often, in a defining relative clause, no relative pronoun is used.

...the pages she was looking at.
I'd be wary of anything Matt is involved with.

In formal English, the preposition comes in front of the relative pronoun **whom** or **which**.

I have at last met John Parr's tenant, about whom I have heard so much.
He was asking questions to which there were no answers.

> ## ! BE CAREFUL
>
> If the verb in a relative clause is a **phrasal verb** ending with a preposition, you cannot move the preposition to the beginning of the clause. For example, you cannot say ~~'all the things with which I have had to put up'~~. You have to say 'all the things I've had to put up with'.
>
> *...the delegates she had been looking after.*
> *Everyone I came across seemed to know about it.*

A non-defining relative clause can begin with a preposition, **which**, and a noun. The only common expressions of this kind are **in which case**, **by which time**, and **at which point**.

It may be that your circumstances are different, in which case we can ensure that you have taken the right action.
Leave the mixture to cool down for two hours, by which time the spices should have flavoured the vinegar.

11 'of whom' and 'of which'

Words such as **some**, **many**, and **most** can be put in front of **of whom** or **of which** at the beginning of a non-defining relative clause. You do this to give information about part of the group just mentioned.

We were greeted by the teachers, most of whom were middle-aged.
It is a language shared by several cultures, each of which uses it differently.

Numbers can be put in front of **of whom** or **of which** or, more formally, after these phrases.

They act mostly on suggestions from present members (four of whom are women).
Altogether 1,888 people were prosecuted, of whom 1,628 were convicted.

12 'whose' in relative clauses

When you want to talk about something belonging or relating to a person, thing, or group, you use a defining or non-defining relative clause beginning with **whose** and a noun.

...workers whose bargaining power is weak.
According to Cookson, whose book is published on Thursday, most disasters are avoidable.

Some people think it is incorrect to use **whose** to show that something belongs or relates to a thing.

→ See **whose**

13 'when', 'where', and 'why'

When, **where**, and **why** can be used in defining relative clauses after certain nouns. **When** is used after **time** and other time words, **where** is used after **place** or place words, and **why** is used after **reason**.

This is one of those occasions when I regret not being able to drive.
That was the room where I did my homework.
There are several reasons why we can't do that.

When and **where** can be used in non-defining relative clauses after expressions of time and place.

This happened in 1977, when I was still a baby.
She has just come back from a holiday in Crete, where Alex and I went last year.

14 referring to the future

In a defining relative clause, you sometimes use the present simple and sometimes use **will** when referring to the future.

→ See **The Future**

---

relax

When you **relax**, you make yourself calmer and less worried or tense.

Make the room dark, get into bed, close your eyes, and relax.
Some people can't even relax when they are at home.

Relax is not a reflexive verb. Don't say that you 'relax yourself'.

---

relieve – relief

1 'relieve'

Relieve /rɪˈliːv/ is a verb. If something **relieves** an unpleasant feeling, it makes it less unpleasant.

Anxiety may be relieved by talking to a friend.
The passengers in the plane swallow to relieve the pressure on their eardrums.

If someone or something **relieves** you **of** an unpleasant feeling or difficulty, you no longer have it.

The news relieved him of some of his embarrassment.

Relieve is often used in the passive structure **be relieved**. If you **are relieved**, you feel happy because something unpleasant has stopped or has not happened.

I was relieved when Hannah finally arrived.

Be relieved is often followed by a *to*-infinitive.

He was relieved to find he'd suffered no more than a few scratches.

2 'relief'

Relief /rɪ'liːf/ is a noun. If you feel **relief**, you feel glad because something unpleasant has stopped or has not happened.

I breathed a sigh of relief.
To my relief, he found the suggestion acceptable.

Relief is also money, food, or clothing that is provided for people who are very poor or hungry.

We are providing relief to vulnerable refugees, especially those who are sick.

remain – stay

Remain and **stay** are often used with the same meaning. **Remain** is more formal than **stay**. To **remain** or **stay** in a particular state means to continue to be in that state.

Oliver remained silent.
I stayed awake all night.

If you **remain** or **stay** in a place, you do not leave it.

I was allowed to remain at home.
Fewer women these days stay at home to look after their children.

If something still exists, you can say that it **remains**. Don't say that it 'stays'.

Even today parts of the old wall remain.
The wider problem remains.

If you **stay** in a town, hotel, or house, you live there for a short time.

How long can you stay in Brussels?
She was staying in the same hotel as I was.

❗ BE CAREFUL

Don't use 'remain' with this meaning.

remark

→ See **comment – mention – remark**

remember – remind

1 'remember'

If you **remember** people or events from the past, your mind still has an impression of them and you are able to think about them.

I remember the look on Gary's face as he walked out the door.
He remembered the man well.

You can use either an *-ing* form or a *to*-infinitive after **remember**, but with different meanings. If your mind has an impression of something you did in the past, you say that you **remember doing** it.

I remember asking one of my sons about this.

If you do something that you had intended to do, you can say that you **remember to do** it.

He remembered to turn the gas off.

2 **'remind'**

If you mention to someone that they had intended to do something, don't say that you 'remember' them to do it. Say that you **remind** them to do it.

→ See **remind**

remind

If you **remind** someone **of** a fact or event that they already know about, you say something which causes them to think about it.

She reminded him of two appointments.
You do not need to remind people of their mistakes.

You can **remind** someone **that** something is true.

I reminded him that we had a wedding to go to on Saturday.

If you **remind** someone **to do** something, you tell them again that they should do it, or you mention to them that they had intended to do it.

She reminded me to wear the visitor's badge at all times.
Remind me to speak to you about Davis.

! BE CAREFUL

Don't say that you 'remind someone of doing' something.

If someone or something **reminds** you **of** another person or thing, they are similar to that other person or thing and make you think about them.

Your son reminds me of you at his age.

You must use **of** in a sentence like this.

remove – move

1 **'remove'**

If you **remove** something, you take it away.

The waiter came over to remove the plates.
He removed his hand from the man's collar.

2 **'move'**

If you go to live in a different house, don't say that you 'remove'. Say that you **move**.

Send me your new address if you move.
Last year my parents moved from Marseille to Paris.

In British English, you can also say that you **move house**.

We have just moved house and are planning to paint some of the rooms.

rent

→ See **hire – rent – let**

GRAMMAR FINDER

Reporting

1 direct speech	**14** with past reporting verb
2 reporting structures	**15** referring to the future
3 reporting verbs	**16** modals in reported clauses
4 reporting verbs with a negative	**17** with past reporting verb
5 reported clauses	**18** ability
6 *that*-clauses	**19** possibility
7 mentioning the hearer	**20** permission
8 use of the passive	**21** the future
9 *to*-infinitive clauses	**22** can, may, will
10 *-ing* clauses	**23** obligation
11 reported questions	**24** prohibiting
12 tense of reporting verb	**25** using reporting verbs for
13 tense of verb in reported clause	politeness

1 direct speech

One way of reporting what someone has said is to repeat their actual words. When you do this, you use a **reporting verb** such as **say**.

I said, 'Where are we?'
'I don't know much about music,' Judy said.

Sentences like these are called **direct speech** or **quote structures**. Direct speech is used more in stories than in conversation.

→ See **Reference** section **Punctuation**

In stories, you can put the reporting verb after the quote. The subject is often put after the verb.

'I see', <u>said John</u>.

! BE CAREFUL

However, when the subject is a pronoun, it must go in front of the verb.

'Hi there!' <u>he said</u>.

The reporting verb you typically use in conversation is **say**. In very informal situations, people sometimes use **go** or **be like** when they are quoting what someone said.

...and he went 'What's the matter with you?'
'I'm like 'What happened?' and he's like 'I reversed into a lamp-post.'

In stories you can show what kind of statement someone made using reporting verbs such as **ask**, **explain**, or **suggest**.

'What have you been up to?' he <u>asked</u>.
'It's a disease of the blood,' <u>explained</u> Kowalski.
'Perhaps,' he <u>suggested</u>, 'it was just an impulse.'

You can also use verbs such as **add**, **begin**, **continue**, and **reply** to show when one statement occurred in relation to another.

'I want it to be a surprise,' I <u>added</u>.
'Anyway,' she <u>continued</u>, 'it's quite out of the question.'
She <u>replied</u>, 'My first thought was to protect him.'

In a story, if you want to show the way in which something was said, you can use a reporting verb such as **shout**, **wail**, or **scream**.

'Jump!' shouted the oldest woman.
'Get out of there,' I screamed.

The following verbs show the way in which something is said:

babble	growl	roar	storm
bellow	hiss	scream	thunder
call	howl	shout	wail
chant	lisp	shriek	whine
chorus	mumble	sing	whisper
cry	murmur	splutter	yell
drawl	mutter	squeal	
exclaim	purr	stammer	

You can use a verb such as **smile**, **grin**, or **frown** to show the expression on someone's face while they are speaking.

'I'm awfully sorry.' – 'Not at all,' I smiled.
'You're late,' he frowned.

2 reporting structures

In conversation, you normally give an idea of what someone said using your own words in a **reporting structure**, rather than quoting them directly. You also use reporting structures to report people's thoughts.

She said it was quite an expensive one.
They thought that he should have been locked up.

Reporting structures are also often used in writing.

A reporting structure consists of two parts: a **reporting clause** and a **reported clause**.

3 reporting verbs

The **reporting clause** contains the **reporting verb** and usually comes first.

I told him that nothing was going to happen to me.
I asked what was going on.

The reporting verb with the widest meaning and use is **say**. You use **say** when you are simply reporting what someone said and do not want to imply anything about their statement.

He said that you knew his family.
They said the prison was surrounded by police.

→ See **say** for more information on its use, and the difference between it and other verbs referring to speaking

You can use a reporting verb such as **answer**, **explain**, and **suggest** to show what kind of statement you think the person was making.

She explained that her friend had been arrested.
I suggested that it was time to leave.

You can also show your own personal opinion of what someone said by using a reporting verb such as **claim** or **admit**. For example, if you say that someone **claimed** that they did something, you are implying that you think they may not be telling the truth. If you say that someone **admitted** something, you are implying that they are telling the truth.

He claims he knows more about the business now.
She admitted she was very much in love with you once.

4 reporting verbs with a negative

With a small number of reporting verbs, you usually make the reporting clause negative rather than the reported clause. For example, you would usually say 'I don't think Mary is at home' rather than 'I think Mary is not at home'.

I don't think I will be able to afford it.
I don't believe we can enforce a total ban.

The following reporting verbs are often used with a negative in this way:

believe	feel	propose	think
expect	imagine	suppose	

5 reported clauses

The second part of a reporting structure is the **reported clause**.

She said that she had been to Belgium.
The man in the shop told me how much it would cost.

There are several types of reported clause. The type used depends on whether a statement, order, suggestion, or question is being reported.

6 *that*-clauses

A report clause beginning with the conjunction **that** is used after a reporting verb to report a statement or someone's thoughts.

He said that the police had directed him to the wrong room.
He thought that Vita needed a holiday.

Some common reporting verbs used in front of a *that*-clause are:

accept	concede	hint	realize
admit	conclude	hope	recommend
agree	confess	imagine	remark
allege	decide	imply	remember
announce	declare	insist	reply
answer	deny	joke	report
argue	discover	know	reveal
assert	emphasize	mention	say
assume	expect	notice	stress
believe	explain	observe	suggest
claim	feel	point out	swear
comment	guarantee	predict	think
complain	guess	promise	warn

That is often omitted from a *that*-clause.

They said I had to see a doctor first.
I think there's something wrong.

However, **that** is nearly always used after some verbs, for example **answer**, **argue**, **complain**, **explain**, **recommend**, and **reply**.

He answered that the price would be three pounds.

A *that*-clause can contain a modal, especially when someone makes a suggestion about what someone else should do.

He proposes that the Government should hold an enquiry.

7 mentioning the hearer

After some reporting verbs that refer to speech, the hearer must be mentioned as the direct object. **Tell** is the most common of these verbs.

He told me that he was a farmer.
I informed her that I could not come.

The following verbs must have the hearer as direct object:

assure	inform	persuade	remind
convince	notify	reassure	tell

You can also choose to mention the hearer as object with **promise**, **remind** and **warn**.

I promised that I would try to phone her.
I reminded Myra I'd be home at seven.

With many other reporting verbs, if you want to mention the hearer, you do so in a prepositional phrase beginning with **to**.

I explained to her that I had to go home.
I mentioned to Tom that I was thinking of resigning.

The following verbs need the preposition **to** if you mention the hearer:

admit	confess	mention	suggest
announce	explain	reply	swear
boast	hint	report	whisper
complain	lie	reveal	

8 use of the passive

Verbs such as **tell** and **inform** can be used in the passive, with the hearer as the subject.

She was told that there were no tickets left.

A passive form of other reporting verbs is sometimes used to avoid saying whose opinion or statement is being reported, or to imply that it is an opinion that is generally held. This use of the passive is formal. You can use **it** as the subject with a *that*-clause, or you can use an ordinary subject with a *to*-infinitive clause.

It is now believed that foreign languages are most easily taught to young children.
He is said to have died a natural death.

9 *to*-infinitive clauses

You use a *to*-infinitive clause after a reporting verb such as **tell**, **ask**, or **advise** to report an order, a request, or a piece of advice. The person being addressed, who is going to perform the action, is mentioned as the object of the reporting verb.

Johnson told her to wake him up.
He ordered me to fetch the books.
He asked her to marry him.

Some common reporting verbs used after an object in front of a *to*-infinitive clause are:

advise	dare	instruct	remind
ask	direct	invite	request
beg	encourage	nag	tell
challenge	forbid	order	urge
command	implore	persuade	warn

The following verbs referring to saying, thinking, or discovering are always or usually used in the passive when followed by a *to*-infinitive.

allege	discover	learn	say
assume	estimate	prove	see
believe	feel	reckon	think
claim	find	report	understand
consider	know	rumour	

The *to*-infinitive that follows them is most commonly **be** or **have**.

The house was believed to be haunted.
Over a third of the population was estimated to have no access to the health service.

You can also use a *to*-infinitive after some reporting verbs that are not used with an object. The person who speaks is also the person who will perform the action.

agree	demand	propose	volunteer
ask	guarantee	refuse	vow
beg	offer	swear	
consent	promise	threaten	

They offered to show me the way.
He threatened to arrest me.

When you are reporting an action that the speaker intends to perform, you can sometimes use either a *to*-infinitive or a *that*-clause.

I promised to come back.
She promised that she would not leave hospital until she was better.

Don't use a *to*-infinitive if the hearer is being mentioned.

I promised her I would send her the money.
I swore to him that I would not tell anyone.

Claim and **pretend** can also be used with these two structures. For example, 'He claimed to be a genius' has the same meaning as 'He claimed **that** he was a genius'.

He claimed to have witnessed the accident.
He pretended that he had found the money in the cupboard.

Several verbs which show someone's intentions, wishes, or decisions, such as **intend**, **want**, and **decide**, are used with a *to*-infinitive clause.

10 *-ing* clauses

When reporting a suggestion about doing something, it is possible to use one of the reporting verbs **suggest**, **advise**, **propose**, or **recommend** followed by an *-ing* clause.

Barbara suggested going to another coffee house.
The committee recommended abandoning the original plan.

Note that you only **propose doing** actions that you yourself will be involved in.

Daniel proposed moving to New York.

11 reported questions

You use the reporting verb **ask** when reporting a question. You can mention the hearer as the direct object if you need to or want to.

He asked if I had a message for Cartwright.
I asked her if she wanted them.

Inquire and **enquire** also mean 'ask', but these are fairly formal words. You cannot mention the hearer as the object of these verbs.

An *if*-clause or a *whether*-clause is used when reporting *yes/no* questions. **Whether** is used especially if there is a choice of possibilities.

She asked him if his parents spoke French.
I was asked whether I wanted to stay at a hotel or at his home.

A reported clause beginning with a *wh*-word is used to report a *wh*-question.

He asked where I was going.
She enquired why I was so late.

! BE CAREFUL

The word order in a reported question is the same as that of a statement, not that of a question. For example, you say 'She asked me what I had been doing'. Don't say 'She asked me what had I been doing'.

Don't use a question mark when you write reported questions.

If the *wh*-word in a reported question is the object of a preposition, the preposition comes at the end of the clause, with no noun after it.

She asked what they were looking for.
He asked what we lived on.

Other verbs which refer to speech or thought about uncertain things can be used in front of clauses beginning with *wh*-words or with **if** or **whether**.

She doesn't know what we were talking about.
They couldn't see how they would manage without her.

A *to*-infinitive clause beginning with a *wh*-word or **whether** can be used to refer to an action that someone is uncertain about doing.

I asked him what to do.
I've been wondering whether to retire.

12 tense of reporting verb

You usually use a past tense of the reporting verb when you are reporting something said in the past.

She said you threw away her sweets.
Brody asked what happened.

However, you can use a present tense of the reporting verb, especially if you are reporting something that is still true.

She says she wants to see you this afternoon.
My doctor says it's nothing to worry about.

13 tense of verb in reported clause

If you are using a present tense of the reporting verb, you use the same tense in the reported clause as you would use for an ordinary, direct statement. For example, if a woman says 'He hasn't arrived yet', you could report this by saying 'She says he hasn't arrived yet'.

He knows he's being watched.
He says he has never seen a shark.
He says he was very worried.

14 with past reporting verb

If you are using a past tense of the reporting verb, you usually put the verb in the reported clause into a tense that is appropriate at the time that you are speaking.

If the event or situation described in the reported clause was in the past when the statement was made, you use the past perfect. You can sometimes use the past simple instead when you do not need to relate the event to the time that the statement was made.

Minnie said she had given it to Ben.
A journalist said he saw the couple at the airport.

You can also use the present perfect if the event or situation is recent or relevant to the present situation.

He said there has been a 56 per cent rise in bankruptcies in the past 12 months.

When reporting a habitual past action or a situation that no longer exists, you can use **used to**.

He said he used to go canoeing on rivers and lakes.

If the event or situation described in the reported clause was happening at the time when it was mentioned, you use the past simple or the past progressive.

Dad explained that he had no money.
She added that she was working too hard.

A past tense is usually used for the verb in the reported clause even if the reported situation still exists. For example, you say 'I told him I was eighteen' even if you are still eighteen. You are concentrating on the situation at the past time that you are talking about.

He said he was English.
I said I liked sleeping on the ground.

A present tense is sometimes used, however, to emphasize that the situation still exists or to mention a situation that often occurs among a group of people.

I told him that I don't go out very often.
A social worker explained that some children live in three or four different foster homes in one year.

15 referring to the future

If the event or situation was in the future at the time of the statement or is still in the future, you usually use a **modal**. See the section below on **modals in reported clauses**.

However, you use a present tense in reported questions and similar *wh*-clauses referring to a future event when the event will happen at about the same time as the statement or thought.

I'll telephone you. If I say it's Hugh, you'll know who it is.

If the future event will happen after the statement, you use **will** in the reported question.

I'll tell you what I will do.

16 modals in reported clauses

If the verb in the reporting clause is in a present tense, you use modals as you would use them in an ordinary, direct statement.

Helen says I can share her flat.
I think some of the sheep may die this year.
I don't believe he will come.
I believe that I could live very comfortably here.

See the individual Usage entries for modals for information on their uses.

17 with past reporting verb

If the verb in the reporting clause is in a past tense or has **could** or **would** as an auxiliary verb, you usually use **could**, **might**, or **would** in the reported clause, rather than **can**, **may**, or **will**, in the ways explained below.

18 ability

When you want to report a statement (or question) about someone's ability to do something, you normally use **could**.

They believed that war could be avoided.
Nell would not admit that she could not cope.

19 possibility

When you want to report a statement about possibility, you normally use **might**.

They told me it might flood here.
He said you might need money.

If the possibility is a strong one, you use **must**.

I told her she must be mistaken.

20 permission

When you want to report a statement giving permission or a request for permission, you normally use **could**. **Might** is used in more formal English.

I told him he couldn't have it.
Madeleine asked if she might borrow a pen and some paper.

21 the future

When you want to report a prediction, promise, or expectation, or a question about the future, you normally use **would**.

She said they would all miss us.
He insisted that reforms would save the system, not destroy it.

22 'can', 'may', 'will', and 'shall'

You can use **can**, **may**, **will**, and **shall** when you are using a past tense of the reporting verb, if you want to emphasize that the situation still exists or is still in the future.

He claimed that childhood problems may cause psychological distress in later life.
A spokesman said that the board will meet tomorrow.

23 obligation

When you want to report a statement in the past about obligation, it is possible to use **must**, but the expression **had to** is more common.

He said he really had to go back inside.
Sita told him that he must be especially kind to the little girl.

You use **have to**, **has to**, or **must** if the reported situation still exists or is in the future.

He said the Government must come clean on the issue.
A spokesman said that all bomb threats have to be taken seriously.

When you want to report a statement or thought about what is morally right, you can use **ought to** or **should**.

He knew he ought to help.
I felt I should consult my family.

24 prohibiting

When you want to report a statement prohibiting something, you normally use **mustn't**.

He said they mustn't get us into trouble.

25 using reporting verbs for politeness

Reporting verbs are often used to say something in a polite way. For example, if you want to contradict someone or to say something which might be unwelcome to them, you can avoid sounding rude by using a reporting verb such as **think** or **believe**.

I think it's time we stopped.
I don't think that will be necessary.
I believe you ought to leave now.

request

Request can be a noun or a verb.

1 used as a noun

When someone asks for something to be done or provided, you can say that they make a **request**.

My friend made a polite request.
The Minister had granted the request.

You say that someone makes a **request for** something.

He agreed to my request for help.

2 used as a verb

When someone **requests** something, they ask for it.

The President requested an emergency meeting of the United Nations.
The pilot had requested permission to land immediately at the airport.

! BE CAREFUL

When **request** is a verb, don't use 'for' after it. Don't say, for example, 'The President requested for an emergency meeting'.

In conversation and in less formal writing, you usually use **ask for** instead of 'request'.

I'm not afraid to ask for help and support when needed.

→ See **ask**

require

If you **require** something, you need it or want it.

Is there anything you require?
We cannot guarantee that any particular item will be available when you require it.

Require is a formal word. You do not usually use it in conversation or in less formal writing. Instead, you use **need** or **want**.

I won't need that book any more.
All they want is a holiday.

If something **is required**, it must be obtained so that something else can be done.

Parliamentary approval would be required for any scheme.
An increase in funds may be required.

If you **are required to** do something, you must do it, for example because of a rule or law.

All the boys were required to study religion.

research

Research is work that involves studying something and trying to discover facts about it. You say that someone **does**, **conducts**, or **carries out research**.

I had come to India to do some research into Anglo-Indian literature.

You can refer to the **research** that someone is doing as their **research** or their **researches**. You normally only use **researches** after a possessive form such as **my**, **his**, or **Gordon's**.

Soon after, Faraday began his researches into electricity.

! BE CAREFUL

Don't talk about 'a research'.

responsible

1 'responsible for'

If you are **responsible for doing** something, it is your job or duty to do it.

The children were responsible for cleaning their own rooms.

! BE CAREFUL

Don't say that someone is 'responsible to do' something.

If you are **responsible for** something bad that has happened, it is your fault.

They were charged with being responsible for the death of two policemen.

Don't use any preposition except **for** after **responsible** in a sentence like this.

2 **used after a noun**

Responsible can also be used after a noun. If you talk about 'the person **responsible**', you mean 'the person who is responsible for what has happened'.

I hope they police find the man responsible.
The company responsible refused to say what happened.

3 **used in front of a noun**

However, if you use **responsible** in front of a noun, it has a completely different meaning. A **responsible** person is someone who can be trusted to behave properly and sensibly.

Responsible adults wouldn't leave poisons lying around for their children to play with.

Responsible behaviour is sensible and correct.

I thought it was a very responsible decision.

---

rest

If you are talking about something that cannot be counted, the verb following **rest** is singular.

The rest of the food was delicious.

If you are talking about several people or things, the verb is plural.

The rest of the boys were delighted.

---

result – effect

1 **'result'**

A **result** of something is an event or situation that happens or exists because of it.

The result of this announcement was that the share price of the company rose by 10 per cent.
I nearly missed the flight as a result of getting stuck in traffic.
I cut my own hair – often with disastrous results.

2 **'effect'**

When something produces a change in a thing or person, don't refer to this change as a 'result' on the thing or person. The word you use is **effect**.

Diet has a significant effect on your health.

---

return

1 **going back**

When someone **returns** to a place, they go back there after they have been somewhere else.

I returned to my hotel.
Mr Platt returned from Canada in 1995.

! BE CAREFUL

Don't say that someone 'returns back' to a place.

Return is a fairly formal word. In conversation and in less formal writing, you usually use **go back**, **come back**, or **get back**.

I went back to the kitchen and poured my coffee.
I have just come back from a trip to Seattle.
I've got to get back to London.

Return is also a noun. When someone goes back to a place, you can refer to their arrival there as their **return**.

The book was published only after his return to Russia in 1917.

In writing, if you want to say that something happens immediately after someone returns to a place, you can use a phrase beginning with **on**. For example, you can say '**On his return** to London, he was offered a job'.

On her return she wrote the last paragraph of her autobiography.

2 giving or putting something back

When someone **returns** something they have taken or borrowed, they give it back or put it back.

He borrowed my best suit and didn't return it.
We returned the books to the shelf.

! BE CAREFUL

Don't say that someone '~~returns something back~~'.

3 'bring back'

When people start using a practice or method that was used in the past, don't say that they 'return' the practice or method. Say that they **bring** it **back** or **reintroduce** it.

He thought they should bring back hanging as a punishment for murderers.
They reintroduced a scheme to provide housing for refugees.

→ See **critic – critical – critique**

---

ride

1 'ride'

When you **ride** an animal, bicycle, or motorcycle, you control it and travel on it.

Every morning he used to ride his horse across the fields.
I learned how to ride a bike when I was seven.

The past tense of **ride** is **rode**. The *-ed* participle is **ridden**.

He usually rode to work on a motorbike.
He was the best horse I have ever ridden.

2 'ride on'

You can also say that someone **rides on** an animal, bicycle, or motorcycle.

She rode around the campus on a bicycle.

3 'drive'

When someone controls a car, lorry, or train, don't say that they 'ride' it. Say that they **drive** it.

It was her turn to drive the car.
Pierre has never learned to drive.

However, if you are a passenger in a vehicle, you can say that you **ride in** it.

We rode back in a taxi.
He prefers travelling on the train to riding in a limousine.

ring – call

1 'ring'

In British English, when you **ring** someone, you dial their phone number and speak to them by phone. The past tense of **ring** is **rang**.

I rang Aunt Jane this evening.

The *-ed* participle is **rung**.

Have you rung Dad yet?

You can say that someone **rings** a place.

You must ring the hospital.

In conversation, people often use **ring up**, instead of 'ring'. There is no difference in meaning.

He had rung up Emily and told her all about it.

! BE CAREFUL

Don't use 'to' after **ring** or **ring up**.

2 'call'

American speakers don't usually use **ring** in this sense. The word they use is **call**. British speakers also say **call**.

He promised to call me soon.

→ See **call**

rise – raise

Rise and **raise** are usually verbs.

1 'rise'

Rise is an intransitive verb. If something **rises**, it moves upwards.

Thick columns of smoke rise from the chimneys.

The other forms of **rise** are **rises**, **rising**, **rose**, **risen**.

A few birds rose noisily into the air.
The sun had risen behind them.

If an amount **rises**, it increases.

Commission rates are expected to rise.
Prices rose by more than 10%.

When someone who is sitting **rises**, they raise their body until they are standing. This use of **rise** occurs mainly in stories.

Dr Willoughby rose to greet them.

In conversation and in less formal writing, don't say that someone 'rises'. Say that they **stand up**.

I put down my glass and stood up.

You can also use **rise** to say that someone gets out of bed in the morning. This use of **rise** also occurs mainly in stories, especially when the author is mentioning the time at which someone gets out of bed.

They had risen at dawn.

In conversation and in less formal writing, don't use 'rise' to say that someone gets out of bed. Say that they **get up**.

Mike decided it was time to get up.

2 'raise'

Raise is a transitive verb. If you **raise** something, you move it to a higher position.

He raised the cup to his lips.
She raised her eyebrows in surprise.

3 used as nouns

Rise and **raise** can also be nouns. A **rise** is an increase in an amount or quantity.

The price rises are expected to continue.
There has been a rise in crime.

In British English, a **rise** is also an increase in someone's wages or salary.

He asked his boss for a rise.

 In American English, and sometimes in British English, people refer to this as a **raise**.

She got a 5% raise.

---

risk

Risk can be a noun or a verb.

1 used as a noun

If there is a **risk** of something unpleasant, there is a possibility that it will happen.

There is very little risk of infection.
The law allows police to stop people if they believe there is a serious risk of violence.

2 used as a verb

If someone **risks doing** something, it may happen as a result of something else they do.

He risked breaking his leg when he jumped.

You can also say that someone **risks doing** something when they do it even though they know it might have unpleasant consequences.

If you have an expensive rug, don't risk washing it yourself.

! BE CAREFUL

Don't say that someone 'risks to do' something.

rob – steal

1 'rob'

The verb **rob** is often used in stories and newspaper reports.

If someone takes something that belongs to you without intending to return it, you can say that they **rob you of** it.

Pirates boarded the ships and robbed the crew of money and valuables.
The two men were robbed of more than £700.

If something that belongs to you has been stolen, you can say that you have **been robbed**.

He was robbed on his way home.

If someone takes several things from a building without intending to return them, you say that they **rob** the building.

He told the police he robbed the bank to buy a car.

2 'steal'

When someone takes something without intending to return it, you do not say that they 'rob' it. You say that they **steal** it.

His first offence was stealing a car.

→ See **steal**

robber

→ See **thief – robber – burglar**

role – roll

These words are both pronounced /rəʊl/.

1 'role'

Your **role** is your position and what you do in a situation or society.

What is the role of the university in modern society?
He had played a major role in the formation of the United Nations.

A **role** is also one of the characters that an actor or singer plays in a film, play, opera, or musical.

She played the leading role in The Winter's Tale.

2 'roll'

A **roll** is a very small loaf of bread.

The soup is served with a roll and butter.

A **roll** of something such as cloth or paper is a long piece of it wrapped many times around itself or around a tube.

I bought a roll of wallpaper.

rotary

→ See **roundabout**

round

→ See **around – round – about**

---

roundabout

In British English, a **roundabout** is a circular area at a place where several roads meet. You drive round it until you come to the road you want.

Take the second exit at the roundabout onto the A140.

 In American English, an area like this is called a **traffic circle** or a **rotary**.

The traffic circle has successfully slowed down vehicle traffic.

In British English, a **roundabout** is also a circular platform in a play park that children sit or stand on. People push the platform to make it spin round.

Children were playing happily on the roundabout, slide and swings.

In American English, this is called a **merry-go-round**.

---

rubbish

In British English, waste food and other unwanted things that you throw away are called **rubbish**.

Illegal dumping of household rubbish was very common.

 In American English, waste food is called **garbage** and other things that are thrown away are called **trash**.

There were rotting piles of garbage everywhere.
They dumped their trash on the street.

Ss

's

1 used to form possessives

When a singular noun refers to a person or animal, you form the possessive by adding **'s**.

I heard Elena's voice.
They asked the boy's name.
Everyone admired the princess's dress.
She patted the horse's nose.

When a plural noun ends in s, you form the possessive by adding an apostrophe **'**.

I try to remember my friends' birthdays.
He borrowed his parents' car.

When a plural noun does not end in s, you form the possessive by adding **'s**.

She campaigned for women's rights.
The children's toys go in this box.

When a name ends in s, you usually form the possessive by adding **'s**.

We went to Carlos's house.
I'm in Mrs Jones's class.

In formal writing, the possessive of a name ending in s is sometimes formed by adding an apostrophe **'**.

This is a statue of Prince Charles' grandfather, King George VI.

You don't usually add **'s** to nouns that refer to things. For example, don't say 'the building's front'. Say 'the front **of the building**'.

We live at the bottom of the hill.
She'll be back at the end of August.

2 pronouns

You can add **'s** to the following pronouns:

another	everybody	no-one	somebody
anybody	everyone	one	someone
anyone	nobody	other	

Sometimes it helps to talk about one's problems.
One of the boys was riding on the back of the other's bike.

The possessive forms of other pronouns, for example **my**, **your**, and **her**, are called **possessive determiners**.

→ See **Possessive determiners**

3 other uses of possessives

In British English, you can add **'s** to a person's name to refer to the house where they live. For example, 'I met him at **Lisa's**' means 'I met him at Lisa's house'.

She was invited to a party at Ravi's.

British speakers also use words ending in **'s** to refer to shops and places offering services. For example, they talk about a **butcher's**, a **dentist's**, or a **hairdresser's**.

There's a newsagent's on the corner of the street.
I went to the doctor's because I kept getting headaches.

You can use **be** and a short noun phrase ending in **'s** to say who something belongs to. For example, if someone says 'Whose is this coat?', you can say 'It**'s my mother's**'.

One of the cars was his wife's.
Why are you wearing that ring? It's Tara's.

> **!** BE CAREFUL
>
> Don't use this construction in formal writing. Instead use **belong to**. You also use **belong to** with a longer noun phrase. For example, say 'It **belongs to** the man next door'. Don't say 'It is the man next door's'.
>
> *The painting belongs to someone I knew at university.*

4 other uses of 's

Apart from its use in possessives, **'s** has three other uses:

▶ It can be a shortened form of **is**, especially after pronouns.

He's a novelist.
It's fantastic.
There's nothing to worry about.

▶ It can be a shortened form of **has** when **has** is an auxiliary verb.

He's got a problem.
She's gone home.

▶ It can be a shortened form of **us** after **let**.

Let's go outside.
Let's not argue.

→ See **let's – let us**

---

safe – secure

1 'safe'

Safe /seɪf/ as an adjective has two main meanings.

If someone is **safe**, they are not in danger or cannot be harmed.

We're safe now. They've gone.
Thank goodness the children are safe.

> **!** BE CAREFUL
>
> When **safe** is used to describe people, it is never used in front of a noun. Don't say, for example, 'the safe children'.

You can say that you are **safe from** something or someone to mean that you cannot be harmed by them.

They want to keep their families safe from crime.
She realised with relief that she was safe from him now.

You can also say that something is **safe** to mean that it is not dangerous or risky.

Is the water safe to drink?
You should always keep your passport in a safe place.

2 'secure'

Something that is **secure** is protected so that nobody can get into it, steal it, or commit a crime involving it.

The hotel has 24-hour secure parking.
A secure password should contain a mixture of numbers, symbols, and letters.

You can also use **secure** to talk about a feeling of confidence that something is likely to continue or succeed.

To enjoy life you have to be financially secure.
The new job offered him a more secure future.

salad – lettuce

1 'salad'

A **salad** is a mixture of cold or uncooked vegetables. You can eat it on its own or with other foods.

For lunch she had a salad of tomato, onion and cucumber.
I made some potato salad for the picnic.

2 'lettuce'

A salad usually includes the large green leaves of a vegetable called a **lettuce** /'letɪs/. Don't refer to this vegetable as a 'salad'.

Tear the lettuce into small pieces and mix it with the dressing.

salary – wages

Salary and **wages** are both used to refer to the money paid to someone regularly for the work they do.

1 'salary'

Professional people such as teachers are usually paid a **salary**. Their **salary** is the total amount of money that they are paid each year, although this is paid in twelve parts, one each month.

She earns a high salary as an accountant.
My salary is paid into my bank account at the end of the month.

2 'wages'

If someone gets money each week for the work they do, you refer to this money as their **wages**.

On Friday afternoon the men are paid their wages.
He was working shifts at the factory and earning good wages.

3 'wage'

You can refer in a general way to the amount that someone earns as a **wage**.

It is hard to bring up children on a low wage.
The government introduced a legal minimum wage.

You can also talk about someone's hourly, weekly, or monthly **wage** to mean the money that they earn each hour, week, or month.

Her hourly wage had gone up from £5.10 to £5.70.
The suit cost £40, more than twice the average weekly wage at that time.

sale

1 'sale'

The **sale** of something is the act of selling it, or the occasion on which it is sold.

They introduced stricter controls on the sale of weapons.
Our agency can help you with the sale of your house.

A **sale** is an event in which a shop sells things at a reduced price.

The shoe shop is having a sale.
I got this jacket for only £25 in the sale.

2 'for sale'

If something is **for sale** or **up for sale**, its owner is trying to sell it.

I asked whether the car was for sale.
Their house is up for sale.

3 'on sale'

A product that is **on sale** is available for people to buy.

There were no English newspapers on sale.
Their new album is now on sale.

 In American English, if something is **on sale**, it is available at a reduced price.

On sale. Slacks marked down from $39.95 to $20.00.
I usually buy whichever brand of toothpaste is on sale.

salute – greet

1 'salute'

When members of the armed forces **salute** someone, they raise their right hand as a formal sign of greeting or respect.

The men saluted the General.

2 'greet'

Don't use 'salute' to say that someone says or does something to express friendliness when they meet someone else. Use **greet**.

He greeted his mother with a hug.
He hurried to greet his guests.

same – similar

Same is almost always used with **the**.

1 'the same'

If two or more things are **the same**, they are alike.

All the streets look the same in the fog.
Essentially, all computers are the same.

2 'the same as'

You say that one thing is **the same as** another thing.

He was not the same as the other boys.
The next day was the same as the one before.

! BE CAREFUL

Don't use any preposition except **as** after **the same** in sentences like these. Don't say, for example, 'He was not the same like the other boys'.

You can put a noun between **the same** and **as**. You can say, for example, 'She goes to **the same school as** her sister'.

Her dress was the same colour as her eyes.
I'm in the same type of job as you.

You can also use **the same as** to compare actions. For example, you can say 'She did **the same as** her sister did', or just 'She did **the same as** her sister'.

He said exactly the same as you did.
They've got to earn a living, the same as anybody else.

3 adverbs used with 'the same'

The following adverbs are often used in front of **the same**:

exactly	almost	virtually
nearly	practically	

The next time I saw him he looked exactly the same.
Their policies are practically the same as those of the previous government.

4 'similar'

If two people or things are **similar**, each one has some features that the other one has.

The two friends look remarkably similar.
Our ideas are basically very similar.

You say that one thing is **similar to** another thing.

It is similar to her last book.
My dress is similar to that, only longer.

You can use **similar** in front of a noun when you are comparing a person or thing to someone or something else that has just been mentioned.

Many of my friends have had a similar experience.
Put them in a jar, bowl, or other similar container.

5 adverbs used with 'similar'

The following adverbs are often used in front of **similar**:

broadly	rather	roughly	surprisingly
quite	remarkably	strikingly	very

Their proposals were rather similar.
My problems are very similar to yours.

savings

→ See **economics**

say

1 'say'

When you **say** something, you use your voice to produce words. The past tense and -ed participle of **say** is **said** /sed/.

You use **say** when you are quoting directly the words that someone has spoken.

'I feel so happy,' she _said_.
'The problem,' he _said_, 'is that Mr Sanchez is very upset.'

In writing, you can use many other verbs instead of **say** when you are quoting someone's words.

→ See **Reporting**

 In spoken English, you usually use **say**.

He _said_ to me, 'What shall we do?'

! BE CAREFUL

In speech, you mention the person and **say** before quoting their words. Don't say, for example, '~~What shall we do?' he said to me~~' in spoken English.

You can use **it** after **said** to refer to the words spoken by someone.

You could have _said it_ a bit more politely.
I just _said it_ for something to say.

If you are referring in a general way to what someone has expressed, rather than their actual words, use **so**, not 'it'. For example, say 'I disagree with him and I **said so**'. Don't say '~~I disagree with him and I said it~~'.

If you wanted more to eat, why didn't you _say so_ earlier?
I know she liked it because she _said so_.

You can report what someone has said without quoting them directly using **say** and a that-clause.

She _said_ she hadn't slept very well.
They _said_ that smoking wasn't permitted anywhere in the building.

Don't use 'say' with an indirect object. For example, don't say '~~She said me that Mr Rai had left~~'. Say 'She **said** that Mr Rai had left' or 'She **told me** that Mr Rai had left.'

2 'tell'

If you are mentioning the hearer as well as the speaker, you usually use **tell**, rather than 'say'. The past tense and -ed participle of **tell** is **told**. For example, instead of saying 'I said to him that his mother had arrived', say 'I **told** him that his mother had arrived'.

'I have no intention of resigning,' he _told_ the press.
She _told_ me to sit down.

→ See **tell**

You say that someone **tells** a story, lie, or joke.

You're telling lies now.
Dad told jokes and stories.

! BE CAREFUL

Don't say that someone 'says' a story, lie, or joke. Don't say, for example 'You're saying lies now'.

3 'ask'

Don't say that someone 'says' a question. Say that they **ask** a question.

Luka asked me a lot of questions about my job.
I asked what time it was.

→ See **ask**

4 'give'

Don't say that someone 'says' an order or instruction. Say that they **give** an order or instruction.

Who gave the order for the men to shoot?
She had given clear instructions about what to do while she was away.

5 'call'

If you want to say that someone describes someone else in a particular way, you can use **say** followed by a *that*-clause. For example, you can say 'He **said** that I was a liar'. You can also say that someone **calls someone something**. For example, you can say 'He **called** me a liar'.

She called me lazy and selfish.

→ See **call**

6 'talk about'

· Don't use **say** to mention what someone is discussing. Don't say, for example, 'He said about his business'. Say 'He **talked about** his business'.

Lucy talked about her childhood and her family.

---

scarce – scarcely

Both **scarce** and **scarcely** are fairly formal words. They have completely different meanings.

1 'scarce'

Scarce is an adjective. If something is **scarce**, very little of it is available.

Good quality land is scarce.
The desert is a place where water is scarce.

2 'rare'

Don't use 'scarce' to say that something is not common, and is therefore interesting. Use **rare**.

This flower is so rare that few botanists have ever seen it.
Deepak's hobby is collecting rare books.

3 'scarcely'

Scarcely is an adverb that means the same as 'hardly'. If something is **scarcely** true, it is almost not true. If something **scarcely** exists, it almost does not exist.

The smell was so bad I could <u>scarcely</u> bear it.
The woman was <u>scarcely</u> able to walk.

! BE CAREFUL

Don't use 'not' with **scarcely**. Don't say, for example, 'I ~~do not scarcely have enough money to live~~'. Say 'I scarcely have enough money to live'.

If you use an auxiliary verb or modal with **scarcely**, put the auxiliary verb or modal first. Say, for example, 'I **could scarcely** stand'. Don't say 'I ~~scarcely could stand~~'.

I <u>can scarcely</u> remember what we ate.
He <u>could scarcely</u> be blamed for his reaction.

Scarcely is sometimes used to emphasize that one thing happened immediately after another.

We had <u>scarcely</u> arrived when it was time to leave again.

Use **when**, not 'than', in sentences like these. Don't say, for example, '~~We had scarcely arrived than it was time to leave again~~'.

In literary writing, **scarcely** is sometimes put at the beginning of a sentence, followed by **had** or the verb **be** and the subject.

<u>Scarcely had she</u> put down the receiver when the phone rang again.
<u>Scarcely were the words</u> spoken when he began to regret them.

→ See **Broad negatives**

scene – sight – view – landscape – scenery

1 'scene'

The noun **scene** has several meanings.

It can refer to a part of a play, film, or novel.

Do you know the balcony <u>scene</u> from 'Romeo and Juliet'?
It was like a <u>scene</u> from a Victorian novel.

The **scene** of an accident or crime is the place where it happened.

They were only a few miles from the <u>scene</u> of the crime.

You can describe something as a **scene** of a particular kind when you are giving your impression of the things that are happening there at a particular time.

I entered the room to be greeted by a <u>scene</u> of domestic tranquillity.
The sun rose over a <u>scene</u> of terrible destruction.

2 'sight'

You use **sight** to give your impression of the appearance of a particular thing or person.

A volcano erupting is a spectacular <u>sight</u>.
With his ragged clothes and thin face, he was a pitiful <u>sight</u>.

You can use the plural form **sights** to refer to the interesting things that there are to see in a particular place.

Did you have time to see the <u>sights</u> while you were in Moscow?
A guide offered to show us the <u>sights</u>.

There are some other nouns that are commonly used to refer to things that people see:

3 'view'

View is used to refer to what you can see from a window or high place.

Her bedroom window looked out on to a superb <u>view</u> of London.
From the top of the hill there is a fine <u>view</u>.

4 'landscape'

The **landscape** is what you can see around you when you are travelling through an area of land. You can use this word whether the area is attractive or not.

The <u>landscape</u> around here is very flat.
The train passed through the industrial <u>landscape</u> of eastern Massachusetts.

5 'scenery'

Scenery refers to what you see around you in an attractive part of the countryside.

We stopped on the way to admire the <u>scenery</u>.
I think Scotland has the most beautiful <u>scenery</u> in the world.

> **! BE CAREFUL**
>
> **Scenery** is an uncountable noun. Don't talk about '~~sceneries~~' or '~~a scenery~~'.

school – university

1 used as countable nouns

In both British and American English, a **school** is a place where children are educated, and a **university** is a place where students study for degrees.

The village had a church and a <u>school</u>.
Heidelberg is a very old <u>university</u>.

2 used as uncountable nouns

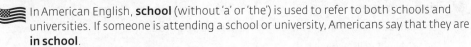 In American English, **school** (without 'a' or 'the') is used to refer to both schools and universities. If someone is attending a school or university, Americans say that they are **in school**.

All the children were <u>in school</u>.
She is doing well <u>in school</u>.

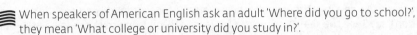 When speakers of American English ask an adult 'Where did you go to school?', they mean 'What college or university did you study in?'.

In British English, **school** refers only to schools for children. If someone is attending a school, British speakers say they are **at school**. If they are attending a university, British speakers say they are **at university**.

I was <u>at school</u> with Joty, but I haven't seen her since I was 16.
She is studying medicine <u>at university</u>.

→ See **student**

scissors

Scissors are a small tool consisting of two sharp blades joined together, used for cutting things such as paper, cloth, or hair.

Scissors is a plural noun. Don't talk about '~~a scissors~~'. Instead say **some scissors** or **a pair of scissors**.

I need some scissors to get this label off.
She took a pair of scissors and cut his hair.

search

Search can be a verb or a noun.

1 used as a verb

If you **search** a place or person, you examine them thoroughly because you are trying to find something.

Police searched the building and found weapons.
He stood with his arms outstretched while the guard searched him.

! BE CAREFUL

Don't say that you 'search' the thing you are trying to find. You can say that you **search for** it, but you usually say that you **look for** it.

He's looking for his keys.

2 used as a noun

A **search** is an attempt to find something or someone by looking for them carefully.

I found the keys after a long search.
The search for survivors of the earthquake continues.

see

The verb **see** is used with several different meanings. Its past tense is **saw**. Its -ed participle is **seen**.

1 using your eyes

If you **can see** something, you are aware of it through your eyes.

I can see a light in her window.

! BE CAREFUL

You usually use **can** in sentences like these. You say, for example, 'I **can see** the sea'. You don't say '~~I see the sea~~'. Don't use a progressive form. Don't say '~~I am seeing the sea~~'.

To say that someone was aware of something in this way in the past, you usually use **could see**.

He could see Amir's face in the mirror.

To say that someone became aware of something, use **saw**.

We suddenly saw a ship through a gap in the fog.

Don't confuse **see** with **look at** or **watch**.

→ See **see – look at – watch**

2 meeting someone

See is often used to mean 'visit' or 'meet by arrangement'.

You should see a doctor.

If two people are meeting regularly, for example because they are in love, you can say that they **are seeing** each other. When **see** has this meaning, it is usually used in a progressive form.

How long have Daniel and Ayeisha been seeing each other?

3 understanding

See is very commonly used to mean 'understand'.

I don't see why she was so angry.
The situation could be complicated, if you see what I mean.

People often say '**I see**' to show that they have understood something.

'He doesn't have any children.' – 'I see.'

When **see** means 'understand', you can use **can** or **could** with it.

I can see why they're worried.
I could see his point.

! BE CAREFUL

Don't use a progressive form when **see** means 'understand'. Don't say, for example, '~~I am seeing why they're worried~~'.

see – look at – watch

1 'see'

When you **see** something, you are aware of it through your eyes, or you notice it.

We saw black smoke coming from the building.
I waved, but nobody saw me.

→ See **see**

2 'look at'

When you **look at** something, you direct your eyes towards it.

He looked at the food on his plate.
People looked at her in astonishment.

→ See **look**

3 'watch'

When you **watch** something, you pay attention to it using your eyes, because you are interested in what it is doing, or in what may happen.

We watched the sunset.
They just stood and watched while she carried all the bags inside.

4 entertainment and sport

Both **see** and **watch** are used when you are talking about entertainment or sport.

When you go to the theatre or cinema, you say that you **see** a play or film.

I saw that movie when I was a child.
We saw him in 'Hamlet'.

Don't say that someone 'looks at' a play or film. Don't say, for example '~~I looked at that movie~~'.

You say that someone **watches** television. You can say that someone **watches** or **sees** a particular programme.

He spends hours <u>watching</u> television.
He <u>watched</u> a rugby match on television.
I <u>saw</u> his speech on the news.

Similarly, you say that someone **watches** a sport such as football, but you can say that they **watch** or **see** a particular match.

More people <u>are watching</u> cricket than ever before.
Did you <u>watch</u> the game last night?
Millions of people <u>saw</u> the World Cup Final.

seem

You use **seem** to say that someone or something gives a particular impression.

1 used with adjectives

Seem is usually followed by an adjective. If someone gives the impression of being happy, you can say that they **seem** happy. You can also say that they **seem to be** happy. There is no difference in meaning.

Even minor problems <u>seem</u> important.
You <u>seem to be</u> very interested.

If the adjective is a non-gradable adjective such as **alone** or **alive**, you usually use **seem to be**. For example, you say 'He **seemed to be** alone'. You don't say '~~He seemed alone~~'.

She <u>seemed to be</u> asleep.

In order to say who has an impression of someone or something, use **seem** followed by an adjective and the preposition **to**.

He always <u>seemed old to me</u>.
This idea <u>seems ridiculous to most people</u>.

2 used with noun phrases

Instead of an adjective, you can use a noun phrase after **seem** or **seem to be**. For example, instead of saying 'She seemed nice', you can say 'She **seemed a nice person**' or 'She **seemed to be a nice person**'. In conversation and in less formal writing, people often say 'She **seemed like a nice person**'.

It <u>seemed a long time</u> before the food came.
She <u>seems to be a very good boss</u>.
It <u>seemed like a good idea</u>.

! BE CAREFUL

Don't use 'as' after **seem**. Don't say, for example, '~~It seemed as a good idea~~'.

If the noun phrase contains a determiner such as **the** or **a** but not an adjective, you must use **seem to be**. For example, say 'He **seemed to be the owner** of the car'. Don't say '~~He seemed the owner of the car~~'.

At first the seal <u>seemed to be a rock</u>.
What <u>seems to be the trouble</u>?

3 **used with verbs**

You can use other *to*-infinitives besides 'to be' after **seem**. For example, you can say 'He **seemed to need** help'. You can also say '**It seemed that he needed** help' or '**It seemed as though he needed** help'.

The experiments <u>seem to prove</u> that sugar is bad for you.
It <u>seemed to me that she was</u> right.
It <u>seemed as though the war had ended</u>.

seldom

Seldom is a formal or literary word. It is used to say that something does not happen very often.

1 **position in clause**

▶ If there is no auxiliary verb, **seldom** usually goes in front of the verb, unless the verb is **be**.

He <u>seldom laughed</u>.
It <u>seldom rains</u> there.

▶ **Seldom** goes after **be**.

She <u>was seldom</u> late for work.

▶ If there is an auxiliary verb, **seldom** goes after it.

These birds <u>are seldom seen</u>.
They <u>can seldom agree</u> on anything.

▶ If there is more than one auxiliary verb, **seldom** goes after the first one.

I <u>have seldom been</u> asked such difficult questions.

▶ In literary writing, **seldom** is sometimes put at the beginning of a sentence, followed by an auxiliary verb and the subject.

<u>Seldom did he</u> ask me questions about our finances.
<u>Seldom can there</u> have been such a happy couple.

2 **'hardly ever'**

 Seldom is not normally used in conversation. Instead people say **hardly ever**.

It <u>hardly ever</u> rains there.
I've <u>hardly ever</u> been asked anything like that.

→ See **Adverbs and adverbials** for a graded list of words used to indicate frequency

select

→ See **choose**

send – sent

'send'

Send and **sent** are different forms of the same verb. Because they sound similar, they are sometimes confused. **Send** /send/ is the base form. If you **send** something to someone, you arrange for it to be taken and delivered to them, for example by post.

They <u>send</u> me a card every year for my birthday.
I always re-read my emails before I <u>send</u> them.

Sent /sent/ is the past tense and -*ed* participle of **send**.

I sent you a text – didn't you get it?
He had sent some flowers to Elena.

sensible – sensitive

1 'sensible'

A **sensible** person makes good decisions and judgements based on reason rather than emotion.

She was a sensible girl and did not panic.

2 'sensitive'

Sensitive has two meanings.

A **sensitive** person is easily upset or offended by other people's remarks or behaviour.

He is quite sensitive about his weight.
A sensitive child can get very upset by people arguing.

If someone is **sensitive**, they show awareness or understanding of other people's feelings.

It would not be very sensitive to ask him about his divorce.
His experiences helped him become less selfish and more sensitive.

GRAMMAR FINDER

Sentence connectors

1 position

Sentence connectors are words and phrases that show a connection between one clause or sentence and another. They are usually put at the beginning of the clause, or after the subject or the first auxiliary verb.

Many species have survived. The effect on wild flowers, however, has been enormous.
He has seen it all before and consequently knows what will happen next.

2 adding information

Some sentence connectors are used to show that you are adding an extra point or piece of information.

also	at the same time	furthermore	on top of that
as well	besides	moreover	too

His first book was published in 1932, and it was followed by a series of novels. He also wrote a book on British cathedrals.
It is difficult to find good quality materials. Smaller organizations, moreover, cannot afford them.

→ See **also – too – as well**

3 giving a parallel

Other Sentence connectors are used to show that you are giving another example of the same point, or that you are using the same argument in two different cases.

| again | equally | likewise |
| by the same token | in the same way | similarly |

This is an immensely difficult subject. But, <u>by the same token</u>, it is a highly important one.
I still clearly remember the time and place where I first saw a shooting star. <u>Similarly</u>, I remember
the first occasion when I saw a peacock spread its tail.

4 contrasting

Another group of sentence connectors are used to show that you are making a
contrast or giving an alternative.

all the same	even so	nonetheless	still
alternatively	however	on the contrary	then again
by contrast	instead	on the other hand	though
conversely	nevertheless	rather	

They were too good to allow us to score, but <u>all the same</u> they didn't play that well.
I would not have been surprised if she had cried. <u>Instead</u>, she sank back in her chair, helpless
with laughter.
He always had good manners. He was very quiet, <u>though</u>.

→ See **although – though** for information on the position of though

5 showing a result

Some sentence connectors are used to show that the situation you are about to
mention exists because of the fact you have just mentioned.

| accordingly | consequently | so | therefore |
| as a result | hence | thereby | thus |

Sales are still lower than a year ago. <u>Consequently</u> stocks have grown.
The room is modern and simply furnished, and <u>thus</u> easy to clean.

So is always put at the beginning of the clause.

His father had been a Member of Parliament. <u>So</u>, Sir Charles Baring's own life was dominated by
public service.

6 showing sequence

Adverbials of time are often used to link two sentences by showing that one event
took place after another.

afterwards	finally	next	suddenly
at last	immediately	presently	then
at once	instantly	since	within minutes
before long	last	soon	within the hour
eventually	later	soon after	
ever since	later on	subsequently	

Philip and Simon had lunch together in the campus restaurant. <u>Afterwards</u>, Simon went back to
his office.

→ See **after – afterwards – later**, **eventually – finally**, **last – lastly**, **soon**

Some adverbials of time are used to indicate that one event took place or will take
place before another.

| beforehand | first | meanwhile |
| earlier | in the meantime | previously |

Then he went out to the island to meet the directors. Arrangements had been made <u>beforehand</u>, of course.

→ See **first – firstly**

A few adverbials are used to show that an event took place at the same time as another event.

at the same time	meanwhile	simultaneously	throughout

Ask the doctor to come as soon as possible. <u>Meanwhile</u>, give first-aid treatment.

shadow – shade

1 'shadow'

A **shadow** is a dark shape made on a surface when something stands between a light and the surface.

The tree cast a <u>shadow</u> over the garden.

If a place is dark because something prevents light from reaching it, you can say that it is **in shadow**.

The whole valley is <u>in shadow</u>.

2 'shade'

You refer to an area that is dark and cool because the sun cannot reach it as **the shade**.

They sat in <u>the shade</u> and read.
I moved my chair into <u>the shade</u>.

shall – will

1 'shall' and 'will'

Shall and **will** are used to make statements and ask questions about the future.

Shall and **will** are not usually pronounced in full after a pronoun. When writing down what someone has said, the contraction **'ll** is usually used after the pronoun, instead of writing **shall** or **will** in full.

He'll come back.
'They'll be late,' he said.

 Shall and **will** have the negative forms **shall not** and **will not**. In speech, these are usually shortened to **shan't** /ʃɑːnt/ and **won't** /wəʊnt/. **Shan't** is rather old-fashioned, and is rarely used in American English.

I <u>shan't</u> ever do it again.
You <u>won't</u> need a coat.

It used to be considered correct to write **shall** after **I** or **we**, and **will** after any other pronoun or noun phrase. Now, most people write **will** after **I** and **we**, and this is not regarded as incorrect, although **I shall** and **we shall** are still sometimes used.

I hope some day I <u>will</u> meet you.
We <u>will</u> be able to help.
I <u>shall</u> be out of the office on Monday.

There are a few special cases in which you use **shall**, rather than 'will':

2 **suggestions**

You can make a suggestion about what you and someone else should do by asking a question beginning with '**Shall we...?**'

Shall we go out for dinner?

You can also suggest what you and someone else should do by using a sentence that begins with '**Let's...**' and ends with '**...shall we?**'

Let's have a cup of tea, shall we?

3 **asking for advice**

You can use **shall I** or **shall we** when you are asking for suggestions or advice.

What shall I give them for dinner?
Where shall we meet?

4 **offering**

You can say '**Shall I... ?**' when you are offering to do something.

Shall I shut the door?

Will also has some special uses:

5 **requests**

You can use **will you** to make a request.

Will you take these upstairs for me, please?
Don't tell anyone, will you?

→ See **Topic** entry **Requests, orders, and instructions**

6 **invitations**

You can also use **will you** or the negative form **won't you** to make an invitation. **Won't you** is very formal and polite.

Will you stay to lunch?
Won't you sit down, Sir?

→ See **Topic** entry **Invitations**

7 **ability**

Will is sometimes used to say that someone or something is able to do something.

This will get rid of your headache.
The car won't start.

! **BE CAREFUL**

You don't normally use 'shall' or 'will' in clauses beginning with words and expressions such as **when**, **before**, or **as soon as**. Instead you use the present simple. Don't say, for example, 'I'll call as soon as I shall get home'. Say 'I'll call as soon as I **get** home'.

shave

When a man **shaves**, he cuts hair from his face using a razor.

He shaved and dressed, and went downstairs.

! **BE CAREFUL**

Shave is not usually a reflexive verb. You don't normally say that a man ~~shaves himself~~.

💬 In conversation, you usually say that a man **has a shave**, rather than that he 'shaves'.

I can't remember when I last had a shave.

Shave can also be used as a transitive verb, meaning that someone removes hair from a particular part of their body using a razor.

Marta had a shower and shaved her legs.
He was starting to go bald, so he decided to shave his head.

sheep – lamb

1 'sheep'

A **sheep** is a farm animal with a thick woolly coat. The plural of **sheep** is **sheep**.

The farmer has six hundred sheep.
A flock of sheep was grazing on the hill.

2 'lamb'

A **lamb** is a young sheep.

The field was full of little lambs.

The meat of a young sheep is called **lamb**. When it is used with this meaning, **lamb** is an uncountable noun.

For dinner, we had lamb and potatoes.

The meat of an adult sheep is called **mutton**, but this meat is less common in Britain and America than **lamb**. Don't use 'sheep' to refer to the meat of a sheep.

ship

→ See **boat – ship**

shop – store

In British English, a building or part of a building where goods are sold is usually called a **shop**.

Are there any shops near here?

In American English, this kind of building is usually called a **store**, and **shop** is only used to mean a very small store that has just one type of goods.

Mom has gone to the store.
I got it from a little antiques shop in Princeton.

In British English, very large shops are sometimes called **stores**.

They've opened a new DIY store on the outskirts of town.

In both British and American English, a large shop that has separate departments selling different types of goods is called a **department store**.

She works in the furnishings department of a large department store.

1 'shop' used as a verb

Shop can also be a verb. When people **shop**, they go to shops and buy things.

I usually shop on Saturdays.

2 'shopping'

You usually say that someone **goes shopping**, rather than that they 'shop'.

They went shopping after lunch.

When someone goes to the shops to buy things that they need regularly, such as food, you say that they **do the shopping** or **do their shopping**.

Who's going to do the shopping?
She went to the next town to do her shopping.

Shopping can be used without 'do' or 'go' to refer to the activity of buying things from shops.

I don't like shopping.

Shopping can also refer to the things that someone has just bought from a shop or shops.

She put her shopping away in the kitchen.

Shopping is an uncountable noun. Don't talk about 'a shopping' or someone's 'shoppings'.

shore

→ See **beach – shore – coast**

short – shortly – briefly

1 'short'

Short is an adjective. You usually use it to say that something does not last for a long time.

Let's take a short break.
She made a short speech.

2 'shortly'

Shortly is an adverb. If something is going to happen **shortly**, it is going to happen soon. This is a slightly old-fashioned use.

They should be returning shortly.

If something happened **shortly** after something else, it happened soon after it.

She died shortly afterwards.
Very shortly after I started my job, I got promoted.

3 'briefly'

Don't use 'shortly' to say that something lasts or is done for a short time. Don't say, for example, 'She told them shortly what had happened'. Use **briefly**.

She told them briefly what had happened.

shorts

→ See **pants – shorts**

should – ought to

1 expectation

You use **should** or **ought to** to say that you expect something to happen.

We should be there by dinner time.
It ought to get easier with practice.

You use **should** or **ought to** with **have** and an *-ed* participle to say that you expect something to have happened already.

You should have heard by now that I'm O.K.
It's ten o'clock, so they ought to have reached the station.

You also use **should** or **ought to** with **have** and an *-ed* participle to say that something was expected to happen, but did not happen.

Bags which should have gone to Rome were sent to New York.
The project ought to have finished by now.

! BE CAREFUL

You must use **have** and an *-ed* participle in sentences like these. Don't say, for example, 'The project ought to finish by now'.

2 moral rightness

You use **should** or **ought to** to say that something is morally right.

Crimes should be punished.
I ought to call the police.

3 giving advice

You can say **you should** or **you ought to** when you are giving someone advice.

I think you should go see your doctor.
I think you ought to try a different approach.

4 negative forms

Should and **ought to** have the negative forms **should not** and **ought not to**.

This should not be allowed to continue.
They ought not to have said anything.

The **not** is not usually pronounced in full. When you write down what someone says, you write **shouldn't** or **oughtn't to**.

You shouldn't dress like that, Andrew.
They oughtn't to mention it.

 When you make a negative statement with **ought** in American English, you can omit **to**:

You oughtn't answer the door without your shirt on.

shout

1 'shout'

When you **shout**, you speak as loudly as you can.

I can hear you – there's no need to shout.
'Stop it!' he shouted.

2 'shout to'

If you **shout to** someone who is a long way away, you speak very loudly so that they can hear you.

'What are you doing down there?' he shouted to Robin.
People waved and shouted to us as our train passed.

3 'shout at'

If you speak very loudly to someone who is near to you, for example because you are angry with them, don't say that you 'shout to' them. Say that you **shout at** them.

The captain shouted at him, 'Get in! Get in!'
Dad shouted at us for making a mess.

You can use a *to*-infinitive with **shout to** or **shout at**. If you **shout to** someone **to do** something, or **shout at** them **to do** it, you tell them to do it by shouting.

A neighbour shouted to us from a window to stop the noise.
She shouted at him to go away.

show

→ See **indicate – show**

shut

→ See **close – closed – shut**

sick

1 'sick'

A **sick** person has an illness or some other problem with their health.

She was at home looking after her sick baby.
He looked sick.

→ See **ill – sick**

2 'be sick'

In British English, to **be sick** usually means to bring up food through your mouth from your stomach.

I think I'm going to be sick.

 In American English, to **be sick** means to be ill.

I was sick last week and couldn't go to work.

> **!** BE CAREFUL
>
> **Be sick** meaning 'be ill' cannot be used in progressive forms. 'George is being sick' means 'George is bringing up food from his stomach'.

3 'vomit' and 'throw up'

If you **vomit**, you bring up food through your mouth from your stomach. **Vomit** is a fairly formal word.

She had a pain in her stomach and began to vomit.

In conversation, some people say **throw up** instead of 'be sick'.

I think I'm going to throw up.

4 'feel sick'

In British English, to **feel sick** means to feel that you want to vomit.

Being on a boat always makes me feel sick.

 In American English, if someone **feels sick**, they feel ill.

Maya felt sick and was sent home from school.

sight

→ See **scene – sight – view – landscape – scenery**

similar

→ See **same – similar**

since

1 'since'

You use **since** to say that something has been true from a particular time in the past until now.

Exam results have improved since 2001.
I've been wearing glasses since I was three.

! BE CAREFUL

In sentences like these you use a perfect form with **since**. Don't say 'Exam results improved since 2001' or 'I am wearing glasses since I was three'.

You can also use **since** to say how long ago something happened. When you use **since** like this, use a simple form. For example, instead of saying 'I last saw him five years ago', you can say 'It's five years **since** I last saw him'.

It's three months since Kathy left.
It's years since I heard that song.

2 'for'

If you want to say how long something has been true, use **for**, not 'since'.

We've been married for seven years.
I've known Adeel for ages.

→ See **for**

3 'during' and 'over'

To say how long something has been happening, use **during** or **over**.

A lot of rain has fallen during the past two days.

Things have become worse <u>over</u> the past few months.

→ See **during, over**

4 **'from ... to'**

To say when something began and finished, use **from** and **to**.

Mr Ito was headmaster <u>from</u> 1998 <u>to</u> 2007.

Instead of 'to', you can use **till** or **until**.

The noise continued <u>from</u> nine in the morning <u>till</u> 5 p.m.

! **BE CAREFUL**

Don't use 'since' and 'to'. Don't say, for example, '~~He was headmaster since 1998 to 2007~~'.

5 **used to mean 'because'**

Since can also be used to mean 'because'.

Aircraft noise is a problem here <u>since</u> we're close to Heathrow Airport.

→ See **because**

---

sit

1 **describing a movement**

When you **sit** or **sit down**, you lower your body until your bottom is resting on something. The past tense and *-ed* participle of **sit** is **sat**.

You usually use **sit** rather than 'sit down' when you mention the place where someone sits.

A woman came and <u>sat next to her</u>.
<u>Sit on this chair</u>, please.

If you are not mentioning the place, use **sit down**.

She <u>sat down</u> and poured herself a cup of tea.

2 **saying where someone is**

If you **are sitting** somewhere, your bottom is resting on something such as a chair. In standard English, don't say that someone '~~is sat~~' somewhere.

They <u>are sitting</u> at their desks.
She <u>was sitting</u> on the edge of the bed.

---

size

→ See **Reference** section **Measurements**

---

skilful – skilled

1 **'skilful'**

Someone who is **skilful** at something does it very well.

They are a great team with a lot of <u>skilful</u> players.
As an artist, he was very <u>skilful</u> with a pencil.

 Skilful is spelled **skillful** in American English.

2 'skilled'

Use **skilled** in front of a noun to describe someone who has been trained to do a particular kind of work and does it very well.

It takes four years to train a skilled engineer.
We need more skilled workers in this country.

You also use **skilled** in front of a noun to describe work that can only be done by a skilled person.

He was only interested in highly-paid, skilled work.
Weaving was a very skilled job, requiring a five-year apprenticeship.

sleep – asleep

1 'sleep'

Sleep can be a noun or a verb. The past tense and -*ed* participle of the verb is **slept**.

Sleep is the natural state of rest in which you are unconscious with your eyes closed.

I haven't been getting enough sleep recently.

To **sleep** means to be in this state of rest.

He was so excited he could hardly sleep.
I had not slept for three days.

2 'asleep'

If someone is in this state, you can use the progressive form and say they **are sleeping**, but it is more common to say that they **are asleep**. Don't say, for example, 'He sleeps'.

She was asleep when we walked in.
I thought someone had been in the house while I was sleeping.

To say how long someone was in this state, or to talk about where or how someone usually sleeps, use **sleep** rather than **asleep**.

She slept for almost ten hours.
Where does the baby sleep?

! BE CAREFUL

Asleep is only used after a verb. Don't use it in front of a noun. Don't, for example, say 'an asleep child'. Instead use **sleeping**.

I glanced down at the sleeping figure.
She was carrying a sleeping baby.

Don't say that someone is 'very asleep' or 'completely asleep'. Instead say that they are **sound asleep** or **fast asleep**.

The baby is still sound asleep.
You were fast asleep when I left.

3 'go to sleep'

When someone changes from being awake to being asleep, you say that they **go to sleep**.

Both the children had gone to sleep.
Go to sleep and stop worrying about it.

4 **'fall asleep'**

When someone goes to sleep suddenly or unexpectedly, you say that they **fall asleep**.

The moment my head touched the pillow I fell asleep.
Marco fell asleep watching TV.

5 **'get to sleep'**

When someone goes to sleep with difficulty, for example because of noise or worries, you say that they **get to sleep**.

Could you turn that radio down – I'm trying to get to sleep.
I didn't get to sleep until four in the morning.

6 **'go back to sleep'**

When someone goes to sleep again after being woken up, you say that they **go back to sleep**.

She rolled over and went back to sleep.
Go back to sleep, it's only five a.m.

7 **'send someone to sleep'**

If something causes you to sleep, you say that it **sends** you **to sleep**.

I brought him a hot drink, hoping it would send him to sleep.
I tried to read the books but they sent me to sleep.

slightly

→ See **Adverbs and adverbials** for a graded list of words used to indicate degree

small – little

Small and **little** are both used to say that someone or something is not large. There are some important differences in the ways these words are used.

1 **position in clause**

Small can be used in front of a noun, or after a verb such as **be**.

They escaped in small boats.
She is small for her age.

Little is normally used only in front of nouns. You can talk about 'a **little** town', but you do not say 'The town is little'.

She bought a little table with a glass top.
I picked up a little piece of rock.

2 **used with grading adverbs**

You can use words like **quite** and **rather** in front of **small**.

Quite small changes in climate can have enormous effects.
She cut me a rather small piece of cake.

Don't use these words in front of 'little'.

You can use **very** and **too** in front of **small**.

The trees are full of very small birds.
They are living in houses which are too small.

'Very' or 'too' are not usually used in front of **little** when it is an adjective, except when you are talking about a young child. You don't say, for example, 'I have a very little car', but you can say 'She was a very little girl.'

3 comparatives and superlatives

Small has the comparative and superlative forms **smaller** and **smallest**.

His apartment is smaller than his other place.
She rented the smallest car she could.

The comparative form **littler** and the superlative form **littlest** are mostly used in spoken English and to talk about young children.

The littler kids had been sent to bed.
You used to be the littlest boy in the school.

4 used with other adjectives

You can use other adjectives in front of **little**.

They gave me a funny little hat.
She was a pretty little girl.

! BE CAREFUL

You don't normally use other adjectives in front of 'small'.

---

smell

Smell can be a noun or a verb. The past tense and -*ed* participle of the verb is **smelled**, but **smelt** is also used in British English.

1 used as a noun

The **smell** of something is a quality it has that you are aware of through your nose.

I love the smell of fresh bread.
What's that smell?

2 used as an intransitive verb

If you say that something **smells**, you mean that people are aware of it because of its unpleasant smell.

The fridge is beginning to smell.
His feet smell.

You can say that a place or object **smells of** a particular thing, which can be pleasant or unpleasant.

The house smelled of flowers.
Her breath smelt of coffee.

! BE CAREFUL

You must use **of** in sentences like these. Don't say 'The house smelled freshly baked bread'.

You can say that one place or thing **smells like** another thing, which can be pleasant or unpleasant.

The house smelt like a hospital ward.
I love this shampoo – it smells like lemons.

You can also use **smell** with an adjective to say that something has a pleasant or unpleasant smell.

What is it? It smells delicious.
The room smelled damp.

Don't use an adverb after **smell**. Don't say, for example, 'It smells deliciously'.

3 used as a transitive verb

If you **can smell** something, you are aware of it through your nose.

I could smell the dinner cooking in the kitchen.
Can you smell the ocean?

> **! BE CAREFUL**
>
> You usually use **can** or **could** in sentences like these. You usually say, for example, 'I **can smell** gas' rather than 'I smell gas'. Don't use a progressive form. Don't say 'I am smelling gas'.

SO

So is used in several different ways.

1 referring back

You can use **so** after **do** to refer back to an action that has just been mentioned. For example, instead of saying 'He crossed the street. As he crossed the street, he whistled', you say 'He crossed the street. As he **did so**, he whistled'.

He went to close the door, falling over as he did so.
A signal which should have turned red failed to do so.

You can use **so** after **if** to form a conditional clause. For example, instead of saying 'Are you hungry? If you are hungry, we can eat', you say 'Are you hungry? **If so**, we can eat'.

Do you enjoy romantic films? If so, you will love this movie.
Have you finished? If so, put your pen down.

You often use **so** after a reporting verb such as **think** or **expect**, especially when you are replying to what someone has said. For example, if someone says 'Is Alice at home?', you can say 'I **think so**', meaning 'I think Alice is at home'.

'Are you all right?' – 'I think so.'
'Will he be angry?' – 'I don't expect so.'
'Is it for sale?' – 'I believe so.'

The reporting verbs most commonly used with **so** are **believe**, **expect**, **hope**, **say**, **suppose**, **tell**, and **think**.

→ See **believe, expect, hope, say, suppose, tell, think**

So is also used in a similar way after **I'm afraid**.

'Do you think you could lose?' – 'I'm afraid so.'

→ See **afraid – frightened**

You can also use **so** to say that something that has just been said about one person or thing is true about another. You put **so** at the beginning of a clause, followed by **be**, **have**, an auxiliary verb, or a modal, and then the subject of the clause.

His shoes are brightly polished; so is his briefcase.

Yasmin laughed, and so did I.
'You look upset.' – 'So would you if you'd done as badly as I have.'

2 used for emphasis

You can use **so** to emphasize an adjective. For example, you can say 'It's **so cold** today'.

I've been so busy.
These games are so boring.

However, if the adjective is in front of a noun, use **such**, not 'so'. Say, for example, 'It's **such a cold day** today'.

She was so nice.
She was such a nice girl.
The children seemed so happy.
She seemed such a happy woman.

→ See **such**

If the adjective comes after **the**, **this**, **that**, **these**, **those**, or a possessive, don't use 'so' or 'such'. Don't say, for example 'It was our first visit to this so old town'. You say 'It was our first visit to **this very old town**'.

He had recovered from his very serious illness.
I hope that these very unfortunate people will not be forgotten.

You can also use **so** to emphasize an adverb.

I sleep so well.
Time seems to have passed so quickly.

3 'so...that' used to mention a result

You use **so** in front of an adjective to say that something happens because someone or something has a quality to an unusually large extent. After the adjective, use a *that*-clause.

The crowd was so large that it overflowed the auditorium.
We were so angry we asked to see the manager.

! BE CAREFUL

Don't use 'so' in the second clause. Don't say, for example, 'We were so angry so we asked to see the manager'.

You can use **so** in a similar way in front of an adverb.

He dressed so quickly that he put his boots on the wrong feet.
She had fallen down so often that she was covered in mud.

Instead of using **so** in front of an adjective, you can use **such** in front of a noun phrase containing the adjective. For example, instead of saying 'The car was **so old** that we decided to sell it', you can say 'It was **such an old car** that we decided to sell it'.

The change was so gradual that nobody noticed it.
This can be such a gradual process that you are not aware of it.

You can use **so**, **and so**, or **so that** to introduce the result of a situation that you have just mentioned.

He speaks very little English, so I talked to him through an interpreter.
There was no answer and so I asked again.
My suitcase had been damaged, so that the lid would not close.

4 **'so that' in purpose clauses**

You also use **so that** to say that something is done for a particular purpose.

He has to earn money so that he can pay his rent.

so – very – too

So, **very**, and **too** can all be used to intensify the meaning of an adjective, an adverb, or a word like **much** or **many**.

1 **'very'**

Very is a simple intensifier, without any other meaning.

The room was very small.
We finished very quickly.

→ See **very**

2 **'so'**

So can suggest an emotion in the speaker, such as pleasure, surprise, or disappointment.

Juan makes me so angry!
Oh, thank you so much!

So can also refer forward to a result clause introduced by **that**.

The traffic was moving so slowly that he arrived three hours late.

3 **'too'**

Too suggests an excessive or undesirable amount.

The soup is too salty.
She wears too much make-up.

Too can be used with a *to*-infinitive or with **for** to say that a particular result does not or cannot happen.

He was too late to save her.
The water was too cold for swimming.

→ See **too**

soccer

→ See **football**

social – sociable

1 **'social'**

The adjective **social** is used in front of a noun. Its usual meaning is 'relating to society'.

We collect statistics on crime and other social problems.
They discussed the government's social and economic policy.

Social can also be used to describe things that relate to a people meeting or communicating with each other for pleasure, as a leisure activity.

We've met at social and business functions.
Social networking sites such as Facebook and Twitter became incredibly popular.

2 'sociable'

Don't use 'social' to describe people who are friendly and enjoy talking to other people. Use **sociable**.

Kaito was an outgoing, <u>sociable</u> man.
She's very <u>sociable</u> and has lots of friends.

society

1 used as an uncountable noun

Society refers to people in general, considered as a large organized group.

Women must have equal status in <u>society</u>.
The whole structure of <u>society</u> is changing.

When **society** has this meaning, don't use 'a' or 'the' in front of it.

2 used as a countable noun

A **society** refers to the people of a particular country, considered as an organized group.

We live in a multi-cultural <u>society</u>.
Industrial <u>societies</u> became increasingly complex.

A **society** is also an organization for people who share an interest or aim.

The gardens are owned by the Royal Horticultural <u>Society</u>.
He was a member of the National <u>Society</u> of Film Critics.

some

1 used as a determiner

You use **some** in front of the plural form of a noun to talk about a number of people or things, without saying who or what they are, or how many of them there are.

<u>Some children</u> were playing in the yard.
I have <u>some important things</u> to tell them.

You can also use **some** in front of an uncountable noun to talk about a quantity of something, without saying how much of it there is.

She had a piece of pie and <u>some coffee</u>.
I have <u>some information</u> that might help.

When you use **some** in front of the plural form of a noun, you use a plural form of a verb with it.

Some cars <u>were</u> damaged.
Here <u>are</u> some suggestions.

When you use **some** in front of an uncountable noun, you use a singular form of a verb with it.

Some action <u>is</u> necessary.
There'<u>s</u> some cheese in the fridge.

! BE CAREFUL

Don't use **some** as part of the object of a negative sentence. Don't say, for example, 'I don't have some money'. You say 'I don't have **any** money'.

I hadn't had <u>any</u> breakfast.
It won't do <u>any</u> good.

2 used as a quantity word

You use **some of** in front of a plural noun phrase beginning with **the**, **these**, **those**, or a possessive. You do this to talk about a number of people or things belonging to a particular group.

<u>Some of the smaller companies</u> have gone out of business.
<u>Some of these people</u> have young children.
We read <u>some of Edgar Allen Poe's stories</u>.

You use **some of** in front of a singular noun phrase beginning with **the**, **this**, **that**, or a possessive to talk about a part of something.

We did <u>some of the journey</u> by bus.
He had lost <u>some of his money</u>.

You can use **some of** like this in front of plural or singular pronouns.

<u>Some of these</u> are mine.
<u>Some of it</u> is very interesting.

Don't use 'we' or 'they' after **some of**. Use **us** or **them**.

<u>Some of us</u> found it difficult.
<u>Some of them</u> went for a walk.

3 used as a pronoun

Some can itself be a plural or singular pronoun.

Some activities are very dangerous and <u>some</u> are not so dangerous.
'You'll need some graph paper.' – 'Yeah, I've got <u>some</u> at home.'

4 used in questions

In questions, you can use either **some** or **any** as part of an object. You use **some** when you are asking someone to confirm that something is true. For example, if you think someone wants to ask you some questions, you might ask 'Do you have **some** questions?' But if you do not know whether they want to ask questions or not, you would ask 'Do you have **any** questions?'

Sorry – have I missed out <u>some</u> names?
Were you in <u>any</u> danger?

5 duration

You use **some** with **time** or with a word such as **hours** or **months** to say that something lasts for a fairly long time.

You will be unable to drive for <u>some time</u> after the operation.
I did not meet her again for <u>some years</u>.

To refer to a fairly short period of time, don't use 'some'. Say **a short time** or use **a few** in front of a word such as **hours** or **months**.

Her mother died only <u>a short time</u> later.
You'll be feeling better in <u>a few days</u>.

someone – somebody

1 used in statements

You use **someone** or **somebody** to refer to a person without saying who you mean.

Carlos sent someone to see me.
There was an accident and somebody got hurt.

 There is no difference in meaning between **someone** and **somebody**, but **somebody** is more common in spoken English, and **someone** is more common in written English.

! **BE CAREFUL**

You don't usually use 'someone' or 'somebody' as part of the object of a negative sentence. Don't say, for example, 'I don't know someone who lives in York'. You say 'I don't know **anyone** who lives in York'.

There wasn't anyone there.
There wasn't much room for anybody else.

2 used in questions

In questions, you can use **someone**, **somebody**, **anyone**, or **anybody** as part of the object. You use **someone** or **somebody** when you are expecting the answer 'yes'. For example, if you think I met someone, you might ask me 'Did you meet **someone**?' If you do not know whether I met someone or not, you would ask 'Did you meet **anyone**?'

Marit, did you have someone in your room last night?
Was there anyone you knew at the party?

! **BE CAREFUL**

Don't use 'someone' or 'somebody' with **of** in front of the plural form of a noun. Don't say, for example, 'Someone of my friends is an artist'. You say '**One of** my friends is an artist'.

One of his classmates won a national poetry competition.
'Where have you been?' one of them asked.

3 'some people'

Someone and **somebody** do not have plural forms. If you want to refer to a group of people without saying who you mean, you say **some people**.

Some people tried to escape through a window.
This behaviour may be annoying to some people.

---

someplace

→ See **somewhere**

---

something

1 used in statements

You use **something** to refer to an object, situation, etc without saying exactly what it is.

I saw something in the shadows.
There's something strange about her.

❗ BE CAREFUL

You don't usually use 'something' as part of the object of a negative sentence. Don't say, for example, 'We haven't had something to eat'. You say 'We haven't had **anything** to eat'.

I did not say anything.
He never seemed to do anything at all.

2 used in questions

In questions, you can use **something** or **anything** as part of the object. You use **something** when you are expecting the answer 'yes'. For example, if you think I found something, you might ask 'Did you find **something**?' If you do not know whether I found something or not, you would ask 'Did you find **anything**?'

Has something happened?
Did you buy anything?

sometimes – sometime

1 'sometimes'

You use **sometimes** to say that something happens on some occasions, rather than all the time.

The bus was sometimes completely full.
Sometimes I wish I was back in Africa.

→ See **Adverbs and adverbials** for a graded list of words used to indicate frequency

2 'sometime'

Don't confuse **sometimes** with **sometime**. **Sometime** means 'at a time in the past or future that is unknown or has not yet been decided'.

Can I come and see you sometime?

Sometime is often written as **some time**.

He died some time last year.

somewhat

→ See **fair – fairly**

somewhere

You use **somewhere** to talk about a place without saying exactly where you mean.

They live somewhere near Brighton.
I'm not going home yet. I have to go somewhere else first.

❗ BE CAREFUL

You don't usually use 'somewhere' in negative sentences. Don't say, for example, 'I can't find my hat somewhere'. Say 'I can't find my hat **anywhere**'.

I decided not to go anywhere at the weekend.
I haven't got anywhere to sit.

In questions, you can use **somewhere** or **anywhere**. If you are expecting the answer 'yes', you usually use **somewhere**. For example, if you think I am going on holiday this summer, you might ask 'Are you going **somewhere** this summer?' If you do not know whether I am going on holiday or not, you would ask 'Are you going **anywhere** this summer?'

Are you taking a trip somewhere?
Is there a spare seat anywhere?

 Some American speakers say **someplace** instead of 'somewhere'.

She had seen it someplace before.
Why don't you boys sit someplace else?

Someplace is sometimes written as **some place**.

Why don't we go some place quieter?

soon

1 talking about the future

You use **soon** to say that something will happen in a short time from now.

Dinner will be ready soon.
He may very soon be leaving the team.

2 talking about the past

You use **soon** to say that something happened a short time after something else in the past.

The mistake was very soon corrected.
The situation soon changed.

3 position in sentence

▶ **Soon** is often put at the beginning or end of a sentence.

Soon unemployment will start rising.
I will see you soon.

▶ You can also put **soon** after the first auxiliary verb in a verb phrase. For example, you can say 'We **will soon** be home'. Don't say 'We soon will be home'.

It will soon be Christmas.
The show was soon being watched by more than 16 million viewers.

▶ If there is no auxiliary verb, you put **soon** in front of the verb, unless the verb is **be**.

I soon forgot about our conversation.
I soon discovered that this was not true.

If the verb is **be**, you put **soon** after it.

She was soon asleep.

4 'how soon'

You use **how soon** when you are asking how long it will be before something happens.

How soon do I have to make a decision?
How soon are you returning to Paris?

5 **'as soon as'**

You use **as soon as** to say that one event happens immediately after another.

As soon as she got out of bed, the telephone stopped ringing.
As soon as we get the tickets, we'll send them to you.

sorry

You say '**Sorry**' or '**I'm sorry**' as a way of apologizing for something you have done.

'You're giving me a headache with that noise.' – 'Sorry.'
I'm sorry I'm so late.

! **BE CAREFUL**

Sorry is an adjective, not a verb. Don't say 'I sorry'.

→ See **Topic** entry **Apologizing**

→ See **regret – be sorry**

sort

Sort is used as a noun to talk about a class of people or things. **Sort** is a countable noun. After words like **all** and **several**, you use **sorts**.

There are all sorts of reasons why this is true.
They sell several sorts of potatoes.

After **sorts of** you can use either the plural or singular form of a noun. For example, you can say 'They sell most sorts of **shoes**' or 'They sell most sorts of **shoe**'. The singular form is more formal.

There were five different sorts of biscuits.
They attract two main sorts of investor.

After **sort of** you use the singular form of a noun.

I know you're interested in this sort of thing.
'What sort of car did she get?' – 'A sports car.'

In conversation, **these** and **those** are often used with **sort**. For example, people say 'I don't like these sort of jobs' or 'I don't like those sort of jobs'. This use is generally thought to be incorrect. Instead, you should say 'I don't like **this sort of job**' or 'I don't like **that sort of job**'.

They never fly in this sort of weather.
I've had that sort of experience before.

In more formal English, you can also say 'I don't like jobs **of this sort**'.

A device of that sort costs a lot of money.

You can also use **like this**, **like that**, or **like these** after a noun. For example, instead of saying 'this sort of weather', you can say 'weather **like this**'.

I don't know why people say things like that.
Cafés like these are found in every town in Britain.

Kind is used in a similar way to **sort**.

→ See **kind**

You can also use **sort of** to describe something in a vague or uncertain way.

→ See **sort of – kind of**

sort of – kind of

In conversation and in less formal writing, people use **sort of** or **kind of** in front of a noun to say that something could be described as being a particular thing.

It's a sort of dictionary of dictionaries.
I'm a kind of anarchist, I suppose.

People also use **sort of** or **kind of** in front of adjectives, verbs, and other types of word to mean 'a little' or 'in some way', or with very little meaning.

I felt kind of sorry for him.
I've sort of heard of him, but I don't know who he is.

sound

1 'sound'

You use **sound** as a verb in front of an adjective phrase when you are describing something that you hear.

The helicopter sounded worryingly close.
The piano sounds really beautiful.

You can also use **sound** in front of an adjective phrase to describe the impression you have of someone when they speak.

José sounded a little disappointed.
I don't know where she comes from, but she sounds foreign.

You also use **sound** to describe the impression you have of someone or something that you have just heard about or read about.

'They have a little house in the mountains.' – 'That sounds nice.'
The instructions sound a bit complicated.

! BE CAREFUL

Don't use a progressive form. Don't say, for example, 'That is sounding nice'.

Sound is followed by an adjective, not an adverb. Don't say 'That sounds nicely'.

2 'sound like'

You can use **sound like** and a noun phrase to say that something has a similar sound to something else.

The bird's call sounds like a whistle.
Her footsteps sounded like pistol shots.

You can also use **sound like** and a noun phrase to say that someone is talking the way another person usually talks.

He sounded like a little boy being silly.
Stop telling me what to do – you sound just like my mother.

You can use **sound like** and a noun phrase to say that you think you can recognize what something is, because of its sound.

They were playing a piece that sounded like Mozart.
Someone left a message – it sounded like your husband.

You can also use **sound like** and a noun phrase to express an opinion about something that someone has just described to you.

That sounds like a lovely idea.
It sounds like something we should seriously consider.

sound – noise

1 used as countable nouns

A **sound** is something that you can hear. A **noise** is an unpleasant or unexpected sound. You say that machinery makes a **noise**. People and animals can also make **noises**.

A sudden noise made Bela jump.
The birds were making screeching noises.

2 used as uncountable nouns

Sound and **noise** can both be uncountable nouns.

Sound is the general term for what you hear as a result of vibrations travelling through the air, water, etc.

The aircraft could go faster than the speed of sound.

! BE CAREFUL

When you use **sound** with this meaning, don't say 'the sound'.

Don't use expressions such as 'much' or 'a lot of' with **sound**. Don't say, for example, 'There was a lot of sound'. Say 'There was **a lot of noise**'.

Is that the wind making all that noise?
Try not to make so much noise.

south

1 'south'

The **south** /saʊθ/ is the direction that is on your right when you are looking towards the direction where the sun rises.

From the hilltop you can see the city to the south.
To the south, an hour's drive away, was the coast.

A **south** wind blows from the south.

A warm south wind was blowing.

The **south** of a place is the part that is towards the south.

Antibes is in the south of France.

South is part of the names of some countries, states, and regions.

I am from the Republic of South Korea.
She is a senator from South Carolina.

2 'southern'

You don't usually talk about a 'south' part of a country or region. You talk about a **southern** /'sʌðən/ part.

The island is near the southern tip of South America.
The southern part of England is more heavily populated.

Don't talk about 'south England' or 'south Europe'. You say **southern** England or **southern** Europe.

Granada is one of the great cities of southern Spain.

southwards – southward

→ See **-ward – -wards**

souvenir – memory

1 **'souvenir'**

A **souvenir** /suːvəˈnɪə/ is an object that you buy or keep to remind you of a holiday, place, or event.

He kept the spoon as a souvenir of his journey.
They bought some souvenirs from the shop at the airport.

2 **'memory'**

Don't use 'souvenir' to talk about something that you remember. Use **memory**.

One of my earliest memories is my first day at school.
She had no memory of what had happened.

Your **memory** is your ability to remember things.

He's got a really good memory for names.
Meeting him as a child really stands out in my memory.

speak – say – tell

1 **'speak'**

When you **speak**, you use your voice to produce words. The past tense of **speak** is **spoke**. The -ed participle is **spoken**.

They spoke very enthusiastically about their trip.
I've spoken to Raja and he agrees with me.

2 **'say'**

Don't use 'speak' to report what someone says. Don't say, for example, 'He spoke that the doctor had arrived'. Say 'He **said** that the doctor had arrived'.

I said that I would like to teach English.
He said it was an accident.

3 **'tell'**

If you mention the person who is being spoken to as well as what was said, use **tell**.

He told me that he was a farmer.
I told her what the doctor had said.

→ See **say, tell**

4 **'talk'**

→ See **speak – talk**

speak – talk

Speak and **talk** have very similar meanings, but there are some differences in the ways in which they are used.

◼ 'speaking' and 'talking'

When saying that someone is using his or her voice to produce words, you usually say that they **are speaking**.

Please be quiet when I am speaking.
He was speaking so quickly I found it hard to understand.

However, if two or more people are having a conversation, you usually say that they **are talking**. You don't say that they 'are speaking'.

I think she was listening to us while we were talking.
They sat in the kitchen drinking and talking.

◼ used with 'to' and 'with'

If you have a conversation with someone, you can say that you **speak to** them or **talk to** them.

I saw you speaking to him just now.
I enjoyed talking to Ana.

 You can also say that you **speak with** someone or **talk with** someone. This use is particularly common in American English.

He spoke with his friends and told them what had happened.
I talked with his mother many times.

When you make a telephone call, you ask if you can **speak to** someone. You don't ask if you can 'talk to' them.

Hello. Could I speak to Sue, please?

◼ used with 'about'

If you **speak about** something, you describe it to a group of people, for example in a lecture.

I spoke about my experiences at University.
She spoke for twenty minutes about the political situation.

 In conversation, you can refer to the thing someone is discussing as the thing they **are talking about**.

You know the book I'm talking about.
I think he was talking about behaviour in the classroom.

You can refer in a general way to what someone is saying as **what** they **are talking about**.

'I saw you at the concert.' – 'What are you talking about? I wasn't there!'

If two or more people are discussing something, you say they **are talking about** it. Don't say they 'are speaking about' it.

The men were talking about some medical problem.
Everybody will be talking about it at school tomorrow.

4 languages

You say that someone **speaks** or **can speak** a language.

They spoke fluent English.
How many languages can you speak?

You don't say that someone 'talks' a language.

! BE CAREFUL

Don't use 'in' when you are talking about someone's ability to speak a language, and don't use a progressive form. Don't say, for example, 'She speaks in Dutch' or 'She is speaking Dutch' to mean that she is able to speak Dutch.

If you hear some people talking, you can say 'Those people **are speaking in** Dutch' or 'Those people **are talking in** Dutch'.

She heard them talking in French.
They are speaking in Arabic.

---

spend – pass

1 'spend'

If someone does something from the beginning to the end of a period of time, you say that they **spend** the period of time doing it.

We spent the evening talking about art.
I was planning to spend all day writing.

! BE CAREFUL

Don't say that someone spends a period of time 'in doing', 'on doing', or 'to do' something. Don't say, for example, 'We spent the evening in talking about art'.

If someone is in a place from the beginning to the end of a period of time, you can say that they **spend** the time there.

He spent most of his time in the library.
We found a hotel where we could spend the night.

You can say that someone **spends** a period of time in another person's company.

I spent an evening with David.

2 'pass'

You don't usually say that you 'pass time' doing something. Don't say, for example, 'We passed the evening talking about art'.

However, if you do something to occupy yourself while you are waiting for something, you say that you do it **to pass the time**.

He had brought a book along to pass the time.
To pass the time they played games.

3 'have'

If you enjoy yourself while you are doing something, don't say that you 'pass' or 'spend' a good time. Say that you **have** a good time.

The kids are having a good time on the beach.
We had a wonderful time visiting our friends.

spite

→ See **in spite of – despite**

spoil

→ See **destroy – spoil – ruin**

spring

Spring is the season between winter and summer.

If you want to say that something happens every year during this season, you say that it happens **in spring** or **in the spring**.

In spring birds nest here.
Their garden is full of flowers in the spring.

> **! BE CAREFUL**
>
> Don't say that something happens 'in the springs' or 'in springs'.

→ See **Reference** section **Days and dates**

stack

→ See **heap – stack – pile**

staff

The people who work for an organization can be referred to as its **staff**.

She was invited to join the staff of the BBC.
The police questioned all the hospital staff.

In British English, you can use a plural or singular form of a verb after **staff**. The plural form is more common.

The staff are very helpful.
The teaching staff is well-qualified and experienced.

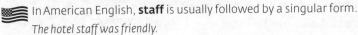 In American English, **staff** is usually followed by a singular form.

The hotel staff was friendly.
Our staff gets bigger every year.

→ See **Nouns** for information on collective nouns

> **! BE CAREFUL**
>
> Don't refer to an individual person who works for an organization as 'a staff'. Refer to him or her as a **member of staff**.
>
> *There are ten students to every member of staff.*
> *All members of staff are expected to attend meetings.*

stand

Stand is usually a verb. Its past tense and -*ed* participle is **stood**.

1 **saying where someone is**

When you **are standing** somewhere, your body is upright, your legs are straight, and your weight is supported by your feet. In standard English you don't say that someone 'is stood' somewhere.

Why is he standing in the middle of the road?
She was standing at the bus stop.

2 **saying where someone goes**

Stand is also used to say that someone moves to a different place and remains standing there.

They stood to one side so that she could pass.
Come and stand next to me.

3 **'stand up'**

Stand is sometimes used to say that someone raises their body to a standing position when they have been sitting.

Everyone stood and applauded.

However, you normally say that someone **stands up**.

The children are supposed to stand up when the teacher comes into the room.
I put down my glass and stood up.

stare

→ See **gaze – stare**

start – begin

1 **used with noun phrases**

If you **start** or **begin** something, you do it from a particular time. There is no difference in meaning.

My father started work when he was fourteen.
We'll begin the meeting as soon as he arrives.

The past tense of **begin** is **began**. The -ed participle is **begun**.

The teacher opened the book and began the lesson.
The company has begun research on a new product.

2 **used with other verbs**

You can use a *to*-infinitive or an *-ing* form after **start** and **begin**.

Rafael started to run.
He started laughing.
I was beginning to feel better.
We began talking about our experiences.

! **BE CAREFUL**

Don't use an *-ing* form after **starting** or **beginning**. Don't say, for example, 'I'm beginning understanding more'. You must say 'I'm beginning to understand more'.

3 **used as intransitive verbs**

Start and **begin** can be intransitive verbs, used to say that something happens from a particular time.

The show starts at 7.
My career as a journalist was about to begin.

4 **special uses of 'start'**

Start has some special meanings. You don't use 'begin' with any of these meanings.

You use **start** to say that someone makes a machine or engine start to work.

She started her car and drove off.
He couldn't get the engine started.

You use **start** to say that someone creates a business or other organization.

He borrowed money to start a restaurant.
Now is a good time to start your own business.

stationary – stationery

Stationary and **stationery** are both pronounced /'steɪʃənəri/. However, their meanings are completely different.

1 **'stationary'**

Stationary is an adjective. If a vehicle is **stationary**, it is not moving.

There was a stationary car in the middle of the street.
Only use the handbrake when your vehicle is stationary.

2 **'stationery'**

Stationery is a noun. It refers to paper, envelopes, pens, and other equipment used for writing.

They sell books and stationery.
Get some envelopes from the office stationery cupboard.

statistics – statistical

1 **'statistics'**

Statistics are facts consisting of numbers, obtained from analysing information.

According to official statistics, 39 million Americans had no health insurance.
The government will publish new unemployment statistics this week.

When **statistics** is used with this meaning, it is a plural noun. You use the plural form of a verb with it.

The statistics are taken from United Nations sources.
Statistics don't necessarily prove anything.

Statistics is also the branch of mathematics dealing with these facts.

She is a Professor of Statistics.

When you use **statistics** with this meaning, it is an uncountable noun. You use a singular form of a verb with it.

Statistics has never been taught here before.

2 'statistical'

Don't use 'statistic' as an adjective to mean 'relating to statistics'. Use **statistical**.

Statistical techniques are used to analyse the data.
The report contains a lot of statistical information.

stay

→ See **remain – stay**

steal

When someone **steals** something, they take it without permission and without intending to return it.

He tried to steal a car from the car park.
She was accused of stealing a necklace.

The past tense of **steal** is **stole**. The *-ed* participle is **stolen**.

Armed raiders stole millions of dollars.
My phone was stolen from my bag.

! BE CAREFUL

When you are speaking about the object that has been stolen, use **steal** or **take**. When the object of the verb is a person or a building, use **rob**.

I had stolen my father's money.
I know who took my watch.
They robbed him and took his laptop.
The gang were accused of robbing a bank.

→ See **rob – steal**

still

Still is most commonly used to say that a situation continues to exist.

1 position in sentence

▶ You usually put **still** after the first auxiliary verb in a verb phrase. For example, you say 'He **was still** waiting'. Don't say 'He still was waiting'.

He could still get into serious trouble.
I've still got $10 left.

▶ If there is no auxiliary verb, you put **still** in front of the verb, unless the verb is **be**.

She still lives in London.
I still need more money.

▶ If the verb is **be**, you put **still** after it.

She was still beautiful.
There is still a chance the plan could fail.

▶ In conversation, **still** is sometimes put at the end of a sentence.

We have a lot to do still.

Don't use 'still' with this meaning at the beginning of a sentence. Don't say, for example 'Still we have a lot to do'.

2 used with 'even if'

Still is often used in sentences that begin with **even if** or **even though**.

Even if they change the system, they've still got a problem to solve.

→ See **even**

3 used in negative clauses

You can use **still** in a negative clause for emphasis. **Still** goes in front of the first auxiliary verb in the clause.

I still don't understand.
I still didn't know her name.

Don't use 'still' in a negative clause simply to say that something has not happened up to the present time. The word you use is **yet**. **Yet** goes after **not** or at the end of the clause.

I haven't yet met his wife.
It isn't dark yet.

→ See **yet**

sting – bite

1 'sting'

Sting is usually a verb. Its past tense and *-ed* participle is **stung**.

If a creature such as a bee, wasp, or scorpion **stings** you, it pricks your skin and pushes poison into your body.

Bees do not normally sting without being provoked.
Felipe had been stung by a wasp.

2 'bite'

Don't say that a mosquito or ant 'stings' you. You say that it **bites** you. The past tense and *-ed* participle of **bite** are **bit** and **bitten**.

A mosquito landed on my arm and bit me.
An ant had bitten her on the foot.

You also say that a snake **bites** you.

In Britain you are very unlikely to get bitten by a snake.

stop

You usually use the verb **stop** to say that someone no longer does something. After **stop**, you can use either an *-ing* form or a *to*-infinitive, but with different meanings.

1 'stop doing'

If you **stop doing** something at a particular time, you no longer do it after that time.

We all stopped talking.
He couldn't stop crying.

2 'stop to do'

If you **stop to do** something, you interrupt what you are doing in order to do something else. For example, if someone stops while they are walking somewhere, admires the view, then continues walking, you can say 'She **stopped to admire** the view'.

The man recognized him and <u>stopped to speak</u> to him.
I <u>stopped to tie</u> my shoelace.

3 'stop somebody doing something'

If you are prevented from doing something, you can say that something **stops you doing** it or **stops you from doing** it.

They tried to <u>stop me coming</u>.
How do you <u>stop a tap dripping</u>?
Nothing was going to <u>stop Elena from being a writer</u>.

> **!** **BE CAREFUL**
>
> Don't say that something 'stops somebody to do' something. Don't say, for example 'How do you stop a tap to drip?'

store

→ See **shop – store**

storey – floor

1 'storey'

You refer to the different levels in a building as its **storeys** or **floors**. If you are saying how many levels a building has, you usually use **storeys**.

They live in a house with <u>four storeys</u>.
The school is a <u>single-storey</u> building.

 'Storey' is spelled **story** in American English. The plural of **story** is **stories**.

The hospital is a <u>six-story</u> building.
The hotel towers are each 30 <u>stories</u> high.

2 'floor'

If you are talking about a particular level in a building, you usually use **floor**, not 'storey'. Don't say that something is on a particular 'storey'. You say that it is on a particular **floor**.

My office is on the second <u>floor</u>.
She rents a ground <u>floor</u> apartment.

story – storey

1 'story'

A **story** is a description of imaginary people and events, written or told in order to entertain people. The plural of **story** is **stories**.

Tell me a <u>story</u>.
Her <u>stories</u> about the boy wizard have sold millions of copies.

A description of a series of real events can also be called a **story**.

We sold the <u>story</u> of the expedition to the Daily Express.

 In American English, a **story** is also one of the floors or levels in a building.

The house was four <u>stories</u> high.

2 'storey'

In British English, one of these floors is called a **storey**.

The house was three storeys high.

→ See **storey – floor**

---

strange – unusual

1 'strange'

You use **strange** to say that something is unfamiliar or unexpected in a way that makes you puzzled, uneasy, or afraid.

The strange thing was that she didn't remember anything about the evening.
It was strange to hear her voice again.

2 'unusual'

If you just want to say that something is not common, you use **unusual**, not 'strange'.

He had an unusual name.
It is unusual for such a small hotel to have a restaurant.

---

stranger

A **stranger** is someone who you have never met before.

A stranger appeared.
Antonio was a stranger to all of us.

! BE CAREFUL

Don't use 'stranger' to talk about someone who comes from a country that is not your own. You can refer to him or her as a **foreigner**, but this word can sound rather impolite. It is better to say, for example, 'someone **from abroad**' or 'a person **from overseas**'.

We have some visitors from abroad coming this week.
Most universities have many postgraduate students from overseas.

---

street – road – lane

1 'street'

A **street** is a road in a town or large village, usually with houses or other buildings built alongside it.

The two men walked slowly down the street.
They went into the café across the street.

2 'road'

Road is a very general word for a paved way in a town or between towns. You can use **road** in almost any context where **street** is used. For example, you can say 'They walked down the **street**' or 'They walked down the **road**'. You can also use **road** for paved ways in the countryside.

The road to the airport was blocked.
They drove up a steep, twisting mountain road.

3 'lane'

A **lane** is a narrow road, usually in the countryside.

There's a cottage at the end of the lane.
He rode his horse down a muddy lane.

A **lane** is also one of the parts of a large road such as a motorway, which has more than one line of traffic going in each direction.

She accelerated into the fast lane.
Are taxis allowed to use the bus lane?

---

strongly

You use **strongly** when you are talking about people's feelings or attitudes. For example, if you **strongly** object to something, you object to it very much.

I feel very strongly that we have a duty to help.
Supporters of Green parties are usually strongly against nuclear power.

You can say that you **strongly advise** or **strongly recommend** something to mean that you believe very definitely that someone should do it, use it, etc.

I strongly advise you to get someone to help you.
I would strongly recommend a Vitamin B supplement.

! BE CAREFUL

Don't use 'strongly' to describe the way someone holds something. Instead, use **tightly** or **firmly**.

He gripped the railing tightly in his right hand.
He held her arm firmly.

Don't say that a person works 'strongly'. Say that they work **hard**.

He had worked hard all his life.

---

student

1 'student'

In British English, a **student** is usually someone who is studying or training at a university or college.

The doctor was accompanied by a medical student.
They met when they were students at Edinburgh University.

In American English, anyone who studies at a school, college, or university can be referred to as a **student**. People studying at a school are also sometimes called **students** in British English.

She teaches math to high school students.
Not enough secondary school students are learning a foreign language.

2 'schoolchildren'

In British English, children attending schools are often referred to generally as **schoolchildren**, **schoolboys**, or **schoolgirls**.

Each year the museum is visited by thousands of schoolchildren.
A group of schoolgirls were walking along the road.

3 'pupils'

In Britain, the children attending a particular school are usually referred to as its **pupils**.

The school has more than 1300 pupils.
Some pupils' behaviour was causing concern.

GRAMMAR FINDER

The subjunctive

The **subjunctive** is a structure that is not very common in English and that is usually regarded as formal or old-fashioned. Using the subjunctive involves using the base form of a verb instead of a present or past tense, or instead of 'should' and a base form.

1 'whether' and 'though'

The subjunctive can be used instead of a present tense in a conditional clause beginning with **whether** or a clause containing **though**.

The change must be welcomed, if only because it will come whether it be welcomed or not.
The church absorbs these monuments, large though they be, in its own immense scope.

2 'that'

The subjunctive can be used in a *that*-clause when making a suggestion or giving an order.

Someone suggested that they break into small groups.
It was his doctor who suggested that he change his job.
He ordered that the books be burnt.

3 subjunctive use of 'were'

In writing and sometimes in conversation, **were** is used instead of 'was' in conditional clauses referring to a situation that does not exist or that is unlikely. This use of **were** is also a type of subjunctive use.

If I were you I'd see a doctor.
He would be persecuted if he were sent back.
If I were asked to define my condition, I'd say 'bored'.

→ See **were**

Were is also often used instead of 'was' in clauses beginning with **as though** and **as if**.

You talk as though he were already condemned.
Margaret looked at me as if I were crazy.

GRAMMAR FINDER

Subordinate clauses

1 subordinate clauses	**6** place clauses
2 position of adverbial clauses	**7** purpose clauses
3 concessive clauses	**8** reason clauses
4 conditional clauses	**9** result clauses
5 manner clauses	**10** time clauses

A **subordinate clause** is a clause that adds to or completes the information given in a main clause. Most subordinate clauses begin with a **subordinating conjunction** such as **because**, **if**, or **that**.

Many subordinate clauses are **adverbial clauses**. These clauses give information about the circumstances of an event. The different types of adverbial clause are described in detail below.

→ See **Relative clauses**, **Reporting** for information about other kinds of subordinate clause, *-ing* **forms**, *-ed* **participles**

1 position of adverbial clauses

The usual position for an adverbial clause is just after the main clause.

Her father died when she was young.
They were going by car because it was more comfortable.

However, most types of adverbial clause can be put in front of the main clause when you want to draw attention to the adverbial clause.

When the city is dark, we can move around easily.
Although crocodiles are inactive for long periods, on occasion they can run very fast indeed.

Occasionally, an adverbial clause is put in the middle of another clause, especially a relative clause.

They made claims which, when you analyse them, are not supported by facts.

2 concessive clauses

Concessive clauses contain a fact that contrasts with the main clause. These are the main conjunctions used to introduce concessive clauses:

although	though	while
even though	whereas	whilst

I used to read a lot although I don't get much time for books now.
While I did well in class, I was a poor performer at games.

 Whilst is a formal word, and is not used at all in American English, which uses only **while**.

▶ words in front of 'though'

You can put a complement in front of **though** for emphasis in formal English. For example, instead of saying 'Though he was ill, he insisted on coming to the meeting', you can say 'Ill though he was, he insisted on coming to the meeting'.

Astute businessman though he was, Philip was capable of making mistakes.
I had to accept the fact, improbable though it was.

When the complement is an adjective, you can use **as** instead of **though**.

Stupid as it sounds, I was so in love with her that I believed her.

You can also put an adverb such as **hard** or **bravely** in front of **though**.

We couldn't understand him, hard though we tried.

▶ 'much as'

When you are talking about a strong feeling or desire, you can use **much as** instead of using 'although' and 'very much'. For example, instead of saying 'Although I like Venice very much, I couldn't live there', you can say 'Much as I like Venice, I couldn't live there'.

Much as he admired her, he had no wish to marry her.

3 conditional clauses

Conditional clauses are used to talk about possible situations. The event described in the main clause depends on the condition described in the subordinate clause. Conditional clauses usually begin with **if** or **unless**.

→ See **if**, **unless**

When using a conditional clause, you often use a **modal** in the main clause. You always use a modal in the main clause when talking about a situation which does not exist.

If you weren't here, she would get rid of me in no time.
If anybody had asked me, I could have told them what happened.

▶ inversion

In formal speech and writing, instead of using 'if' or 'unless', you can use **inversion**: that is, you can put the verb before the subject. For example, instead of saying 'If I'd been there, I would have stopped them', you can say 'Had I been there, I would have stopped them'.

Should ministers demand an enquiry, we would accept it.

▶ imperatives

People sometimes use an imperative clause followed by **and** or **or** instead of a conditional clause. For example, instead of saying 'If you keep quiet, you won't get hurt', they say 'Keep quiet and you won't get hurt'.

→ See **Topic** entries **Advising someone**, **Warning someone**

▶ less common conjunctions

You use **provided**, **providing**, **as long as**, or **only if** to begin a conditional clause referring to a situation that is a necessary condition for the situation referred to in the main clause.

Ordering is quick and easy provided you have access to the internet.
As long as you write clearly you don't have to learn any new typing skills.

When you use **only if**, the subject and verb in the main clause are inverted.

Only if these methods are followed correctly will the results be accurate.

To show that a situation is not affected by another possible situation, you use **even if**.

Even if you've never studied English before, you can take this course.
I would have married her even if she had been poor.

To show that a situation is not affected by any of several possibilities, you use **whether** and **or**.

Some children always have a huge appetite, whether they're well or sick, calm or worried.

To show that a situation is not affected by either of two opposite possibilities, you can use **whether or not**.

A parent should talk over the child's problems with the teacher, whether or not these problems are connected with school.
He will have to pay the bill whether he likes it or not.

4 **manner clauses**

Manner clauses describe someone's behaviour or the way that something is done. The following conjunctions are used to introduce manner clauses:

as	as though	the way
as if	like	

I don't understand why he behaves as he does.
Is she often rude and cross like she's been this last month?
Joyce looked at her the way a lot of girls did.

→ See **like – as – the way**

As if and **as though** are used to say that something is done as it would be done if something else were the case. Note that a past tense is used in the subordinate clause.

Presidents can't dispose of companies as if people didn't exist.
She treats him as though he was her own son.

In formal or literary English, **were** is sometimes used instead of 'was'.

He spoke as though his father were already dead.

5 **place clauses**

Place clauses show the location or position of something. Place clauses usually begin with **where**.

He said he was happy where he was.
He left it where it lay.

You use **wherever** to say that something happens in every place where something else happens.

Flowers grew wherever there was enough light.
Wherever I looked, I found patterns.

Everywhere can be used instead of 'wherever'.

Everywhere I went, people were angry or suspicious.

 Informally, speakers of American English also use **everyplace** instead of 'everywhere'.

Everyplace her body touched the seat began to itch.

6 **purpose clauses**

Purpose clauses show the intention someone has when they do something. The most common type of purpose clause is a *to*-infinitive clause.

All information in this brochure has been checked as carefully as possible to ensure that it is accurate.
Carol had brought the subject up simply to annoy Sandra.

In formal writing and speech, **in order** followed by a *to*-infinitive clause is often used instead of a simple *to*-infinitive clause.

They bought more land in order to extend the church.

You can also use **so as** followed by a *to*-infinitive clause.

We put up a screen so as to let in the fresh air and keep out the flies.

> **!** **BE CAREFUL**
>
> You cannot use 'not' with a simple *to*-infinitive clause when indicating a negative purpose. For example, you cannot say 'He slammed on his brakes to not hit it'. Instead, you must use **to avoid** followed by an *-ing* form, or **in order** or **so as** followed by **not** and a *to*-infinitive.
>
> *He had to hang on to avoid being washed overboard.*
> *I would have to give myself something to do in order not to be bored.*
> *They went on foot, so as not to be heard.*

Other purpose clauses are introduced by **so**, **so that**, or **in order that**. You usually use a modal in these purpose clauses.

She said she wanted to be ready at six so she could be out by eight.
I have drawn a diagram so that my explanation will be clearer.
Many people have to learn English in order that they can study a particular subject.

7 reason clauses

Reason clauses explain why something happens or is done. They are usually introduced by **because**, **since**, or **as**.

I couldn't feel angry because I liked him too much.
I didn't know that she had been married, since she seldom talked about herself.

You use **in case** or **just in case** when you are mentioning a possible future situation that is someone's reason for doing something. In the reason clause, you use the present simple.

I'll take my phone with me just in case you need to contact me.

When you are talking about someone's reason for doing something in the past, you use the past simple in the reason clause.

Sam took a coat with him in case it rained.

8 result clauses

Result clauses show the result of an event or situation. Result clauses are introduced by the conjunctions **so that** or **so**. They always come after the main clause.

He persuaded Nichols to turn it into a film so that he could play the lead.
The young do not have the money to save and the old are spending their savings, so it is mainly the middle-aged who are saving money.

That-clauses (with or without **that**) can also be used as result clauses when **so** or **such** has been used in the main clause.

They were so surprised they didn't try to stop him.
These birds have such small wings that they cannot fly even if they try.

→ See **so**

9 time clauses

Time clauses show the time of an event. The following conjunctions are used to introduce time clauses:

after	once	till	whilst
as	since	until	
as soon as	the minute	when	
before	the moment	while	

We arrived _as they were leaving_.
When the jar was full, he turned the water off.

More information on the uses of the words listed above can be found in the entry for each word.

▶ tenses in time clauses

When talking about the past or the present, the verb in a time clause has the same tense that it would have in a main clause or a simple sentence. However, if the time clause refers to the future, you use the present simple. Don't use 'will'.

As soon as I get back, I'm going to call my lawyer.
He wants to see you before he _dies_.

When mentioning an event in a time clause which will happen before an event referred to in the main clause, you use the present perfect in the time clause. Don't use 'will have'.

We won't be getting married until we've _saved_ enough money.
Let me know as soon as you _have finished the report_.

When reporting a statement or thought about such an event, you use the past simple or the past perfect in the time clause.

I knew he would come back as soon as I _was_ gone.
He argued that violence would continue until political oppression _had ended_.

→ See **since** for information on the use of tenses with **since** in a time clause

▶ omitting the subject

If the subject of the main clause and the time clause are the same, the subject in the time clause is sometimes omitted and a participle is used as the verb. This is done especially in formal English.

I read the book _before going to see the film_.
The car was stolen _while parked in a London street_.

When, **while**, **once**, **until**, or **till** can be used in front of a noun phrase, an adjective group, or an adverbial.

While in Venice, we went to the theatre every night.
Steam or boil them _until just tender_.

▶ regular occurrences

If you want to say that something always happens or happened in particular circumstances, you use a clause beginning with **when** or, more emphatically, **whenever**, **every time**, or **each time**.

When he talks about his work, he sounds so enthusiastic.
Whenever she had a cold, she ate only fruit.
Every time I go to that class I panic.
He flinched _each time she spoke to him_.

subway – underground – metro

1 'subway'

A **subway** is a path for pedestrians under a busy road.

You feel worried if you walk through a subway.

 In some American cities, **the subway** is a railway system in which electric trains travel below the ground in tunnels. In other cities this is called **the metro**.

I don't ride the subway at night.
You can take the metro to the Smithsonian museums.

2 'underground'

Some speakers of British English also use **subway** to refer to a British railway system like this, but the London and Glasgow systems are usually called **the underground**. The London system is also called **the tube**.

He crossed London by underground.
You can take the tube to Green Park and then walk.

---

such

1 referring back

Such a thing or person means a thing or person like the one that has just been described, mentioned, or experienced.

We could not believe such a thing.

> **!** **BE CAREFUL**
>
> Don't use 'such' when you are talking about something that is present, or about the place where you are. For example, if you are admiring someone's watch, don't say 'I'd like such a watch'. Say 'I'd like a watch **like that**'. Don't say about the town where you are living 'There's not much to do in such a town'. Say 'There's not much to do in a town **like this**'.
>
> *We have chairs like these at home.*
> *It's hard living alone in a place like this.*

2 'such as'

You use **such as** between two noun phrases when you are giving an example of something.

They played games such as bingo.
Mammals such as dogs and elephants give birth to live young.

The first noun phrase is sometimes put between **such** and **as**. This use is more common in formal or literary English.

We talked about such subjects as the weather.
She spent a lot of time buying such things as clothes and linen.

3 'such' used for emphasis

Such is sometimes used to emphasize the adjective in a noun phrase. For example, instead of saying 'He's a nice man', you can say 'He's **such a nice man**'.

She seemed such a happy woman.
It was such hard work.

> **!** **BE CAREFUL**
>
> Use **a** when the noun phrase is singular and countable. Don't say, for example, ~~'She seemed such happy woman'~~. Also, don't say ~~'She seemed a such happy woman'~~.

💬 In conversation, for greater emphasis, some people say **ever such** instead of 'such'.

I think that's <u>ever such a nice photo</u>.

Don't use 'ever such' in writing.

You can use **such** to refer to something or someone that has just been described or mentioned and to emphasize a quality that they have. For example, instead of saying 'It was a very old car. I was surprised to see her driving it', you can say 'I was surprised to see her driving **such an old car**'.

I was impressed to meet <u>such a famous actress</u>.
You really shouldn't tell <u>such obvious lies</u>.

4 **'such...that': mentioning a result**

You can also use **such** in front of a noun phrase when you are saying that something happens because someone or something has a quality to an unusually large extent. After the noun phrase, you use a *that*-clause.

This can be <u>such a gradual process that</u> you are not aware of it happening.
Sometimes the children are <u>such hard work that</u> she's relieved when the day is over.

---

suggest

When you **suggest** something, you mention it as a plan or idea for someone to consider.

Your doctor will probably <u>suggest</u> time off work.
We have to <u>suggest</u> a list of possible topics for next term's seminars.

> **!** **BE CAREFUL**
>
> **Suggest** is not usually followed directly by a noun or pronoun referring to a person. You usually have to put the preposition **to** in front of it. You don't ~~'suggest someone something'~~; you **suggest something to someone**.

Laura first <u>suggested this idea to me</u>.

Don't ~~'suggest someone to do something'~~ when you mean that you advise them to do it. You **suggest that someone does something**.

I <u>suggest that he writes her a letter</u>.
I'm not <u>suggesting we leave her here</u>.

In sentences like these, you can also use an infinitive without *to* in the *that*-clause. This is a fairly formal use.

He <u>suggested she talk</u> to a psychologist.

The modals **might** and **should** are sometimes used. This is a formal use.

He <u>suggested we might go</u> there straight after dinner.
His wife <u>suggested that he should start</u> a school.

Don't confuse **suggest** and **advise**. If you **suggest** something, you mention it as an idea or plan for someone to think about. If you **advise** someone to do something, you tell them what you think they should do.

I <u>advised him to leave</u> as soon as possible

→ See **Topic** entries **Advising someone**, **Suggestions**

suitcase

→ See **bag**

summer

Summer is the season between spring and autumn.

If you want to say that something happens every year during this season, you say that it happens **in summer** or **in the summer**.

The room is stifling hot in summer and freezing in winter.
The town is full of tourists in the summer.

> **!** BE CAREFUL
>
> Don't say that something happens 'in the summers' or 'in summers'.

supper

Some people call a large meal they eat in the early part of the evening their **supper**. Other people use **supper** to refer to a small meal eaten just before going to bed at night.

Jane invited us to have supper at her house.
She usually has a piece of fruit for supper.

→ See **Topic** entry **Meals**

support

If you **support** someone or **support** their aims, you agree with their aims and want them to succeed.

Parents support the headteacher and approve of what she is trying to do.
Most voters did not support the war.

If you **support** a sports team, you want them to win.

He has supported Arsenal all his life.

If you **support** someone, you provide them with money or the things they need.

He has three children to support.

> **!** BE CAREFUL
>
> Don't use 'support' in any of the following ways:
>
> Don't use 'support' to say that someone accepts pain or an unpleasant situation. Say that they **bear** it, **put up with** it, or **tolerate** it.
>
> *It was painful of course but I bore it.*
> *You have to put up with small inconveniences.*
>
> Don't use 'support' to say that someone allows something that they do not approve of. You say that they **put up with** it or **tolerate** it.
>
> *I've put up with his bad behaviour for too long.*
> *We will not tolerate bullying in this school.*
>
> If someone does not allow something that they do not approve of, you can also say that they **won't stand for** it.
>
> *I won't stand for any disobedience.*

If you do not like something at all, don't say that you 'can't support' it. Say that you **can't bear** it or **can't stand** it.

I _can't bear_ this music.
She _can't stand_ being kept waiting.

→ See **bear**

---

suppose

1 'suppose'

If you **suppose** that something is true, you think it is probably true.

I _suppose_ it was difficult.
I _suppose_ he left fairly recently.

2 'don't suppose'

Instead of saying that you **suppose** something is **not** true, you usually say that you **don't suppose that it is** true.

I _don't suppose_ anyone cares much whether he stays or goes.
I _don't suppose_ you've ever seen anything like this before!

You can use **I don't suppose** as a very polite way of asking or suggesting something.

I _don't suppose_ you'd like to come out for a drink?

3 'I suppose so'

If someone says that something is true, or asks you whether something is true, you can say '**I suppose so**' as a way of agreeing with them or saying 'yes' but showing that you are not very certain or enthusiastic.

'It was good, wasn't it?' – '_I suppose so._'
'Shall we go' – '_I suppose so._'

! BE CAREFUL

Don't say '~~I suppose it~~'.

4 'I suppose not'

Similarly, you can agree with a negative statement or question in a way that shows you are not very certain by saying '**I suppose not**'.

'It doesn't often happen.' – 'No, _I suppose not._'
'You don't want this, do you?' – '_I suppose not._'

5 'suppose' used as a conjunction

You can use **suppose** as a conjunction when you are considering a possible situation or action and trying to think what effects it would have.

Suppose we don't tell anyone, and somebody finds out about it.
Suppose you had a million dollars, what would you do?

Supposing can be used in a similar way.

Supposing something should go wrong, what would you do then?
Supposing he's right, it could be very serious.

6 'be supposed to'

If something **is supposed to** be done, it should be done because of a rule, instruction, or custom.

You are supposed to report it to the police as soon as possible.
I'm not supposed to talk to you about this.

If something **is supposed to** be true, people generally think that it is true.

The house was supposed to be haunted by a ghost.
She was supposed to be a very good actor.

> **!** **BE CAREFUL**
> Don't say that something 'is suppose to' be done or be true. Don't say, for example, ~~'The house is suppose to be haunted'~~.

sure

→ See **certain – sure**

surely – definitely – certainly – naturally

1 'surely'

You use **surely** for emphasis when you are objecting to something that has been said or done.

'I can have it ready for next week.' – 'Surely you can get it done sooner than that?'
Their lawyers claim that they have not broken any rules, but surely this is not good practice.

2 'definitely' and 'certainly'

Don't use 'surely' simply to give strong emphasis to a statement. Use **definitely**.

They were definitely not happy.
The call definitely came from your phone.

In British English, you don't use 'surely' when you are agreeing with something that has been said, or confirming that something is true. Use **certainly**.

Ellie was certainly a student at the university but I'm not sure about her brother.
'You like him, don't you?' – 'I certainly do.'

 American speakers use both **surely** and **certainly** to agree with requests and statements.

'It is still a difficult world for women.' – 'Oh, certainly.'
Surely, yes, I agree with that.

Don't use 'surely' to say emphatically that something will happen in the future. Use **definitely** or **certainly**.

The conference will definitely be postponed.
If nothing is done, there will certainly be problems.

3 'naturally'

Don't use 'surely' to emphasize that something is what you would expect in particular circumstances. Use **naturally**.

His sister was crying, so naturally Sam was upset.
Naturally, some of the information will be irrelevant.

surgery

1 used as an uncountable noun

In both British and American English, **surgery** is medical treatment in which a person's body is cut open so that a surgeon can deal with a diseased or damaged part.

He underwent surgery to repair a torn knee ligament.
She may have to have more surgery on her wrist.

2 used as a countable noun

A **surgery** can be used to refer to a particular medical operation. This meaning is used more in American English than British English.

He has had five knee surgeries.
She was told she would have to have another surgery.

In British English, a doctor's or dentist's **surgery** is the building or room where he or she works and where people go to receive advice and minor treatment.

I called the surgery to make an appointment.

 In American English, a building or room like this is called the doctor's or dentist's **office**.

Dr Patel's office was just across the street.

---

surprise

Surprise can be a verb or a noun.

1 used as a verb

If something **surprises** you, you did not expect it.

What you say surprises me.
Her decision to resign had surprised everybody.

Don't use a progressive form of **surprise**. Don't say, for example, '~~What you say is surprising me~~'.

2 used as a noun

If something is a **surprise**, it surprises someone.

The result came as a surprise to everyone.
It was a great surprise to find out I had won.

In stories, expressions such as **to my surprise** and **to her surprise** are sometimes used to show that someone is surprised by something.

To her surprise he said no.

! BE CAREFUL

Don't use any preposition except **to** in these expressions. Don't say, for example, '~~For her surprise he said no~~'.

3 'surprised'

Surprised is an adjective. If you are **surprised to see** something or **surprised to hear** something, you did not expect to see it or hear it.

I was surprised to see her return so soon.
You won't be surprised to learn that I disagreed with this.

BE CAREFUL

Don't say that someone is 'surprised at seeing' or 'surprised at hearing' something. Don't say that someone is 'surprise to' see or hear something. Don't say, for example, ~~'I was surprised at seeing her return'~~ or ~~'I was surprise to see her return'~~.

sweetcorn

→ See **corn**

sweets – candy

'sweets'

In British English, small, sweet things that you eat, such as toffees and chocolates, are called **sweets**.

She did not allow her children to eat too many sweets.

 In American English, sweet things like these are called **candy**. **Candy** is an uncountable noun.

You eat too much candy. It's bad for your teeth.

Tt

take

Take is one of the commonest verbs in English. It is used in many different ways. Its other forms are **takes**, **taking**, **took**, **taken**.

1 actions and activities

Most commonly, **take** is used with a noun that refers to an action.

She took a shower.
He liked taking long walks in the country.

→ See **have – take**

2 moving things

If you **take** something from one place to another, you carry it there.

Don't forget to take your umbrella.
He has to take the boxes to the office every morning.

→ See **carry – take**

! BE CAREFUL

Don't confuse **take** with **bring** or **fetch**.

→ See **bring – take – fetch**

3 exams and tests

When someone completes an exam or test, you say that they **take** the exam or test.

Have you taken your driving test yet?
She took her degree last year.

4 time

If something **takes** a certain amount of time, you need that amount of time in order to do it.

How long will it take?
It may take them several weeks to get back.

take place

You say that an event **takes place**.

The wedding took place on the stage of the Sydney Opera House.
Elections will take place in November.

Happen and **occur** have a similar meaning, but they can only be used for talking about events which were not planned. You can use **take place** to talk about either planned or unplanned events.

The talks will take place in Vienna.
The accident took place on Saturday morning.

> **!** **BE CAREFUL**
>
> **Take place** is an intransitive verb. Don't say that something 'was taken place'.

talk

Talk can be a verb or a noun.

1 used as a verb

When you **talk**, you say things.

Nancy's throat was so sore that she could not talk.

Don't use 'talk' to report what someone says. Don't say, for example, 'He talked that the taxi had arrived'. Say 'He **said** that the taxi had arrived'.

I said that I would like to teach English.

If you mention the person who is being spoken to, you use **tell**.

He told me that Sheldon would be arriving in a few days.

→ See **say**, **tell**

Don't confuse **talk** with **speak**.

→ See **speak – talk**

2 used as a countable noun

If you **give a talk**, you speak for a period of time to an audience.

Colin Blakemore came here and gave a talk a couple of years ago.

3 used as an uncountable noun

If there is **talk about** something, people are discussing it.

There was a lot of talk about me getting married.

4 used as a plural noun

Talks are formal discussions intended to produce an agreement, usually between different countries or between employers and employees. People **hold** talks.

Government officials held talks with union leaders yesterday.

tall

→ See **high – tall**

tea

1 the drink

Tea is a drink made with boiling water and the dried leaves of the tea bush. Many people add milk to the drink, and some add sugar.

She poured herself another cup of tea.
Brian went into the kitchen to make a fresh pot of tea.

2 meals

Tea is also the name of two different types of meal.

In Britain, some people use **tea** to refer to a light meal that they eat in the afternoon. This meal usually consists of sandwiches and cakes, with tea to drink. It is sometimes called **afternoon tea**.

I'll make sandwiches for tea.

Some British people use **tea** to refer to a main meal that they eat in the early evening.

At five o'clock he comes home for his tea.

→ See **Topic** entry **Meals**

teach

1 teaching a subject

If you **teach** a subject, you explain it to people so that they know about it or understand it. The past form and *-ed* participle of **teach** is **taught**.

I taught history for many years.
English will be taught in primary schools.

When **teach** has this meaning, it often has an indirect object. The indirect object can go either in front of the direct object or after it. If it goes after the direct object, you put **to** in front of it.

That's the man that taught us Geography at school.
I found a job teaching English to a group of adults in Paris.

2 teaching a skill

If you **teach** someone **to do** something, you give them instructions so that they know how to do it.

He taught me to sing a song.
His dad had taught him to drive.

When **teach** is used with a *to*-infinitive like this, it must have a direct object. Don't say, for example, 'His dad had taught to drive'.

Instead of using a *to*-infinitive, you can sometimes use an *-ing* form. For example, instead of saying 'I taught them to ski', you can say 'I taught them **skiing**'. You can also say 'I taught them **how to ski**'.

She taught them singing.
My mother taught me how to cook.

team

→ See **Nouns** for information on collective nouns

tell

Tell is a common verb which is used in several different ways. Its past form and *-ed* participle is **told**.

1 information

If someone **tells** you something, they give you some information. You usually refer to this information by using a *that*-clause or a *wh*-clause.

Tell Dad the electrician has come.
I told her what the doctor had said.

You can sometimes refer to the information that is given by using a noun phrase as the direct object of **tell**. When the direct object is not a pronoun, you put the indirect object first.

She told <u>him the news</u>.
I never told <u>her a thing</u>.

When the direct object is a pronoun, you usually put it first. You put **to** in front of the indirect object.

I've never told <u>this to anyone else</u> in my whole life.

When you are referring back to information that has already been mentioned, you use **so** after **tell**. For example, you say 'I didn't agree with him and I **told him so**'. Don't say '<s>I didn't agree with him and I told him it</s>'.

She knows that I might be late. I have <u>told her so</u>.
'Then how do you know she's well?' – 'She <u>told me so</u>.'

2 stories, jokes, lies

You say that someone **tells** a story or a joke.

She <u>told me the story</u> of her life.
He's extremely funny when he <u>tells a joke</u>.

You can also say that someone **makes** or **cracks** a joke.

→ See **joke**

You say that someone **tells** a lie.

We <u>told a lot of lies</u>.

If someone is not lying, you say that they are **telling the truth**.

We knew that he was <u>telling the truth</u>.
I wondered why I <u>hadn't told</u> Mary <u>the truth</u>.

When you use **tell** to talk about stories, jokes, or lies, the indirect object can go either after the direct object or in front of it.

His friend <u>told me this story</u>.
Many hours had passed when Karen finished <u>telling her story to Kim</u>.

3 orders

If you **tell** someone **to do** something, you order or instruct them to do it. When **tell** has this meaning, it is followed by an object and a *to*-infinitive.

Tell Martha <u>to come</u> to my office.
They <u>told us to put on</u> our seat-belts.

> **! BE CAREFUL**
>
> Don't use **tell** like this without an object. Don't say, for example, '<s>They told to put on our seat-belts</s>'.

4 recognizing the truth

If you **can tell** what is happening or what is true, you are able to judge correctly what is happening or what is true.

I <u>can usually tell</u> when someone's lying to me.
I <u>couldn't tell</u> what they were thinking.

When **tell** has this meaning, you usually use **can**, **could**, or **be able to** with it.

5 'inform'

Inform means the same as **tell**, but it is more formal, and is used in slightly different ways. You can **inform** someone **of** something, or **inform** someone **that** something is the case.

The public is informed of the financial benefits that are available.
It was his duty to inform the king that his country was in danger.

In conversation and in less formal writing, you usually use **tell**.

temperature

→ See **Reference** section **Measurements**

terrible – terribly

1 'terrible'

The adjective **terrible** is used in two ways. In conversation and in less formal writing, you use it to say that something is very unpleasant or of very poor quality.

I know this has been a terrible shock to you.
His eyesight was terrible.

In writing or conversation, you use **terrible** to say that something is very shocking or distressing.

That was a terrible air crash last week.

2 'terribly'

The adverb **terribly** is sometimes used for emphasizing how shocking or distressing something is.

My son has suffered terribly. He has lost his best friend.
The wound bled terribly.

However, **terribly** is much more commonly used as a stronger word than 'very' or 'very much'.

I'm terribly sorry.
We all miss him terribly and are desperate for him to come home.
It's a terribly dull place.

! **BE CAREFUL**

Don't use 'terribly' like this in formal writing.

test

A **test** is a series of questions that you answer to show how much you know about a subject. You say that someone **takes** or **does** this type of test.

All candidates will be required to take an English language test.
We did another test.

A **test** is also a series of actions that you do to show how well you are able to do something. You say that someone **takes** a test of this kind.

She's not yet taken her driving test.

! BE CAREFUL

Don't use 'make' with **test**. Don't say, for example, 'She's not yet made her driving test'.

If someone is successful in a test of either kind, you say that they **pass** it.

I _passed_ my driving test in Holland.

To **pass** a test always means to succeed in it. It does not have the same meaning as **take** or **do**.

If someone is unsuccessful in a test, you say that they **fail** it.

I think I've _failed_ the test.

→ See **exam – examination**

---

than

1 **'than' used with comparatives**

Than is mainly used after comparative adjectives and adverbs.

I am happier _than I have ever been_.
They had to work harder _than expected_.

If you use a personal pronoun on its own after **than**, it must be an object pronoun such as **me** or **him**.

My brother is younger than _me_.
Lamin was shorter than _her_.

However, if the pronoun is the subject of a clause, you use a subject pronoun.

They knew my past much better than _she did_.
He's taller than _I am_.

2 **'than ever'**

You can also use **ever** or **ever before** after **than**. For example, if you say that something is 'bigger **than ever**' or 'bigger **than ever before**', you are emphasizing that it has never been as big as it is now, although it has always been big.

Bill worked harder _than ever_.
He was now managing a bigger team _than ever before_.

! BE CAREFUL

Don't use 'than' when you are making comparisons using **not as** or **not so**. Don't say, for example, 'He is not as tall than his sister'. You say 'He is not as tall **as** his sister'.

→ See **as ... as**

→ See **Comparative and superlative adjectives**, **Comparative and superlative adverbs**

3 **'more than'**

You use **more than** to say that the number of people or things in a group is greater than a particular number.

We live in a city of _more than_ a million people.
There are _more than_ two hundred and fifty species of shark.

→ See **more**

You can also use **more than** in front of some adjectives as a way of emphasizing them. For example, instead of saying 'If you can come, I shall be very pleased', you can say 'If you can come, I shall be **more than** pleased'. This is a fairly formal use.

I am more than satisfied with my achievements in Australia.
You would be more than welcome.

4 'rather than'

You use **rather than** when you want to compare something that is the case with something that is not.

The company's offices are in London rather than in Nottingham.
She was angry rather than afraid.

→ See **rather**

thank

1 'thank you'

Thank is mainly used in the expressions **Thank you** and **Thanks**.

Thank you very much! The flowers are so pretty!
Thanks a lot, Suzie. You've been great.

! BE CAREFUL

Don't say '~~Thanks you~~' or '~~Thanks you a lot~~'.

→ See **Topic** entry **Thanking someone**

2 'thank' used as a verb

Thank is also a verb. If you **thank** someone, you show that you are grateful for something they have done or something they have given you.

She smiled at him, thanked him, and drove off.

You say that you **thank** someone **for** something.

I thanked Jenny for her time, patience and sense of humour.
He thanked me for what I had done.

You can also **thank** someone **for doing** something.

He thanked the audience for coming.
He thanked me for bringing the sandwiches.

! BE CAREFUL

Don't use 'to'. Don't say, for example, '~~He thanked me to bring the sandwiches~~'.

that

That has three main uses:

1 used for referring back

You use it in various ways to refer to something that has already been mentioned or that is already known. When **that** is used like this, it is always pronounced /ðæt/.

I was so proud of that car!
How about natural gas? Is that an alternative?

→ See **that – those**

2 used in *that*-clauses

That is used at the beginning of a special type of clause called a *that*-clause. In *that*-clauses, **that** is usually pronounced /ðət/.

He said that he was sorry.
Mrs Kaul announced that the lecture would now begin.

→ See **That-clauses**, **Reporting**

3 used in relative clauses

That is also used at the beginning of another type of clause called a **defining relative clause**. In defining relative clauses, **that** is usually pronounced /ðət/.

I reached the gate that opened onto the lake.

→ See **Relative clauses**

GRAMMAR FINDER

That-clauses

A *that*-clause is a clause beginning with **that** which is used to refer to a fact or idea.

1 reporting

That-clauses are commonly used to report something that is said.

She said that she'd been married for about two months.
Sir Peter recently announced that he is to retire at the end of the year.

→ See **Reporting**

2 after adjectives

You can use a *that*-clause after adjectives that show someone's feelings or beliefs to say what fact those feelings or beliefs relate to.

She was sure that he meant it.
He was frightened that something terrible might be said.

The following adjectives often have a *that*-clause after them:

afraid	determined	horrified	scared
amazed	disappointed	insistent	shocked
angry	disgusted	jealous	sorry
annoyed	dismayed	keen	sure
anxious	doubtful	lucky	surprised
ashamed	eager	nervous	suspicious
astonished	envious	optimistic	terrified
astounded	fearful	pessimistic	thankful
aware	fortunate	pleased	unaware
certain	frightened	positive	uncertain
concerned	furious	proud	unconvinced
confident	glad	puzzled	unhappy
conscious	grateful	relieved	unlucky
convinced	happy	sad	upset
definite	hopeful	satisfied	worried

You can use a *that*-clause after **it is** and an adjective to comment on a situation or fact.

It is extraordinary that we have never met.

→ See **it**

3 after nouns

Nouns such as **assumption**, **feeling**, and **rumour**, which refer to what someone says or thinks, can be followed by a *that*-clause.

Our strategy has been based on the assumption that the killer is just one man.
I had a feeling that no-one thought I was good enough.
There is no truth in the rumour that he is resigning.

The following nouns are often followed by a *that*-clause:

accusation	criticism	impression	remark
admission	decision	information	reminder
advice	declaration	insistence	report
agreement	demand	judgement	request
allegation	denial	knowledge	rule
announcement	excuse	message	rumour
argument	expectation	news	saying
assertion	explanation	notion	sense
assumption	fear	observation	statement
assurance	feeling	opinion	suggestion
belief	generalization	point	superstition
charge	guarantee	prediction	theory
claim	guess	principle	thought
comment	hint	promise	threat
concept	hope	proposal	view
conclusion	hypothesis	question	warning
contention	idea	realization	wish
conviction	illusion	recognition	

4 after 'be'

A *that*-clause can be used as a complement after **be**.

Our hope is that this time all parties will co-operate.
The important thing is that we love each other.

5 omitting 'that'

That is sometimes omitted in all of the above cases, especially in spoken English.

He knew the attempt was hopeless.
She is sure Henry doesn't mind.
I have the feeling I've read this book already.

6 'the fact that'

In very formal English, a *that*-clause is sometimes used as the subject of a sentence.

That people can achieve goodness is evident through all of history.

However, if the main verb is a reporting verb or **be**, it is much more usual to have **it** as the subject, with the *that*-clause coming later.

It cannot be denied that this view is justified.

In other cases, it is more usual to use a structure consisting of **the fact** and a *that*-clause as the subject.

The fact that he is always late should make you question how reliable he is.

Structures beginning with **the fact that** are also used as the object of prepositions and of verbs which cannot be followed by a simple *that*-clause.

We expect acknowledgement of the fact that we were treated badly.
We overlooked the fact that the children's emotional development had been affected.

that – those

That and **those** are used in different ways when you are referring to people, things, events, or periods of time. They can both be determiners or pronouns. In this use, **that** is pronounced /ðæt/. **Those** is the plural form of **that**.

1 referring back

You can use **that** or **those** to refer to people, things, or events that have already been mentioned or that are already known about.

I knew that meeting would be difficult.
'Did you see him?' – 'No.' – 'That's a pity.'
Not all crimes are committed for those reasons.
There are still a few problems with the software, but we're working hard to remove those.

2 things you can see

You can also use **that** or **those** to refer to people or things that you can see but that are not close to you.

Look at that bird!
Don't be afraid of those people.

3 'that', referring to a person

However, you don't usually use **that** as a pronoun to refer to a person. You only use it when you are identifying someone or asking about their identity.

'Who's the woman in the red dress?' – 'That's my wife.'
Who's that?

→ See **Topic** entry **Telephoning**

4 saying when something happened

When you have been describing an event, you can use **that** with a word like **day**, **morning**, or **afternoon** to say that something else happened during the same day.

There were no classes that day.
Paula had been shopping that morning.

You can also use **that** with **week**, **month**, or **year** to show that something happened during the same week, month, or year.

There was a lot of extra work to do that week.
Later that month they attended another party at Maidenhead.

5 'this' and 'these'

This and **these** are used in some similar ways to **that** and **those**.

→ See **this – that**

the

1 basic uses

The is called the **definite article**. You use **the** at the beginning of a noun phrase to refer to someone or something that has already been mentioned or that is already known to the hearer or reader.

A man and a woman were walking on the beach. The man wore shorts, a T-shirt, and sandals. The woman wore a bright dress.

You can add a prepositional phrase or a relative clause when you need to show which person or thing you are talking about.

I've no idea about the geography of Scotland.
That is a different man to the man that I knew.

You use **the** with a singular noun to refer to something of which there is only one.

They all sat in the sun.
The sky was a brilliant blue.

2 types of thing or person

You can use **the** with the singular form of a countable noun when you want to make a general statement about all things of a particular type.

The computer allows us to deal with a lot of data very quickly.
My father's favourite flower is the rose.

! BE CAREFUL

You can make a similar statement using a plural form. If you do this, don't use 'the'.

It is then that computers will have their most important social effects.
Roses need to be watered frequently.

Don't use 'the' with an uncountable noun when it is used with a general meaning. For example, if you are talking about pollution in general, you say '**Pollution** is a serious problem'. Don't say 'The pollution is a serious problem'.

We continue to fight crime.
People are afraid to talk about disease and death.

You can use **the** with words such as **rich**, **poor**, **young**, **old**, or **unemployed** to refer to all people of a particular type.

Only the rich could afford his firm's products.
They were discussing the problem of the unemployed.

When you use one of these words like this, don't add '-s' or '-es' to it. Don't say, for example, 'the problem of the unemployeds'.

3 nationalities

You can use **the** with some nationality adjectives to refer to the people who live in a particular country, or to a group of people who come from that country.

They depend on the support of the French.

→ See **Reference** section **Nationality words**

4 systems and services

You use **the** with a singular countable noun to refer to a system or service.

I don't like using the phone.
How long does it take on the train?

5 institutions

You don't usually use 'the' between a preposition and a word like **church**, **college**, **home**, **hospital**, **prison**, **school**, or **university**.

Will we see you in church tomorrow?
I was at school with her.

→ See **church**, **college**, **home**, **hospital**, **prison**, **school – university**

6 meals

You don't usually use 'the' in front of the names of meals.

I open the mail immediately after breakfast.
I haven't had dinner yet.

→ See **Topic** entry **Meals**

7 used instead of a possessive

You sometimes use **the** instead of a possessive determiner, particularly when you are talking about something being done to a part of a person's body.

She touched him on the hand.
He took her by the arm and began pulling her away.

→ See **Possessive determiners**

8 used with superlatives and comparatives

You usually use **the** in front of superlative adjectives.

We saw the smallest church in England.

You don't usually use 'the' in front of superlative adverbs.

They use the language they know best.

You don't usually use 'the' in front of comparative adjectives or adverbs.

The model will probably be smaller
I wish we could get it done quicker

However, there are a few exceptions to this.

→ See **Comparative and superlative adjectives**, **Comparative and superlative adverbs**

their

→ See **there**

them

1 referring to a plural noun

Them can be the object of a verb or preposition. You use **them** to refer to people or things that have just been mentioned or whose identity is known.

Those children are now getting ready for school; some of them are only four years old.
She gathered the last few apples and put them into a bag.

> **! BE CAREFUL**
>
> Don't use 'them' as the object of a clause when you are referring to the same people as the subject. Instead, use **themselves**.
>
> *Your children should be old enough now to dress themselves.*

2 meaning 'him or her'

You can use **them** instead of 'him or her' to refer to a person whose sex is not known or not stated.

If anyone phones, tell them I'm out.

→ See **he – she – they**

---

there

There has two main uses. You use it in front of a verb such as **be**, or you use it as an adverb to refer to a place.

1 used in front of 'be'

You use **there** in front of **be** to say that something exists or happens, or that something is in a particular place. When **there** is used like this, it is usually pronounced /ðe/ or /ðə/. In slow or careful speech, it is pronounced /ðeə/.

There must be a reason.
There was a new cushion on one of the sofas.

After **there**, you use a singular form of **be** in front of a singular noun phrase, and a plural form in front of a plural noun phrase.

There is a fire on the fourth floor.
There are several problems with this method.

> In conversation, some people use **there's** in front of a plural noun phrase.
> For example, they say 'There's several problems with this method'. This use is generally regarded as incorrect, and you shouldn't use it in formal speech or in writing.

> **! BE CAREFUL**
>
> Don't use 'there is' or 'there are' with **since** to say how long ago something happened. Don't say, for example, 'There are four days since she arrived in London'. Say '**It's** four days since she arrived in London' or 'She arrived in London four days **ago**'.
>
> *It's three months since you were here last.*
> *Her husband died four years ago.*

2 used as an adverb

In its other main use, **there** is used for referring to a place which has just been mentioned. When **there** is used like this, it is always pronounced /ðeə/.

I must get home. Bill's there on his own.
Come into the kitchen. I spend most of my time there now.

> **! BE CAREFUL**
>
> Don't use 'to' in front of **there**. Don't say, for example, 'I like going to there'. Say 'I like going **there**'.

My family live in India. I still go there often.

Also, don't use 'there' to introduce a subordinate clause. Don't say, for example, '~~I went back to the park, there my sister was waiting~~'. Say 'I went back to the park, **where** my sister was waiting'.

The accident took place in Oxford, where he and his wife lived.

3 **'their'**

Don't confuse **there** with **their**, which is also pronounced /ðeə/. You use **their** to show that something belongs or relates to particular people, animals, or things.

I looked at their faces.
What would they do when they lost their jobs?

these

→ See **this – these**

they

They can be the subject of a verb. You use **they** to refer to people or things that have just been mentioned or whose identity is known.

All universities have chancellors. They are always rather senior people.
The women had not expected a visitor and they were in their everyday clothes.

→ See **Pronouns**

! BE CAREFUL

When the subject of a sentence is followed by a relative clause, don't use 'they' in front of the main verb. Don't say, for example, '~~The people who live next door, they keep chickens~~'. Say 'The people who live next door keep chickens'.

Two children who were rescued from a fire are now in hospital.
The girls who had been following him suddenly stopped.

They can refer to people in general, or to a group of people whose identity is not actually stated.

They say that former nurses make the worst patients.
Mercury is the stuff they put in thermometers.

→ See **one – you – we – they**

You can also use **they** instead of 'he or she' to refer to an individual person whose sex is not known or not stated.

I was going to stay with a friend, but they were ill.

→ See **he – she – they**

! BE CAREFUL

Don't use 'they' with **are** to say that a number of things exist or are in a particular place. Don't say, for example, '~~They are two bottles of juice in the fridge~~'. Say '**There are** two bottles of juice in the fridge'.

There are always plenty of jobs to be done.

→ See **there**

thief – robber – burglar

Anyone that steals can be called a **thief**. A **robber** often uses violence or the threat of violence to steal things from places such as banks or shops.

They caught the armed <u>robber</u> who raided a supermarket.

A **burglar** breaks into houses or other buildings and steals things.

The average <u>burglar</u> spends just two minutes inside your house.

think

The verb **think** is used in several different ways. Its past tense and *-ed* participle is **thought**.

1 used with a *that*-clause

You can use **think** with a *that*-clause when you are giving your opinion about something or mentioning a decision that you have made.

I <u>think</u> you should go.
I <u>thought</u> I'd wait.

 When you use **think** like this, you usually use a simple form, but in conversation you can use a progressive form, especially if you want to emphasize that your opinion or decision might change.

I have too many books. I'<u>m thinking</u> I might sell some of them.

Instead of saying that you think something is not the case, you usually say that you **don't think** it **is** the case.

I <u>don't think</u> this will work.
I <u>don't think</u> there is any doubt about that.

2 'I think so'

If someone asks you whether something is the case, you can express your opinion that it is probably the case by saying '**I think so**'. Don't say 'I think it'.

'Do you think my mother will be all right?' – '<u>I think so</u>.'

If you want to reply that something is probably not the case, you usually say '**I don't think so**'.

'I have another friend, Barbara Robson. Do you know her?' – '<u>I don't think so.</u>'
'Are you going to be sick?' – '<u>I don't think so.</u>'

3 using a progressive form

When someone **is thinking**, they are considering something. When you use **think** with this meaning, you often use a progressive form.

I'll fix us both a sandwich while I'<u>m thinking</u>.
You <u>have been thinking</u>, haven't you?

You also use a progressive form when you are talking about what is in someone's mind at a particular time.

That's what I <u>was thinking</u>.
It's very difficult to guess what the other people <u>are thinking</u>.

You can say that someone **is thinking about** something or someone, or **is thinking of** something or someone.

I spent hours <u>thinking about</u> the letter.
She <u>was thinking of</u> her husband.

If you are considering doing something, you can say that you **are thinking of doing** it.
I <u>was thinking of leaving</u> home.

> **!** **BE CAREFUL**
>
> Don't say '~~I was thinking to leave home~~'.

---

this – that

This and **that** are determiners or pronouns. The plural form of **this** is **these**. The plural form of **that** is **those**.

→ See **this – these, that – those**

This entry deals with the similarities and differences between the ways in which these words are used.

1 referring back

This, **these**, **that**, and **those** are all used for referring to people, things, or events that have already been mentioned. It is more common to use **this** and **these** than **that** and **those**.

New machines are more expensive and <u>this</u> is something one has to consider.
So, for all <u>these</u> reasons, my advice is to be very, very careful.

You use **that** or **those** when you are referring to something for the second time in a sentence, using the same noun.

I know that what I say to a <u>person</u> is seldom what <u>that person</u> hears.
Students suggest <u>books</u> for the library, and normally we're quite happy to get <u>those books</u>.

You usually use **that**, rather than 'this', to refer to a statement that someone has just made.

'She was terribly afraid of offending anyone.' – '<u>That's</u> right.'
'<u>That's</u> a good point,' he said in response to my question.

2 present and past

You can use **this** or **that** to talk about events or situations.

You use **this** to refer to a situation that is continuing to exist, or to an event that is continuing to take place.

'My God,' I said, '<u>This</u> is awful.'
<u>This</u> whole business has gone on too long.

You use **that** to refer to an event or situation that has taken place recently.

I knew <u>that</u> meeting would be difficult.
<u>That</u> was a terrible air crash last week.

3 closeness

You use **this** or **these** to refer to people or things that are very near to you. For example, you use **this** to refer to an object you are holding in your hand, or something on a desk or table in front of you.

'What is this?' she said, picking up the parcel on my desk.
Wait a minute. I just have to sort these books out.

You use **that** or **those** to refer to people or things that you can see or hear, but that are not very near to you, so that, for example, you cannot put out your hand and touch them.

Look at that bird!
Can you move those boots off there?

When you are comparing two things and one of them is nearer to you than the other, you can use **this** to refer to the one that is nearer and **that** to refer to the one that is further away.

This one's nice but I don't like that one much.

this – these

This and **these** are used in different ways when you are referring to people, things, situations, events, or periods of time. They can both be determiners or pronouns. **These** is the plural form of **this**.

1 referring back

You can use **this** or **these** to refer to people, things, or events that have just been mentioned.

He's from the Institute of English Language in Bangkok. This institute has been set up to serve language teachers in the area.
Tax increases may be needed next year to do this.
These particular students are extremely bright.

Don't use 'this' as a pronoun to refer to a person who has just been mentioned. Instead you use **he** or **she**.

He was known to everyone as Eddie.
'Bye,' Mary said as she drove away.

 In conversation, many people use **this** and **these** as determiners even when they are mentioning people or things for the first time.

Then this guy came to the door of the class and he said, 'Mary, you're wanted out here in the hall.'
At school we had to wear these awful white cotton hats.

2 closeness

You can use **this** or **these** to refer to people or things that are very near to you. For example, if you are holding a book, you refer to it as '**this** book'.

The colonel handed him the bag. 'This is for you,' he said.
Get these kids out of here.

'This' is not usually used as a pronoun to refer to a person. You only use it when you are identifying someone or asking them about their identity. For example, you use **this** when you are introducing someone. Note that when you are introducing more than one person, you use **this**, not 'these'.

This is Bernadette, Mr Zapp.
This is my brother Andrew and his wife Claire.

You also use **this** to say who you are when you phone someone.

Sally? This is Martin Brody.

3 present situations

You can use **this** to refer to a situation that exists now or to an event that is happening now.

You know a lot about this situation.

4 'this' and 'these' in time expressions

This is used in the following ways in time expressions:

You use it with **morning**, **afternoon**, or **evening** to refer to the morning, afternoon, or evening of the present day.

I was here this afternoon. Have you forgotten?

However, don't say 'this day'. You say **today**.

I had a letter today from my solicitor.

Also, don't say 'this night'. You refer to the previous night as **last night**. You refer to the night of the present day as **tonight**.

We left our bedroom window open last night.
I think I'll go to bed early tonight.

This week, **month**, or **year** means the present week, month, or year.

They're talking about going on strike this week.

You usually use **this** with **weekend** or with the name of a day, month, or season to refer to the next weekend or to the next day, month, or season with that name.

Come down there with me this weekend.
Let's fix a time. This Sunday. Four o'clock.

However, you can also use **this** with one of these words to refer to the previous weekend, or the previous day, month, or season with that name.

This summer they spent £15 million on emergency shelters for the homeless.

These days means 'at the present time'.

The prices these days are absolutely ridiculous.

5 'that' and 'those'

That and **those** are used in some similar ways to **this** and **these**.

→ See **this – that** for an explanation of the differences

---

those

→ See **that – those**

---

though

→ See **although – though**

---

thousand

A thousand or **one thousand** is the number 1,000.

You can say that there are **a thousand** things or **one thousand** things.

We'll give you a thousand dollars for the story.
There was a ship about one thousand yards off shore.

> ❗ **BE CAREFUL**

Don't say that there are 'thousand' things.

Don't change the word **thousand** when you put another number in front of it. Don't say, for example, 'five thousands'. Say 'five **thousand**'.

I'll pay you seven thousand dollars.
We have five thousand acres.

→ See **Reference** section **Numbers and fractions**

till

→ See **until – till**

time

→ See **Topic** entry **Time** for information on telling the time, and on prepositions and adverbs used to talk about time

1 'time'

Time is what we measure in hours, days, years, etc.

It seemed like a long period of time.
More time passed.

You don't usually use **time** when you are saying how long something takes or lasts. Don't say, for example, 'The course took two years' time' or 'Each song lasts ten minutes' time'. Say 'The course took **two years**' or 'Each song lasts **ten minutes**'.

The whole process probably takes twenty-five years.
The tour lasts 4 hours.

You can, however, use **time** when you are saying how long it will be before something happens. For example, you can say 'We are getting married **in two years' time**'.

The exchange ends officially in a month's time.
In a few days' time, she may change her mind.

Time is usually an uncountable noun, so don't use 'a' with it. Don't say, for example, 'I haven't got a time to go shopping'. Say 'I haven't got **time** to go shopping'.

I didn't know if we'd have time for tea.

2 'a...time'

However, you can use **a** with an adjective and **time** when you are showing how long something takes or lasts. You can say, for example, that something takes **a long time** or takes **a short time**.

The proposal would take quite a long time to discuss in detail.
After a short time one of them said 'It's all right, we're all friends here.'

You can also use expressions like these, with or without **for**, as adverbial phrases.

He's going to have to wait a very long time.
They worked together for a short time.
You've only been in the firm quite a short time.

If you are enjoying yourself while you are doing something, you can say, for example, that you **are having a good time**.

Downstairs, Aneesa was having a wonderful time.
Did you have a good time in Edinburgh?

You must use **a** in sentences like these. Don't say, for example, 'Aneesa was having wonderful time'.

3 meaning 'occasion'

Time is used with **the** or **that** and a qualifier to refer to the occasion when something happened or will happen.

By the time the waiter brought their coffee, she was almost asleep.
Do you remember that time when Adrian phoned up?

When **time** has this meaning, you can use words like **first** or **last** in front of it.

It was the first time she spoke.
When was the last time I saw you?

Expressions such as **the first time** and **the next time** are often adverbial phrases.

The next time he would offer to pay.
The second time I hired a specialist firm.

Next time (without 'the') is also an adverbial.

You'll see a difference next time.
Next time you will do everything right.

4 'on time'

If something happens **on time**, it happens at the right time or punctually.

He turned up on time for guard duty.
Their planes usually arrive on time.

5 'in time'

Don't confuse **on time** with **in time**. If you are **in time** for a particular event, you are not late for it.

We're just in time.
He returned to his hotel in time for a late supper.

If something such as a job or task is finished **in time**, it is finished at or before the time when it should be finished.

I can't do it in time.

In time has another meaning. You use it to say that something happens eventually, after a lot of time has passed.

In time the costs will decrease.
In time I came to see how important this was.

title – headline

1 'title'

The **title** of a book, play, painting, or piece of music is its name.

He wrote a book with the title 'The Castle'.
'Walk under Ladders' is the title of her new play.

2 'headline'

Don't refer to the words printed in large letters at the top of a newspaper report as a 'title'. You call them a **headline**.

All the <u>headlines</u> are about the Ridley affair.

to

To is used in several different ways as a preposition. Its usual pronunciation is /tə/. However, when it is followed by a word beginning with a vowel sound, it is pronounced /tu/ and when it comes at the end of a clause, it is pronounced /tuː/.

1 destination

You use **to** when you mention the place where someone goes.

I'm going with her <u>to Australia</u>.
The children have gone <u>to school</u>.
I made my way back <u>to my seat</u>.

Don't use 'to' in front of **here** or **there**. Don't say, for example, '~~We go to there every year~~'. Say 'We go **there** every year'.

Before I came <u>here</u>, there were a few offers from other clubs.
His mother was from New Orleans and he went <u>there</u> every summer.

Also, don't use 'to' in front of **home**.

I want to go <u>home</u>.
I'll pick the parcels up on my way <u>home</u>.

2 direction

You can use **to** to show the place that a person is intending to arrive at.

We're sailing <u>to Europe</u>.
We used to go through Yugoslavia on our way <u>to Greece</u>.

However, don't use 'to' to show the general direction in which someone or something is moving. Don't say, for example, '~~The boat was drifting to the shore~~'. You say 'The boat was drifting **towards** the shore'.

He saw his mother running <u>towards him</u>.
We turned to fly back <u>towards Heathrow</u>.

Toward is sometimes used instead of **towards**.

They walked along the pathway <u>toward the house</u>.

You also say that someone looks **towards** or **toward** something.

She glanced <u>towards the mirror</u>.
He stood looking <u>toward the back of the restaurant</u>.

3 position

You can use **to** to show the position of something. For example, if something is **to** your left, it is nearer your left side than your right side.

My father was in the middle, with me <u>to his left</u> carrying the umbrella.
<u>To the west</u> lies Gloucester.

You can also use **to** to show where something is tied or attached, or what it is touching.

I locked my bike to a fence.
He clutched the parcel to his chest.

4 time

To is sometimes used with a similar meaning to 'until'.

Breakfast was from 9 to 10.
Only ten shopping days to Christmas.

5 indirect objects

You put **to** in front of the indirect object of some verbs when the indirect object comes after the direct object.

He showed the letter to Barbara.

→ See **Verbs** for information on ditransitive verbs

6 used in infinitives

To is used for introducing a special kind of clause called a *to*-infinitive clause.

He was doing this to make me more relaxed.
She began to cry.

→ See **Infinitives**

! **BE CAREFUL**

Don't confuse **to** with **too** or **two**, both of which are pronounced /tuː/.

You use **too** to show that what has just been said applies to someone or something else.

I'm on your side. Mike is too.

You also use **too** when you want to say that an amount or degree of something is more than is desirable or acceptable.

Eggs shouldn't be kept in the fridge, it's too cold.

→ See **too**

! **BE CAREFUL**

Two is the number 2.

The two boys glanced at each other.

today

Today means the day on which you are speaking or writing.

How are you feeling today?
Today is Thursday.

Don't use 'today' in front of **morning**, **afternoon**, or **evening**. Instead, use **this**.

His plane left this morning.
Can I take it with me this afternoon?
Come and have dinner with me this evening.

toilet

1 'toilet'

A **toilet** is a large bowl connected to the plumbing and used by people to get rid of waste from their bodies.

British speakers also use **toilet** or **bathroom** to refer to a room containing a toilet. When this room is in a house, they might also refer to it as the **lavatory**, the **loo**, or the **WC**. **Lavatory** and **WC** are rather old-fashioned, more formal words. **Loo** is only used in conversation. A downstairs toilet in a house is sometimes called a **cloakroom**.

Annette ran and locked herself in the toilet.
On the ground floor there is a large living room, a kitchen, a dining room and a cloakroom.
Can I use your loo?

 In American English, the room in a house containing a toilet is called the **bathroom**. **Washroom** is also used.

She had gone in to use the bathroom.

2 'conveniences'

In British English, a group of toilets in a public place are called **public toilets**, but you might see **public conveniences**, **WC**, or simply **toilets** on signs. They can also be referred to as **the ladies** and **the gents**.

Where are the nearest public toilets?
She made a quick visit to the ladies to re-apply lipstick.

 In American English, a room with toilets in a public place can be referred to as a **restroom**, a **comfort station**, or a **washroom**. It can also be referred to as **the ladies' room** and **the men's room**.

He walked into the men's restroom and looked at himself in the mirror.

---

tolerate

→ See **bear**

---

too

Too can be an adverb or a grading adverb.

1 used as an adverb

You use **too** as an adverb to show that what has just been said applies to or includes someone or something else.

Of course, you're a teacher too, aren't you?
Hey, where are you from? Brooklyn? Me too!

→ See also – **too** – **as well**

2 used as a grading adverb

You use **too** in front of an adjective or adverb to say that an amount or degree of a quality is more than is needed or wanted.

By then he was far too tall for his little bed.
I realized my mistake too late.

Don't use 'very' in front of **too**. Don't say, for example, '~~The hat was very too small for her~~'. Say 'The hat was **much** too small for her' or 'The hat was **far** too small for her'.

That may seem <u>much too expensive</u>.

You can use **rather**, **slightly**, or **a bit** in front of **too**.

The dress was <u>rather too small</u> for her.
His hair had grown <u>slightly too long</u> over his ears.
I'm afraid the price may just be <u>a bit too high</u>.

! **BE CAREFUL**

Don't use 'fairly', 'quite', or 'pretty' in front of **too**.

You don't normally use **too** with an adjective in front of a noun. Don't say, for example, '~~These are too big boots~~'. You say 'These boots **are too big**'.

However, **too** is sometimes used with an adjective in front of a noun in formal or literary English. **A** or **an** is put after the adjective. For example, you can say 'This is **too complex a problem** to be dealt with here'. Don't say '~~This is a too complex problem to be dealt with here~~'.

That's <u>too easy an answer</u>.
Somehow, Vadim seems <u>too nice a man</u> for the job.

3 **used as an intensifier**

Some people use **too** in front of words like **kind** to say how grateful they are. This is fairly formal.

You're <u>too kind</u>.

However, you don't usually use 'too' in front of an adjective or adverb simply to emphasize it. Don't say, for example, '~~I am too pleased with my new car~~'. The word you use is **very**.

She was upset and <u>very angry</u>.
Think <u>very carefully</u>.

→ See **very**

4 **'too much' and 'too many'**

You can use **too much** with an uncountable noun to say that there is more of something than is needed or wanted.

They said I was earning <u>too much money</u>.

You can also say that there is **too little** of something.

There would be <u>too little moisture</u> for the plants to grow.

You can use **too many** with a countable noun to say that there are more people or things than are needed or wanted.

I was making <u>too many mistakes</u>.

You can also say that there are **too few** people or things.

<u>Too few people</u> nowadays are interested in literature.

You can use **much too much** or **far too much** with an uncountable noun to say that there is very much more of something than is necessary or desirable.

This would leave <u>much too much power</u> in the hands of the judges.
These people are getting <u>far too much attention</u>.

You can use **far too many** with a countable noun to say that there is a much larger number of people or things than is necessary or desirable. Don't say that there are 'much too many' of them.

Every middle-class child gets far too many toys.

> **!** BE CAREFUL
>
> Don't use **too much** or **much too much** in front of an adjective which is not followed by a noun. Don't say, for example, 'It's too much hot to play football'. Say 'It's **too hot** to play football' or 'It's **much too hot** to play football'.

toward – towards

→ See **to** section on direction

traffic

You use **traffic** to refer to all the vehicles moving along a road.

In many areas rush-hour traffic lasted until 11am.

Traffic is an uncountable noun. Don't talk about 'traffics' or 'a traffic'.

traffic circle

→ See **roundabout**

transport – transportation

1 'transport'

In British English, vehicles that you travel in are referred to generally as **transport**.

It's easier to travel if you have your own transport.
You can get to the museum by public transport.

Transport is an uncountable noun. Don't refer to a single vehicle as 'a transport'.

British speakers also use **transport** to refer to the moving of goods or people from one place to another.

The goods were ready for transport and distribution.
High transport costs make foreign goods too expensive.

2 'transportation'

 American speakers usually use **transportation** to refer both to vehicles and to the moving of goods or people.

Do you two children have transportation home?
Long-distance transportation will increase the price of the product.

trash

→ See **rubbish**

travel

 Travel can be a verb or a noun. The other forms of the verb are **travels**, **travelling**, **travelled** in British English, and **travels**, **traveling**, **traveled** in American English.

1 used as a verb

If you make a journey to a place, you can say that you **travel** there.

I travelled to work by train.

When you **travel**, you go to several places, especially in foreign countries.

They brought news from faraway places in which they travelled.
You have to have a passport to travel abroad.

2 used as a noun

Travel is the act of travelling. When **travel** has this meaning, it is an uncountable noun.

They arrived after four days of hard travel.
Air travel is so easy these days.
We used to dream about space travel.

3 'travels'

When someone has made several journeys to different places, especially places a long way from their home, you can refer to these journeys as their **travels**.

Stasya told us all about her travels.
It is a collection of rare plants and trees collected during lengthy travels in the Far East.

! BE CAREFUL

Don't talk about 'a travel'. Instead you talk about a **journey**, a **trip**, or a **voyage**.

→ See **journey – trip – voyage – excursion**

trip

→ See **journey – trip – voyage – excursion**

trouble

1 used as an uncountable noun

Trouble is most commonly an uncountable noun. If something causes you **trouble**, you have difficulty dealing with it.

The weather was causing more trouble than the enemy.
This would save everyone a lot of trouble.

You can say that someone **has trouble doing** something.

Did you have any trouble finding your way here?

! BE CAREFUL

Don't say 'Did you have any trouble to find your way here?'

2 'troubles'

Your **troubles** are the problems in your life.

It helps me forget my troubles and relax.

> **!** BE CAREFUL
>
> You don't usually refer to a single problem as 'a trouble'.

3 'the trouble'

If a particular aspect of something is causing problems, you can refer to this as **the trouble**.

It's getting a bit expensive now, that's the trouble.
The trouble is there's a shortage of suitable property.

---

trousers

Trousers are a piece of clothing that covers your body from the waist downwards, and covers each leg separately. **Trousers** is a plural noun. You use a plural form of a verb with it.

His trousers were covered in mud.

Don't talk about 'a trousers'. You say **some trousers** or **a pair of trousers**.

It's time I bought myself some new trousers.
Umar was dressed in a pair of black trousers.

You usually use a singular form of a verb with **a pair of trousers**.

There was a pair of trousers in his carrier-bag.

The form **trouser** is often used in front of another noun.

The waiter took a handkerchief from his trouser pocket.
Hamo was rolling up his trouser leg.

 In American English, more common words for this item of clothing are **pants** or **slacks**.

---

truck

→ See **carriage – car – truck – wagon, lorry – truck**

---

true – come true

1 'true'

A **true** story or statement is based on facts, and is not invented or imagined.

The story about the murder is true.
Unfortunately it was true about Sylvie.

2 'come true'

If a dream, wish, or prediction **comes true**, it actually happens.

Remember that some dreams come true.
The worst of the predictions might come true.

> **!** BE CAREFUL
>
> Don't say that something 'becomes true'.

---

trunk

→ See **boot – trunk**

try – attempt

Both these words can be verbs or nouns. The other forms of **try** are **tries**, **trying**, **tried**.

1 'try' used as a verb

If you **try to do** something, you make an effort to do it.

My sister tried to cheer me up.
He was trying his best to understand.

You can also **try and do** something. There is no difference in meaning, but **try and do** is used in conversation and less formal writing. In formal English, use **try to do**.

Try and see how many of these questions you can answer.
Please try and help me to cope with this.
We must try and understand.

> **!** **BE CAREFUL**
>
> You can only use **and** after the base form of **try** – that is, when you are using it as an imperative or infinitive, or after a modal. You cannot say, for example, 'I was trying and help her' or 'I was trying and helping her'.

If you **try doing** something, you do it in order to find out how useful, effective, or enjoyable it is.

He tried changing the subject.
Have you ever tried painting?

2 'attempt' used as a verb

If you **attempt to do** something, you try to do it. **Attempt** is a more formal word than **try**.

Some of the crowd attempted to break through the police lines.
Rescue workers attempted to cut him from the crashed vehicle.

> **!** **BE CAREFUL**
>
> You don't say 'The crowd attempted and break through' or 'The crowd attempted breaking through'.

3 'try' and 'attempt' used as nouns

When someone tries to do something, you can refer to what they do as a **try** or an **attempt**. **Try** is normally used only in conversation and less formal writing. In formal English, you usually talk about an **attempt**.

After a few tries they gave up.
The young birds manage to fly several kilometres at their first attempt.

You say that someone **has a try at** something or **gives** something **a try**.

You've had a good try at it.
'I'll go and see him in the morning.' – 'Yes, give it a try.'

You say that someone **makes an attempt to do** something.

He made an attempt to call Courtney; she wasn't in.
Two recent reports made an attempt to assess the success of the project.

type

Type is a noun used for talking about a class of people or things. **Type** is a countable noun. After words like **all** and **many**, you use **types**, not 'type'.

There were hundreds of ships of every size and type.
We work in hospitals of all types.
Elderly people need many types of public service.

After **types of** you can use either the plural or singular form of a noun. You can say 'He eats most types of **vegetables**' or 'He eats most types of **vegetable**'. The singular form is more formal.

How many types of people live in these households?
This only happens with certain types of school.

If you use a number in front of **types of**, you should use a singular form after it.

There are three types of muscle in the body.
They run two types of playgroup.

After **type of** you use the singular form of a noun.

He was an unusual type of actor.
This type of problem is common in families.

 In conversation, **these** and **those** are often used with **type**. For example, people say 'These type of books are boring' or 'Those type of books are boring'.

This use is generally thought to be incorrect, and you should avoid it in writing. Instead you should say '**This type of book** is boring' or '**That type of book** is boring'.

This type of person has very little happiness.
I could not be happy in that type of household.

Uu

---

under – below – beneath

1 **'under'**

Under is almost always a preposition. You use **under** to say that one thing is at a lower level than another, and that the other thing is directly above it. For example, you might say that an object on the floor is **under** a table or chair.

There's a cupboard under the stairs.
A path runs under the trees.

2 **'underneath'**

Underneath can be a preposition with a similar meaning to **under**.

We sat at a table underneath some olive trees.

Underneath can also be an adverb.

Let's pull up the carpet and see what's underneath.

3 **'below'**

Below can be a preposition. You normally use it to say that one thing is at a much lower level than another.

There's a tunnel 100 metres below the surface.

Below can also be an adverb.

They stood at the top of the mountain and looked at the valley below.

4 **'beneath'**

Beneath can be a preposition with a similar meaning to **under** or **below**. **Beneath** is more formal.

He could feel the soft ground beneath his feet.

Beneath can also be an adverb.

He stared out of the window at the courtyard beneath.

---

understand – realize

1 **'understand'**

If you can **understand** someone or can **understand** what they are saying, you know what they mean.

His lecture was confusing; no one could understand the terminology.
Her accent was hard to understand.

If you say that you **understand** that something is true, you mean that you have been told that it is true.

I understand he's been married before.
There was no definite evidence, I understand.

2 'realize'

Don't use **understand** to say that someone becomes aware of something. Don't say, for example, 'Until he stopped working he hadn't understood how late it was'. You say 'Until he stopped working he **hadn't realized** how late it was'.

As soon as I saw him, I realized that I'd seen him before.

understanding

→ See **comprehension – understanding**

university

→ See **school – university**

unless

You usually use **unless** to say that something can only happen or be true in particular circumstances. For example, instead of saying 'I will go to France only if the firm pays my expenses', you can say 'I will **not** go to France **unless** the firm pays my expenses'. When you are talking about the future, you use the present simple after **unless**.

We cannot understand disease unless we understand the person who has the disease.

When you are talking about a situation in the past, you use the past simple after **unless**.

She wouldn't go with him unless I came too.

! BE CAREFUL

Don't use a future form after **unless**. Don't say, for example, 'I will not go to France unless the firm will pay my expenses'.

You also use **unless** to mention the only circumstances in which something will not happen or be true. For example, instead of saying 'If we are not told to stop, we will carry on selling the furniture', you can say 'We will carry on selling the furniture **unless** we are told to stop'.

The mail will go by air unless it is quicker by other means.
We might as well stop unless you've got something else you want to talk about.

Don't use 'unless' to say that something would happen or be true if particular circumstances did not exist. For example, if you have a cold, don't say 'I would go to the party unless I had this cold'. You say 'I would go to the party **if I didn't have** this cold'.

She'd be pretty if she didn't wear so much make-up.

until – till

Until and **till** can be prepositions or conjunctions. There is no difference in meaning between **until** and **till**. **Till** is more common in conversation, and is not used in formal writing.

1 used as prepositions

If you do something **until** or **till** a particular time, you stop doing it at that time.

He continued to teach until his death in 1960.
I said I'd work till 4 p.m.

If you want to emphasize that something does not stop before the time you mention, you can use **up until**, **up till**, or **up to**.

Up until 1950 coal provided over 90% of our energy needs.
Eleanor had not up till then taken part in the discussion.
Up to now they've had very little money.

If something does not happen **until** or **till** a particular time, it does not happen before that time.

Details will not be available until January.
We didn't get back till two.

2 used with 'after'

You can use **until** or **till** with phrases beginning with **after**.

He decided to wait until after Christmas to propose to Gertrude.
We didn't get home till after midnight.

> ❗ **BE CAREFUL**
>
> Don't use 'until' or 'till' to say that something will have happened before a particular time. Don't say, for example, 'The work will be finished until four o'clock'. You say 'The work will be finished **by** four o'clock'.
>
> *By 8.05 the groups were ready.*
> *Total sales reached 1 million by 2010.*

3 used with 'from'

From is often used with **until** or **till** to say when something finishes and ends.

The ticket office will be open from 10.00am until 1.00pm.
They worked from dawn till dusk.

 In sentences like these, you can use **to** instead of 'until' or 'till'. Some American speakers also use **through**.

Open daily 1000-1700 from 23rd March to 3rd November.
I was in college from 1985 through 1990.

> ❗ **BE CAREFUL**
>
> You only use **until** or **till** when you are talking about time. Don't use these words to talk about position. Don't say, for example, 'She walked until the post office'. You say 'She walked **as far as** the post office'.
>
> *They drove as far as the Cantabrian mountains.*

4 used as conjunctions

Instead of a noun phrase, you can use a subordinate clause after **until** or **till**. You often use the present simple in the subordinate clause.

They concentrate on one language until they go to university.
Stay here with me till help comes.

You can also use the present perfect in the subordinate clause.

I'll wait here until you have had your breakfast.

When you are talking about events in the past, you use the past simple or the past perfect in the subordinate clause.

The plan remained secret until it was exposed by the press.
He continued watching until I had driven off in my car.

> **!** **BE CAREFUL**
>
> Don't use a future form in the subordinate clause. Don't say, for example 'Stay here ~~with me till help will come~~' or '~~I'll wait here until you will have had your breakfast~~'.

up

1 'up'

Up can be a preposition. You usually use it to show that someone or something moves towards a higher place or position.

I carried my suitcase up the stairs behind her.
The heat goes straight up the chimney.

Up can also be an adverb. It is often used in phrasal verbs to show that someone or something moves towards a higher place or position.

The coffee was sent up from the kitchen below.
Bill put up his hand.

You also use **up** as an adverb to show that someone or something is in a high place.

He was up in his bedroom.
They live in a house up in the hills.

2 'up to'

You can say that someone goes **up to** a higher place.

I went up to the top floor.

You also say that someone goes **up to** a place when it is further north than the place they started from.

I thought of going up to New York.
Why did you come up to Edinburgh?

British speakers sometimes use **up to** instead of 'to' for no special reason.

The other day I went up to the supermarket.
We all went up to the pub.

upwards – upward

→ See -ward – -wards

us

Us can be the object of a verb or preposition. You use **us** to refer to yourself and one or more other people.

Why didn't you tell us?
There wasn't room for us all.

> **!** **BE CAREFUL**
>
> In standard English, don't use 'us' as the object of a sentence when **we** is the subject. Don't say, for example, '~~We bought us some drinks~~'. You say 'We bought **ourselves** some drinks'.
>
> *After the meeting we introduced ourselves.*

used to

1 main meaning

If something **used to** /juːs tuː, juːs tə/ happen, it happened regularly in the past but does not happen now. Similarly, if something **used to** be true, it was true in the past but is not true now.

She used to go swimming every day.
I used to be afraid of you.

2 'used to' in negative structures

In conversation, you can say that something **didn't use to** happen or **didn't use to** be true.

The house didn't use to be so clean.

> **!** **BE CAREFUL**
>
> Many people use the form **didn't used to** instead of **didn't use to**. However, some people think that this use is incorrect.
>
> *They didn't used to mind what we did.*

You can also say that something **never used to** happen or be true.

Where I lived before, we never used to have posters on the walls.
Snooker and darts never used to be shown on television.

You can also say that something **used not to** happen or be true. This is a fairly formal use.

It used not to be taxable, but now it will be subject to tax.

In standard English you don't say that something 'usedn't to' happen or be true.

3 'used to' in questions

You form *yes/no*-questions with **used to** by putting **did** in front of the subject, followed by **use to**.

Did you use to do that, when you were a kid?

> **!** **BE CAREFUL**
>
> Many people use the form **used to** instead of **use to** in questions. However, some people think that this use is incorrect.
>
> *Did you used to live here?*

Used to can also be used in *wh*-questions. If the *wh*-word is the subject of the clause, or part of the subject, you put **used to** after it, without an auxiliary verb.

What used to annoy you most about him?

If the *wh*-word is the object of the clause, or part of the object, you use the auxiliary verb **do** after it, followed by the subject and **used to**.

What did you used to do on Sundays?

4 familiarity

Used to has another meaning. If you are **used to** something, you have become familiar with it and you accept it. With this sense, **used to** is preceded by the verb **be** or **get**, and is followed by a noun or an *-ing* form.

It doesn't frighten them. They're <u>used to it</u>.
I'm <u>used to getting up</u> early.
It's very noisy here, but you'll <u>get used to it</u>.

→ See **accustomed to**

---

usual – usually

1 'usual'

Usual is used to describe the thing that happens most often, or that is done or used most often, in a particular situation.

They are not taking the <u>usual</u> amount of exercise.
He sat in his <u>usual</u> chair.

⚠ BE CAREFUL

Usual normally comes after **the** or a possessive such as **my** or **his**. Don't use it after 'a'. Don't say, for example, 'T̶h̶e̶y̶ ̶a̶r̶e̶ ̶n̶o̶t̶ ̶t̶a̶k̶i̶n̶g̶ ̶a̶ ̶u̶s̶u̶a̶l̶ ̶a̶m̶o̶u̶n̶t̶ ̶o̶f̶ ̶e̶x̶e̶r̶c̶i̶s̶e̶'.

You can say that it is **usual for** a person or animal **to do** something.

It is <u>usual for</u> staff <u>to meet</u> regularly.
It was quite <u>usual for</u> the horses <u>to wander</u> short distances.

Don't use 'that'. Don't say, for example, 'I̶t̶ ̶i̶s̶ ̶u̶s̶u̶a̶l̶ ̶t̶h̶a̶t̶ ̶s̶t̶a̶f̶f̶ ̶m̶e̶e̶t̶ ̶r̶e̶g̶u̶l̶a̶r̶l̶y̶'.

2 'ordinary'

Don't use 'usual' to say that something is not of a special kind. Don't say, for example, 'I̶ ̶h̶a̶v̶e̶n̶'̶t̶ ̶g̶o̶t̶ ̶a̶n̶y̶ ̶c̶h̶o̶c̶o̶l̶a̶t̶e̶ ̶b̶i̶s̶c̶u̶i̶t̶s̶,̶ ̶o̶n̶l̶y̶ ̶u̶s̶u̶a̶l̶ ̶o̶n̶e̶s̶'. You say 'I haven't got any chocolate biscuits, only **ordinary** ones'.

These children should be educated in an <u>ordinary</u> school.
It was furnished with <u>ordinary</u> office furniture.

3 'usually'

You use the adverb **usually** when you are mentioning the thing that most often happens in a particular situation.

She <u>usually</u> found it easy to go to sleep at night.
We <u>usually</u> eat in the kitchen.

4 'as usual'

When something happens on a particular occasion and it is the thing that most often happens in that situation, you can say that it happens **as usual**.

Nina was late, <u>as usual</u>.
She wore, <u>as usual</u>, her black dress.

⚠ BE CAREFUL

Don't say that something happens 'a̶s̶ ̶u̶s̶u̶a̶l̶l̶y̶'.

Vv

---

vacation

→ See **holiday – vacation**

GRAMMAR FINDER

Verb forms

→ See **Reference** section **Verb forms** formation of

1 uses

You use different **verb forms** to show roughly what time you are referring to. **Simple forms** are used to refer to situations, habitual actions, and single completed actions.

I like him very much.
He always gives both points of view.
He walked out of the kitchen.

The progressive is used when talking about temporary situations at a particular point in time.

Inflation is rising.
We believed we were fighting for a good cause.

Some verbs are not usually used in the progressive.

→ See **The Progressive form**

Perfect forms are used when relating an action or situation to the present or to a moment in the past.

Football has become international.
She did not know how long she had been lying there.

The passive is used when the subject of a clause is the person or thing affected by an action. The passive is formed by using an appropriate form of **be** and the *-ed* participle of the main verb.

The earth is baked by the sun into a hard, brittle layer.
They had been taught to be critical.

→ See **The passive**

→ See **The Future**, **The Past**, **The Present** for more information on the uses of verb forms

Sometimes the verb form used in a subordinate clause is not what you would expect:

→ See **The Future**, **Reporting**, **Subordinate clauses**

2 present and past tenses

The table on the following pages shows present and past verb forms.

Active	Passive
present simple	
base form *I want a breath of air.* (3rd person singular) -s form *Flora laughs again.*	present simple of **be** + -ed participle *It is boiled before use.*
present progressive	
present simple of **be** + -ing form *Things are changing.*	present progressive of **be** + -ed participle *My advice is being ignored.*
present perfect	
present simple of **have** + -ed participle *I have seen this before.*	present perfect of **be** + -ed participle *You have been warned.*
present perfect progressive	
present perfect of **be** + -ing form *Howard has been working hard.*	present perfect progressive of **be** + -ed participle (not common)
past simple	
past form *I resented his attitude.*	simple past of **be** + -ed participle *He was murdered.*
past progressive	
past simple of **be** + -ing form *I was sitting on the rug.*	past progressive of **be** + -ed participle *We were being watched.*
past perfect	
had + -ed participle *Everyone had liked her.*	past perfect of **be** + -ed participle *Raymond had been rejected.*
past perfect progressive	
had been + -ing form *Miss Gulliver had been lying.*	past perfect progressive of **be** + -ed participle (not common)

3 future forms

There are several ways of referring to the future in English. The commonest way is to use the modal **will** or **shall**.

→ See **shall – will**

Verb phrases in which **will** and **shall** are used to talk about the future are sometimes called **future forms**.

The following table shows future forms.

Active	Passive
future	
will or **shall** + base form *They will arrive tomorrow.*	**will be** or **shall be** + *-ed* participle *More land will be destroyed.*
future progressive	
will be or **shall be** + *-ing* form *I shall be leaving soon.*	**will be being** or **shall be being** + *-ed* participle (not common)
future perfect	
will have or **shall have** + *-ed* participle *They will have forgotten you.*	**will have been** or **shall have been** + *-ed* participle *By the end of the year, ten projects will have been approved.*
future perfect progressive	
will have been or **shall have been** + *-ing* form *By March, I will have been doing this job for six years.*	**will have been being** or **shall have been being** + *-ed* participle (very rare)

→ See **The Future**

GRAMMAR FINDER

Verbs

1 verb forms	**9** reciprocal verbs
2 uses of verb forms	**10** verbs with object or prepositional
3 intransitive verbs	phrase
4 transitive verbs	**11** verbs with two objects
5 reflexive verbs	(ditransitive verbs)
6 delexical verbs	**12** linking verbs
7 transitive or intransitive	**13** compound verbs
8 ergative verbs	**14** other verbs

A **verb** is a word which is used with a subject to say what someone or something does, what they are, or what happens to them. This entry explains the different verb forms and then gives information about different types of verbs.

1 verb forms

Regular verbs have the following forms:

▶ a base form, for example **walk**

▶ an -s form, for example **walks**

▶ an -ing form, for example **walking**

▶ a past form, for example **walked**

In the case of regular verbs, the past form is used for the past tense and is also used as the -ed participle. However, with many **irregular verbs** there are two past forms:

▶ a past tense form, for example **stole**

▶ a -ed participle form, for example **stolen**

→ See **Reference** section **Irregular verbs**

→ See **Auxiliary Verbs** for the forms of the common irregular verbs **be**, **have**, and **do**

Sometimes there is a spelling change when the -s, -ing, and -ed endings are added, as shown in the table on page 763 of the Reference Section.

2 uses of verb forms

The base form is used for the present simple, the imperative, and the infinitive, and is used after modals.

I hate him.
Go away.

He asked me to send it to him.
He asked if he could take a picture.

The -s form is used for the third person singular of the present simple.
She likes you.

The -ing form is used for the progressive, -ing adjectives, verbal nouns, and some non-finite clauses.

→ See **-ing forms**

The attacks are <u>getting</u> worse.
...the <u>increasing</u> complexity of industrial societies.
She preferred <u>swimming</u> to tennis.
'So you're quite recovered now?' she said, <u>smiling</u> at me.

The past form is used for the past simple, and for the *-ed* participle of regular verbs.

I <u>walked</u> down the garden with him.
She had <u>walked</u> out without speaking.

The *-ed* participle is used for perfect forms, the passive, *-ed* adjectives, and some non-finite clauses.

→ See *-ed* **participles**

Two countries have <u>refused</u> to sign the document.
It was <u>stolen</u> weeks ago.
He became quite <u>annoyed</u>.
The cargo, <u>purchased</u> all over Europe, included ten thousand rifles.

→ See **Verb forms**

3 **intransitive verbs**

Some verbs do not have an object. These verbs are called **intransitive verbs**. Intransitive verbs often describe actions or events which do not involve anyone or anything other than the subject.

Her whole body <u>ached</u>.
The gate <u>squeaked</u>.

Some intransitive verbs always or typically have a preposition after them.

I'm <u>relying on</u> Bill.
The land <u>belongs to</u> a rich family.

These are some of the commonest:

amount to	depend on	object to	resort to
apologize for	hint at	pay for	sympathize with
aspire to	hope for	qualify for	wait for
believe in	insist on	refer to	
belong to	lead to	relate to	
consist of	listen to	rely on	

You will find information on what preposition to use after a particular verb in many of the entries for individual words in this book.

4 **transitive verbs**

Some verbs describe events that must, in addition to the subject, involve someone or something else. These verbs are called **transitive verbs**. They have an **object**, that is, a noun phrase which is put after the verb.

He <u>closed the door</u>.
Some of the women <u>noticed me</u>.

Some transitive verbs always or typically have a particular preposition after their object.

The police <u>accused</u> him <u>of</u> murder.
The judge <u>based</u> her decision <u>on</u> constitutional rights.
He managed to <u>prevent</u> the bottle <u>from</u> falling.

These are some of the commonest:

accuse of	entitle to	regard as	swap for
attribute to	mistake for	remind of	trust with
base on	owe to	return to	view as
dedicate to	pelt with	rob of	
deprive of	prevent from	subject to	

Some transitive verbs have a complement after their object when used with a particular meaning, as in 'They make me angry'.

→ See **Complements**

Most transitive verbs can be used in the passive. However, a few, such as **have**, **get**, and **let**, are rarely or never used in the passive.

→ See **The passive**

5 **reflexive verbs**

A **reflexive verb** is a transitive verb that is normally or often used with a **reflexive pronoun** such as **myself**, **himself**, or **themselves** as its object. The following verbs are often reflexive verbs:

amuse	distance	express	prepare
apply	dry	help	restrict
blame	enjoy	hurt	strain
compose	excel	introduce	teach
cut	exert	kill	

Sam amused himself by throwing branches into the fire.
'Can I borrow a pencil?' – 'Yes, help yourself.'

The verbs **busy**, **content**, and **pride** must be used with a reflexive pronoun.

He had busied himself in the laboratory.
He prides himself on his tidiness.

! **BE CAREFUL**

Reflexive pronouns are not used as much in English as in some other languages when talking about actions that you normally do to yourself. You only use a reflexive pronoun to emphasize that a person is doing the action himself or herself.

She washed very quickly and rushed downstairs.
Children were encouraged to wash themselves.

6 **delexical verbs**

A number of very common verbs can be used with an object referring to an action simply to show that the action takes place. They are called **delexical verbs**. The verbs most commonly used in this way are:

do	have	take
give	make	

The noun which is the object of the delexical verb is usually countable and singular, although it can sometimes be plural.

We were having a joke.
She gave an amused laugh.
They took regular walks along the beach.

In a few cases, an uncountable noun is used after a delexical verb.

We have made progress in both science and art.
A nurse is taking care of him.

→ See **do**, **give**, **have – take**, **make** for information on the nouns used with delexical verbs

7 transitive or intransitive

Many verbs are transitive when used with one meaning and intransitive when used with another meaning.

She runs a hotel.
The hare runs at enormous speed.

It is often possible to use a verb intransitively because the object is known or has already been mentioned.

I don't own a car. I can't drive.
Both dresses are beautiful. I can't choose.
Come and eat.

Even verbs which are almost always followed by a direct object can occasionally be used intransitively, when you are making a very general statement.

Some people build while others destroy.
She was anxious to please.

8 ergative verbs

An **ergative verb** can be used either transitively to focus on the person who performs an action, or intransitively to focus on the thing affected by an action.

When I opened the door, there was Laverne.
Suddenly the door opened.
The driver stopped the car.
The big car stopped.
He slammed the door with such force that a window broke.
They threw stones and broke the windows of buses.

Many ergative verbs refer to change or movement:

age	darken	improve	spoil
alter	decrease	increase	spread
balance	diminish	move	stand
begin	disperse	open	start
bend	dissolve	quicken	steady
bleach	double	rest	stick
break	drop	ripen	stop
bruise	drown	rock	stretch
burn	dry	rot	swing
burst	empty	shake	tear
change	end	shatter	thicken
close	fade	shrink	turn
continue	fill	shut	vary
cool	finish	slow	widen
crack	freeze	snap	worsen
crash	grow	spin	
crumble	heal	split	

I shattered the glass.
Wine bottles had shattered all over the pavement.

Verbs which refer to cooking are usually ergative verbs.

bake	cook	melt	thaw
boil	freeze	simmer	
brown	marinate	steam	

While the water boiled, I put the shopping away.
Residents have been advised to boil their tap water or drink bottled water.

So are verbs which refer to driving or controlling vehicles.

anchor	halt	sink	swerve
back	reverse	start	
capsize	sail	stop	

The boys reversed their car and set off down the road.
The jeep reversed at full speed.

The following verbs are used ergatively with one or two nouns only:

▶ **catch** (an article of clothing)

▶ **fire** (a gun, rifle, pistol)

▶ **play** (music)

▶ **ring** (a bell, the alarm)

▶ **show** (an emotion such as fear, anger)

▶ **sound** (a horn, the alarm)

She always plays her music too loudly.
Music was playing in the background.

The following ergative verbs usually have an adverbial after them when they are used intransitively:

clean	handle	polish	stain
freeze	mark	sell	wash

I like my new car. It handles beautifully.
Wool washes well if you treat it carefully.

9 reciprocal verbs

A **reciprocal verb** describes an action or process that involves two or more people doing the same thing to each other, having a relationship, or participating jointly in an action or event.

Reciprocal verbs have two basic patterns:

▶ They can be used with a plural subject – that is, a subject consisting of a plural noun phrase. When they are used with this plural subject, the meaning is that the people, groups, or things involved are interacting with each other. For example, two people can **argue**, can **have a chat**, or can **meet**.

Their children are always arguing.
He came out and we hugged.
Their eyes met.

▶ They can be used with a subject that refers to one of the participants, and an object, prepositional object, or adverbial which refers to the other participant, as in 'She agreed with her sister', 'I had a chat with him' and 'I met him at university'.

He argued with his father.
I hugged him.
His eyes met hers.

To emphasize that the participants are equally involved in the action, **each other** or **one another** can be put after the verb phrase.

We embraced each other.
It was the first time they had touched one another.

The following reciprocal verbs can be followed by **each other** or **one another**:

cuddle	embrace	hug	match
date	engage	kiss	meet
divorce	fight	marry	touch

With some verbs it is necessary to use a preposition, usually **with**, in front of **each other** and **one another**.

You've got to be able to communicate with each other.
Third World countries are competing with one another for a restricted market.

The following reciprocal verbs can be used with a plural subject or can be followed by **with**:

agree	communicate	dance	mate
alternate	compete	differ	merge
argue	conflict	disagree	mix
bicker	connect	draw	negotiate
chat	consult	engage	quarrel
clash	contend	fight	row
coincide	contrast	flirt	speak
collaborate	converse	gossip	struggle
collide	co-operate	integrate	talk
combine	correspond	joke	wrangle

Her parents never argued.
He is always arguing with his girlfriend.
Owen and his boss are still negotiating.
They are negotiating with union leaders.

You can also use **against** after **compete** and **fight**, and **to** after **correspond** and **talk**. You use **from** after **part** and **separate**. You use **to** after **relate**.

Engage and **fight** can be used either transitively or with a preposition.

10 verbs with object or prepositional phrase

A small group of verbs can be followed by either an object or a prepositional phrase. For example, you can say either 'He tugged her sleeve' or 'He tugged at her sleeve'. There is usually little difference in meaning between using the verb on its own and using a preposition after it.

Her arm brushed my cheek.
Something brushed against the back of my neck.
We climbed the mountain.
I climbed up the tree.

The following verbs can be used with an object or a prepositional phrase:

boo (at)	fight (against)	jeer (at)	rule (over)
brush (against)	fight (with)	juggle (with)	sip (at)
check (on)	gain (in)	mock (at)	sniff (at)
distinguish	gnaw (at)	mourn (for)	tug (at)
(between)	hiss (at)	nibble (at)	twiddle (with)
enter (for)	infiltrate (into)	play (against)	

11 verbs with two objects

Some verbs can have two objects: a **direct object** and an **indirect object**. These verbs are called **ditransitive verbs**. The indirect object usually refers to the person who benefits from the action or receives something as a result. When the indirect object is a short noun phrase such as a pronoun, or **the** and a noun, you often put it in front of the direct object.

I gave him the money.
Sheila showed the boy her new bike.
I taught myself French.

! BE CAREFUL

You don't usually put a preposition in front of the indirect object when it is in this position. For example, don't say 'I gave to him the money'.

Instead of putting the indirect object in front of the direct object, it is possible to put it in a prepositional phrase that comes after the direct object.

He handed his passport to the policeman.

It is normal to use this prepositional structure when the indirect object is long, or when you want to emphasize it.

I've given the key to the woman who lives in the house next door to the garage.
I bought that for you.

You must use a preposition when the direct object is a personal pronoun and the indirect object is not. Don't say, for example 'He bought his wife it'.

He got a glass from the cupboard, filled it and gave it to Atkinson.
Then Stephen bought it for his wife.

If both the direct object and the indirect object are personal pronouns, you should use a preposition in writing. A preposition is also often used in conversation.

He gave it to me.
Save it for me.

However, some people do not use a preposition in conversation. Sometimes the direct object follows the indirect object, and sometimes the indirect object follows the direct object. For example, someone might say either 'My mother bought me it' or, in British English 'My mother bought it me'.

With the following verbs, you use **to** to introduce the indirect object.

accord	deliver	grant	mail
advance	donate	hand	offer
award	export	lease	owe
bequeath	feed	leave	pass
bring	forward	lend	pay
deal	give	loan	post

present	rent	send	supply
quote	repay	serve	teach
read	sell	show	

I lent my car to a friend for the weekend.
We picked up shells and showed them to each other.

You can sometimes use **to** to introduce the indirect object of **tell**.

→ See **tell**

With the following verbs, you use **for** to introduce the indirect object.

book	design	knit	prepare
build	fetch	make	reserve
buy	find	mix	save
cash	fix	order	secure
collect	get	paint	set
cook	guarantee	pick	spare
cut	keep	pour	win

They booked a place for me.
She painted a picture for her father.

With the following verbs, you can use either **to** or **for** to introduce the indirect object, depending on the meaning you want to express.

bring	play	take
leave	sing	write

Mr Schell wrote a letter the other day to the New York Times.
Once, I wrote a play for the children.

With a few ditransitive verbs, the indirect object almost always comes in front of the direct object rather than being introduced by 'to' or 'for'.

allow	cause	draw	promise
ask	charge	envy	refuse
begrudge	cost	forgive	
bet	deny	grudge	

The radio cost me three quid.
The man had promised him a job.

In passive sentences either the direct object or the indirect object can become the subject. For example, you can say either 'The books will be sent to you next week' or 'You will be sent the books next week'.

A seat had been booked for him on the 6 o'clock flight.
I was given two free tickets.

Most of the verbs listed above as ditransitive verbs can be used with the same meaning with just a direct object.

He left a note.
She fetched a jug from the kitchen.

A few verbs can be used with a direct object referring to the person who benefits from the action, or receives something.

ask	feed	pay
envy	forgive	teach

I *fed the baby* when she awoke.
I *forgive you*.

12 linking verbs

A **linking verb** is a verb that is followed by a **complement** rather than an object. The complement gives more information about the subject, and can be an adjective or a noun phrase. The linking verbs are:

appear	feel	measure	smell
be	form	pass	sound
become	get	prove	stay
come	go	rank	taste
comprise	grow	remain	total
constitute	keep	represent	turn
equal	look	seem	weigh

I *am* proud of these people.
She *was getting* too old to play tennis.

→ See **Complements** for information on which linking verbs are used with which kind of complement

Some linking verbs are often followed by **be** and an adjective, instead of immediately by an adjective.

appear	get	look	seem
come	grow	prove	

Mary was breathing quietly and *seemed to be asleep*.
The task *proved to be very interesting*.

13 compound verbs

Compound verbs consist of two words that are normally linked by a hyphen.

It may soon become economically attractive to *mass-produce* hepatitis vaccines.
Somebody *had short-changed* him.
Send it to the laundry. Don't *dry-clean* it.

Only the second part of a compound verb changes to show tense and number.

dry-clean – dry-cleans – dry-cleaning – dry-cleaned

force-feed – force-feeds – force-feeding – force-fed

14 other verbs

→ See **Reporting** for information on verbs followed by a reported clause, **-ing forms**, **Infinitives** for information on verbs followed by an -ing form or an infinitive, **Phrasal verbs**

very

1 basic use

You use **very** to emphasize an adjective or adverb.

She is a *very tall* woman.

That's <u>very nice</u> of you.
Think <u>very carefully</u>.

2 used with -ed words

You can use **very** to emphasize adjectives ending in *-ed*, especially when they refer to a state of mind or emotional condition. For example, you can say 'I was **very bored**' or 'She was **very frightened**'.

He seemed <u>very interested</u> in everything.
Joe must have been <u>very worried</u> about her.

However, don't use 'very' to emphasize *-ed* words when they are part of a passive construction. Don't say, for example, '~~He was very liked~~'. You say 'He was **well liked**'. Similarly, don't say '~~She was very admired~~'. You say 'She was **very much admired**' or 'She was **greatly admired**'.

Argentina were <u>well beaten</u> by Italy in the first round.
I was <u>greatly influenced</u> by his work.
He is <u>very much resented</u> by his colleagues.

Don't say that someone is '~~very awake~~'. You say that they are **wide awake** or **fully awake**.

He was <u>wide awake</u> by the time we reached the hotel.
He was not <u>fully awake</u>.

Don't say that someone is '~~very asleep~~'. You say that they are **sound asleep** or **fast asleep**.

Chris is still <u>sound asleep</u> on the sofa.
Charlotte had been <u>fast asleep</u> when he left her.

Don't say that two things are '~~very apart~~'. You say that they are **far apart**.

His two hands were <u>far apart</u>.

Also, don't use 'very' with adjectives which already describe an extreme quality. Don't say, for example, that something is '~~very enormous~~'. Here is a list of adjectives of this kind:

absurd	essential	massive	unique
awful	excellent	perfect	wonderful
brilliant	furious	splendid	
enormous	huge	terrible	

3 comparatives and superlatives

Don't use 'very' with comparatives. Don't say, for example, '~~Tom was very quicker than I was~~'. You say 'Tom was **much quicker** than I was' or 'Tom was **far quicker** than I was'.

It was <u>much colder</u> than before.
This is a <u>far better</u> picture than the other one.

→ See **far**

You can use **very** in front of **best**, **worst**, or any superlative which ends in *-est*.

It's one of Shaw's <u>very best</u> plays.
We must deal with the <u>very worst</u> crimes.
They use the <u>very latest</u> technology.

However, don't use 'very' with superlatives that begin with **the most**. Instead you use **much**, **by far**, or **far and away**.

He is much the most likely winner.
The last exam was by far the most difficult.
This is far and away the most important point.

4 used with 'first', 'next', and 'last'

You can use **very** in front of **first**, **next**, or **last** to emphasize that something is the first, next, or last thing of its kind.

I was their very first guest.
We left the very next day.
Those were his very last words.

! BE CAREFUL

Don't use 'very' to say that something happens because someone or something has a quality to an unusually large extent. Don't say, for example, '~~He looked very funny that we couldn't help laughing~~'. You say 'He looked **so** funny that we couldn't help laughing'.

We were so angry we asked to see the manager.
He had shouted so hard that his throat was sore.

→ See **so**

5 prepositions

Don't use 'very' in front of prepositions such as **ahead of**, **above**, or **behind**. Instead you use **well** or **far**.

Figures are well above average.
David was following not far behind us.

6 prepositional phrases

Don't use 'very' in front of prepositional phrases. Don't say, for example, '~~He was very in love with Kate~~'. Instead, you use **very much** or **greatly**.

The findings were very much in line with previous research.
I was greatly in awe of Jane at first.

---

very much

→ See **much**

---

vest

In British English, a **vest** is a piece of clothing that you wear on the top half of your body underneath a shirt, blouse, or dress in order to keep warm.

She wore a woollen vest under her blouse.

In American English, a piece of clothing like this is called an **undershirt**.

When it's cold I always wear an undershirt.

In American English, a **vest** is a piece of clothing with buttons and no sleeves, which a man wears over his shirt and under his jacket. In British English, a piece of clothing like this is called a **waistcoat**.

Under his jacket he wore a navy blue vest with black buttons.
The men wore evening suits and waistcoats.

In both British and American English, a **vest** is a piece of clothing that you wear on the top part of your body for a particular purpose.

The police officers had to wear bulletproof vests.
Cyclists should always wear a helmet and a reflective vest.

victim – casualty

1 'victim'

You refer to someone as a **victim** when they have suffered as the result of a crime or natural disaster.

They offered financial aid for flood victims.
We have been the victims of a terrible crime.

2 'casualty'

You don't usually use 'victim' to refer to someone who has been injured or killed in a war or accident. The word you use is **casualty**.

There were heavy casualties on both sides.
The casualties were taken to the nearest hospital.

visit

1 used as a verb

If you **visit** a place, you go there for a short time.

He had arranged to visit a number of museums in Paris.
She'll visit four cities on her trip.

If you **visit** someone, you go to see them at their home or where they are staying, or you stay with them there for a short time.

She visited some of her relatives for a few days.
When my dad was in hospital, I visited him every day.

You can also **visit** a professional person such as a doctor or lawyer, in order to get treatment or advice.

He persuaded me to visit a doctor.
You might need to visit a solicitor before thinking seriously about divorce.

 Some American speakers use **visit with** instead of 'visit'.

She wanted to visit with her family for a few weeks.

 However, in American English, to **visit with** someone you know well usually means to chat to them.

You and I could visit with each other undisturbed.

2 used as a noun

Visit is also a noun. You can **make** a visit to a place or **pay** a visit to someone.

He made a visit to the prison that day.
It was after nine o'clock, too late to pay a visit to Sally.

> **!** **BE CAREFUL**
>
> Don't say that someone 'does a visit'.

voyage

→ See **journey – trip – voyage – excursion**

Ww

wages

→ See **salary – wages**

wagon

→ See **carriage – car – truck – wagon**

waist – waste

These words are both pronounced /weɪst/.

3 'waist'

Waist is a noun. Your **waist** is the middle part of your body, above your hips.

She tied a belt around her waist.
He was naked from the waist up.

4 'waste' used as a verb

Waste is most commonly a verb. If you **waste** time, money, or energy, you use it on something that is unimportant or unnecessary.

You're wasting time asking him to help – he won't.
We wasted money on a computer that didn't work.

5 'waste' used as a noun

You can also say that something is **a waste of** time, money, or energy.

I'll never do that again. It's a waste of time.
It's a waste of money buying a new washing machine when we could repair the old one.

Waste also refers to material that has been used and is no longer wanted, for example because the useful part has been removed.

The river was full of industrial waste.
Your kidneys help to remove waste from your body.

waistcoat

→ See **vest**

wait

1 'wait'

You use the verb **wait** to say that someone remains in the same place, or avoids doing something, until something happens or someone arrives.

Please wait here until he is ready to see you.
She had been waiting to buy some stamps.

2 **'wait for'**

You can say that someone **waits for** something or someone.

I stayed at home, <u>waiting for</u> her call.
If he's late, I'll <u>wait for</u> him.

You can also say that someone **waits for** a person or thing **to do** something.

She <u>waited for</u> me <u>to say something</u>.
I <u>waited for</u> Dad <u>to come home</u>.

 BE CAREFUL

Wait is never a transitive verb. Don't say, for example, '~~I was waiting her call~~'. You must use **wait for**.

→ See **await**

---

wake – waken

→ See **awake**

---

wallet

A **wallet** is a small, flat case made of leather or plastic, in which someone, especially a man, keeps banknotes and other small things such as credit cards.

 In American English, a man's wallet is sometimes called a **billfold**, and a woman's wallet is sometimes called a **pocketbook**. A small bag for carrying money is called a **change purse** or a **coin purse**.

In British English, a woman's wallet is usually called a **purse**.

→ See **purse**

---

want

1 **basic use**

If you **want** something, you feel a need for it or a desire to have it.

Do you <u>want</u> a cup of coffee?
All they <u>want</u> is some sleep.

In informal conversation, people sometimes use present progressive and past progressive forms of **want**.

I think someone <u>is wanting</u> to speak to you.
They <u>were</u> all <u>wanting</u> to be on the team.

 BE CAREFUL

Don't use present progressive or past progressive forms of **want** in formal speech or writing.

However, **want** can be used in the present perfect progressive, the past perfect progressive and the future progressive, in both formal and informal English.

John <u>had been wanting</u> to resign for months.
These new phones are getting very popular – soon everyone <u>will be wanting</u> one.

2 used with a *to*-infinitive

You can say that someone **wants to do** something.

They wanted to go shopping.
I want to ask you a favour, Sara.

! BE CAREFUL

Don't say that someone '~~wants to not do something~~' or '~~wants not to do something~~'. Say that they **don't want to do** it.

I don't want to discuss this.
He didn't want to come.

Instead of using a *to*-infinitive clause, you can sometimes use **to** on its own after **don't want**. For example, instead of saying 'I was asked to go, but I didn't want to go', you would normally say 'I was asked to go, but I **didn't want to**'. Don't say '~~I was asked to go, but I didn't want it~~' or '~~I was asked to go, but I didn't want~~'.

I could do it faster, but I just don't want to.
He should not be forced to eat it if he doesn't want to.

You can say that you **want** someone else **to do** something.

I want him to learn to read.
The little girl wanted me to come and play with her.

Don't use a *that*-clause after **want**. Don't say, for example, '~~I want that he should learn to read~~'.

3 requests

You don't normally use 'want' when you are making a request. It is not polite, for example, to say in a shop 'I want a box of matches, please'. You should say 'Could I have a box of matches, please?' or just 'A box of matches, please.'

→ See **Topic** entry **Requests, orders, and instructions**

4 another meaning of 'want'

In British English, in conversation and in less formal writing, **want** has another meaning. If something **wants doing**, there is a need for it to be done.

We've got a few jobs that want doing in the garden.
The windows wanted cleaning.

! BE CAREFUL

Don't use a *to*-infinitive in sentences like these. Don't say, for example, '~~We've got a few jobs that want to be done in the garden~~'.

5 'be about to'

Don't use 'want to' to say that someone is going to do something very soon. Use the expression **be about to**. Don't say, for example, '~~I was just wanting to leave when the phone rang~~'. Say 'I **was just about to** leave when the phone rang'.

Her father is about to retire soon.
I can't talk now, because I'm just about to go to work.

-ward – -wards

1 '-wards' in adverbs

-wards is a suffix that forms adverbs showing direction. For example, if you move or look **backwards**, you move or look in the direction your back is facing. If you move or look **northwards**, you move or look towards the north.

Ryan walked forwards a couple of steps.
I looked out the window and could see eastwards as far as the distant horizon.
She stretched upwards to the cupboard above the sink.

Here are some common adverbs ending in **-wards**:

backwards	forwards	northwards	southwards
downwards	homewards	onwards	upwards
eastwards	inwards	outwards	westwards

However, you can be creative and add **-wards** to other nouns in order to show direction. For example, if you look **skywards**, you look in the direction of the sky. If you move **seawards**, you move in the direction of the sea.

2 '-ward' in adverbs

 In American English, and sometimes in British English, **-ward** is used instead of '-wards' to form adverbs of direction. For example, instead of saying 'He looked upwards', American speakers usually say 'He looked **upward**'.

I began to climb upward over the steepest ground.
They marched westward.

3 '-ward' in adjectives

In both British and American English, **-ward** is used to form adjectives showing direction. For example, you say 'a **backward** glance' and 'a **homeward** journey'. These adjectives are usually used in front of nouns.

There were plans for the eastward expansion of London.
His announcement was followed by silence and downward glances.
She arrived in London and started preparing for her onward journey to Paris.

> **!** **BE CAREFUL**
>
> Both **afterwards** and **afterward** are always adverbs, not adjectives. **Afterward** is more common in American English.
>
> *They got married not long afterwards.*
> *I left soon afterward.*

→ See **after – afterwards – later**

> **!** **BE CAREFUL**
>
> Both **towards** and **toward** are always prepositions, not adjectives or adverbs.
>
> *He saw his mother running towards him.*
> *She glanced toward the door.*

→ See **to**

wardrobe

→ See **cupboard – wardrobe – closet**

wash

1 used as a transitive verb

If you **wash** something, you clean it with water and usually with soap or detergent.

He got a job washing dishes in a pizza parlour.
She washes and irons their clothes.

You can **wash** a part of your body.

First wash your hands.
She combed her hair and washed her face.

2 used without an object

If someone **washes**, they wash parts of their body, especially their hands and face. This is a formal or literary use. In conversation and in less formal writing, you usually say that someone **has a wash**.

She rose early and washed.
He went upstairs to have a wash.

3 'wash up'

 In American English, if someone **washes up**, they wash parts of their body, especially their hands and face.

I'll just go wash up before dinner.

In British English, if someone **washes up**, they wash the pans, plates, cups, and cutlery which have been used in cooking and eating a meal.

I cooked, so you can wash up.

---

washroom

→ See **toilet**

---

waste

→ See **waist – waste**

---

way

1 'way'

You use **way** to refer to the thing or series of things that someone does in order to achieve a particular result. You can talk about a **way of doing** something or a **way to do** it. There is no difference in meaning.

This is the most effective way of helping the unemployed.
What is the best way to help a child with reading problems?

! BE CAREFUL

If you use a possessive with **way**, you must use **of** and an *-ing* form after it.

I have to fit in with her way of doing things.
They are part of the author's way of telling his story.

Don't use a *to*-infinitive. Don't say, for example, '~~I have to fit in with her way to do things~~'.

2 'means'

You don't usually use a noun after 'way of' when you are saying how something is done or achieved. For example, you don't refer to something as a 'way of transport'. The word you use is **means**.

The main means of transport on the island was the donkey.
Drums can be used as a means of communication.

3 used for describing manner

You can say that something is done **in** a particular **way**.

The play was performed in a very interesting way.
She smiled in a friendly way.

You usually say **this way** or **that way** without using 'in'.

Let's do it this way.
It's easier to do it that way.

You can also omit 'in' when you are using **the** or a possessive.

We don't look at things the same way.
I'm going to handle this my way.

4 used with relative clauses

When **the way** is followed by a defining relative clause, this clause can be either a *that*-clause or a clause beginning with **in which**. For example, you can say '**the way** she told the story', '**the way that** she told the story', or '**the way in which** she told the story'. There is no difference in meaning.

It's the way they used to do it.
I was shocked by the way in which they treated their animals.

---

we

You use **we** to refer to yourself together with one or more other people. **We** is the subject of a verb.

We could hear the birds singing.
We both sat down.

You can use **we** to include the person or people you are speaking or writing to.

If you like, we could have dinner together.

! BE CAREFUL

Don't say 'you and we' or 'we and you'. Instead of saying 'You and we must go', you say '**We** must go'.

You can also use **we** to refer to people in general, including yourself.

We need to stop polluting the planet.
Nowadays we like to think of ourselves as rational and scientific.

→ See **one – you – we – they**

wear

1 'wear'

When you **wear** something, you have it on your body. You can **wear** clothes, shoes, a hat, gloves, jewellery, make-up, or a pair of glasses. The past tense of **wear** is **wore**. The -ed participle is **worn**.

She was small and wore glasses.
I've worn this dress so many times.

2 'dressed in'

You can also say that someone is **dressed in** particular clothes.

All the men were dressed in grey suits.

However, don't say that someone is 'dressed in' a hat, shoes, gloves, jewellery, make-up, or glasses.

→ See **dress**

3 'in'

You can use **in** to mention the clothes, shoes, hat, or gloves someone is wearing. **In** usually goes immediately after a noun phrase.

With her was a small girl in a blue T-shirt.
The bar was full of men in baseball caps.

You can use **in** as part of an adverbial phrase.

I saw you walking along in your old jeans.
She stood at the top of the stairs in her pyjamas.

In is sometimes used to mean 'wearing only'. For example, 'George was **in** his underpants' means 'George was wearing only his underpants'.

He was standing in the hall in his swimming shorts.
She opened the door in her dressing gown.

weather – whether

1 'weather'

If you are talking about the **weather**, you are saying, for example, that it is raining, cloudy, sunny, hot, or cold.

The weather was good for the time of year.
The trip was cancelled because of bad weather conditions.

! BE CAREFUL

Weather is an uncountable noun. Don't use 'a' with it. Don't say, for example, 'We are expecting a bad weather'. Say 'We are expecting **bad weather**'.

They completed the climb despite appalling weather.
The wedding took place in perfect May weather.

Don't tell someone what the weather is like by saying, for example, 'It's lovely weather'. Say 'The weather **is lovely**'.

The weather was awful. It hardly ever stopped raining.

2 'whether'

Do not confuse **weather** with **whether**. You use **whether** when you are talking about two or more alternatives.

I don't know whether to go out or stay at home.
She asked whether I wanted more coffee.

→ See **whether**

wedding

→ See **marriage – wedding**

week

A **week** is a period of seven days. A week is usually regarded as beginning on a Monday, or sometimes on a Sunday.

She will be back next week.
It will take several weeks to repair the damage.

If something happens **in the week** or **during the week**, it happens on weekdays, which are the days when people usually go to work or school, rather than at the weekend.

In the week, we get up at seven.
I never have time to cook during the week.

→ See **last – lastly**, **next**, **this – that**

→ See **Reference** section **Days and dates**

weekday

A **weekday** is any of the days of the week except Saturday or Sunday. **Weekdays** are the days that most people in Europe, North America, and Australia go to work or school.

She spent every weekday at meetings.
You don't need to reserve a table if you come on a weekday.

You can say that something happens **on weekdays**.

I visited them on weekdays for lunch.
We have to get up early on weekdays.

 American speakers sometimes omit the 'on'.

Weekdays after six, I'd go fetch him for dinner.

weekend

1 'weekend'

A **weekend** consists of a Saturday and the Sunday that comes after it. Sometimes Friday evening is also considered to be part of the weekend. The weekend is the time when most people in Europe, North America, and Australia do not go to work or school.

I spent the weekend at home.
Did you have a good weekend?

2 regular events

British English speakers say that something takes place **at weekends**.

The beach gets very crowded at weekends.

 American speakers usually say that something takes place **weekends** or **on weekends**.

He often studies evenings and weekends.
On weekends I usually sleep late.

3 single events

You can say that an event takes place **during** a particular weekend.

Will you be visiting relatives during the holiday weekend?

On a weekday, **the weekend** or **this weekend** can refer either to the previous weekend or the following weekend. You can use **at**, **during**, or **over** in front of **the weekend**. Don't use any preposition in front of **this weekend**.

Her new film came out at the weekend.
I'll call you over the weekend.
My birthday was this weekend.
We might be able to go skiing this weekend.

---

weep

→ See **cry – weep**

---

welcome

Welcome can be a verb, a noun, or an adjective. It can also be a greeting.

1 used as a verb

If you **welcome** someone, you greet them in a friendly way when they arrive at the place where you are.

He went to the door to welcome his visitor.

2 used as a noun

If you want to describe the way in which someone is welcomed to a place, you can use **welcome** as a noun. For example, you can say that someone is given **a warm welcome**.

He was given a warm welcome by the President himself.
We always get a friendly welcome from the hotel staff.

3 'you're welcome'

You can say '**you're welcome**' as a response when someone thanks you.

'Thanks for the coffee.' – 'You're welcome.'

→ See **Topic** entry **Thanking someone**

You can say that someone **is welcome to do something** or **is welcome to something**, meaning that you are happy for them to do it or have it if they want.

She is welcome to stay with us while she finds a place to live.
We don't have a bath, only a shower, but you're welcome to it.

In different contexts, and with different intonation, you can say that someone **is welcome to something** to mean that they can have it because you do not want it and are happy to get rid of it.

If he wants my job, he's <u>welcome to it</u>!

4 used as a greeting

When someone arrives at the place where you are, you can greet them by saying '**Welcome**' to them.

<u>Welcome</u> to Beijing.
<u>Welcome</u> home, Marta.

---

well

1 used before a statement

In conversation, people sometimes say **well** when they are about to make a statement. **Well** can show that someone is hesitating or uncertain, but sometimes it has no meaning at all.

'Is that right?' – '<u>Well</u>, I think so.'

In conversation, people also use **well** when they are correcting something they have just said.

We walked along in silence; <u>well</u>, not really silence, because she was humming.
It took me years, <u>well</u> months at least, to realise that he'd lied to me.

2 used as an adverb

Well is very commonly an adverb.

You use **well** to say that something is done to a high standard or to a great extent.

He handled it <u>well</u>.
The strategy has worked very <u>well</u> in the past.

You use **well** to emphasize some *-ed* participles when they are part of a passive construction.

You seem to be <u>well liked</u> at work.

When **well** is used with an *-ed* participle like this to make a compound adjective that comes before a noun, the compound usually has a hyphen.

She was seen having dinner with a <u>well-known</u> actor.
This is a very <u>well-established</u> custom.

When the compound adjective comes after a verb, don't use a hyphen.

The author is <u>well known</u> in his native country of Scotland.
Their routine of a morning walk was <u>well established</u>.

You also use **well** in front of some prepositions such as **ahead of** and **behind**.

The candidate is <u>well ahead of</u> his rivals in the opinion polls.
The border now lay <u>well behind</u> them.

When **well** is an adverb, its comparative and superlative forms are **better** and **best**.

People are <u>better</u> housed than ever before.
What works <u>best</u> is a balanced, sensible diet.

3 used as an adjective

Well is also an adjective. If you are **well**, you are healthy and not ill.

She looked well.
'How are you?' – 'I'm very well, thank you.'

 Most British speakers do not use **well** in front of a noun. They don't say, for example, '~~He's a well man~~'. They say 'He's **well**'. However, American and Scottish speakers sometimes use **well** in front of a noun.

When **well** is an adjective, it does not have a comparative form. However, you can use **better** to say that the health of a sick person has improved. When **better** is used like this, it means 'less ill'.

He seems better today.

Better is more commonly used to say that someone has completely recovered from an illness or injury.

I hope you'll be better soon.
Her cold was better.

→ See **better**

4 'as well'

You use **as well** when you are giving more information about something.

Fresh fruit is healthier than tinned fruit. And it tastes nicer as well.
The woman laughed, and Jayah giggled as well.

→ See also – **too – as well**

were

1 used to talk about the past

Were is the plural form and the second person singular form of the past tense of **be**.

They were only fifty miles from the coast.
You were about twelve at the time.

2 used in conditional clauses

Were has a special use in conditional clauses when these clauses are used to mention situations that do not exist, or events that are unlikely to happen. When the subject of the clause is **I**, **he**, **she**, **it**, **there**, or a singular noun, **were** is sometimes used instead of 'was', especially in formal writing.

If I were in his circumstances, I would do the same.
If the law were changed, it would not benefit women.

In conversation and in less formal writing, people usually use **was**.

If I was an architect, I'd re-design this house.
If the business was properly run this wouldn't happen.

Both **was** or **were** are now considered correct in clauses like this and are acceptable even in formal writing.

The fixed phrase 'If I were you' almost always contains **were**, even in informal English. Don't say '~~If I was you~~'.

If I were you, I'd start looking for a new job.

> **!** **BE CAREFUL**
>
> Don't confuse **were** /wə/ with **where** /weə, weə/. You use **where** to make statements or ask questions about place or position.
>
> *Where is the nearest train station?*

→ See **where**

---

west

◼1 'west'

The **west** is the direction which you look towards in order to see the sun set.

The village is fifty miles to the west of Oxford.
We watched the sun set behind the hills in the west.

A **west** wind blows from the west.

A warm west wind was blowing.

The **west** of a place is the part that is towards the west.

They live in a remote rural area in the west of Ireland.

West is used in the names of some states and regions.

He was a coal miner from West Virginia.
Benin is a country in West Africa.

◼2 'western'

You don't usually talk about a 'west' part of a country or region. You talk about a **western** part.

There will be rain in northern and western parts of the United Kingdom.

Similarly, you don't talk about 'west Europe' or 'west France'. Say **western** Europe or **western** France.

They were studying the history of western Europe.
She was born in western Australia.

You can use **Western** to describe people and things connected with the United States, Canada, the countries of western Europe, and sometimes other industrialized countries.

The US and other Western governments criticized the move.
He discussed the problems of Western society.

---

westwards – westward

→ See **-ward – -wards**

GRAMMAR FINDER

Wh-words

Wh-words are a set of adverbs, pronouns, and determiners that all, with the exception of **how**, begin with *wh*. They are:

▶ the adverbs **how**, **when**, **where**, and **why**

▶ the pronouns **who**, **whom**, **what**, **which**, and **whose**

▶ the determiners **what**, **which**, and **whose**

Wh-words are used in questions.
Why are you smiling?

→ See **Questions**

They are also used in reported questions.
He asked me where I was going.

→ See **Reporting**

With the exception of 'how' and 'what', *wh*-words can be used to begin relative clauses.
...nurses who have trained for two years.

That is also used to begin relative clauses, although it is not used for questions and reported questions.

→ See **Relative clauses**, **Wh-clauses** for information on the use of *wh*-words to begin clauses used as subjects and prepositional objects

You will find information on how to use each *wh*-word in the Usage entry for that word.

what

1 asking for information

You use **what** when you are asking for information about something. You can use **what** as a pronoun or a determiner.

When you use **what** as a pronoun, it can be the subject, object, or complement of a verb. It can also be the object of a preposition.

What happened to the crew?
What is your name?

When **what** is the object of a verb, it is followed by an auxiliary verb, the subject, and then the main verb. When **what** is the object of a preposition, the preposition usually goes at the end of the question.

What did she say then?
What did he die of?

2 used as a determiner

When you use **what** as a determiner, it usually forms part of the object of a verb.

What books can I read on the subject?
What car do you drive?

> **!** BE CAREFUL
>
> Don't use 'what' when your question involves a choice from a limited number of people or things. For example, if someone has hurt their finger, don't ask '~~What finger have you hurt?~~' Say '**Which** finger have you hurt?'
>
> *When you get your daily paper, which page do you read first?*
> *Which department do you want?*

You use **what** when you are asking about the time.

What time is it?
What time does their flight get in?

3 used in reported clauses

What is often used in reported clauses.

I asked her what had happened.
I find it difficult to understand what people are saying.

→ See **Reporting**

4 'what...for'

You use **what** with **for** when you are asking about the purpose of something. You put **what** at the beginning of the question and **for** at the end of it. For example, '**What** is this tool **for**?' means 'What is the purpose of this tool?'

What are those lights for?

> In conversation, you can also use **what** with **for** to ask about the reason for something. You can say, for example, '**What** are you looking at me **for**?' This means 'Why are you looking at me?'
>
> *What are you asking him for?*

5 'what if'

You use **what if** to ask what should be done if a particular difficulty occurs. For example, '**What if** the bus doesn't come?' means 'What shall we do if the bus doesn't come?'

What if it's really bad weather?
What if this doesn't work out?

6 'what about'

You use **what about** to remind someone of something, or to draw their attention to something. **What about** is followed by a noun phrase.

What about the other names on the list?
What about your breakfast?

> **!** BE CAREFUL
>
> When you ask someone a question beginning with **what about** you are often expecting them to do something, rather than answer your question.
>
> *What about this bag – aren't you taking it?*

7 used in relative clauses

What is sometimes used at the beginning of a special kind of relative clause called a **nominal relative clause**. This kind of clause functions like a noun phrase; it can be the subject, object, or complement of a verb, or the object of a preposition. In a nominal relative clause, **what** means 'the thing which' or 'the things which'.

What he said was perfectly true.
They did not like what he wrote.
I am what is known as a light sleeper.
That is a very good account of what happened.

People often use a nominal relative clause in front of **is** or **was** to focus attention on the thing they are about to mention.

What I need is a lawyer.
What impressed me most was their sincerity.

A similar type of clause consists of **what** followed by the subject and **do**. After a clause like this, you use **be** and an infinitive structure with or without *to*. For example, instead of saying 'I wrote to George immediately', you can say '**What I did** was to write to George immediately'.

What Stefan did was to interview a lot of people.
What you need to do is choose five companies to invest in.

> **!** | **BE CAREFUL**
>
> Don't use 'what' in defining or non-defining relative clauses. Don't say, for example, '~~The man what you met is my brother~~' or '~~The book what you lent me is very good~~'. Use **who**, **which**, or **that**, or don't use a relative pronoun at all. For example, say 'The man who you met is my brother' or 'The man you met is my brother'.

→ See **Relative clauses**

8 used to mean 'whatever'

What can be used with the same meaning as 'whatever', both as a pronoun and a determiner.

Do what you like.
They shared what food they had.

→ See **whatever**

9 used in exclamations

What is often used in exclamations.

What a great idea!
What nonsense!

→ See **Topic** entry **Reactions**

whatever

Whatever can be a pronoun, a determiner, or an adverb.

1 used as a pronoun or determiner

You use **whatever** as a pronoun or determiner to refer to anything or everything of a particular kind.

I read whatever I could find about the course.
You can buy whatever ingredients you need from the market.

You can also use **whatever** to say that something is true in all possible circumstances.

Whatever happens, I'll be back by five.
Whatever type of garden you have, you can have fun growing your own vegetables.

2 **used as an adverb**

You use **whatever** after **nothing** or after a noun phrase beginning with **no** to emphasize that there is nothing of a particular kind.

He knew <u>nothing whatever</u> about it.
There is <u>no scientific evidence whatever</u> to support this view.

3 **used in questions**

Whatever is sometimes used in questions to express surprise.

<u>Whatever</u> is the matter?
<u>Whatever</u> do you want to go up there for?

However, many people consider this form to be incorrect, and it is better to write **what ever** as two separate words.

<u>What ever</u> does it mean?

4 **used as an informal response**

In informal conversation, people sometimes use **whatever** as a response, to show that they do not care or have no opinion about something. This use can sound rude.

'Shall we get a pizza tonight?' – 'Whatever. I don't mind.'
'You really should try to be more organized with your schoolwork.' – 'Yeah, whatever.'

when

1 **used in questions**

You use **when** to ask about the time that something happened or will happen.

<u>When</u> did you arrive?
'They're getting married.' – '<u>When?</u>' – 'Next month.'

2 **used in time clauses**

You use **when** in time clauses to say that something happened, happens, or will happen at a particular time.

He left school <u>when he was sixteen</u>.
<u>When I have free time</u>, I always spend it fishing.

If you are talking about the future, use the present simple in the time clause, not a future form. For example, say 'Stop when you **feel** tired'. Don't say '~~Stop when you will feel tired~~'.

When you <u>get</u> to the hotel, go to reception and give your name.
I'll come when I <u>finish</u> work.

3 **'when', 'as', and 'while'**

If you want to say what was happening at the time that an event occurred, you can begin by saying what was happening, then add a clause beginning with **when**.

I was just going out <u>when there was a knock at the door</u>.
We were at our desks working <u>when we heard the explosion</u>.

You can also use **as** or **while** to say what was happening when an event occurred. When you use one of these words, you describe the event in the main clause and say what was happening in the clause beginning with **as** or **while**.

<u>As I was out walking one day</u>, I saw a very unusual bird.
<u>While I was standing at the bus stop,</u> Raul came by.

If you want to say that two events are continuing to happen at the same time, you usually use **while**.

What were you thinking about <u>while he was talking to you</u>?
I don't like music playing <u>while I am working</u>.

4 used with 'why'

When has another use which is not related to time. You can add a clause beginning with **when** to a question which begins with **why**, as a way of expressing surprise or disagreement. The *when*-clause shows the reason for your surprise or disagreement.

Why should I help him <u>when he refused to help me</u>?
Why worry her <u>when there's nothing she can do about it</u>?

---

whenever

1 used in time clauses

You use **whenever** in time clauses to say that something always happens or is always true when something else happens or is true.

<u>Whenever she lost a game</u>, she used to cry.
She always comes to see me <u>whenever she is in the area</u>.

If you are talking about the future, you use the present simple tense in the time clause, not a future form.

You can talk to me whenever you <u>feel</u> depressed.

Every time and **each time** can be used in a similar way to 'whenever'.

<u>Every time I want to catch that bus</u> it's late.
He frowned <u>each time she spoke</u>.

2 used with 'possible'

You can use **whenever** with **possible** instead of using a time clause. For example, instead of saying 'She met him ~~whenever it was possible for her to meet him~~', you simply say 'She met him **whenever possible**'.

I avoided arguments <u>whenever possible</u>.
It is better to tell the truth <u>whenever possible</u>.

---

where

1 used in questions

You use **where** to ask questions about place or position.

<u>Where</u>'s Dad?
<u>Where</u> does she live?

You also use **where** to ask about the place that someone or something is coming from or going to.

<u>Where</u> are you going?
<u>Where</u> does all this anger come from?

2 used in place clauses

You use **where** in place clauses when you are talking about the place or position in which someone or something is.

He said he was happy _where he was_.
He dropped the ball and left it _where it lay_.

A place clause usually goes after the main clause. However, in stories, the place clause can be put first.

Where the house had once stood, there was an empty space.
Where the sun touched the water it shone like gold.

3 used in reported clauses

Where is often used in reported clauses.

I think I know _where we are_.
I asked someone _where the nearest hotel was_.

→ See **Reporting**

4 used in relative clauses

Where is often used in non-defining relative clauses.

He comes from Canterbury, _where the famous cathedral is_.
She went into the art room, _where the brushes and paint had been set out_.

Where can also be used in defining relative clauses after **place** or after a word such as **room** or **street**.

Will you show me _the place where you work_?
The room where I did my homework was too noisy.

Where can also be used in defining clauses after words such as **situation** and **stage**.

We have _a situation where people feel afraid of going out_.
I've reached _the point where I'm ready to retire_.

→ See **Relative clauses**

5 used with 'possible' and 'necessary'

Where is sometimes used in front of adjectives such as **possible** and **necessary**. When it is used like this, it has a similar meaning to 'when' or 'whenever'.

Where possible, friends will be put in the same class.
Help must be given _where necessary_.

wherever

1 used in place clauses

You use **wherever** in place clauses to say that something happens or is true in every place where something else happens or is true.

These plants grow _wherever there is enough light_.
Wherever I looked, I saw broken glass.

You can also use **wherever** to say that something is true and that it does not matter what place is involved.

Wherever it is, I can't find it.

2 used with 'possible'

Wherever is sometimes used in front of adjectives such as **possible** and **practicable**. When it is used like this, it has a similar meaning to 'when' or 'whenever'.

Experts agree that, _wherever possible_, children should enjoy learning.

3 **used in questions**

Wherever is sometimes used when asking a question, to express surprise.

Wherever did you get that idea?
Wherever have you been?

However, many people consider this form to be incorrect, and it is better to write **where ever** as two separate words.

Where ever did you get that hat?

whether

Whether is used in reported clauses and conditional clauses.

1 **used in reported clauses**

You can use a clause beginning with **whether** after a reporting verb such as **know**, **ask**, or **wonder**. You use **whether** when you are mentioning two or more alternatives. You put **whether** in front of the first alternative, and **or** in front of the second one.

I don't know whether he's in or out.
I was asked whether I wanted to stay at a hotel or at his home.

When the two alternatives are opposites, you don't need to mention both of them. For example, instead of saying 'I don't know whether he's in or out', you can simply say 'I don't know **whether he's in**'.

Lucy wondered whether Rita had been happy.
I asked Professor Gupta whether he agreed.

2 **'whether...or not'**

You can also mention the second alternative using **or not**. You put **or not** either at the end of the sentence or immediately after **whether**.

I didn't know whether to believe him or not.
She didn't ask whether or not we wanted to come.

3 **'if'**

If can be used instead of 'whether', especially when the second alternative is not mentioned.

I asked her if I could help her
I rang up to see if I could get seats.

4 **reporting uncertainty**

If someone is uncertain about doing a particular thing, or uncertain how to respond to a situation, you can report this using a clause consisting of **whether** and a to-infinitive.

I've been wondering whether to look for another job.
He didn't know whether to feel glad or sorry that she was leaving.

5 **used in conditional clauses**

You can add a clause containing **whether** and **or not** to a sentence to indicate that something is true in any of the circumstances you mention.

He's going to buy a house whether he gets married or not.

6 'weather'

Do not confuse **whether** with **weather**, which is pronounced the same way. If you say that it is raining, windy, hot, or cold, you are talking about the **weather**.

The wet weather lasted all weekend.

→ See **weather – whether**

---

which

Which can be a determiner or a pronoun.

1 asking for information

You use **which** when you are asking for information about one of a limited number of things or people. A noun phrase beginning with **which** or consisting of the pronoun **which** can be the subject, object, or complement of a verb. It can also be the object of a preposition.

Which type of oil is best?
Which is her room?

! BE CAREFUL

When the noun phrase is the object of a verb or preposition, you put an auxiliary verb after the object, followed by the subject and the main verb. When the noun phrase is the object of a preposition, the preposition usually goes at the end of the clause.

Which hotel did you want?
Which station did you come from?

2 used in reported clauses

Which is often used in reported clauses.

Do you remember which country he played for?
I don't know which to believe.

→ See **Reporting**

3 used in relative clauses

Which can be a relative pronoun in both defining and non-defining relative clauses. In relative clauses, **which** always refers to things, never to people.

We heard about the awful conditions which exist in some prisons.
I'm teaching at the local college, which is just over the road.

In relative clauses, you can use either **which** or **who** after a collective noun such as **family**, **committee**, or **group**. After **which** you use a singular verb. After **who** you usually use a plural verb.

He is on the committee which makes decisions about planning.
They are a separate ethnic group who have their own language.

! BE CAREFUL

When **which** is the subject of a non-defining clause, don't use another pronoun after it. Don't say, for example, 'He stared at the painting, which it was completely ruined'. You say 'He stared at the painting, **which** was completely ruined'.

→ See **Relative clauses**

while

1 used in time clauses

If one thing happens **while** another thing is happening, the two things happen at the same time.

He stayed with me while he was looking for a new house.
While I was out she was trying to reach me on the phone.

2 'while' in concessive clauses

While has a special use which is not related to time. You use it to introduce a clause that contrasts with something else that you are saying.

Miguel loved sports while Julio preferred to read a book.
While I have some sympathy for these people, I think they went too far.

3 'a while'

A while is a period of time.

After a while, my eyes got used to the darkness.
Let's just sit down for a while.

---

who – whom

Who and **whom** are pronouns.

1 asking for information

You use **who** when you are asking about someone's identity. **Who** can be the subject, object, or complement of a verb. It can also be the object of a preposition.

Who invited you?
Who are you?

> **!** **BE CAREFUL**
>
> When **who** is the object of a verb or preposition, it is followed by an auxiliary verb, the subject, and then the main verb. When **who** is the object of a preposition, the preposition must go at the end of the clause. Don't use a preposition in front of **who**.

Who are you going to invite?
Who did you dance with?

Whom is a formal word which is sometimes used instead of 'who'. **Whom** can only be the object of a verb or preposition.

Whom shall we call?
By whom are they elected?

When **whom** is the object of a preposition, the preposition must go in front of **whom**. Don't use it at the end of a clause. Don't say, for example 'Whom are they elected by?'

2 used in reported clauses

Who is often used in reported clauses.

She didn't know who I was.
We have to find out who did this.

→ See **Reporting**

3 **used in relative clauses**

Who and **whom** are used in both defining and non-defining relative clauses.

He's the man who I saw last night.
Joe, who was always early, was there already.
The writer was Philip Pullman, for whom I have great respect.

In relative clauses, you can use either **who** or **which** after a collective noun such as **family**, **committee**, or **group**. After **who** you usually use a plural verb. After **which** you use a singular verb.

It is important to have a family who love you.
He is a member of a group which does a lot of charitable work.

! **BE CAREFUL**

When **who** is the subject of a non-defining clause, don't use another pronoun after it. Don't say, for example, 'He told his mother, who she was very shocked'. Say 'He told his mother, **who** was very shocked'.

whoever

1 **used in statements**

You use **whoever** to refer to any person involved in the kind of situation you are describing.

You can have whoever you like to visit you.
Whoever is the last to leave should lock the door.

You also use **whoever** to refer to someone whose identity you do not know.

Whoever answered the telephone was a very charming woman.

You also use **whoever** to say that the identity of someone will not affect a situation.

Whoever you vote for, prices will go on rising.

2 **used in questions**

Whoever is sometimes used when asking questions, in order to express surprise.

Whoever could that be, calling so late?

However, many people consider this form to be incorrect, and it is better to write **who ever** as two separate words.

Who ever told you that?

whole

1 **'the whole of' and 'whole'**

When you talk about **the whole of** something, you mean all of it.

We were there for the whole of July.
I felt pain throughout the whole of my body.

Instead of using **the whole of** in front of a noun phrase beginning with **the**, you can simply use **whole** after **the**. For example, instead of saying 'The whole of the house was on fire', you can say '**The whole house** was on fire'.

I spent the whole day in the library.
They're the best team in the whole world.

You can use **whole** in a similar way after **this**, **that**, or a possessive.

I just want to say how sorry I am about this whole business.
I've never seen anything like this in my whole life.

You use **whole** after **a** to emphasize that you mean all of something of a particular kind.

We worked on the project for a whole year.
I drank a whole pot of coffee, and I still felt tired.

You can also use **whole** like this in front of the plural form of a noun.

There were whole paragraphs in the article that I didn't understand.

! BE CAREFUL

In front of plurals, **whole** does not have the same meaning as **all**. If you say 'All the buildings have been destroyed', you mean that every building has been destroyed. If you say '**Whole** buildings have been destroyed', you mean that some buildings have been destroyed completely.

2 **'as a whole'**

You use **as a whole** after a noun to emphasize that you are talking about all of something and regarding it as a single unit.

Is this true just of some classes, or of the school as a whole?
In the country as a whole, average house prices went up by 19%.

3 **'on the whole'**

You add **on the whole** to a statement to show that what you are saying is true in general but may not be true in every case.

I didn't enjoy the food because on the whole I don't really like fish.
On the whole it's not a good idea to ask him questions.

whom

→ See **who – whom**

whose

1 **used in relative clauses**

You use a noun phrase containing **whose** /huːz/ at the beginning of a relative clause to show who or what something belongs to or is connected with. **Whose** is used in both defining and non-defining clauses.

A noun phrase containing **whose** can be the subject or object of a verb, or the object of a preposition.

It is a story whose purpose is to entertain.
This was one of the students whose work I had seen.

When **whose** is the object of a preposition, the preposition can come at the beginning or end of the clause.

You should consider the people in whose home you are staying.
It was an article whose subject I have never heard of.

2 used in questions

You use **whose** in questions when you are asking who something belongs to or is connected with. **Whose** can be a determiner or a pronoun.

Whose fault is it?
Whose is this?

3 used in reported clauses

Whose is also used in reported clauses.

It would be interesting to know whose idea it was.
Do you know whose fault it is?

→ See **Reporting**

! BE CAREFUL

Don't confuse **whose** with **who's**, which is also pronounced /huːz/. When you write down what someone says, you can write 'who is' or 'who has' as **who's**. Don't write them as 'whose'.

'Edward drove me here.' – 'Who's Edward?'
Who's left these boots here?

why

1 used in questions

You use **why** when you are asking a question about the reason for something.

'I had to say no.' – 'Why?'
Why did you do it, Marta?

2 used when no answer is expected

You sometimes use **why** in questions without expecting an answer. For example, you can make a suggestion by asking a question beginning with **Why don't**.

Why don't we all go?
Why don't you write to her yourself?

You can emphasize that there is no reason for something to be done by asking a question beginning with **Why should**.

Why would he be angry with you?
'Will you say sorry?' – 'No, why should I?'

You can emphasize that there is no reason why something should not be done by asking a question beginning with **Why shouldn't**.

Why shouldn't he go to college?

You can suggest that an action is pointless by using **why** followed by an infinitive without *to*.

Why tell the police? It won't do any good.

3 used in reported clauses

Why is often used in reported clauses.

He wondered why she had come.
You never really told me why you don't like him.

Why can be used on its own instead of a reported clause, if it is clear what you mean. For example, instead of saying 'She doesn't like him. I don't know why she doesn't like him', you can say 'She doesn't like him, I don't know **why**'.

They refuse to come – I don't know <u>why</u>.
He's certainly cheerful, though I can't think <u>why</u>.

4 used in relative clauses

Why is sometimes used in relative clauses with the word **reason**.

That is one reason <u>why they were such a successful team</u>.

→ See **reason**

wide – broad

Something that is **wide** or **broad** measures a large distance from one side to the other. You can say that something such as a street or river is **wide** or **broad**.

They live on a <u>wide</u>, tree-lined street.
The streets of this town are <u>broad</u>.

 Wide is more common in conversation than 'broad'.

The river was so <u>wide</u> I couldn't jump over it.

When you are talking about objects, you usually say that they are **wide** rather than 'broad'.

In the centre of the room was a <u>wide</u> bed.
The men came out through a <u>wide</u> doorway.

When you are talking about parts of someone's body, you usually use **broad** rather than 'wide'.

He was tall, with <u>broad</u> shoulders.
She gave me a <u>broad</u> smile.

widow – widower

1 'widow'

You say that a woman is a **widow** when her husband has died and she has not married again.

I had been a <u>widow</u> for five years.

When a man has died, you can refer to his wife as **his widow**.

His property had been left to <u>his widow</u>.
He visited the <u>widow of</u> an old school friend.

2 'widower'

You say that a man is a **widower** when his wife has died and he has not married again.

He's a <u>widower</u> in his late forties.

When a woman has died, you can refer to her husband as **her widower**.

Ten years later <u>her widower</u> remarried.
The ceremony was attended by the <u>widower of</u> the Pulitzer Prize-winning author Carol Shields.

will

→ See **shall – will**

win – defeat – beat

1 'win'

If you **win** a war, fight, game, or contest, you defeat your opponent. The past tense and -ed participle of **win** is **won** /wʌn/.

We won the game easily.
The party had won a great victory.

2 'defeat' and 'beat'

Don't say that someone 'wins' an enemy or opponent. In a war or battle, you say that one side **defeats** the other.

The French defeated the English troops.

In a game or contest, you say that one person or side **defeats** or **beats** the other.

He defeated his rival in the semi-finals and went on to win the tournament.
She beat him at chess.

wind

Wind can be a noun or a verb.

1 used as a noun

The **wind** /wɪnd/ is a current of air moving across the earth's surface.

An icy wind brought clouds of snow.
Leaves were being blown along by the wind.

2 used as a verb

The verb **wind** /waɪnd/ has a completely different meaning. If a road or river **winds** in a particular direction, it goes in that direction with a lot of bends.

The river winds through miles of beautiful countryside.

The past tense and -ed participle of this verb is **wound**, pronounced /waʊnd/.

The road wound across the desolate plain.

You can also **wind** /waɪnd/ something around something else. For example, you can **wind** a wire around a stick. This means that you wrap the wire around the stick several times.

She started to wind the bandage around her arm.
He had a long scarf wound round his neck.

When you **wind** /waɪnd/ something such as a watch or a clock, you turn a knob or handle several times in order to make it operate.

I hadn't wound my watch so I didn't know the time.

3 'wound'

Wound can also be pronounced /wuːnd/. When it is pronounced like this, it is a noun or a verb, and it has a completely different meaning. A **wound** is damage to a part of your body, caused by a weapon.

They treated a soldier with a leg <u>wound</u>.

If someone **wounds** you, they damage your body using a weapon.

Her father was badly <u>wounded</u> in the war.

winter

Winter is the season between autumn and spring. In winter, the weather is cold.

A lot of plants and wild animals died during the harsh <u>winter</u>.
It was a dark <u>winter's</u> night.

If you want to say that something happens every year during this season, you say that it happens **in winter** or **in the winter**.

The park closes earlier <u>in winter</u>.
<u>In the winter</u> the path can be icy.

> **!** **BE CAREFUL**
>
> Don't say that something happens 'in the winters' or 'in winters'.

→ See **Reference** section **Days and dates**

wish

Wish can be a noun or a verb.

1 used as a noun

A **wish** is a longing or desire for something, often something that is difficult to obtain or achieve.

She told me of her <u>wish</u> to have a baby.
They are motivated by a <u>wish</u> for more freedom.

2 used as a verb

When **wish** is a verb, it is usually followed by a *that*-clause. If you **wish** that something was the case, you would like it to be the case, although you know it is unlikely or impossible.

I <u>wish</u> I lived nearer London.
We never have enough time and we <u>wish</u> we had more.

> **!** **BE CAREFUL**
>
> Use a past tense in the *that*-clause, not a present tense. Don't say, for example, 'I wish I have more friends'. Say 'I wish I **had** more friends'. Don't say 'I wish I have sold my car'. You say 'I wish I **had sold** my car'.
>
> *I wish I <u>could</u> help you, but I can't.*
> *I envy you. I wish I <u>was going</u> away too.*

You use the same tense in the *that*-clause when you are talking about the past as you would use if you were talking about the present. For example, you say 'She wished she **lived** in Tuscany' and 'She wishes she **lived** in Tuscany'.

The woman wished she <u>could</u> help them.
He wished he <u>had phoned</u> for a taxi.

When the subject of the *that*-clause is a singular pronoun such as **I** or **he** or a singular noun phrase, you can use either **was** or **were** after it. This use of **were** is rather formal, especially in British English.

Sometimes, I wish I was back in Africa.
My sister occasionally wished that she were a boy.

→ See **were**

You can also use **could** in the *that*-clause.

I wish I could paint.
He wished he could believe her.

If you **wish** that something **would** happen, you want it to happen, and you are annoyed or worried because it has not happened already.

I wish he would hurry up!
I wish someone would explain it to me.

If you say to someone that you **wish** they **would** do something, you want them to do it, and you are annoyed or disappointed because they have not done it already.

I wish you would leave me alone.
I wish you would find out the facts before you start accusing people.

! BE CAREFUL

Don't use 'wish' with a *that*-clause simply to express a wish for the future. Don't say, for example, 'I wish you'll have a nice time in Finland'. Say 'I **hope you'll have** a nice time in Finland' or 'I **hope you have** a nice time in Finland'.

I hope I'll see you before you go.
I hope you enjoy the play.

However, you can sometimes express a wish for the future using **wish** as a transitive verb with two objects.

May I wish you luck in writing your book.
He wished the newly wed couple every possible happiness.

with

1 basic uses

If one person or thing is **with** another, they are together in one place.

I stayed with her until she fell asleep.
The dictionaries go on that shelf with the other reference books.

If you do something **with** a tool or object, you do it using that tool or object.

Clean the floor with a mop.
He pushed back his hair with his hand.

2 used to mention an opponent

You use **with** after verbs like **fight** or **argue**. For example, if two people are fighting, you can say that one person is fighting **with** the other.

He was always fighting with his brother.
Judy was arguing with Brian.

Similarly, you can use **with** after nouns like **fight** or **argument**.

I had a disagreement <u>with my friend</u>.
She won a legal battle <u>with her employer</u>.

3 used in descriptions

You can use **with** immediately after a noun phrase to mention a physical feature that someone or something has.

He was an old man <u>with a beard</u>.
They lived in a house <u>with white walls and a red roof</u>.

You can use **with** like this to identify someone or something. For example, you can refer to someone as 'the tall man **with** red hair'.

Who's that girl <u>with the gold earrings?</u>
Our house is the one <u>with the blue shutters</u>.

You don't usually use 'with' to mention what someone is wearing. Instead you use **in**.

I noticed a smart woman <u>in a green dress</u>.
The office was full of men <u>in suits</u>.

→ See **wear**

---

woman – lady

1 used as a noun

You usually refer to an adult female person as a **woman** /ˈwʊmən/.

His mother was a tall, dark-haired <u>woman</u>.

The plural of **woman** is **women** /ˈwɪmɪn/.

There were men and <u>women</u> working in the fields.

You can use **lady** as a polite way of referring to a woman, especially if the woman is present.

We had a visit from an American <u>lady</u>.
There is a <u>lady</u> here who wants to speak to you.

> ❗ **BE CAREFUL**
>
> It is almost always better to refer to someone as an **old lady** or an **elderly lady**, rather than an 'old woman'.
>
> *I helped an <u>old lady</u> to carry her shopping.*
> *She is an <u>elderly lady</u> living on her own.*

If you are addressing a group of women, you call them **ladies**, not 'women'.

<u>Ladies</u>, could I have your attention, please?
Good evening, <u>ladies</u> and gentlemen.

2 'woman' and 'women' used as modifiers

Woman is sometimes used in front of other nouns.

She said that she would prefer to see a <u>woman doctor</u>.

You use **women** in front of plural nouns, not 'woman'.

<u>Women drivers</u> can get cheaper car insurance.

> **!** **BE CAREFUL**
>
> Normally, you just refer to a female doctor, writer etc as a **doctor** or a **writer**. Only use **woman doctor**, **woman writer** etc if it is necessary to make it clear that you are referring to a woman.

→ See **female – feminine**

wonder

1 basic use

The verb **wonder** is usually used to say that someone thinks about something and tries to guess or understand more about it.

I have been <u>wondering</u> about her strange behaviour.

2 used with *wh*-clauses

Wonder is often used with *wh*-clauses.

I <u>wonder what she looks like</u>.
I <u>wonder which hotel it was</u>.

3 used with 'if' and 'whether'

Wonder is also used with **if** or **whether**. If you **wonder if** something is true, you ask yourself whether it is true.

He <u>wondered if she remembered him</u>.
He was beginning to <u>wonder whether it had really happened</u>.

> **!** **BE CAREFUL**
>
> Don't use a *that*-clause in sentences like these. Don't say, for example, '~~He wondered that she remembered him~~'.

Wonder is sometimes used with **if** to make an invitation.

→ See **Topic** entry **Invitations**

wood

1 'wood'

Wood is the material which forms the trunks and branches of trees, and which is used to make things such as furniture.

He made a shelf out of a piece of <u>wood</u>.
The <u>wood</u> of the window frames was all rotten.

> **!** **BE CAREFUL**
>
> Don't refer to a piece of wood as 'a wood'.

2 'wooden'

You don't usually use 'wood' in front of a noun to say that something is made of wood. Use **wooden**.

She kept their toys in a <u>wooden</u> box.
They were all sitting at a long <u>wooden</u> table.

work

Work can be a verb or a noun.

1 used as a verb

People who **work** have a job which they are paid to do.

You need to save money for when you stop working.
I work in a hotel.

You can use **as** with **work** to say what a person's job is.

Maria works as a nurse.

! BE CAREFUL

You use the progressive *-ing* form of **work** to talk about a temporary job, but simple forms to talk about a permanent job. For example, if you say 'I'm working in London', this suggests that the situation is temporary and you may soon move. If you say 'I work in London', this suggests that London is your permanent place of work.

He was working as a truck driver because his business venture had failed.

2 used as a noun

If you have **work**, you have a job which you are paid to do.

There are many people who can't find work.
The website has information on many different types of work.

When someone has a job, you can say that they are **in work**.

Fewer and fewer people are in work.

When someone does not have a job, you can say that they are **out of work**.

Her father had been out of work for six months.

Work is also used to talk about the place where someone works.

He drives to work by car.
I can't leave work till five.

worse

Worse is the comparative form of **bad** and the usual comparative form of **badly**.

→ See **bad – badly**

worst

Worst is the superlative form of **bad** and the usual superlative form of **badly**.

→ See **bad – badly**

worth

Worth can be a preposition or a noun.

1 used as a preposition

If something is **worth** an amount of money, that is the amount you would get for it if you sold it.

His yacht is <u>worth</u> $1.7 million.
They own a two-bedroom house <u>worth</u> £350,000.

> **!** **BE CAREFUL**
>
> **Worth** is not a verb. Don't say ~~'His yacht worths $1.7 million'~~.

2 used as a noun

You use **worth** as a noun after words like **pounds** or **dollars** to show how much money you would get for an amount of something if you sold it.

I can't believe we're arguing over fifty pence <u>worth</u> of chocolate.
Twelve million pounds <u>worth</u> of gold and jewels were stolen.

Don't talk about the 'worth' of something that someone owns. Don't say, for example, ~~'The worth of his house has greatly increased'~~. You say 'The **value** of his house has greatly increased'.

What will happen to the <u>value</u> of my car?
The <u>value</u> of the land is now over £1 million.

---

would

1 form and pronunciation

Would is a modal. It is used in a number of different ways.

When **would** comes after a pronoun, it is not usually pronounced in full. When you write down what someone says, you usually represent 'would' as **'d** and add it to the end of the pronoun. For example, instead of writing '**I would** like that', you write' **I'd** like that'.

Would has the negative form **would not**. The **not** is not usually pronounced in full. When you write down what someone says, you usually write **wouldn't**. For example, instead of writing 'He **would not** do that', you write 'He **wouldn't** do that'.

2 talking about the past

You can use **would** to talk about something that happened regularly in the past but no longer happens.

We <u>would</u> normally spend the winter in Miami.
She <u>would</u> often hear him singing.

Used to has a similar meaning.

She <u>used to</u> visit them every Sunday.
In the afternoons, I <u>used to</u> read.

However, **used to** can also be used to talk about states and situations that existed in the past but no longer exist. You cannot use 'would' like this. You can say, for example, 'She **used to** work there'. Don't say ~~'She would work there'~~

I <u>used to</u> be quite overweight.

You use **would have** to talk about actions and events that were possible in the past, although they did not in fact happen.

It <u>would have</u> been unfair if we had won.
I <u>would have</u> said yes, but Julia persuaded me to stay at home.

When **would not** is used to talk about something that happened in the past, it means that someone refused to do something.

They just would not believe what we told them.
I asked him to come with me, but he wouldn't.

Would is sometimes used in stories to talk about someone's thoughts about the future.

He thought to himself how wonderful it would taste.
Would he ever be successful?

3 used in conditional sentences

You use **would** in a conditional sentence when you are talking about a situation that you know does not exist. Use **would** in the main clause. In the conditional clause, use the past simple, the past progressive, or **could**.

If I had enough money, I would buy the car.
If he was coming, he would call.
I would work if I could.

! BE CAREFUL

Don't use 'would' in the conditional clause in sentences like these. Don't say, for example, 'If I would have enough money, I would buy the car'.

When you are talking about the past, you use **would have** in a conditional sentence to mention an event that might have happened but did not happen. In this kind of sentence, you use the past perfect in the conditional clause and **would have** in the main clause.

If he had realized, he would have told someone.
If she had not been wearing her seat belt, she would have been killed.

4 used in reported clauses

Would is also used in reported clauses.

He asked if I would answer some questions.
I felt confident that everything would be all right.

→ See **Reporting**

5 requests, orders, and instructions

You can use **would** to make a request.

Would you do something for me?
Would someone carry this?

You can also use **would** to give an order or instruction.

Pour me a cup of coffee, would you?
Would you sit down, please?

→ See **Topic** entry **Requests, orders,** and **instructions**

6 offers and invitations

You can say '**Would you...?**' when you are offering something to someone, or making an invitation.

Would you like a drink?
Would anyone care for some ice cream?

→ See **Topic** entries **Offers, Invitations**

write

1 'write' and 'write down'

When you **write** something or **write** it **down**, you use a pen or pencil to make words, letters, or numbers on a surface. The past tense of **write** is **wrote**. The -ed participle is **written**.

I wrote down what the boy said.
Her name was written on the back of the photograph.

2 writing a letter

When you **write** a letter to someone, you write information or other things in a letter and send it to the person. When you use **write** like this, it has two objects. If the indirect object is a pronoun, it usually goes in front of the direct object.

We wrote them a little note to say thanks.
I wrote him a very nice letter.

If the indirect object is not a pronoun, it usually goes after the direct object, with **to** in front of the indirect object.

I wrote a letter to my sister asking her to come.
She wrote a note to the teacher.

You can also omit the direct object. If you **write to** someone, you write a letter to them.

She wrote to me last summer.
I wrote to the manager and complained.

 American speakers often omit the 'to'.

If there is anything you want, write me.
She wrote me that she was feeling much better.

You can put '**I am writing...**' at the beginning of a letter to introduce the topic you are writing about.

Dear Sir, I am writing to enquire about job opportunities in your organization.

! **BE CAREFUL**

Don't put 'I write...' Don't say, for example, 'I write to enquire about job opportunities'.

Yy

yard

The noun **yard** has two main meanings.

1 measurement

A **yard** is a unit of length in the imperial system of measurement. It is equal to thirty-six inches, or approximately 91.4 centimetres.

Jack was standing about ten <u>yards</u> away.

In Britain it is becoming more common to give measurements in metres, rather than yards.

→ See **Reference** section **Measurements**

2 area around a house

 In both British and American English, a **yard** is an area of ground attached to a house. In British English, it is a small area behind a house, with a hard surface and usually a wall round it. In American English, it is an area on any side of a house, usually with grass growing on it. In British English, a fairly large area like this is called a **garden** or **back garden**.

year

A **year** is a period of 365 or 366 days, beginning on the first day of January and ending on the last day of December.

We had an election last <u>year</u>.

A **year** is also any period of twelve months.

The school has been empty for ten <u>years</u>.

You can use **year** when you are mentioning the age of a person or thing.

She is now <u>seventy-four years old</u>.
My house is <u>about 300 years old</u>.

! BE CAREFUL

When you use **year** to talk about age, you must use **old** after it. Don't say, for example, 'She is now seventy-four years'.

→ See **Topic** entry **Age**

→ See **old**

yes

You use **yes** to agree with someone, to say that something is true, or to accept something.

'We need to talk.' – '<u>Yes</u>, you're right.'
'Is that true?' – '<u>Yes</u>.'
'Tea?' – '<u>Yes</u>, thanks.'

> ⚠️ **BE CAREFUL**
>
> When someone asks a negative question, you must say **yes** if you want to give a positive answer. For example, if someone says 'Aren't you going out this evening?', you say '**Yes**, I am'. Don't say 'No, I am'. Similarly, if someone says 'Haven't you met John?', you say, '**Yes**, I have'.
>
> *'Haven't you got any clothes with you?' – 'Yes, in that suitcase.'*
> *'Didn't you buy him a present?' – 'Yes, I did.'*
>
> Similarly, you say **yes** if you want to disagree with a negative statement. For example, if someone says 'He doesn't want to come', you can say '**Yes**, he does'. Don't say 'No, he does'.
>
> *'That isn't true.' – 'Oh yes, it is.'*

---

yesterday

Yesterday means the day before today.

It was hot yesterday.
We spent yesterday in Glasgow.

You refer to the morning and afternoon of the day before today as **yesterday morning** and **yesterday afternoon**.

Yesterday morning I went for a run.
Heavy rain fell here yesterday afternoon.

You can also talk about **yesterday evening**, but it is more common to refer to the previous evening as **last night**.

I met your husband last night.
I've been thinking about what you said last night.

You can also use **last night** to refer to the previous night.

We left our bedroom window open last night.

> ⚠️ **BE CAREFUL**
>
> Don't talk about 'yesterday night'.

---

yet

1 used in negative sentences

You use **yet** in negative sentences to say that something has not happened up to the present time, although it probably will happen. In conversation and in less formal writing, you usually put **yet** at the end of a clause.

It isn't dark yet.
I haven't decided yet.

In formal writing, you can put **yet** immediately after **not**.

Computer technology has not yet reached its peak.
They have not yet set a date for the election.

2 'have yet to'

Instead of saying that something 'has not yet happened', you can say that it **has yet to happen**. People often use this structure to show that they do not expect something to happen.

I have yet to meet a man I can trust.
Whether it will be a success has yet to be seen.

3 used in questions

You often use **yet** in questions when you are asking if something has happened. You put **yet** at the end of the clause.

Have you done that yet?
Have you had your lunch yet?

 Many American speakers and some British speakers use the past simple in questions like these. They say, for example, '**Did** you **have** your lunch yet?'

4 'already'

Don't confuse **yet** with **already**. You use **already** at the end of a question to express surprise that something has happened sooner than expected.

Is he there already?
You mean you've been there already?

→ See **already**

5 'still'

Don't use 'yet' to say that something is continuing to happen. Don't say, for example, '~~I am yet waiting for my luggage~~'. The word you use is **still**.

He still doesn't understand.
Brian's toe is still badly swollen.

→ See **still**

6 'just yet'

If you don't intend to do something **just yet**, you don't intend to do it immediately.

It is too risky to announce an increase in our charges just yet.
I'm not ready to retire just yet.

you

You use **you** to refer to the person or people that you are speaking or writing to. **You** can be the subject or object of a verb, or the object of a preposition.

Have you got any money?
I have nothing to give you.
I want to come with you.

If you want to make it clear that you are talking to more than one person, you can use a phrase such as **you two**, **you all**, **both of you**, or **you guys**. These phrases can be the subject or object of a verb, or the object of a preposition. **You guys** is informal.

As you all know, this is a challenge.
You guys have helped me so much!
I'd like to invite both of you for dinner on Saturday.
I need to talk to you two.

You guys and **you two** can be used as vocatives.

Hey! You guys! Come over here!
Don't stay up late, you two.

→ See **Topic** entry **Addressing someone**

You can also be used to refer to people in general, rather than to a particular person or group. **You** is often used like this in this book.

→ See **one – you – we – they**

your – you're

1 'your'

You use **your** /jə/ or /jɔː/ to show that something belongs or relates to the person or people that you are speaking to.

Can I borrow your pen?
Where's your father?

2 'you're'

You are is also sometimes pronounced /jɔː/. When you write down what someone says, you write this as **you're**. Don't write it as 'your'.

You're quite right.
You're not an expert.

yourself – yourselves

When **you** is the subject of a verb and refers to one person, you use **yourself** as the object of the verb or of a preposition in the clause to refer to the same person.

Are you feeding yourself properly?
You're making a fool of yourself.

When **you** refers to more than one person, you use **yourselves** as the object of the verb or preposition.

I hope you both behaved yourselves.
Are you looking after yourselves?

Yourself and **yourselves** are often used in imperative structures.

Control yourself.
Please help yourselves to another drink.

Yourself and **yourselves** can also be used to emphasize the subject of a clause.

You don't even know it yourself.
You must sort this out yourselves.

If you do something **yourself**, you do it without any help from anyone else.

Did you write this yourself?

When you are using **you** to refer to people in general, the reflexive form is **yourself**, not 'yourselves'.

If you find yourself in debt you must start dealing with it immediately.

Zz

zero

Zero is the number 0.

Visibility dropped to <u>zero</u>.
Participants rated the products on a scale of <u>zero</u> to five.

In conversation, British speakers often say **nought** or **oh** instead of 'zero'.

How good was the hotel, on a scale of <u>nought</u> to ten?
You arrive at Palma at <u>oh</u> two thirty-five.

American speakers usually use **zero**, in both conversation and writing.

The group is for infants between <u>zero</u> and three.

→ See **Reference** section **Numbers and fractions**

TOPICS

TOPICS

Section A: Subject areas

Age

> 1 asking about age
> 2 exact age
> 3 approximate age
> 4 similar ages
> 5 age when something happens
> 6 showing the age of a thing

1 asking about age

When you want to ask about the age of a person or thing, you use **How old** and the verb **be**.

'How old are you?' – 'Thirteen.'
'How old is he?' – 'About sixty-five.'
'How old's your house?' – 'I think it was built about 1950.'

There are several ways in which you can say how old someone or something is. You can be exact, or you can be less precise and show their approximate age.

2 exact age

When you want to say how old someone is, you use the verb **be** followed by a number.

I was nineteen, and he was twenty-one.
I'm only 63.

You can put **years old** after the number if you want to be more emphatic.

She is twenty-five years old.

You can also put **years of age** after the number, but this is more formal and is more usual in written English.

He is 28 years of age.

> **!** **BE CAREFUL**
>
> Don't use 'have' to talk about age. For example, don't say ~~'He has thirteen years'~~.
> You say 'He **is thirteen**' or 'He **is thirteen years old**'.

 When you are mentioning someone, you can show their exact age using **of** or **aged**, or, in American English, **age** after the noun that refers to them, followed by a number.

...a man of thirty.
...two little boys aged nine and eleven.
They have twin daughters, age 18.

You can also mention someone's age using a compound adjective in front of a noun. For example, you can refer to a **five-year-old** boy. Note that the noun referring to the period of time, such as **year**, is always singular, even though it comes after a number. The compound adjective is usually hyphenated.

...a twenty-two-year-old student.
...a five-month-old baby.

You can also refer to someone using a compound noun such as **ten-year-old**.

All the six-year-olds are taught by one teacher.
...Melvin Kalkhoven, a tall, thin thirty-five-year-old.

3 approximate age

If you are not sure exactly how old someone is, or you do not want to state their exact age, you can use the verb **be** followed by **about**, **almost**, **nearly**, **over**, or **under**, and a number.

I think he's about 60.
He must be nearly thirty.
She was only a little over forty years old.
There weren't enough people who were under 25.

You can also use a number with the suffix '**-ish**' to give an approximate age.

The nurse was fiftyish.

You can also use **above the age of** or **below the age of** followed by a number. This is more formal.

55 percent of them were below the age of twenty-one.

You can show that someone's age is between 20 and 29 by saying '**He's in his twenties**' or '**She's in her twenties**'. You can use **thirties**, **forties**, and so on in the same way. People aged 13 to 19 are said to be **in their teens**.

Note that you use **in** and a possessive determiner in these structures.

He was in his sixties.
...when I was in my teens.

Another way of showing approximate age is to use **something** after a number that ends in zero.

A table of thirty-something guys.
She was twenty-something.

You can use **early**, **mid-**, **middle**, or **late** to show approximately where someone's age comes in a particular ten-year period (or eight-year period in the case of 'teens').

Jane is only in her early forties.
She was in her mid-twenties.
He was then in his late seventies.

You can put most of the above structures after a noun such as **man** or **woman** to show someone's approximate age.

They provide help for ladies over 65.
She had four children under the age of five.
...a woman in her early thirties.

Don't use **about**, **almost**, or **nearly** immediately after a noun. For example, don't say '~~He is a man about 60~~'. Say 'He is a man **of** about 60'.

 In British English, you can refer to a group of people whose age is more or less than a particular number using a compound noun which consists of **over** or **under** followed by the plural form of the number. This usage is understood but not used in American English.

The over-sixties do not want to be turned out of their homes.
Schooling for the under-fives should be expanded.

4 similar ages

If you want to show that someone's age is similar to someone else's, you can use the verb **be** followed by expressions such as **my age**, **his own age**, and **her parents' age**.

I wasn't allowed to do that when I was her age.
He guessed the policeman was about his own age.

To show the age of a person you are mentioning, you can use these expressions after the noun which refers to the person, or after the noun and **of**.

I know a bit more literature than <u>most girls my age</u>.
It's easy to make friends because you're with <u>people of your own age</u>.

5 age when something happens

There are several ways of showing how old someone was when something happened.

You can use a clause beginning with **when**.

I left school <u>when I was thirteen</u>.
Even <u>when I was a child</u> I was frightened of her.

You can use **at the age of** or **at**, followed by a number showing the person's age.

She had finished college <u>at the age of 20</u>.
All they want to do is leave school <u>at sixteen</u> and get a job.

Aged followed by a number is also used, mainly in writing, especially when talking about someone's death.

Her husband died three days ago, <u>aged only forty-five</u>.

As is used with a noun phrase such as **a girl** or **a young man** to show that someone did something when they were young. This structure occurs mainly in writing.

She suffered from bronchitis <u>as a child</u>.
<u>As teenagers</u> we used to stroll round London during lunchtime.

If you want to show that someone does something before they reach a particular age, you can say that they do it, for example, **before the age of four** or **by the age of four**.

He maintained that children are not ready to read <u>before the age of six</u>.
It set out the things he wanted to achieve <u>by the age of 31</u>.

If you want to show that someone does something after they reach a particular age, you can say that they do it, for example, **after the age of four**.

<u>After the age of five</u>, your child will be at school full time.

6 showing the age of a thing

If you want to say how old something is, you use the verb **be** followed by a number, followed by **years old**.

Most of the coral is some <u>2 million years old</u>.
The house <u>was about thirty years old</u>.

! BE CAREFUL

You can't just use 'be' and a number, as you can when stating the age of a person. Don't say, for example, '~~The house was about thirty~~'.

The usual way of showing the age of something you are mentioning is to use a compound adjective in front of the noun referring to it. For example, you can refer to a **thirty-year-old** house. As with compound adjectives showing the age of a person, the noun **year** is always singular and the adjective is usually hyphenated.

...a rattling, <u>ten-year-old</u> car.
...a violation of a <u>six-year-old</u> agreement.

You can also use a number, especially a large number, and **years old** after a noun referring to a thing.

They found rocks <u>200 million years old</u>.

You can show the approximate age of something by using an adjective that shows the period in history in which it existed or was made.

...a splendid <u>Victorian</u> building.
...a <u>medieval</u> castle.

You can show the century when something existed or was made by using a modifier consisting of an ordinal number and **century**.

...a <u>sixth-century</u> church.
...life in <u>fifth-century</u> Athens.

Meals

1 'breakfast'	**6** 'for' and 'to'
2 'dinner', 'lunch'	**7** 'have'
3 'tea' and 'supper'	**8** 'make'
4 more formal terms	**9** 'a' with meals
5 'at' and 'over'	**10** meal times

The meanings of words referring to meals, and the ways that these words are used, are explained below. Some words for meals are used by different people to refer to different meals.

1 'breakfast'

Breakfast is the first meal of the day. You eat it in the morning, just after you get up.

I always have cereal for <u>breakfast</u>.

2 'dinner', 'lunch', and 'luncheon'

Dinner, for most people, is the name of the main evening meal. However, in some regions, the word **dinner** is used for the meal people have in the middle of the day. These people call their evening meal **tea** or **supper**, depending on where they come from.

People who call their evening meal **dinner** usually refer to a meal eaten in the middle of the day as **lunch**.

We went out for <u>dinner</u> on Tuesday night.
Workers started at 9am and finished at 5pm with an hour for <u>lunch</u>.

3 'tea' and 'supper'

Tea can be a light meal eaten in the afternoon, usually consisting of sandwiches and cakes, with tea to drink. The expression **afternoon tea** is often used in hotels and restaurants.

I invited him for <u>tea</u> that afternoon.
Traditional <u>afternoon tea</u> is served.

Tea can also be a main meal that is eaten in the early evening.

Katie had some friends round for <u>tea</u> after school.

 'Tea' is not used to talk about meals in American English.

Some people call a large meal they eat in the early part of the evening **supper**. Other people use **supper** to refer to a small meal eaten just before going to bed at night.

We had eaten a light <u>supper</u> at six.
I had some toast for <u>supper</u>, then went to bed.

4 more formal terms

You can refer to a meal that you eat in the middle of the day as a **midday meal**.
Similarly, you can refer to a meal that you eat in the evening as an **evening meal**.
However, these terms are not normally used in conversation to refer to meals eaten at
home, only to meals provided for you, for example at school or in a hotel.

5 'at' and 'over'

You show that someone does something while they are having a meal using the
preposition **at**.

He had told her at lunch that he couldn't take her to the game tomorrow.
Isaac sat next to me at dinner.

However, you usually use **over** when talking about an event that takes some time,
especially when saying that people discuss something while having a meal.

It's often easier to discuss difficult ideas over lunch.
He said he wanted to reread it over lunch.

6 'for' and 'to'

When you talk about what a meal consists of, you say what you have **for** breakfast,
lunch, and so on.

They had hard-boiled eggs for breakfast.
What's for dinner?

When you invite someone to have a meal with you, for example at your house, you say
that you ask them **for** the meal or **to** the meal.

Why don't you join me and the girls for lunch, Mr Jordache?
Stanley invited me to lunch on Sunday.

7 'have'

You often use **have** to say that someone eats a meal. You can say, for example, that
someone **has breakfast** or **has their breakfast**.

When we've had breakfast, you can phone for a taxi.
That Tuesday, Lo had her dinner in her room.

! BE CAREFUL

Don't say that someone 'has a breakfast' or 'has the breakfast'.

8 'make'

When someone prepares a meal, you can say, for example, that they **make breakfast**,
make the breakfast, or **make their breakfast**.

I'll go and make dinner.
He makes the breakfast every morning.
She had been making her lunch when he arrived.

! BE CAREFUL

Don't that someone 'makes a breakfast'.

9 'a' with meals

Words referring to meals can be used either as uncountable nouns or as countable
nouns. However, these words are not generally used with 'a'. For example, don't say
'I had a lunch with Deborah' or 'I had a dinner early'. You say 'I had **lunch** with Deborah'
or 'I had **dinner** early'. You can, however, use **a** when you are describing a meal.

They had a quiet dinner together.
He was a big man and needed a big breakfast.

🔟 meal times

When you want to refer to the period of the day when a particular meal is eaten, you can use a compound noun consisting of a word referring to a meal and the word **time**. The compound noun can be hyphenated or written as two separate words.

I shall be back by dinner-time.
It was almost lunch time.

 The forms **dinnertime**, **lunchtime**, **suppertime**, and **teatime** are also used, and are preferred in American English. **Breakfast time** is never written as one word.

He had a great deal to do before lunchtime.

Money

1️⃣ writing amounts of money	5️⃣ expressing a rate
2️⃣ saying amounts of money	6️⃣ expressing quantity by cost
3️⃣ asking and stating the cost of something	7️⃣ American currency
4️⃣ notes and coins	8️⃣ other currencies

British currency consists of **pounds** and **pence**. There are a hundred pence in a pound.

1️⃣ writing amounts of money

When you write amounts of money in figures, the pound symbol **£** is shown in front of the figures. For example, **two hundred pounds** is written as **£200**. **Million** is sometimes abbreviated to **m**, and **billion** to **bn**. **k** and **K** are sometimes used as abbreviations for **thousand** when people's salaries are being mentioned.

About £20m was invested in the effort.
...revenues of £6bn.
...Market Manager, £30K + bonus + car.

If an amount of money consists only of pence, you put the letter **p** after the figures. For example, **fifty pence** is written as **50p**.

If an amount of money consists of both pounds and pence, you write the pound symbol and separate the pounds and the pence with a full stop. Don't write 'p' after the pence. For example, 'two pounds fifty pence' is written as **£2.50**.

2️⃣ saying amounts of money

When saying aloud an amount of money that consists only of pence, you say the word **pence** or the letter **p** (pronounced like 'pea') after the number.

When saying aloud an amount of money that consists of pounds and pence, you don't usually say the word 'pence'. For example, you say **two pounds fifty**.

❗ BE CAREFUL

 In conversation, people sometimes say **pound** not 'pounds'. For example, they say 'I get ten **pound** a week'. However, many people regard this as incorrect, so you should say **pounds**.

TOPICS

The words 'pounds' and 'pence' are often left out when it is clear which you are referring to.

At the moment they're paying £2 for their meal, and it costs us three.
'I've come to pay an account.' – 'All right then, fine, that's four seventy-eight sixty then, please.'

In informal speech, **quid** is often used instead of 'pound' or 'pounds'.

'How much did you have to pay?' – 'Eight quid.'

3 asking and stating the cost of something

When you ask or state the cost of something, you use the verb **be**. You begin a question about cost with **How much...**.

How much is that?
The cheapest is about eight pounds.

You can also use the verb **cost**. This is slightly more formal.

How much will it cost?
They cost several hundred pounds.

You can mention the person buying something by adding a pronoun or other noun phrase after **cost**.

It would cost me around six hundred.

4 notes and coins

You use **notes** to refer to paper money. In British currency, there are notes worth five, ten, twenty, and fifty pounds.

You didn't have a five-pound note, did you?
Several paid on the spot in notes.

! BE CAREFUL

Don't say 'a five-pounds note'.

You use **coins** to refer to metal money. In British currency, there are coins worth one, two, five, ten, twenty, and fifty pence, one pound, and two pounds.

You should make sure that you have a ready supply of coins for making phone calls.

If you want to refer to a coin that is worth a particular amount, you usually use the word **piece**.

That fifty pence piece has been there all day.
The machine wouldn't take 10p pieces.

You can refer to coins that you have with you as **change**.

He rattled the loose change in his pocket.

5 expressing a rate

When you want to express the rate at which money is spent or received, you use **a** or **per** after the amount. **Per** is more formal.

He gets £180 a week.
Farmers spend more than half a billion pounds per year on pesticides.

Per annum is sometimes used instead of 'per year'.

...staff earning less than £11,500 per annum.

6 expressing quantity by cost

You can talk about a quantity of something by saying how much it costs using **worth of**.

He owns some 20 million pounds worth of property in Mayfair.

7 American currency

American currency consists of **dollars** and **cents**. There are a hundred cents in a dollar. Americans use the word **bill** to refer to paper money. There are bills worth one, two, five, ten, twenty, fifty, and a hundred dollars. Bills larger than this are used only between banks.

Ellen put a five-dollar <u>bill</u> and three ones on the counter.

There are coins worth one, five, ten, twenty-five and fifty cents. These are often referred to by the special words **penny**, **nickel**, **dime**, **quarter**, and **half-dollar**.

I only had a dollar bill, a <u>quarter</u>, two <u>dimes</u> and a <u>nickel</u>, and three <u>pennies</u>.

In informal speech, **buck** is often used instead of 'dollar'.

I got 500 <u>bucks</u> for it.

When writing amounts of money, you use the dollar symbol **$**, or **c** for cents. For example, **two hundred dollars** is written as **$200**, **fifty cents** is written as **50c**, and **two dollars fifty cents** is written as **$2.50**.

When saying aloud an amount of money that consists of dollars and cents, you don't usually say the word 'cents'. For example, you say **two dollars fifty** or simply **two fifty**.

8 other currencies

Many countries use the same units for their currencies. If you need to show clearly which country's currency you are talking about, you use a nationality adjective.

...a contract worth 200 million <u>Canadian dollars</u>.
It cost me about thirteen hundred <u>Swiss francs</u>.

Note that some currencies have some units in common, but also have some different units. For example, Britain uses **pounds** and **pence**, but Egypt uses **pounds** and **piastres**.

When talking about exchange rates, you say how many units of one currency there are **to the** other unit of currency.

The rate of exchange while I was there was 1.10 euros <u>to the</u> pound.

Names and titles

1 kinds of names	**8** referring to a family
2 short forms	**9** using a determiner with names
3 nicknames	**10** titles
4 spelling	**11** titles of relatives
5 initials	**12** titles before 'of'
6 referring to someone	**13** very formal titles
7 referring to relatives	

This entry gives basic information about names and titles, and explains how you use them when talking or writing about people.

You also use a person's name or title when you talk or write to them.

→ See **Topic** entries **Addressing someone**, **Letter writing**, **Emailing**

1 kinds of names

People in English-speaking countries have a **first name** (also called a **given name**), which is chosen by their parents, and a **surname** (also called a **family name** or **last name**), which is the last name of their parents or one of their parents.

Many people also have a **middle name**, which is also chosen by their parents. This name is not generally used in full, but the initial (first letter) is sometimes given, especially in the United States.

...the assassination of John F. Kennedy.

Christians use the term **Christian name** to refer to the names they choose for their children. On official forms, the term **first name** or **forename** is used.

→ See **Usage** entry **first name – forename – given name – Christian name**

In the past, married women always used their husband's surname. Nowadays, some women continue to use their own surname after getting married.

2 short forms

People often use an informal and usually shorter form of someone's first name, especially in conversation. Many names have traditional short forms. For example, if someone's first name is **James**, people may call him **Jim** or **Jimmy**.

3 nicknames

Sometimes a person's friends invent a name for him or her, for example a name that describes them in some way, such as **Lofty** (meaning 'tall'). This kind of name is called a **nickname**.

4 spelling

People's names begin with a capital letter.

...John Bacon.
...Jenny.
...Dr. Smith.

In names beginning with **Mac**, **Mc**, or **O'**, the next letter is often a capital.

...Maggie McDonald.
... Mr Manus O'Riordan.

In Britain, some people's surnames consist of two names joined by a hyphen or written separately.

...John Heath-Stubbs.
...Ralph Vaughan Williams.

5 initials

Someone's **initials** are the capital letters that begin their first name, middle name, and surname, or just their first name and middle name. For example, if someone's full name is 'Elizabeth Margaret White', you can say that her initials are **EMW**, or that her surname is 'White' and her initials are **EM**. Sometimes a dot is put after each initial: **E.M.W.**

6 referring to someone

When you refer to someone, you use their first name if the person you are talking to knows who you mean.

John and I have discussed the situation.
Have you seen Sarah?

If you need to make it clear who you are referring to, or do not know them well, you usually use both their first name and their surname.

If Matthew Davis is unsatisfactory, I shall try Sam Billings.

You use their **title** and their surname if you do not know them as a friend and want to be polite. People also sometimes refer to people much older than themselves in this more polite way.

Mr Nichols can see you now.
We'd better not let Mrs Townsend know.

Information on **titles** is given later in this entry.

You don't generally use someone's title and full name in conversation. However, people are sometimes referred to in this way in broadcasting and formal writing.

The machine was developed by Professor Jonathan Allen at the Massachusetts Institute of Technology.

In general, you only use someone's initials and surname in writing, not in conversation. However, some well-known people (especially writers) are known by their initials rather than their first name, for example **T.S. Eliot** and **J.G. Ballard**.

You can refer to famous writers, composers, and artists using just their surname.

...the works of Shakespeare.

7 referring to relatives

Nouns such as **father**, **mum**, **grandpa**, and **granny**, which refer to your parents or grandparents, are also used as names. When they are used as names, they are written with a capital letter.

Mum will be pleased.
You can stay with Grandma and Grandpa.

8 referring to a family

You can refer to a family or a married couple with the same surname by using **the** and the plural form of that name.

...some friends of hers called the Hochstadts.

9 using a determiner with names

When you use a person's name, you usually use it without a determiner. However, in formal or business situations, you can put **a** in front of someone's name when you do not know them or have not heard of them before.

You don't know a Mrs Burton-Cox, do you?

You can check that someone actually means a well-known person, or simply express surprise, using **the** /ðiː/ emphatically.

You actually met the George Harrison?

10 titles

A person's **title** shows their social status or job.

You use a person's title and surname, or their title, first name, and surname, as explained above. The titles that are most commonly used are **Mr** for a man, **Mrs** for a married woman, and **Miss** for an unmarried woman. **Ms** /məz/ or /mɪz/ can be used for both married and unmarried women. The following titles are also used in front of someone's surname, or first name and surname:

Ambassador	Cardinal	Imam	Professor
Archbishop	Congressman	Inspector	Rabbi
Archdeacon	Constable	Judge	Representative
Baron	Councillor	Justice	Senator
Baroness	Doctor	Nurse	Superintendent
Bishop	Father	Police Constable	
Canon	Governor	President	

I was interviewed by Inspector Flint.
...representatives of President Anatolijs Gorbunovs of Latvia.

Titles showing rank in the armed forces, such as **Captain** and **Sergeant**, are also used in front of someone's surname, or first name and surname.

General Haven-Hurst wanted to know what you planned to do.
...his nephew and heir, Colonel Richard Airey.

11 titles of relatives

The only words that are generally used in modern English in front of names when referring to relatives are **Uncle**, **Aunt**, **Auntie**, **Great Uncle**, and **Great Aunt**. You use them in front of the person's first name. People who have two living grandmothers or grandfathers may distinguish them by using a name after them.

...Aunt Jane.
She's named after my granny Kathryn.

Father is used as the title of a priest, **Brother** as the title of a monk, and **Mother** or **Sister** as the title of a nun, but these words are not used in front of the names of relatives.

Mother Teresa spent her life caring for the poor.
Sister Joseann is from a large Catholic family.

12 titles before 'of'

A title can sometimes be followed by **of** to show what place, organization, or part of an organization the person with the title has authority over.

...the President of the United States.
...the Prince of Wales.
...the Bishop of Birmingham.

The following titles can be used after **the** and in front of **of**:

Archbishop	Duke	Marchioness	Prince
Bishop	Earl	Marquis	Princess
Chief Constable	Emperor	Mayor	Queen
Countess	Empress	Mayoress	
Dean	Governor	President	
Duchess	King	Prime Minister	

13 very formal titles

When you refer formally to someone important such as a king or queen, an ambassador, or a judge, you use a title consisting of a possessive determiner in front of a noun. For example, if you want to refer to the Queen, you can say **Her Majesty the Queen** or **Her Majesty**. The possessive determiner is usually spelled with a capital letter.

Her Majesty must do an enormous amount of travelling each year.
His Excellency is occupied.

Pieces and amounts

1 substances		**4** typical pieces and amounts	
2 liquids		**5** measurements and containers	
3 food			

There are many words which are used in front of **of** and an uncountable noun to refer to a piece of something or a particular amount of something. The most common words are given here.

1 substances

Some words can be used to refer to a piece or amount of many kinds of substance:

atom	fragment	piece	sliver
ball	heap	pile	speck
bit	hunk	pinch	splinter
block	lump	ring	stick
chunk	mass	roll	strip
crumb	molecule	scrap	trace
dab	mound	sheet	tuft
dash	mountain	shred	wad
dollop	patch	slab	wedge
flake	particle	slice	wodge

She threw another bit of wood into the fire.
The soup was delicious, with lumps of chicken, and chunks of potato and cabbage.

2 liquids

Some words are used to refer to an amount of a liquid:

dash	globule	puddle	trickle
dribble	jet	splash	
drop	pool	spot	

Rub a drop of vinegar into the spot where you were stung.
One fireman was kneeling down in a great pool of oil.

3 food

Helping, **portion**, and **serving** are used when talking about the amount of a particular kind of food that you are given at a meal.

He had two helpings of ice-cream.
I chose a large portion of local salmon.

You can refer to a very small piece of food as a **morsel** of food.

He had a morsel of food caught between one tooth and another.

TOPICS

TOPICS

4 typical pieces and amounts

The following table shows you which word is typically used to refer to a piece or amount of something of a particular kind. Where more than one word is given, the meanings are often very different. Use a COBUILD dictionary if you are unsure of the differences.

bread	a loaf/slice of bread
butter	a knob (British)/pat (American) of butter
cake	a slice/piece of cake
chocolate	a bar/piece/square of chocolate
cloth	a bolt/length/piece of cloth
coal	a lump of coal
corn	an ear/sheaf of corn
dust	a speck/particle/cloud of dust
fog	a wisp/bank/patch of fog
glass	a sliver/splinter/pane of glass
grass	a blade of grass
hair	a lock/strand/wisp/tuft/mop/shock of hair
hay	a bale of hay
land	a piece/area of land
light	a ray/beam/shaft of light
medicine	a dose of medicine
money	a sum of money
paper	a piece/sheet/scrap of paper
rice	a grain of rice
rope	a coil/length/piece of rope
salt	a grain/pinch of salt
sand	a grain of sand
smoke	a cloud/blanket/column/puff/wisp of smoke
snow	a flake/blanket of snow
soap	a bar/cake of soap
stone	a slab/block of stone
string	a ball/piece/length of string
sugar	a grain/lump of sugar
sweat	a bead/drop/trickle of sweat
thread	a reel/strand of thread
wheat	a grain/sheaf of wheat
wire	a strand/piece/length of wire
wool	a ball of wool

5 measurements and containers

You can also refer to an amount of something using a measurement noun such as **pound** or **metre**, or a noun referring to a container such as **bottle** or **box**.

→ See **Reference** section **Measurements**

Places

1	asking about someone's home	**7**	used after nouns
2	place names	**8**	prepositions with parts and areas
3	modifier use	**9**	adverbs: position
4	adverbials	**10**	adverbs: direction or destination
5	prepositions: position	**11**	used after nouns
6	prepositions: destination and direction	**12**	modifier use
		13	indefinite place adverbs

TOPICS

1 asking about someone's home

If you want to know where someone's home is, you say '**Where do you live?**' or '**Whereabouts do you live?**' You use **whereabouts** if you know approximately where they live, and you want more precise information.

'Where do you live?' – 'I have a little studio flat, in Chiswick.'
'I actually live near Chester.' – '<u>*Whereabouts?*</u>*'*

If you want to know where someone spent their early life, you can say '**What part of the country are you from?**' You can also say, '**Where do you come from?**' or '**Where are you from?**', especially if you think they spent their early life in a different country.

'Where do you come from?' – 'India.'

2 place names

Place names such as **Italy** and **Amsterdam** are a type of proper noun and are spelled with a capital letter.

The table on this page and the following page shows ways of referring to different types of places. Those marked with a star are less common.

Continents	proper noun	Africa Asia
Areas and regions	**the** + proper noun	the Arctic the Midlands
	adjective + proper noun	Eastern Europe North London
	the + **North, South, East, West**	the East the South of France
Oceans, seas, deserts	**the** + modifier + **Ocean, Sea, Desert**	the Indian Ocean the Gobi Desert
	the + proper noun	the Pacific the Sahara
Countries	proper noun	France Italy
	*****the** + type of country	the United States the United Kingdom the Netherlands
Counties and states	proper noun	Surrey California
	*****proper noun + **County** (*American*)	Butler County

TOPICS

Islands	proper noun	Malta
	proper noun + **Island**	Easter Island
	the Isle of + proper noun	the Isle of Wight
Groups of islands	**the** + modifier + **Islands/Isles**	the Channel Islands
		the Scilly Isles
	the + plural proper noun	the Bahamas
Mountains	**Mount** + proper noun	Mount Everest
	proper noun	Everest
Mountain ranges	*__the__ + proper noun	the Matterhorn
	the + plural proper noun	the Andes
	the + modifier + **Mountains**	the Rocky Mountains
Rivers	**the** + **River** + proper noun	the River Thames
	the + proper noun	the Thames
	*__the__ + proper noun + **River** (*not British*)	the Colorado River
Lakes	**Lake** + proper noun	Lake Michigan
Capes	**Cape** + proper noun	Cape Horn
	*__the__ + **Cape** + proper noun	the Cape of Good Hope
Other natural places	**the** + modifier + place noun	the Grand Canyon
		the Bering Strait
	modifier + place noun	Sherwood Forest
		Beachy Head
	the + place noun + **of** + proper noun	the Gulf of Mexico
		the Bay of Biscay
Towns	proper noun	London
Buildings and structures	proper noun + place noun	Durham Cathedral
		London Zoo
	the + modifier + place noun	the Severn Bridge
		the Tate Gallery
	the + place noun + **of** + proper noun/ noun	the Church of St. Mary
		the Museum of Modern Art
Cinemas, theatres, pubs, hotels	**the** + proper noun	the Odeon
		the Bull
Railway stations	proper noun	Paddington
	proper noun + **station**	Paddington Station
Streets	modifier + **Road, Street, Drive**, etc	Downing Street
	*__the__ + proper noun	the Strand
	*__the__ + modifier + **Street** or **Road**	the High Street

Most place names are used with a singular verb form. Even place names that look like plural nouns, for example **The United States** and **The Netherlands**, are used with a singular verb form.

Canada still <u>has</u> large natural forests.
Milan <u>is</u> the most interesting city in the world.
...when the United States <u>was</u> prospering.

However, the names of groups of islands or mountains are usually used with a plural verb form.

...one of the tiny Comoro Islands that <u>lie</u> in the Indian Ocean midway between Madagascar and Tanzania.
The Andes <u>split</u> the country down the middle.

The name of a country or its capital city is often used to refer to the government of that country.

<u>Britain</u> and <u>France</u> jointly suggested a plan.
<u>Washington</u> had put a great deal of pressure on <u>Berlin</u>

You can also sometimes use the name of a place to refer to the people who live there. You use a singular verb form even though you are talking about a group of people.

<u>Europe</u> <u>was</u> sick of war.
<u>Poland</u> <u>needs</u> additional imports.

→ See **Reference** section **Nationality words**

Place names can also be used to refer to a well-known event that occurred in that place, such as a battle or a disaster.

After <u>Waterloo</u>, trade and industry surged again.
...the effect of <u>Chernobyl</u> on British agriculture.

3 modifier use

You can use a place name as a modifier to show that something is in a particular place, or that something comes from or is characteristic of a particular place.

...a <u>London</u> hotel.
She has a <u>Midlands</u> accent.

4 adverbials

Many adverbials are used to talk about place.

→ See **Grammar** entry **Adverbs and adverbials** for information on where to put these adverbs and adverbials in a clause

5 prepositions: position

The main prepositions used to show position are **at**, **in**, and **on**.

Sometimes we went to concerts <u>at</u> the Albert Hall.
I am back <u>in</u> Rome.
We sat <u>on</u> the floor.

→ See **Usage** entries **at**, **in**, **on**

→ See **by** for the difference in use between **by** and **near**

Here is a full list of prepositions which are used to show position:

aboard	at	in	over
about	away from	in between	past
above	before	in front of	through
across	behind	inside	throughout
against	below	near	under
ahead of	beneath	near to	underneath
all over	beside	next to	up
along	between	off	upon
alongside	beyond	on	with
amidst (AM amid)	by	on top of	within
among	close by	opposite	
around	close to	out of	
astride	down	outside	

6 prepositions: destination and direction

The main preposition used to show a destination is **to**.

I went to the door.
She went to Australia in 1970.

At is not usually used to show a person's destination. It is used to show what someone is looking towards, or what they cause an object to move towards.

They were staring at a garage roof.
Supporters threw petals at his car.

→ See **Usage** entries **into**, **onto**

Here is a full list of prepositions which are used to show where something goes:

aboard	below	inside	round
about	beneath	into	(AM around)
across	beside	near	through
ahead of	between	near to	to
all over	beyond	off	towards
along	by	on	(AM toward)
alongside	down	onto	under
around	from	out of	underneath
at	in	outside	up
away from	in between	over	
behind	in front of	past	

As you can see from the above lists, many prepositions can be used to show both place and direction.

The bank is just across the High Street.
I walked across the room.
We live in the house over the road.
I stole his keys and escaped over the wall.

7 used after nouns

Prepositional phrases are used after nouns to show the location of the thing or person referred to by the noun.

The table in the kitchen had a tablecloth over it.
The driver behind me began shouting.

8 prepositions with parts and areas

If you want to say explicitly which part of something else an object is nearest to, or exactly which part of an area it is in, you can use **at**, **by**, **in**, **near**, or **on**. **To** and **towards** (**toward** in American English), which are usually used to show direction, are used to express position in a more approximate way.

You use **at**, **near**, and **towards** with the following nouns:

back	centre	foot	side
base	edge	front	top
bottom	end	rear	

She waited at the bottom of the stairs.
The old building of University College is near the top of the street.
He was sitting towards the rear.

You can also use **to** with **rear** and **side**.

Some troops were moved to the rear.
There was one sprinkler in front of the statue and one to the side of it.

You use **on** or **to** with **left** and **right**, and **in** with **middle**. You can also use **on** instead of **at** with **edge**.

The church is on the left and the town hall and police station are on the right.
To the left were the kitchens and staff quarters.
My mother stood in the middle of the road, watching.
He lives on the edge of Sefton Park.

You use **to** or **in** with the following nouns:

east	(AM northeast)	south	south-west
north	north-west	south-east	(AM southwest)
north-east	(AM northwest)	(AM southeast)	west

To the south-west lay the city.
The National Liberation Front forces were still active in the north.

You use **at** or **by** with the following nouns:

bedside	kerbside	quayside	seaside
dockside	(AM curbside)	ringside	waterside
fireside	lakeside	riverside	
graveside	poolside	roadside	

She stood crying at the graveside.
We found him sitting by the fireside.

You generally use **the** with the nouns in the three previous lists.

I ran up the stairs. Wendy was standing at the top.
To the north are the main gardens.

However, you can also use a possessive determiner with the nouns in the first list above (**back**, **base**, etc), and with **left**, **right**, and **bedside**.

We reached another cliff face, with trees and bushes growing at its base.
There was a gate on our left leading into a field.
I was at his bedside when he died.

In front of and **on top of** are fixed phrases, without a determiner.

She stood in front of the mirror.
I fell on top of him.

9 adverbs: position

There are many adverbs that show position. Many of these show that something is near a place, object, or person that has already been mentioned.

Seagulls were circling overhead.
Nearby, there is another restaurant.
This information is summarized below.

Here is a list of the main adverbs which are used to show position:

aboard	ahead	away	beside
about	aloft	behind	beyond
above	alongside	below	close by
abroad	ashore	beneath	close to

down	inside	outside	underground
downstairs	near	over	underneath
downstream	nearby	overhead	underwater
downwind	next door	overseas	up
here	off	round	upstairs
in	offshore	(AM around)	upstream
in between	opposite	there	upwind
indoors	out of doors	throughout	
inland	outdoors	underfoot	

A small group of adverbs of position are used to show how wide an area something exists in:

globally	locally	nationally	widely
internationally	regionally	universally	worldwide

Everything we used was bought <u>locally</u>.
Western culture was not <u>universally</u> accepted.

Unlike most other adverbs of position, these adverbs (with the exception of **worldwide**) can't be used after 'be' to state the position of something.

The adverbs **deep**, **far**, **high**, and **low**, which show distance as well as position, are usually followed by another adverb or phrase showing position, or are modified or qualified in some other way.

Many of the eggs remain buried <u>deep among the sand grains</u>.
One plane, flying <u>very low</u>, swept back and forth.

Deep down, **far away**, **high up**, and **low down** are often used instead of the adverbs on their own.

The window was <u>high up</u>, miles above the rocks.
Sita scraped a shallow cavity <u>low down</u> in the wall.

10 adverbs: direction or destination

There are also many adverbs which show direction or destination.

They went <u>downstairs</u> hand in hand.
Go <u>north</u> from Leicester Square up Wardour Street.
She walked <u>away</u>.

Here is a list of the main ones:

aboard	downtown	near	south
abroad	downwards	next door	southwards
ahead	east	north	there
along	eastwards	northwards	underground
anti-clockwise	forwards	on	up
(AM counter-	heavenward	onward	upstairs
clockwise)	here	out of doors	uptown
around	home	outdoors	upwards
ashore	homeward	outside	west
back	in	overseas	westwards
backwards	indoors	right	
clockwise	inland	round	
close	inside	(AM around)	
down	inwards	sideways	
downstairs	left	skyward	

Note that American English normally uses a form of these adverbs ending in **'-ward'** where British speakers use the form ending in **'-wards'**.

You move forward and backward by leaning slightly in those directions.
We were drifting backwards and forwards.

→ See **Usage** entry **-ward – -wards**

11 used after nouns

Place adverbs can be used after nouns to give more information.

The stream runs through the sand to the ocean beyond.
My suitcase had become damaged on the journey home.

12 modifier use

Some place adverbs can be used in front of nouns as modifiers.

Gradually the underground caverns fill up with deposits.
There will be some variations in your heart rate as you encounter uphill stretches or increase your pace on downhill sections.

The following place adverbs can be used as modifiers:

anti-clockwise (AM counter-clockwise)	downstairs	outside	uphill
	eastward	overhead	upstairs
	inland	overseas	westward
backward	inside	southward	
clockwise	nearby	underground	
downhill	northward	underwater	

13 indefinite place adverbs

There are four indefinite adverbs of position and direction: **anywhere**, **everywhere**, **nowhere**, and **somewhere**.

 In informal American English **someplace** and **anyplace** are also used, as well as **no place** and **every place**.

No-one can find Howard or Barbara anywhere.
There were bicycles everywhere.
I thought I'd seen you somewhere.
I suggested they stay someplace else.

→ See **Usage** entry **somewhere**

Nowhere makes a clause negative.

I was to go nowhere without an escort.

In writing, you can put **nowhere** at the beginning of a clause for emphasis. You put the subject of the verb after an auxiliary or a form of **be**.

Nowhere have I seen any serious mention of this.
Nowhere are they overwhelmingly numerous.

You can put a *to*-infinitive clause after **anywhere**, **somewhere**, or **nowhere** to show what you want to do in a place.

I couldn't find anywhere to put it.
We mentioned that we were looking for somewhere to live.
There was nowhere for us to go.

You can also put a relative clause after these adverbs. You don't usually use a relative pronoun.

I could go anywhere I wanted.
Everywhere I went, people were angry or suspicious.

You can use **else** after an indefinite place adverb to show a different or additional place.

We could hold the meeting somewhere else.
More people die in bed than anywhere else.

Elsewhere can be used instead of 'somewhere else' or 'in other places'.

It was obvious that he would rather be elsewhere.
Elsewhere in the tropics, rainfall is variable.

Time

1 clock times	**5** adverbs showing time
2 prepositions showing time	**6** times as modifiers
3 approximate times	**7** time adverbials after nouns
4 periods of the day	

→ See **Reference** section **Days and dates** for information on referring to days and longer periods of time

→ See **Grammar** entry **Subordinate clauses** for information on time clauses

1 clock times

When you want to know the time at the moment you are speaking, you say '**What time is it?**' or '**What's the time?**'

'What time is it?' – 'Three minutes past five.'
'What's the time now?' – 'Twenty past.'

When asking about the time of an event, you usually use **when**.

'When did you come?' – 'Just after lunch.'

You can also use '**What time**'.

'What time did you get back to London?' – 'Ten o'clock.'
'What time do they shut?' – 'Half past five.'

When you tell someone the time, you say '**It's...**'.

It's ten to eleven now.

The table opposite shows different ways of referring to times.

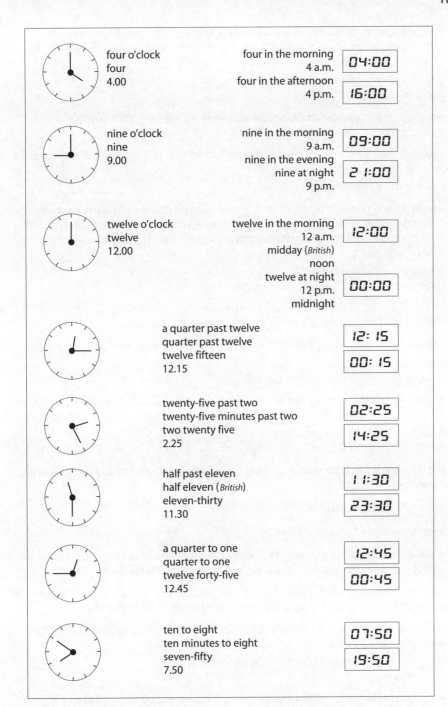

	four o'clock four 4.00	four in the morning 4 a.m.	`04:00`
		four in the afternoon 4 p.m.	`16:00`
	nine o'clock nine 9.00	nine in the morning 9 a.m.	`09:00`
		nine in the evening nine at night 9 p.m.	`21:00`
	twelve o'clock twelve 12.00	twelve in the morning 12 a.m. midday (*British*) noon	`12:00`
		twelve at night 12 p.m. midnight	`00:00`
	a quarter past twelve quarter past twelve twelve fifteen 12.15		`12:15` `00:15`
	twenty-five past two twenty-five minutes past two two twenty five 2.25		`02:25` `14:25`
	half past eleven half eleven (*British*) eleven-thirty 11.30		`11:30` `23:30`
	a quarter to one quarter to one twelve forty-five 12.45		`12:45` `00:45`
	ten to eight ten minutes to eight seven-fifty 7.50		`07:50` `19:50`

Note the following points:

▶ The twenty-four hour clock is used on some digital clocks and on timetables. In this system, five o'clock in the afternoon, for example, is expressed as 17.00.

 In the United States, the 24-hour clock is not very common, and timetables use the 12-hour system, with a.m. and p.m.

▶ You can use **o'clock** only when saying exact hours, not times between hours. For example, you can say **five o'clock**, but you don't say 'ten past five o'clock' or 'a quarter past five o'clock'.

Come round at five o'clock.
I must leave by eight o'clock.

Note that when using **o'clock**, people usually write the number as a word (for example **five**), not a figure ('5').

You don't have to use 'o'clock' when referring to an exact hour. People often just use a number.

I used to get up every morning at six.

▶ When saying times between hours, you can use **past** and **to**. You use **past** and a number when referring to a time thirty minutes or less after a particular hour. You use **to** and a number when referring to a time less than thirty minutes before a particular hour.

It's twenty past seven.
He returned to the house at half past four.
He got to the station at five to eleven.

You don't normally use the word 'minutes' in these expressions.

 Speakers of American English often use **after** instead of 'past', and **of** instead of 'to'.

It was twenty after eight.
At a quarter of eight, he called Mrs. Curry.

▶ You only use the word **minutes** when you are talking about times between sets of five minutes, or when you want to show that you are being accurate and precise.

It was twenty-four minutes past ten.
We left Grosvenor Crescent at five minutes to ten.

▶ If it is clear what hour you are talking about, you don't need to add the hour after **past** or **to**.

'What time is it?' – 'It's eighteen minutes past.'
It's quarter past.
'What time's break?' – 'Twenty-five to.'

▶ You can also express a time by saying the hour first and then the number of minutes past the hour. For example, you can say **7.35** as **seven thirty-five**.

If the number of minutes is less than 10, many people say 'o' as **oh** before the number of minutes. For example, **7.05** can be said as **seven oh five** or **seven five**.

 You put a full stop after the hour when writing a time like this. Some people, especially Americans, use a colon instead.

At 6.30 each morning, the partners meet to review the situation.
The door closes at 11:15.

▶ You can make it clear when a time occurs, if necessary, by adding a prepositional phrase. Note that you say **in the morning**, **in the afternoon**, and **in the evening**, but you say **at night**, not 'in the night'.

It was about four o'clock in the afternoon.
They worked from seven in the morning until five at night.

→ See **Usage** entries **afternoon**, **evening**, **morning**, **night**

You can also add **a.m.** to indicate a time between midnight and midday, or **p.m.** to indicate a time between midday and midnight. These abbreviations are not generally used in conversation in British English.

The doors will be opened at 10 a.m.
We will be arriving back in London at 10.30 p.m.

! **BE CAREFUL**

Don't use 'a.m.' or 'p.m.' with 'o'clock'.

2 **prepositions showing time**

The commonest preposition used to show the time when something happens is **at**.

The taxi arrived at 7.30.
They'd arranged to leave at four o'clock.
I'll be back at four.

Other prepositions are used in the following ways to show when something happens:

▶ If something happens **after** a particular time, it happens during the period that follows that time.

It's a very quiet place with little to do after ten at night.

▶ If something happens **before** a particular time, it happens earlier than that time.

I was woken before six by the rain hammering against my bedroom window.

▶ If something happens **by** a particular time, it happens at or before that time.

I have to get back to town by four o'clock.

▶ If something happens **until** a particular time, it stops at that time. **Till** is often used instead of 'until' in conversation.

I work until three.
I didn't get home till five.

▶ If something has been happening **since** a particular time, it started at that time and it is still happening.

He had been up since 4 a.m.

For information on other uses of these words, see separate Usage entries at each word.

3 **approximate times**

You can show that a time is approximate by using **about** or **around** in front of the time.

We were woken up at about four o'clock in the morning.
The device, which exploded at around midnight on Wednesday, severely damaged the fourth-floor bar.

At is sometimes left out.

He left about ten o'clock.

In conversation, people sometimes show an approximate time by adding '**-ish**' to the time.

Shall I call you about nine-ish?

You can say that something happens **just after** or **just before** a particular time. You can also use **shortly after** or **shortly before**.

We drove into Jerusalem just after nine o'clock.
He came home just before six o'clock and lay down for a nap.
Shortly after nine, her husband appeared.

When saying what the time is or was, you can also use **just gone** in British English, or **just after**.

It was just gone half past twelve.
It was just after 9pm on a cold October night.

4 periods of the day

The main periods of the day are:

morning	afternoon	evening	night

You can use the prepositions **in** or **on** with words referring to periods of the day. You can also use **last**, **next**, **this**, **tomorrow**, and **yesterday** in front of these words to form adverbial phrases.

I'll ring the agent in the morning.
On Saturday morning all flights were cancelled to and from Glasgow.
I spoke to him this morning.
He is going to fly to Amiens tomorrow morning.

For detailed information on how to use these words and which prepositions to use with them, see Usage entry at each word.

→ See **Usage** entries **last – lastly, next, this – that**

There are also several words that refer to the short period when the sun rises or sets:

dawn	first light	dusk	sunset
daybreak	sunrise	nightfall	twilight

You use **at** with these words when showing that something happens during the period they refer to.

At dawn we landed in Tunisia.
Draw the curtains at sunset.

5 adverbs showing time

The adverbs and adverbials in the two lists below are used to show that something happened in the past. Note that all these adverbials can be put after the first auxiliary in a verb phrase.

The following adverbials can be used with past tenses and with the present perfect:

in the past	lately	recently
just	previously	

It wasn't very successful in the past.
Her husband had recently died in an accident.

The following adverbials can be used with past tenses but not normally with the present perfect:

at one time	earlier on	once	sometime
earlier	formerly	originally	then

The cardboard folder had been blue originally but now the colour had faded to a light grey.
The world was different then.

Before is not used with the present perfect when simply showing that a situation existed in the past. However, it is used with the present perfect to show that this is not the first time that something has happened.

I'm sure I've read that before.

 The tenses used with **already** are different in American English and British English.

→ See **Usage** entry **already**

You use the following adverbials when referring to the future:

afterwards	in a minute	later on	sometime
at once	in a moment	one day	soon
before long	in future	one of these days	sooner or later
eventually	in the future	shortly	within minutes
immediately	later	some day	within the hour

We'll be free soon.
I'll remember in a minute.
In future when you visit us you must let us know in advance.

These adverbials are usually put at the end or beginning of the clause.

 '**Momentarily**' is used when referring to the future in American English, but not in British English.

→ See **Usage** entry **momentarily**

You use the following adverbials to contrast the present with the past or the future, or to show that you are talking about a temporary situation in the present:

at the moment	just now	presently
at present	now	right now
currently	nowadays	these days

Biology is their great passion at the moment.
Well, we must be going now.

These adverbials are usually put at the end or beginning of the clause.

Note that **today** is used, mainly in newspapers and broadcasting, to refer to the present time in history as well as to the day on which you are speaking.

...the kind of open society which most of us in the Western world enjoy today.

→ See **Usage** entry **now**

Note that **already** is used when referring to a present situation, as well as when referring to the past.

I'm already late.

→ See **Usage** entry **already**

6 **times as modifiers**

Clock times and periods of the day can be used as modifiers.

Every morning he would set off right after the eight o'clock news.
He was usually able to catch the six thirty-five train from Euston.
But now the sun was already dispersing the morning mists.

People often refer to a train or bus by the time it leaves a particular place. They talk, for example, about **the six-eighteen**, meaning 'the train that leaves at six-eighteen'.

He knew Alan caught <u>the seven-thirty-two</u> most days.

Possessive forms of periods of the day can also be used as modifiers, when talking about a particular day.

It was Jim Griffiths, who knew nothing of <u>the morning's</u> happenings.

They are also used when saying how long an activity lasts.

He still had <u>an afternoon's</u> work to get done.

7 time adverbials after nouns

You can use a time adverbial after a noun, in order to give more information about events or periods of time.

I'm afraid the meeting <u>this afternoon</u> tired me badly.
No admissions are permitted in the hour <u>before closing time</u>.

Transport

1 prepositions

You can use **by** with most forms of transport when you are talking about travel using that form of transport.

Most visitors to these parts choose to travel <u>by bicycle</u>.
I never go <u>by car</u>.
It is cheaper to travel to London <u>by coach</u>.

! BE CAREFUL

Don't use a determiner after **by**. For example, don't say '~~I never go by a car~~'. Also, don't use 'by' when you are giving more detail about the vehicle. For example, don't say '~~I came by Tom's car~~'. You say 'I came **in** Tom's car'.

If you want to emphasize that someone walks somewhere, you usually say that they go **on foot**.

They'd have to go <u>on foot</u>.

You can also use **in** when you are talking about travel using a car, taxi, ambulance, lorry, small boat, or small plane. Similarly, you can use **in** or **into** when talking about entering one of these vehicles and **out of** when talking about leaving one of them.

I always go back <u>in a taxi</u>.
She and Oliver were put <u>into a lorry</u>.
I saw that he was already <u>out of the car</u>.

However, you usually use **on**, **onto**, and **off** when you are talking about other forms of transport, such as buses, coaches, planes, trains, and ships.

...your trip <u>on planes, ships and cross-channel ferries</u>.
He got <u>onto the bus</u> and we waved until it drove out of sight.
Sheila looked very pretty as she stepped <u>off the train</u>.

You can also say that someone is **aboard** or **on board** these other forms of transport, especially planes and ships.

He fled the country <u>aboard a US Air Force plane</u>.
He hauled the fish <u>on board his boat</u>.

2 verbs

You usually use the verb **get** followed by a preposition to say that someone enters or leaves a vehicle.

Then I stood up to get off the bus.
They got on the wrong train.

The verbs **board**, **embark**, and **disembark** are used in formal English.

You use **board** to talk about getting on a bus, train, large plane, or ship.

He was the first to board the plane.

You can also use **embark on** to talk about getting on a ship and **disembark from** to talk about getting off a ship.

Even before they embarked on the ferry at Southampton she was bored.
They disembarked from the QE2 after their trip.

When you are talking about travel by public transport, you can use **take** instead of 'go by'. For example, instead of saying that you will 'go by' bus, you can say that you will **take** a bus.

We then took a boat downriver.
'I could take a taxi,' I said.

Section B: Communication skills

Addressing someone

1 position of vocatives	5 addressing relatives
2 writing vocatives	6 addressing a group of people
3 addressing someone you do not know	7 vocatives showing dislike
	8 vocatives showing affection
4 addressing someone you know	9 other vocatives

When you talk to someone, you sometimes use their name. You can sometimes use their title, if they have one. Sometimes you use a word that shows how you feel about them, for example **darling** or **idiot**. Words used to address people are called **vocatives**.

1 position of vocatives

If you use a vocative, you usually use it at the end of a sentence.

I told you he was okay, Phil.
Where are you staying, Mr Swallow?

When you want to get someone's attention, you use a vocative at the beginning of a sentence.

John, how long have you been at the university?
Dad, why have you got that suit on?

A vocative can also be used between clauses or after the first group of words in a clause. People often do this to emphasize the importance of what they are saying.

I regret to inform you, Mrs West, that your husband is dead.
Don't you think, John, it would be wiser to wait?

2 writing vocatives

When you are writing speech down, you separate a vocative from words in front of it or after it using a comma.

Don't leave me, Jenny.
Professor Schilling, do you think that there are dangers associated with this policy?

3 addressing someone you do not know

In British English, if you want to say something to someone you do not know, for example in the street or in a shop, you don't usually use a vocative at all. You say '**Excuse me**' if you need to attract their attention.

→ See **Topic** entry **Apologizing**

> **!** **BE CAREFUL**
>
> In modern British English, the titles **Mr**, **Mrs**, **Miss**, and **Ms** are only used in front of names. Don't use them on their own to address people you do not know. Also, don't address someone as 'gentleman' or 'lady'.

In British English, it is usually considered old-fashioned to use a word that shows the person's job, such as **officer** (to a policeman). However, this is commonly used in American English. **Doctor** and **nurse** can be used in this way in British and American English.

Is he all right, doctor?

Some people use **you** to address someone whose name they do not know, but this is very impolite.

4 addressing someone you know

If you know the surname of the person you are talking to, you can address them using their title (usually **Mr**, **Mrs**, **Miss**, or **Ms**) and surname.

Thank you, Ms Jones.
Goodbye, Dr Kirk.

Titles showing a person's rank can be used without a surname after them.

I'm sure you have nothing to worry about, Professor.
Is that clear, Sergeant?

Mr and **Madam** are sometimes used in front of the titles **President**, **Chairman**, **Chairwoman**, and **Chairperson**.

No, Mr President.

→ See **Topic** entry **Names and titles**

> **!** **BE CAREFUL**
>
> People do not usually address other people using their first name and surname. Don't say, for example, '~~Thank you, Henry Smith~~'. Say 'Thank you, Henry' or 'Thank you, Mr Smith'.

If you know someone well, you can address them using their first name. However, people do not usually do this in the course of an ordinary conversation, unless they want to make it clear who they are talking to.

What do you think, John?
Shut up, Simon!

Short, informal forms of people's names, such as **Jenny** and **Mike**, are sometimes used as vocatives. However, you should not use a form like this unless you are sure that the person does not object to it.

5 addressing relatives

People usually address their parents and grandparents using a noun that shows their relationship to them.

Someone's got to do it, <u>mum</u>.
Sorry, <u>Grandma</u>.

The following list shows the commonest nouns that people use to address their parents and grandparents:

Mother:

in British English, **Mum**, **Mummy**, **Mother**

in American English, **Mom**, **Mommy**, and especially for young children, **Mama** or **Momma**

Father:

in British English, **Dad**, **Daddy**, **Father**

in American English, **Dad**, **Daddy**, and sometimes **Pop**

Grandmother:

in British English, **Gran**, **Granny**, **Grandma**, **Nan**, **Nanna**

in American English, **Granny** or **Grandma**

Grandfather:

in British English, **Grandad** or **Grandpa**

in American English, **Grandad** or **Grandpa**

Aunt and **Uncle** are also used as vocatives, usually in front of the person's first name.

This is Ginny, <u>Aunt Bernice</u>.
Goodbye, <u>Uncle Harry</u>.

! **BE CAREFUL**

Nouns showing other family relationships, such as 'daughter', 'brother', and 'cousin' are not used as vocatives.

6 addressing a group of people

If you want to address a group of people formally, for example at a meeting, you say **ladies and gentlemen** (or **ladies** or **gentlemen**, if the group is not mixed).

Good evening, <u>ladies and gentlemen</u>.

If you want to address a group of people informally, you can use **everyone** or **everybody**, although it is not necessary to use any vocative. You can also use **guys** to address a group of people informally, whether they are male or female.

I'm so terribly sorry, <u>everybody</u>.
Hi <u>guys</u>, how are you doing?

If you want to address a group of children or young people, you can use **kids**. You can use **boys** or **girls** if the group is not mixed.

Come and meet our guest, <u>kids</u>.
Give Mr Hooper a chance, <u>boys</u>.

The use of **children** as a vocative is formal.

7 vocatives showing dislike

People show dislike, contempt, or impatience using nouns and combinations of nouns and adjectives as vocatives, usually with **you** in front of them.

Shut your big mouth, you stupid idiot.
Give it to me, you silly girl.

8 vocatives showing affection

Vocatives showing affection are usually used by themselves.

Goodbye, darling.
Come on, love.

! BE CAREFUL

Some people use **my** or the person's name in front of affectionate vocatives, but this usually sounds old-fashioned or humorous.

We've got to go, my dear.
Oh Harold darling, why did he die?

9 'sir', 'madam', and 'ma'am'

People who are serving in shops, or providing a service to the public, sometimes politely call male customers or clients **sir** and female ones **madam**.

In American English the abbreviation **ma'am** is used.

Are you read to order, sir?
'Thank you very much.' – 'You're welcome, madam.'

In British English, 'sir' or 'madam' are normally only used to address customers or clients. However, in American English, some people use **sir** and **ma'am** when speaking politely to a man or woman whose name they do not know.

What does your father do, sir?
Do you need assistance getting that to your car, ma'am?

Advising someone

1 general advice

There are many ways of giving someone advice.

In conversation, or in informal writing such as letters to friends, you can use '**I would**', or '**I'd**'.

I would try to talk to him about how you feel.
I'd buy tins of one vegetable rather than mixtures.

People often emphasize these expressions with **if I were you**.

If I were you, I'd just take the black one.
I should let it go if I were you.

You can also say '**You ought to...**' or '**You should...**'. People often say '**I think**' first, in order not to sound too forceful.

You should explain this to him at the outset.
I think maybe you ought to try a different approach.

You can say to someone which course of action or choice is likely to be most successful by using the informal expression '**Your best bet is...**' or '**...is your best bet**'.

Well, your best bet is to book online.
I think Boston's going to be your best bet.

2 firm advice

If you want to give advice firmly, especially if you are in a position of authority, you can say '**You'd better...**'. This way of giving advice can also be used as a kind way of telling someone to do something that will benefit them.

You'd better write it down.
Perhaps you'd better listen to him.
I think you'd better sit down.

When you are talking to someone you know well, you can use an imperative form.

Make sure you note that down.
Take no notice of him.

People sometimes add **and** followed by a good consequence of taking the advice, or **or** followed by a bad consequence. These structures are similar in meaning to conditional sentences.

Stay with me and you'll be okay.
Now hold onto the chain, or you'll hurt yourself.

And and **or** are also used like this in threats. In threats, both **and** and **or** are followed by bad consequences.

Just try – and you'll have a real fight on your hands.
Drop that gun! Drop it or I'll kill you!

Imperative forms are also used by experts to give advice: see the section on professional advice later in this entry.

3 serious advice

A more formal and serious way of giving advice is to say '**I advise you to...**'.

'What shall I do about it?' – 'I advise you to consult a doctor, Mrs Smedley.'
I strongly advise you to get professional help.

A very strong way of giving advice is to say '**You must...**'.

You must tell the pupils what it is you want to do, so that they feel involved.
You must maintain control of the vehicle at all times.

You can also use '**You've got to...**' or '**You have to...**' with the same meaning.

If somebody makes a mistake you've got to say so.
You have to put all these things behind you.

4 professional advice

There are other ways of giving advice which are used mainly in books, articles, and broadcasts.

One common way is to use an imperative form.

Clean one room at a time.
If you don't have a freezer, keep bread in a bread-bin.

Another way of advising that is used mainly in writing and broadcasting is to say '**It's a good idea to...**'.

It's a good idea to spread your savings between several building societies.
It's a good idea to get a local estate agent to come and value your house.

Another expression that is used is '**My advice is...**' or '**My advice would be...**'. Again, this is used especially by professionals or experts, who have knowledge on which to base their advice.

My advice is to look at all the options before you buy.
My advice would always be: find out where local people eat, and go there.

The expression '**A word of advice**' is sometimes used to introduce a piece of advice.

A word of advice – start taking your children to the dentist as soon as they get teeth.

→ See **Topic** entries **Suggestions**, **Warning someone** for information on how to advise someone not to do something

Agreeing and disagreeing

1 asking for agreement	**5** expressing ignorance or
2 expressing agreement	uncertainty
3 strong agreement	**6** expressing disagreement
4 partial agreement	**7** strong disagreement

1 asking for agreement

You can ask someone if they agree with your opinion of something or someone by using a question tag. When you do this, you usually expect them to agree with you.

That's an extremely interesting point, isn't it?
It was really good, wasn't it, Andy?

People sometimes use question tags like this and carry on talking because they think a reply is unnecessary. You can also use a question tag to ask someone if they agree that something is a fact.

Property in France is quite expensive, isn't it?
You don't have a television, do you?

You can also show that you want someone to express agreement by using a negative yes/no-question, or by saying a statement as if it were a question.

So there's no way you could go back to work?
He's got a scholarship?

You can use the tag **don't you**? after a clause in which you say that you like or dislike something, or think it is good or bad. The pronoun **you** is stressed.

I adore it, don't you?
I think this is one of the best things, don't you?

In formal situations, people sometimes use expressions such as '**Don't you agree...?**' and '**Would you agree...?**'

Don't you agree with me that it is rather an impossible thing to do after all this time?
Would you agree with that analysis?

2 expressing agreement

When you want to show that you agree with someone or something, the simplest way is to say **yes**. People often say something further, especially in more formal discussions.

'That was probably the border.' – 'Yes.'
'It's quite a nice school, isn't it?' – 'Yes, it's well decorated and there's a nice atmosphere there.'

You can add an appropriate tag such as **I do** or **it is** to **Yes**. This tag is often followed by a question tag.

'That's fantastic!' – 'Yes, _it is, isn't it?_'
'I was really rude to you at that party.' – 'Yes, _you were_. But I deserved it.'

You can also just add a question tag to **Yes**, or use a question tag by itself. You do not expect a reply.

'He's a completely changed man.' – 'Yes, _isn't he?_'
'What a lovely evening!' – '_Isn't it?_'

> **!** **BE CAREFUL**
>
> If you want to express agreement with a negative statement, you say **No**, not 'Yes'.
>
> 'I don't think it's as good now.' – '_No_, it isn't really.'
> 'That's not very healthy, is it?' – '_No._'

You can also express agreement using expressions such as '**That's right**', '**That's true**', or '**True**', when agreeing that something is a fact. You say '**That's true**' or '**True**' when you think a good point has been made.

'Most teenagers are perfectly all right.' – '_That's right_, yes.'
'You don't have to be poor to be lonely.' – '_That's true._'
'They're a long way away.' – '_True._'

People sometimes say '**Sure**' when accepting what someone has said in a discussion.

'You can earn some money as well.' – '_Sure_, you can make quite a bit.'

The expression '**I agree**' is quite formal.

'It's a catastrophe.' – '_I agree._'

When someone has made a statement about what they like or think, you can show that you share their opinion by saying '**So do I**' or '**I do too**'.

'I find that amazing.' – '_So do I._'
'I like basketball.' – 'Yes, _I do too._'

When you want to show that you share someone's negative opinion, you can say '**Nor do I**', '**Neither do I**', or '**I don't either**'.

'I don't like him.' – '_Nor do I._'
'Oh, I don't mind where I go as long as it's sunny.' – 'No, _I don't either._'

3 strong agreement

You can show strong agreement by using expressions such as the ones shown in the examples below. Most of these sound rather formal. '**Absolutely**' and '**Exactly**' are less formal.

'I thought June Barry's performance was the best.' – '_Absolutely_. I thought she was wonderful.'
'It's good exercise and it's good fun.' – '_Exactly._'
'They earn far too much money.' – 'Yes, _I couldn't agree more._'
'We reckon that this is what he would have wanted us to do.' – '_I think you're absolutely right._'

 The expressions that use **quite** are used in British English, but would not be used in American English.

'I must do something, though.' – 'Yes, _I quite agree._'
'The public showed that by the way they voted.' – '_That's quite true._'

TOPICS

4 partial agreement

If you agree with someone, but not entirely or with reluctance, you can reply '**I suppose so**'.

'I must get a job.' – 'Yes, I suppose so.'
'We need to tell Simon.' – 'I suppose so.'

If you are replying to a negative statement, you say '**I suppose not**'.

'Some of these places haven't changed a bit.' – 'I suppose not.'

→ See **Usage** entry **suppose**

5 showing that you do not know something

If you do not know enough to agree or disagree with a statement, you say '**I don't know**'.

'He was the first Australian Prime Minister, wasn't he?' – 'Perhaps. I don't know.'

If you are not sure of a particular fact, you say '**I'm not sure**'.

'He was world champion one year, wasn't he?' – 'I'm not sure.'

6 expressing disagreement

Rather than simply expressing complete disagreement, people usually try to disagree politely using expressions which soften the contradictory opinion they are giving. '**I don't think so**' and '**Not really**' are the commonest of these expressions.

'You'll change your mind one day.' – 'Well, I don't think so. But I won't argue with you.'
'It was a lot of money in those days.' – 'Well, not really.'

The expressions shown below are also used.

'You'll need bolts', he said. 'Actually, no,' I said.
'I know he loves you.' – 'I don't know about that.'
'It's all over now, anyway.' – 'No, I'm afraid I can't agree with you there.'

People often say '**Yes**' or '**I see what you mean**', to show partial agreement, and then go on to mention a point of disagreement, introduced by **but**.

'It's a very clever film.' – 'Yes, perhaps, but I didn't like it.'
'They ruined the whole thing.' – 'I see what you mean, but they didn't know.'

7 strong disagreement

The following examples show stronger ways of expressing disagreement. You should be very careful when using them, in order to avoid offending people.

'That's very funny.' – 'No it isn't.'
'You were the one who wanted to buy it.' – 'I'm sorry, but you're wrong.'

The expressions of disagreement shown in the following examples are more formal.

'University education does divide families in a way.' – 'I can't go along with that.'
'There would be less of the guilt which characterized societies of earlier generations.' – 'Well, I think I would take issue with that.'

In formal situations, people sometimes use '**With respect...**' to make their disagreement seem more polite.

'We ought to be asking the teachers some tough questions.' – 'With respect, Mr Graveson, you should be asking pupils some questions as well, shouldn't you?'

When people are angry, they use very strong, impolite words and expressions to disagree.

'He's absolutely right.' – *'Oh, <u>come off it</u>! He doesn't know what he's talking about.'*
'They'll be killed.' – *'<u>Nonsense</u>.'*
'He wants it, and I suppose he has a right to it.' – *'<u>Rubbish</u>.'*
'He said you plotted to get him removed.' – *'<u>That's ridiculous</u>!'*
'He's very good at his job, isn't he?' – *'<u>You must be joking</u>! He's absolutely useless!'*

With people you know well, you can use expressions like these in a casual, light-hearted way.

 Note that the word 'rubbish' is not used in this way in American English.

Apologizing

1	saying sorry	**4**	saying something wrong
2	interrupting, approaching, or leaving someone	**5**	formal apologies
		6	apologies on notices
3	doing something embarrassing	**7**	accepting an apology

1 saying sorry

There are several ways of apologizing and accepting apologies. You apologize when you have upset someone or caused trouble for them in some way.

The commonest way of apologizing is to say '**Sorry**' or '**I'm sorry**'. When using '**I'm sorry**', you can use adverbs such as '**very**', '**so**', '**terribly**', and '**extremely**' to be more emphatic.

'Stop that, please. You're giving me a headache.' – *'<u>Sorry</u>.'*
<u>Sorry</u> I'm late.
<u>I'm sorry</u> about this morning.
<u>I'm sorry</u> if I've distressed you by asking all this.
<u>I'm very sorry</u>, but these are vital.
<u>I'm terribly sorry</u> – we shouldn't have left.

When apologizing for accidentally doing something, for example stepping on someone's foot, some people say '**I beg your pardon**' instead of 'Sorry'. This is rather old-fashioned.

She bumped into someone behind her. '<u>I beg your pardon</u>,' she said.

 Speakers of American English usually say '**Excuse me**' in the above situations.

2 interrupting, approaching, or leaving someone

You use '**Excuse me**' to apologize politely to someone when you are disturbing or interrupting them, or when you want to get past them. This is also the expression to use when you want to speak to a stranger.

<u>Excuse me</u> for disturbing you at home.
<u>Excuse me</u> butting in.
<u>Excuse me</u>, but is there a fairly cheap restaurant near here?
<u>Excuse me</u>, do you mind if I move your bag slightly?

 The expression '**Pardon me**' is used by some speakers of American English.

<u>Pardon me</u>, Sergeant, I wonder if you'd do me a favour?

When you are disturbing or interrupting someone, you can also say '**I'm sorry to disturb you**' or '**I'm sorry to interrupt**'.

I'm sorry to disturb you again but we need some more details.
Sorry to interrupt, but I've some forms to fill in.

You also say '**Excuse me**' when you have to leave someone for a short time in order to do something.

Excuse me. I have to make a telephone call.
Will you excuse me a second?

3 doing something embarrassing

You can use '**Excuse me**' or '**I beg your pardon**' to apologize when you have done something slightly embarrassing or impolite, such as burping, hiccupping, or sneezing.

4 saying something wrong

You say '**I beg your pardon**' to apologize for making a mistake in what you are saying, or for using the wrong word. You can also say '**sorry**'.

It is treated in a sentence as a noun – I beg your pardon – as an adjective.
It's in the southeast, sorry, southwest corner of the USA.

5 formal apologies

When you want to apologize in a formal way, you can say explicitly '**I apologize**'.

I apologize for my late arrival.
How silly of me. I do apologize.
I really must apologize for bothering you with this.

Another formal expression, used especially in writing, is '**Please accept my apologies**'.

Please accept my apologies for this unfortunate incident.

You can use **forgive** in polite expressions like '**Forgive me**' and '**Forgive my ignorance**' to reduce the directness of what you are saying, and to apologize in a mild way for saying something that might seem rude or silly.

Look, forgive me, but I thought we were going to talk about my book.
Forgive my ignorance, but who is Jennifer Lopez?

6 apologies on notices

Regret is often used in public notices and formal announcements.

London Transport regrets any inconvenience caused by these repairs.
The notice said: 'Dr. Beamish has a cold and regrets he cannot meet his classes today.'

7 accepting an apology

To accept an apology, you normally use a short fixed expression such as '**That's okay**', '**That's all right**', '**Forget it**', '**Don't worry about it**', or '**It doesn't matter**'.

'I'm sorry about this, sir.' – 'That's all right. Don't let it happen again.'
'I apologize for my outburst just now.' – 'Forget it.'
She spilt his drink and said 'I'm sorry.' 'Don't worry about it,' he said, 'no harm done.'
'I'm sorry to ring at this late hour.' – 'I'm still up. It doesn't matter.'

Some words and expressions that are used to apologize are also used to ask someone to repeat something that they just said.

→ See **Topic** entry **Asking for repetition**

Asking for repetition

You ask someone to repeat what they have said when you have not heard them or when you have not understood them. You can also ask someone to repeat what they have said when you feel that what they have said is surprising or impolite.

1 asking informally

In an informal situation, you usually ask someone to repeat what they have said using a short fixed expression such as '**Sorry?**', '**I'm sorry?**', or '**Pardon?**'

'Have you seen my book anywhere?' – 'Sorry?' – ' seen my book?'
'Well, what about it?' – 'I'm sorry?' – 'What about it?'
'How old is she?' – 'Pardon?' – 'I said how old is she?'

Some people say 'Come again?'

'It's on Monday.' – 'Come again?' – 'Monday.'

 In American English, '**Excuse me?**' is also used in this way. Some people say '**Pardon me?**'
'You do see him once in a while, don't you?' – 'Excuse me?' – 'I thought you saw him sometimes.'

Some people use '**What?**', '**You what?**', or '**Eh?**' to ask someone to repeat something, but these expressions are impolite.

'Do you want another coffee?' – 'What?' – 'Do you want another coffee?'

You can use a *wh*-word to check part of what someone has said.

'Can I speak to Nikki, please?' – 'Who?' – 'Nikki.'
'We've got a special offer in April for Majorca.' – 'For where?' – 'Majorca.'
'I don't like the tinkling.' – 'The what?' – 'The tinkling.'

If you think you heard what someone said but are not sure, or are surprised, you can repeat it, or repeat part of it, making it sound like a question.

'I just told her that rain's good for her complexion.' – 'Rain?'
'I have a message for you?' – 'A message?'

You add **again** to the end of a question when you are asking someone to repeat something that they told you a little while ago and which you have forgotten.

What's his name again?
Where are we going again?

2 asking more formally

When talking to someone you do not know well, you use longer expressions such as '**Sorry, what did you say?**', '**I'm sorry, I didn't quite catch that**', '**I'm sorry, I didn't hear what you said**', '**I'm sorry, would you mind repeating that again?**', and '**Would you repeat that, please?**'

'What about tomorrow at three?' – 'Sorry, what did you say?' – 'I said, What about meeting tomorrow at three?'
Would you repeat that, I didn't quite catch it.

The expressions '**Beg your pardon?**' and '**I beg your pardon?**' are sometimes used, but they are fairly formal and old-fashioned.

'Did he listen to you?' – 'Beg your pardon?' – 'Did he listen to you?'
'Did they have a dog?' – 'I beg your pardon?' – 'I said did they have a dog?'

'**I beg your pardon?**' (but not 'Beg your pardon?') is also used to show that you find what someone says surprising or offensive. The word **beg** is stressed.

TOPICS

TOPICS

'Where the devil did you get her?' – '*I beg your pardon?*'

 Speakers of American English also use '**Excuse me**' in this way, but it is important that you strongly stress the second syllable of **excuse** to make the meaning clear.

Complimenting and congratulating someone

1	clothes and appearance	**4**	achievements
2	meals	**5**	accepting compliments and
3	skills		congratulations

1 clothes and appearance

If you know someone quite well, or are talking to someone in an informal situation, you can compliment them on their clothes or appearance using an expression such as '**That's a nice coat**', '**What a lovely dress**', or '**I like your jacket**'.

That's a beautiful dress.
What a pretty dress.
I like your haircut.
I love your shoes. Are they new?

You can also say something like '**You look nice**' or '**You're looking very smart today**'. If you want to be more emphatic, you can use adjectives such as **great** or **terrific**.

You're looking very glamorous.
You look terrific.

You can also compliment someone on their appearance by saying that what they are wearing suits them.

I love you in that dress, it really suits you.

2 meals

You can compliment someone on a meal by saying something like '**This is delicious**' during the meal or '**That was delicious**' after the meal.

This is delicious, Ginny.
He took a bite of meat, chewed it, savoured it, and said, 'Fantastic!'
Mm, that was lovely.

3 skills

You can compliment someone on doing something skilfully or well using an exclamation.

What a marvellous memory you've got!
Oh, that's true. Yes, what a good answer!
'Look – there's a boat.' – 'Oh yes – well spotted!'

A teacher might praise a pupil who has given a correct answer by saying '**Good**'.

'What sort of soil do they prefer?' – 'Acid soil.' – 'Good.'

4 achievements

You can say '**Congratulations**' to someone to congratulate them on achieving something.

Well, congratulations, Fernando. You've done it.
Congratulations to all three winners.

You can also say '**Congratulations**' to someone when something nice has happened to them.

'*Congratulations*,' *the doctor said*. '*You have a son.*'

→ See **Topic** entry **Reactions**

There are several more formal ways of congratulating someone.

I must congratulate you on your new job.
Let me offer you my congratulations on your success.
Let me be the first to congratulate you on a wise decision, Mr Dorf.
May I congratulate you again on your excellent performance.

You can congratulate someone informally by saying '**Well done**'.

'*You did very well today. Well done*'.

5 accepting compliments and congratulations

You can accept compliments with several different expressions.

Oh, thanks!
It's very nice of you to say so.
I'm glad you think so.

You can also respond by saying how old it is, or how or where you got it.

'*That's a nice top.*' – '*Haven't you seen this before? I've had it for years.*'
'*That's a nice piece of jewellery.*' – '*Yeah, my husband bought it for me.*'

If someone compliments you on your skill, you can say something modest that implies that what you did was not very difficult or skilful.

Oh, there's nothing to it.
'*Terrific job.*' – '*Well, I don't know about that*'.

When someone congratulates you, you usually say '**Thanks**' or '**Thank you**'.

'*Congratulations on publication.*' – '*Thanks very much.*'
'*Congratulations to both of you.*' – '*Thank you.*'

Criticizing someone

1 mild criticism

People do not usually express criticism strongly unless they know the person they are criticizing well.

If you want to criticize someone for doing something badly, you can say something like '**That's not very good**' or '**I think that's not quite right**'.

What answer have you got? Oh dear. Thirty-three. That's not very good.
I think your answer's wrong.

2 stronger criticism

If you want to criticize someone for doing something wrong or stupid, you can use a question beginning '**Why did you...?**' or '**Why didn't you...?**' Questions like this can be used to express great anger or distress, or merely exasperation.

Why did you lie to me?
Why did you do it?
Why didn't you tell me?

You can be more direct and say '**You shouldn't have...**' or '**You should have...**'.

You shouldn't have given him money.
You should have asked me.

Some people say '**How could you?**' when they feel very strongly that someone has been thoughtless.

How could you? You knew I didn't want anyone to know!
How could you be so stupid?

Emailing

Emails are often fairly informal or neutral in tone, but there are still rules to follow, and a certain degree of good manners is expected between people who do not know each other well.

If you are communicating with someone for the first time, the language you use in your email should be fairly formal. Even if you are writing to someone with whom you have already established a relationship, a formal style might be appropriate.

Examples of cases where a more formal style might be preferred are:

▶ if the person is much older than you

▶ if the person has a higher rank than you in your company

▶ if the person is from a country or culture where relations between people of different ages or different ranks in a company are more formal than in your own.

Once you have built a relationship, and you feel that it is appropriate, you can use a more informal style. It is also useful to pay attention to the style of the emails you receive from people. If a contact uses an informal style, then you can do the same in your reply. Emails to colleagues and people you know tend to be less formal, but should still be polite. If you are unsure about which style to use, keep it more formal.

1 key points

It is important to keep emails clear, concise, and polite. You can do this by following the suggestions below.

▶ Remember that busy people receive a lot of correspondence. For this reason, you should avoid sending long emails. Try to tell them your points quickly and clearly.

▶ Ensure that the first sentence introduces the topic of the email clearly, and in a few words.

▶ Write short paragraphs. This will make the information easier to understand. Leave a space between each paragraph.

▶ If the email is long, consider numbering your points, using bullet points, or using headings. The reader will find this useful when responding to particular points.

▶ Write your emails carefully. Emails that are written very quickly and carelessly can seem unfriendly and rude.

▶ Contractions (*I'm*, *he's*, *can't*, *we'd*, etc) are acceptable in emails.

2 the subject line

The subject line should clearly show the main point of your email. For example, if you are emailing a company to ask for information about a product, use the subject line to give the name of the product, and to mention the fact that you need information:

Subject: Balance bike (ref: N765) information required

Here are some more examples of subject lines:

Subject: Meeting Room changed to 307
Subject: Lunch (Fri 9 Oct) cancelled
Subject: Feb sales figures
Subject: Reminder: conference agenda due

3 salutations (= words or phrases for saying hello)

Formal emails are similar to formal letters, and the same salutations can be used.

If you decide to use the more formal salutation 'Dear Mr Sanchez' or 'Dear Ms Sanchez', remember to make sure that you use the title, e.g. Mr, Miss, Mrs, Ms, Dr, etc with surnames, not first names.

Dear Mr Sanchez
Dear Mrs O'Neill
Dear Miss Lee
Dear Dr Armstrong

In less formal emails, you can be more familiar. If the sender of the message has used his or her first name only, it is acceptable to use their first name when you reply. When you are communicating regularly with colleagues or business contacts, you can start with 'Hello' or 'Hi'.

Hello James
Hi Akiko
Hello
Hi

4 ending an email

There is often a short sentence that links the main part of the email and the sign-off (= the part that says goodbye). What you write will, of course, depend on the purpose of your email, but here are a few typical sentences that are often used:

I hope to hear from you soon.
I look forward to hearing from you.
Thanks again for this.
Many thanks in advance.
Thank you for taking the time to answer my questions.
I hope this helps.
Please get in touch if you have any more queries.
Let me know what you think.

It is polite to finish an email with a sign-off. There are no fixed rules for the type of sign-off that you use. The phrases below are some of the most common ones.

Many thanks.
Thank you.
Thanks again.
Thanks.
Best
Regards
Best regards
Kind regards
Warm regards
Best wishes
With best wishes

TOPICS

TOPICS

5 attachments

An attachment is a file that you send with your email. You can refer to attachments by using these expressions.

Please find attached...
I am attaching...
I'm sending you a copy of...
I attach...

6 dealing with technical problems

Occasionally, emails or attachments do not reach the person they were intended for. Here are some expressions you can use to check whether someone has received an email or to ask someone to send an attachment again.

Did you get my last email, sent on ...?
I'm afraid I can't open the attachment.
The attachment doesn't seem to have come through. Could you possibly re-send it?

Greetings and goodbyes

1	greetings	4	replying to a greeting
2	informal greetings	5	greetings on special days
3	formal greetings	6	goodbyes

This entry deals with ways of greeting someone when you meet them, and with ways of saying goodbye.

→ See **Topic** entries **Introducing yourself and other people**, **Telephoning**

1 greetings

The usual way of greeting someone is to say '**Hello**'. You can add '**How are you?**' or another comment or question.

Hello there, Richard, how are you today?
Hello, Lucy. Had a good day?

Note that the greeting 'How do you do?' is used only by people who are meeting each other for the first time.

→ See **Topic** entry **Introducing yourself and other people**

2 informal greetings

A more informal way of greeting someone is to say '**Hi**' or '**Hiya**'. In American English, '**hey**' is also sometimes used in this way.

'Hi,' said Brody. 'Come in.'
'Hey! How are ya?'

If you meet someone in a place where you did not expect to see them, you can say '**Fancy seeing you here**'.

'Well, I never, Mr Delfont! Fancy seeing you here!'

3 formal greetings

When you greet someone formally, the greeting you use depends on what time of day it is. You say '**Good morning**' until about noon. '**Good afternoon**' is normal from about noon until about six o'clock, or until it is dark in the winter. After six o'clock, or after dark, you say '**Good evening**'.

Good morning, everyone.
Good evening. I'd like a table for four, please.

These greetings are often used by people who are making formal telephone calls, or introducing a television programme or other event.

'*Good afternoon*. William Foux and Company.' – '*Good afternoon*. Could I speak to Mr Duff, please?'
Good evening. I am Brian Smith and this is the second of a series of programmes about the University of Sussex.

You can make these expressions less formal by omitting 'Good'.

Morning, Alan.
Afternoon, Maria.

> **!** **BE CAREFUL**
>
> You only say '**Goodnight**' when you are leaving someone in the evening or going to bed. Don't use 'Goodnight' to greet someone.

'**Good day**' is old-fashioned and rather formal in British and American English, although the short form '**g'day**' is more common in Australian English.

 '**Welcome**' can be used to greet someone who has just arrived. It is quite formal in British English, but is normal in American English.

Welcome to Peking.
Welcome home, Marsha.
Welcome back.

4 replying to a greeting

The usual way of replying to a greeting is to use the same word or expression.

'Hello, Sydney.' – '*Hello*, Yakov! It's good to see you.'
'Good afternoon, Superintendent. Please sit down.' – '*Good afternoon*, sir.'

If the other person has also asked you a question, you can just answer the question.

'Hello, Barbara, did you have a good shopping trip?' – '*Yes, thanks*.'
'Good evening. May I help you?' – '*Yes, I'd like a table for two, please*.'

If someone says '**How are you?**' to you, you say something brief like '**Fine, thanks**', unless they are a close friend and you know they will be interested in details of your life and health. It is polite to add '**How are you?**' or '**And you?**'

'Hello John. How are you?' – 'All right. And you?' – 'Yeah, fine.'
'How are you?' – 'Good. You?' – 'So-so.'

5 greetings on special days

There are particular expressions which you use to give someone your good wishes on special occasions such as Christmas, Easter, or their birthday.

At Christmas, you say '**Happy Christmas**' or '**Merry Christmas**'. At New Year, you say '**Happy New Year**'. At Easter, you say '**Happy Easter**'. You reply by repeating the greeting, or saying something like '**And a happy Christmas to you too**' or '**And you!**'

If it is someone's birthday, you can say '**Happy Birthday**' to them, or '**Many happy returns**'. When someone says this to you, you reply by saying '**Thank you**'.

6 goodbyes

You say '**Goodbye**' or, more informally, '**Bye**' to someone when you or they are leaving.

'*Goodbye*, Doctor. Thank you for your help,' Miss Saunders said. *see you about seven*. *Bye*.

'**Bye-bye**' is even more informal. It is used between close relatives and friends, and to children.

Bye-bye, darling; see you tomorrow.

If you expect to meet the other person again soon, you can say things like '**See you**', '**See you later**', '**See you soon**', '**See you around**', or '**I'll be seeing you**'.

Must go now. See you tomorrow.
See you in the morning, Pedro.

Some people say '**So long**'.

'Well. So long.' He turned and walked back to the car.

You can say '**Take care**' or '**Look after yourself**' when you are saying goodbye to a friend or relative.

'Take care.' – 'Bye-bye.'
'Look after yourself, Ginny.' – 'You, too, Dad.'

'**Cheers**' and '**cheerio**' are used in informal British English.

See you at six, then. Cheers!
I'll tell Marcus you called. Cheerio.

At night, you can say '**Goodnight**' or, more informally, '**Night**', to say goodbye.

'Well, I must be off.' – 'Goodnight, Mrs Kendall.'
'Night, Jim.' – 'Night, Rita.'

People also say '**Goodnight**' to people in the same house before they go to bed.

! BE CAREFUL

In modern English, 'Good morning', 'Good afternoon', and 'Good evening' are not used to say goodbye.

 Many speakers of American English use the expression '**Have a nice day**' to say goodbye to people they do not know as friends. For example, employees in some shops and restaurants say it to customers.

'Have a nice day.' – 'Thank you.'

When you are saying goodbye to someone you do not know very well, you can use a more formal expression such as '**I look forward to seeing you again soon**' or '**It was nice meeting you**'.

I look forward to seeing you in Washington. Goodbye.
It was nice meeting you, Dimitri. Hope you have a good trip back.

Intentions

1 general intentions	**4** expressing intentions formally
2 vague intentions	**5** involuntary actions
3 firm intentions	

1 general intentions

When you want to express an intention, especially one relating to an immediate action, you can say '**I'm going to…**'.

I'm going to call my father.
I'm going to have a bath.

You can also say '**I think I'll...**'.

I think I'll finish this later.
I think I'll go to sleep now.

You can use the present progressive when you regard your intention as a fixed plan or have already made the necessary arrangements.

I'm taking it back to the library soon.
I'm going away.

The future progressive is also sometimes used.

I'll be waiting outside.

You can also express an intention by saying '**I've decided to...**'.

I've decided to clear this place out.
I've decided to go away this weekend.

To express a negative intention, you say '**I'm not going to...**' or '**I've decided not to...**'.

I'm not going to make it easy for them.
I've decided not to take it.

2 vague intentions

If your intention is not a firm one, you can say '**I'm thinking of...**'.

I'm thinking of going to the theatre next week.
I'm thinking of giving it up altogether.
I'm thinking of writing a play.

You can also say '**I might...**' or '**I may...**'.

I might stay a day or two.
I may come back to Britain, I'm not sure.

If you feel that your intention might surprise the person you are talking to, or are not sure that they will approve of it, you say '**I thought I might...**'.

I thought I might buy a house next year.
I thought I might invite him over to dinner one evening.

To express a vague negative intention, you can say '**I might not...**'.

I might not go.

3 firm intentions

You use '**I'll**' to express a firm intention, especially when making arrangements or reassuring someone.

I'll do it this afternoon and call you back.
I'll explain its function in a minute.

To express a firm negative intention, you can say '**I won't...**'.

I won't go.
I won't let my family suffer.

4 expressing intentions formally

A more formal way of expressing an intention is to say '**I intend to...**'.

I intend to carry on with it.
I intend to go into this in rather more detail this term.

I intend is also occasionally followed by an *-ing* form.

I intend retiring to Florence.

The emphatic expression '**I have every intention of...**', followed by an *-ing* form, is also sometimes used. You use this expression if you think the person you are addressing does not believe you will do something, or does not want you to do it.

I have every intention of buying it.

Even more formal expressions are '**My intention is to...**' and '**It is my intention to...**'.

My intention is to summarize previous research in this area.
It is still my intention to resign if they choose to print the story.

To express a negative intention formally, you can say '**I don't intend to...**'.

I don't intend to investigate that at this time.
I don't intend to stay too long.

You can also say '**I have no intention of...**', followed by an *-ing* form. This is more emphatic.

I have no intention of retiring.
I've no intention of marrying again.

5 **involuntary actions**

'**Be going to**', '**might**', '**may**', and '**will**' are also used to make statements about involuntary future actions.

If you keep interrupting I'm going to make a mistake.
I might not be able to find it.
I may have to stay there for a while.
If I don't have lunch, I'll faint.

Introducing yourself and other people

1 introducing yourself	**4** more casual introductions
2 introducing other people	**5** responding to an introduction
3 more formal introductions	

1 **introducing yourself**

When you meet someone for the first time, and they do not already know who you are, you can introduce yourself by saying who you are. You may need to say '**Hello**' or make a remark first.

'I'm Helmut,' said the boy. 'I'm Edmond Dorf,' I said.
I had better introduce myself. I am Doctor Marc Rodin.
You must be Kirk. My name's Linda Macintosh.

In formal situations, people sometimes say '**How do you do?**' when introducing themselves.

I'm Nigel Jessop. How do you do?

2 **introducing other people**

If you are introducing people who have not met each other before, you say '**This is...**'. You introduce each person, unless you have already told one of them who they are going to meet.

'This is Bernadette, Mr Zapp,' said O'Shea.

You use an appropriate form of each person's name, depending on how formal the occasion is.

→ See **Topic** entry **Names and titles**

Note that 'these' is rarely used, although you might say, for example, '**These are my children**' or '**These are my parents**'. When you are introducing a couple, you can use **this** once instead of repeating it.

This is Mr Dixon and Miss Peel.

You can just say the name of the person or people you are introducing, showing with your hand which one you mean.

3 **more formal introductions**

If you need to be more formal, you first say something like '**May I introduce my brother**', '**Let me introduce you to my brother**', or '**I'd like to introduce my brother**'.

By the way, may I introduce my wife? Karin – Mrs Stannard, an old friend.
Bill, I'd like to introduce Charlie Citrine.

You can also say '**I'd like you to meet...**'.

Officer O'Malley, I'd like you to meet Ted Peachum.

4 **more casual introductions**

A more casual way of introducing someone is to say something like '**You haven't met John Smith, have you?**', '**You don't know John, do you?**', or '**I don't think you know John, do you?**'

'I don't think you know Ingrid.' – 'No. I don't think we've met. How do you do?'

If you are not quite sure whether an introduction is necessary, you can say something like '**Have you met...?**' or '**Do you two know each other?**'

'Do you know my husband, Ken?' – 'Hello. I don't think I do.'

If you are fairly sure that the people have met each other before, you say something like '**You know John, don't you?**' or '**You've met John, haven't you?**'

Hello, come in. You've met Paul.

5 **responding to an introduction**

When you have been introduced to someone, you both say '**Hello**'. If you are in an informal situation, you can say '**Hi**'. If you are in a formal situation, you can say '**How do you do?**'

'Francis, this is Father Sebastian.' – 'Hello, Francis,' Father Sebastian said, offering his hand.
How do you do? Elizabeth has spoken such a lot about you.

People sometimes say '**Pleased to meet you**' or '**Nice to meet you**'.

Pleased to meet you, Doctor Floyd.
It's so nice to meet you, Edna. Freda's told us so much about you.

TOPICS

Invitations

1 polite invitations	**6** indirect invitations
2 informal invitations	**7** inviting someone to ask you for
3 persuasive invitations	something
4 very emphatic invitations	**8** responding to an invitation
5 casual invitations	

There are several ways of inviting someone to do something or to come to a place.

1 polite invitations

The usual polite way to invite someone to do something is to say '**Would you like to...?**'

Would you like to come up here on Sunday?
Would you like to look at it, Ian?

Another polite form of invitation is **please** with an imperative. This form of invitation is used mainly by people who are in charge of a situation.

Please help yourselves to another drink.
Sit down, please.

2 informal invitations

In informal situations, you can use an imperative form without 'please'. However, you should only do this if it is clear that you are giving an invitation rather than an order.

Come and have a drink, Max.
Sit down, sit down. I'll order tea.
Stay as long as you like.

3 persuasive invitations

You can make your invitation more persuasive or firm by putting **do** in front of the imperative. You do this especially when the other person seems reluctant to do what you are inviting them to do.

Do sit down.
What you said just now about Seaford sounds intriguing. Do tell me more.

You can also say '**Wouldn't you like to...?**' when you want to be persuasive.

Wouldn't you like to come with me?

When you want to be very polite and persuasive, you can say '**Won't you...?**'

Won't you take off your coat?
Won't you sit down, Mary, and have a bite to eat?

4 very emphatic invitations

If you know the person you are inviting well, and you want to make your invitation very emphatic, you can say '**You must...**', '**You have to...**' or '**You've got to...**'. You use this form of invitation when inviting someone to do something in the future, rather than immediately.

You must come and stay.
You have to come down to the office and see all the technology we have.

5 **casual invitations**

A casual, non-emphatic way of inviting someone to do something is to say '**You can...**' or '**You could...**'. You can add '**if you like**'.

Well, when I get my flat, <u>you can</u> come and stay with me.
<u>You can</u> tell me about your project, <u>if you like</u>.

'**You're welcome to...**' is another way of starting a casual invitation, but is more friendly.

<u>You're welcome to</u> live with us for as long as you like.
The cottage is about fifty miles away. But <u>you're very welcome to</u> use it.

Another way of making an invitation seem casual is to say '**I was wondering if...**'.

<u>I was wondering if</u> you'd like to come over next weekend.
<u>I was wondering if</u> you're free for lunch.

6 **indirect invitations**

An invitation can be indirect. For example, you can invite someone to do something in the future by saying '**I hope you'll...**'. You use this form of invitation especially when you are not confident that the other person will accept your invitation.

<u>I hope</u> you'll be able to stay the night. We'll gladly put you up.
<u>I hope</u>, Kathy, you'll come and see me again.

You can also invite someone indirectly using '**How would you like to...?**' or '**Why don't you...?**'

<u>How would you like to</u> come and work for me?
<u>Why don't you</u> come to the States with us in November?

You can also use a question beginning with '**How about**' followed by an *-ing* form or a noun.

Now, <u>how about</u> coming to stay with me, at my house?
<u>How about</u> some lunch?

You can also use a statement that begins with '**You'll**' and ends with the tag '**won't you?**' This implies that you are expecting the other person to accept.

You'll bring Angela up for the wedding, <u>won't you?</u>

7 **inviting someone to ask you for something**

You can invite someone else to ask you for something by saying '**Don't hesitate to...**'. This form of invitation is polite and emphatic, and is usually used between people who do not know each other well. It is often used in formal or business correspondence.

Should you have any further problems, please <u>do not hesitate to</u> telephone.
When you want more, <u>don't hesitate to ask me</u>.

8 **responding to an invitation**

If you want to accept an invitation, you say '**Thank you**' or, more informally, '**Thanks**'. You can also say something like '**Yes, I'd love to**' or '**I'd like that very much**'.

'You could come and stay with us for a few days.' – '<u>Yes, I'd love to</u>.'
'Won't you join me and the girls for lunch, Mr Jordache?' – '<u>Thanks</u>, Larsen. <u>I'd like that very much</u>.'

If you want to decline an invitation to visit someone or go somewhere with them, you can say something like '**I'm sorry, I can't**', '**I'm afraid I'm busy then**', or '**I'd like to, but...**'.

'I was wondering if you'd like to come round on Sunday.' – *'I'm afraid I'm busy that day.'*
'Would you like to stay for dinner?' – *'I'd like to, but I have to get back home.'*

You can also decline an invitation by saying '**No, thanks**', '**Thanks, but...**', or '**I'm all right, thanks**'.

'How about dinner?' – *'Thanks, but I've eaten already.'*
'Would you like to lie down?' – *'No, I'm all right.'*

Letter writing

1 formal letters	**6** address and date
2 address and date	**7** beginning an informal letter
3 beginning a formal letter	**8** ending an informal letter
4 ending a formal letter	**9** addressing an envelope
5 informal letters	

When you are writing a letter, the language you use and the layout of the letter will depend on how formal the letter is.

1 formal letters

If you are writing a formal letter, such as a business letter or an application for a job, you use formal language, as in the example below.

---

80 Green Road
Moseley
Birmingham
B13 9PL

29/4/12

The Personnel Manager
Cratex Ltd.
21 Fireside Road
Birmingham
B15 2RX

Dear Sir

I am writing in response to your advertisement for the position of Team Leader in *The Times* (28/4/12). Could you please send me an application form and details about the position. I have recently graduated from Southampton University in Mechanical Engineering.
I look forward to hearing from you soon.

Yours faithfully
James Laker
James Laker

---

2 address and date

You put your address in the top right-hand corner. You can put a comma at the end of each line, and a full stop at the end of the last one, but this is not necessary. Don't put your name above the address.

You put the date under your address. If you are using headed notepaper, you put the date above the address of the person you are writing to or at the right-hand side of the page. You can write the date in several different ways, for example **29.4.04**, **29/4/04**, **29 April 2004**, or **April 29th, 2004**.

 In American English the month is put in front of the day, for example **4/29/04**.

→ See **Reference** section **Day and dates**

You put the name or job title and the address of the person you are writing to on the left-hand side of the page, usually starting on the line below the date.

3 **beginning a formal letter**

You begin a formal letter with the person's title and surname, for example **Dear Mr Jenkins**, **Dear Mrs Carstairs**, or **Dear Miss Stephenson**.

→ See **Topic** entry **Names and titles**

If you do not know whether the woman you are writing to is married or not, you can use the title **Ms**. If you are writing a very formal letter, or do not know the person's name, you use **Dear Sir** or **Dear Madam**. If you are not sure whether the person you are writing to is a man or a woman, it is safest to write **Dear Sir or Madam**.

 When writing to a company, **Dear Sirs** is used in British English and **Gentlemen** in American English. It is also acceptable in American English to address a company as if it were a person when you do not have a name or person to send your letter to: **Dear AT&T**.

 People writing in the formal American style put a colon after the 'Dear...' expression, for example **Dear Mr. Jones:**. If you are writing in the British style, you can either use a comma or have no punctuation.

4 **ending a formal letter**

If you begin the letter using the person's title and surname (for example **Dear Mrs Carstairs**), you finish with **Yours sincerely**. If you want to be less formal, you can finish with **Yours**. If you begin your letter with **Dear Sir**, **Dear Madam**, or **Dear Sirs**, you finish with **Yours faithfully**.

 In American English, the usual way of finishing a letter is with the expression **Sincerely yours** or, more formally, **Very truly yours**. You write your signature underneath the expression you finish with. You can type your name (or write it in capitals) underneath your signature. If you are writing a business letter, you can also put your job title.

5 **informal letters**

If you are writing a letter to a friend or relative, you use informal language, as in the example on the next page.

63 Pottery Row
Birmingham
B13 8AS
18/4/12

Dear Mario

How are you? Thanks for the letter telling me that you'll be coming over to England this summer. It'll be good to see you again. You must come and stay with me in Birmingham.

I'll be on holiday when you're here as the University will be closed, so we can have some days out together. Write or phone me to tell me when you want to come and stay.

All the best,

Dave

6 address and date

You put your address and the date, or just the date, in the top right-hand corner. Don't put the address of the person you are writing to at the top of the letter.

7 beginning an informal letter

You normally begin an informal letter to a friend using **Dear** and the person's first name, for example **Dear Louise**. When people are writing to a relative, they use the person's 'relative' title, for example **Dear Dad**, **Dear Grandpa**, or **Dear Grandma**.

8 ending an informal letter

There are various ways in which you can end an informal letter. You can use **Love** or **Lots of love** when writing to close friends or relatives. When writing to someone you know less well, you can use **Yours**, **Best wishes**, or **All the best**.

9 addressing an envelope

The example below shows how to write the name and address on an envelope. In British English, some people put a comma at the end of each line, and a full stop after the county or country.

Miss S. Wilkins
13 Magpie Close
Guildford
Surrey
GL4 2PX

You usually use the title, initial or initials, and surname of the person you are writing to.

You can also use the person's title, first name, and surname: **Miss Sarah Wilkins**. When the letter is informal, you can just use their first name and surname, or their initial (or initials) and surname: **Sarah Wilkins** or **S Wilkins**.

If you are writing to someone who is temporarily staying with someone else or staying in a particular place, you put their name first and then, on the line below, put **c/o** in front of the name of the other person or the place, as in the example below. **c/o** stands for **care of**.

> Mr JL Martin
> c/o Mrs P Roberts
> 28 Fish Street
> Cambridge
> CB2 8AS

 When sending a letter to a place in Britain, you should put the **postcode** (the set of letters and numbers at the end of the address) on a separate line. The American equivalent is a **zip code**, and needn't be on a separate line.

Offers

1 offering something to someone	**5** less confident or firm offers
2 other ways of offering something	**6** offers to a customer
3 offering to help or do something	**7** replying to an offer
4 confident offers	

1 offering something to someone

There are several ways of offering something to someone.

A polite way of offering something is to say '**Would you like...?**'

Would you like another biscuit?
I was just making myself some tea. Would you like some?

When talking to someone you know well, you can use the less polite form '**Do you want...?**'

Do you want a biscuit?
Do you want a coffee?

If you know the other person well, and you want to be persuasive, you can use the imperative form **have**.

Have some more tea.
Have a chocolate biscuit.

You can also use just a noun phrase, making it sound like a question.

'Tea?' – 'Yes, thanks.'
Ginger biscuit?

TOPICS

2 other ways of offering something

If what you are offering is not immediately available, you can say something like '**Can I get you something?**' or '**Let me get you something to eat**'.

Can I get you anything?
Sit down and let me get you a cup of tea or a drink or something.

If you want the other person to take what they need, you say '**Help yourself**'.

Help yourself to sugar.
'Do you suppose I could have a drink?' – 'Of course. You know where everything is. Help yourself.'

A casual, non-emphatic way of offering something is to say '**You can have...**' or, if appropriate, '**You can borrow...**'.

You can borrow my pen if you like.

A British person might say '**Fancy some coffee?**' or '**Fancy a biscuit?**' as a way of informally offering something.

3 offering to help or do something

If you want to offer to help someone or to do something for them, you say '**Shall I...?**' You can use this kind of question whether you are offering to do something immediately or at some time in the future.

Shall I fetch another doctor?
'What's the name?' – 'Khulaifi. Shall I spell that for you?'

4 confident offers

If you are fairly sure that the other person wants to have something done for them at that moment, you can say '**Let me...**'.

Let me buy you a coffee.
Let me help.

If you want to make an offer in a firm but friendly way, you say '**I'll...**'.

Leave everything, I'll clean up.
Come on out with me. I'll buy you dinner.

5 less confident or firm offers

If you are not sure whether the other person wants you to do something, you can say '**Do you want me to...?**', '**Should I...?**' or, more politely, '**Would you like me to...?**' However, this can sound as if you are rather reluctant to do what you are offering to do.

Do you want me to check his records?
Should I go in?
Would you like me to drive you to the station?

You can also say '**Do you want...?**', '**Do you need...?**', or, more politely, '**Would you like...?**', followed by a noun referring to an action. Although you do not say directly that you are offering to do something, that is what you are implying.

Do you want a lift?
Are you all right, Alan? Need any help?

'**Can I...?**' is also sometimes used, by people who know each other slightly or have just met.

Can I give you a lift anywhere?

Another way of making an offer when you are not sure that it is necessary is to add '**if you want**' or '**if you like**' after using '**I'll**' or '**I can**'.

I'll drive you home if you want.
I can show it to you now if you like.

6 offers to a customer

Employees of a shop or company sometimes say '**Can I...**' or '**May I...**' when they are politely offering to help a customer on the phone or in person.

Flight information, can I help you?
Morgan Brown, Janine speaking, how may I help you?

7 replying to an offer

The usual way of accepting an offer is to say '**Yes, please**'. You can also say '**Thank you**' or, informally, '**Thanks**'.

'Shall I read to you?' – 'Yes, please.'
'Have a cup of coffee.' – 'Thank you very much.'
'You can take the jeep.' – 'Thanks.'

If you want to show that you are very grateful for an offer, especially an unexpected one, you can say something like '**Oh, thank you, that would be great**' or '**That would be lovely**'. You can also say '**That's very kind of you**', which is more formal.

'Shall I run you a bath?' – 'Oh, yes, please! That would be lovely.'
'I'll have a word with him and see if he can help.' – 'That's very kind of you.'

The usual way of refusing an offer is to say '**No, thank you**' or, informally, '**No, thanks**'.

'Would you like some coffee?' – 'No, thank you.'
'Do you want a biscuit?' – 'No, thanks.'

You can also say things like '**No, I'm fine, thank you**', '**I'm all right, thanks**', or '**No, it's all right**'.

'Is the sun bothering you? Shall I draw the curtains?' – 'No, no, I'm fine, thank you.'
'Do you want a lift?' – 'No, it's all right, thanks, I don't mind walking.'

! **BE CAREFUL**

Don't refuse an offer by just saying '~~Thank you~~'.

Opinions

1 showing type of opinion	**7** showing honesty
2 being cautious	**8** showing form of statement
3 showing degree of certainty	**9** explicitly labelling a thought
4 showing that something is obvious	**10** explicitly labelling a statement
5 emphasizing truth	**11** drawing attention to what you are about to say
6 showing personal opinion	

People often use expressions that show their attitude to what they are saying.

If you want to show how certain you are that what you are saying is true, you can use a **modal**.

→ See **Usage** entries **can – could – be able to**, **might – may**, **must**, **shall – will**, **should**

There are many adverbs which are used to show your attitude to what you are saying. These adverbs, which are sometimes called **sentence adverbials**, are explained below. Most of them are usually put first in a clause. They can also come at the end of a clause, or within a clause.

1 showing type of opinion

There are many sentence adverbials that you can use to show your opinion of the fact or event you are talking about, for example whether you think it is surprising or is a good thing or not. The following adverbs are commonly used in this way:

absurdly	incredibly	oddly	surprisingly
astonishingly	interestingly	of course	typically
characteristically	ironically	paradoxically	unbelievably
coincidentally	luckily	predictably	understandably
conveniently	mercifully	remarkably	unexpectedly
curiously	miraculously	sadly	unfortunately
fortunately	mysteriously	significantly	unhappily
happily	naturally	strangely	

Luckily, I had seen the play before so I knew what it was about.
It is fortunately not a bad bump, and Henry is only slightly hurt.

A small number of adverbs are often used in front of **enough**.

curiously	interestingly	strangely
funnily	oddly	

Funnily enough, lots of people seem to love bingo.
Interestingly enough, this proportion has not increased.

You can show what you think of someone's action using one of the following adverbs:

bravely	correctly	kindly	wrongly
carelessly	foolishly	rightly	
cleverly	generously	wisely	

She very kindly arranged a beautiful lunch.
Paul Gayner is rightly famed for his menu for vegetarians.
Foolishly, we had said we would do the decorating.

These adverbs typically come after the subject or the first auxiliary of the clause. They can be put in other positions for emphasis.

2 being cautious

You can use one of the following adverbials to show that you are making a general, basic, or approximate statement:

all in all	estimate	fundamentally	on the whole
all things	basically	generally	overall
considered	broadly	in essence	ultimately
altogether	by and large	in general	
as a rule	essentially	on average	
at a rough	for the most part	on balance	

Basically, the more craters a surface has, the older it is.
I think on the whole we did a good job.

You can also use the expressions **broadly speaking**, **generally speaking**, and **roughly speaking**.

We are all, broadly speaking, in favour of the idea.
Roughly speaking, the problem appears to be confined to the tropics.

You can use one of the following adverbials to show that your statement is not completely true, or only true in some ways:

almost	in effect	to all intents and	virtually
in a manner of	more or less	purposes	
speaking	practically	to some extent	
in a way	so to speak	up to a point	

It was <u>almost</u> a relief when the race was over.
<u>In a way</u> I liked her better than Mark.
Rats eat <u>practically</u> anything.

Almost, **practically**, and **virtually** are not used at the beginning of a clause, unless they relate to a subject beginning with a word like **all**, **any**, or **every**.

<u>Practically all schools</u> make pupils take examinations.

3 showing degree of certainty

You can show how certain or definite you are about what you are saying by using one of the following adverbials. They are arranged from 'least certain' to 'most certain'.

conceivably
possibly
perhaps, maybe
hopefully
probably
presumably
almost certainly
no doubt, doubtless, undoubtedly
definitely, surely

She is <u>probably</u> right.
<u>Perhaps</u> they looked in the wrong place.
He knew that if he didn't study, he would <u>surely</u> fail.

Maybe is normally used at the beginning of a sentence.

<u>Maybe</u> you ought to try a different approach.

Definitely is hardly ever used at the beginning of a sentence.

I'm <u>definitely</u> going to get in touch with these people.

You can imply that you do not have personal knowledge of something, or responsibility for it, by using **it seems that** or **it appears that**.

I'm so sorry. <u>It seems that</u> we're fully booked tonight.
<u>It appears that</u> he followed my advice.

You can also use the adverb **apparently**.

<u>Apparently</u> they had a row.

4 showing that something is obvious

You can use the following adverbials to show that you think it is obvious that what you are saying is right:

clearly	obviously	plainly
naturally	of course	

<u>Obviously</u> I can't do the whole lot myself.
Price, <u>of course</u>, is a critical factor.

5 emphasizing truth

You can emphasize the truth of your statement using the following adverbials:

actually	certainly	indeed	truly
believe me	honestly	really	

I was so bored I actually fell asleep.
Believe me, if you get robbed, the best thing to do is forget about it.
I don't mind, honestly.
I really am sorry.

Use **indeed** at the end of a clause only when you have used **very** in front of an adjective or adverb.

I think she is a very stupid person indeed.

→ See **Usage** entry **indeed**

You can use **exactly**, **just**, and **precisely** to emphasize the correctness of your statement.

They'd always treated her exactly as if she were their own daughter.
I know just how you feel.
It is precisely his originality that makes his work unpopular.

6 showing personal opinion

If you want to emphasize that you are expressing an opinion, you can use one of the following adverbials:

as far as I'm	for my money	in my opinion	personally
concerned	(*informal*)	in my view	to my mind

The city itself is brilliant. For my money, it's better than Manchester.
In my opinion it was probably a mistake.
There hasn't, in my view, been enough research done on mob violence.
Personally, I don't think we should hire him.
She succeeded, to my mind, in living up to her legend.
As far as I'm concerned, it would be a moral duty.

7 showing honesty

You can show that you are making an honest statement using **frankly** or **in all honesty**.

Frankly, the more I hear about him, the less I like him.
In all honesty, I would prefer to stay at home.

Another way of showing this is to use **to be** followed by **frank**, **honest**, or **truthful**.

I don't really know, to be honest.
To be perfectly honest, he was a tiny bit frightened of them.
'How do you rate him as a photographer?' – 'Not particularly highly, to be frank.'

These types of adverbial often act as a kind of warning or apology that you are going to say something rather impolite or controversial.

8 showing form of statement

You can use **to put it** followed by an adverb to draw attention to the fact that you are making your statement in a particular way.

To put it crudely, all unions have got the responsibility of looking after their members.
Other social classes, to put it simply, are either not there or are only in process of formation.

You can use **to put it mildly** or **to say the least** to show that what you are saying is an understatement.

Most students have, to put it mildly, concerns about the plans.
The history of these decisions is, to say the least, worrying.

9 explicitly labelling a thought

You can use **I** with a verb that refers to having an opinion or belief in order to show how strongly you hold an opinion. If you just say **I think** or **I reckon**, this often has the effect of softening your statement and making it less definite. By using **I suppose**, you often imply that you are not really convinced about what you are saying. If you use **I trust**, you mean that you quite strongly believe what you are saying. The following verbs are used like this:

agree	guess	realize	trust
assume	hope	reckon	understand
believe	imagine	suppose	
fancy	presume	think	

A lot of that goes on, I imagine.
He was, I think, in his early sixties when I first met him.
I reckon you're right.
I suppose she might have done it, but I don't really see why.

You can use **I'm** with the following adjectives to show that you strongly hold an opinion.

certain	convinced	positive	sure

I'm sure he'll win.
I'm convinced that it is the best way of teaching.
I'm quite certain they would have made a search and found him.

10 explicitly labelling a statement

You can explicitly show what kind of thing you are saying by using **I** and one of the following verbs:

acknowledge	contend	predict	tell
admit	demand	promise	vow
assure	deny	propose	warn
claim	guarantee	submit	
concede	maintain	suggest	
confess	pledge	swear	

I admit there are problems about removing these safeguards.
It was all in order, I assure you.
I guarantee you'll like my work.

I can't deny and **I don't deny** are used much more often than **I deny**.

I can't deny that you're upsetting me.

People often use **say**, for example with modals, to show that they are thinking carefully about what they are saying, or to show that they are only giving a personal opinion.

I must say I have a good deal of sympathy with Dr Pyke.
All I can say is that it's extraordinary how similar they are.
What I'm really saying is, I'm delighted they've got it.
I would even go so far as to say that we are on the brink of a revolution.

Let me, **May I**, and **I would like** are used with various verbs to introduce explicitly a point or question.

Let me give you an example.
May I make one other point.
I would like to ask you one question.

11 drawing attention to what you are about to say

You can use a structure consisting of **the**, a noun (or adjective and noun), and **is** to classify what you are about to say, in a way that draws attention to it and shows that you think it is important. The nouns most commonly used in this structure are:

answer	point	rule	tragedy
conclusion	problem	solution	trouble
fact	question	thing	truth

The fact is they were probably right.
The point is, why should we let these people do this to us?
The only trouble is it's rather noisy.
Well, you see, the thing is she's gone away.
The crazy thing is, most of us were here with him on that day.

Note that **that** can be used after **is**, unless the next clause is a question.

The important thing is that she's eating normally.
The problem is that the demand for health care is unlimited.

You can also use a clause beginning with **what** as the subject.

What's particularly impressive, though, is that they use electronics so well.
But what's happening is that each year our old machinery becomes less adequate.

→ See **Usage** entry **what**

Permission

There are several ways of asking, giving, and refusing permission.

1 asking permission

If you want to ask permission to do something, you can use '**Can I...?**' or '**Could I...?**' (You use **we** instead of **I** if you are speaking on behalf of a group.) '**Could I...?**' is more polite.

Can I light the fire? I'm cold.
Could we put this fire on?
Could I stay at your place for a bit, Rob?

You can add **please** to be more polite.

David, can I look at your notes please?
Good afternoon. Could I speak to Mr Duff, please.
Could you ask for them to be taken out, please.

You can also make your request very polite by adding **perhaps** or **possibly** after '**Could I**' or '**May I**'.

Could I perhaps bring a friend with me?
May I possibly have a word with you?

You can ask permission in a stronger way by using **can't** or **couldn't** instead of 'can' or 'could'. You do this if you think you may not be given the permission you want.

Can't I come?
Couldn't we stay here?

2 indirect ways

There are other, more indirect, ways of asking for permission to do something. You can use expressions such as '**Would it be all right if I...?**' and, more informally, '**Is it okay if I...?**'

Would it be all right if I used your phone?
Is it all right if I go to the bathroom?
Is it okay if I go home now?

In very informal situations, these expressions are often shortened so that they start with the adjective. This sounds more casual, as if you are assuming the other person will give their permission.

Okay if I smoke?

An even more indirect way is to say something like '**Would it be all right to...?**', using a *to*-infinitive.

Would it be all right to take this?

A more polite way is to say '**Do you mind if I...?**' or '**Would you mind if I...?**'

Do you mind if we discuss this later?
Would you mind if I just ask you some routine questions?

Again, these expressions are shortened in very informal situations.

Mind if I bring my bike in?

You can also say '**I was wondering if I could...**' or '**I wonder if I could...**'.

I was wondering if I could go home now.
I wonder if I could have a few words with you.

In formal situations, you can add **if I may** after stating your intention to do something. You do this when you do not think it is really necessary to ask permission but want to appear polite.

I'll take a seat if I may.

3 giving someone permission

There are many words and expressions that you can use to give someone permission to do something when they have just asked you for it.

In informal situations, you can say '**OK**' or '**All right**'.

'Could I have a word with him?' – 'OK.'
'I'll be back in a couple of minutes, okay?' – 'All right'

'**Sure**' is slightly more emphatic, and is used especially by American speakers.

'Can I go with you?' – 'Sure.'

'**Of course**', '**Yes, do**', and '**By all means**' are more formal, and emphatic.

'Could I make a telephone call?' – 'Of course.'
'Do you mind if I look in your cupboard for extra blankets?' – 'Yes, do.'
'May I come too?' – 'By all means.'

If you are not very certain or enthusiastic about giving permission, you can say '**I don't see why not**'.

'Can I take it with me this afternoon?' – 'I don't see why not.'

You can give someone permission to do something when they have not asked for it by saying '**You can...**'. If you want to be more formal, you say '**You may...**'.

You can go off duty now.
You may use my wardrobe.

4 refusing permission

The commonest way of refusing someone permission is to use an expression such as '**Sorry**', '**I'm sorry**', or '**I'm afraid not**', and give an explanation.

'I was wondering if I could borrow a book for the evening.' – 'Sorry, I haven't got any with me.'
'Could I see him – just for a few minutes?' – 'No, I'm sorry, you can't. He's very ill.'
'I wonder if I might see him.' – 'I'm afraid not, sir. Mr Wilt is in a meeting all afternoon.'

If you know the other person very well, you can simply say '**No**' or '**No, you can't**', but this is impolite. In informal situations, people sometimes use even more impolite and emphatic expressions to refuse permission, such as '**No way**' and '**No chance**'.

You can show that you do not really want someone to do something by saying '**I'd rather you didn't**'. You say this when you cannot in fact prevent them from doing it.

'May I go on?' – 'I'd rather you didn't.'

In British English, you can refuse someone permission to do something when they have not asked for it by saying '**You can't...**' or '**You mustn't...**'.

You can't go.
You mustn't open it until you get home.

 Speakers of American English do not usually use '**You mustn't...**'. They say '**Don't...**' instead. British people also use '**Don't...**'.

Don't eat all the cookies.

You can also use '**You're not**' and an *-ing* form. This is informal and emphatic.

You're not putting that thing on my boat.

Reactions

1 exclamations	7 expressing relief
2 'how'	8 expressing annoyance
3 'what'	9 expressing disappointment or
4 exclamations in question form	distress
5 expressing surprise or interest	10 expressing sympathy
6 expressing pleasure	

There are several ways of expressing your reaction to something you have been told or something you see.

1 exclamations

You often use an **exclamation** to express your reaction to something. An exclamation may consist of a word, a group of words, or a clause.

Wonderful!
Oh dear!
That's awful!

In speech, you say an exclamation emphatically. When you write down an exclamation, you usually put an exclamation mark (!) at the end of it.

2 'how'

How and **what** are sometimes used to begin exclamations. **How** is normally used with an adjective and nothing else after it.

'They've got free hotels run by the state specially for tourists.' – 'How marvellous!'
'He's been late every day this week.' – 'How strange!'

3 'what'

What is used in front of a noun phrase.

'I'd have loved to have gone.' – 'What a shame!'
'...and then she died in poverty.' – 'Oh dear, what a tragic story.'
What a marvellous idea!
What rubbish!
What fun!

! BE CAREFUL

You must use **what** and **a** (or **an**) if you are using a singular countable noun. For example, you say '**What an** extraordinary experience!' Don't say 'What extraordinary experience!'

You can put a *to*-infinitive such as **to say** or **to do** after the noun phrase, if it is appropriate.

'If music dies, we'll die.' – 'What an awful thing to say!'
What a terrible thing to do!

4 exclamations in question form

You can express a reaction by using an exclamation in the form of a question beginning with '**Isn't that**'.

'University teachers seem far bolder here than they are over there.' – 'Isn't that interesting.'
'It was a big week for me. I got a letter from Paris.' – 'Oh, isn't that nice!'

A few common exclamations have the same form as positive questions.

Alan! Am I glad to see you!
Well, would you believe it. They won.
'How much?' – 'A hundred million.' – 'Are you crazy?'

5 expressing surprise or interest

You can express surprise or interest by saying '**Really?**' or '**What?**'

'It only takes 35 minutes from my house.' – 'Really? To Oxford Street?'
'He's gone to borrow a gun.' – 'What?'

'**My God**' is also used to express surprise or interest. However, you should not use it if you are with religious people who might be offended by it.

My God, what are you doing here?

You can also express surprise or interest using a short question with the form of a question tag.

'He gets free meals.' – 'Does he?'
'They're starting up a new arts centre there.' – 'Are they?'
'I got the job.' – 'Did you? Good for you.'

To express very great surprise, you can use a short statement that contradicts what you have just heard, although you do in fact believe it.

'I just left him there and went home.' – 'You didn't!'

You can also express surprise, and perhaps annoyance, by repeating part of what has just been said, or checking that you have understood it.

'Could you please come to Ira's right now and help me out?' – 'Now? Tonight?'
'We haven't found your husband.' – 'You haven't?'

You can also use **That's** or **How** with an adjective such as **strange** or **interesting** to express surprise or interest.

'Is it a special sort of brain?' – 'Probably.' – 'Well, that's interesting.'
'He said he hated the place.' – 'How strange! I wonder why.'

You can say '**Strange**', '**Odd**', '**Funny**', '**Extraordinary**', or '**Interesting**' to express your reaction to something.

'They invented the whole story?' – 'That's right.' – 'Extraordinary.'
'They both say they saw it.' – 'Mmm. Interesting.'

You can also say '**What a surprise!**'

Tim! Why, what a surprise!
'Felicity? How are you?' – 'Oh, Alan! What a surprise to hear you! Where are you?'

In informal situations, you can use expressions such as '**No!**', '**You're joking!**', or '**I don't believe it!**' to show that you find what someone has said very surprising. '**You're kidding**' is a more informal way of saying '**You're joking**'.

'Gertrude's got a new boyfriend!' – 'No! Who is he?' – 'Tim Reede!' – 'You mean the guy who works in accounts? You're joking!'
You've never sold the house! I don't believe it!
'They'll be allowed to mess about with it.' – 'You're kidding!'

In very informal English, some people use expressions like '**Bloody Hell!**' to express surprise. However, this may cause offence, and should be avoided.

Some people use expressions beginning with '**Fancy**' and an -ing form to express surprise.

Fancy seeing you here!
Fancy choosing that!

6 **expressing pleasure**

You can show that you are pleased about a situation or about what someone has said by saying something like '**That's great**' or '**That's wonderful**', or just using the adjective.

'I've arranged the flights.' – 'Oh, that's great.'
'We can give you an idea of what the prices are.' – 'Great.'

You can also say things like '**How marvellous**' or '**How wonderful**'.

'I've just spent six months in Italy.' – 'How lovely!'
Oh, Robert, how wonderful to see you.

! BE CAREFUL

However, don't say 'How great'.

In a formal situation, you can say '**I'm glad to hear it**', '**I'm pleased to hear it**', or '**I'm delighted to hear it**' when someone tells you something.

'He took me home, so I was well looked after.' – 'I'm glad to hear it.'

These expressions are often used to show in a humorous way that you would have been annoyed if something had not been the case.

'I have a great deal of respect for you.' – 'I'm delighted to hear it!'

You can also show that you are pleased about something by saying something like **'That is good news'** or **'That's wonderful news'**.

'My contract's been extended for a year.' – 'That is good news.'

7 **expressing relief**

You can express relief when you are told something by saying **'Oh good'** or **'That's all right then'**.

'I think he will understand.' – 'Oh good.'
'They're all right?' – 'They're perfect.' – 'Good, that's all right then.'

You can also say **'That's a relief'** or **'What a relief!'**

'He didn't seem to notice much.' – 'Well, that's a relief, I must say.'
'It's nothing like as bad as that.' – 'What a relief!'

When you are very relieved, you can say **'Thank God'**, **'Thank goodness'**, **'Thank God for that'**, or **'Thank heavens for that'**.

'He's arrived safely in Moscow.' – 'Thank goodness.'
Thank God you're safe!

In formal situations, you should say something like **'I'm relieved to hear it'**.

'Is that the truth?' – 'Yes.' – 'I am relieved to hear it!'
'I certainly did not support Captain Shays.' – 'I am relieved to hear you say that.'

 People sometimes use sounds rather than words to express relief. In writing, this is usually represented by the words **phew** (in British English) or **whew** (American English).

Phew. I'm glad that's sorted out.
Whew, what a relief!

8 **expressing annoyance**

You can express annoyance by saying **'Oh no'** or **'Bother'**. **'Bother'** is slightly old-fashioned.

'We're going to be late.' – 'Oh no!'
Bother. I forgot to eat my sandwiches before I came here.

People often use swear words to express annoyance. **Damn** and **hell** are mild swear words used in this way. However, you should not use even these words when you are with people you do not know well. Words like **fuck** and **shit** are stronger swear words, and you should avoid using them, as they may cause offence.

Damn. It's nearly ten. I have to get down to the hospital.
'It's broken.' – 'Oh, hell!'

 Some people use words such as **sugar** or **flipping** in British English, and **darn**, **dang** or **shoot** in American English, to avoid using swear words in situations where they might cause offence.

I can't flipping believe it.
Oh shoot, I don't have a can opener.

You can also say **'What a nuisance'** or **'That's a nuisance'**.

He'd just gone. What a nuisance!

People often say things like '**Great**' or '**Oh, that's marvellous**' to express annoyance in a sarcastic way. Usually the way they say these things makes it clear that they are annoyed, not pleased.

'I phoned up about it and they said it's a mistake.' – 'Marvellous.'

9 expressing disappointment or distress

You can show that you are disappointed or upset at something by saying '**Oh dear**'.

'We haven't got any results for you yet.' – 'Oh dear.'
Oh dear, I wonder what's happened.

You can also say '**That's a pity**', '**That's a shame**', '**What a pity**', or '**What a shame**'.

'They're going to demolish it.' – 'That's a shame. It's a nice place.'
'Perhaps we might meet tomorrow?' – 'I have to leave Copenhagen tomorrow, I'm afraid. What a pity!'

People often just say '**Pity**'.

'Do you play the violin by any chance?' – 'No.' – 'Pity. We could have tried some duets.'

You can also say '**That's too bad**'.

'We don't play that kind of music any more.' – 'That's too bad. David said you were terrific.'

You can express great disappointment or distress by saying '**Oh no!**'

'Johnnie Frampton has had a nasty accident.' – 'Oh no! What happened?'

10 expressing sympathy

When someone has just told you about something bad that has happened to them, you can express sympathy by saying '**Oh dear**'.

'First of all, it was pouring with rain.' – 'Oh dear.'

You can also say things like '**How awful**' or '**How annoying**'.

'He's ill.' – 'How awful. So you aren't coming home?'
'We never did find the rest of it.' – 'Oh, how dreadful!'

You can also say '**What a pity**' or '**What a shame**'.

'It took four hours, there and back.' – 'Oh, what a shame.'

You can express sympathy more formally by saying '**I'm sorry to hear that**'.

'I was ill on Monday.' – 'Oh, I'm sorry to hear that.'

If what has happened is very serious, for example if a relative of the other person has died, you can express strong sympathy by saying '**I'm so sorry**' or, more informally, '**That's terrible**'.

'You remember Gracie, my sister? She died last autumn.' – 'Oh, I'm so sorry.'
'My wife's just been sacked.' – 'That's terrible.'

If someone has failed to achieve something, you can say '**Bad luck**' or '**Hard luck**', which implies that the failure was not their fault. If they can make a second attempt, you can say '**Better luck next time**'.

'I failed my driving test again.' – 'Oh, hard luck.'
Well, there we are, we lost this time, but better luck next time.

Replies

This entry explains how to reply to *yes/no*-questions and *wh*-questions that are being used to ask for information.

→ See **Topic** entries **Agreeing and disagreeing**, **Apologizing**, **Complimenting and congratulating someone**, **Greetings and goodbyes**, **Invitations**, **Offers**, **Requests**, **orders**, **and instructions**, **Suggestions**, **Thanking someone** for other ways of replying to things that people say

1 replying to *yes/no*-questions

When you reply to a positive *yes/no*-question, you say '**Yes**' if the situation referred to exists and '**No**' if the situation does not exist.

'Did you enjoy it?' – '*Yes, it was very good.*'
'Have you decided what to do?' – '*Not yet, no.*'

You can add an appropriate tag such as **I have** or **it isn't**. Sometimes the tag is said first.

'Are they very complicated?' – '*Yes, they are. They have quite a number of elements.*'
'Did you have a look at the shop when you were there?' – '*I didn't, no.*'

 Some speakers, particularly Irish and some Americans, answer with a tag question only, without using 'yes' or 'no'.

'You do believe me?' – '*I do.*'

Some people say '**Yeah**' /jeə/ instead of 'Yes' when speaking informally.

'Have you got one?' – '*Yeah.*'

People sometimes make the sound '**Mm**' instead of saying 'Yes'.

'Is it very expensive?' – '*Mm, it's quite pricey.*'

Sometimes you can answer a question with an adverb of degree.

'Did she like it?' – '*Oh, very much, she said it was marvellous.*'
'Has he talked to you?' – '*A little. Not much.*'

If you feel a 'No' answer is not quite accurate, or you want to be more polite, you can say **not really** or **not exactly** instead or as well.

'Right, is that any clearer now?' – '*Not really, no.*'
'Have you thought at all about what you might do?' – '*No, not really.*'
'Has Davis suggested that?' – '*Not exactly, but I think he'd be glad to get away.*'

Often when people ask a question, they do not want just a 'Yes' or 'No' answer; they want detailed information of some kind. In reply to questions like this, people sometimes do not say 'Yes' or 'No' but just give the information, often after **well**.

'Do you have any plans yourself for any more research in this area?' – '*Well, I hope to look more at mixed ability teaching.*'

2 replying to negative *yes/no*-questions

Negative *yes/no*-questions are usually used when the speaker thinks the answer will be, or should be, 'Yes'.

You should reply to questions of this kind with '**Yes**' if the situation does exist and '**No**' if the situation does not exist, just as you would reply to a positive question. For example, if someone says '**Hasn't James phoned?**', you reply '**No**' if he hasn't phoned.

'Haven't they just had a conference or something?' – '*Yes, that's right.*'
'Didn't you like it, then?' – '*Not much.*'

TOPICS

If you are replying to a negative statement which is said as a question, you reply '**No**' if the statement is true.

'*So you've never been guilty of physical violence?*' – '<u>*No.*</u>'
'*You didn't mind me coming in?*' – '<u>*No*</u>, *don't be daft.*'

If you are replying to a positive statement said as a question, you reply '**Yes**' if the statement is true.

'*He liked it?*' – '<u>*Yes*</u>, *he did.*'
'*You've heard me speak of Angela?*' – '<u>*Oh, yes.*</u>'

③ replying when uncertain

If you do not know the answer to a *yes/no*-question, you say '**I don't know**' or '**I'm not sure**'.

'*Did they print the list?*' – '<u>*I don't know.*</u>'
'*Is there any chance of you getting away this summer?*' – '<u>*I'm not sure.*</u>'

If you think the situation probably exists, you say '**I think so**'.

'*Do you understand?*' – '<u>*I think so.*</u>'

 American speakers often say '**I guess so**'.

'*Can we go inside?*' – '<u>*I guess so.*</u>'

If you are making a guess, you can also say '**I should think so**', '**I would think so**', '**I expect so**', or '**I imagine so**'.

'*Will Sarah be going?*' – '<u>*I would think so*</u>, *yes.*'
'*Did you say anything when I first came up to you?*' – '*Well,* <u>*I expect so*</u>, *but how on earth can I remember now?*'

If you are rather unenthusiastic or unhappy about the situation, you say '**I suppose so**'.

'*Are you on speaking terms with them now?*' – '<u>*I suppose so.*</u>'

If you think the situation probably does not exist, you say '**I don't think so**'.

'*Did you ever meet Mr Innes?*' – '*No,* <u>*I don't think so.*</u>'

If you are making a guess, you can also say '**I shouldn't think so**', '**I wouldn't think so**', or '**I don't expect so**'.

'*Would Nick mind, do you think?*' – '*No,* <u>*I shouldn't think so.*</u>'
'*Is my skull fractured?*' – '<u>*I shouldn't think so.*</u>'

④ replying to *either/or*-questions

If the question has **or** in it, you reply with a word or group of words that shows what the situation is. You only use a whole clause for emphasis or if you want to make your answer really clear.

'*Do you want to pay by cash or card?*' – '<u>*Cash.*</u>'
'*Are they undergraduate courses or postgraduate courses?*' – '<u>*Mainly postgraduate.*</u>'
'*Are cultured pearls synthetic or are they real pearls?*' – '<u>*They are real pearls*</u>, *but a tiny piece of mother-of-pearl has been inserted in each oyster.*'

⑤ replying to *wh*-questions

In replying to *wh*-questions, people usually use one word or a group of words instead of a full sentence.

'*How old are you?*' – '<u>*Thirteen.*</u>'
'*How do you feel?*' – '<u>*Strange.*</u>'

'Where are we going?' – 'Up the coast.'
'Why did you leave?' – 'Because Michael lied to me.'

Sometimes, however, a full sentence is used, for example when giving the reason for something.

'Why did you argue with your wife?' – 'She disapproved of what I'm doing.'

If you do not know the answer, you say '**I don't know**' or '**I'm not sure**'.

'What shall we do?' – 'I don't know.'
'How old were you then?' – 'I'm not sure.'

Requests, orders, and instructions

1 asking for something	**6** signs and notices
2 asking as a customer	**7** instructions on how to do
3 asking someone to do something	something
4 orders and instructions	**8** replying to a request or order
5 emphatic orders	

When you make a **request**, you ask someone for something or ask them to do something. If you have authority over someone or know them well, you give them an **order** or an **instruction**, that is you tell them to do something rather than asking them to do something. You can also give someone **instructions** on how to do something or what to do in a particular situation.

→ See **Topic** entry **Permission** for information on how to request permission to do something

Information on how to reply to a request or order is given at the end of this entry.

1 **asking for something**

The simplest way to ask for something is to say '**Can I have...?**' (You use **we** instead of **I** if you are speaking on behalf of a group.) You can add **please** in order to be more polite.

Can I have some tomatoes?
Can we have something to wipe our hands on, please?

It is more polite to use **could**.

Could I have another cup of coffee?

Requests with **may** sound very polite and formal, and requests with **might** sound old-fashioned.

May we have something to eat?

You use **can't** or **couldn't** instead of 'can' or 'could' to make a request sound more persuasive, if you think you may not get what you are asking for.

Can't we have some music?

You can use '**Have you got...?**', '**You haven't got...**', or '**You don't have...**' and a question tag, to ask for something in an informal, indirect way.

Have you got a piece of paper or something I could write it on?
You haven't got a spare pen, have you?

An indirect way of asking for something you think you might not get is to say '**Any chance of...?**' This is very informal and casual.

Any chance of a bit more cash in the New Year?

2 asking as a customer

If you want to ask for something in a shop, bar, café, or hotel, you can simply use a noun phrase followed by **please**.

A packet of crisps, please.
Two black coffees, please.

You can also say '**I'd like...**'.

As I'm here, doctor, I'd like a prescription for some aspirins.
I'd like a room, please. For one night.

If you are not sure whether a particular thing is available, you say '**Have you got...?**' or '**Do you have...?**'.

Have you got any brochures on Holland?
Do you have any information on that?

When you are in a restaurant or bar, you can say '**I'll have...**'. You can also say this when you are offered something to eat or drink in someone's house. You can also say '**I'd like...**'.

The waitress brought their drinks and said, 'Ready to order?' 'Yes,' said Ellen. 'I'll have the shrimp cocktail and the chicken.'
I'd like some tea.

3 asking someone to do something

You can ask someone to do something by saying '**Could you...?**' or '**Would you...?**' This is fairly polite. You can add **please** to be more polite.

Could you just switch the projector on behind you?
Could you tell me, please, what time the flight arrives?
Would you tell her that Adrian phoned?
Would you take the call for him, please?

You can make a request even more polite by adding **perhaps** or **possibly** after '**Could you**'.

Morris, could you possibly take me to the station on your way to work this morning?

If you want to be very polite, you can say '**Do you think you could...?**' or '**I wonder if you could...?**'

Do you think you could help me?
I wonder if you could look after my garden for me while I'm away?

You can also use '**Would you mind...?**' and an -*ing* form.

Would you mind fetching another chair?
Would you mind waiting a moment?

In formal letters and speech, you use very polite expressions such as '**I would be grateful if...**', '**I would appreciate it if...**', or '**Would you kindly...**'.

I would be grateful if you could let me know.
I would appreciate it if you could deal with this issue promptly.
Would you kindly call to see us next Tuesday at eleven o'clock?

Note that these very polite expressions are in fact sometimes used as indirect ways of telling someone to do something.

In informal situations, you can say '**Can you...?**' or '**Will you...?**'

Can you give us a hand?
Can you make me a copy of that?
Will you post this for me on your way to work?
Will you turn on the light, please, Henry?

If you think it is unlikely that the person you are asking will agree to your request, you use '**You wouldn't...would you?**', or '**You couldn't...could you?**' You also use these structures when you realize that you are asking them to do something which is difficult or will involve a lot of work.

You wouldn't sell it to me, would you?
You couldn't give me a lift, could you?

You can also use '**I suppose you couldn't...**' or '**I don't suppose you would...**'.

I suppose you couldn't just stay an hour or two longer?
I don't suppose you'd be prepared to stay in Edinburgh?

People sometimes use expressions such as '**Would you do me a favour?**' and '**I wonder if you could do me a favour**' to show that they are about to ask you to do something for them.

'Oh, Bill, I wonder if you could do me a favour.' – 'Depends what it is.' – 'Could you ring me at this number about eleven on Sunday morning?'
'Do me a favour, Grace. Don't say anything about this to Sally.' – 'All right.'

4 orders and instructions

People often ask someone to do something, rather than telling them to do it, even when they have authority over them, because this is more polite. More direct ways of telling someone to do something are explained below.

In an informal situation, you can use an imperative clause. This is a direct and forceful way of giving an order.

Pass the salt.
Let me see it.
Don't touch that!
Hurry up!
Look out! There's a car coming.

It is not very polite to use imperative clauses like this in speech and you mainly use them when talking to people you know well, or in situations of danger or urgency.

However, imperative forms are quite often used to invite someone to do something, in phrases such as '**Come in**' and '**Take a seat**'.

→ See **Topic** entry **Invitations**

You can use **please** to make orders more polite.

Go and get the file, please.
Wear rubber gloves, please.

You can use the question tag **will you?** to make an order sound less forceful and more like a request.

Come into the kitchen, will you?
Don't mention them, will you?

People also use **will you?** to make an order more forceful when they are angry.

TOPICS

See section below on **emphatic orders**.

You can also use the tag **won't you?** to make an order more like a request, unless you are giving a negative order.

See that she gets safely back, won't you?

You can say '**I would like you to...**' or '**I'd like you to...**' as an indirect, polite way of telling someone to do something, especially someone you have authority over.

John, I would like you to get us the files.
I'd like you to read this.
I shall be away tomorrow, so I'd like you to chair the weekly meeting.

5 emphatic orders

You use **do** in front of an imperative form to add emphasis when you are telling someone to do something that will be for their own benefit, or when you are friendly with them.

Do be careful.
Do remember to tell William about the change of plan.

You use '**You must...**' to emphasize the importance and necessity of the action.

You must come at once.
You mustn't tell anyone.

 You can also use '**You have to...**' or '**You can't...**' for this usage, and these forms are preferred in American English.

You have to come and register now.
You can't tell anyone about this place.

You can also add emphasis to an order by putting **you** in front of an imperative form. However, this is very informal and sometimes shows impatience.

You take it.
You get in the car.

You use '**Will you...?**' to give an order in a forceful and direct way, either to someone you have authority over or when you are angry or impatient.

Will you pack everything, please, Maria.
Will you stop yelling!

People also add the tag **will you?** to an imperative clause when they are angry.

Just listen to me a minute, will you?

People say '**Can't you...?**' when they are very angry. This is very impolite.

Really, can't you show a bit more consideration?
Look, can't you shut up about it?

Adding the question tag **can't you?** to an imperative clause is also impolite and shows annoyance.

Do it quietly, can't you?

People use '**You will...**', with stress on **will**, to emphasize the fact that the other person has no choice but to carry out the order. This is a very strong form of order, and is only used by people who have unquestionable authority.

You will go and get one of your parents immediately.
You will give me those now.

6 **signs and notices**

On signs and notices, negative orders are sometimes expressed by **no** and an *-ing* form.

No Smoking.

Must be is sometimes used for positive orders.

Children <u>must be</u> accompanied by an adult at all times.

7 **instructions on how to do something**

You can use an imperative clause to give instructions on how to do something. This is not impolite.

Turn right off Broadway into Caxton Street.
Fry the chopped onion and pepper in the oil.

Imperative clauses are especially common in written instructions. Verbs that usually have an object are often not given an object in instructions, when it is clear what the instructions refer to. For example, you might see **Store in a dry place** on a packet of food, rather than 'Store this food in a dry place'. Similarly, determiners are often left out. You might read in a recipe **Peel and core apples** rather than 'Peel and core the apples'.

Must be is used to show what you should do with something. **Should be** is used in a similar way, but is less strong.

Mussels <u>must be</u> bought fresh and cooked on the same day.
No cake <u>should be</u> stored before it is quite cold.

→ See **Topic** entry **Advising someone**

In conversation and informal writing, you can also use **you** and the present simple to give instructions. We use **you** like this in this book.

First <u>you take</u> a few raisins and soak them overnight in water.
Note that in sentences like these <u>you use</u> an infinitive without to after 'would rather'.

8 **replying to a request or order**

You can agree to someone's request informally by saying '**OK**', '**All right**', or '**Sure**'.

'Do them as fast as you can.' – 'Yes, <u>OK</u>.'
'Don't do that.' – '<u>All right</u>, I won't.'
'Could you give me lift?' – '<u>Sure</u>.'

If you want to be more polite, you can say '**Certainly**'.

'Could you make out my bill, please?' – '<u>Certainly</u>, sir.'

You can refuse someone's request by saying something like '**I'm sorry, I'm afraid I can't**' or by giving the reason why you are unable to do what they want.

'Put it on the bill.' – '<u>I'm afraid I can't do that</u>.'
'Could you phone me back later?' – '<u>No, I'm going out in five minutes</u>.'

Note that it is impolite just to say 'No'.

TOPICS

Structuring your ideas

A discourse marker is a word or expression that (1) shows a speaker's attitude, or (2) connects a sentence to what comes before or after it.

1 focusing on the speaker's attitude

There are several ways that speakers can focus on their attitude towards what they are saying, and who they are talking to.

▶ indicating your opinion

One way of showing your reaction to, or your opinion of, the fact or event you are talking about is by using **commenting adverbials**, which comment on the whole message given in a sentence.

Surprisingly, I found myself enjoying the play.
Luckily, I had seen the play before so I knew what it was about.
It was, fortunately, not a bad accident, and Henry is only slightly hurt.
Interestingly, the solution adopted in these two countries was the same.

The following adverbials are commonly used in this way:

absurdly	fortunately	oddly	true
admittedly	happily	of course	typically
alas	incredibly	paradoxically	unbelievably
anyway	interestingly	please	understandably
astonishingly	ironically	predictably	unexpectedly
at least	luckily	remarkably	unfortunately
characteristically	mercifully	sadly	unhappily
coincidentally	miraculously	significantly	unnecessarily
conveniently	mysteriously	strangely	
curiously	naturally	surprisingly	

One of the uses of 'at least' and 'anyway' is to show that you are pleased about a particular fact, although there may be other less desirable facts.

At least we're agreed on something.
I like a challenge anyway, so that's not a problem.

There are a few commenting adverbials that are often followed by 'enough' when used to show your opinion of what you are talking about:

curiously	interestingly	strangely
funnily	oddly	

Oddly enough, she'd never been abroad.
Funnily enough, I was there last week.

▶ distancing

There are several commenting adverbials that have the effect of showing that you are not completely committed to the truth of your statement.

Rats eat practically anything.
It was almost a relief when the race was over.
They are, in effect, prisoners in their own homes.
In a way I liked her better than Mark.

The following adverbials are used in this way:

almost	in effect	to all intents and	virtually
in a manner of	more or less	purposes	
speaking	practically	to some extent	
in a way	so to speak	up to a point	

Note that 'almost', 'practically', and 'virtually' are not used at the beginning of a clause.

▶ indicating a quality shown by the performer of an action

Another group of commenting adverbials is used to show a quality you think someone showed by doing an action. They are formed from adjectives that can be used to describe people, and are often placed after the subject of the sentence and in front of the verb.

The League of Friends generously provided about five thousand pounds.
The doctor had wisely sent her straight to hospital.
She very kindly arranged a delicious lunch.
Foolishly, we said we would do the decorating.

The following adverbials are used in this way:

bravely	correctly	helpfully	wisely
carelessly	foolishly	kindly	wrongly
cleverly	generously	rightly	

▶ mentioning your justification for a statement

If you are basing your statement on something that you have seen, heard, or read, you can use a commenting adverbial to show this. For example, if you can see that an object has been made by hand, you might say 'It is obviously made by hand.'

His friend was obviously impressed.
Higgins evidently knew nothing about their efforts.
Apparently they had a row.

These are some common adverbials used in this way:

apparently	evidently	obviously	unmistakably
clearly	manifestly	plainly	visibly

▶ showing that you assume your hearer agrees

People often use commenting adverbials to persuade someone to agree with them. In this way, they show that they are assuming that what they are saying is obvious.

Obviously I can't do the whole lot myself.
Price, of course, is an important factor.

The following adverbials are often used in this way:

clearly	obviously	plainly
naturally	of course	

▶ indicating reality or possibility

Some adverbials are used to show whether a situation actually exists or whether it seems to exist, or might exist.

She seems confident, but actually she's quite shy.
They could, conceivably, be right.
Extra cash is probably the best present.

The following adverbials are used like this:

actually	in practice	possibly	apparently
certainly	in reality	presumably	ostensibly
conceivably	in theory	probably	potentially
definitely	maybe	really	seemingly
doubtless	no doubt	unofficially	supposedly
hopefully	officially	~	theoretically
in fact	perhaps	allegedly	undoubtedly

The adverbials in the second group are often used in front of adjectives.

We drove along apparently empty streets.
It would be theoretically possible to lay a cable from a satellite to Earth.

▶ indicating your attitude

If you want to make it clear what your attitude is to what you are saying, you can use a commenting adverbial.

Frankly, the more I hear about him, the less I like him.
In my opinion it was probably a mistake.

Here is a list of some of the common adverbials used in this way:

as far as I'm concerned	in all honesty	in retrospect	to my mind
	in fairness	on reflection	
frankly	in my opinion	personally	
honestly	in my view	seriously	

▶ using infinitive clauses

Another way of showing the sort of statement you are making is to use 'to be' followed by an adjective, or 'to put it' followed by an adverb.

I don't really know, to be honest.
To put it bluntly, someone is lying.

2 connecting sentences

Sentence connectors are used to show what sort of connection there is between one sentence and another.

▶ indicating an addition

In the course of speaking or writing, you can introduce a related comment or an extra supporting piece of information using one of the following adverbials:

also	at the same time	furthermore	on top of that
as well	besides	moreover	too

I cannot apologize for his comments. Besides, I agree with them.
Moreover, new reserves continue to be discovered.
His first book was published in 1932, and it was followed by a series of novels. He also wrote a book on British poetry.

▶ indicating a similar point

You can show that you are adding a fact that illustrates the same point by using one of the following adverbials:

again	equally	likewise
by the same token	in the same way	similarly

Every baby's face is different from every other's. In the same way, every baby's pattern of development is different.
Never feed your rabbit raw potatoes that have gone green—they contain a poison. Similarly, never feed it rhubarb leaves.

▶ **contrasts and alternatives**

When you want to add a sentence that contrasts with the previous one or gives another point of view, you can use one of the following adverbials:

all the same	even so	nonetheless	still
alternatively	however	on the contrary	then again
by contrast	instead	on the other hand	though
conversely	nevertheless	rather	yet

I had forgotten that there was a rainy season in the winter months. It was, however, a fine, soft rain and the air was warm.
Her aim is to punish the criminal. Nevertheless, she is not convinced that imprisonment is always the answer.
Her children are very tiring. She never loses her temper with them though.

▶ **causes**

When you want to say that the fact you are mentioning exists *because of* the fact or facts previously given, you link your statements using one of the following adverbs:

accordingly	consequently	so	therefore
as a result	hence	thereby	thus

It isn't giving any detailed information. Therefore it isn't necessary.
We want a diverse press and we haven't got it. I think as a result a lot of options are closed to us.

▶ **putting points in order**

In formal writing and speech, people often want to say what stage they have reached in writing or speaking. They do this using the following sentence connectors:

first	secondly	finally	then
firstly	third	in conclusion	to sum up
second	thirdly	lastly	

What are the advantages of geothermal energy? Firstly, there's no fuel required, the energy already exists. Secondly, there's plenty of it.
Finally, I want to say something about the heat pump.

▶ **linking parts of a conversation together**

Sometimes people want to avoid abruptness when they are changing the topic of conversation, or when they are starting to talk about a different aspect of it. They do this by using a particular group of sentence connectors.

The following adverbials are commonly used in this way:

actually	incidentally	okay	well
anyhow	look	right	well now
anyway	now	so	well then
by the way	now then	then	you know

Here are some examples showing sentence connectors being used to change the topic of a conversation:

Actually, Dan, before I forget, she asked me to tell you about my new job.

Well now, we've got a very big task ahead of us.

Here are some examples showing sentence connectors being used to start talking about a different aspect of the same topic:

What do you sell there anyway?
This approach, incidentally, also has the advantage of being cheap.

Some sentence connectors are used at the beginning of a clause to introduce a fact, often one that corrects the statement just made. They can also be used at the end of a clause, and elsewhere, to emphasize the fact.

actually	as it happens	indeed
as a matter of fact	I mean	in fact

Note that 'actually' is used here to add information on the same topic, whereas in the previous paragraph it indicated a change of topic.

Actually, I do know why he wrote that letter.

I'm sure you're right. In fact, I know you're right.

Suggestions

1 neutral suggestions		**6** less firm suggestions
2 firm suggestions		**7** very firm suggestions
3 less firm suggestions		**8** suggestions about what would be
4 more formal suggestions		best
5 suggesting doing something together		**9** replying to a suggestion

1 neutral suggestions

There are many ways of suggesting a course of action to someone.

You can say '**You could...**'.

You could phone her and ask.
'Well, what shall we do?' – 'You could try Ebury Street.'

You can also use '**How about...?**' or '**What about...?**', followed by an *-ing* form.

How about taking him outside to have a game?
What about becoming an actor?

You can also use '**How about...?**' or '**What about...?**' with a noun phrase, to suggest that someone has a drink or some food, usually with you, or to suggest an arrangement.

How about a pizza?
What about a drink?
'I'll explain when I see you.' – 'When will that be?' – 'How about after work?'

A more indirect way of suggesting a course of action is to use '**Have you thought of...?**', followed by an *-ing* form.

Have you thought of asking what's wrong with Henry?

2 firm suggestions

A firmer way of making a suggestion is to say '**Couldn't you...?**', '**Can't you...?**', or '**Why not...?**'

Couldn't you get a job in one of the smaller colleges around here?

Can't you just tell him?
Why not write to her?

You can also use '**Try...**', followed by an *-ing* form or a noun phrase.

Try advertising in the local papers.
Try a little methylated spirit.

A very firm way of making a suggestion is to say '**I suggest you...**'.

I suggest you leave this to me.

If you want to suggest persuasively but gently that someone does something, you can say '**Why don't you...?**'

Why don't you think about it and decide later?
Why don't you go to bed?

→ See **Topic** entry **Advising someone** for other ways of saying firmly what course of action someone should take

3 less firm suggestions

If you do not feel strongly about what you are suggesting, but cannot think of anything better that the other person might do, you can say '**You might as well...**' or '**You may as well...**'.

You might as well drive back by yourself.
You may as well go home and come back in the morning.

4 more formal suggestions

More formal ways of making suggestions are expressions like '**You might like to...**' and '**It might be a good idea to...**'.

Alternatively, you might like to consider discussing your insurance problems with your bank manager.
You might consider moving to a smaller house.
You might want to have a separate heading for each point.
It might be a good idea to rest on alternate days between running.

5 suggesting doing something together

There are several ways of making a suggestion about what you and someone else might do.

If you want to make a firm suggestion which you think the other person will agree with, you say '**Let's...**'.

Come on, let's go.
Let's be practical. How can we help?

You can make the suggestion seem persuasive rather than firm and forceful by adding the tag **shall we?**

Let's discuss this later, shall we?
Let's meet at my office at noon, shall we?

For a negative suggestion, you say '**Let's not...**'.

Let's not talk here.
We have twenty-four hours. Let's not panic.
Let's not go jumping to conclusions.

 Speakers of American English sometimes say '**Let's don't...**' instead of 'Let's not...' in informal speech.

Let's don't talk about it.

Another way of making a firm suggestion is to say '**We'll...**'.

We'll talk later, Paula.
'What do you want to do with Ben's boat?' – 'We'll leave it here till tomorrow.'

Again, you can make the suggestion persuasive rather than forceful by adding the tag **shall we?**

We'll leave somebody else to clear up the mess, shall we?
All right, we'll change things around a bit now, shall we?

Another firm way of suggesting is to say '**I suggest we...**'.

I suggest we discuss this elsewhere.
I suggest we go to the hospital right away.

Another way of making a suggestion is to say '**Shall we...?**' You can make a suggestion like this sound firm or less firm by altering your tone of voice.

Shall we go and see a film?
Shall we make a start?
Shall we sit down?

6 less firm suggestions

When you want to make a suggestion without being too forceful, you use '**We could...**'. You use this form of suggestion when the issue of what to do has already been raised.

I did ask you to have dinner with me. We could discuss it then.
'I'm tired.' – 'Too tired for a walk, even? We could go to see a movie instead.'

You can also make a non-forceful suggestion in an indirect way, using '**I thought we...**' or '**I wonder if we...**' and a modal.

I thought we might have some lunch.
In the meantime, I wonder if we can just turn our attention to something you mentioned a little earlier.
I wonder whether we could have a little talk, after the meeting.

If you are unenthusiastic about your own suggestion, but cannot think of a better course of action, you say '**We might as well...**'.

We might as well go in.
We might as well go home.

7 very firm suggestions

 If you want to make a very firm and forceful suggestion, which you feel is very important, you say '**We must...**'. In American English, '**We've got to...**' or '**We have to...**' are more common with this meaning.

We must be careful.
We've got to go, now!
We have to hurry.

8 suggestions about what would be best

When you are suggesting doing something that you think is the sensible thing to do, you say '**We ought to...**' or '**We'd better...**'. People often soften this form of suggestion by saying **I think** or **I suppose** first, or adding the tag **oughtn't we?** or **hadn't we?**

We ought to tell Dad.
Come on, we'd better try and find somebody.

I think we'd better leave.
I suppose we'd better finish this later.
We ought to order, oughtn't we?
We'd better get going, hadn't we?

'**I think we should…**' is also used.

I think we should go back.
I think we should change the subject.

 If you are not sure that your suggestion will be accepted without argument, you say '**Shouldn't we…?**' or '**Oughtn't we to…?**'. Note that in American English, '**Oughtn't we…**' is followed by an infinitive without *to*.

Shouldn't we have supper first?
Shouldn't we be on our way?
Oughtn't we to phone for the police?

You can also say '**Don't you think we should…?**' or '**Don't you think we'd better…?**'

Don't you think we'd better wait and see what he says?

9 replying to a suggestion

The usual way of replying to a suggestion that you agree with is to say '**All right**' or '**OK**'. You can also say something like '**Good idea**' or '**That's a good idea**'.

'Let's not do that. Let's play cards instead.' – 'That's all right with me.'
'Try up there.' – 'OK.'
'Let's sit down for a while.' – 'Good idea.'

You can reply '**Yes, I could**' to a suggestion starting with '**You could**'.

'You could get a job over there.' – 'Oh yes, I could do that, couldn't I?'

A more casual way of replying is to say '**Why not?**'

'Shall we take a walk?' – 'Why not?'

People also sometimes say '**Fine**' or '**That's fine by me**' when replying to a suggestion about doing something together. If they are very enthusiastic, they say '**Great**'.

'What about Tuesday?' – 'Fine.'

If you do not agree with the suggestion, you can say '**I don't think that's a good idea**', '**No, I can't**', or '**No, I couldn't**'.

'You could ask her.' – 'I don't think that's a very good idea.'
'Well, can you not make synthetic ones?' – 'We can't, no.'

You can also give a reason for not accepting the suggestion.

'I'll ring her up when I go out to lunch.' – 'Why not do it here and save money?' – 'I like my calls private.'

Telephoning

In the examples in this entry, A is the person answering the phone, and B is the person who is making the phone call.

1 answering the phone

There are several ways of answering the telephone when someone phones you. Most people answer the telephone by saying '**Hello**'.

A: *Hello*.
B: *Hello. It's me.*

You can also give your name or, if you are at work, you can give the name of your organization or department. You can say '**Good morning**' or '**Good afternoon**' instead of 'Hello'.

A: *Parkfield Medical Centre*.
B: *Hello. I'd like to make an appointment to see one of the doctors this morning please.*

A: *Hello. Tony Parsons speaking*.
B: *Oh, hello. It's Tom Roberts here.*

A: *Good morning*.
B: *Good morning. Who am I speaking to?*
A: *Er, my name is Alan Fentiman*.

Some people say '**Yes?**' when answering a phone call, especially one within an organization, but this can sound abrupt and rude.

If you recognize the person's voice when they say 'Hello', you can say '**Hello**' followed by their name.

A: *Hello*.
B: *Hello, Jim.*
A: *Hello, Alex, how are you?*

If you don't recognize the caller's voice, you can ask who it is. If you are at home, you say '**Sorry, who is it?**' or '**Who is this?**'

A: *Hello*.
B: *Hello.*
A: *Sorry, who is it?*
B: *It's me, Terry.*

If you think you know who the caller is, you say, for example, '**Is that James?**' or '**That's James, isn't it?**'

A: *Hello*.
B: *Hello. Can I speak to John?*
A: *I'm afraid he's just gone out. Is that Sarah?*
B: *Yes.*

If you are at work, and the caller wants to speak to someone else, you say '**Who's calling?**' or '**Who's speaking?**'

B: *Hello, could I speak to Mrs George, please?*
A: *Who's calling?*
B: *The name is Pearce.*
A: *Hold on a minute, please.*

If the caller has got through to the wrong number, you say something like '**I think you've got the wrong number**' or '**Sorry, wrong number**'.

A: *Hello*.
B: *Mrs Clough?*
A: *No, you've got the wrong number*.
B: *I'm sorry.*

2 telephoning someone

When you are phoning a friend or relative, you can just say '**Hello**' when they answer the phone, if you think they will recognize your voice. You can add their name.

TOPICS

A: *Hello.*
B: <u>*Hello!*</u> *I just thought I'd better ring to let you know what time I'll be arriving.*
A: *Hello.*
B: <u>*Hello, Alan*</u>.
A: *Hello, Mark, how are you?*
B: *Well, not so good.*

After saying '**Hello**' friends and relatives normally ask each other how they are.

If you need to make it clear who you are when you phone someone, you say '**It's**' or '**This is**' and your name.

A: *Hello.*
B: *Hello.* <u>*It's Jenny*</u>.
A: *Hello.*
B: *Hello, Alan.* <u>*This is Eila*</u>.

You can also say '**It's ... here**'.

A: *Hello.*
B: <u>*It's Maggie Turner here*</u>.

Sometimes you do not need to give your name, for example when you are asking for general information.

A: *Citizen's Advice Bureau.*
B: *Hello. I'd like some advice about a dispute with my neighbours.*

If you are not sure who has answered the phone, you say '**Who am I speaking to?**' or, informally, '**Who's that?**'

A: *Hello.*
B: *Hello.* <u>*Who am I speaking to, please?*</u>
A: *Yes?*
B: *I want to speak to Mr Taylor.*
A: *I'm afraid Mr Taylor's not in the office right now.*
B: <u>*Who's that?*</u>

You can check that you have the right person, organization, or number by saying '**Is that...?**', or by just saying the name or number like a question.

A: *Hello.*
B: <u>*Is that Mrs Thompson?*</u>
A: *Er, yes it is.*
B: *This is Kaj Mintti from Finland.*
A: *Hello.*
B: *Hello?* <u>*435 1916?*</u>
A: *Yes?*

 Note that American speakers usually say '**Is this...?**' instead of 'Is that...?'

A: *Hello.*
B: *Hello.* <u>*Is this the Casa Bianca restaurant?*</u> *I want to speak with Anna. Anna di Pietro.*

3 **asking to speak to someone**

If the person who answers the phone is not the person you want to speak to, you say, for example, '**Can I speak to Paul, please?**' or '**Is Paul there?**'

A: *Hello.*
B: <u>*Can I speak to Sue, please?*</u>
A: *Hang on – I'm sorry, but she's not in at the moment.*
B: *Can I leave a message?*

A: Yes.
B: Would you tell her that Adrian phoned?

If you are making a business call, you say, for example, '**Could I speak to Mr Green, please?**' or just say the name of the person or department you want, followed by **please**.

A: William Foux and Company.
B: Er, good afternoon. Could I speak to Mr Duff, please?
A: Oh, I'm sorry, he's on another line at the moment. Can you hold?
B: No, it's all right. I'll ring later.
A: British Gas.
B: Customer services, please.
A: I'll put you through.

If the person you are speaking to is in fact the person you want, they sometimes say '**Speaking**'.

A: Personnel.
B: Could I speak to Mr Wilson, please.
A: Speaking.
B: Oh, right. I wanted to ask you a question about sick pay.

4 ending a phone call

When you end a phone call, you say '**Goodbye**' or, informally, '**Bye**'.

A: I'm afraid I can't talk right now.
B: OK, I'll phone back after lunch.
A: OK. Goodbye.
B: Goodbye.
A: I'll just check. Yes, it's here.
B: Oh, OK. Thanks. Bye.

People sometimes also say '**Speak to you soon**' or '**Thanks for ringing**'.

Thanking someone

1 basic ways of thanking	**6** thanking someone for an enquiry
2 emphatic ways of thanking	**7** thanking someone in a letter or
3 more formal ways of thanking	email
4 thanking someone for an offer	**8** replying to thanks
5 thanking someone for a present	

1 basic ways of thanking

You thank someone when they have just done something for you or given you something. You say '**Thank you**' or, more casually, '**Thanks**'.

'I'll take over here.' – 'Thank you.'
'Don't worry, Caroline. I've given you a marvellous reference.' – 'Thank you, Mr Dillon.'
'There's your receipt.' – 'Thanks.'
'Would you tell her that Adrian phoned and that I'll phone at eight?' – 'OK.' – 'Thanks.'

Some speakers, especially speakers of British and Australian English, say '**Cheers**' to thank someone in a casual way.

→ See **Usage** entry **cheers**

Some British speakers also say '**Ta**' /tɑː/.

'*You're pretty good at this.*' – '*Cheers, mate.*'
'*This is all the material you need.*' – '*Ta.*'

If you need to say why you are thanking the other person, you say '**Thank you for...**' or '**Thanks for...**'.

Thank you for a delicious lunch.
Well, then, good-night, and thanks for the lift.
Thanks for helping out.

2 emphatic ways of thanking

People often add **very much** or **very much indeed** to be more emphatic.

'*Here you are.*' – '*Thank you very much.*'
'*I'll ring you tomorrow morning.*' – '*OK. Thanks very much indeed.*'

> **!** **BE CAREFUL**
>
> You can say '**Thanks a lot**', but you can't say '~~Thank you a lot~~' or '~~Thanks lots~~'.
>
> '*All right, then?*' – '*Yes, thanks a lot.*'

If you want to show that you are very grateful, you can say something like '**That's very kind of you**' or '**That's very good of you**'.

'*Any night when you feel a need to talk, you will find me here.*' – '*That's very kind of you.*'
'*Would you give this to her?*' – '*Sure. When I happen to see her.*' – '*That's very good of you, Nicole.*'

You can also say something like '**That's wonderful**' or '**Great**'.

'*I'll see if she can be with you on Monday.*' – '*That's wonderful!*'
'*Do them as fast as you can.*' – '*Yes. OK.*' – '*Great.*'

Even more emphatic ways of thanking are shown below.

'*All right, Sandra?*' – '*Thank you so much, Mr Atkinson; you've been wonderful. I just can't thank you enough.*'
'*She's safe.*' – '*I don't know how to thank you.*'
I can't tell you how grateful I am to you for having listened to me.

3 more formal ways of thanking

People sometimes thank someone more formally by saying '**I wanted to thank you for...**' or '**I'd like to thank you for...**', especially when expressing thanks for something that was done or given a little while ago.

I wanted to thank you for the beautiful necklace.
I want to thank you all for coming.
We learned what you did for Ari and I want to tell you how grateful I am.
I'd like to thank you for your patience and your hard work.

You can also express thanks more formally by saying things like '**I'm very grateful to you**' or '**I really appreciate it**'.

I'm grateful for the information you've given me on Mark Edwards.
Thank you for coming to hear me play. I do appreciate it.

4 thanking someone for an offer

You can say '**Thank you**' or '**Thanks**' when accepting something that is offered.

'*Have a cake.*' – '*Thank you.*'

You say '**No, thank you**' or '**No, thanks**' when refusing something that is offered.
'*There's one biscuit left. Do you want it?*' – '*No, thanks.*'

> ! **BE CAREFUL**
> Don't refuse something by just saying '~~Thank you~~'.

→ See **Topic** entry **Offers**

5 **thanking someone for a present**

When you have been given a present, you say '**Thank you**', or something like '**It's lovely**'.
'*Here's a little gift for your birthday.*' – '*Oh, thank you! It's lovely.*'

People sometimes say '**You shouldn't have**' as a polite way of showing that they are very grateful.
'*Here. This is for you.*' – '*Joyce, you shouldn't have.*'

6 **thanking someone for an enquiry**

You also say '**Thank you**' or '**Thanks**' when replying to someone who has asked how you are or how a member of your family is, or if you have had a nice weekend or holiday.
'*How are you?*' – '*Fine, thank you.*'
'*Did you have a nice weekend?*' – '*Lovely, thank you.*'

7 **thanking someone in a letter or email**

When thanking someone in a letter or email, you most commonly say '**Thank you for...**'. In a formal business letter, you can say '**I am grateful for...**'.

Dear Madam, Thank you for your letter replying to our advertisement for an assistant cashier.
I am grateful for your prompt reply to my request.

If the letter or email is to a friend, you can say '**Thanks for...**'.
Thanks for writing.

8 **replying to thanks**

When someone thanks you for handing them something or doing a small service for them, it is acceptable not to say anything in reply in Britain.

 However, people in the United States, especially employees in shops, often say something like '**You're welcome**' or '**No problem**'. When someone thanks you for helping them or doing them a favour, you reply '**That's all right**', '**Don't mention it**', or '**That's OK**'.

'*Thank you, Charles.*' – '*That's all right, David.*'
'*Thanks. This is really kind of you.*' – '*Don't mention it.*'
'*Thanks. I really appreciate it.*' – '*That's okay.*'

If you want to be both polite and friendly, you can say '**It's a pleasure**', '**My pleasure**', or '**Pleasure**'.

'*Thank you very much for talking to us about your research.*' – '*It's a pleasure.*'
'*Thank you for the walk and the conversation.*' – '*Pleasure.*'
'*Thanks for sorting it out.*' – '*My pleasure.*'

'**Any time**' is more casual.
'*You've been very helpful.*' – '*No problem. Any time.*'

If someone thanks you in a very emphatic way, you can reply using the expressions below.

'He's immensely grateful for what you did for him.' – 'It was no trouble.'
'Thanks, Johnny. Thanks for your help.' – 'It was nothing.'
'I'm enormously grateful to you for telling me.' – 'Not at all.'

Warning someone

1	warnings	**4**	more formal warnings
2	strong warnings	**5**	warnings on products and notices
3	explicit warnings	**6**	immediate warnings

1 warnings

There are several ways of warning someone not to do something.

In conversation, you can say '**I wouldn't … if I were you**'.

I wouldn't drink that if I were you.

A weaker way of warning is to say '**I don't think you should…**' or '**I don't think you ought to…**'.

I don't think you should try to make a decision when you are so tired.
I don't think you ought to turn me down quite so quickly, before you know a bit more about it.

You can also warn someone indirectly not to do something by saying what will happen if they do it.

You'll fall down and hurt yourself if you're not careful.

You can warn someone not to do something by accident or because of carelessness by saying '**Be careful not to…**' or '**Take care not to…**'.

Be careful not to keep the flame in one place too long, or the metal will be distorted.
Well, take care not to get arrested.

2 strong warnings

'**Don't**' is used in strong warnings.

Don't put more things in the washing machine than it will wash.
Don't open the door for anyone.

You can emphasize **don't** with **whatever you do**.

Whatever you do don't overcrowd your greenhouse.
Don't get in touch with your wife, whatever you do.

You can mention the consequences of not doing what you say by adding **or** and another clause.

Don't say another word or I'll leave.

3 explicit warnings

People sometimes say '**I warn you**' or '**I'm warning you**' when warning someone, especially when preparing them for something they are going to experience.

I warn you it's going to be expensive.
I must warn you that I have advised my client not to say another word.
It'll be very hot, I'm warning you.

These expressions are also used as threats.

I'm warning you, if you do that again there'll be trouble.

4 more formal warnings

Never is used with an imperative in more formal warnings.

Never put antique china into a dishwasher.
Even if you are desperate to get married, never let it show.

'**Beware of...**' is used to warn against doing something, or to warn about something that might be dangerous or unsatisfactory.

Beware of becoming too complacent.
I would beware of companies which depend on one product.

The expression '**A word of warning**' is sometimes used to introduce a warning. So are '**Warning**' and '**Caution**', in books and articles.

A word of warning: Don't have your appliances connected by anyone who is not a specialist.
Warning! Keep all these liquids away from children.
Caution. Keep the shoulders well down when doing this exercise.

5 warnings on products and notices

'**Warning**' and '**Caution**' are also used on products and notices. '**Danger**' and '**Beware of...**' are used on notices.

Warning: Smoking can seriously damage your health.
CAUTION: This helmet provides limited protection.
DANGER – RIVER.
Beware of Falling Tiles.

6 immediate warnings

When you want to warn someone about something that they might be just about to do, you say '**Careful**' or '**Be careful**', or, more informally, '**Watch it**'.

Careful! You'll break it.
He sat down on the bridge and dangled his legs. 'Be careful, Tim.'
Watch it! There's a rotten floorboard somewhere just here.

In British English, you can also use '**Mind**', followed by a noun referring to something the other person might hit, fall into, or harm, or a clause referring to something they must be careful about.

Mind the pond.
Mind you don't slip.

'**Watch**' is sometimes used in a similar way, especially with a clause.

Watch where you're putting your feet.

 Other warning expressions are '**Look out**' and '**Watch out**'. '**Look out**' is used only in urgent situations of danger. '**Watch out**' is used for urgent situations and for situations that are going to arise or might arise, or, in American English, as '**Mind...**' is used in British English.

Look out. There's someone coming.
Watch out for that tree!
'I think I'll just go for a little walk.' – 'Watch out – it's a very large city to take a little walk in.'

REFERENCE

Abbreviations

An **abbreviation** is a shortened form of a word, compound, or phrase, made by leaving out some of the letters or by using only the first letter of each word. For example, **g** is an abbreviation for **gram** in an expression of weight such as **25g**, and **BBC** is an abbreviation for **British Broadcasting Corporation**. Some abbreviations are more commonly used than the full form.

You have to follow the accepted way of abbreviating, although with certain words there can be more than one way. For example, you can use either **cont.** or **contd.** as an abbreviation for **continued**.

In general, if a word begins with a capital letter, its abbreviation also begins with a capital letter. For example, the title **Captain** is written with a capital letter when used in front of a name, so the abbreviation **Capt** is also written with a capital letter.

There are five basic types of abbreviation.

1 abbreviating one word

The first three types are used for abbreviating a single word.

▶ The first type consists of the first letter of the word. When read aloud, the abbreviation is usually pronounced like the full word.

m = metre

p. = page

F = Fahrenheit

N = North

▶ The second type consists of the first few letters of the word. When read aloud, the abbreviation is usually pronounced like the full word.

cont. = continued

usu. = usually

vol. = volume

Brit. = British

Thurs. = Thursday

▶ The third type consists of the word with several letters missed out. When read aloud, the abbreviation is pronounced like the full word.

asst. = assistant

dept. = department

km = kilometre

tbsp. = tablespoonful

Sgt = sergeant

Note that the abbreviations for **headquarters** and **television** are of this type but consist of capital letters: **HQ** and **TV**. You say each letter separately. In the case of some units of measurement, the second letter is a capital. For example, the abbreviation for **kilowatt** or **kilowatts** is **kW**.

2 abbreviating more than one word

The fourth and fifth types of abbreviation are used for abbreviating a compound noun or a phrase.

▶ The fourth type consists of the first letter of each word. You usually say each letter separately, with the main stress on the last letter.

MP = Member of Parliament

CD = compact disc

USA = United States of America

VIP = very important person

rpm = revolutions per minute

The choice of **a** or **an** before an abbreviation of this type depends on the pronunciation of the first letter of the abbreviation. For example, you say **an MP** not 'a MP' because the pronunciation of 'M' begins with a vowel sound: /em/.

→ See **Usage** entry **a – an**

Note that abbreviations of compound nouns usually consist of capital letters even when the full words do not begin with capital letters. However, abbreviations of phrases usually consist of lowercase letters.

A few abbreviations of this type also include the second letter of one of the words, which is not written as a capital. For example, the abbreviation for **Bachelor of Science** (someone who has a science degree) is **BSc**.

▶ The fifth type of abbreviation uses the first letter of each word to form a new word. This type of abbreviation is called an **acronym**. You pronounce an acronym as a word, rather than saying each letter.

OPEC /'əʊpek/ = Organization of Petroleum-Exporting Countries

SARS /sɑːrz/ = severe acute respiratory syndrome

TEFL /'tefl/ = teaching English as a foreign language

Most acronyms consist of capital letters. When an acronym is written with lowercase letters, for example **laser** (= light amplification by stimulated emission of radiation), it is regarded as an ordinary word.

3 full stops with abbreviations

You can put a full stop at the end of the first three types of abbreviation, or after each letter of the fourth kind of abbreviation. However, people often do not put in full stops nowadays, especially between capital letters.

b. = born

Apr. = April

St. = Saint

D.J. = disc jockey

Full stops are more commonly put at the end of abbreviations in American writing than in British writing. The abbreviations commonly used before a person's name (**Mr.**, **Mrs.**, **Ms.** and **Dr.**) always have full stops in American English.

REFERENCE

Full stops are not usually used when writing abbreviations that are pronounced as words.

NATO /'neɪtəʊ/ = North Atlantic Treaty Organization

AIDS /eɪdz/ = acquired immune deficiency syndrome

4 plurals of abbreviations

If you want to make an abbreviation plural, you usually add a small '**s**' to the singular abbreviation.

hr	→	hrs
MP	→	MPs
UFO	→	UFOs

However, the plural of **p** (= page) is **pp**.

With words that refer to units of measurement, you usually use the same abbreviation for the singular and the plural. For example, **ml** is the abbreviation for both **millilitre** and **millilitres**.

Capital letters

1 obligatory capital letter

You must use a capital letter for the first word of a sentence or a piece of direct speech.

→ See **Reference** section **Punctuation**

You must also start the following words and word groups with a capital letter:

▶ names of people, organizations, books, films, and plays (except for short, common words like **of**, **the**, and **and**)

...Miss Helen Perkins, head of management development at PriceWaterhouse.
Troilus and Cressida and Coriolanus are the greatest political plays that Shakespeare wrote.

You spell even short, common words with a capital letter when they come at the beginning of the title of a book, film, or play.

...his new book, 'A Future for Socialism'.

▶ names of places

Dempster was born in India in 1941.
The strongest wind was recorded at Berry Head, Brixham, Devon.

▶ names of days, months, and festivals

The trial continues on Monday.
It was mid-December and she was going home for Christmas.

▶ nouns referring to people of a particular nationality

The Germans and the French move more of their freight by rail or water than the British.
I had to interview two authors – one an American, one an Indian.

▶ names of people used to refer to art, music, and literature created by them

In those days you could buy a Picasso for £300.
I listened to Mozart.

▸ nouns referring to products produced by a particular company

I bought a second-hand Volkswagen.
...a cleansing powder which contains bleach (such as Vim).

▸ titles used in front of someone's name

There has been no statement so far from President Bush.
The tower was built by King Henry II in the 12th century.

▸ adjectives showing nationality or place

...a French poet.
...the Californian earthquake.

▸ adjectives showing that something is associated with or resembles a particular person

...his favourite Shakespearean sonnet.
...in Victorian times.

2 **'I'**

The personal pronoun **I** is always written as a capital letter.

I thought I was alone.

! **BE CAREFUL**

The words **me**, **my**, **mine**, and **myself** are not written with a capital letter, unless they come at the beginning of a sentence.

3 **optional capital letter**

You can use either a lowercase letter or a capital letter at the beginning of

▸ words referring to directions such as **North** and **South**

We shall be safe in the north.
The home-ownership rate in the South East of England is higher than in the North.

▸ words referring to decades

It was very popular in the seventies.
Most of it was done in the Seventies.

▸ names of seasons

I planted it last autumn.
In the Autumn of 1948 Caroline returned to the United States.

 Note that in American English, a lowercase letter is used unless the word is part of a title.

Construction is expected to begin next spring.
...Rachel Carson's book 'Silent Spring'.

▸ titles of people (especially when used to refer to a type of person)

...the great prime ministers of the past.
...one of the greatest Prime Ministers who ever held office.
...portraits of the president.
...the brother of the President.

Days and dates

1 days	**9** decades and centuries
2 special days	**10** part of a decade or century
3 months	**11** using prepositions
4 saying years	**12** using other adverbials
5 'AD' and 'BC'	**13** indefinite dates
6 writing dates	**14** modifying nouns
7 saying dates	**15** regular events
8 seasons	

→ See **Topic** entry **Time** for information on how to indicate the time or part of the day when something happens

1 days

These are the days of the week:

Monday	Wednesday	Friday	Sunday
Tuesday	Thursday	Saturday	

Days of the week are always written with a capital letter. They are usually used without a determiner.

I'll see you on Monday.

However, if you are referring generally to any day with a particular name, you put **a** in front of the day.

It is unlucky to cut your nails on a Friday.

If you want to say that something happened or will happen on a particular day of a particular week, especially when making a contrast with other days of that week, you put **the** in front of the day.

He died on the Friday and was buried on the Sunday.
We'll come and see you on the Sunday.

Saturday and Sunday are often referred to as **the weekend**, and the other days as **weekdays**.

I went down and fetched her back at the weekend.
The Tower is open 9.30 to 6.00 on weekdays.
They are open weekdays and Saturday mornings.

When people say that something happens **during the week**, they mean that it happens on weekdays, not on Saturday or Sunday.

I never have time for breakfast during the week.

2 special days

A few days in the year have special names, for example:

New Year's Day (1st January)

Valentine's Day (14th February)

April Fool's Day (1st April)

Good Friday (not fixed)

Easter Sunday (not fixed)

Easter Monday (not fixed; not used in the USA)

May Day (1st May)

Fourth of July (4th July; not used in Britain)

Labor Day (first Monday in September; not used in Britain)

Hallowe'en (31st October)

Guy Fawkes Night (5th November; not used in the USA)

Thanksgiving (fourth Thursday in November; not used in Britain)

Christmas Eve (24th December)

Christmas Day (25th December)

Boxing Day (26th December; not used in the USA)

New Year's Eve (31st December)

3 months

These are the months of the year:

January	April	July	October
February	May	August	November
March	June	September	December

Months are always written with a capital letter. They are usually used without a determiner.

I wanted to leave in September.

In a date, months can be represented by a number. January is represented by 1, February by 2, and so on. You can use **early**, **mid**, and **late** to specify part of a month.

You can't use 'middle' like this, although you can use **the middle of**.

I should very much like to come to California in late September or early October.
We must have five copies by mid February.
By the middle of June the campaign already had more than 1000 members.

4 saying years

When you are speaking, you refer to a year before 2000 in two parts. For example, '1970' is said as **nineteen seventy**, and '1820' is said as **eighteen twenty**.

In the case of years ending in '00', you say the second part as **hundred**. For example, '1900' is said as **nineteen hundred**.

For years ending in '01' to '09', such as '1901', you can say, for example, **nineteen oh one** or **nineteen hundred and one**.

You refer to years between 2000 and 2009 as **two thousand** (2000) or **two thousand and eight** (2008), for example.

Years after 2009 are said as either **two thousand and ten** (2010), **two thousand and eleven** (2011), etc or as **twenty ten** (2010), **twenty eleven** (2011), etc.

5 'AD' and 'BC'

To be more specific, for example in historical dates, **AD** is added before or after the numbers for years after Jesus is believed to have been born: '1650 AD', 'AD 1650', 'AD 1650-53', '1650-53 AD'. Some writers who prefer to avoid referring to religion use **CE**, which stands for 'the Common Era': '1650 CE'.

REFERENCE

BC (which stands for 'Before Christ') is added after the numbers for years before Jesus is believed to have been born: '1500 BC', '12-1500 BC'. An alternative abbreviation that does not refer to religion is **BCE**, which stands for 'Before the Common Era': '800 BCE'.

6 writing dates

When writing a date, you use a number to show which day of the month you are talking about. There are several different ways of writing a date:

20 April

20th April

April 20

April 20th

the twentieth of April

If you want to give the year as well as the day and the month, you put it last.

I was born on December 15th, 1933.

You can write a date entirely in figures:

20/4/03

20.4.03

 Americans put the month in front of the day when writing the date in figures, so the date above would be written **4/20/03** or **4.20.03**.

This way of writing dates is often used for the date at the top of a letter, and for dates on forms. Dates within a piece of writing are not usually written entirely in figures.

7 saying dates

You say the day as an ordinal number, even when it is written in figures as a cardinal number. Speakers of British English say **the** in front of the number. For example, 'April 20' is said as **April the twentieth**.

 Speakers of American English usually say **April twentieth**.

When the month comes after the number, you use 'of' in front of the month. For example, '20 April' would be said as **the twentieth of April**.

You can omit the month when it is clear which month you are referring to.

So Monday will be the seventeenth.
Valentine's Day is on the fourteenth.

When you want to tell someone today's date, you use **It's**.

'What's the date?' – 'It's the twelfth.'

8 seasons

These are the four seasons of the year:

spring	summer	autumn	winter

Seasons are sometimes written with a capital letter in British English, but it is more usual to use a lowercase letter. They are written with a lowercase letter in American English.

I was supposed to go last summer.
I think it's nice to get away in the autumn.

REFERENCE

In American English, **fall** is usually used instead of 'autumn'.

They usually give a party in the fall and in the spring.

Springtime, **summertime**, and **wintertime** are also used to refer generally to particular times of year.

> ! **BE CAREFUL**
>
> Note that there is no word 'autumntime'.

→ See **Usage** entries **spring**, **summer**, **autumn**, **winter**

9 **decades and centuries**

A decade is a period of ten years. A century is a period of a hundred years. Decades are usually thought of as starting with a year ending in zero and finishing with a year ending in nine. For example, the decade from 1960 to 1969 is referred to as **the 1960s**.

In the 1950s, synthetic hair was invented.
He wrote most of his poetry in the 1840s.

When you are talking about a decade in the twentieth century, you don't have to say the century. For example, you can refer to the 1920s as **the 20s**, **the '20s**, **the twenties**, or **the Twenties**.

...the depression of the twenties and thirties.
Most of it was done in the Seventies.

> ! **BE CAREFUL**
>
> You can't refer to the first or second decade of a century in the way described above. Instead you can say, for example, **the early 1800s** or **the early nineteenth century**. Some people refer to the first decade of the twenty-first century as **the noughties**.

Centuries are considered by many people to start with a year ending in 00 and finish with a year ending in 99. Ordinals are used to refer to them. The **first century** was from 0AD to 99AD, the **second century** was 100Ad to 199 AD, and so on, so the period 1800–1899AD was the **nineteenth century** and the current century is the **twenty-first century** (2000–2099 AD). Centuries can also be written using numbers: **the 21st century**.

This style of architecture was very popular in the eighteenth century.
That practice continued right through the 19th century.

Note that some people think that centuries start with a year ending in 01, so, for example, the twenty-first century is 2001-2100.

You can add **BC** or **AD**, or **CE** or **BCE**, after the name of a century.

The great age of Greek sport was the fifth century BC.

You can also refer to a century using the plural form of its first year. For example, you can refer to the eighteenth century as **the 1700s** or **the seventeen hundreds**.

The building goes back to the 1600s.
...furniture in the style of the early eighteen hundreds.

10 **part of a decade or century**

You can use **early**, **mid**, and **late** to specify part of a decade or century. Note that you can't use 'middle' like this, although you can use **the middle of**.

His most important writing was done in the late 1920s and early 1930s.

REFERENCE

...the wars of <u>the late nineteenth century</u>.
In <u>the mid 1970s</u> forecasting techniques became more sophisticated.
The next major upset came in <u>the middle of the nineteenth century</u>.

11 using prepositions

You use particular prepositions when mentioning the day, date, or time of year of an event.

▶ You use **at** with:

religious festivals: at Christmas, at Easter

short periods: at the weekend, at the beginning of March

In American English you say **on the weekend** not 'at the weekend'.

▶ You use **in** with:

months: in July, in December

seasons: in autumn, in the spring

long periods: in wartime, in the holidays

years: in 1985, in the year 2000

decades: in the thirties

centuries: in the nineteenth century

▶ You use **on** with:

days: on Monday, on weekdays, on Christmas Day, on the weekend

In British English you say **at the weekend** not 'on the weekend'.

dates: on the twentieth of July, on June 21st, on the twelfth

Note that American speakers sometimes omit 'on' with days and dates.

Can you come <u>Tuesday</u>?

To show that something happened at some time in a particular period, or throughout a period, you can use **during** or **over**.

There were 1.4 million enquiries <u>during</u> 1988 and 1989 alone.
More than 1,800 government soldiers were killed in fighting <u>over</u> Christmas.

12 using other adverbial phrases

You can show when something happens using the adverbs **today**, **tomorrow**, and **yesterday**.

One of my children emailed me <u>today</u>.

You can also use a noun phrase consisting of a word like **last**, **this**, or **next** combined with a word like **week**, **year**, or **month**. Don't use prepositions with these time expressions.

They're coming <u>next week</u>.

→ See **Usage** entries **last – lastly**, **this – these**, **next** for detailed information on the use of these expressions

REFERENCE

If you say that you did something **the week before last**, you mean that you did it in the week just before the week that has just passed.

Eileen went to visit friends made on a camping trip the year before last in Spain.
I saw her the Tuesday before last.

If you say that something happened **a week ago last Tuesday**, you mean that it happened exactly one week before the previous Tuesday.

If you say that you will do something **the week after next**, you mean that you will do it in the week after the week that comes next.

I was appointed a week ago last Friday.
He wants us to go the week after next.

In British English, if you say that something is going to happen **Thursday week**, you mean that it is going to happen exactly one week after the next Thursday.

'When will it open?' – 'Monday week.'

 This construction is not used in American English, where you have to say **a week from Thursday**.

I'm leaving a week from Wednesday.

If you say that something will happen **three weeks on Thursday**, you mean that it will happen exactly three weeks after the next Thursday.

England's first game takes place five weeks on Sunday.

13 indefinite dates

→ See **Topic** entry **Time** for information on how to indicate an indefinite date

14 modifying nouns

If you want to show that you are referring to something that occurred or will occur on a particular day or in a particular period, you use **-'s** after a noun phrase referring to that day or period.

How many of you were at Tuesday's lecture?
...yesterday's triumphs.
...next week's game.
...one of this century's most controversial leaders.

You can use the name of a day or period of the year as a modifier if you are referring to a type of thing.

Some of the people in the Tuesday class had already done a ten or twelve hour day.
I had summer clothes and winter clothes.
Lee had spent the Christmas holidays at home.

When showing what season a day occurs in, you use the name of the season as a noun modifier. You can also use **-'s** with **summer** and **winter**.

...a clear spring morning.
...wet winter days.
...a summer's day.

15 regular events

If something happens regularly, you can say that it happens **every day**, **every week**, and so on.

I call my parents every Sunday.
Every weekend we went camping.

You can also use an adverb such as **daily** or **monthly**. This is more formal and less common.

It was suggested that we give each child an allowance <u>yearly</u> or <u>monthly</u> to cover all he or she spends.

If you want to say that something happens regularly on a particular day of the week, you can use **on** and the plural form of the day instead of using 'every' and the singular form of the day. You do this when you are simply saying when something happens, rather than emphasizing that it is a regular event.

He went there <u>on Mondays and Fridays</u>.

 In American English, the 'on' is often omitted in this meaning.

My father came out to the farm <u>Saturdays</u> to help his father.

If something happens at intervals of two days, two weeks, and so on, you can say that it happens **every other day**, **every other week**, and so on.

We wrote <u>every other day</u>.

A less common way of showing an interval is to say that something happens **on alternate days**, **in alternate weeks**, and so on.

Just do some exercises <u>on alternate days</u> at first.

You can also indicate an interval by saying that something happens **every two weeks**, **every three years**, and so on.

The World Cup is held <u>every four years</u>.
Take two tablets <u>every six hours</u>.

You can also show that something happens regularly by saying that it happens, for example, **once a week**, **once every six months**, or **twice a year**.

The group met <u>once a week</u>.
...in areas where it only rains <u>once every five or ten years</u>.
You only have a meal <u>three times a day</u>.

Irregular verbs

An **irregular verb** has a past form or an *-ed* participle that is not formed by adding *-ed*.

A few irregular verbs have regular past forms, but two *-ed* participle forms, one of which is irregular. The commoner one is given first.

base form	past form	*-ed* participle
mow	mowed	mowed, mown
prove	proved	proved, proven
sew	sewed	sewed, sewn
show	showed	showed, shown
sow	sowed	sowed, sown
swell	swelled	swelled, swollen

Some irregular verbs have two past forms and two *-ed* participle forms. The form more commonly used is given first in the following table; note that some of the verbs have no regular forms, only irregular ones.

base form	past form	-ed participle
bid	bid, bade	bid, bidden
burn	burned, burnt	burned, burnt
bust	busted, bust	busted, bust
dream	dreamed, dreamt	dreamed, dreamt
dwell	dwelled, dwelt	dwelled, dwelt
hang	hanged, hung	hanged, hung
kneel	kneeled, knelt	kneeled, knelt
lean	leaned, leant	leaned, leant
leap	leaped, leapt	leaped, leapt
lie	lied, lay	lied, lain
light	lit, lighted	lit, lighted
smell	smelled, smelt	smelled, smelt
speed	sped, speeded	sped, speeded
spell	spelled, spelt	spelled, spelt
spill	spilled, spilt	spilled, spilt
spoil	spoiled, spoilt	spoiled, spoilt
weave	wove, weaved	woven, weaved
wet	wetted, wet	wetted, wet
wind	wound, winded	wound, winded

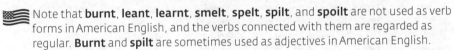 Note that **burnt**, **leant**, **learnt**, **smelt**, **spelt**, **spilt**, and **spoilt** are not used as verb forms in American English, and the verbs connected with them are regarded as regular. **Burnt** and **spilt** are sometimes used as adjectives in American English.

With a few verbs, different forms are used for different meanings. For example, the past form and the -ed participle of the verb **hang** is **hung** for most of its meanings. However, **hanged** is used when it means 'executed by hanging'.

→ See **Usage** entries **lay – lie, speed – speed up, wind**

The following table shows verbs that have irregular past forms and -ed participles.

base form	past form	-ed participle	base form	past form	-ed participle
arise	arose	arisen	catch	caught	caught
awake	awoke	awoken	choose	chose	chosen
bear	bore	born	cling	clung	clung
beat	beat	beaten	come	came	come
become	became	become	cost	cost	cost
begin	began	begun	creep	crept	crept
bend	bent	bent	cut	cut	cut
bet	bet	bet	deal	dealt	dealt
bind	bound	bound	dig	dug	dug
bite	bit	bitten	draw	drew	drawn
bleed	bled	bled	drink	drank	drunk
blow	blew	blown	drive	drove	driven
break	broke	broken	eat	ate	eaten
breed	bred	bred	fall	fell	fallen
bring	brought	brought	feed	fed	fed
build	built	built	feel	felt	felt
burst	burst	burst	fight	fought	fought
buy	bought	bought	find	found	found
cast	cast	cast	flee	fled	fled

base form	past form	-ed participle	base form	past form	-ed participle
fling	flung	flung	shed	shed	shed
fly	flew	flown	shine	shone	shone
forbear	forbore	forborne	shoe	shod	shod
forbid	forbade	forbidden	shoot	shot	shot
forget	forgot	forgotten	shrink	shrank	shrunk
forgive	forgave	forgiven	shut	shut	shut
forsake	forsook	forsaken	sing	sang	sung
forswear	forswore	forsworn	sink	sank	sunk
freeze	froze	frozen	sit	sat	sat
get	got	got	slay	slew	slain
give	gave	given	sleep	slept	slept
go	went	gone	slide	slid	slid
grind	ground	ground	sling	slung	slung
grow	grew	grown	slink	slunk	slunk
hear	heard	heard	speak	spoke	spoken
hide	hid	hidden	spend	spent	spent
hit	hit	hit	spin	spun	spun
hold	held	held	spread	spread	spread
hurt	hurt	hurt	spring	sprang	sprung
keep	kept	kept	stand	stood	stood
know	knew	known	steal	stole	stolen
lay	laid	laid	stick	stuck	stuck
lead	led	led	sting	stung	stung
leave	left	left	stink	stank	stunk
lend	lent	lent	strew	strewed	strewn
let	let	let	stride	strode	stridden
lose	lost	lost	strike	struck	struck
make	made	made	string	strung	strung
mean	meant	meant	strive	strove	striven
meet	met	met	swear	swore	sworn
pay	paid	paid	sweep	swept	swept
plead	pled	pled	swim	swam	swum
put	put	put	swing	swung	swung
quit	quit	quit	take	took	taken
read	read	read	teach	taught	taught
rend	rent	rent	tear	tore	torn
ride	rode	ridden	tell	told	told
ring	rang	rung	think	thought	thought
rise	rose	risen	throw	threw	thrown
run	ran	run	thrust	thrust	thrust
saw	sawed	sawn	tread	trod	trodden
say	said	said	understand	understood	understood
see	saw	seen	wake	woke	woken
seek	sought	sought	wear	wore	worn
sell	sold	sold	weep	wept	wept
send	sent	sent	win	won	won
set	set	set	wring	wrung	wrung
shake	shook	shaken	write	wrote	written

 Note that **gotten** is often used instead of 'got' as the -ed participle of **get** in American English.

→ See **Usage** entry **gotten**

Measurements

1 metric and imperial measurements	**8** distance and position
2 size	**9** weight
3 size of circular objects and areas	**10** temperature
4 size by dimensions	**11** speed, rates, and ratios
5 area	**12** measurements used before and after nouns
6 volume	**13** size of something abstract
7 distance	**14** measurement nouns before 'of'

You can refer to a size, area, volume, weight, distance, speed, or temperature by using a number or general determiner in front of a **measurement noun**.

...blocks of stone weighing up to a hundred tons.
They may travel as far as 70 kilometres in their search for fruit.
Reduce the temperature by a few degrees.

1 metric and imperial measurements

In Britain, two systems of measurement are used – the **metric system** and the **imperial system**. The metric system is now commonly used for most purposes, but the imperial system is still used for people's heights and weights, drinks in pubs, distances on road signs, and sports such as cricket, football, and horseracing.

Each system has its own measurement nouns, as shown in the table below. Their abbreviations are shown in brackets.

	metric units		imperial units	
size/distance	millimetre	(mm)	inch	(in or ")
	centimetre	(cm)	foot	(ft or ')
	metre	(m)	yard	(yd)
	kilometre	(km)	mile	(m)
area	hectare	(ha)	acre	(a)
volume	millilitre	(ml)	fluid ounce	(fl oz)
	centilitre	(cl)	pint	(pt)
	litre	(l)	quart	(q)
			gallon	(gal)
weight	milligram	(mg)	ounce	(oz)
	gram	(g)	pound	(lb)
	kilogram	(kg)	stone	(st)
	tonne	(t)	hundredweight	(cwt)
			ton	(t)

If you are using metric units, you use decimal numbers. For example, you say that something is **1.68 metres long** or **weighs 4.8 kilograms**. With imperial units, fractions are often used instead, for example **six and three-quarter inches** or **one and a half tons** of wheat.

Kilo is sometimes used instead of 'kilogram', and **metric ton** instead of 'tonne'.

REFERENCE

In the United States, the metric system is not commonly used, except for military, medical, and scientific purposes. The spellings **meter** and **liter** are used instead of 'metre' and 'litre'. The terms 'stone' and 'hundredweight' are very rarely used. Note that U.S. **pints**, **quarts**, and **gallons** are slightly smaller than British ones.

2 size

When you want to state the size of something, you usually use a number, a measurement noun, and an adjective. The verb you use is **be**.

The water was fifteen feet deep.
One of the layers is six metres thick.

As well as the plural form **feet**, the singular form **foot** can be used with numbers.

The spears were about six foot long.

If you are expressing size using feet and inches, and using the form **foot**, you don't have to say 'inches'. For example, you can say that something is **two foot six long**. However, don't say 'two feet six' or 'two foot six inches'.

I'm five foot three.
He's immensely tall, six feet six inches.

The following adjectives can be used after measurement nouns showing size:

deep	long	thick
high	tall	wide

! BE CAREFUL

Don't use adjectives such as 'narrow', 'shallow', 'low', or 'thin'.

When mentioning someone's height, you can use the adjective **tall** or leave it out.

She was six feet tall.
He was six foot six.

! BE CAREFUL

Don't use the adjective 'high' for people. Use **long** for babies, not 'tall'.

When describing how wide something is, you can use **across** instead of 'wide'.

The squid was 21 metres long with eyes 40 centimetres across.

Instead of using an adjective when stating size, you can use one of the following prepositional phrases after the measurement noun.

in depth	in length	in width
in height	in thickness	

They are thirty centimetres in length.
He was five feet seven inches in height.

When asking a question about the size of something, you use **how** and the adjectives listed earlier. You can also use the less specific adjective **big**.

How tall is he?
How big is it going to be?

3 size of circular objects and areas

If you are talking about the size of a circular object or area, you can give its circumference (edge measurement) or diameter (width) using **in circumference** or

in diameter. You can also say that something has a **radius** (half the diameter) of a particular length. However, don't say 'in radius'.

Some of the lakes are <u>ten or twenty kilometres in circumference</u>.
They are about <u>nine inches in diameter</u>.
It had <u>a radius of fifteen kilometres</u>.

4 size by dimensions

If you want to describe the size of an object or area fully, you can give its **dimensions**; that is, you can give the measurements for its length and width, or length, width, and depth. When you give the dimensions of an object or area, you separate the figures using **and**, **by**, or the multiplication sign **x** (pronounced 'by'). You use the verb **be** or **measure**. You can use adjectives such as **long** and **wide** or leave them out.

Each frame was <u>four metres tall and sixty-six centimetres wide</u>.
The island measures about <u>25 miles by 12 miles</u>.
The box measures approximately <u>26 inches wide x 25 inches deep x 16</u> inches high.

5 area

Area is often expressed by using **square** in front of units of length. For example, a **square metre** has the same area as a square whose sides are one metre long.

He had cleared away about <u>three square inches</u>.
They are said to be as little as <u>300 sq cm</u>.

If you are talking about a square object or area, you can give the length of each side followed by the word **square**.

Each family has only one room <u>eight or ten feet square</u>.
...an area that is <u>25 km square</u>.

When talking about large areas of land, the words **hectare** and **acre** are often used.

In 1975 there were <u>1,240 million hectares</u> under cultivation.
His land covers <u>twenty acres</u>.

6 volume

The volume of an object is the amount of space it occupies or contains.

Volume is usually expressed by using **cubic** in front of units of length. For example, you can say **10 cubic centimetres** or **200 cubic feet**.

Its brain was close to <u>500 cubic centimetres (49 cubic inches)</u>.

Units of volume such as **litre** and **gallon** are used to refer to quantities of liquids and gases.

Wine production is expected to reach <u>4.1 billion gallons</u> this year.
The amount of air being expelled is about <u>1,000 to 1,500 mls</u>.

7 distance

You can show the distance from one thing to another by using a number and measurement noun in front of **from**, **away from**, or **away**.

The hotel is <u>60 yds from the beach</u>.
These offices were approximately <u>nine kilometres away from the city centre</u>.
She sat down about <u>a hundred metres away</u>.

Distance can also be shown by stating the time taken to travel it.

It is <u>half an hour from the Pinewood Studios</u> and <u>forty-five minutes from London</u>.
They lived only <u>two or three days away from Juffure</u>.

The method of travelling can be stated to be more precise.

It is less than an hour's drive from here.
It's about five minutes' walk from the bus stop.

If you want to know the distance to a place, you use **how far**, usually with **from**, or with impersonal **it** and **to**.

How far is Chester from here?
How far is it to Charles City?

! **BE CAREFUL**

'Far' is not used when stating distances.

→ See **Usage** entry **far**

8 **distance and position**

To show both the distance and the position of something in relation to another place or object, the distance can be stated in front of the following prepositions:

above	beneath	off	under
across	beyond	out of	underneath
along	down	outside	up
behind	inside	over	
below	into	past	

He guessed that he was about ten miles above the surface.
Maurice was only a few yards behind him.

All the words in the list above, except 'across', 'into', 'over', and 'past', can be used as adverbs after the distance. The adverbs **apart**, **in**, **inland**, **offshore**, **on**, and **out** can also be used.

These two fossils had been lying about 50 feet apart in the sand.
We were now forty miles inland.
A few metres further on were other unmistakable traces of disaster.

The distance can also be stated in front of phrases such as **north of**, **to the east of**, and **to the left**.

He was some miles north of Ayr.
It had exploded 100 yards to their right.

9 **weight**

When you want to state how much an object or animal weighs, you use the verb **weigh**.

The statue weighs fifty or more kilos.
The calf weighs 50 lbs.

When you want to state how much a person weighs, you can use **weigh** or **be**. In Britain, you usually use the singular form **stone**.

He weighs about nine and a half stone.
You're about ten and a half stone.

If you express weight using stones and pounds, you can leave out the word 'pounds'. For example, you can say that someone weighs **twelve stone four**. Don't say 'two pounds heavy', but you can say 'two pounds in weight'.

I put on nearly a stone in weight.

In the United States, all weights are normally expressed in **pounds** or **tons**. 'Stone' is very rarely used.

REFERENCE

Philip Swallow weighs about 140 pounds.

 Americans often omit the words 'hundred' and 'pounds' when talking about a person's weight.

I bet he weighs one seventy, at least.

When asking about the weight of something or someone, you can use **how much** and **weigh**.

How much does the whole thing weigh?

You can also use **how heavy**.

How heavy are they?

10 temperature

You express temperature using either degrees centigrade (often written **5°C**), or degrees Fahrenheit (often written **5°F**). In everyday language the metric term **centigrade** is used, whereas in scientific language **Celsius** is used to refer to the same scale of measurement.

The temperature was still 23 degrees centigrade.
It was 95°C, and felt much colder.

If the scale is known, **degrees** can be used by itself.

It's 72 degrees down here and we've had a dry week.

 In cold weather, temperatures are often stated as **degrees below freezing** or **degrees below zero**. Note that in Britain **below zero** usually means below zero Celsius, but in the US **below zero** means below zero Fahrenheit, which is much colder.

...when the temperature is fifteen degrees below freezing.
It's amazingly cold: must be twenty degrees below zero.

11 speed, rates, and ratios

You talk about the speed of something by saying how far it travels in a particular unit of time. To do this, you use a noun such as **kilometre** or **mile**, followed by **per**, **a**, or **an**, and a noun referring to a length of time.

Wind speeds at the airport were 160 kilometres per hour.
He'd been driving at 10 miles an hour.

When writing about speeds, rates, or pressures, you can use the symbol ' **/** ' instead of 'per' between abbreviations for the units of measurement.

...a velocity of 160 km/sec.

Per, **a**, and **an** are also used when talking about other rates and ratios.

...a heart rate of 70 beats per minute.
He earns thirty dollars an hour.

Per can also be used in front of a word that does not refer to a length of time or a unit of measurement.

In Indonesia there are 18,100 people per doctor.
I think we have more paper per employee in this department than in any other.

Per head or **a head** are often used instead of 'per person' or 'a person'.

The average cereal consumption per head per year in the U.S.A. is 900 kg.

You can also use **to the** when you are talking about rates and ratios.

The exchange rate would soon be $2 to the pound.

REFERENCE

12 measurements used before and after nouns

Expressions showing size, area, volume, distance, and weight can be used as modifiers in front of a noun.

...a 5 foot 9 inch bed.
15 cm x 10 cm posts would be ideal.
...a 2-litre engine.

You can use adjectives like 'long' and 'high', but you do not have to.

If the expression consists simply of a number and a measurement noun, it is often hyphenated.

...a five-pound bag of lentils.
We finished our 500-mile journey at 4.30 p.m. on the 25th September.

> ! **BE CAREFUL**
>
> The measurement noun is singular, not plural, even though it comes after a number. For example, don't say 'a ten-miles walk'. Say **a ten-mile walk**.

However, the plural form is used in athletics, because the measurement is really the name of a race. For example, 'the 100 metres record' means 'the record for the 100 metres (race)'.

He won the 100 metres breaststroke.

You can use measurement expressions, usually ending in an adjective or a phrase beginning with **in**, after a noun.

There were seven main bedrooms and a sitting-room fifty feet long.
...a giant planet over 30,000 miles in diameter.

You can also show the area or weight of something using -ing forms such as **covering**, **measuring**, or **weighing**.

...a large park covering 40,000 square feet.
...a square area measuring 900 metres on each side.
...an iron bar weighing fifteen pounds.

You can also show the area or volume of something using a phrase beginning with **of**.

...industrial units of less than 15,000 sq ft.
...vessels of 100 litres.

13 size of something abstract

If you want to show how great something abstract such as an area, speed, or increase is, you use **of**.

...speeds of nearly 100 mph.
...an average annual temperature of 20 50.
...an increase of 10 per cent.

You can also sometimes use a modifier, for example when talking about percentages or salaries.

...a 71 per cent increase in earnings.
...his £ 25,000-a-year salary.

14 measurement nouns before 'of'

Measurement nouns are often used in front of **of** to refer to an amount of something which is a particular length, area, volume, or weight.

...20 yds of nylon.

→ See **Grammar** entry **Quantity**

→ See **Topic** entry **Pieces and amounts**

Nationality words

1 basic forms		**5** combining nationality adjectives	
2 referring to a person		**6** language	
3 referring to the people		**7** cities, regions, and states	
4 country as modifier			

1 basic forms

When talking about people and things from a particular country, you use one of three types of words:

▶ an adjective showing the country, such as **French** in **French wine**

▶ a noun referring to a person from the country, such as **Frenchman**

▶ a noun preceded by **the** which refers to all the people of the country, such as **the French**

In many cases, the word for a person who comes from a particular country is the same as the adjective, and the word for all the people of the country is the plural form of this. Here are some examples:

country	adjective	person	people
America	American	an American	the Americans
Australia	Australian	an Australian	the Australians
Belgium	Belgian	a Belgian	the Belgians
Canada	Canadian	a Canadian	the Canadians
Chile	Chilean	a Chilean	the Chileans
Germany	German	a German	the Germans
Greece	Greek	a Greek	the Greeks
India	Indian	an Indian	the Indians
Italy	Italian	an Italian	the Italians
Mexico	Mexican	a Mexican	the Mexicans
Norway	Norwegian	a Norwegian	the Norwegians
Pakistan	Pakistani	a Pakistani	the Pakistanis

All nationality adjectives that end in '**-an**' follow this pattern. All nationality adjectives that end in '**-ese**' also follow this pattern. However, the plural form of these words is the same as the singular form. For example:

country	adjective	person	people
China	Chinese	a Chinese	the Chinese
Portugal	Portuguese	a Portuguese	the Portuguese
Vietnam	Vietnamese	a Vietnamese	the Vietnamese

A form ending in '**-ese**' is in fact not commonly used to refer to one person. For example, people tend to say **a Portuguese man** or **a Portuguese woman** rather than 'a Portuguese'.

REFERENCE

Swiss also follows this pattern.

There is a group of nationality words where the word for all the people of a country is the plural of the word for a person from that country, but the adjective is different. Here are some examples:

country	adjective	person	people
Czech Republic	Czech	a Czech	the Czechs
Denmark	Danish	a Dane	the Danes
Finland	Finnish	a Finn	the Finns
Iceland	Icelandic	an Icelander	the Icelanders
New Zealand	New Zealand	a New Zealander	the New Zealanders
Poland	Polish	a Pole	the Poles
Slovakia	Slovak	a Slovak	the Slovaks
Sweden	Swedish	a Swede	the Swedes
Turkey	Turkish	a Turk	the Turks

Another group of nationality words have a special word for the person who comes from the country, but the adjective and the word for the people are the same. Here are some examples:

country	adjective	person	people
Britain	British	a Briton	the British
England	English	an Englishman	the English
		an Englishwoman	
France	French	a Frenchman	the French
		a Frenchwoman	
Holland	Dutch	a Dutchman	the Dutch
		a Dutchwoman	
Ireland	Irish	an Irishman	the Irish
		an Irishwoman	
Spain	Spanish	a Spaniard	the Spanish
Wales	Welsh	a Welshman	the Welsh
		a Welshwoman	

 Briton is used only in writing, and is not common in British English, but is the standard term for someone from the UK in American English.

The adjective relating to **Scotland** is **Scottish**. A person from Scotland is **a Scot**, **a Scotsman**, or **a Scotswoman**. You usually refer to all the people in Scotland as **the Scots**.

2 referring to a person

Instead of using a nationality noun to refer to a person from a particular country, you can use a nationality adjective followed by a noun such as **man**, **gentleman**, **woman**, or **lady**.

...an Indian gentleman.
...a French lady.

People usually use nationality adjectives rather than nouns after **be**. For example, you would say **He's Polish** rather than 'He's a Pole'.

Spike is <u>American</u>. You can tell from the accent.

3 referring to the people

When you are saying something about a nation, you use a plural form of the verb, even when the nationality word you are using does not end in '-s'.

The British are worried about the prospect of cheap imports.

You can use plural nouns ending in '-s' on their own to refer to the people of a particular country.

There is no way in which Italians, for example, can be prevented from entering Germany or France to seek jobs.

You can use a general determiner, a number, or an adjective in front of a plural noun to refer to some of the people of a particular country.

Many Americans assume that the British are stiff and formal.
There were four Germans with Dougal.

! BE CAREFUL

You can't use nationality words which do not end in '-s' like this. For example, you can't say 'many French' or 'four French'.

You can also use the name of a country to mean the people who belong to it or who are representing it officially. You use a singular form of a verb with it.

...the fact that Britain has been excluded from these talks.

4 country as modifier

If there is no adjective that shows what country someone or something belongs to, you can use the name of the country as a modifier.

...the New Zealand government.

5 combining nationality adjectives

You can usually combine nationality adjectives by putting a hyphen between them when you want to show that something involves two countries.

...He has dual German-American citizenship.
...the Italian-Swiss border.

There are a few special adjectives that are only used in this sort of combination, in front of the hyphen.

Anglo- (England or Britain)

Euro- (Europe)

Franco- (France)

Indo- (India)

Italo- (Italy)

Russo- (Russia)

Sino- (China)

...Anglo-American trade relations.

6 language

Many nationality adjectives can be used to refer to the language that is spoken in a particular country or that was originally spoken in a particular country.

She speaks French so well.
There's something written here in Greek.

REFERENCE

7 **cities, regions, and states**

There are a number of nouns that are used to refer to a person from a particular city, region, or state.

...a 23-year-old New Yorker.
Perhaps Londoners have simply got used to it.
Their children are now like other Californians.

Similarly, there are a number of adjectives that show that a person or thing comes from or exists in a particular city or state.

...a Glaswegian accent.
...a Californian beach.

Numbers and fractions

1 numbers		**12** ordinals as modifiers	
2 expressing numbers		**13** ordinals as pronouns	
3 position		**14** fractions	
4 agreement		**15** agreement of fractions	
5 numbers as pronouns		**16** fractions as pronouns	
6 numbers in compound adjectives		**17** decimals	
7 'one'		**18** percentages	
8 'zero'		**19** approximate numbers	
9 Roman numerals		**20** minimum numbers	
10 ordinal numbers		**21** maximum numbers	
11 written forms		**22** showing a range of numbers	

REFERENCE

0	zero, nought, nothing, oh	26	twenty-six
1	one	27	twenty-seven
2	two	28	twenty-eight
3	three	29	twenty-nine
4	four	30	thirty
5	five	40	forty
6	six	50	fifty
7	seven	60	sixty
8	eight	70	seventy
9	nine	80	eighty
10	ten	90	ninety
11	eleven	100	a hundred
12	twelve	101	a hundred and one
13	thirteen	110	a hundred and ten
14	fourteen	120	a hundred and twenty
15	fifteen	200	two hundred
16	sixteen	1000	a thousand
17	seventeen	1001	a thousand and one
18	eighteen	1010	a thousand and ten
19	nineteen	2000	two thousand
20	twenty	10,000	ten thousand
21	twenty-one	100,000	a hundred thousand
22	twenty-two	1,000,000	a million
23	twenty-three	2,000,000	two million
24	twenty-four	1,000,000,000	a billion
25	twenty-five		

1 numbers

The table on the previous page shows the names of numbers. These numbers are sometimes called **cardinal numbers**. You can see from the numbers in this table how to form all the other numbers.

! BE CAREFUL

When you use **hundred**, **thousand**, **million**, or **billion**, they remain singular even when the number in front of them is greater than one.

...six hundred miles.
Most of the coral is some 2 million years old.

Don't use 'of' after these words when referring to an exact number. For example, don't say 'five hundred of people'; say 'five **hundred** people'.

See also the section on **approximate numbers** later in this entry.

Dozen is used in a similar way to these words. It is used to refer to twelve things.

→ See **Usage** entry **dozen**

2 expressing numbers

Numbers over 100 are generally written in figures. However, if you want to say them aloud, or want to write them in words rather than figures, you put **and** in front of the number expressed by the last two figures. For example, **203** is said or written as **two hundred and three** and **2840** is said or written as **two thousand, eight hundred and forty**.

Four hundred and eighteen men were killed and a hundred and seventeen wounded.

'And' is usually omitted in American English.

...one hundred fifty dollars.

If you want to say or write in words a number between 1000 and 1,000,000, there are various ways of doing it. For example, the number **1872** is usually said or written in words as **one thousand, eight hundred and seventy-two** when it is being used to refer to a quantity of things.

Four-figure numbers ending in **oo** can also be said or written as a number of hundreds. For example, **1800** can be said or written as **eighteen hundred**.

If the number **1872** is being used to identify something, it is said as **one eight seven two**. You always say each figure separately like this with telephone numbers.

In British English, if a telephone number contains a double number, you use the word **double**. For example, **1882** is said as **one double eight two**. In American English, it is more common to repeat the number: **one eight eight two**.

If you are mentioning the year **1872**, you usually say **eighteen seventy-two**.

→ See **Reference** section **Days and dates**

When numbers over 9999 are written in figures, a comma is usually put after the fourth figure from the end, the seventh figure from the end, and so on, dividing the figures into groups of three, for example **15,000** or **1,982,000**. With numbers between 1000 and 9999, a comma is sometimes put after the first figure, for example **1,526**.

3 position

When you use a determiner and a number in front of a noun, you put the determiner in front of the number.

REFERENCE

...the three young men.
All three candidates are coming to Blackpool later this week.

When you put a number and an adjective in front of a noun, you usually put the number in front of the adjective.

...two small children.
...fifteen hundred local residents.
...three beautiful young girls.

However, you can put a few adjectives such as **following** and **only** after numbers.

→ See **Grammar** entry **Adjectives**

4 **agreement**

When you use any number except 'one' in front of a noun, you use a plural noun and a plural verb.

...a hundred years.
Seven soldiers were wounded.
There were ten people there, all men.

However, when you are talking about an amount of money, a period of time, or a distance, speed, or weight, you usually use a singular verb.

Three hundred pounds is a lot of money.
Ten years is a long time.
90 miles an hour is much too fast.

5 **numbers as pronouns**

When it is clear what sort of thing you are referring to, you can use a number without a noun following it. Numbers can be used on their own or with a determiner.

They bought eight companies and sold off five.
These two are quite different.

You use **of** to show the group that a number of people or things belong to.

I saw four of these programmes.
All four of us wanted to leave.

6 **numbers in compound adjectives**

Numbers can be used as part of **compound adjectives**. These adjectives are usually hyphenated.

He took out a five-dollar bill.
I wrote a five-hundred-word essay.

! **BE CAREFUL**

Note that the noun remains singular even when the number is two or more. Don't say, for example, 'I wrote a five-hundred-words essay'. Also, compound adjectives formed like this can't be used as complements. For example, don't say 'My essay is five-hundred-word'. Instead you would probably say 'My essay is five hundred **words long**.'

7 **'one'**

One is used as a number in front of a noun to emphasize that there is only one thing or to show that you are being precise. It is also used when you are talking about a particular member of a group. **One** is followed by a singular noun and is used with a singular verb.

REFERENCE

There was only one gate into the palace.
One member declared that he would never vote for such a proposal.

When no emphasis or precision is wanted, you use **a** instead.

A car came slowly up the road.

8 'zero'

The number 0 is not used in ordinary English to show that the number of things you are talking about is zero. Instead the determiner **no** or the pronoun **none** is used, or **any** is used with a negative.

She had no children.
Sixteen people were injured but luckily none were killed.
There weren't any seats.

→ See **Usage** entries **no**, **none**

There are several ways of expressing the number 0:

▶ as **zero**, especially when expressing numerical values, for example temperatures, taxes, and interest rates

It was fourteen below zero when they woke up.
...zero tax liability.
They lent capital to their customers at low or zero rates of interest.

▶ as **nought**, when expressing some numerical values in British English. For example, 0.89 can be said as **nought point eight nine**.

 American English uses **zero** for this kind of number.

x equals nought.
...linguistic development between the ages of nought and one.
...babies from ages zero to five years.

▶ as **nothing**, when talking informally about calculations

Subtract nothing from that and you get a line on the graph like that.
'What's the difference between this voltage and that voltage?' – 'Nothing.'

▶ like **oh** or the letter O, when reading out numbers figure by figure. For example, the telephone number **021 4620** can be said as **oh two one**, **four six two oh**; and the decimal number **.089** can be said as **point oh eight nine**.

▶ as **nil**, in sports scores.

 This word is not commonly used in American English, which uses **nothing** in sports scores.

Leeds United won four-nil.
Harvard won thirty-six to nothing.

9 Roman numerals

In a few situations, numbers are expressed in Roman numerals. Roman numerals are in fact letters:

I = 1	C = 100
V = 5	D = 500
X = 10	M = 1000
L = 50	

These letters are used in combination to express all numbers. A smaller Roman numeral is subtracted from a larger one if put in front of it. It is added to a larger numeral if put after it. For example, **IV** is 4 and **VI** is 6.

Roman numerals are used after the name of a king or queen when other kings or queens have had the same name.

...Queen Elizabeth II.

This would be said as **Queen Elizabeth the Second**.

Roman numerals are often used to number chapters and sections of books, plays, or other pieces of writing.

Chapter IV: Summary and Conclusion.
We read Act I of Macbeth.

Roman numerals are also sometimes used to express dates formally, for example at the end of films and television programmes. For example, **1992** can be written as **MCMXCII**.

10 ordinal numbers

If you want to identify or describe something by showing where it comes in a series or sequence, you use an **ordinal number**.

Quietly they took their seats in the first three rows.
Flora's flat is on the fourth floor of this five-storey block.

The following table shows the ordinal numbers.

1st	first	26th	twenty-sixth
2nd	second	27th	twenty-seventh
3rd	third	28th	twenty-eighth
4th	fourth	29th	twenty-ninth
5th	fifth	30th	thirtieth
6th	sixth	31st	thirty-first
7th	seventh	40th	fortieth
8th	eighth	41st	forty-first
9th	ninth	50th	fiftieth
10th	tenth	51st	fifty-first
11th	eleventh	60th	sixtieth
12th	twelfth	61st	sixty-first
13th	thirteenth	70th	seventieth
14th	fourteenth	71st	seventy-first
15th	fifteenth	80th	eightieth
16th	sixteenth	81st	eighty-first
17th	seventeenth	90th	ninetieth
18th	eighteenth	91st	ninety-first
19th	nineteenth	100th	hundredth
20th	twentieth	101st	hundred and first
21st	twenty-first	200th	two hundredth
22nd	twenty-second	1000th	thousandth
23rd	twenty-third	1,000,000th	millionth
24th	twenty-fourth	1,000,000,000th	billionth
25th	twenty-fifth		

11 written forms

As shown in the table, ordinals can be written in abbreviated form, especially in dates.

He lost his job on January 7th.
Write to HPT, 2nd Floor, 59 Piccadilly, Manchester.

12 ordinals as modifiers

Ordinals are used in front of nouns, preceded by a determiner. They are not usually used after linking verbs like 'be'.

He took the lift to the sixteenth floor.
...on her twenty-first birthday.

They are used after verbs such as **come** or **finish** when giving the results of a race or competition.

I came second in the poetry competition.
He was third in the 100m race.

Ordinals are included in the small group of adjectives that are put in front of cardinal numbers, not after them.

The first two years have been very successful.

13 ordinals as pronouns

When it is clear what sort of thing you are referring to, you can use an ordinal number without a noun following it. Note that you must use a determiner.

A second pheasant flew up. Then a third and a fourth.
There are two questions to be answered. The first is 'Who should do what?' The second is 'Who should be accountable?'

You use **of** to show the group that the person or thing belongs to.

This is the third of a series of programmes from the University of Sussex.
Tony was the second of four sons.

14 fractions

When you want to show how large a part of something is compared to the whole of it, you use a **fraction**, such as **a third** or **two fifths**, followed by **of** and a noun phrase referring to the whole thing. Most fractions are based on ordinal numbers. The exceptions are the words **half** (one of two equal parts) and **quarter** (one of four equal parts).

You can write a fraction in figures. For example, 'a half' can be written as **4½**, 'a quarter' as **4¼**, 'three-quarters' as **4¾**, and 'two thirds' as **4⅔**.

When referring to one part of something, you usually use **a**. You only use **one** in formal speech and writing or when you want to emphasize the amount.

This state produces a third of the nation's oil.
...one quarter of the total population.

Plural fractions are often written with a hyphen.

More than two-thirds of the globe's surface is water.
He was not due at the office for another three-quarters of an hour.

You can put an adjective in front of a fraction, after **the**.

...the southern half of England.
...the first two-thirds of this century.

When you use **a half** and **a quarter** in combination with whole numbers, they come in front of the plural noun you are using.

...*one and a half acres of land*.
...*five and a quarter days*.

However, if you are using **a** instead of the number 'one', the noun modified by **a** is singular and comes in front of the fraction word.

...*an acre and a half of woodland*.
...*a mile and a quarter of motorway*.

15 agreement of fractions

When you talk about part of a single thing, you use a singular form of a verb.

Half of our work is to design programmes.
Two fifths of the forest was removed.

However, when you talk about part of a group of things, you use a plural form of the verb.

Two fifths of the houses have more than six people per room.
A quarter of the students were seen individually.

16 fractions as pronouns

When it is clear who or what you are referring to, you can use fractions without 'of' and a noun phrase.

Most were women and about half were young with small children.
One fifth are appointed by the Regional Health Authority.

17 decimals

Decimals are a way of expressing fractions. For example, 0.5 is the same as 4½ and 1.4 is the same as 1⅗.

...*an increase of 16.4 per cent*.
The library contains over 1.3 million books.

You say the dot as **point**. For example, **1.4** is said as **one point four**.

! BE CAREFUL

Don't use a comma in decimal numbers in English.

Numbers that look like decimal numbers are used when referring to one of a number of sections, tables, or illustrations that are closely connected.

... *see section 3.3*.
The normal engineering drawing is quite unsuitable (figure 3.4).

18 percentages

Fractions are often given a special form as a number of hundredths. This type of fraction is called a **percentage**. For example, 'three hundredths', expressed as a percentage, is **three per cent**. This is often written as **3%**.

About 20 per cent of student accountants are women.
...*interest at 10% per annum*.

In American English, 'per cent' is written as a single word **percent**.

In 1980, only 29 percent of Americans were Republicans.

19 **approximate numbers**

You can refer to a large number imprecisely by using **several**, **a few**, or **a couple of** in front of **dozen**, **hundred**, **thousand**, **million**, or **billion**.

...several hundred people.
A few thousand cars have gone.

You can be even more imprecise, and emphasize how large the number is, by using **dozens**, **hundreds**, **thousands**, **millions**, or **billions**, followed by **of**.

That's going to take hundreds of years.
We travelled thousands of miles across Europe.

People often use plural forms when they are exaggerating.

I was meeting thousands of people every day.
Do you have to fill in hundreds of forms before you go?

The following expressions are used to show that a number is approximate and that the actual figure could be larger or smaller:

about	odd	roughly
approximately	or so	some
around	or thereabouts	something like

You put **about**, **approximately**, **around**, **roughly**, **some**, and **something like** in front of a number.

About 85 students were there.
It costs roughly $10,000 a year to educate an undergraduate.
I found out where this man lived, and drove some four miles inland to see him.

This use of **some** is quite formal.

You put **odd**, **or so**, and **or thereabouts** after a number or the noun that follows a number.

...a hundred odd acres.
The car should be here in ten minutes or so.
Get the temperature to 3050C or thereabouts.

20 **minimum numbers**

The following expressions show that a number is a minimum figure and that the actual figure may be larger:

a minimum of	from	more than	over
at least	minimum	or more	plus

You put **a minimum of**, **from**, **more than**, and **over** in front of a number.

He needed a minimum of 26 votes.
...a 3 course dinner from £15.
...a school with more than 1300 pupils.
The British have been on the island for over a thousand years.

You put **or more**, **plus**, and **minimum** after a number or after the noun that follows a number.

...a choice of three or more possibilities.
This is the worst disaster I can remember in my 25 years plus as a police officer.
They should be getting £180 a week minimum.

REFERENCE

Plus is sometimes written as the symbol '**+**', for example in job advertisements.

2+ years' experience of market research required.

You usually put **at least** in front of a number.

She had at least a dozen biscuits.
It was a drop of at least two hundred feet.

However, this expression is sometimes put after a number or noun. This position is more emphatic.

I must have slept twelve hours at least.
He was fifty-five at least.

21 maximum numbers

The following expressions show that a number is a maximum figure and that the actual figure is or may be smaller:

almost	at the most	nearly	under
a maximum of	fewer than	no more than	up to
at most	less than	or less	
at the maximum	maximum	or under	

You put **almost**, **a maximum of**, **fewer than**, **less than**, **nearly**, **no more than**, **under**, and **up to** in front of a number.

The company now supplies almost 100 of Paris's restaurants.
We managed to finish the entire job in under three months.

You put **at the maximum**, **at most**, **at the most**, **maximum**, **or less**, and **or under** after a number or the noun that follows a number.

They might have IQs of 40, or 50 at the maximum.
The area would yield only 200 pounds of rice or less.

22 showing a range of numbers

You can show a range of numbers using **between** and **and**, or **from** and **to**, or just **to**.

Most of the farms are between four and five hundred years old.
My hospital groups contain from ten to twenty patients.
Many owned two to five acres of land.

Anything is used in front of **between** and **from** to emphasize how great a range is.

An average rate of anything between 25 and 60 per cent is usual.
It is a job that takes anything from two to five weeks.

A dash is used between two figures to show a range. It is said as **to**.

Allow to cool for 10–15 minutes.
These figures were collected in 1965–9.
...the Tate Gallery (open 10 a.m.–6 p.m., Sundays, 2–6).

When mentioning two numbers that follow each other in a range or sequence, you can use the symbol '**/**'. This is said aloud as **slash** or **to**. In British English it is sometimes said aloud as **stroke**.

Earnings increased in 1975/6.
Write for details to 41/42 Berners Street, London.

Plural forms of nouns

The following table shows the basic ways of forming the plurals of countable nouns.

	singular form	plural form
		add -s (/s/ or /z/)
regular	hat tree	hats trees
		add -s (/iz/)
ending in -se ending in -ze ending in -ce ending in -ge	rose prize service age	roses prizes services ages
		add -es (/iz/)
ending in -sh ending in -ch ending in -ss ending in -x ending in -s	bush speech glass box bus	bushes speeches glasses boxes buses
		change -y to -ies
ending in consonant + -y	country lady	countries ladies
		add -s
ending in vowel + -y	boy valley	boys valleys

Nouns ending with a long vowel sound and the sound /θ/ have their plural forms pronounced as ending in /ðz/. For example, the plural of **path** is pronounced /pɑːðz/ and the plural of **mouth** is pronounced /maʊðz/.

House is pronounced /haʊs/, but its plural form **houses** is pronounced /ˈhaʊzɪz/.

Note that, if the 'ch' at the end of a noun is pronounced as /k/, you add 's', not 'es', to form the plural. For example, the plural of **stomach** /ˈstʌmək/ is **stomachs**.

stomach	→	stomachs
monarch	→	monarchs

1 **nouns with no change in form**

Some nouns have the same form for both singular and plural.

...*a sheep*.
...*nine sheep*.

Many of these nouns refer to animals or fish.

bison	goldfish	moose	sheep
cod	greenfly	mullet	shellfish
deer	grouse	reindeer	trout
fish	halibut	salmon	whitebait

REFERENCE

Even when a noun referring to an animal has a plural form ending in '**s**', it is quite common to use the form without 's' to refer to a group of the animals in the context of hunting.

Zebra are a more difficult prey.

Similarly, when you are referring to a large number of trees or plants growing together, you can use the form without 's'. However, this is used like an uncountable noun, not a plural form.

...the rows of willow and cypress that lined the creek.

The following nouns also have the same form for singular and plural:

aircraft	gallows	insignia	series
crossroads	grapefruit	mews	spacecraft
dice	hovercraft	offspring	species

2 nouns ending in 'f' or 'fe'

There are several nouns ending in '**f**' or '**fe**' where you form the plural by substituting '**ves**' for 'f' or 'fe'.

calf	→	calves
elf	→	elves
half	→	halves
knife	→	knives
leaf	→	leaves
life	→	lives
loaf	→	loaves
scarf	→	scarves
sheaf	→	sheaves
shelf	→	shelves
thief	→	thieves
wife	→	wives
wolf	→	wolves

The plural of **hoof** can be **hoofs** or **hooves**.

3 nouns ending in 'o'

With many nouns ending in '**o**', you just add '**s**' to form the plural.

photo	→	photos
radio	→	radios

However, the following nouns have plurals ending in '**oes**':

domino	embargo	negro	tomato
echo	hero	potato	veto

The following nouns ending in '**o**' can have plurals ending in either '**os**' or '**oes**':

buffalo	ghetto	memento	stiletto
cargo	innuendo	mosquito	tornado
flamingo	mango	motto	torpedo
fresco	manifesto	salvo	volcano

4 irregular plurals

A few nouns have special plural forms, as shown below:

child	→	children
foot	→	feet
goose	→	geese
louse	→	lice
man	→	men
mouse	→	mice
ox	→	oxen
tooth	→	teeth
woman	→	women

> **!** **BE CAREFUL**
>
> Note that the first syllable of **women** /'wɪmɪn/ is pronounced differently from that of **woman** /'wʊmən/.

Most nouns that refer to people and that end with '**man**', '**woman**', or '**child**' have plural forms ending with '**men**', '**women**', or '**children**'.

postman	→	postmen
Englishwoman	→	Englishwomen
grandchild	→	grandchildren

However, the plural forms of **German**, **human**, **Norman**, and **Roman** are **Germans**, **humans**, **Normans**, and **Romans**.

5 plurals of compound nouns

Most compound nouns have plurals formed by adding '**s**' to the end of the last word.

down-and-out	→	down-and-outs
swimming pool	→	swimming pools
tape recorder	→	tape recorders

However, in the case of compound nouns that consist of a noun ending in '**er**' and an adverb such as **on** or **by** and that refer to a person, you add '**s**' to the first word to form the plural.

passer-by	→	passers-by
hanger-on	→	hangers-on

Compound nouns consisting of three or more words have plurals formed by adding '**s**' to the first word when the first word is a noun identifying the type of person or thing you are talking about.

REFERENCE

| brother-in-law | → | brothers-in-law |
| bird of prey | → | birds of prey |

6 plurals of foreign words

There are words in English that are borrowed from other languages, especially Latin, and that still form their plurals according to the rules of those languages. Many of them are technical or formal, and some are also used with a regular '**s**' or '**es**' plural ending in non-technical or informal contexts. You may need to check these in a dictionary.

Some nouns ending in '**us**' have plurals ending in '**i**'.

nucleus	→	nuclei
radius	→	radii
stimulus	→	stimuli

However, other nouns ending in '**us**' have different plurals.

| corpus | → | corpora |
| genus | → | genera |

Nouns ending in '**um**' often have plurals ending in '**a**'.

| aquarium | → | aquaria |
| memorandum | → | memoranda |

Some nouns ending in '**a**' have plurals formed by adding '**e**'.

| larva | → | larvae |
| vertebra | → | vertebrae |

Nouns ending in '**is**' have plurals in which the '**is**' is replaced by '**es**'.

analysis	→	analyses
crisis	→	crises
hypothesis	→	hypotheses

Nouns ending in '**ix**' or '**ex**' often have plurals ending in '**ices**'. Some of these have two plural forms, one formed with '**s**' and one formed in a different way. Usually the form with '**s**' is used in less formal English.

appendix	→	appendices or appendixes
index	→	indices or indexes
matrix	→	matrices
vortex	→	vortices

Nouns borrowed from Greek that end in '**on**' have plurals in which the '**on**' is replaced by '**a**'.

| criterion | → | criteria |
| phenomenon | → | phenomena |

The following words borrowed from French have the same written form for the plural as for the singular. The '**s**' at the end is not pronounced for the singular but is pronounced /**z**/ for the plural.

bourgeois	corps	précis
chassis	patois	rendezvous

Punctuation

1 full stop		**10**	brackets
2 question mark		**11**	square brackets
3 exclamation mark		**12**	apostrophe
4 comma		**13**	hyphen
5 optional comma		**14**	slash or stroke
6 no comma		**15**	direct speech
7 semi-colon		**16**	titles and quoted phrases
8 colon		**17**	italics
9 dash		**18**	other uses of punctuation

The first section of this entry deals with the punctuation of ordinary sentences.

See also the sections on **direct speech** and **titles and quoted phrases** later in this entry.

1 full stop (.)

You start a sentence with a capital letter. You put a **full stop** at the end of a sentence, unless it is a question or an exclamation.

It's not your fault.
Cook the rice in salted water until just tender.

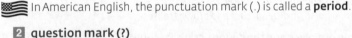 In American English, the punctuation mark (.) is called a **period**.

2 question mark (?)

If a sentence is a question, you put a **question mark** at the end.

Why did you do that?
Does any of this matter?
He's certain to be elected, isn't he?

You put a question mark at the end of a question even if the words in the sentence are not in the normal question order.

You know he doesn't live here any longer?

People occasionally do not put a question mark at the end of a sentence in question form if, for example, it is really a request.

Would you please call my office and ask them to collect the car.

! BE CAREFUL

You put a full stop, not a question mark, after a reported question or an indirect question.

He asked me where I was going.
I wonder what's happened.

3 exclamation mark (!)

If a sentence is an exclamation, that is, something said with strong emotion, you put an **exclamation mark** at the end. In informal writing, people also put an exclamation mark at the end of a sentence which they feel is exciting, surprising, or very interesting.

How awful!
Your family and children must always come first!
We actually heard her talking to them!

 In American English, the punctuation mark (!) is called an **exclamation point**.

4 comma (,)

You must put a **comma**

▶ after or in front of a vocative

Jenny, I'm sorry.
Thank you, Adam.
Look, Jenny, can we just forget it?

▶ between items in a list, except ones separated by **and** or **or**. You can choose whether or not to put a comma after the last item, before **and** or **or**.

We ate fish, steaks, and fruit.
...political, social and economic equality.
The men hunted and fished, kept cattle and sheep, made weapons, and occasionally fought.
...educational courses in accountancy, science, maths or engineering.

▶ between three or more descriptive adjectives in front of a noun, without **and**

...in a cool, light, feminine voice.
Eventually the galleries tapered to a long, narrow, twisting corridor.

▶ after a name or noun phrase, before a description or further information

...Carlos Barral, the Spanish publisher and writer.
...a broad-backed man, baldish, in a cream coat and brown trousers.

▶ between the name of a place and the county, state, or country it is in. A comma is usually put after the county, state, or country as well, unless it is at the end of a sentence.

She was born in Richmond, Surrey, in 1913.
There he met a young woman from Cincinnati, Ohio.

▶ after or in front of an adjective which is separate from the main part of the sentence, or after a separate participle

She nodded, speechless.
I left them abruptly, unwilling to let them have anything to do with my project.
Shaking, I crept downstairs.

▶ before a non-defining relative clause (a clause that gives more information about someone or something but is not needed to identify them)

She wasn't like David, who cried about everything.
The only decent room is the living room, which is rather small.
He told us he was sleeping in the wood, which seemed to me a good idea.

▶ before a question tag

That's what you want, isn't it?
You've noticed, haven't you?

5 optional comma

You can put a comma, for emphasis or precision,

▶ after the first of two qualitative adjectives used in front of a noun

We had long, involved discussions.
...a tall, slim girl with long, straight hair.

Note that **young**, **old**, and **little** do not usually have commas in front of them.

...a huge, silent young man.
...a sentimental old lady.
...a charming little town.

▶ after or in front of a word or group of words that adds something to the main part of the sentence. If you put a comma in front of the word or group, you should also put one after it, unless it comes at the end of the sentence.

In 1880, he founded a large furniture company.
Obviously, it is not always possible.
There are links between my work and William Turnbull's, for instance.
They were, in many ways, very similar in character and outlook.
The ink, surprisingly, washed out easily.

Long groups of words are usually separated with commas.

He is, with the possible exception of Robert de Niro, the greatest screen actor in the world.

A comma is put after or in front of an adverbial if its meaning is otherwise likely to be misunderstood.

'No,' she said, surprisingly.
Mothers, particularly, don't like it.

▶ in front of **and**, **or**, **but**, or **yet**, when giving a list or adding a clause

...a dress-designer, some musicians, and half a dozen artists.
...if you suffer from fear, stress, or anxiety.
I tried to help, but neither of them could agree.
Her remarks shocked audiences, yet also improved her reputation.

▶ after a subordinate clause

When the fish is cooked, strain off the liquid.
Even if he survives, he may be disabled permanently.

It is usually best to put a comma after a subordinate clause, although many people do not put commas after short subordinate clauses.

You don't normally put a comma in front of a subordinate clause, unless it contains something such as an afterthought, contrast, or exception.

Don't be afraid of asking for simple practical help when it is needed.
Switch that thing off if it annoys you.
The poor man was no threat to her any longer, if he ever really had been.
He was discharged from hospital, although he was homeless and had nowhere to go.

If you do put a comma in front of a clause, you should also put a comma after it if it does not come at the end of the sentence.

This is obviously one further incentive, if an incentive is needed, for anybody who needs to take slimming a little more seriously.

▶ in front of a participle which is separate from the main part of the sentence

Maurice followed, laughing.
Marcus stood up, muttering incoherently.

▶ after a noun being used in front of someone's name

...that marvellous singer, Jessye Norman.
She had married the gifted composer and writer, Paul Bowles.

6 no comma

Don't put a comma

▶ in front of **and**, **or**, **but**, and **yet** when these words are being used to link just two nouns, adjectives, or verbs

We had a lunch of fruit and cheese.
...when they are tired or unhappy.

▶ between a qualitative adjective and a classifying adjective, or between two classifying adjectives

...a large Victorian building.
...a medieval French poet.

▶ after the subject of a clause, even if it is long

Even this part of the Government's plan for a better National Health Service has its risks.
Indeed, the amount of support for the proposal surprised ministers.

▶ in front of a *that*-clause or a reported question

His brother complained that the office was not business-like.
Georgina said she was going to bed.
She asked why he was so silent all the time.

▶ in front of a defining relative clause (a clause that identifies someone or something)

I seem to be the only one who can get close enough to him.
Happiness is all that matters.
The country can now begin to develop a foreign policy which serves national interests.

7 semi-colon (;)

The **semi-colon** is used in more formal writing to separate clauses that are closely related and could be written as separate sentences, or that are linked by **and**, **or**, **but**, or **yet**.

I can see no remedy for this; one can't order him to do it.
He knew everything about me; I knew nothing about his recent life.
He cannot easily bring interest rates down; yet a failure to do so would almost certainly push the economy into recession.

It is also sometimes used between items in a list, especially if the list items are phrases or clauses, or if they contain internal punctuation.

He wrote about his life: his wife, Louise; their three children; the changes that he saw in the world around him.

8 colon (:)

The **colon** is used

▶ in front of a list or explanation

The clothes are all made of natural materials: cotton, silk, wool and leather.
Nevertheless, the main problem remained: what should be done with the two murderers?

▶ between two main clauses that are connected, mainly in more formal writing

Be patient: this particular cruise has not yet been advertised.

▶ after introductory headings

Cooking time: About 5 minutes.

▶ in front of the second part of a book title

...a volume entitled Farming and Wildlife: A Study in Compromise.

A colon is also sometimes used in front of quotes. See below at **direct speech**.

9 **dash (–)**

A spaced **dash** (i.e. with a single space before and after it) is used

▶ in front of a list or explanation

They need simple things – building materials, clothing, household goods, and agricultural implements.
...one of his most basic motives – commercialism.

▶ after and in front of a group of words or a clause that adds something to the main sentence but could be removed

Many species will take a wide variety of food – insects, eggs, and fruit – but others will only take the leaves of particular trees.

▶ in front of an adverbial, clause, or other group of words, for emphasis

I think Ruth was right – in theory and practice.
Let Tess help her – if she wants help.
My family didn't even know about it – I didn't want anyone to know.

! BE CAREFUL

Spaced dashes are not used in very formal writing.

An unspaced dash (i.e. with no space before or after it) is used

▶ to show a range

... see pages 15–60.

▶ between two adjectives or noun modifiers that show that two countries or groups are involved in something or that an individual has two roles or aspects

...German–French relations.
...the United States–Canada free trade pact
...a mathematician–philosopher

▶ to show that something such as a plane or a train goes between two places

...the Anguilla–St Kitts flight.
...the New York–Montreal train.

10 **brackets ( )**

Brackets, also called **parentheses**, are used after and in front of a word, group of words, or clause that adds something to the main sentence, or explains it, but could be removed.

This is a process which Hayek (a writer who came to rather different conclusions) also observed.
A goat should give from three to six pints (1.7 to 3.4 litres) of milk a day.
This is more economical than providing heat and power separately (see section 3.2 below).

REFERENCE

Full stops, question marks, exclamation marks, and commas go after the second bracket, unless they apply only to the words in the brackets.

I ordered two coffees and an ice cream (for her).
We had sandwiches (pastrami on rye and so on), salami, coleslaw, fried chicken, and potato salad.
In the face of unbelievable odds (the least being a full-time job!) Gladys took the six-hour exam – and passed.

11 square brackets [ ]

Square brackets are used, usually in books and articles, when supplying words that make a quotation clearer or comment on it, although they were not originally said or written.

Mr Runcie concluded: 'The novel is at its strongest when describing the dignity of Cambridge [a slave] and the education of Emily [the daughter of an absentee landlord].'

12 apostrophe (')

You use an **apostrophe**

▶ in front of an '**s**' added to a noun or pronoun, or after a plural noun ending in '**s**', to show a relationship such as possession.

...my friend's house.
...someone's house.
...friends' houses.

→ See **Usage** entry '**s**

→ See **Topic** entry **Possession and other relationships**

▶ in front of contracted forms of **be**, **have**, and modals, and between '**n**' and '**t**' in contracted forms with '**not**'.

I'm terribly sorry.
I can't see a thing.

→ See **Grammar** entry **Contractions**

▶ in front of '**s**' for the plurals of letters and, sometimes, numbers

Rod asked me what grades I got. I said airily, 'All A's, of course.'
There is a time in people's lives, usually in their 40's and 50's, when they find themselves benefiting from their investments.

▶ in front of two figures referring to a year or decade

...souvenirs from the '68 campaign.
He worked there throughout the '60s and the early '70s.

An apostrophe sometimes shows that letters are missing from a word. Often the word is never written in full in modern English. For example, **o'clock** has been reduced from 'of the clock', but it is never written in full.

She left here at eight o'clock this morning.

! BE CAREFUL

Don't use an apostrophe in front of the 's' of a plural word like **apples** or **cars**. Also, don't use an apostrophe in front of the 's' of the possessive pronouns **yours**, **hers**, **ours**, and **theirs**, or the possessive determiner **its**.

13 hyphen (-)

→ See **Reference** section **Spelling** for information on the use of the hyphen in compound words

14 slash or stroke (/)

A **slash**, **stroke**, or **oblique** is used

▶ between two words or numbers that are alternatives

Write here, and/or on a card near your telephone, the number of the nearest hospital with a casualty ward.
...the London Hotels Information Service (telephone 629 5414/6).

▶ in rations and ranges

He was driving at 100 km/h.
... the 2010/11 academic year.

▶ in website addresses

... http://www.harpercollins.com

▶ between two words describing something that is in fact two things, as in **a washer/drier** or **a clock/radio**

Each apartment has a sizeable lounge/diner with colour TV.

15 direct speech (' ' or " ")

You put **inverted commas**, also called **quotation marks** or **quotes**, at the beginning and end of direct speech. You start the direct speech with a capital letter.

'Thank you,' I said.
"What happened?"

 British writers use both single and double inverted commas (' ' and " "), but American writers tend to use double inverted commas (" ").

If you put something like **he said** after the direct speech, you put a comma in front of the second inverted comma, not a full stop. However, if the direct speech is a question or an exclamation, you put a question mark or an exclamation mark instead.

'We have to go home,' she told him.
'What are you doing?' Sarah asked.
'Of course it's awful!' shouted Clarissa.

If you then give another piece of direct speech said by the same person, you start it with a capital letter and put inverted commas round it.

'Yes, yes,' he replied. 'He'll be all right.'

If you put something like **he said** within a sentence in direct speech, you put a comma after the first piece of direct speech and after **he said**, and you start the continuation of the direct speech with inverted commas. Don't give the first word of the continuation a capital letter, unless it would have one anyway.

'Frankly darling,' he murmured, 'it's none of your business.'
'Margaret,' I said to her, 'I'm so glad you came.'

If you put something like **he said** in front of the direct speech, you put a comma in front of the direct speech and a full stop, question mark, or exclamation mark at the end of it.

She added, 'But it's totally up to you.'
He smiled and asked, 'Are you her grandson?'

People sometimes put a colon in front of the direct speech, especially to show that what follows is important.

I said: 'Perhaps your father was right.'

A dash is used to show that someone who is speaking hesitates or is interrupted.

'Why don't I – ' He paused a moment, thinking.
'It's just that – circumstances are not quite right for you to come up just now.'
'Oliver, will you stop babbling and – ' 'Jennifer,' I interrupted, 'the man is a guest!'

A line of dots (usually three) is used to show that someone hesitates or pauses.

'I think they may come soon. I...' He hesitated, reluctant to add to her trouble.
'Mother was going to join us but she left it too late...'

Note that sometimes what a person thinks is directly quoted in front of a comma or after it, rather than in inverted commas.

My goodness, I thought, Tony was right.
I thought, what an extraordinary childhood.

When you are writing a conversation, for example in a story, you start a new line for each new piece of direct speech.

! **BE CAREFUL**

When the direct speech takes up more than one line, don't put an opening inverted comma at the beginning of each line, only at the beginning of the direct speech. If you are giving more than one paragraph of direct speech, you put inverted commas at the beginning of each paragraph but not at the end of any paragraph except the last one.

16 titles and quoted phrases

When you are mentioning the title of a book, play, film, etc, you can put inverted commas round it, although people quite often do not, especially in informal writing. In books and articles, titles are often written without inverted commas, or in **italics** (sloping letters). The titles of newspapers, especially, are not usually written in inverted commas.

...Robin Cook's novel 'Coma'.
...Follett's most recent novel, Hornet Flight.

When you are mentioning a word, or quoting a few words that someone said, you put the word or words in inverted commas.

The manager later described the incident as 'unfortunate'.
He has always claimed that the programme 'sets the agenda for the day'.

In British English you don't usually put the punctuation of your sentence within the inverted commas.

Mr Wilson described the price as 'fair'.
What do you mean by 'boyfriend'?

However, when people are quoting a whole sentence, they often put a full stop in front of the closing inverted comma, rather than after it.

You have a saying, 'Four more months and then the harvest.'

If they want to put a comma after the quote, the comma comes after the closing inverted comma.

The old saying, 'A teacher can learn from a student', happens to be literally true.

In American English, a full-stop or comma is put in front of the closing inverted comma, not after it.

There was a time when people were divided roughly into children, "young persons," and adults.

If you are quoting someone who is also quoting, you need to use a second set of inverted commas. If you begin with a single inverted comma, you use double inverted commas for the second quote. If you begin with double inverted commas, you use single inverted commas for the second quote.

'What do they mean,' she demanded, 'by a "population problem"?'
"One of the reasons we wanted to make the programme," he explains, "is that the word 'hostage' had been used so often that it had lost any sense or meaning."

People sometimes put inverted commas round a word or expression which they think is inappropriate.

He was badly injured after a 'friend' had jokingly poured petrol over him and set fire to it.

A line of dots (usually three) is used to show that you are giving an incomplete quotation, for example from a review.

'A creation of singular beauty...magnificent.' Washington Post.

17 italics

You will see **italics** (sloping letters) used in printed books and articles, for example to mention titles or foreign words, and emphasize or highlight other words. Italics are not used in this way in handwriting. When mentioning titles, use inverted commas, or have no special punctuation at all. When mentioning foreign words, use inverted commas. In informal writing, you can underline words to emphasize them.

18 other uses of punctuation

→ See **Reference** sections **Abbreviations**, **Days and dates**, **Numbers and fractions**, **Measurements**

→ See **Topic** entry Time

Spelling

1 short vowel or long vowel	**15** '-oul' and '-ol'
2 doubling final consonants	**16** '-re' and '-er'
3 omitting final 'e'	**17** 'ae' or 'oe' and 'e'
4 changing final 'y' to 'i'	**18** '-ise' and '-ize'
5 'ie' or 'ei'	**19** small groups
6 '-ically'	**20** individual words
7 '-ful'	**21** two words or one word
8 '-ible'	**22** hyphens: compound nouns
9 '-able'	**23** compound adjectives
10 '-ent' and '-ant'	**24** compound verbs
11 silent consonants	**25** phrasal verbs
12 difficult words	**26** numbers
13 doubling consonants	**27** other points
14 '-our' and '-or'	

Some spellings are explained in more detail at other entries in this book.

→ See **Grammar** entries **Comparative and superlative adjectives**, **Contractions**

REFERENCE

→ See **Topic** entries **Abbreviations, Names and Titles**

→ See **Reference** sections **Capital letters, Irregular verbs, Plural forms of nouns, Verb forms** formation of

1 short vowel or long vowel

If a one-syllable word has a short vowel, it usually does not have '**e**' at the end. The most common exceptions to this rule are the words **have** and **give**. If it has a long vowel represented by a single letter, the word usually does have an '**e**' at the end. For example:

▸ /fæt/ is spelled **fat** and /feɪt/ is spelled **fate**.

▸ /bɪt/ is spelled **bit** and /baɪt/ is spelled **bite**.

▸ /rɒd/ is spelled **rod** and /rəʊd/ is spelled **rode**.

2 doubling final consonants

If a one-syllable word ends in a single vowel and consonant, you double the final consonant before adding a suffix that begins with a vowel.

run	→	runner
set	→	setting
stop	→	stopped
wet	→	wettest

If the word has more than one syllable, you usually only double the final consonant if the final syllable is stressed.

admit	→	admitted
begin	→	beginner
refer	→	referring
motor	→	motoring
open	→	opener
suffer	→	suffered

However, in British English, you double the final '**l**' of verbs like **travel** and **quarrel**, even though the last syllable is not stressed.

| travel | → | travelling |
| quarrel | → | quarrelled |

In British English, and sometimes in American English, the final consonant of the following verbs is doubled, even though the last syllable is not stressed.

| hiccup | kidnap | program | worship |

The final '**p**' of **handicap** is also doubled.

3 omitting final 'e'

If a final '**e**' is silent, you omit it before adding a suffix beginning with a vowel.

bake	→	baked
blame	→	blaming
fame	→	famous
late	→	later

nice	→	nicest
secure	→	security

Don't omit the final '**e**' of words like **courage** or **notice** when forming words like **courageous** /kə'reɪdʒəs/ and **noticeable** /'nəʊtɪsəbl/, because the '**e**' shows that the preceding '**g**' is pronounced /dʒ/ and the preceding '**c**' is pronounced /s/. Compare **analogous** /ən'æləgəs/ and **practicable** /'præktɪkəbl/. You sometimes omit the silent final '**e**' in front of suffixes that begin with a consonant. For example **awful** is formed from **awe**, and **truly** is formed from **true**. However, you don't always omit the '**e**': **useful** is formed from **use**, and **surely** is formed from **sure**.

4 changing final 'y' to 'i'

If a word ends in a consonant and '**y**', you usually change '**y**' to '**i**' before adding a suffix.

carry	→	carries
early	→	earlier
lovely	→	loveliest
try	→	tried

However, don't change '**y**' to '**i**' when adding *ing*.

carry	→	carrying
try	→	trying

You don't usually change the final '**y**' of one-syllable adjectives like **dry** and **shy**.

dry	→	dryness
shy	→	shyly

5 'ie' or 'ei'

When the sound is /iː/, the spelling is often '**ie**'. Here is a list of the commonest words in which /iː/ is spelled '**ie**':

achieve	field	priest	shield
belief	grief	relief	siege
believe	grieve	relieve	thief
brief	niece	reprieve	wield
chief	piece	retrieve	yield

In **mischief** and **sieve** the '**ie**' is pronounced /ɪ/.

After '**c**', when the sound is /s/, the spelling is usually '**ei**'.

ceiling	conceive	deceive	receipt
conceit	deceit	perceive	receive

In some words, '**c**' is followed by '**ie**', but the sound of '**ie**' is not /iː/: for example, **efficient** /ɪ'fɪʃnt/, **science** /'saɪəns/, and **financier** /fɪ'nænsɪə/.

In the following words '**ei**' is pronounced /eɪ/:

beige	freight	sleigh	weight
deign	neighbour	veil	
eight	reign	vein	
feign	rein	weigh	

The '**ei**' in **either** and **neither** can be pronounced /aɪ/ or /iː/. Note also the pronunciation of '**ei**' in **height** /haɪt/, **foreign** /'fɒrɪn/, and **sovereign** /'sɒvrɪn/.

6 '-ically'

With adjectives ending in '**ic**', you add '**ally**' to form adverbs, for example, **artistically**, **automatically**, **democratically**, **specifically**, and **sympathetically**. Don't add 'ly', although the '**ally**' ending is often pronounced like 'ly'. However, **publicly** is an exception.

7 '-ful'

You form some adjectives by adding '**ful**' to a noun, for example, **careful**, **harmful**, **useful**, and **wonderful**. Don't add 'full'.

8 '-ible'

Many adjectives end in '**ible**', but there is a fixed set of them, and new words are not formed by adding 'ible'. Here is a list of the most common adjectives ending in '**ible**'.

accessible	discernible	indestructible	permissible
admissible	edible	indivisible	plausible
audible	eligible	inexhaustible	possible
collapsible	fallible	inexpressible	reducible
combustible	feasible	intelligible	reprehensible
compatible	flexible	invincible	responsible
comprehensible	forcible	irascible	reversible
contemptible	gullible	irrepressible	sensible
convertible	horrible	irresistible	susceptible
credible	inadmissible	legible	tangible
crucible	incorrigible	negligible	terrible
defensible	incorruptible	ostensible	visible
digestible	indelible	perceptible	

Negative forms are only included in the above list if the positive form is rarely used. You can add a negative prefix to many of the positive forms in the list, for example, **illegible**, **impossible**, **invisible**, **irresponsible**, and **unintelligible**.

9 '-able'

Many adjectives end in '**able**'. There is no fixed set of them, and new words are often formed by adding '**able**' to verbs. Here is a list of the most common adjectives ending in '**able**':

acceptable	desirable	miserable	respectable
available	fashionable	probable	suitable
capable	formidable	profitable	valuable
comfortable	inevitable	reasonable	
comparable	invaluable	reliable	
considerable	liable	remarkable	

You can add a negative prefix to most of the positive forms in the list, for example, **incapable** and **uncomfortable**.

10 '-ent' and '-ant'

You cannot usually tell from the sound of a word whether it ends in '**ent**' or '**ant**', both pronounced /ənt/. These are the commonest adjectives ending in '**ent**':

absent	different	intelligent	silent
confident	efficient	magnificent	sufficient
consistent	evident	patient	urgent
convenient	frequent	permanent	violent
current	independent	present	
decent	innocent	prominent	

REFERENCE

These are the commonest adjectives ending in '**ant**':

abundant	expectant	militant	resistant
arrogant	extravagant	poignant	resonant
brilliant	exuberant	predominant	self-reliant
buoyant	fragrant	pregnant	significant
defiant	hesitant	radiant	tolerant
distant	ignorant	redundant	vacant
dominant	important	relevant	vigilant
elegant	intolerant	reluctant	

These are the commonest nouns ending in '**ent**':

accident	development	government	present
achievement	element	investment	president
agent	employment	management	punishment
agreement	environment	moment	statement
apartment	equipment	movement	student
argument	establishment	parent	treatment
department	excitement	parliament	unemployment

Note that nouns referring to actions and processes, such as **assessment** and **improvement**, end in '**ment**', not 'mant'.

These are the commonest nouns ending in '**ant**':

accountant	descendant	merchant	protestant
applicant	giant	migrant	sergeant
attendant	immigrant	occupant	servant
commandant	infant	pageant	tenant
confidant	informant	participant	tyrant
consultant	instant	peasant	
defendant	lieutenant	pheasant	

Note that many of these words refer to people.

Adjectives ending in '**ent**' have related nouns ending in '**ence**' or '**ency'**. Here are some other common nouns ending in '**ence**' or '**ency**':

agency	currency	influence	sentence
audience	deterrence	licence	sequence
coincidence	emergency	preference	subsistence
conference	essence	presidency	tendency
conscience	existence	reference	
consequence	experience	residence	
constituency	incidence	science	

Adjectives ending in '**ant**' have related nouns ending in '**ance**' or '**ancy**'. Here are some other common nouns ending in '**ance**' or '**ancy**':

acceptance	assurance	inheritance	resemblance
acquaintance	balance	instance	substance
alliance	disturbance	insurance	tenancy
allowance	entrance	maintenance	
appearance	guidance	nuisance	
assistance	infancy	performance	

REFERENCE

11 silent consonants

Many words are spelled with consonants that are not pronounced. Here are the main rules about silent consonants.

silent 'b' (followed by 't' in the same syllable)	debt doubt subtle	/det/ /daʊt/ /'sʌtl/
silent b (after 'm' at end of syllable)	bomb climb lamb	/bɒm/ /klaɪm/ /læm/
silent d	sandwich	/'sænwɪdʒ/
silent g (in front of 'm' or 'n' at start/end of syllable)	foreign gnat phlegm sign	/'fɒrɪn/ /næt/ /flem/ /saɪn/
silent h (at start of word)*	heir honest honour hour	/eə/ /'ɒnɪst/ /'ɒnə/ /aʊə/
silent h (after vowel at the end of word)	hurrah oh	/hə'rɑː/ /oʊ/
silent h (between vowels)	annihilate vehicle	/ən'aɪəleɪt/ /'viːɪkl/
silent h (after 'r')	rhythm rhubarb	/'rɪðəm/ /'ruːbɑːb/
silent k (at start of word followed by 'n')	knee know	/niː/ /nəʊ/
silent l (between 'a' and 'f', 'k', or 'm')	half talk palm	/hɑːf/ /tɔːk/ /pɑːm/
silent l (between 'ou' and 'd')	should would	/ʃʊd/ /wʊd/
silent n (at end of word, after 'm')	column hymn	/'kɒləm/ /hɪm/
silent p (in front of 'n', 's', or 't' at start of words of Greek origin)	pneumatic psychology pterodactyl	/njuː'mætɪk/ /saɪk'ɒlədʒi/ /ˌterə'dæktɪl/
silent r (in standard British, when followed by a consonant or a silent 'e', or at the end of a word) **	farm more stir	/fɑːm/ /mɔː/ /stɜː/
silent s	island	/'aɪlənd/
silent s (in many words of French origin)	debris viscount	/'debri/ /'vaɪkaʊnt/
silent t	listen thistle	/'lɪsn/ /'θɪsl/
silent t (at the end of words of French origin)	buffet chalet	/'bʊfeɪ/ /'ʃæleɪ/
silent w (at the start of words, in front of 'r')	wreck write	/rek/ /raɪt/
silent w	answer sword two	/'ɑːnsə/ /sɔːd/ /tuː/

12 difficult words

Many people find some words especially hard to spell. Here is a list of some common problem words:

accommodation	exceed	medicine	referred
acknowledge	February	necessary	science
across	fluorescent	occasion	secretary
address	foreign	occurred	separate
allege	gauge	parallel	skilful (AM skillful)
argument	government	parliament	succeed
awkward	harass	precede	supersede
beautiful	inoculate	privilege	surprise
bureau	instalment	proceed	suspicious
bureaucracy	(AM installment)	professor	threshold
calendar	language	pronunciation	tomorrow
cemetery	library	psychiatrist	vegetable
committee	manoeuvre	pursue	vehicle
conscience	(AM maneuver)	recommend	Wednesday
embarrass	mathematics	reference	withhold

13 doubling consonants

 In American English, when you add a suffix to a two-syllable word whose final syllable is not stressed, you don't double the 'l'. For example, American English uses the spellings **traveling** and **marvelous**, whereas British English uses the spellings **travelling** and **marvellous**.

If the final syllable is stressed, the final consonant is doubled in both British and American English. For example, both use the spellings **admitting** and **admitted**.

A few verbs have a single consonant in the base form and -s form in British English, but a double consonant in American English. For example, British English uses the spellings **appal** and **appals**, but American English uses **appall** and **appalls**. Both British and American English use the spellings **appalling** and **appalled**.

appal	enrol	fulfil	instil
distil	enthral	instal	

Note also the British spellings **skilful** and **wilful**, contrasted with the American spellings **skillful** and **willful**.

 Note that a few words have a double consonant in British English, and a single consonant in American English.

carburettor	→	carburetor
chilli	→	chili
jeweller	→	jeweler
jewellery	→	jewelry
programme	→	program
tranquillize	→	tranquilize
woollen	→	woolen

14 '-our' and '-or'

 Many words, mostly abstract nouns of Latin origin, have their ending spelled '**our**' in British English, but '**or**' in American English.

armour	→	armor
behaviour	→	behavior
colour	→	color
demeanour	→	demeanor
favour	→	favor
flavour	→	flavor
honour	→	honor
humour	→	humor
neighbour	→	neighbor
odour	→	odor
tumour	→	tumor
vapour	→	vapor

15 '-oul' and '-ol'

 Some words spelled with '**oul**' in British English are spelled with '**ol**' in American English.

mould	→	mold
moult	→	molt
smoulder	→	smolder

16 '-re' and '-er'

 Many words, mostly of French origin, have their ending spelled '**re**' in British English and '**er**' in American English.

calibre	→	caliber
centre	→	center
fibre	→	fibre
meagre	→	meager
reconnoitre	→	reconnoiter
sombre	→	somber
spectre	→	specter
theatre	→	theater

17 'ae' or 'oe' and 'e'

 Many words, mostly of Greek or Latin origin, are spelled with '**ae**' or '**oe**' in British English, but '**e**' in American English. However, the American spellings are now sometimes used in British English as well.

aesthetic	→	esthetic
amoeba	→	ameba
diarrhoea	→	diarrhea
gynaecology	→	gynecology
mediaeval	→	medieval

Note that **manoeuvre** is spelled **maneuver** in American English.

18 '-ise' and '-ize'

 Many verbs can end in either '**ise**' or '**ize**'. For example, **authorise** and **authorize** are alternative spellings of the same verb. The '**ise**' ending is more common in British English than American English, but British people are increasingly using the '**ize**' ending. In this book, we use the '**ize**' ending.

Note that for the following verbs you can only use the 'ise' ending in both American and British English:

advertise	compromise	improvise	surprise
advise	despise	promise	televise
arise	devise	revise	
chastise	excise	supervise	
circumcise	exercise	surmise	

19 small groups

 Note also the following small groups of words that are spelled differently in British and American English. The British spelling is given first.

analyse	→	analyze
breathalyse	→	breathalyze
catalyse	→	catalyze
paralyse	→	paralyze
analogue	→	analog
catalogue	→	catalog
dialogue	→	dialog
defence	→	defense
offence	→	offense
pretence	→	pretense

Vice is spelled **vise** in American English when it refers to the tool used to hold a piece of wood or metal firmly.

→ See **Usage** entry **practice – practise**

20 individual words

 Some individual words are spelled differently in British English and American English. In the list below, the British spelling is given first.

axe – ax	distension –	glycerin	pyjamas –
chequer – checker	distention	grey – gray	pajamas
dependence –	gelatine – gelatin	nought – naught	sceptic – skeptic
dependance	glycerine –	plough – plow	tyre – tire

→ See **Usage** entries **assure – ensure – insure**, **disc – disk**, **story – storey**

With the following pairs there is also a slight change of pronunciation:

aluminium /ˌælʊˈmɪniəm/	→	aluminum /əˈluːmɪnəm/
furore /fjʊˈrɔːri/	→	furor /ˈfjʊərɔːr/
speciality /ˌspeʃiˈælɪti/	→	specialty /ˈspeʃəlti/

REFERENCE

21 two words or one word

 In British English, some items are usually written as two words, but in American English they can be written as one word.

any more	→	anymore
de luxe	→	deluxe
per cent	→	percent

22 hyphens: compound nouns

Compound nouns can often be written as two separate words or with a hyphen. There are many differences between British and American practice, and you should check a COBUILD dictionary to be sure. In general, American English has fewer hyphenated compounds than British English. Speakers of American English are more likely to spell a compound as one word, or as two words without a hyphen.

At seven he was woken by the <u>alarm clock</u>.
She's the kind of sleeper that even the <u>alarm-clock</u> doesn't always wake.

You must always use a hyphen in words referring to relatives, for example **great-grandmother** and **mother-in-law**. You usually use a hyphen in compound nouns such as **T-shirt**, **U-turn**, and **X-ray** where the first part consists of only one letter. Words used together as compound nouns are often hyphenated when they are used to modify another noun, in order to make the meaning clearer. For example, you would refer to the **sixth form** in a school, but use a hyphen for a **sixth-form class**.

The <u>stained glass</u> above the door cast beautiful colours upon the floor.
...a <u>stained-glass window</u>.
I did a lot of drawing in my <u>spare time</u>.
I teach cookery as a <u>spare-time occupation</u>.

23 compound adjectives

Compound adjectives can usually be written with a hyphen or as one word.

...any <u>anti-social</u> behaviour such as continuous lateness.
...the activities of <u>antisocial</u> groups.

Some adjectives are generally written with a hyphen in front of a noun and as two words after **be**.

He was wearing a <u>brand-new</u> uniform.
His uniform was <u>brand new</u>.

Prefixes that are used in front of a word beginning with a capital letter always have a hyphen after them.

...a wave of <u>anti-British</u> feeling.
...from the steps of the <u>neo-Byzantine</u> cathedral.

When you are describing something that is two colours, you use **and** between two adjectives, with or without hyphens.

...an ugly <u>black and white</u> swimming suit.
...a <u>black-and-white</u> calf.

If you are talking about a group of things, it is best to use hyphens if each thing is two colours.

...fifteen <u>black-and-white</u> police cars.

If each thing is only one colour, don't use hyphens.

...<u>black and white</u> dots.

REFERENCE

24 compound verbs

Compound verbs are usually written with a hyphen or as one word.

Take the baby along if you can't find anyone to <u>baby-sit</u>.
I can't come to London, because Mum'll need me to <u>babysit</u> that night.

25 phrasal verbs

Phrasal verbs are written as two (or three) words, without a hyphen.

She <u>turned off</u> the radio.
They <u>broke out of</u> prison on Thursday night.

However, nouns and adjectives that are related to phrasal verbs are written with a hyphen, if the first part ends in -*ing*, -*er*, -*ed*, or -*en*.

Finally, he monitors the <u>working-out</u> of the plan.
One of the boys had stopped a <u>passer-by</u> and asked him to phone an ambulance.
Gold was occasionally found in the <u>dried-up</u> banks and beds of the rivers.
He fixed <u>broken-down</u> second-hand cars.

Other nouns and adjectives related to phrasal verbs are written with a hyphen or as one word, or can be written in either way. For example, **break-in** is always written with a hyphen, **breakthrough** is always written as one word, and **takeover** can also be written as **take-over**.

 In American English, the solid form without a hyphen is more common than in British English.

Abbey National had fought off a <u>take-over</u> bid from Lloyds TSB.
They failed to reach a <u>takeover</u> deal.

26 numbers

Numbers between twenty and a hundred are usually written with a hyphen, as in **twenty-four** and **eighty-seven**. Fractions are also often written with a hyphen, as in **one-third** and **two-fifths**. However, when you use **a** instead of 'one' don't use a hyphen: **a third**.

Some headaches can last <u>twenty-four</u> hours or more.
<u>Two-fifths</u> of the world economy is now in recession.
<u>A third</u> of the cost went into technology and services.

27 other points

 In British English, if a word has two clear parts and the first letter of the second part is the same as the last letter of the first part, people usually use a hyphen, especially if the letter is a vowel. For example, they write **pre-eminent** and **co-operate**. In American English, the hyphen is now usually omitted, for example in **preeminent** and **cooperate**.

He agreed to <u>co-operate</u> with the police investigation.
Both companies said they would <u>cooperate</u> with the government.

When people are using a pair of hyphenated words that have the same second part, they sometimes just write the first part of the first word. However, it is clearer to write each word in full.

Their careers bridged the <u>pre- and post-war</u> eras.
...<u>long- and short-term</u> economic planning.

Compound words that are formed with the prefixes *anti-*, *non-*, and *semi-* are usually spelled with a hyphen in British English, but without it in American English. Adjectives formed by adding -*like* to a word are spelled without a hyphen in American English, unless the first part of the word is a proper noun or is rather long.

| anti-nuclear – antinuclear | non-aggression – nonaggression | semi-literate – semiliterate | cloud-like – cloudlike |

See a COBUILD dictionary for information on the usual way to write a particular compound word.

→ See **Reference** section **Punctuation**

Verb forms (formation of)

Sometimes there is a spelling change when the -*s*, -*ing*, and -*ed* endings are added, as shown in the table below.

	base form	-*s* form	-*ing* form or -*ing* participle	past form and -*ed* participle
		add -*s*	add -*ing*	add -*ed*
	join	joins	joining	joined
ending in -*sh* **ending in -*ch*** **ending in -*ss*** **ending in -*x*** **ending in -*z*** **ending in -*o***	finish reach pass mix buzz echo	add -*es* finishes reaches passes mixes buzzes echoes	finishing reaching passing mixing buzzing echoing	finished reached passed mixed buzzed echoed
ending in -*e*	dance	dances	omit -*e* before adding -*ing* or -*ed* dancing	danced
ending in -*ie*	tie	ties	change -*ie* to -*y* before adding -*ing* tying	omit -*e* before adding -*ed* tied
ending in consonant + -*y*	cry	change -*y* to -*ies* cries	crying	change -*y* to -*ied* cried
one syllable ending in single vowel + consonant	dip	dips	double final consonant before adding -*ing* or -*ed* dipping	dipped
last syllable stressed	refer	refers	double final consonant before adding -*ing* or -*ed* referring	referred
ending in -*ic*	panic	panics	add -*k* before adding -*ing* or -*ed* panicking	panicked

REFERENCE

In the following verbs ending in *e*, you just add *-ing* in the normal way to form the *-ing* form. For example, the *-ing* form of **age** is **ageing**.

age	dye	hoe	singe
agree	eye	knee	tiptoe
disagree	free	referee	

You don't double the final consonant of verbs ending in *w*, *x*, or *y* when forming the *-ing* form or past form.

row	→	rowing	→	rowed
box	→	boxing	→	boxed
play	→	playing	→	played

In British English, you double the final *l* of verbs like **travel** and **quarrel**, even though the last syllable is not stressed.

travel	→	travelling	→	travelled
quarrel	→	quarrelling	→	quarrelled

You don't double the final *l* in American English. In British English, and sometimes in American English, the final consonant of the following verbs is doubled, even though the last syllable is not stressed.

handicap	kidnap	worship
hiccup	program	

Glossary of grammatical terms

Glossary of grammatical terms

abstract noun a noun used to describe a quality, idea, or experience rather than something that is physical or concrete; e.g. *joy, size, language*. Compare with **concrete noun**. See **Grammar** entry **Nouns**.

active used for describing verb phrases such as 'gives', 'took', and 'has made', where the subject is the person or thing doing the action or responsible for the action; e.g. *The storm destroyed dozens of trees*. Compare with **passive**.

adjectival clause another name for **relative clause**.

adjective a word used to tell you more about a thing, such as its appearance, colour, size, or other qualities; e.g. *...a pretty blue dress*. See **Grammar** entry **Adjectives**.

adverb a word that gives more information about when, how, where, or in what circumstances something happens; e.g. *quickly, now*.
adverb of degree an adverb that indicates the amount or extent of a feeling or quality; e.g. *I enjoyed it enormously..., She felt extremely tired*.
adverb of duration an adverb that indicates how long something lasts; e.g. *He smiled briefly*.
adverb of frequency an adverb that indicates how often something happens; e.g. *I sometimes regret it*.
adverb of manner an adverb that indicates the way in which something happens or is done; e.g. *She watched him carefully*.
adverb of place an adverb that gives more information about position or direction; e.g. *Come here*.
adverb of time an adverb that gives more information about when something happens; e.g. *I saw her yesterday*. See **Grammar** entry **Adverbs and adverbials**.

adverbial a word or combination of words that is added to a clause in order to give more information about time, place, or manner; e.g. *She laughed nervously..., No birds or animals came near the body*. Also called 'adjunct'. See also **sentence adverbial**. See **Grammar** entry **Adverbs and adverbials**.

adverbial clause a subordinate clause that gives more information about the event described in the main clause. See **Grammar** entry **Subordinate clauses**.

adverb phrase two adverbs used together; e.g. *She spoke very quietly*.

affirmative an affirmative clause is one that does not contain a negative word. Compare with **negative**.

affix a letter or group of letters that is added to the beginning or end of a word to make a different word; e.g. *anti-communist, harmless*. See also **suffix**, **prefix**.

agent another name for **performer**.

agreement the relationship between a subject and its verb, or between a number or determiner and its noun; e.g. *I look/She looks..., This book is mine/These books are mine..., one bell/three bells*. Also called 'concord'.

apostrophe s an ending ('s) added to a noun to mark possession; e.g. *...Harriet's daughter..., the professor's husband..., the Managing Director's secretary*. See **Usage** entry **'s**.

article See **definite article**, **indefinite article**.

aspect the use of verb forms to show whether an action is still continuing, is repeated, or is finished.

attributive used for describing adjectives when they are used in front of a noun; e.g. *classical music, outdoor shoes, woollen socks*. Compare with **predicative**.

auxiliary verb one of the verbs 'be', 'have', and 'do' when they are used with a main verb to form tenses, negatives, questions, and so on. Also called 'auxiliary'. **Modals** are also auxiliary verbs. See **Grammar** entries **Auxiliary verbs**, **Modals**.

bare infinitive another name for **infinitive without 'to'**.

base form the form of a verb that has no letters added to the end and is not a past form; e.g. *walk, go, have, be*. The base form is the form you look up in a dictionary.

broad negative adverb one of a small group of adverbs, including 'barely' and 'seldom', that are used to make a statement almost negative. e.g. *I barely knew her*. See **Grammar** entry **Broad negatives**.

cardinal number a number used for counting; e.g. *one, seven, nineteen*. See **Topic** entry **Numbers and fractions**.

classifying adjective an adjective that is used to identify something as being of a particular type; e.g. *Indian, wooden, mental*. Compare with **qualitative adjective**. See **Grammar** entry **Adjectives**.

clause a group of words containing a verb. See **main clause**, **subordinate clause**. See **Grammar** entry **Clauses**.

clause of manner another name for **manner clause**.

collective noun a noun that refers to a group or set of people or things; e.g. *committee, team, family*. See **Grammar** entry **Nouns**.

colour adjective an adjective that indicates what colour something is; e.g. *red, blue, scarlet*. See **Grammar** entry **Adjectives**.

common noun a noun used to refer to a kind of person, thing, or substance; e.g. *sailor, computer, glass*. Compare with **proper noun**.

comparative an adjective or adverb with '-er' on the end or 'more' in front of it; e.g. *friendlier, more important, more carefully*. See **Grammar** entries **Comparative and superlative adjectives**, **Comparative and superlative adverbs**.

complement a noun phrase or adjective that comes after a linking verb such as 'be', and gives more information about the subject or object of the clause; e.g. *She is a teacher..., She is tired*. See **Grammar** entry **Complements**. See also **object complement**.

complex sentence a sentence consisting of a main clause and a subordinate clause;

e.g. *She wasn't thinking very quickly because she was tired*. See **Grammar** entry **Clauses**.

compound a combination of two or more words that function as a unit. For example, 'self-centred' and 'free-and-easy' are compound adjectives, 'bus stop' and 'state of affairs' are compound nouns, and 'dry-clean' and 'roller-skate' are compound verbs.

compound sentence a sentence consisting of two or more main clauses linked by a coordinating conjunction; e.g. *They picked her up and took her into the house*. See **Grammar** entry **Clauses**.

concessive clause a subordinate clause, usually introduced by 'although', 'though', or 'while', that contrasts with a main clause. e.g. *Although I like her, I find her hard to talk to*. See **Grammar** entry **Subordinate clauses**.

concord another name for **agreement**.

concrete noun a noun that refers to something you can touch or see; e.g. *table, dress, flower*. Compare with **abstract noun**. See **Grammar** entry **Nouns**.

conditional clause a subordinate clause usually starting with 'if' or 'unless'. The event described in the main clause depends on the condition described in the subordinate clause; e.g. *If it rains, we'll go to the cinema..., They would be rich if they had taken my advice*. See **Grammar** entry **Subordinate clauses**.

conjunction a word that links together two clauses, groups, or words. There are two kinds of conjunction: **coordinating conjunctions**, which link parts of a sentence which are the same grammatical type ('and', 'but', 'or'), and **subordinating conjunctions**, which begin subordinate clauses ('although', 'because', 'when'). See **Grammar** entry **Subordinate clauses**.

continuous another name for **progressive**.

contraction a shortened form in which an auxiliary verb and 'not', or a subject and an auxiliary verb, are joined together and function as one word; e.g. *aren't, she's*. See **Grammar** entry **Contractions**.

coordinating conjunction a word such as 'and', 'but', or 'or' that joins together two clauses, phrases, or words of the same grammatical type. See **Grammar** entry **Subordinate clauses**.

coordination the linking of words or groups of words which are of the same grammatical type, or the linking of clauses which are of equal importance. See **Grammar** entries **Conjunctions**, **Adjectives**.

copula another name for **linking verb**.

countable noun a noun that has a singular form and a plural form; e.g. *dog/dogs*, *lemon/lemons*, *foot/feet*. Also called 'count noun'. See **Grammar** entry **Nouns**.

defining relative clause a relative clause that identifies the person or thing that is being talked about; e.g. *I wrote down everything that she said*. Compare with **non-defining relative clause**. See **Grammar** entry **Relative clauses**.

definite article the determiner 'the'.

definite determiner a determiner that is used when referring to someone or something that has already been mentioned, or whose identity is obvious. e.g. *the, that, my*. See **Grammar** entry **Determiners**.

delexical verb a verb that has very little meaning in itself and is used with an object to describe an action. 'Give', 'have', and 'take' are commonly used as delexical verbs; e.g. *She gave a small cry*..., *I've had a bath*. See **Grammar** entry **Verbs**.

demonstrative one of the words 'this', 'that', 'these', and 'those'. They are used as determiners. e.g. *...this woman...*, *that tree*. They are also used as pronouns. e.g. *That looks interesting...*, *This is fun*. See **Usage** entries **that - those**, **this - these**.

dependent clause another name for **subordinate clause**.

determiner one of a group of words including 'the', 'a', 'some', and 'my', which are used at the beginning of a noun phrase. See **Grammar** entry **Determiners**.

direct object a noun phrase referring to the person or thing directly affected by an action, in a clause with an active verb;

e.g. *She wrote her name...*, *I shut the windows*. Compare with **indirect object**. See **Grammar** entry **Objects**.

direct speech speech reported in the words actually spoken by someone, without any changes in tense, person, and so on. See **Grammar** entry **Reporting**.

ditransitive verb a verb such as 'give', 'take', or 'sell' that can have both an indirect and a direct object; e.g. *She gave me a kiss*. See **Grammar** entry **Verbs**.

dynamic verb a verb such as 'run', 'fight', or 'sing' which describes an action. Compare with **stative verb**. See **Grammar** entry **The progressive form**.

-ed participle a verb form such as 'broken' or 'watched', which is used to make perfect forms and passives. Also called **past participle**. See **Grammar** entry **-ed participles**.

ellipsis leaving out words because they are obvious from the context. See **Grammar** entry **Ellipsis**.

emphasizing adjective an adjective such as 'complete', 'utter', or 'total' which stresses how strongly you feel about something; e.g. *I feel a complete fool*. See **Grammar** entry **Adjectives**.

emphasizing adverb an adverb that adds emphasis to a verb or adjective; e.g. *I simply can't do it...*, *I was absolutely amazed*. See **Grammar** entries **Adjuncts**, **Adverbs**.

ergative verb a verb that can be used either transitively to focus on the person who performs an action, or intransitively to focus on the thing affected by the action; e.g. *He had boiled a kettle...*, *The kettle had boiled*. See **Grammar** entry **Verbs**.

exclamation a sound, word, or sentence that is spoken suddenly and loudly in order to express surprise, anger, and so on; e.g. *Oh Gosh!* See **Topic** entry **Reactions**.

finite a finite verb is inflected according to person or tense rather than being an infinitive or a participle; e.g. *He loves gardening...*, *You can borrow that pen if you want to*. Compare with **non-finite**.

first person See **person**.

focusing adverb a sentence adverbial that indicates the most relevant thing involved;

e.g. *only, mainly, especially*. See **Grammar** entry **Adverbs and adverbials**.

future the use of 'will' or 'shall' with the base form of the verb to refer to future events; e.g. *She will come tomorrow*. See **Grammar** entry **Future time**.

future continuous another name for **future progressive**.

future perfect 'will have' or 'shall have' with an *-ed* participle, used to refer to future events. e.g. *I will have finished* by tomorrow. See **Grammar** entry **Future time**.

future perfect continuous another name for **future perfect progressive**.

future perfect progressive 'will have been' or 'shall have been' with an *-ing* participle, used to refer to future events. Also called **future perfect continuous**; e.g. *I will have been walking* for three hours by then. See **Grammar** entry **The progressive form**.

future progressive 'will be' or 'shall be' with an *-ing* participle, used to refer to future events. Also called **future continuous**; e.g. *She will be going* soon. See **Grammar** entries **Future time**, **The progressive form**.

gerund another name for *-ing* noun.

gradable a gradable adjective can be used with a word such as 'very' or in a comparative or superlative form, in order to say that the person or thing referred to has more or less of a quality. **Qualitative adjectives** such as 'big' and 'good' are gradable; e.g. *very boring, less helpful, the best*.

idiom a group of two or more words with a special meaning that cannot be understood by taking the meaning of each individual word. e.g. *to go like a bomb, a free-for-all*.

if-clause a **conditional clause**, or a clause used to report a *yes/no* question.

imperative the base form of the verb without a subject, used especially for giving commands, orders, and instructions. It is also used for making offers and suggestions; e.g. *Come here…*, *Take two tablets every four hours…*, *Enjoy yourself*. See **Grammar** entry **The imperative**.

impersonal 'it' 'It' is called an impersonal subject when it is used to introduce or comment on a fact; e.g. *It's raining*. See **Usage** entry **it**.

indefinite article the determiners 'a' and 'an'.

indefinite determiner a determiner that is used when you are talking about people or things in a general or indefinite way. e.g. *a, some*. See **Grammar** entries **Determiners**, **Quantity**.

indefinite place adverb one of a small group of adverbs including 'anywhere' and 'somewhere' which are used to indicate location or destination in a general or vague way. See **Topic** entry **Places**.

indefinite pronoun one of a small group of pronouns including 'someone' and 'anything' which are used to refer to a person or thing in a general or vague way. See **Grammar** entry **Pronouns**.

indirect object a second object, used with a transitive verb to show who or what benefits from an action, or receives something as a result of it. e.g. *She gave me a rose*. See **Grammar** entry **Verbs**.

indirect question another name for **reported question**.

indirect speech another name for **reported speech**.

infinitive the base form of a verb. It is often used with 'to' in front of it; e.g. *(to) take, (to) see, (to) bring*. See **Grammar** entries **Infinitives**, **To-infinitive clauses**.

infinitive without 'to' the infinitive of the verb without 'to'; e.g. *Let me think*.

inflection the variation in the form of a verb, noun, pronoun, or adjective to show differences in tense, number, case, and degree; e.g. *come/came, cat/cats, small/smaller/smallest*.

-ing clause a clause beginning with an *-ing* form; e.g. *Realising that something was wrong, I stopped*. See **Grammar** entry **-ing forms**.

-ing form a verb form ending in *-ing* which is used, for example, to make progressive structures; e.g. *swimming, laughing*. See **Grammar** entry **-ing forms**.

-*ing* noun a noun that has the same form as the *-ing* form of a verb; e.g. *Swimming is a great way to get fit*. See **Grammar** entry **-*ing* forms**.

-*ing* participle a verb form ending in *-ing*, which is used to make progressive structures. Also called **present participle**; e.g. *They were all laughing at me*. See **Grammar** entry **-*ing* forms**.

intensifier a grading adverb that is used to reinforce an adjective and make it more emphatic; e.g. *very, exceptionally*.

interjection another name for **exclamation**.

interrogative adverb one of the adverbs 'how', 'when', 'where', and 'why' when they are used to ask questions; e.g. *How do you know that?* See **Grammar** entries **Questions**, **Reporting**.

interrogative a clause in the interrogative has part or all of the verb phrase in front of the subject. Most questions are in the interrogative; e.g. *Is it still raining?* See **Grammar** entry **Questions**.

interrogative pronoun one of the pronouns 'who', 'whose', 'whom', 'what', and 'which' when they are used to ask questions; e.g. *Who did you talk to?* See **Grammar** entries **Questions**, **Reporting**.

intransitive verb a verb that is used to talk about an action or event that only involves the subject and so does not have an object; e.g. *She arrived...*, *I was yawning*. Compare with **transitive verb**. See **Grammar** entry **Verbs**.

inversion changing the word order in a sentence, especially changing the order of the subject and the verb. See **Grammar** entry **Inversion**.

irregular used for describing a verb, noun, or adjective that does not follow the normal rules for inflection. An irregular verb has a past form and/or *-ed* participle that is formed in a different way from the regular *-ed* ending. See **Grammar** entries **Comparative and superlative adjectives**, **Comparative and superlative adverbs**. See **Reference** sections **Irregular verbs**, **Plural forms of nouns**.

lexical verb another name for **main verb**.

linking verb a verb that links the subject and complement of a clause. Also sometimes called 'copula'; e.g. *be, become, seem, appear*. See **Grammar** entries **Complements**, **Verbs**.

main clause a clause that is not dependent on, or is not part of, another clause. See **Grammar** entry **Clauses**.

main verb any verb that is not an auxiliary verb. Also called **lexical verb**.

manner clause a subordinate clause, usually introduced with 'as', 'like', or 'the way', which describes the way in which something is done; e.g. *She talks like her mother used to*. See **Grammar** entry **Subordinate clauses**.

mass noun a noun that is usually an uncountable noun, but that can be used as a countable noun when it refers to quantities or types of something; e.g. *...two sugars..., cough medicines*. See **Grammar** entry **Nouns**.

measurement noun a noun that refers to a unit of size, volume, weight, speed, temperature, etc; e.g. *metre, pound*. See **Topic** entry **Measurements**.

modal an auxiliary verb that is used with the base form of another verb to express a particular attitude, such as possibility, obligation, prediction, or deduction. Also called 'modal auxiliary' or 'modal verb'; e.g. *can, could, may, might*. See **Grammar** entry **Modals**.

modifier a word or group of words that comes in front of a noun and describes it in some way; e.g. *...a beautiful sunny day..., a psychology conference*. See **Grammar** entry **Modifiers**.

negative a negative clause uses a word such as 'not', 'never', or 'no-one' to indicate the absence or opposite of something, or to say that something is not the case. e.g. *I don't know you.*, *I'll never forget*. Compare with **affirmative**. See **Usage** entries **not, no, none, no-one, nothing, nowhere, never**.

negative word a word such as 'never', 'no-one', and 'not' which makes a clause negative.

nominal relative clause a clause beginning with a *wh*-word, which functions as a noun phrase; e.g. *I wrote down what she said*.

non-defining relative clause a relative clause that gives more information about someone or something, but which is not needed to identify them; e.g. *That's Mary, who was at university with me*. Compare with **defining relative clause**. See **Grammar** entry **Relative clauses**.

non-finite a non-finite verb is a verb that is not inflected according to person or tense. Infinitives and a participles are non-finite; e.g. *to go, do, being*. Compare with **finite**.

non-finite clause a subordinate clause that is based on a participle or an infinitive. Non-finite clauses do not show the time at which something happened; they have no tense. See **Grammar** entries *To*-**infinitive clauses**, *-ing* **forms**, *-ed* **participles**, **Ellipsis**.

noun a word that refers to people, things, and abstract ideas such as feelings and qualities; e.g. *woman, Harry, guilt*. See **Grammar** entry **Nouns**.

noun phrase a group of words that acts as the subject, complement, or object of a clause, or as the object of a preposition.

noun modifier a noun used in front of another noun, as if it were an adjective; e.g. *...a car door..., a steel works*. See **Grammar** entry **Noun modifiers**.

number the way in which differences between singular and plural are shown; e.g. *flower/flowers, that/those*. See also **cardinal number**, **ordinal number**.

object a noun phrase that refers to a person or thing, other than the subject, which is involved in or affected by the action of a verb. See also **direct object**, **indirect object**. Prepositions are also followed by objects. See **Grammar** entry **Objects**.

object complement a complement that is used to describe the object of a clause, and that occurs with verbs such as 'make' and 'find'; e.g. *It made me tired..., I found her asleep*. See **Grammar** entry **Complements**.

object pronoun a personal pronoun that is used as the object of a verb or preposition. The object pronouns are 'me', 'us', 'you', 'him', 'her', 'it', and 'them'; e.g. *Can you help me?..., I'd like to talk to them*. See **Grammar** entry **Pronouns**.

ordinal number a number that is used to show where something comes in an order or sequence; e.g. *first, fifth, tenth, hundredth*. See **Reference** section **Numbers and fractions**.

participle a verb form used for making different tenses. See *-ed* **participle**, *-ing* **participle**.

particle an adverb or preposition that combines with verbs to make phrasal verbs; e.g. *out, on*.

partitive a word that is used before 'of' to give information about the amount of a particular thing; e.g. *pint, loaf, portion*. See **Grammar** entry **Quantity**.

passive verb forms such as 'was given', 'were taken', 'had been made', where the subject is the person or thing that is affected by the action. e.g. *Dozens of trees were destroyed*. Compare with **active**. See **Grammar** entry **The passive**.

past continuous another name for **past progressive**.

past form the form of a verb, often ending in *-ed*, which is used for the past simple.

past participle another name for *-ed* **participle**. See **Grammar** entry *-ed* **participles**.

past simple the past form of a verb, used to refer to past events and situations; e.g. *They waited*. See **Grammar** entry **The past**.

past progressive the use of 'was' or 'were' with an *-ing* participle, used to refer to past events. Also called **past continuous**; e.g. *They were worrying about it yesterday*. See **Grammar** entries **The past**, **The progressive form**.

past perfect the use of 'had' with an *-ed* participle, used to refer to past events; e.g. *She had finished*. See **Grammar** entry **The past**.

past perfect continuous another name for **past perfect progressive**.

past perfect progressive the use of 'had been' with an -*ing* participle, used to refer to past events; e.g. *He had been waiting for hours*. See **Grammar** entries **The past**, **The progressive form**.

performer the person who performs an action. Also called 'agent'.

person a term used to refer to the three classes of people who are involved in something that is said. They are called the first person (the person who is speaking or writing), the second person (the person who is being addressed), and the third person (people or things that are being talked about).

personal pronoun one of a group of words including 'I', 'you', 'me', and 'they', which are used to refer back to the people or things you are talking about. See **Grammar** entry **Pronouns**.

phrasal verb a combination of a verb and an adverb and/or preposition, which together have a single meaning; e.g. *back down, hand over, look forward to*. See **Grammar** entry **Phrasal verbs**.

phrase a set of words that is smaller than a clause, and that is based around a particular word class. See **noun phrase**, **prepositional phrase**, **verb phrase**. Also sometimes used to refer to any group of words.

place clause a subordinate clause that is used to talk about where something is; e.g. *I left it where it fell*. See **Grammar** entry **Subordinate clauses**.

plural the form of a countable noun or verb that is used to talk about more than one person or thing. e.g. *Puppies chew everything..., The women were ouside*. Compare with **singular**. See **Reference** section **Plural forms of nouns**.

plural noun a noun that is used only in the plural form; e.g. *trousers, scissors, vermin*. See **Grammar** entry **Nouns**.

positive another name for **affirmative**.

possessive determiner a determiner such as 'my', 'your', 'his', 'her', 'its', 'our', and 'their', which show who or what something belongs to or is connected with. Also called 'possessive adjective'. See **Grammar** entry **Possessive determiners**.

possessive pronoun one of the words 'mine', 'yours', 'hers', 'his', 'ours', and 'theirs'. See **Grammar** entry **Pronouns**.

postdeterminer one of a small group of adjectives that can be used after a determiner and in front of any other adjectives to make a reference clear and precise; e.g. *The following brief description*. See **Grammar** entry **Adjectives**.

predeterminer a word that comes in front of a determiner, but is still part of the noun phrase; e.g. *...all the boys..., double the trouble..., such a mess*.

predicative used for describing the position of adjectives when they are used after a linking verb such as 'be'; e.g. *alive, asleep, sure*. Compare with **attributive**.

prefix a letter or group of letters added to the beginning of a word in order to make a new word; e.g. *semi-circular*. Compare with **affix** and **suffix**.

preposition a word such as 'by', 'with', or 'from' that is always followed by a noun phrase or an -*ing* form. See **Grammar** entry **Prepositions**.

prepositional phrase a structure consisting of a preposition and its object; e.g. *...on the table..., by the sea*.

present continuous another name for **present progressive**.

present participle another name for -*ing* form.

present perfect the use of 'have' or 'has' with an -*ed* participle, used to refer to past events that affect the present; e.g. *She has loved him for ten years*. See **Grammar** entry **The past** .

present perfect continuous another name for **present perfect progressive**.

present perfect progressive the use of 'has been' or 'have been' with a present participle, used to refer to past situations that still exist in the present. Also called **present perfect continuous**; e.g. *We have been sitting here for hours*. See **Grammar** entries **The progressive form**, **The past**.

present progressive the use of 'am', 'are', or 'is' with an -*ing* participle, used to refer to present events; e.g. *Things are improving*.

See **Grammar** entries **The present**, **The progressive form**.

present simple the use of the base form or the s form of a verb, usually to refer to present events and situations; e.g. *I like bananas...*, *My sister hates them*. See **Grammar** entry **The present**.

progressive a verb form that contains a form of the verb 'be' and an *-ing* participle; e.g. *She was laughing...*, *They had been playing tennis*. Also called 'continuous'. See **Grammar** entry **The progressive form**.

pronoun a word used instead of a noun, when you do not want to name someone or something directly; e.g. *it, you, none*. See **Grammar** entry **Pronouns**.

proper noun a noun that refers to a particular person, place, or institution; e.g. *Maria, Edinburgh, January*. Compare with **common noun**. See **Grammar** entry **Nouns**.

purpose clause a subordinate clause, usually introduced by 'in order to', 'to', 'so that', or 'so', which indicates the purpose of an action; e.g. *I came here in order to help you*. See **Grammar** entry **Subordinate clauses**.

qualitative adjective an adjective that is used to indicate a quality, and that is gradable; e.g. *funny, intelligent, small*. Compare with **classifying adjective**. See **Grammar** entry **Adjectives**.

question a structure that typically has the verb in front of the subject and that is used to ask someone about something; e.g. *Have you lost something?...*, *When did she leave?*. Also called 'interrogative'. See **Grammar** entry **Questions**.

question tag a structure consisting of an auxiliary verb followed by a pronoun, used at the end of a statement in order to form a question; e.g. *She's quiet, isn't she?*

quote structure a structure containing a reporting clause and a quote; used in **direct speech**; e.g. *She said 'I'll be late'*. Compare with **reporting structure**. See **Grammar** entry **Reporting**.

reason clause a subordinate clause, usually introduced by 'because', 'since', or 'as', which gives the reason for something;

e.g. *Since you're here, we'll start*. See **Grammar** entry **Subordinate clauses**.

reciprocal pronoun the pronouns 'each other' and 'one another', used to show that two people do or feel the same thing. e.g. *They loved each other*.

reciprocal verb a verb that describes an action involving two people doing the same thing to each other. e.g. *They met in the street*.

reflexive pronoun a pronoun ending in '-self' or '-selves', such as 'myself' or 'themselves', used as the object of a verb when the person affected by an action is the same as the person doing it. See **Grammar** entry **Pronouns**.

reflexive verb a verb that is typically used with a reflexive pronoun; e.g. *Can you amuse yourself until dinner?* See **Grammar** entry **Verbs**.

relative clause a subordinate clause that gives more information about someone or something mentioned in the main clause. See also **defining relative clause**, **non-defining relative clause**. See **Grammar** entry **Relative clauses**.

relative pronoun a *wh*-word such as 'who' or 'which', used to introduce a relative clause. e.g. *...the girl who was carrying the bag*.

reported clause the part of a reporting structure that describes what someone has said; e.g. *She said that she couldn't see me*.

reported question a question that is reported using a reporting structure rather than the exact words used by the speaker. Also called 'indirect question'. See **Grammar** entry **Reporting**.

reported speech speech which is reported using a report structure rather than the exact words used by the speaker. Also called 'indirect speech'.

reporting clause a clause that contains a reporting verb, used to introduce what someone has said; e.g. *They asked if I could come*.

reporting structure a structure that reports what someone has said by using a reporting clause and a reported clause rather than repeating their exact words;

e.g. *She told me she'd be late.* Compare with **quote structure**. See **Grammar** entry **Reporting**.

reporting verb a verb that describes what people say or think; e.g. *suggest, say, wonder.*

result clause a subordinate clause introduced by 'so', 'so that', or 'such that', which gives the result of something; e.g. *The house was severely damaged, so that it is now uninhabitable.* See **Usage** entries **so**, **such**.

second person See **person**.

semi-modal the verbs 'dare', 'need', and 'used to', which behave rather like modals.

sentence a group of words that expresses a statement, question, or command. A sentence usually has a verb and a subject, and may consist of one clause, or two or more clauses. A sentence in writing has a capital letter at the beginning and a full stop, question mark, or exclamation mark at the end.

sentence adverbial an adverb or adverbial expression that applies to the whole clause, rather than to just a part of it; e.g. *Fortunately, he wasn't seriously injured.* See **Topic** entry **Opinions**.

sentence connector a sentence adverbial that is used to introduce a comment or to reinforce what is said; *moreover, besides*

s form the base form of a verb with s on the end, used in the present simple. e.g. *She likes reading.*

singular the form used to talk about one person or thing; e.g. *dog, woman*. Compare with **plural**.

singular noun a noun that is typically used in the singular form; e.g. *sun, moon*. See **Grammar** entry **Nouns**.

stative verb a verb that describes a state; e.g. *be, live, know.* Compare with **dynamic verb**. See **Grammar** entry **The progressive form**.

subject the noun phrase that comes before the verb in a statement, and agrees with the verb in person and number. In active sentences, the subject usually refers to the person or thing that does the action expressed by the verb; e.g. *We were going shopping.* See **Grammar** entry **Subjects**.

subject pronoun a personal pronoun that is used as the subject of a clause. The subject pronouns are 'I', 'we', 'you', 'he', 'she', 'it', and 'they'. See **Grammar** entry **Pronouns**.

subjunctive a verb form that is used to express attitudes such as wishing, hoping, and doubting. The subjunctive is not very common in English, and is used mainly in conditional clauses such as 'If I were you...'. See **Grammar** entry **The subjunctive**.

subordinate clause a clause that begins with a subordinating conjunction such as 'because' or 'while', and that must be used with a main clause. Also called 'dependent clause'. See **Grammar** entry **Subordinate clauses**.

suffix a letter or group of letters added to the end of a word in order to make a different word, tense, case, or word class; e.g. *slowly, childish*. Compare with **affix** and **prefix**.

superlative an adjective or adverb with '-est' on the end or 'most' in front of it. e.g. *thinnest, quickest, most wisely*. See **Grammar** entries **Comparative and superlative adjectives**, **Comparative and superlative adverbs**.

tense the verb form that shows whether you are referring to the past or the present. See **Grammar** entries **The past**, **The present**.

that-clause a clause starting with 'that', used mainly when reporting what someone has said. 'That' can be omitted when the clause is used after a reporting verb; e.g. *She said that she'd wash up for me*. See **Grammar** entry **That-clauses**.

third person See **person**.

time clause a subordinate clause that indicates the time of an event; e.g. *I'll phone you when I get back*. See **Grammar** entry **Subordinate clauses**.

title a word used before a person's name to show their position or status; e.g. *Mrs, Lord, Queen*. See **Topic** entry **Names and titles**.

to-infinitive the base form of a verb preceded by 'to'; e.g. *to go, to have, to jump.*

transitive verb a verb used to talk about an action or event that involves more than one person or thing, and so is followed by an object; e.g. *She's <u>wasting</u> her money*. Compare with **intransitive verb**. See **Grammar** entry **Verbs**.

uncountable noun a noun that refers to a general kind of thing rather than to an individual item, and so does not have a plural form; e.g. *money, furniture, intelligence*. Also called 'uncount noun'. See **Grammar** entry **Nouns**.

verb a word used with a subject to say what someone or something does, or what happens to them; e.g. *sing, spill, die*. See **Grammar** entry **Verbs**.

verb phrase a main verb, or a main verb preceded by one or more auxiliary verbs, which combines with a subject to say what someone or something does, or what happens to them; e.g. *I'll <u>show</u> them...*, *She's <u>been</u> sick*.

vocative a word used when speaking to someone, just as if it were their name; e.g. *darling, madam*. See **Topic** entry **Addressing someone**.

***wh*-clause** a clause starting with a *wh*-word. See **Grammar** entry **Reporting**.

***whether*-clause** a clause beginning with *whether*, used to report a *yes/no*-question. e.g. *I asked her <u>whether she'd seen him</u>*. See **Grammar** entry **Reporting**.

***wh*-question** a question that expects an answer mentioning a particular person, place, thing, amount, and so on, rather than just 'yes' or 'no'. Compare with ***yes/no*-question**. See **Grammar** entry **Questions**.

***wh*-word** one of a group of words starting with 'wh-', such as 'what', 'when', or 'who', which are used in *wh*-questions. 'How' is also called a *wh*-word because it behaves like the other *wh*-words. See **Grammar** entry **Wh- words**.

***yes/no*-question** a question that can be answered simply with either 'yes' or 'no'. e.g. *Would you like some more tea?* Compare with ***wh*-question**. See **Grammar** entry **Questions**.

Index

Index

A

a 1
a bit 2
a few 222
a little 307
a lot 36
a.m. 41
Abbreviations 706
ability 2
able 2
about 3, 55
above 3
absent 4
accept 5
acceptable 5
accommodation 6
accompany 6
accord 6
according to 6
accuse 7
accustomed to 7
actual 8
actually 8
Addressing someone 643
Adjectives 9
Adverbs and adverbials 15
advertisement 45
advice 24
advise 24
Advising someone 646
affect 25
afford 25
afloat 26
afraid 26
after 27
after all 28
afternoon 28
afterward 29
afterwards 27, 29
Age 616
aged 29
ago 30
agree 30
Agreeing and disagreeing 648
aim 31
alight 31

alike 32
alive 32
all 32
all right 34
allow 34
almost 34
alone 35
along 36
aloud 36
already 36
alright 37
also 37
alternate 38
alternately 39
alternative 38
alternatively 39
although 39
altogether 40
always 40
among 41
amount 42
an 1, 42
and 42
angry 45
anniversary 45
announcement 45
annoyed 346
another 46
answer 47
anxious 47, 346
any 48
any more 49
any time 50
anybody 49
anyone 49
anyplace 50
anything 50
anyway 51
anywhere 51
apart 51
apartment 228
apologize 52
Apologizing 651
appeal 52
appear 52
apply 53
appreciate 53

approach 54
approve 54
argument 177
arise 54
armchair 54, 116
army 55
around 55
arrange 319
arrival 56
arrive 56
as 57, 306
as ... as 58
as if 59
as long as 61
as soon as 62
as though 63
as usual 63
as well 37, 63
as well as 63
ashamed 59
ask 60
Asking for repetition 653
asleep 61, 486
assignment 62
assist 62
assure 63
at 64
at first 65
at last 65
athletic 65
athletics 65
attempt 66, 551
attendant 66
attention 66
audience 66
aural 66
autumn 67
Auxiliary verbs 67
avoid 68
await 69
awake 69
away 70

B

back 71
back yard 72
backwards 72
bad 72

badly 72
bag 73
baggage 73, 314
bake 73
band 73
bank 74
banknote 74
bar 74, 421
bare 74, 80
barely 74
base 75
bass 75
bath 75
bathe 75
be 76
be able to 79, 107
be born 93
be present 62
be sorry 439
beach 79
bear 79, 80
beat 80, 600
because 80
become 81
before 82
begin 83, 504
behaviour 83
behind 83
believe 84
belong 84
below 85, 553
bench 74
beneath 85, 553
beside 85
besides 85
best 85
better 86
between 86
beware 87
bid 87
big 87
bill 88, 356
billfold 89
billion 89
birthday 45
bit 89
bite 90, 507
blame 90
blind 91
blow up 91, 214
board 91

boat 92
bonnet 92
bookshop 304
boot 92
border 92
bore 93
borrow 93
bosom 94, 97
both 94
bottom 96
boundary 92, 96
boxcar 96
brackets 96
brake 96, 97
brand 96
break 97
breakfast 97
breast 97
breath 98
breathe 98
briefly 98, 481
bring 98
bring up 99
Britain 99
British 99
Briton 99
broad 100, 599
Broad negatives 100
broken 101
bum 101
burglar 101, 538
burglarize 101
burgle 101
burst 101
bus 102
business 102
bust 97, 102
but 103
butt 104
buttocks 104
buy 104
by 104
by far 105

C
café 106
call 106, 459
called 107
camp bed 107, 156
can 107
cancel 110, 167
candy 110, 523

cannot 110
capability 2, 110
capable 2
capacity 2, 110
Capital letters 708
car 110, 112
car park 389
care 111
carefree 111
careful 111
careless 111
carriage 112
carry 112
case 113
cast 114
casualty 114, 573
cause 114
certain 114
certainly 115, 521
chair 116, 117
chairman 117
chairperson 117
chairwoman 117
chance 117, 368
charge 7, 117
cheap 118
cheaply 118
check 88, 118, 120
checkroom 118, 125
cheerful 118, 244
cheers 119
chef 119
chemist 119
chemist's 119
cheque 120
chief 119, 120
childish 120
childlike 120
chips 120
choose 121
chord 121
Christian name 122, 227
church 122
cinema 122
class 122
classic 123
classical 123
Clauses 124
client 125, 162
cloakroom 125
close 125, 342

closed 125
closet 126, 160
cloth 126
clothes 126
clothing 126
co-operate 127, 155
coach 102, 126
coast 79, 126
coat 126
coffee 106, 127
cold 127
collaborate 127
college 127
colour 128
come 128
come from 129
come true 550
come with 129
comic 129
comical 129
comment 130
commentary 130
committee 130
common 130
company 131
Comparative and superlative adjectives 131
Comparative and superlative adverbs 136
compare 137
complain 137
complement 137
Complements 138
complete 140
completely 141
compliment 137, 141
Complimenting and congratulating someone 654
composed 141
comprehensible 141
comprehension 142
comprehensive 141, 142
comprise 142
concentrate 143
concerned 143
concert 144
concerto 144
confidant 144
confident 144
conform 144

Conjunctions 144
conscience 145
conscientious 145
conscious 145
consciousness 145
consider 146
considerably 146
consist of 146
constant 146
constantly 147
constitute 147
consult 147
content 147
continent 148
continual 146, 149
continually 149
continuous 146, 149
Contractions 149
contrary 152
control 152
convince 153
convinced 153
cook 153, 155
cooker 155
cord 121, 155
corn 155
corner 156
cost 156, 410
cot 156
could 107, 156
council 156
counsel 156
country 157
couple 157, 387
course 157
craft 158
credible 158
creditable 158
credulous 158
crib 156, 158
crime 158
crisps 158
criterion 159
critic 159
critical 159
Criticizing someone 655
cry 159
cup 160
cupboard 160
curb 161
curiosity 161

currant 162
current 162
custom 162, 251
customer 162
cut 162

D

dare 163
data 164
day 164
Days and dates 710
dead 166
deal 166
defeat 600
definitely 167, 521
delay 167
demand 167
deny 168
depend 168
describe 169
desert 170
despite 170, 284
dessert 170
destroy 170
detail 170
details 170
Determiners 171
die 172
difference 172
different 173
difficulty 173
dinner 174
direct 174
directly 174
disabled 175
disagree 176
disappear 176
disc 176
discover 177
discuss 177
discussion 177
disease 177, 272
disk 176, 177
dislike 177
dispose of 178
distance 178
distinction 172, 178
disturb 178
disturbed 178
do 179
doubt 180
downwards 181

dozen 181
dream 181
dress 182
drink 183
drugstore 119,184
during 184
duty 184,367

E

each 185
each other 186
earn 240
easily 186,187
east 186
eastwards 187
easy 187
economic 188
economical 188
economics 188
economies 189
economy 189
-*ed* participles 189
educate 99,190
effect 25,190,457
effective 190
efficient 190,191
effort 191
either 191
either ... or 192
elderly 192
electric 192
electrical 192
electronic 192
elevator 193,305
Ellipsis 193
else 195
Emailing 656
embarrassed 59,196
emigration 196
enable 34,197
end 197
endure 197
enjoy 198
enough 198
ensure 63,200
entirely 200
equally 200
equipment 200
error 201
especially 201
even 201
evening 202

eventually 203
ever 204
every 205
every day 206
everybody 206
everyday 206
everyone 206
evidence 207
exam 207
examination 207
example 208
except 5,208
excited 209
exciting 209
excursion 210,291
excuse 210
exhausted 211
exhausting 211
exhaustive 211
exist 211
expect 212
expensive 213
experience 213
experiment 213
explain 214

F

fabric 215
fact 215
factory 215,320
fair 216,217
fairly 216
fall 217
familiar 218
far 218
fare 217,219
fault 90,220
favourite 220
feel 220
female 221
feminine 221
fetch 98,222
few 222
fewer 223
film 223
finally 203,223
find 223
fine 225
finely 225
finish 225
first 226
first floor 227,248

first name 227
firstly 226
fit 227
flat 228
floor 228,508
foot 229
football 229
for 230
forename 227,231
forget 231
form 122,231
former 300
fortnight 231
forward 231
forwards 231
free 232
freely 232
frequently 232
friend 232
friendly 233
fries 233
frighten 26,233
frightened 26,233
from 234
front 234
frontier 92,235
fruit 235
full 235
fun 236
funny 129,236
furniture 236
Future time 237

G

gain 240
garbage 240
gas 240
gaze 240
generally 241
gently 241
get 241
get into 246
get off 247
get on 246
get out 247
get rid of 178
get to 242
get up 242
give 242,370
given name 227,243
glad 244
glass 160

glasses 244
go 244
go into 246
go on 247
go out 247
go with 248
good 246
gotten 247
government 248
grade 122, 248
great 87, 248
greatly 248
greet 466
Greetings and goodbyes 658
grill 248
ground 228
ground floor 248
grow 248
grow to 242
guess 249
gymnasium 249

H

habit 251
hair 251
half 251
half of 251
hand 252
handicapped 175
happen 253
happy 244, 313
hard 253
hardly 253
have 254, 256
have got 257
have got to 258
have to 258
he 258
headache 259
headline 259, 543
heap 259
hear 260
hear 262
help 260
her 261
here 261, 262
high 262
high school 262
him 262
hire 263
holiday 263

home 264
homework 62, 265
hood 92, 265
hope 265
hospital 266
house 266
housework 265, 266
how 266
how much 268
however 267
hundred 268
hurt 269
hyphen 269

I

I 270
if 270
ill 271
illness 272
imagine 272
immediately 272
immigrant 273
immigration 196, 273
important 274
in 274
in case 276
in front of 283
in spite of 284
indicate 276
indoor 276
indoors 276
industrial 276
industrious 276
Infinitives 277
inform 279
information 279
-ing forms 279
injured 283
inside 283
insist 284
instead 284
instead of 284
insure 63, 285
intention 285, 325
Intentions 660
interested 285
interesting 285
into 286
Introducing yourself and other people 662
Inversion 289
Invitations 664

invite 286, 370
involved 287
Irregular verbs 716
irritated 287, 346
it 287
it's 288
its 288

J

jam 291, 321
jelly 321
job 291, 403
joke 291
journal 291
journey 291
just 292
just now 293

K

keep 294
kerb 161, 294
kind 294
kind of 498
know 295

L

lack 297
lady 297, 603
lamb 480
landscape 297, 470
lane 509
large 87, 297
last 297
lastly 297
late 299
lately 299
later 27, 300
latter 300
lay 300
learn 301
lend 93, 301
less 302
let 34, 263, 303
let us 304
let's 304
Letter writing 666
lettuce 304, 465
library 304
lie 300, 304
lift 305
like 305, 306
likely 306
listen to 307

little 307, 487
live 308
lonely 35
long 309
look 310
look after 311
look at 473
look for 311
look forward to 311
loose 311
lorry 312
lose 311, 312
lot 312
loudly 36, 313
love 313
lucky 313
luggage 314
lunch 174, 314

M

machinery 315
mad 315
made from 315
made of 315
made out of 315
magazine 316
mail 316, 405
mainly 241
majority 316
make 96, 317
make up 318
male 318
man 319
manage 319
mankind 319
manufacture 320
many 320
marmalade 321
marriage 321
married 321
marry 321
masculine 318, 322
match 322
math 322
mathematics 322
maths 322
matter 322
may 323, 326
me 323
Meals 619
mean 324
meaning 325

Measurements 719
media 325
meet 325
memory 326, 500
mention 130, 326
merry-go-round 326
metro 517
might 326
migrant 328
migrate 328
migration 196, 328
mill 215, 328
million 328
mind 328
mistake 329
Modals 330
Modifiers 331
moment 332
money 332, 621
more 332
morning 334
most 335
move 446
movie 336
much 336
mug 160
must 338

N

named 107, 341
Names and titles 623
nation 341
nationality 341
Nationality words 725
naturally 521
nature 341
near 342
nearly 34, 343
necessary 343
need 343
neither 345
neither ... nor 345
nervous 346
never 346
news 279, 347
next 348
night 350
no 350
no one 352
nobody 351
noise 351, 499
none 351

nor 353
normally 353
north 353
northern 353
northwards 354
not 354
not like 177
not only 357
note 356
nothing 356
Noun modifiers 357
Nouns 358
now 364
nowhere 365
number 365
Numbers and fractions 728

O

object 366
Objects 366
obligation 367
obtain 367
occasion 368
occasionally 368
occur 368
of 369
offer 370
Offers 669
often 371
old 372
on 373
once 374
one 374, 375
one another 186, 376
only 376
onto 378
open 378
opinion 325, 379, 401
Opinions 671
opportunity 368, 404
opposite 379
or 381
or else 382
oral 66, 382
ordinary 382
other 382
ought to 383, 482
out 383
outdoor 383
outdoors 383
outside 384
over 3, 384

overseas 385
own 385

P

package 387, 389
packet 387, 389
pair 387
pants 388
paper 388
parcel 389
pardon 389
parking 389
part 390
partly 390
party 390
pass 390, 502
past 392
pay 394
people 395
per cent 395
percentage 395
permission 396
Permission 676
permit 34, 396
person 395, 396
persuade 153, 396
petrol 240, 396
pharmacist 119, 397
pharmacy 119, 397
phone 397
Phrasal modals 397
Phrasal verbs 397
pick 398
Pieces and amounts 627
pile 259, 399
place 399
Places 629
plant 215
play 400
Plural forms of nouns 737
point 400
point of view 401
police 402
policy 402
politely 241
political 402
politics 402
position 403
Possessive determiners 403
possibility 404
possible 405

possibly 405
post 403, 405
postpone 167, 406
power 406
practically 406
practice 406
practise 406
prefer 407
Prepositions 407
present 409
press 410
previous 410
price 410
principal 411
principle 411
prison 411
prize 410, 411
probably 412
problem 412
produce 413
product 413
professor 413
program 414
programme 414
progress 414
Pronouns 416
proper 419
protest 420
prove 420
provide 421
pub 421
public 422
public house 422
Punctuation 741
pupil 422
purse 422
put off 167, 422
put up with 422

Q

quality 423
Quantity 423
Question tags 432
Questions 429
quiet 432
quite 432, 433

R

raise 99, 434, 459
rarely 434
rather 434
reach 56, 435

Reactions 678
read 435
ready 435
realize 436, 438, 553
really 436
reason 436
receipt 437
receive 437
recipe 437
recognize 438
recommend 438
recover 439
regret 439
relation 440
relationship 440
relative 440
Relative clauses 440
relax 444
relief 444
relieve 444
remain 445
remark 130, 445
remember 445
remind 445, 446
remove 446
rent 263, 446
Replies 683
Reporting 447
request 455
Requests, orders, and instructions 685
require 456
research 456
responsible 456
rest 457
result 457
return 457
ride 458
ring 459
rise 54, 459
risk 460
road 509
rob 461
robber 461, 538
role 461
roll 461
rotary 461
round 55, 462
roundabout 462
rubbish 462
ruin 170

S

's 463
safe 464
salad 465
salary 465
sale 466
salute 466
same 466
savings 468
say 468, 500
scarce 469
scarcely 469
scene 470
scenery 470
school 471
scissors 472
search 472
seat 74
secure 464
see 472, 473
seem 474
seldom 475
select 475
send 475
sensible 476
sensitive 476
sent 475
Sentence connectors 476
shade 478
shadow 478
shall 478
shave 479
she 258
sheep 480
ship 92, 480
shop 316, 480
shore 79, 481
short 481
shortly 481
shorts 388, 482
should 482
shout 483
show 276, 483
shut 125, 483
sick 271, 483
sight 470, 484
similar 466, 484
since 484
sit 485
size 485
skilful 485

skilled 485
sleep 486
slightly 487
small 487
smell 488
so 489, 491
soccer 491
sociable 491
social 491
society 492
some 492
somebody 494
someone 494
someplace 494
something 494
sometime 495
sometimes 495
somewhat 495
somewhere 495
soon 496
sorry 497
sort 497
sort of 498
sound 498, 499
south 499
southward 500
southwards 500
souvenir 500
speak 500, 501
specially 201
Spelling 749
spend 502
spite 503
spoil 170, 503
spring 503
stack 259, 503
staff 503
stand 503
stare 240, 504
start 504
stationary 505
stationery 505
statistical 505
statistics 505
stay 445, 506
steal 461, 506
still 506
sting 507
stop 507
store 480, 508
storey 508

story 508
strange 509
stranger 509
street 509
strength 406
strongly 510
Structuring your ideas 690
student 510
Subordinate clauses 512
subway 517
such 517
suggest 518
Suggestions 694
suit 227
suitcase 519
summer 519
supper 519
support 519
suppose 520
sure 114, 521
surely 521
surgery 522
surprise 522
sweetcorn 523
sweets 523

T

take 98, 112, 256, 524
take place 524
talk 501, 525
tall 262, 525
tape 73
tea 525
teach 526
teacher 413
team 526
Telephoning 697
tell 500, 526
temperature 528
terrible 528
terribly 528
test 420, 528
than 529
thank 530
Thanking someone 700
that 530, 533, 539
That-clauses 531
the 534
The imperative 273
The passive 391
The past 393
The present 409

The progressive form 414
The subjunctive 511
the way 306
their 535
them 535
there 536
these 537, 540
they 258, 375, 537
thief 538
think 538
this 539, 540
those 533, 541
though 39, 541
thousand 541
till 542, 554
time 542
Time 636
title 543
to 544
today 545
toilet 546
tolerate 546
too 37, 491, 546
toward 548
towards 548
traffic 548
traffic circle 548
transport 548
Transport 642
transportation 548
trash 548
travel 549
trip 291, 549
trouble 549
trousers 550
truck 112, 312, 550
true 550
trunk 92, 550
try 551
type 552

U

under 553
underground 517
understand 553
understanding 142, 554
university 471, 554
unless 554
until 554
unusual 509
'n 556
'rd 556

upwards 556
us 556
use 196
used to 557
usual 558
usually 558

V

vacation 263, 559
Verb forms 559
Verb forms (formation of)
  760
Verbs 562
very 491, 570
very much 572
vest 572
victim 573
view 401, 470
visit 573
voyage 291, 574

W

wages 465, 575
wagon 112, 575
waist 575
waistcoat 575
wait 575
wake 576
waken 576
wallet 576
want 576
-ward 578
wardrobe 160, 578
-wards 578
Warning someone 703
wash 579
washroom 579
waste 575, 579
watch 473
way 579
we 375, 580
wear 581
weather 581
wedding 321, 582
week 582
weekday 582
weekend 582
weep 159, 583
welcome 583
well 246, 584
were 585
west 586

westward 586
westwards 586
Wh-words 587
what 587
whatever 589
when 590
whenever 591
where 591
wherever 592
whether 581
whether 593
which 594
while 595
who 595
whoever 596
whole 596
whom 595, 597
whose 597
why 598
wide 599
widow 599
widower 599
will 478, 600
win 600
wind 600
winter 601
wish 601
with 602
woman 603
wonder 604
wood 604
work 605
works 215
worse 605
worst 605
worth 605
would 606
write 608

Y

yard 609
year 122, 609
yes 609
yesterday 610
yet 610
you 375, 611
you're 612
your 612
yourself 612
yourselves 612

Z

zero 613